DIVERSIFICATION AND PORTFOLIO MANAGEMENT OF MUTUAL FUNDS

Also edited by Greg N. Gregoriou

ADVANCES IN RISK MANAGEMENT
ASSET ALLOCATION AND INTERNATIONAL INVESTMENTS
PERFORMANCE OF MUTUAL FUNDS

Diversification and Portfolio Management of Mutual Funds

Edited by

GREG N. GREGORIOU

palgrave
macmillan

First published 2007 by
PALGRAVE MACMILLAN
Houndmills, Basingstoke, Hampshire RG21 6XS and
175 Fifth Avenue, New York, N.Y. 10010
Companies and representatives throughout the world

PALGRAVE MACMILLAN is the global academic imprint of the Palgrave Macmillan division of St. Martin's Press, LLC and of Palgrave Macmillan Ltd. Macmillan® is a registered trademark in the United States, United Kingdom and other countries. Palgrave is a registered trademark in the European Union and other countries.

ISBN–13: 978–0–230–01915–7
ISBN–10: 0–230–01915–3

This book is printed on paper suitable for recycling and made from fully managed and sustained forest sources.

A catalogue record for this book is available from the British Library.

Library of Congress Cataloging-in-Publication Data
Diversification and portfolio management of mutual funds / edited by Greg N. Gregoriou.
p. cm.
Includes bibliographical references and index.
ISBN 0-230-01915-3 (cloth)
1. Mutual funds. 2. Portfolio management. I. Gregoriou, Greg N., 1956–
HG4530.D575 2006
332.63'27—dc22 2006043574

10 9 8 7 6 5 4 3 2 1
16 15 14 13 12 11 10 09 08 07

Transferred to Digital Printing 2011

To my mother Evangelia and in loving memory of my father Nicholas

Contents

Acknowledgments

I would like to thank Stephen Rutt, Publishing Director, and Alexandra Dawe, Assistant Editor at Palgrave Macmillan, for their suggestions, efficiency and helpful comments throughout the production process, as well as Keith Povey (with Paul Dennison and Nick Fox) for copy-editing and editorial supervision of the highest order. In addition, I would like to thank the numerous anonymous referees in the US and Europe during the review and selection process of the articles proposed for this volume.

Notes on the Contributors

The Editor

Greg N. Gregoriou is Associate Professor of Finance and coordinator of faculty research in the School of Business and Economics at the State University of New York (Plattsburgh). He obtained his PhD (Finance) from the University of Quebec at Montreal and is the hedge fund editor for the peer-reviewed journal *Derivatives Use, Trading and Regulation* published by Palgrave Macmillan based in the UK. He has authored over 50 articles on hedge funds, and managed futures in various US and UK peer-reviewed publications, including the *Journal of Portfolio Management*, the *Journal of Futures Markets*, the *European Journal of Finance*, the *Journal of Asset Management*, the *European Journal of Operational Research*, and *Annals of Operations Research*. He has published four books with John Wiley & Sons Inc. and four with Elsevier.

The Contributors

Paul U. Ali is an Associate-Professor in the Faculty of Law, University of Melbourne, Australia. Paul was previously a finance lawyer in Sydney. Paul has published several books and journal articles on finance and investment law, including, most recently, *Opportunities in Credit Derivatives and Synthetic Securitization* (London, 2005) and articles in *Derivatives Use, Trading and Regulation, Journal of Alternative Investments, Journal of Banking Regulation* and *Journal of International Banking Law and Regulation*. He is currently co-editing a book on corporate governance.

Sergio Sanfilippo Azofra is Assistant Professor of Finance at the University of Cantabria. He teaches also in some postgraduate courses in banking and financial markets. After taking his BS in economics, he completed his PhD in finance at the University of Cantabria. He has been a visiting researcher at Cass Business School (City University of London). He has research interests in banking and corporate finance and he has published several papers in academic journals and presented several papers at national and international conferences.

Wolfgang Breuer is a Professor of Finance at the RWTH Aachen University, Germany's leading Technical University. From October 1995 to February 2000 he was a Professor of Finance at the University of Bonn. He earned his PhD degree in February 1993 and his habilitation degree in July 1995, both at the University of Cologne. After his diploma in 1989 he worked one year in Frankfurt as a consultant at McKinsey & Co., Inc., before he continued his academic career. He has written about a dozen books, more than 30 articles in books and numerous peer-reviewed journal articles comprising a great variety of topics in the field of finance. His current research interests focus on portfolio management issues and in particular performance evaluation for mutual funds as well as behavioral corporate finance and international financial management.

Mercer Bullard is an Assistant Professor of Law at the University of Mississippi School of Law and founder and President of Fund Democracy, a nonprofit advocacy group for mutual fund shareholders. As one of the nation's leading advocates for investors, Professor Bullard has submitted comment letters, organized rule-making petition drives, litigated issues, requested hearings on exemptions, drafted and edited legislation, and testified before House, Senate, Department of Labor, and state committees on mutual funds, 529 plans, 401(k) plans and other regulatory issues. He was named by *Investment News* in March 2001 as one of the 25 most powerful voices in the financial services industry, cited by *BusinessWeek* for leading the fight for shareholders' rights, named by a mutual fund trade publication as one of four "Fund Titans" for 2003, and listed by *Registered Rep.* magazine as one of "Ten to Watch" for 2004. Professor Bullard has also been widely quoted on mutual fund issues in major newspaper and financial media, been featured in *Business Week, Ticker Magazine, Research Magazine, Worth, TheStreet.com,* and other publications, and appeared on NBC Nightly News with Tom Brokaw, CBS Evening News, CNBC, CNN, Wall Street Week, the NewsHour with Jim Lehrer, and on other broadcasts. Following a clerkship with Judge Will Garwood on the US Court of Appeals, Fifth Circuit, Professor Bullard practiced securities law in Washington DC with Wilmer, Cutler and Pickering, and served as an Assistant Chief Counsel with the Securities and Exchange Commission. He received his BA from Yale, his MA from Georgetown, and his JD from Virginia.

Radu Burlacu is Associate Professor of Finance at the University Pierre Mendés France, Grenoble. His thesis entitled "Issuing Convertible Bonds: A Signal of Firms' Quality" obtained the prize of the Best Thesis in Finance – 2001, awarded by EURONEXT Stock Exchange and the French Finance Association. His research fields are in asset pricing (information asymmetry, rational expectations equilibrium), portfolio management (mutual fund performance, ethical investment) and investment decisions with hybrid securities. He has published several articles in these different fields.

Rachel Campbell completed her PhD on risk management in international financial markets at Erasmus University, Rotterdam, in 2001. She currently works at the University of Maastricht as an Assistant Professor of Finance. Her work has been published in a number of leading journals, including the *Journal of International Money and Finance*, the *Journal of Banking and Finance*, *Financial Analysts Journal*, the *Journal of Portfolio Management*, the *Journal of Risk*, and *Derivatives Weekly*. She teaches for Euromoney Financial Training on art investment, and works as an independent economic advisor for the Fine Art Fund in London, and for Fine Art Wealth Management, UK.

Carlo Fiorio holds a PhD in economics from the London School of Economics. He is currently an Assistant Professor (Ricercatore) in the Department of Economics at Milan State University. He is also a Research Fellow of Econpubblica at Bocconi University, a research centre on public sector economics. His research interests are in microeconometrics and the analysis of fiscal policy through micro-simulation.

Patrice Fontaine is Professor of Finance at the University Pierre Mendés France, and formerly President of the French Finance Association. His PhD thesis entitled "Arbitrage Theory and International Pricing Financial Assets" obtained the prize for the Best Thesis in Finance from the French Stocks Markets' Society. He is the author of several books on international financial markets, arbitrage theory and exchange risk management. He has published more than 30 articles on issues related to arbitrage pricing theory, financial integration, international portfolio management, asset pricing and financial crises.

Giampaolo Gabbi is Professor of Banking and Risk Management at the University of Siena, Italy, and senior teacher at SDA Bocconi Milan, where he coordinates several executive courses on financial forecasting, and risk management. He is Head of the financial areas of Masters in Economics of the University of Siena. Professor Gabbi holds a PhD in banking and corporate management. He has published many books and articles in referred journals, including *Decision Technologies for Computational Management Science*, *MTA Journal*, *Managerial Finance*, and the *European Journal of Finance*.

Alexei P. Goriaev received his BA in mathematical economics in 1997 at Moscow State University and his MA in finance in 1998 at Tilburg University (both cum laude). He earned his PhD in finance in 2002 at Tilburg University with the thesis "On the Behavior of Mutual Fund Investors and Managers". Since September 2002, Alexei Goriaev has been Assistant Professor in Finance at the New Economic School. His general research interests are in financial econometrics, and his recent research focuses on dynamic strategies and forecasting of future performance of US and Russian mutual funds as well as risk factors (in particular, political risks) and corporate financial policy in emerging markets.

Guangxi Jia is an LLM candidate at the Washington University School of Law in St Louis. He is a 1991 graduate of Xiamen University, where he earned a Bachelor of Laws, and a 1997 graduate of Sun Yat-sen University, where he earned an LLM. Mr Jia has been a partner in Hao Li Wen PRC Attorneys in Shanghai and worked as in-house counsel for Coca-Cola (China) and as an attorney in the Guangzhou office of Brand Farrar Buxbaum, LLP, a US law firm based in Los Angeles.

Sonia Jimenez-Garces is Associate Professor of Finance at the Institut National Polytechnique de Grenoble. Her PhD thesis, "Asset Pricing in Multi-Asset Markets with Informational Asymmetry: A General Equilibrium Framework", obtained the prize Best Thesis in Finance – 2005 from the French Finance Association and the Fondation Nationale pour l'Enseignement de la Gestion des Entreprises. She has specialized in rational expectations models, and her publications are mainly in the field of asset pricing and portfolio management with asymmetrically informed investors.

Roman Kräussl obtained his Masters in Economics with a specialization in financial econometrics at the University of Bielefeld, Germany, in 1998. He completed his PhD on the "Role of Credit Rating Agencies in International Financial Markets" at Johann Wolfgang Goethe-University, Frankfurt/Main, Germany, in 2002. As the Head of Quantitative Research at Cognitrend GmbH, he was closely involved with the financial industry. Currently he is Assistant Professor of Finance at Vrije Universiteit Amsterdam and Research Fellow with the Centre for Financial Studies, Frankfurt/Main.

Júlio Lobão is a doctoral student in Management Sciences at the University of Minho. He has an MSc in finance and was an undergraduate in economics at Faculdade de Economia, University of Porto (Portugal). Previously he worked as a financial analyst and Lecturer at the Instituto de Estudos Superiores Financeiros e Fiscais (Portugal).

Carlos López-Gutiérrez is Assistant Professor of Finance at the University of Cantabria. He also teaches in some postgraduate courses in banking and financial markets. He holds a PhD in finance and a Bachelor degree and a Diploma in Business. Professor López is author of several papers on corporate financial distress and efficiency of the bankruptcy law, and he has taken part in several prestigious national and international professional meetings presenting this work.

Claudio Marsala is quantitative portfolio manager for Ras Asset Management, and prior to this he spent several years at the risk management department of Ras Asset Management, that he joined in 2001. His main focus is on the practical application of econometric models to portfolio management. He studied economics and econometrics in Pisa and holds a Masters in Finance from CORIPE, University of Turin.

Clark L. Maxam is currently the Director of Research at Braddock Financial Corporation. As former Director of Research and Portfolio Manager at New York Life Asset Management and Professor of Finance at Colorado College, Dr Maxam combines his 21 years of proprietary fixed income, equity and derivatives trading experience with a PhD in finance from the Indiana University Kelley School of Business. At New York Life, he led product development in both equities and fixed income and managed or co-managed over $1 billion in assets for their $6 billion quantitative strategies group. His market experience includes proprietary fixed income and derivative arbitrage and market-making as Senior Vice-President at Security Pacific Global Trading and NatWest Capital Markets. He is a past member of both the Chicago Board of Trade and the Chicago Mercantile Exchange and was Senior Vice-President of financial futures floor trading and sales from 1988–93. In 1993, Dr Maxam left Chicago to obtain a PhD in finance from Indiana University which he completed in 1996. Dr Maxam now specializes in quantitative financial modeling of domestic and international equity and fixed income markets. As both an academic trained in the latest techniques in financial modeling and an experienced trader and portfolio manager, Dr Maxam brings a unique perspective to the development and implementation of quantitative techniques that always emphasize practicality and the realities of a dynamic marketplace.

Jin Meng received a Bachelor's degree of law from Shanghai University of Finance and Economy in 2004, and has worked as a legal assistant for a Chinese information technology company. She is currently an LLM candidate at Washington University in St Louis.

Manuel Moreno holds a PhD in economics from the Universidad Carlos III of Madrid and a BSc in mathematics from the Universidad Complutense of Madrid. He is currently Assistant Professor of Financial Economics and Accounting at the University of Castilla La-Mancha at Toledo (Spain), Associate Editor of *Revista de Economía Financiera* and a member of GARP

(Global Association of Risk Professionals). He has previously held teaching and research positions at the Financial Option Research Centre (Warwick Business School), Universidad Carlos III de Madrid, IESE Business School and Instituto de Empresa Business School. In the past, he was the Co-Director of the Masters in Finance program at the University Pompeu Fabra in Barcelona (Spain). His research interests focus on finance in continuous time with a special emphasis on derivatives markets, financial engineering applications, pricing of derivatives, empirical analysis of different pricing models, portfolio management and term structure models. His research has been published in a number of academic journals including *Review of Derivatives Research* and the *Journal of Futures Markets*, as well as in professional volumes. He has presented his work at different international conferences and has given invited talks in many academic and non-academic institutions.

Andreas Oehler is Professor of Finance at Bamberg University and has held a Chair in Management, Business Administration and Finance there since 1994. He received his MSc (diploma) and his Doctoral degree in economics, business administration and finance from Mannheim University 1985 and 1989, and his Habilitation (postdoctoral degree) in economics and finance from Hagen University 1994. During his academic career he has worked as a senior and managing consultant at Pricewaterhouse and other companies. His major fields of research are empirical, experimental and behavioral finance, risk management, and banking and financial institutions.

Seow Eng Ong is an Associate Professor in the Department of Real Estate, National University of Singapore and his research includes securitized real estate, price discovery and housing finance issues. Seow Eng sits on the editorial board of six international real estate journals such as the *Journal of Real Estate Finance and Economics* and the *Journal of Property Research*. He was the 2002–03 President of the Asian Real Estate Society and is currently President-elect of the International Real Estate Society. He was the recipient of the 2005 International Real Estate Society achievement award for outstanding research, education and practice at the international level.

Massimiliano Pallotta joined the risk management team of Ras Asset Management in 1997, working on the quantitative and technological aspects of the development of the company's internal model. In June 2004 he joined the quantitative portfolio management unit. He studied mathematics in Milan and he has practical experience on the more advanced technological aspects of the risk management and portfolio management process.

Marco Percoco, PhD, is a Research Fellow in the Department of Economics at Bocconi University (Milan, Italy) where he teaches several graduate courses in the field of applied economics. His main research interests are in public policy, infrastructure finance and economics and sensitivity analysis of economic models.

Joshua Pullan works in the Corporate Alliances department at Sotheby's, London. He is currently writing on art investment in Self-Invested Personal Pensions in the United Kingdom. He has a Masters in Arts Business from Sotheby's Institute of Art, London. Prior to moving to London he graduated from the University of Western Australia with a Bachelor of Laws/Bachelor of Arts with honours. In 2004 he was admitted as a Legal Practitioner in the Supreme Court of New South Wales, Australia.

Ji Qi is an LLM candidate at the Washington University School of Law in St Louis and a 2001 graduate of Nankai University. Mr Qi previously practiced with Sea & Sea Law Firm in Tianjin, where he advised corporate clients and handled contracts, corporate governance and maritime matters. He has also worked for the Wanhuida Intellectual Property agency drafting legal documents for trademark affairs. Mr Qi previously founded China Knowledge M & T Co., Ltd, for which he produced guidelines and detailed reports on M&A in China, and established a Century 21 real estate franchise, for which he provided management consulting and legal services.

Stefano Ricci joined the quantitative portfolio management unit in June 2004 at Ras Asset Management after being in the risk management department for a few months. His focus is on the application of non-linear, non-parametric forecasting models. He previously gained experience in a major Italian bank in pricing complex derivatives. He studied economics and econometrics in Pavia and holds a Masters in finance from CORIPE, University of Turin.

Gonzalo Rubio is Professor of Economics and Finance at the University of the Basque Country (Spain). He holds an MBA from Columbia University and a PhD from the University of California at Berkeley. His research interests have been related to theoretical and empirical topics on asset pricing. He holds the research award of the European Finance Association and has published articles on leading international journals on asset pricing, derivatives, microstructure and corporate finance. He is currently working on the relationship between the yield curve and consumer confidence, the predicting performance of risk-neutral densities adjusted by habit preferences, and the relationship between expected return and risk on internationally integrated markets. He is the editor of the *Spanish Review of Financial Economics* and co-author (with José Marín from the University Pompeu Fabra) of the book *Financial Economics*.

Marco Rummer is currently finishing his PhD in financial economics at the University of Bamberg, Germany. He holds an MSc in economics and finance from the University of York, UK, which was funded by the German Academic Exchange Service, and a BA in management from the Georg-Simon-Ohm Fachhochschule Nuremberg, Germany. His major research interests include empirical and experimental research on financial markets and corporate finance.

Muhammad Akbar Saeed is Assistant Professor of Finance in the Department of Management Sciences at Bahria University (Karachi Campus). Akbar completed his MBA in finance in 1982 and Postgraduate Diploma in computer science in 1989 from the Institute of Business Administration (IBA), University of Karachi. Besides a marine engineering certification, Mr. Saeed is also a Diplomaed Associate of the Institute of Bankers, Pakistan, and an Academic Member, European Corporate Governance Institute, Belgium. Akbar's investment banking career of 17 years (1983–2000) with the Investment Corporation of Pakistan (ICP) covered underwriting of public offerings, project financing, equity research, and culminated in heading ICP's Mutual Funds Department.

Roberto Savona is Assistant Professor of Financial Markets and Institutions at the University of Brescia, Department of Business Studies, Italy. He received his PhD in finance at the University of Udine, Italy (2002). He also teaches at the Master MF of Brescia and collaborates with SDA and Newfin at Bocconi University. His current research interests include mutual funds, hedge funds, performance measurement, and he has presented his works at EFMA, FMA, also organizing the Euro Working Group of Financial Modelling Conference held in Brescia in May 2005.

Ana Paula Serra is an Assistant Professor in the Faculty of Economics, University of Porto (Portugal), where she teaches undergraduate and graduate courses in corporate finance, international finance and investments. She holds a PhD in finance from the London Business School. Her research concentrates on international asset pricing and capital markets, emerging markets and privatization. Previously, she worked at one of the leading Portuguese investment banks, as a research analyst and asset manager.

Olaf Stotz holds a PhD in finance and is Assistant Professor of Finance at RWTH Aachen University, Germany's leading Technical University. His research interests include asset management, behavioral finance, empirical asset pricing, market efficiency and mutual funds. He has written several peer-reviewed research articles in the fields of fund management and the equity risk premium and edited a book on asset allocation. Before his academic career he worked for several years in the finance industry for major financial institutions in Germany.

Nadeem A. Syed completed his MBA (personnel and industrial management) and Doctorate in business administration (general management) from Aquinas University, Philippines in 1997. He possesses over 15 year's corporate experience with national and multinational companies. He is presently serving as Associate Professor and Head of the Department, Management Sciences, at Bahria University, Karachi, Pakistan. He teaches organization behavior and organization development on MBA courses. He is also the Coordinator of the Faculty Research Program at Bahria University. He has authored a number of international conference papers in the areas of HRM systems and practices, e-governance, privatization, and general management.

Begoña Torre-Olmo is Professor of Banking and Finance at the University of Cantabria, and is Assistant Vice-Chancellor of teaching staff for the University of Cantabria and member of the Board of the Public Project Finance Company of Cantabria Regional Government. She is the coordinator of doctorate programs with several important Mexican universities. She has research interests in the mutual funds industry and corporate finance distress, and has published several papers in academic journals.

Thomas Walker is a native of Germany. He received a PhD in finance and an MBA degree in finance and international business from Washington State University (WSU) in Pullman, WA, and a BSc in Wirtschaftsinformatik (management information systems) from the Technical University of Darmstadt, Germany. Dr. Walker joined Concordia University in Montreal, Canada, as an Assistant Professor in 2001. Prior to his academic career, he worked for several years in the German consulting and industrial sector for such firms as Mercedes Benz, Utility Consultants International, Lahmeyer International, Telenet, and KPMG Peat Marwick. His research interests are in IPO underpricing, securities regulation and litigation, institutional ownership, insider trading, and aviation finance.

Stefan Wendt is a doctoral student as well as Research and Teaching Assistant in finance at the University of Bamberg, Germany. He studied international and European business studies at the University of Bamberg and at the Norwegian School of Management BI, Sandvika, Norway, and graduated in 2005. His main research interests include corporate governance and empirical finance.

Craig Wisen is an Assistant professor of Finance at the University of Alaska, Fairbanks School of Management, and is a Chartered Financial Analyst. He received his PhD in finance from the Indiana University Kelley School of Business in 2002. His primary research interests include mutual fund performance evaluation and real estate.

Raffaele Zenti has been Risk Manager at Ras Asset Management from 1997 to June 2004, working on the development of the internal risk model and on the definition and application of risk policies to actively managed portfolios. Since 2004 he has been a quantitative portfolio manager: he supervises a department that manages several portfolios using non-subjective models. He studied economics and statistics in Turin and is Lecturer on the Masters in finance of CORIPE, University of Turin.

Introduction

Chapter 1 discusses the introduction of a number of art funds in the financial marketplace which has led to a number of interesting issues arising in the mutual fund industry. From an investment perspective, art funds provide an alternative avenue down which investors can diversify their portfolios. They also offer investors a market with irregularities and inefficiencies, which art funds may be able to exploit to reap highly attractive returns. Just how interesting an avenue can this be and what benefits exist from investing in art funds, are addressed in this chapter.

Chapter 2 examines the numerous empirical studies that have analysed the individual or aggregate performance of mutual funds. Relatively little work has investigated the effect that the additional management layer funds of mutual funds (FOFs) may have on its risk-adjusted return. The authors compare the risk-adjusted returns of FOFs to those generated by a random selection of mutual funds possessing the same investment objective of the FOFs. FOFs perform no better than their respective benchmarks, and exhibit a propensity for economic underperformance. FOFs tend to invest in funds with lower than average expense ratios, but their total fees exceed those of traditional funds by an average of 0.97 percent suggesting that they are engaged in expense arbitrage: buying low-cost funds and repackaging them as a higher expense fund.

Chapter 3 examines how portfolio selection has been in the focus of financial research for at least thirty years. With hand-collected data containing information about the portfolio structure of private and institutional investors, this chapter gives a brief literature review and sheds light on the home bias effect in Germany from 1990 until 2005. Despite a decline of this effect since the early 1990s, German – in particular private – investors still hold a bigger-than-optimal portion of domestic assets (bonds and equities) in their portfolios compared to the world market portfolio.

Chapter 4 develops a model to estimate the efficiency in international mutual funds. The author interprets returns and volatility spreads with benchmarks and constructs a four-diagram plot to calculate two efficiency ratios and correlate them to monetary policy behavior.

Chapter 5 shows how portfolio construction is a complex phase at the core of any quantitative asset management process. During this phase portfolio managers face topics like use and misuse of constraints, estimation of covariances and other parameters, optimization, and the rebalancing frequency. The authors compare, from a practical point of view, different ways to construct benchmark-relative portfolios of stocks. They further consider various alternatives that a practitioner can face and back-test the associated portfolios, comparing the results.

Chapter 6 observes that households are increasingly using mutual funds as their main long-term investment vehicles. Today, the number of mutual funds available exceeds 17,000 in the United States alone. Market participants are therefore in need of valid, unbiased and straightforward information in order to select mutual funds with the best future prospects. The most well-known fund rating system is provided by Morningstar Inc. This chapter reviews the mid-June 2002 revised Morningstar 5-star rating system, its many attractive features but also its limitations.

Chapter 7 considers theoretically the portfolio selection problem for (private) mean-variance investors and (professional) tracking-error investors and examines the optimal wealth delegation from the former group to the latter (mutual fund flows). Moreover, the authors study empirically the German stockmarket and find (among other things) that fund flows impact benchmark stocks and non-benchmark stocks in different ways. Within the authors' model, their observations can be explained by a private investors' mean-reverting expectation bias regarding mutual fund returns.

Chapter 8 tests for herding by Portuguese mutual funds over the period 1998–2000 using the herding measure suggested by Lakonishok, Schleifer, Thaler and Vishny (1992). The authors find strong evidence of herding behavior for Portuguese mutual funds and the level of herding is four to five times stronger than the herding found in previous studies.

Chapter 9 investigates the popular types of mutual funds worldwide called Exchange Traded Funds (ETFs). In general, they offer lower fees, greater pricing transparency and greater liquidity than other mutual funds following comparable investment strategies. The chapter discusses the dual trading structure of ETFs and the key legal concerns that arise when designing ETFs for a common law market.

Chapter 10 examines the nature of competition for new investor money in the mutual fund industry by analysing how fund flows are affected by their relative performance within different types of categories. The author demonstrates that domestic stock and domestic bond funds should outperform not only their peers with the same stated objective or Morningstar style, but also other funds within the same asset class in order to attract investors.

Chapter 11 examines the increasing globalization and changing market conditions, whereby European mutual fund managers turn more and more towards industry placement. The authors find that momentum strategies based on sector funds provide positive risk-adjusted abnormal returns even after subtracting expenses, loads and redemption fees. Their results represent a challenge for the efficient markets hypothesis.

Chapter 12 provides a comparative overview of mutual fund regulation in the USA and China. The chapter compares each country's approach to key aspects of the regulation of investment pools, including affiliated transactions, corporate governance and sales practices, and offers insights into how China's nascent regulatory regime may evolve in light of the US experience.

Chapter 13 analyses the mutual funds industry in Spain. The empirical evidence reported in this chapter shows striking differences in behavior among management companies when distinguishing among banks, savings banks and independent management companies. One possible explanation may be the universal banking model characterizing the Spanish financing system. As a consequence, a worrying lack of competition in the Spanish mutual fund industry can be observed.

Chapter 14 describes the worldwide escalation of the mutual funds industry over the last two decades by stimulating major players to offer their products beyond national borders. In Italy the role of foreign firms has grown significantly, since it is widely believed that foreigners outperform Italian money managers in almost all investment categories. With the purpose of inspecting this supposed foreign superiority, the author's empirical analyses demonstrate that this common view is due to tax distortion between domestic and non-domestic funds.

Chapter 15 examines the best global practices and codes of corporate governance in the context of mutual funds and then compares them with the practices and the regulatory regime for the mutual fund industry in Pakistan. Historical perspectives of the mutual fund industry in Pakistan are also addressed.

Chapter 16 investigates public spending for pensions, one of the most relevant items in government budgets. Public spending on pensions has become a source of concern for policy-makers as, given the PAYGO system in use in most countries, the ageing of the population as measured by the percentage of individuals in working age is declining and is expected to decline even more. In recent years Italy has undertaken reforms to move towards more sustainable pension systems. The data-set used in this chapter is the Survey of Household Income and Wealth (SHIW) published by the Bank of Italy and based on interviews in 2002. It is found that the probability to underwrite such an instrument is positively correlated with education and negatively with the age of the worker. The fact that younger workers are more willing to join pension funds is crucial for portfolio management, as this situation calls for a long-term investment horizon. The presence of liabilities (in terms of pensions) occurring in the long run will lead the market to demand new instruments, such as long-term indexed bonds, and for a portfolio composition reflecting the constant relative risk-aversion of workers.

Chapter 17 illustrates the moral hazards in the Spanish market of mutual funds that determine manager activity in terms of risk-taking behavior, window-dressing, or follow-up of active or passive management strategies.

Chapter 18 attempts to shed some light on the mutual fund industry from the standpoint of how participants choose these financial products. The authors analyse which factors are most important to investors and find that financial factors and behavioral arguments must both be considered.

CHAPTER 1

Diversification into Art Mutual Funds

Rachel Campbell and Joshua Pullan

1.1 INTRODUCTION

Mutual funds have become a popular structure for investors seeking exposure to financial markets. With thousands of funds in operation, it is unsurprising that mutual funds have become the largest means of investment in the USA, with almost $7.5 trillion of assets held at the beginning of 2004.[1] The structure provides investors with an opportunity to participate in securities markets without having to become money managers themselves. Furthermore, by pooling small amounts of money into a single fund value, individual investors are able to participate in investment strategies that would have otherwise been financially unfeasible.

In the context of art,[2] it seems a novel idea to own a share in a Picasso or a Van Gogh. However, with artworks routinely selling for millions of dollars, art investors are beginning to consider innovative alternatives to obtain some of the financial benefits offered from investing in art. Strictly speaking, the market is currently without an Art Mutual Fund ("AMF").[3] However, there are a number of art investment vehicles ("AIVs") such as limited partnerships, that currently exist, and it is important to examine how these may impact upon the entrance of AMFs.

In this chapter we examine the financial properties of art as an asset class and the complications that arise with such analysis. It also explores the advantages and disadvantages associated with AMFs.

1.2 ART AS AN ASSET

1.2.1 Financial properties of art

Determining the price of an artwork can be difficult. However, an examination of the subject matter, size, medium, provenance and condition of the artwork, as well as the artist's popularity, will all materially contribute to the financial value an artwork is given. While many of these are necessarily objective enquiries, it is ultimately the subjective opinion of the purchaser that will be determinative of the price paid. Therefore, unlike stocks and bonds, the price of an artwork comprises an unquantifiable element: taste. For a collector, taste will play an important role in determining whether an artwork is bought. On the other hand, a pure investor will only be interested in the potential financial performance of the artwork, because they are not intending to derive an aesthetic benefit from the work. For the purposes of our discussion, art will be examined from an investment perspective and accordingly discussion of any aesthetic benefits derived from viewing an artwork will be ignored.

Art may provide an investor with financial returns in the form of a capital gain accruing upon its sale and in limited circumstances, with an income stream generated from rental paid for display of the artwork. When calculating an artwork's return, the costs of ownership needs to be deducted and these typically include insurance premiums and conservation costs. If the price of artwork expected in the following time period, P_{t+1}, where P_t is the actual purchase price, H is the holding costs, and S the potential rental stream, the return on art, r, is simply $R_t = (P_t - P_{t-1} + S_t - H_t)/P_{t-t}$.

Any investment in art will arguably be speculative. John Maynard Keynes, himself an art collector, contrasted speculation "forecasting the psychology of the market" with enterprise "forecasting the prospective yield of an asset". The enterprise value of art will generally be zero because an income stream arising from an artwork's rental will be rare. In fact the yield from enterprise is potentially negative given the costs of storage, insurance and maintenance. Therefore money managers focus upon the speculative qualities of art investment as the primary avenue to generate capital gains. They seek to anticipate changes in public opinion and sentiment rather than the traditional enterprise approach of focussing on earnings, dividends and book values. As a result, the ability of AMF managers to forecast future returns is central to a fund's success.

Asymmetric information between investors and managers is likely to be greater in the art market than in the market for equities. This is largely due to information flows. In the art market information is imperfect, with participants not necessarily as well-informed about the quality, resale value, price and availability of substitutes. Unlike other financial markets, dealers are able to "make the market". AMF's with their greater weight can influence the demand for art by promoting particular artworks and artists. In this regard, the art market differs from traditional investment strategies, as pricing anomalies disappear rapidly in other financial markets, whereas the art market tends to tolerate their existence for greater periods of time. A number of these pricing discrepancies have been investigated in the literature and we highlight some of the evidence for and against them in Table 1.1.

Table 1.1 Art pricing anomalies

Anomaly	Literature	Evidence
Masterpiece effect	Pesando (1993)	No support of masterpieces outperforming the market, uniformly lower returns
	Goetzman (1996)	No effect
	Mei & Moses (2002)	Overbidding tends to occur for master pieces of work. Artworks with high estimates tend to underperform the market
	Pommerehne & Frey (1997)	Museums pay above average prices in auction markets
Burned artworks	Ashenfelter & Graddy (2003)	Artworks not selling first time at auction tend to sell at a higher multiple of their price estimate when put on auction for a second time
Law of one price	Pesando (1993)	***Geographical differences***: Between 1989–92: prices in NY significantly higher than in London and Europe
		Auction house premiums: Sotheby's NY significantly higher prices than Christie's NY; insignificant for London
	Mei & Moses (2002)	***Auction house premiums***: only small differences
Inefficient estimates for art	Ashenfelter (1989)	Action houses are truthful
	Bauwens & Ginsburgh (2000)	Art experts do not seem to take advantage of all the information contained in sales catalogues
	Mei & Moses (2002)	Upward bias for expensive paintings
	Ashenfelter, Graddy & Stevens (2002)	Smaller spread in the price estimate, results in a high reserve price and a greater likelihood of price not reaching the reserve price
Declining prices for repeat items sold	Pesando & Shum (1996)	Evidence for Picasso prints
	Beggs & Graddy (1997)	Evidence for Art

Certainly these inefficiencies present opportunities for exploitation and profit, but conversely represent a danger for uninformed investors. It is the extent to which these inefficiencies and anomalies exist in the art market that determines the positive abnormal returns that can be made by art funds. Naturally, this position is only sustainable in the short term. Once more funds enter the marketplace there will be less room for abnormal profits to be made. Until then the inefficient nature of the market means that if artworks are chosen wisely attractive returns may be made from AIVs and AMFs in the foreseeable future.

Art may also be attractive to investors seeking diversified portfolios. The low correlation between art and other assets means that art may build part of an optimal portfolio allocation. As we see from the correlation statistics for a variety of asset classes in Table 1.2, art and equities are approximately 5 percent correlated over the period 1976–2004. The correlation between

Table 1.2 Asset classes

A. summary statistics
Monthly log returns data 1976/01–2004/12, 348 observations

	MSCI USA	LM AGGR	GSCI	Real estate	AMR 100	AMR US
Average annual return	11.99%	8.53%	8.89%	15.44%	5.73%	7.94%
Average standard deviation	15.14%	5.94%	16.96%	22.20%	8.27%	8.73%
Monthly return	0.010	0.007	0.007	0.013	0.005	0.007
Monthly standard deviation	0.044	0.017	0.049	0.064	0.024	0.025
Skewness	−0.754	0.432	0.027	−0.498	−0.509	−0.343
Kurtosis	3.057	5.307	1.241	2.194	2.857	3.565

B. correlation matrix
Monthly log returns data 1976/01–2004/12, 348 observations

	MSCI USA	LM AGGR	GSCI	Real estate	AMR 100	AMR US
MSCI USA	1.000					
LM AGGR	0.242	1.000				
GSCI	0.013	−0.022	1.000			
Real estate	0.615	0.233	0.018	1.000		
AMR 100	**−0.020**	**−0.049**	**0.107**	**0.002**	**1.000**	
AMR US	**−0.027**	**−0.031**	**0.083**	**0.035**	**0.666**	**1.000**

other asset classes is also low, the highest being between art and commodity futures, and even then only 10 percent correlated.

In focusing upon the potential of expected returns to art, the significant diversification benefits offered by art are often ignored. Arguably this is where the broader appeal of art in an investment strategy lies and the next few years may see its acceptance as a valid financial tool. Mean-variance portfolio optimization also shows this for US art, even after accounting for the high transaction costs prevalent in the art market.[4] It is possible that in the future, a market for a mutual fund of international art funds shall develop for investors who seek a truly diversified investment into art.

1.3 ART MUTUAL FUNDS

1.3.1 History

The first mutual funds developed during the early days of organized stock trading in The Netherlands.[5] In 1774 a fund, aptly named "United Creates Strength", provided small investors with a means of diversifying their holdings into a number of European countries and colonial plantations in Central and South America. In contrast to other financial markets, the art market has yet to witness the development of an operational AMF. Interestingly the Dutch were also leading the way by attempting to develop a fund of art funds. ABN Amro, the Dutch investment bank, endeavoured to launch their product in 2005. However, its introduction seems to have been premature given the small number of art funds currently active for investment purposes. Their efforts must be acclaimed because the fund of funds may have brought greater liquidity to the art market.

Because AMFs are yet to develop in the market it is useful to go back a step and examine the development of other AIVs such as art funds. The first known art fund was a relatively recent phenomenon and was created when French financier André Level set up a fund named *La Peau de l'Ors* (the skin of the bear) in 1904. He convinced 12 other investors to contribute 212 francs each to the fund and over a period of 10 years bought over 100 paintings and drawings (including Picasso and Matisse). The fund closed in 1914 making a return of 400 percent, with some artworks reaping 10 times their original purchase prices.[6]

A historical examination of art funds would not be complete without briefly discussing the most famous art fund, The British Rail Pension Fund, and arguably the most infamous, The BNP Paribas Fund. The British Rail Pension Fund (BRPF) was established in 1974 in an attempt to hedge against a period of rapid inflation and rising interest rates. The BRPF invested £40 million, representing 4 percent of the fund's total portfolio value into art. It diversified its art holdings across Impressionist, Old Master and Chinese art, as well as through a dozen other fields. When the BRPF finished selling the majority of its holdings in 1999 it yielded a nominal annual return of 11.3 percent. Despite the criticism the BRPF received from some segments of the investment community, the art investment achieved its primary objective of diversifying the portfolio.

There was no uncertainty surrounding the performance of the BNP Paribas Fund (BNPPF). It was a disaster. The BNPPF reportedly lost more than 40 percent of its capital invested, which equated to an amount in the region of US$8 million. The failure of the fund was largely attributed to the art buyers overpaying for the artworks and a rigid fund structure that didn't allow for market conditions to be factored in upon the artworks sale.

More recently, the art market has witnessed the unveiling of an unprecedented number of proposed art funds and AIVs. The word "proposed" is crucial in the preceding sentence, because to date, many AIVs have had difficulty making the transition from the developmental, capital raising phase and moving into actively trading artworks.

1.3.2 Advantages

AMFs may offer similar benefits to mutual funds that invest in tradi-tional asset classes. AMF investors will generally be seeking a reduction of risk by holding a diversified portfolio of artworks. A fund is able to hold a variety of artworks, diversifying across artists, countries and categories: a strategy beyond the scope of most individual art investors. By investing in a fund, investors are greatly reducing the specific risk associated with holding artworks directly. Benefits can also be obtained by utilizing the economies of scale of the fund, for example through lower transaction costs with dealers and auction houses. Investors would also benefit from the professional management services and information provided that would otherwise be difficult and expensive to obtain on a fund by fund basis.

In theory the AMF structure may also increase the liquidity of art investment because investors will be able to redeem their shares in the AMF, rather than having to dispose of the artworks themselves. In this sense AMFs allow art investors to make the transition from trading real property (the artworks) to financial instruments (their share in the AMF). However due to the limited number of art funds and AIVs currently in the market and niche appeal that investing in these structures currently has, investors are unlikely to benefit from significantly increased liquidity.

1.3.3 Disadvantages

Evidently AMFs can provide investors with significant financial benefits; however these do not come without a price. As is the case in the general mutual fund industry, management fees are typically performance-oriented and therefore take a sizeable percentage of the fund's profits once the requisite watermark has been reached. Whether this is an acceptable expense will depend upon each investor's assessment of the fund.

At present, investors face significant barriers to entry for investing in art funds. As a result, AMFs are likely to develop and circumvent many of these difficulties. The market for art funds remains unregulated. Funds are not required to report annual performance or even the value of their holdings. Investors may also find the substantial financial contributions required to join the funds problematic. Minimum entrance levels are at present in the realm of £250,000 for the UK and $500,000 for the USA. This is under revision and likely to be reduced in time, but with entrance levels still at around £50,000, art funds will remain largely the domain of high net-worth individuals. The required contribution levels relate to the manner in which the funds are marketed. In the UK, art funds only target institutional or "sophisticated" investors and therefore escape regulation by the Financial Services Authority. This depends on the exact financial form which the AIV takes. There are obvious advantages from having a private equity or a hedge fund structure over a REIT structure. The Securities and Exchange Commission (SEC) requires registration of mutual funds. Therefore AMFs may create greater transparency of fund manager performance and fees in the future. However, whether a potential AMF would meet the registration requirements imposed by the SEC is questionable due to the unregulated nature of the art market.

Although AMFs are yet to become a reality, some sectors of the art market have already been exhausted. However, opportunities to make substantial returns still exist in the middle and emerging markets. AMFs which utilize these sectors, where art prices are likely to continue growing at a faster pace, given the increase in wealth, and repatriation of art to their original countries, are likely to succeed to a greater extent.[7]

1.3.4 Structure

Open-end mutual funds[8] allow new shares to be sold to investors wishing to invest and shares can always be redeemed by investors wanting their money back. In the context of art, a number of issues arise in relation to open-ended mutual funds. Firstly, the share price of an open-ended mutual fund is dependent on the net asset value of the fund. At present there is not enough liquidity for art funds to be open-ended. At best, a second tranch of investment may occur. This behavior is evident amongst current players in the art fund field such as: The Fine Art Fund (founded in 2002), the Indian-based Yatra Fund (founded in 2004) and Fernwood Art Investments (investors shall be able to purchase shares on two occasions per year; planned to launch early in 2006).

As was the case in the early development of the mutual fund industry for equities, closed-end funds were more popular.[9] Investors pooled their money, and shares were issued only once (in an Initial Public Offering) to investors in exchange for their money. Normally it was the case that no further shares were issued or redeemed during the period of the fund. Under this arrangement the fixed number of shares, tradable on the secondary market, determines the share price through supply and demand. In this respect, the price of each share may significantly differ from the price of a share based upon the net asset value of the fund. A potential difficulty for closed-end funds is that there is no secondary market currently available for actively trading the art shares. This prevents the general public from investing into the market for art funds. The structure of a closed fund may be beneficial to existing investors of a fund, since performance tends to deteriorate when funds grow so large that managers have trouble executing their strategies. Although the investor is "locked in" for a period of 5–10 years, research has shown that closed-fund managers tend to put the long-term interests of their investors ahead of their own short-term profit goals. The disadvantage of course being to the fund manager, whose fee is normally calculated as a percentage of the funds growing assets, so there is an internally motivated incentive to make funds open-ended.

Since 1774, the broader financial market for closed-end funds has steadily declined. At present closed-end funds comprise less than 3 percent of the total US fund market. By comparison, open-ended funds have flourished since their introduction to the US market in 1924. Based upon this experience it is likely that closed-end AMFs will appear in the art market in the short term, with open-ended funds likely to be on offer once the market has become more transparent and liquid.

1.4 ART PRICE DATA QUALIFICATIONS

The new vogue in investing in art has received a boost from the availability of art price data. In any market "knowledge is power" and the proliferation of information sources in the art market is a testimony to this. Databases, indices, and market reports are now essential analytical tools with which art investors can assess financial performance. A number of indices have been derived to demonstrate average returns, with data going as far back as the seventeenth century. The difficulty with these tools is that the information upon which they are based is neither consistent nor complete, and therefore arguably distorts results when compared to more transparent markets. It is useful to briefly examine the methods currently employed by these information sources in order to gain an informed perspective on the results they provide.

1.4.1 Data collection

The Mei Moses and Art Market Research art indices are the two most widely quoted indicators of art market performance. Both are reliant on data from sales at the main auction houses. Auction results alone as a measure of art market performance provide an incomplete picture of the market performance because they are only a portion of the whole market. The dealer market is largely ignored due to an absence of obtainable data. There is some disagreement as to the percentage of the market that dealers comprise. Figures from two recent studies range from a 50–50 split between auction houses and dealers to 70–30 split in favor of dealers. In any event, it cannot be denied that dealers have a significant, albeit unquantifiable, impact upon the art market. The absence of dealers' transactions from the art indices may have a bearing upon the rate of return indicated by the indices. Dealers will generally sell at higher prices and buy at lower prices than in general at auction. Investors who trade with dealers will therefore face higher transaction costs, thereby reducing the art investor's rate of return.[10] If so, the average prices derived from sales from auction house data may overestimate the average market return. However it is likely that some art funds, who act more like private dealers, will be able to take a similar strategy and furthermore take account of inefficiencies in the market; likely to produce returns larger than the art market benchmark.

1.4.2 Methodologies

There are four main methodologies for producing art price indices. Geometric means, average prices, repeat sales and hedonic regressions. Chanel, Gerard-Varet and Ginsburgh's study indicates that over long periods the respective methodologies are closely correlated.[11] Issues regarding the various index pricing methodologies are extremely well highlighted in a recent paper by Ginsburgh, Mei and Moses (2006) which compares hedonic to repeat sales regression (RSR).

Ashenfelter and Graddy (2003) also provide an excellent survey of average returns estimated from art price data, currently in the academic literature. We have extended their table with a few additional studies, as shown in Table 1.3.

Average real returns for art are moderately low, as documented in the various studies, with returns above inflation and bonds, but lower than for equities. However, there has been a general upward trend of art price indices in the market. Figure 1.1 presents an overview of how a $1 investment in a variety of assets would have performed over the period 1976–2004.

The survey of art pricing methodologies tends to indicate that the repeat sales methodology provides slightly higher estimates of average returns

Table 1.3 Estimated art returns and standard deviation (as reported by various papers)

Author	Sample	Period	Method	Nominal return	Real return	Standard deviation
Baumol (1986)	Paintings in general	1652–1961	RSR		0.60%	
Frey and	Paintings in general	1635–1949	RSR		1.40%	
Pommerehne (1989)		1653–1987	RSR		1.50%	5.00%
		1950–87	RSR		1.70%	
Buelens and	Paintings in general	1700–1961	Hedonic		0.91%	
Ginsburgh (1992)	Paintings in general	1780–1970	RSR	3.70%	3.00% *	
Goetzmann (1993)	Paintings in general	1716–1986	RSR	3.20%	2.00% *	5.65%
		1850–1986	RSR	6.20%	3.80%	6.50%
		1900–86	RSR	17.50%	13.3%	5.19%
Anderson (1974)	Paintings in general	1780–1960	Hedonic	3.30%	2.60% *	
		1780–1970	RSR	3.70%	3.00% *	
Chanel, Gerard–Varet and Ginsburgh (1996)	Paintings in general	1855–1969 1855–1969	Hedonic Repeat Sales		4.90% 5.00%	
Mei and Moses (2002)	American, Impressionist, and Old Masters	1875–1999	RSR		4.90%	4.28%
		1900–86	RSR		5.20%	3.72%
		1900–99	RSR		5.20%	3.55%
		1950–99	RSR		8.20%	2.13%
		1977–91	RSR		7.80%	2.11%

Goetzmann (1996)	Paintings in general	1907–77	RSR		5.00%		
Fase (1996)	19th century	1946–66		11.00%	7.50%		
		1972–92		10.60%	1.10%		
Stein (1977)	Paintings in general	1946–68	Geometric mean	10.47%			
Barre, Docclo and Ginsburgh (1996)	Great Impressionist	1962–91	Hedonic	12.0%	5.00%	*	
	Other Impressionist	1962–91	Hedonic	8.00%	1.00%	*	
Czujack (1997)	Picasso paintings	1966–94	Hedonic		8.30%		
Deutschman (1991)	Old Masters	1971–91		12.30%	6.04%		
Angnello and Pierce (1996)	19th century US	1971–92		9.30%	3.25%		
Campbell (2005)	Paintings in general	1976–2004	Average prices	5.73%	1.44%		8.27%
	US paintings	1976–2004	Average prices	7.94%	3.66%		8.73%
Pesando (1993)	Modern prints	1977–92	RSR		1.51%		9.94%
Pesando and Shum (1996)	Picasso prints	1977–92	RSR	12.00%	2.10%		23.38%
Frey and Serna (1990)	Old Masters	1981–88	Hedonic	10.59%	3.20%		
Candela and Scorcu (1997)	Modern contemporary paintings	1983–94		3.89%	0.21%		

* Real returns estimated additionally by Ashenfelder and Graddy (2003).

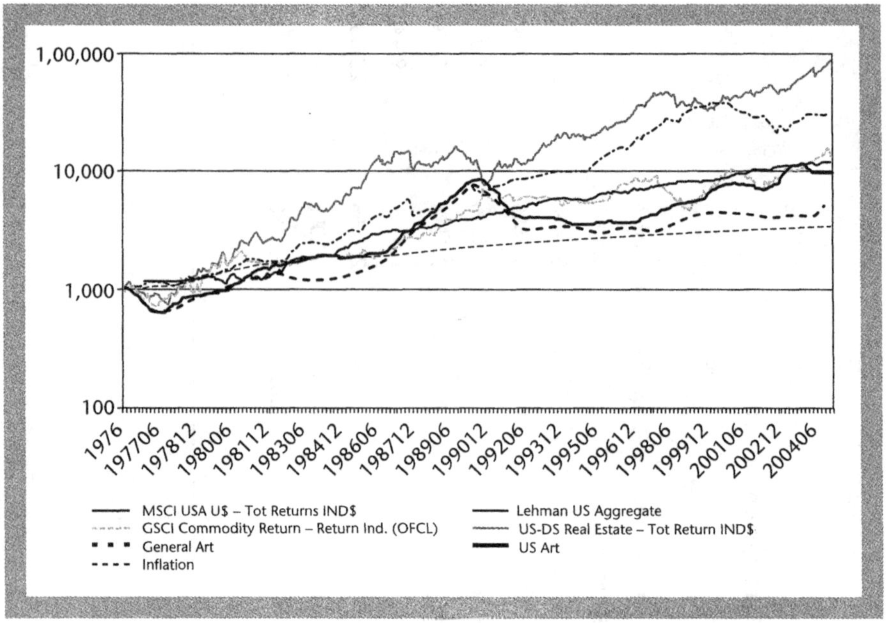

Figure 1.1 Asset performance
Note: $1 invested in various asset classes, using monthly data from January 1976 until December 2004 from global financial data, Datastream and art market research.

than the other methodologies, considering similar time periods. For example Anderson (1974) provides RSR and Hedonic price indices for the periods 1780–1970 and 1780–1960 and Chanel, Gerard-Varet and Ginsburgh (1996) for the period 1855–1969. It is certainly of interest to observe the long run trend in the market, and to see that there have been periods in which returns to art have been substantially higher.

Art market research data is available monthly but only goes as far back as 1976. The Mei Moses series for the All Art Index is available as far back as 1875; however, only on an annual basis and from 1965 on a semi-annual basis. In Table 1.4 we have provided the summary statistics for two types of price index methodology: the Mei Moses All Art Index which is computed using repeat sales and Art Market Research data which use average returns on a 3-month moving average. To be able to compare the two series we use semi-annual data from 1976 up until 2002.[12] The lower frequency increases the annual volatility of the series, and the slightly shorter time period results in a slightly lower average annual return.

Computing the correlation statistics (Table 1.5) for the two price index methodologies shows us that at first glance that the Art 100 methodology from Art Market Research is fairly uncorrelated with the Mei Moses All Art

Table 1.4 Summary statistics

Semi-annual log return data 1976/01–2002/12				
	Average prices			**Repeat sales All Art Index**
	ART 100	**US 100**	**UK 100**	
Annual average return	5.27%	8.26%	5.12%	10.07%
Annual average st. deviation	17.11%	15.86%	11.10%	21.88%
Average	0.026	0.041	0.026	0.050
Standard deviation	0.121	0.112	0.078	0.155
Skewness	−0.837	−0.817	−0.097	−0.277
Kurtosis	1.694	1.029	−1.083	−0.395

Table 1.5 Comparison of average prices and repeat sales data

Correlation matrix A
Semi-annual log return data 1976/01–2002/12

	Average prices			**Repeat sales All Art Index**
	ART 100	**US 100**	**UK 100**	
Art 100	1.000			
US 100	0.822	1.000		
UK 100	0.651	0.565	1.000	
All Art Index	0.210	0.221	0.250	1.000

Correlation matrix B
Semi-annual log returns 2-period moving averages 1976/01–2002/12

	Average prices			**Repeat sales All Art Index**
	ART 100	**US 100**	**UK 100**	
Art 100	1.000			
US 100	0.871	1.000		
UK 100	0.716	0.644	1.000	
All Art Index	0.857	0.714	0.342	1.000

Index, at only 20 percent. However, taking a 2-period moving average for the return series increases the correlation dramatically. This is especially so for the All Art Index and the US 100 indices which has a correlation coefficient of 86 percent. A larger number of observations used in deriving the moving averages provide correlation coefficients above 90 percent.

Stein (1977) and Ginsburgh (2006) acknowledge the selection bias which occurs from only focusing on repeat sales of auction house data: Repeat sales regressions require artworks to be offered for sale at auction more than once to be included as a repeat sale. It is thought that artworks that fall drastically in value tend not to be resold at auction.[13]

The information from databases that collect sales information are therefore problematic for a number of reasons.[14] Ashenfelter and Graddy's (2003) study contends that an empirical discrepancy in one year can materially alter the overall rate of return by up to 5 percent. We also find evidence of this phenomenon for the more recent Mei & Moses All Art Index compared to the General Art Index of Art Market Research for the period 1976–2004. A difference in the estimation of the return after the burst in the art market bubble in 1991, results in a significant difference between the average return figures thereafter. This can be observed in Figure 1.2.

This difference also indicates the importance of liquidity during downturns in the market. The number of art sales is likely to be greatly reduced in downturns, with the market becoming more illiquid during these times. There is a greater degree of liquidity risk facing the art investor than for other financial assets. With artworks not reaching their reservation prices and not being sold, this will have an effect on the prices included in the price indices. Fewer transactions result in large estimation errors occurring in the various price indices. At present there is little information available as to the degree of liquidity over the empirical time series. This problem is especially significant for the case of repeat sales regression estimation for price indices constructed with fewer observations. By definition they are

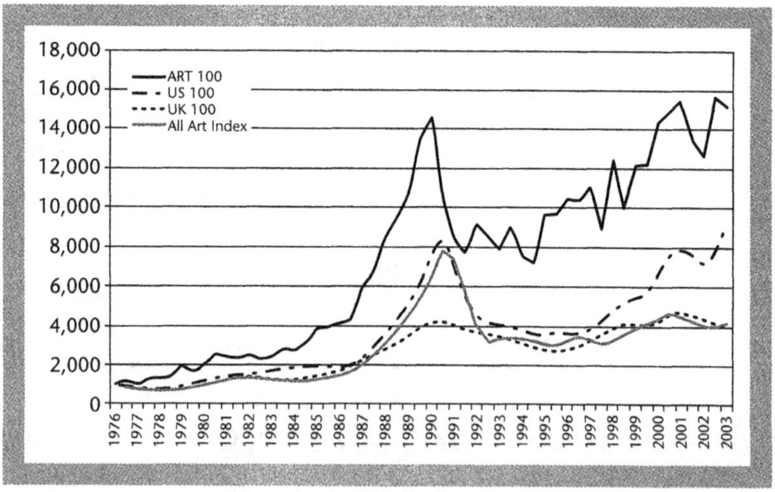

Figure 1.2 Comparison of art price indices, semi-annual data
Note: The figure depicts repeat sales All Art Index vs the average price indices from AMR for the general art market (ART 100), the Top US Artists (US 100), and the Top British Artists (UK 100).

required to be repeated at least once during the time series to be included in the data series. It is likely that the price estimation error which occurs after the art market crash in the early 1990s is underestimated from the repeat sales estimation. Mei and Moses (2002, 2005) also suggest that art does significantly better during wartime, using the example of four US wars this century. During these periods art appears to outperform stocks. This may also be due to the lack of liquidity during these periods and is a highly interesting point that requires further investigation.

There will always be spectacular success and failures in any market. The skill of investing is interpreting the available information, assessing whether the risk–return ratio indicates an acceptable opportunity to prosper, and deciding whether the investment is appropriate in the existing portfolio. Some artworks will never be a suitable investment. Clearly taste adds an additional, unquantifiable element of risk to art investment even after market analysis has been undertaken. Art as a direct investment presents a risky investment opportunity; however, as long as collectors purchase what they like, the aesthetic benefit derived may outweigh any financial benefit or detriment incurred.

When considering art as an indirect investment, where the non-pecuniary benefits are not obtained, then an investor would be more sensible to opt for an AIV or AMF where risk diversification through the securitization of artworks is more likely to result in greater financial returns.

Evidently fundamental problems exist with art databases and indices. However, both are becoming more sophisticated and accurate at providing objective information on what is a notoriously difficult asset to value. Comfort can be taken from the fact that the Standard & Poor's was recently overhauled to reflect a free-float weighting system. Therefore if well-established, traditional investment indices are still tweaking their assumptions, then art indices can be forgiven for refining their models over time.

Although the information provided by the databases and indices is not complete, it is the best market information that is currently available. The information provides us with a good indication of the general trends in the market. Market anomalies and inefficiencies may lead to much higher realized returns.

1.5 CONCLUSION

Faced with underperforming portfolios, investors are seeking increasingly sophisticated solutions to fulfil their financial objectives. Due to the significant diversification benefits arising from placing art in an investment portfolio, investors may consider it an attractive addition to their investment strategy. Similarly, those investors seeking to obtain a relative return from art may consider art funds an attractive strategy as empirical figures suggest that there is a moderate financial return to be made from art from a long-term investment. If art funds were to become more accessible to investors it is possible that a combination of AMFs and directly investing in art may yield optimal results. By using an AMF as the "core" investment vehicle for investing in art, investors gain the benefit of expertise, diversification and potentially lower investment requirements. At the same time, investors may employ direct art investments as "satellites" to their "core" investment in order to potentially increase returns.

It is important to acknowledge ABN Amro's attempt at developing a "fund of art funds" structure. Unfortunately this strategy was largely premature, with the number of available art funds insufficient to put together a fund of funds. However, as the financial community becomes increasingly aware of the investment characteristics of art it seems likely that a fund-of-funds structure may emerge in due course. Based upon similar incremental developments in the hedge fund and real-estate industries in the not so distant past, it is arguably only a matter of time before AMFs emerge.

NOTES

1. See Bogle (2005) for a comparison of the Mutual Fund industry today to 60 years hence.
2. In order to generate meaningful analysis, the discussion of "art" shall be limited to visual fine art: paintings, drawings and sculpture rather than the performing arts.
3. The Mutual Art Fund is a partnership of artists formed as an investment vehicle for their personal pensions.
4. See Campbell (2005).
5. See Rouwenhorst (2004) for an excellent introduction to the origins of mutual funds.
6. See *New Yorker* (2005).
7. See Goodwin (2006) for a global analysis of the art market for both investors and collectors.
8. Open-ended mutual funds are commonly known as Unit Trusts in the UK.
9. Closed ended funds are also referred to as Investment Trusts.
10. Frey and Eichenberger (1995).
11. O Chanel, Gerard-Varet and Ginsburgh (1996).
12. Data is only available until December 2002 on the All Art Index.
13. A similar survivorship bias is also apparent in other financial indices.
14. See Ashenfelter and Graddy (2003).

REFERENCES

Anderson, R.C. (1974) "Paintings as an Investment", *Economic Inquiry*, 12(1): 13–26.

Angnello and Pierce (1996) "Financial Returns, Price Determinants and Genre Effects in American Art Investment", *Journal of Cultural Economics*, 20(4): 359–83.

Ashenfelter, O. (1989) "How Auctions Work for Wine and Art", *Journal of Economic Perspectives*, 3(3): 23–36.

Ashenfelter, O. and Graddy, K. (2003) "Auctions and the Price of Art", *Journal of Economic Literature*, 41(3): 763–88.

Barre de la, M., Ducclo, S. and Ginsburgh, V. (1996) "Returns of Impressionist, Modern and Contemporary European Paintings 1962–1991", *Annales dÉconomie et de Statistique*, 35: 143–81.

Bauer, R., Molesnaar, R. Steenkamp, T. and Vrugt, E. (2004) "Dynamic Commodity Timing Strategies", LIFE Working Paper, no. 04–012.

Baumol, W.J. (1986) "Unnatural Value: Or Art Investment as Floating Crap Game?", *American Economic Review*, 76(2): 10–14.

Bogle, J.C. (2005) "The Mutual Fund Industry 60 Years Later: For Better or Worse?", *Financial Analysts Journal*, 61(1): 15–24.

Buelens, N. and Ginsburgh, V. (1993) "Revisiting Baumol's 'Art as Floating Crap Game'", *European Economic Review*, 37(7): 1351–71.

Campbell, R. (2005) "Art as an Alternative Asset Class", Working Paper, Maastricht University.

Candella, G. and Scorcu, A.E. (1997) "A Price Index for Art Market Auctions: An Application to the Italian Market of Modern and Contemporary Oil Paintings", *Journal of Cultural Economics*, 21: 175–96.

Chanel, O., Gerard-Varet, L.A. and Ginsburgh V. (1996) "The Relevance of Hedonic Price Indices", *Journal of Cultural Economics*, 20(1): 1–24.

Deutschman, A. (1991) "A Calculus of Collectibles", *Fortune*, 124(10): 115–20.

Fase, M.M.G. (1996) "Purchase of Art: Consumption and Investment", *De Economist*, 144(4): 649–69.

Frey, B.R. and Eichenberger, R. (1995) "On the Return of Art Investment Return Analyses", *Journal of Cultural Economics*, 19: 207–20.

Frey, B.S. and Pommerehne, W.W. (1989) *Art Investment: An Empirical Inquiry*, 396–409.

Frey, B.S. and Serna, A. (1990) "Der Preis der Kunst", *Kursbuch*, 99: 105–13.

Genesove, D. and Mayer, C. (2001) "Loss Aversion and Seller Behaviour: Evidence from the Housing Market", *Quarterly Journal of Economics*, 116(4): 1233–60.

Ginsburgh, V., Mei, J. and Moses, M. (2006) "On the Computation of Price Indices", in *Handbook of Economics, Art and Culture* (London: Elsevier).

Goetzmann, W.N. (1993) "Accounting for Taste: Art and the Financial Markets over Three Centuries", *American Economic Review*, 83 (December): 1370–76.

Goetzmann, W.N. (1996) "How Costly is the Fall from Fashion? Survivorship Bias in the Painting Market", in V. Ginsburg and P.-M. Menger (eds), *Economics of the Arts: Selected Essays* (Amsterdam: Elsevier).

Goodwin, J.D. (2005) *The Handbook of Personal Wealth Management* (London: Institute of Directors).

Grampp, W. (1989) *Pricing the Priceless – Art, Artists and Economics* (New York: Basic Books).

Keynes, J.M. (1947) *The General Theory of Employment, Interest and Money* (London: Macmillan, now Palgrave Macmillan).

Kochugovindan, S. (2005) *Barclays Capital Equity Gilt Study* (London: Barclays Bank).

Mei, J.E. and Moses, M. (2002) "Art as an Investment and the Underperformance of Masterpieces", *American Economic Review*, 92(1): 1656–68.

Mei, J. and Moses, M. (2005) "Vested Interest and Biased Price Estimates: Evidence from an Auction Market", *Journal of Finance*, 60(5): 2409–35.

Odean, T. (1998) "Are Investors Reluctant to Realise their Losses?", *Journal of Finance*, 53(5): 1775–98.

Pesando, J.E. (1993) "Art as an Investment: The Market for Modern Prints", *American Economic Review*, 83(5): 1075–89.

Pesando, J.E. and Shum, P. (1996) "Price Anomalies at Auction: Evidence from the Market for Modern Prints", in V. Ginsburgh and P.-M. Menger (eds), *Economics of the Arts: Selected Essays* (Amsterdam: Elsevier).

Rouwenhorst, K.G. (2004) "The Origins of Mutual Funds", Yale ICF Working Paper no. 04-48.

Stein, J.P (1977) "The Monetary Appreciation of Paintings", *Journal of Political Economy*, 85(5): 1021–35.

CHAPTER 2

Funds of Funds: Diversification, Selection or Expense Arbitrage?

*Clark L. Maxam, Seow Eng Ong and Craig Wisen**

2.1 INTRODUCTION

The bull market in the USA during the 1990s resulted in an unprecedented number of investors choosing to invest in equities and in equity mutual funds. As of 30 June 2005 the market value of the stocks held in mutual fund portfolios accounted for nearly 22 percent of total US stockmarket capitalization versus 5 percent at the close of 1985.[1] In response to this trend, and to other incentives, financial intermediaries acting as fund managers are increasingly offering mutual funds based on a basket of other mutual funds. Among companies offering these so-called funds of funds (FOFs) are Fidelity, Goldman Sachs, T. Rowe Price, Schwab and Vanguard.

The growth in the variety of mutual funds available to investors plays an important role in explaining the existence and growth of FOFs. Although the characteristics of individual FOFs account holders are not readily available to the research community, several FOF characteristics are worthy of note based upon cross-sectional comparisons of investment objectives, portfolio holdings, fees, and risk-adjusted returns between FOFs and their traditional counterparts.

The difficulties faced by the average investor in selecting an appropriate mix of mutual funds can be as daunting as the selection of an appropriate mix

* The authors would like to acknowledge invaluable comments from Robert Jennings, James Mehling, Martin Gruber and seminar participants at the European FMA.

of common stocks. At the close of 2004, there were approximately 11,000 equity mutual funds in the USA in comparison to approximately 7,000 companies listed on the American, NASDAQ and New York Stock Exchanges. FOFs are marketed either as providing superior fund selections (Willis, 1997) and market timing decisions (Hensley, 1996) or as simplifying the task of portfolio diversification with the option of buying one fund (Williamson, 1997). In some cases, a FOF may invest in more than 59 different mutual funds. FOFs may also advertise the ability to buy mutual funds that are not available to regular investors. This ability is due to a pre-existing position in a fund that is closed to new investors or due to economies of scale in the case of funds that have large minimum purchase requirements (for example, $500,000).

There are various styles of FOFs currently available in the market, for example passive buy-and-hold FOFs, active market-timing FOFs, stock-oriented or bond-oriented FOFs, and so forth. As of January 2000, the Morningstar Principia database of mutual funds listed 214 FOFs. Of the total, 181, or 85 percent, had inception dates ranging from 1996 to 1999. Although the emerging nature of FOF offerings makes this type of fund interesting, their short operating history confounds traditional statistical evaluation measures. As a result, this chapter uses several methods to calculate risk-adjusted returns of FOFs and analyses the holdings of their portfolios in order to best characterize and assess FOF performance. Though short time series make inferences difficult, we include histories as short as one year to provide a balance between methodological requirements for parameter estimation and the reduction in sample size associated with the paucity of FOFs having longer return histories.

It is widely recognized that a potential problem with FOFs is the likelihood that their multi-layered fees results in higher overall expense ratios. For instance, a management fee may be charged by the fund company that manages the FOFs in addition to the fees for the individual funds in the portfolio. In contrast, some FOFs (for example, T. Rowe Price, Wells Fargo, TIAA-CREF and Vanguard) invest solely in their own family's mutual funds and do not charge additional management fees for bundling their family's funds into a single security. The set of FOFs that re-package in-house funds have fees ranging from zero in many cases to a maximum of 2.19 percent in the case of the Merrill Strategic All-Equity Class B and C Shares. A second group of FOFs select their holdings from families unrelated to the FOF and pass on additional fees often ranging from 0.50 percent to 2.65 percent (PMFM Managed Portfolio Trust). In-house FOFs have an average annual expense ratio of 0.81 percent and a capitalization-weighted annual expense ratio of 0.16 percent, whereas FOFs that select outside funds have an average annual expense ratio of 1.32 percent and a capitalization-weighted expense ratio of 1.14 percent. The lion's share of the FOF market is represented by in-house FOFs; in 2004 they represented 98.3 percent of total FOF capitalization and generated 95.6 percent of total FOF fees. This study investigates whether FOFs as a group perform differently than their traditional counterparts from the perspective of standard performance methodologies, or from the perspective of a randomized selection of funds controlling for the FOF investment objective.

Another possible explanation for the growth of FOF offerings is the relaxation of government regulations. In October 1995, Congress passed the National Security Market Improvement Act that exempts funds investing in their own family from obtaining approval from the Securities Exchange Commission (SEC). In addition, the SEC has expanded the ability of firms to increase their investments in non-affiliated funds beyond the previous limit of 10 percent of fund assets.

Constantinides and Malliaris (1995), Grinblatt and Titman (1995) and Campbell *et al.* (1997) survey the major empirical studies on equity fund performance and asset allocation, but few studies to date have been published that specifically address the performance of funds that charge investors to select and manage other funds. A working paper by Capriles *et al.* (1995) presents an institutional fund of fund problem and reviews several mean-variance optimization techniques for systematically allocating to portfolios across funds. However, it does not assess the cross-sectional performance of FOFs. The purpose of this study is to analyse the risk-adjusted returns and expense characteristics of the subset of funds that are classified as a FOF by Morningstar, Inc. Benchmarks used to evaluate performance are limited to the extent they are representative of the restrictions imposed on the FOF. So we use a variety of benchmarks: simulated benchmarks consisting of randomly selected funds within an equally weighted portfolio, standard capitalization-weighted indices such as the S&P 500 index, and average mutual fund returns by investment objective. We examine the risk–return characteristics of FOFs, controlling for investment objective (Aggressive Growth, Asset Allocation, Balanced, Foreign Stock Growth-Income, Growth, Multi-asset Global, and World Stock) over 1, 3 and 5-year spans using returns net of expenses.[2] In addition, an analysis of the annual expenses across the major types of FOFs is documented and compared to their annual excess risk-adjusted return.

We find that, in general, the performance of FOFs is no better than their respective benchmarks, and when their risk-adjusted returns are statistically significant they are predominantly negative. Moreover, FOFs as mere collections of mutual funds are highly diversified and thus have a tendency to mirror performance in their appropriate index. This confirms previous findings that diversified funds have difficulty outperforming their benchmarks (Jensen, 1968; Grinblatt and Titman, 1989; Ippolito, 1989).

FOFs that select and manage funds external to the FOF's family do not perform well because they generally charge higher fees than the funds held in the FOF portfolio. Apparently managing funds is more costly than managing stocks. Fees are important as evidenced by the fact that FOFs tend to invest in funds with lower than average expense ratios, controlling for investment objective. Nevertheless, the total annual fees of FOFs that select funds from outside the FOF's family exceed fees on traditional mutual funds with similar objectives by an average of 0.97 percent per year suggesting that there may be a type of expense arbitrage employed by FOFs. In other words, they select low-expense funds and sell the bundle in the form of a higher expense FOF. However, while market timing and selectivity measures are statistically inconclusive due to data set constraints, it does appear that FOFs are providing some incremental benefit in that their net returns are no worse than their benchmarks, in essence offsetting their above average fees. Thus, it is possible that FOFs do exhibit some selection and/or timing ability. However, this incremental gain is not passed on to their investors, but rather it is absorbed in the form of higher than average management fees.

Section 2.2 presents additional background on FOFs, Section 2.3 details the data employed and section 2.4 outlines the empirical methodology and benchmarking techniques used. The empirical results are presented in section 2.5 and we conclude with section 2.6.

2.2 FOF BACKGROUND AND DATA

From an individual investor's perspective, a FOF purchase is executed like any other mutual fund trade. The typical investor in FOFs is likely to value the simplification of buying one fund, the selection or timing ability of the FOF manager, or the FOF's fund holdings that would otherwise be inaccessible (for example, closed funds or funds with high minimum purchase requirements). FOFs, like most other funds, use 12b-1 fees (annual fees the mutual fund charges to pay for its marketing, advertising and promotions) to compensate custodians for administering and advertising their funds, but it is unclear the extent to which FOFs collect 12b-1 fees on the funds they hold. Entities who primarily function as brokerage houses, such as Schwab, have also introduced FOFs as have the large mutual fund complexes such as Fidelity, Vanguard and T. Rowe Price.

Data is drawn from CRSP Survivorship Bias Free Mutual Fund database and annual editions of Morningstar's databases. There were 218 FOFs in existence during the three calendar years ending 1999. Of the 218, 82 were excluded due to multiple share classes issued on the same portfolio. Of the remaining 136 FOFs, 39 were terminated prior to the year ending 2004. In the event of fund termination and mergers, the returns of the acquiring fund are used through the end of the analysis. Although small in proportion to the number of all funds, FOFs represents a rapidly growing segment of the mutual fund industry. Approximately 55 percent of all FOFs were established within the last three years, whereas 26 percent of traditional mutual funds were established with the last three years. Figures 2.1 and 2.2 provide histograms of the ages of FOFs and traditional funds at the end of the FOF formation period.

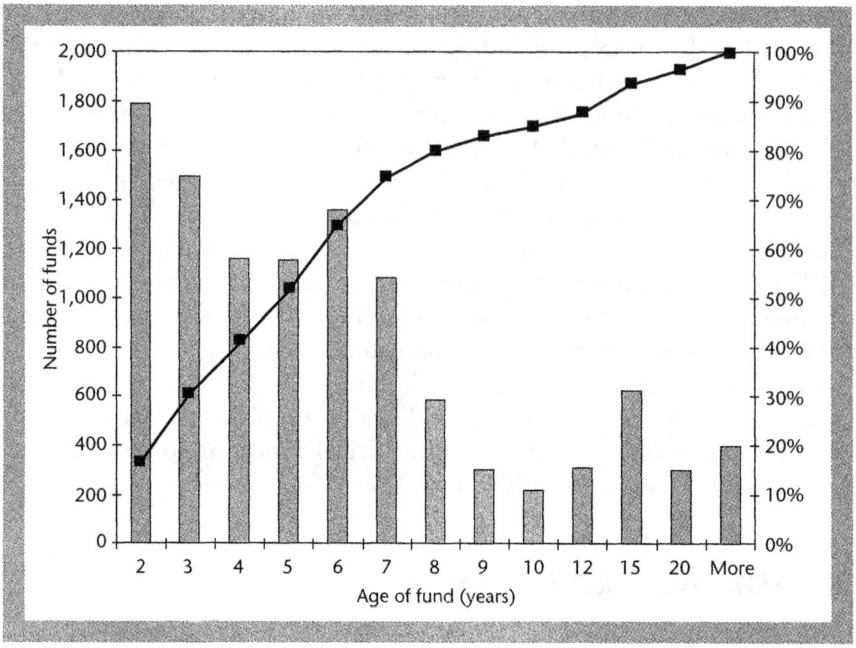

Figure 2.1 Histogram of mutual fund ages excluding FOFs (fund ages are represented by the number of years between the fund inception date and 31 December 1999)

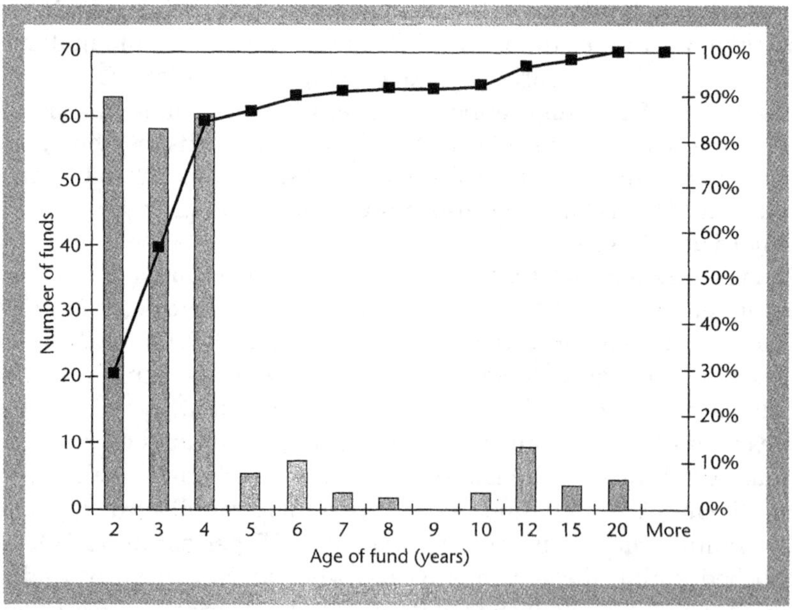

Figure 2.2 Histogram of funds of funds (FOFs) ages (fund ages are represented by the number of years between the fund inception date and 31 December 1999)

Table 2.1 Summary statistics

	Fund of Funds (FOFs)		Mutual Funds excluding FOFs	
Market value (billions)	171		5,709	
Number of funds	1,017		16,394	
Number of distinct portfolios	346		5,958	
Number of funds with inception dates between 1997–99	215		3,626	
Number of distinct portfolios with inception data between 1997–99	73		1,138	
	Average	**Median**	**Average**	**Median**
Size (millions)	185	19	348	40.4
Number of portfolio positions	13	12	163.9	84.0
Percentage of portfolio allocated to largest 10 positions	92	96	36.0	31.7
Portfolio turnover (percent)	30	16	94.0	65.0
5-year percentile rank within investment objective (1 = max)	49	42	51	52
5-year percentile rank within Morningstar category (1 = max)	43	39	50	51
Morningstar star rating	3.2	3.0	2.9	3.0
Age as of 31 Dec. 2004 (years)	3.3	2.4	4.5	2.8

Notes: Data is from CRSP Mutual Fund and Morningstar Principia Plus databases. The number of distinct portfolios figure excludes multiple share classes representing identical portfolios of the same underlying fund. Portfolio statistics were drawn from the most recent semi-annual reporting date as of 31 December 2004.

Table 2.1 presents summary statistics for the FOFs as of 31 December 2004. Appendix A identifies the FOFs and their respective portfolio values as of 31 December 1999 and their 3- and 5-year percentile rank by peer-based objective. As of 31 December 1999 the average FOF size was $197.1 million and the median size was $30.3 million, whereas as of 31 December 2004 the average FOF size was $184.6 and median size was $19.3 million. The distribution of FOF sizes based upon the net asset value of the portfolio is skewed by the large holding sizes of the Fidelity, T. Rowe Price and the Vanguard families of funds. Excluding these three fund families from the FOFs set decreases the average FOF size to $55 million.

A histogram of the ranked market shares of FOFs and mutual funds is provided in Table 2.2. The two largest FOFs (approximately 1% of the total number of FOFs) manage 26.3 percent of total ($43 billion) FOF assets. This

Table 2.2 Concentration of mutual fund assets

Cumulative percent of population of funds		FOFs				Mutual funds excluding FOFs			
From	To	Funds in bin	Cumulative percent of assets managed	Average fund portfolio value (millions)	Average annual expense ratio	Funds in bin	Cumulative percent of assets managed	Average fund portfolio value (millions)	Average annual expense ratio
	0.01	2	0.2627	5,678.65	0.00	56	0.4001	23,942.22	0.80
0.01	0.05	8	0.6372	2,024.06	0.14	224	0.6865	4,284.11	0.96
0.05	0.10	11	0.7562	467.92	0.49	280	0.8041	1,406.86	1.12
0.10	0.15	11	0.8197	249.84	0.75	280	0.8648	726.80	1.15
0.15	0.20	10	0.8609	178.06	0.61	280	0.9033	459.96	1.24
0.20	0.25	11	0.8928	125.20	0.51	280	0.9293	311.88	1.24
0.25	0.33	17	0.9312	97.75	0.73	448	0.9559	198.47	1.26

0.33	0.50	37	0.9755	51.77	0.82	952	0.9844	100.34	1.38
0.67	0.67	36	0.9941	22.29	1.11	952	0.9956	39.45	1.55
0.67	0.75	17	0.9979	9.64	1.12	448	0.9979	17.70	1.67
0.75	0.80	11	0.9990	4.38	0.52	280	0.9989	11.04	1.71
0.80	0.85	10	0.9994	1.97	0.53	280	0.9995	7.26	1.76
0.85	0.90	11	0.9998	1.40	0.47	280	0.9998	4.12	1.73
0.90	0.95	11	1.0000	0.68	1.08	280	1.0000	1.86	1.83
0.95	0.99	8	1.0000	0.20	0.87	224	1.0000	0.50	2.03
0.99	1.00	3	1.0000	0.00	0.47	56	1.0000	0.03	1.30
Total		214				5,600			

Notes: Cumulative percent of population of funds and cumulative percent of assets managed is based on a descending rank of individual fund portfolio values. Average fund portfolio value and average annual expense ratio are calculated as a simple average of funds within each row. Data is for FOFs and mutual funds (excluding FOFs) as of 31 Dec. 1999 that operate with the following investment objectives: Aggressive Growth, Asset Allocation, Balanced, Corp. Bond–General, Equity Income, Foreign Stock, Growth, Growth and Income, Multi-Asset Global, Multi-Sector Bond, Small Company, and World Stock. Total assets of 214 FOFs amounted to $43.2 billion. Total assets of 5,600 mutual funds amounted to $3.406 trillion. Mutual funds excluded from this table consist of 661 funds ($54.965 billion) that did provide annual expense ratios or fund portfolio values. Average annual expense ratio does not include front end or deferred loads.

Table 2.3 Number of fund of funds by investment objective

Prospectus objective	FOFs with inception dates 12/31/96 to 12/31/99		FOFs with inception		Mutual funds excluding FOFs dates prior to 12/31/04		
	Number	Percent	Number	Percent	Number	Percent	Percent excluding all other
Aggressive growth	8	0.037	39	0.038	291	0.018	0.028
Asset allocation	49	0.229	288	0.283	392	0.024	0.037
Balanced	31	0.145	124	0.122	470	0.029	0.045
Corp. bond-general	19	0.089	24	0.024	811	0.049	0.077
Equity income	1	0.005	10	0.010	310	0.019	0.030
Foreign stock	13	0.061	9	0.009	942	0.057	0.090
Growth	50	0.234	255	0.251	4,208	0.256	0.401
Growth and income	25	0.117	196	0.193	1,264	0.077	0.120
Multi-asset global	5	0.023	6	0.006	77	0.005	0.007
Multi-sector bond	2	0.009	4	0.004	198	0.012	0.019
Small company	5	0.023	9	0.009	1,160	0.071	0.111
World stock	6	0.028	17	0.017	367	0.022	0.035
All other*			36	0.035	5,943	0.362	
Total	214	1.000	1,017	1.000	16,433	1.000	1.000

Note: The number of funds includes multiple share classes issued by the funds company on the same underlying portfolio of funds.
* This category includes prospectus objectives such as municipal bond income, government-bond income, sector and index objectives.

Table 2.4 Fund of funds capitalization by investment objective

Prospectus objective	All FOFs inception dates prior to 12/31/99		FOFs with inception dates prior to 12/31/96		Mutual funds		
	Size (millions)	Percent	Size (millions)	Percent	Size (millions)	Percent	Percent excluding all other
Aggressive growth	362	0.008	224	0.006	140,200	0.033	0.041
Asset allocation	16,733	0.387	16,217	0.406	68,570	0.016	0.020
Balanced	11,379	0.263	10,832	0.271	178,754	0.042	0.052
Corp. bond-general	336	0.008	297	0.007	172,101	0.040	0.051
Equity income	1	0.000	1	0.000	125,498	0.029	0.037
Foreign stock	2,862	0.066	2,700	0.068	223,508	0.052	0.066
Growth	6,758	0.156	5,966	0.150	1,183,434	0.275	0.347
Growth and income	1,462	0.034	937	0.023	903,334	0.210	0.265
Multi-asset global	258	0.006	26	0.001	40,175	0.009	0.012
Multi-sector bond	2,597	0.060	2,597	0.065	27,101	0.006	0.008
Small company	301	0.007	2	0.000	172,948	0.040	0.051
World stock	190	0.004	102	0.003	170,123	0.040	0.050
All other*	0	0.000	0	0.000	894,818	0.208	
Total	43,239	1.000	39,898	1.000	4,300,562	1.000	1.000

Notes: Allocation of FOFs and mutual fund (excluding FOFs) capitalization by investment objective. Capitalization (shares outstanding times NAV) is the total portfolio value based on shares outstanding as of 31 December 1999.

* This category includes prospectus objectives such as municipal bond income, government-bond income, sector and index objectives.

compares to the 56 largest mutual funds (1% of their total number) that manage 40.0 percent of the total ($3.4 trillion) assets of 5,600 mutual funds. Mutual funds with dissimilar investment objectives as FOFs have been excluded from this analysis.

Large fund families who offer a FOF product are more likely to place an additional constraint of their FOF's selections. Namely, they select only from their own family of funds. A FOF portfolio that is solely comprised of "in-house" mutual funds is labelled an "inside" FOF. Inside FOFs are often marketed as allowing investors to meet the minimum purchase requirements (for example, $3,000 for most Vanguard funds) while providing the diversification benefits of owning multiple funds with diverse investment objectives. Inside FOFs run by families offering loaded funds such as Goldman Sachs and Smith Barney usually discount load charges on purchases in excess of several hundred thousand dollars. FOFs allow one to consolidate purchases of many funds into a larger initial purchase of one fund thereby gaining access to discounted load charges in this type of fund family.

The number of mutual funds held by FOFs varies substantially, from a minimum of two funds in the case of the Barr Rosenberg Double Alpha Fund to a maximum of 59 in the case of the American Pension Investors Growth Fund. The average and median number of funds held by FOFs was 11.5 and 9.0 respectively. The average and median value of the ten largest positions held by FOFs as a percentage of the FOF total value was 92.0 percent and 98.8 percent respectively. The average age for a FOF is only 3.6 years while the median age is 3.0 years. As a group, these FOFs are an emerging financial product with very limited performance histories. It should not be surprising then that there is little in the way of previous empirical work on FOFs. However, there is a highly developed literature on mutual fund performance. In the interest of brevity, we refer readers to the excellent articles by Carhart (1997), Malkiel (1995) and Grinblatt and Titman (1992).

Tables 2.3 and 2.4 provide details on the relative market share of FOFs as well as the breakdown of FOFs by investment objective. As noted above, FOFs represent a small, but fast growing segment of the overall mutual fund industry. FOFs investment objectives are most heavily concentrated in the Asset Allocation and Balanced categories. Recently created FOFs maintain concentrations in these categories and have added to FOF presence in the Growth category.

2.3 THE DATA

Morningstar's Principia database releases for the years 1997 to 2000 were evaluated for FOF coverage initiations and terminations. During this time span, 66 FOFs were covered prior to the database's 1997 release, two FOFs were dropped by the service, eight FOFs were merged into new FOFs and coverage on 142 FOFs was initiated. Information on the two FOFs dropped by the service was acquired directly from the funds and is included in the current analysis. The eight FOFs that merged during the 1997–2000 time-span were associated with the acquisition of the Qualivest family of funds by First American Investment family. The oldest FOFs covered by Morningstar, Fund Manager Aggressive Growth, Fund Manager Bond and Fund Manager Growth, had inception dates of 1984. Based on Morningstar's data, no FOFs ceased operations over the sample period other than the Qualivest funds. Brown, Goetzmann, Ibbotson and Ross (1992) argue that survivorship bias can be serious in mutual fund performance studies since its presence may falsely indicate a persistency in the predictability of excess returns. It is unlikely that survivorship bias is a problem in our study since the death rate and performance of terminated FOFs is likely to be similar to the death rate and performance of traditional mutual funds. With the exception of a few FOFs created in the early 1960s, no FOFs have been liquidated. Other exclusions to the database's coverage include funds whose net assets are below the standard requirements for electronic distribution (for example, micro mutual funds).

The structure and function of a FOF exists in many alternative forms; consultants who charge annual fees to select money managers, hedge funds, limited partnerships, and so on. Unique to FOFs using open-ended investment companies is the availability and accessibility of information required for standard performance methodologies. While mutual funds represent only one type of financial intermediary generating public performance records, the information provided by mutual funds is broader in most cases, and is less subject to biases found in un-audited or selectively aggregated track records of other investments managed by financial advisors.

FOF returns are computed monthly based on the change in monthly net asset value (NAV) and assumes all income and capital-gains distributions are reinvested. Reinvestments are made on the reinvestment date using the NAV on this date. The illustrations above indicate the impact of restrictions related to fund ages (three years) and multiple share classes on the population of FOFs. FOFs possessing less than 36 months of returns are excluded from Jensen's estimation requirements of metrics generated by ordinary least squares. Many funds have several classes of shares, for example, Class A, B, C, D. Each share class represents an alternative fee structure applied to sub-accounts of a portfolio with identical position weights. Class A and B shares typically have respectively front-end and back-end load fee structures whereas Class C and D shares typically have respectively higher annual fees and higher initial purchase requirements. In order to avoid double counting FOFs with multiple share classes we use a single share class for performance evaluation. In sum, we required three years of returns and excluded multiple share classes. The three-year return requirement reduces the FOFs set from 214 funds to 114 funds. The exclusion of the multiple share classes reduces the 114 FOFs to 73 remaining FOFs. Appendix B identifies the 73 FOFs on which performance analysis is applied, their prospectus objective, and whether the FOF is restricted to "in-house" fund family selections.

2.3.1 Performance evaluation

To evaluate the performance of these FOFs, we employ common performance measures, such as the Sharpe Ratio (SR) and Treynor Ratio (TR).[3] Since FOFs are, by definition, mutual funds who manage a portfolio of mutual funds, these two measures are appropriate for FOF performance evaluation.

In addition, Jensen's alpha for each of the FOFs is computed. The estimated value of alpha has been used to ascertain whether a fund outperforms or underperforms an appropriate benchmark. To compute a fund's Jensen alpha, the intercept of the regression below is estimated using ordinary least squares:

$$R_{it} - R_{ft} = \alpha_i^{OLS} + \beta_i(R_{mt} - R_{ft}) + \varepsilon_{it}$$

where R_{it} = FOF return, R_{ft} = risk-free rate and R_{mt} = benchmark return. A significantly positive (negative) value of alpha indicates that the FOF outperforms (underperforms) a buy-and-hold strategy in the index (of equivalent risk within the confines of the CAPM model; Sharpe, Lintner, Black, etc.). The estimated alpha is computed based on the 1, 3 and 5-year investment horizons. We also compare FOFs alphas with non-FOF alphas.

Fama (1972) suggests that the fund performance should be subdivided into two parts: selectivity skills and timing skills. Jensen (1968) demonstrates that the presence of market timing ability will bias the estimated risk exposure of funds and the fund's estimated alpha. Timing skill is the ability to adjust the proportional mix of a fund's assets thereby enhancing its risk/return profile. Thus, comparisons between the performance of active and passive fund managers can be misleading if market timing is not taken into consideration.

Treynor-Mazuy (1986) and Henriksson-Merton (1981) proposed modified measures of performance that incorporate market timing ability. The Treynor-Mazuy performance index is estimated via the following regression:

$$R_{it} - R_{ft} = \alpha_i^{TM} + \beta_i(R_{mt} - R_{ft}) + \delta_i(R_{mt} - R_{ft})^2 + \varepsilon_{it}$$

A significantly positive estimated value of δ_i indicates that the manager possesses timing skill while a significantly positive value of alpha indicates selectivity skill. Henriksson-Merton (1981) proposed an alternative measure of the fund manager's performance. To compute this measure, the following regression was estimated:

$$R_{it} - R_{ft} = \alpha_i^{HM} + \beta_i \max|0, \{R_{mt} - R_{ft}\}| + \delta_i \min|0, \{R_{mt} - R_{ft}\}| + \varepsilon_{it}$$

The null hypothesis is that β_i equals δ_i against the alternative hypothesis that β_i is greater than δ_i. The intuition is that β_i measures the fund's return sensitivity during up markets while δ_i represents the fund's return sensitivity during down markets. A larger value of β_i relative to δ_i suggests the manager's superior ability to time the fund's portfolio adjustment properly. Once again, a significantly positive alpha indicates superior selectivity skills. In addition to evaluating FOF performance using these measures, we compare the cumulative performance of FOFs relative to non-FOF by investment objective. Since most FOFs impose an additional management fee relative to non FOFs, this analysis provides evidence on the incremental benefit to investors in FOFs.

Note that although more recent mutual fund performance work indicates potential benefits from multi-index methodologies,[4] our short dataset already begs the issue of statistical significance which the introduction of further factors will only exacerbate. Further, with only 66 funds in our sample, implementation of multi-factor models would require further sample sub-division which, again, would lead to even greater problems with inference.

2.3.2 Benchmarking

It is well-documented that effective performance evaluation of mutual fund managers depends crucially on the selection of the appropriate comparative benchmark (Lehman and Modest, 1987; Kothari and Warner, 1998). The current literature frequently relies on indices such as the S&P 500 index as both a market proxy and as a benchmark index. Our study uses this benchmark, and several others to provide robustness. The three additional benchmarks are: Morningstar Inc. "Best-fit" index for each fund; a simulated benchmark consisting of equally weighted, randomly selected portfolios of mutual funds from which the FOF can choose; and the overall average mutual fund performance for each investment objective. These are each discussed below:

Best-fit Benchmark. Morningstar identifies an index that best fits the mutual fund monthly returns over a 3-year horizon (ending December 1999). The best-fit benchmark is defined as the index that results in the highest R-squared value from a single factor market model during the period of 1997 through 1999. The list of these best-fit benchmarks evaluated for FOFs over the 3-year horizon is obtained from Morningstar. This analysis implicitly assumes the best-fit benchmark does not change over time and is the same for all funds within the same investment objective.[5]

Simulated Benchmarks. Since proper benchmarking is crucial to fund performance analysis, we also construct simulated benchmarks for each investment objective category. This is accomplished by taking a random sample of 10 funds[6] from the universe of funds from which the fund can choose and computing the equally weighted average monthly return for the sample. This random sampling is repeated 500 times to obtain an overall simulated average monthly return for each of the investment objective categories (Aggressive Growth, Asset Allocation, Balanced, Growth, Growth and Income, Foreign Stock, Multi-Asset Global and World Stock). This benchmarking method provides a basis for evaluating the selection skills of managers relative to the naïve selection skills generated by a random selection of funds. Since both the T. Rowe Price and Vanguard FOFs are "in-house" FOFs which (since October 1995) have been permitted to invest only in funds from within their group, two separate benchmarks for these funds were constructed using the above methods, but limiting the universe from which the sample was drawn to their respective fund families (excluding Money Funds). Prior to the change in SEC legislation, FOFs were restricted to a maximum allocation of 10 percent to funds within their own group. As a result, we use the overall category benchmark for dates prior to October 1995 and the "family restricted" benchmark for dates after October 1995 for these two funds.

Category Average Benchmark. For each FOF, we also compute an average monthly return for all mutual funds with the same investment objective. This is a very broadbased benchmark for comparison that, again, addresses the selectivity skills of the FOF manager. Obviously, if the FOF cannot better the performance of the average fund in its given objective, the FOF manager is not providing much incremental benefit.

2.4 EMPIRICAL RESULTS

2.4.1 Overall FOF performance

Table 2.5 presents the 5, 3 and 1-year returns for periods ending 31 December 1999 of FOFs in comparison to the performance of mutual funds while controlling for investment objective. FOFs show a tendency to under-perform their respective investment objective average returns with an average annual deficit of 1.0 percent, 1.7 percent and 3.1 percent for the 5, 3 and 1-year investment horizons respectively. Moreover, note that the categories with the most FOFs – equity and equity based mix funds – exhibit a tendency to underperform more consistently and by wider margins than FOFs with fixed income or international orientations. The Asset Allocation and World Stock investment objectives were the two categories in which FOF returns exceeded the returns of mutual funds during these three periods.

2.4.2 FOF performance: Sharpe ratios

The above analysis ignores differences in risk within investment objectives. In order to better address the relative performance of FOF managers versus their non-FOF counterparts, annualized Sharpe ratios by investment objective for the three investment horizons against non-FOF ratios are calculated in Table 2.6. Table 2.6 highlights several interesting characteristics. First, the

Table 2.5 Annual returns by investment objective

Instrument objective	Panel A: 5 years ending 12/31/99					Panel B: 3 years ending 12/31/99					Panel C: 1 year ending 12/31/99				
	Sample size		Returns					Returns			Size		Returns		
	FOFs	Mutual funds	FOFs (A)	Mutual funds (B)	(A)−(B)	FOFs	Mutual funds	FOFs (C)	Mutual funds (D)	(C)−(D)	FOFs	Mutual funds	FOFs (E)	Mutual funds (F)	(E)−(F)
Aggressive growth	1	75	0.197	0.259	−0.062	3	123	0.225	0.288	−0.064	8	148	0.276	0.619	−0.343
Asset allocation	8	114	0.165	0.156	0.009	40	181	0.150	0.132	0.018	48	234	0.165	0.079	0.086
Balanced	5	240	0.136	0.158	−0.022	19	330	0.125	0.132	−0.007	31	415	0.117	0.083	0.035
Corporate bond-general	1	297	0.058	0.068	−0.010	8	406	0.056	0.048	0.009	14	562	0.025	−0.007	0.032
Equity income	0	122		0.178		1	171	0.080	0.137	−0.057	1	227	0.054	0.053	0.000
Foreign stock	0	271		0.142		4	461	0.131	0.179	−0.048	13	683	0.452	0.457	−0.005
Growth	5	660	0.196	0.245	−0.049	24	1,097	0.188	0.243	−0.056	50	1,812	0.219	0.301	−0.083
Growth and income	3	400	0.195	0.221	−0.025	10	590	0.164	0.190	−0.026	25	786	0.146	0.137	0.010
Multi-asset global	2	57	0.158	0.123	0.034	3	83	0.126	0.107	0.019	5	97	0.172	0.204	−0.032

Continued

Table 2.5 Continued

Instrument objective	Panel A: 5 years ending 12/31/99					Panel B: 3 years ending 12/31/99					Panel C: 1 year ending 12/31/99				
	Sample size		Returns					Returns			Size		Returns		
	FOFs	Mutual funds	FOFs (A)	Mutual funds (B)	(A)−(B)	FOFs	Mutual funds	FOFs (C)	Mutual funds (D)	(C)−(D)	FOFs	Mutual funds	FOFs (E)	Mutual funds (F)	(E)−(F)
Multi-sector bond	2	69	0.080	0.074	0.006	2	103	0.053	0.040	0.012	2	133	0.016	0.026	−0.010
Small company	0	288		0.191		1	476	0.124	0.172	−0.048	5	705	0.264	0.361	−0.097
World stock	2	134	0.215	0.186	0.029	2	215	0.242	0.201	0.042	6	297	0.421	0.385	0.036
Average					−0.010					−0.017					−0.031
Index: MSCI AC World			0.168					0.191					0.255		
Index: Russell 2000			0.167					0.131					0.213		
Index: S&P 500			0.285					0.276					0.210		
Index: Wilshire 4500			0.236					0.226					0.349		

Notes: Average buy and hold annualized returns for periods ending 31 December 1999. Returns are net of annual fees but do not include front-end or back-end loads. Mutual fund column excludes FOFs.

Table 2.6 Sharpe Ratios by Investment Objective

Investment objective	Panel A: 5 years ending 12/31/99					Panel B: 3 years ending 12/31/99					Panel C: 1 year ending 12/31/99				
	Sample size		Sharpe ratio					Sharpe ratio			Size		Sharpe ratio		
	FOFs	Mutual funds	FOFs (A)	Mutual funds (B)	(A)−(B)	FOFs	Mutual funds	FOFs (C)	Mutual funds (D)	(C)−(D)	FOFs	Mutual funds	FOFs (E)	Mutual funds (F)	(E)−(F)
Aggressive growth	1	75	1.947	2.119	−0.172	3	123	1.534	1.584	−0.050	8	148	1.362	1.858	−0.496
Asset allocation	8	114	2.706	2.368	0.338	40	181	1.563	1.265	0.298	48	234	0.942	0.276	0.666
Balanced	5	240	2.580	2.443	0.137	19	330	1.401	1.278	0.123	31	415	0.775	0.292	0.483
Corporate bond-general	1	297	0.350	1.039	−0.688	8	406	0.183	−0.058	0.241	14	562	−0.680	−1.932	1.252
Equity income	0	122		2.278		1	171	1.052	1.097	−0.045	1	227	0.157	0.056	0.101
Foreign stock	0	271		1.383		4	461	0.799	1.225	−0.426	13	683	2.267	1.865	0.403
Growth	5	660	2.204	2.460	−0.255	24	1,097	1.501	1.605	−0.104	50	1,812	1.282	1.103	0.179
Growth and income	3	400	2.691	2.596	0.095	10	590	1.560	1.454	0.107	25	786	0.962	0.603	0.359

Continued

Table 2.6 Continued

Investment objective	Panel A: 5 years ending 12/31/99					Panel B: 3 years ending 12/31/99					Panel C: 1 year ending 12/31/99				
	Sample size		Sharpe ratio					Sharpe ratio			Size		Sharpe ratio		
	FOFs	Mutual funds	FOFs (A)	Mutual funds (B)	(A)−(B)	FOFs	Mutual funds	FOFs (C)	Mutual funds (D)	(C)−(D)	FOFs	Mutual funds	FOFs (E)	Mutual funds (F)	(E)−(F)
Multi-asset global	2	57	2.055	1.672	0.383	3	83	1.017	0.850	0.168	5	97	1.069	0.807	0.261
Multi-sector bond	2	69	1.645	1.009	0.636	2	103	0.019	−0.301	0.321	2	133	−0.989	−0.732	−0.257
Small company	0	288		1.600		1	476	0.787	0.913	−0.126	5	705	1.218	0.971	0.247
World stock	2	134	2.661	1.926	0.734	2	215	2.092	1.408	0.684	6	297	1.979	1.575	0.404
Average					0.134					0.099					0.300
Total	29	2,727				117	4,236				208	6,099			
Russell 2000			1.519					0.807					0.908		
S&P 500			3.431					2.205					1.219		
Wilshire 4500			2.287					1.488					1.489		

Notes: Average of annualized Sharpe ratios of monthly returns of FOFs and mutual funds (excluding FOFs) by investment objective

$$\text{Sharpe ratio of } i\text{th } fund = SR_i = \frac{1/T \sum_{t=1}^{T} (R_{it} - R_{ft})}{\sigma_{R_{it}-R_{tf}}}$$

average FOF performance relative to mutual funds improves when using Sharpe ratios rather than annualized returns except for FOFs operating in the aggressive growth investment objective. Since the returns (Table 2.5) indicated average FOF underperformance and the Sharpe ratios (Table 2.6) indicated average FOF out-performance it appears that the risk measured by standard deviation of monthly returns is less for FOFs than it is for traditional mutual funds operating in the same investment objective. There is a general tendency for FOF performance to drop as the time horizon lengthens from one to three years suggesting that the newer FOFs included in the one year horizon might performer better than older FOFs (those with inception years prior to 31 December 1996.

2.5.2 FOF performance: Jensen's alpha

Jensen's alpha is computed using ordinary least-squares estimation.[7] Monthly returns are net of managerial expenses. Table 2.7 shows the Jensen's alpha summary statistics for all FOFs and various benchmarks over the 3 and 5-year investment horizons. In general, average alpha tends to be negative. Moreover, there is a clear pattern for negative alphas using the S&P 500 benchmark regardless of the investment horizon. Not surprisingly, none of the alphas are significant using even generous confidence levels and non-parametric sign tests also confirm this lack of significance. Insignificant results undoubtedly stem from the short time series available for most FOFs (for example, the small number of FOFs with track records longer than 1 year). However, more negative alphas are observed than positive alphas. In fact, the distribution of alphas is substantially negatively skewed. The average proportion of negative alphas across all measures is 62.5 percent. The above results suggest that although FOFs do not significantly underperform or outperform their benchmarks, there is a tendency for FOFs to underperform. Moreover, few would argue that this underperformance is not economically significant despite its failure to pass standard statistical significance tests.

Since the majority of FOFs are constrained to invest only in their investment objective, use of the S&P 500 and best-fit index benchmarks may induce varying degrees of misspecification. As a result, we use the average return of funds with like objectives benchmark and a simulated benchmark to evaluate the sensitivity of the results to a change in benchmarks. Recall that the simulated benchmark samples by investment objective from the universe of mutual funds available. Although there is no clear pattern of the superior or inferior performance using the average category benchmark, FOFs display positive alphas versus the simulated benchmark across all horizons. Thus, FOFs may exhibit some selection capability relative to a random selection, but this capability is neither consistent across benchmarks nor significant.[8]

Another interesting observation is that FOFs appear to exhibit much lower systematic risk components relative to their respective benchmarks.

Table 2.7 FOF Mean Jensen's alpha with different benchmarks and investment horizons

	α	t(α)	β	Percent with negative α	Median α	Number of FOFs
5 year						
S&P500	−.05984	.3882	.6536	60	−.0462	15
best-fit	−.03419	.2130	.6525	60	−.0282	15
Average	−.02288	.1882	.8537	47	.0045	15
simulated	.03557	.1652	.8504	47	.0024	15
3 year						
S&P500	−.16858	.6969	.6453	82*	−.1683	17
best-fit	−.04882	.2134	.6525	71	−.1394	17
Average	.04197	.1974	.8318	53	−.0125	17
simulated	.07689	.3016	.8369	53	−.0015	17
1 year						
S&P500	−.14517	.2944	.6171	66	−.2274	29
best-fit	.07277	.1685	.6341	47	.0175	17
Average	.00195	.0044	.8816	82*	.0119	17
Simulated	.04813	.1005	.8572	82*	.0176	17

Notes: Corrected for heteroscedasticity using White's consistent estimators. We need standard errors of the alphas and betas displayed here, ideally with Newey–West corrections. Let's remove the 1-year measures.

* significant at 5% level.

The average beta for the FOFs above *vis-à-vis* the S&P 500 is 0.63, but varies depending on the benchmark. There are very few FOFs with beta greater than 1. This may be evidence of significant cash holdings, asset mixes that do not fit the specified objective (for example, international stocks in a growth fund), or perhaps measurement or specification problems.[9]

Table 2.8 presents FOF performance based on Jensen's measure. Several FOFs perform worse while none exhibits superior performance when S&P500 is used as the benchmark. The result is less pronounced with the best-fit benchmark. There is only one FOF exhibiting underperformance while one fund also indicates superior performance relative to the best-fit benchmark. However, regardless of the benchmark, the majority of FOFs still do not exhibit significantly superior or inferior performance perhaps because of low power due to small samples.

There are, however, two FOFs that consistently outperform both the Category Average and Simulated benchmarks: the Vanguard STAR and T-Rowe Price Spectrum Growth funds. However, as noted earlier, both

Table 2.8 Sharpe ratios by investment objective of distinct portfolios

Investment objective	Panel A: FOFs that select funds from *outside* their fund family				Panel B: FOFs that select funds from *inside* their fund family				Panel C: Mutual funds excluding FOFs			
	Sample size		Sharpe ratio		Sample size		Sharpe ratio		Sample size		Sharpe ratio	
	No. of funds	Assets (millions)	Simple average	Size wt. average	No. of funds	Assets (millions)	Simple average	Size wt. average	No. of funds	Assets (millions)	Simple average	Size wt. average
Asset allocation	9	621	1.688	1.672	19	15,206	1.670	1.928	105	56,862	2.171	2.235
Balanced	3	112	1.407	1.635	8	9,549	1.394	1.380	176	146,927	1.351	1.373
Growth	4	173	1.506	1.479	8	3,348	1.484	1.410	629	938,977	1.615	2.062

Notes: Annualized Sharpe ratios are for the three years ending 31 December 1999. Simple averages and size-weighted Sharpe ratios of the distinct FOF and mutual fund portfolios for asset allocation, balanced, and growth investment objectives. Investment objectives with fewer than three FOFs that select from either inside or outside their own fund family have been excluded. Distinct portfolios exclude multiple share classes on the same underlying portfolio. Size-weighted averages are based upon the size of each portfolio as of 31 December 1999.

$$\text{Sharpe ratio of } i\text{th fund} = SR_i = \frac{\frac{1}{T}\sum_{t=1}^{T}(R_{it} - R_{ft})}{\sigma_{R_{it}-R_{tf}}}$$

FOFs are restricted to invest only in their respective family and do not charge a separate fee for bundling their family's funds. The earlier simulated benchmark and the category benchmark are inappropriate since they use the universe of existing mutual funds. To account for this potential misspecification, simulated benchmarks and average benchmarks are constructed for these two funds taking into account the restricted set of securities they are allowed to invest in. After re-calibrating the above analysis, we found that the significant alphas for both FOFs disappear.

As a result of this evidence, we derive the same conclusion as the earlier analysis: FOFs, at most, will fare equally well as the market or appropriate benchmarks. Some investors may prefer FOFs to traditional funds due to relatively low FOF betas and standard deviation of returns controlling for investment objective, however these characteristics do not translate into higher risk adjusted returns using traditional metrics such as Jensen alpha.

2.4.4 FOF timing skills

Table 2.9 presents the results of the Treynor and Mazuy (T&M) and Henrikkson and Merton (H&M) market timing performance models using both the S&P500 and the Morningstar Best Fit benchmark market indices. In addition, we report the results of a standard OLS regression of excess returns on market returns (Jensen's alpha approach) for completeness. The summary of timing skill performance parameters for FOFs are reported in Appendix C.

Once again, it is apparent that majority of FOFs neither outperform nor underperform the benchmarks. Regardless of the evaluation model employed, more than 80 percent of FOFs achieve insignificant alpha estimates. However, Table 2.10 clearly shows that the ratio of significant underperformance to significant overperformance is nearly 7 to 1 (a total of 6 FOFs exhibit significant outperformance vs. a total of 40 FOFs with significant underperformance).

These results suggest the possibility that FOFs may be redundant securities. In other words, existing mutual funds already reap diversification benefits from investing in multiple, imperfectly correlated securities and as a consequence some FOFs may be overdiversified. Our results suggest that on average any additional diversification benefit derived from a FOF is exceeded by the incremental expense fees associated with the FOF. Hence, investors seeking diversification should select mutual funds according to their risk preferences. If the goal truly is further diversification, investors are better advised to seek out broadly diversified portfolios that seek to minimize expenses such as passive index funds.

Another interesting finding is the insignificance of the FOF manager's timing skills. We obtain a similar conclusion using either T&M or H&M methodology. Regardless of the investment horizon, the majority of FOFs fare similarly to the benchmarks. However, these two measures clearly

Table 2.9 FOF performance based on various performance models

	S&P 500 Benchmark				Best-fit Benchmark			
	Outperform $t(\alpha) > 1.96$	Insignificant $-1.96 > t(\alpha) > 1.96$	Underperform $t(\alpha) < -1.96$	Total	Outperform $t(\alpha) > 1.96$	Insignificant $-1.96 > t(\alpha) > 1.96$	Underperform $t(\alpha) < -1.96$	Total
5 year								
OLS	0	15	0	15	1	14	0	15
T&M	1	13	1	15	2	11	2	15
H&M	1	13	1	15	0	9	6	15
3 year								
OLS	0	16	1	17	0	16	1	17
T&M	0	15	2	17	1	14	2	17
H&M	0	15	2	17	0	8	9	17
1 year*								
OLS	0	25	4	29	0	16	1	17
T&M	0	26	3	29	0	16	1	17
H&M	0	25	4	29	0	14	3	17

Notes: The fund performance is evaluated using the estimated Jensen's alpha. Jensen's alpha is computed by regressing monthly FOF excess returns against S&P500 and best-fit benchmarks on 5 and 3-year horizons using regular OLS approach and the Treynor-Mazuy (1966) and Henriksson-Merton (1981) timing models:

OLS: $R_{it} - R_{ft} = \alpha_i^{OLS} + \beta_i(R_{mt} - R_{ft}) + \varepsilon_{it}$

TM: $R_{it} - R_{ft} = \alpha_i^{TM} + \beta_i(R_{mt} - R_{ft}) + \delta_i(R_{mt} - R_{ft})^2 + \varepsilon_{it}$

HM: $R_{it} - R_{ft} = \alpha_i^{HM} + \beta_i \max|0, \{R_{mt} - R_{ft}\}| + \delta_i \min|0, \{R_{mt} - R_{ft}\}| + \varepsilon_{it}$

R_i = return of fund i, R_f = risk-free return, R_m = benchmark return

* Note that the total number of FOF with a 1-year horizon under the Morningstar Best-Fit index is reduced to 17 since this index by definition requires a 3-year time horizon.

show that FOFs exhibit inferior selectivity skills by a wide margin over superior selectivity skills.[10]

2.5.5 FOF performance versus non-FOF performance

Table 2.10 reports the number and the percentage of FOFs and non-FOFs that outperform and underperform the benchmarks. Panel A shows that less than 5 percent of both FOFs and non-FOFs perform equally well relative to both benchmarks. However, a larger percentage of non-FOFs performed better than FOFs using the S&P500 benchmark. If we use the best-fit benchmark, then the performance of FOFs is better only over the 3-year horizon (based only on percentage), marginally better over the 5-year investment horizon and worse over the 1-year horizon. Lack of out-performance for FOFs is consistent with empirical results for mutual funds in general which find that funds typically do no better than their appropriate benchmark and often do worse (Jensen, 1968; Grinblatt and Titman, 1989; and Ippolito, 1989).

Though we do not find a clear picture on FOF out-performance, Panel B shows evidence of more FOF under-performance. With the best-fit benchmark and a 3-year investment horizon or the S&P500 benchmark with 1-year horizon, there is a substantially higher percentage of FOFs underperforming the benchmark. Nevertheless, caution should be exercised when interpreting these results due to the insufficient track record length for most FOFs. Only one FOF outperforms the benchmark index for both the 3- and 5-year horizon. At best we can conclude that FOFs perform as well as non-FOFs. However, statistical significance is likely to be elusive regardless of the track record. Brignoli (1989) presents a simple method of determining the measurement interval required to determine whether a portfolio's return exceeds a benchmark's return by at least one standard deviation (for example, level of confidence of 84%) under the assumption of normally distributed returns. Using the standard covariance formula, he shows that a measurement interval of 20 years would be required to determine with 84 percent confidence whether the portfolio's return exceeded the benchmark. This assumes a 20 percent standard deviation for the benchmark and portfolio, an annual alpha of 2.0 percent, and correlation of 0.9 between the benchmark and the portfolio. A full 80 years would be required if the true alpha were 1.0%/yr. Therefore, it is unlikely that the issue of significant performance for FOFs will be determined anytime soon.

Note that when the category average and simulated benchmarks are used to compare the FOFs and non-FOFs, the proportion of FOFs that outperform tends to be lower than that of the non-FOFs for all three time horizons. FOFs, however, do not significantly underperform their investment objective category average and simulated benchmarks over the 3 and 5 year horizons. They do underperform relative to non-FOFs over a 1-year horizon.

Table 2.10 Frequency of FOF under/over-performance

	S&P500 benchmark			Total funds	Best-fit benchmark		
	Outperform $t(\alpha) > 1.96$	Insignificant $-1.96 > t(\alpha) > 1.96$	Underperform $t(\alpha) < -1.96$		Outperform $t(\alpha) > 1.96$	Insignificant $-1.96 > t(\alpha) > 1.96$	Underperform $t(\alpha) < -1.96$
5-year	0	15	0	15	1	14	0
3-year	0	16	1	17	0	16	1
1-year	0	25	4	29	0	16	1
	Category average benchmark			**Total funds**	**Simulated benchmark**		
	Outperform $t(\alpha) > 1.96$	Insignificant $-1.96 > t(\alpha) > 1.96$	Underperform $t(\alpha) < -1.96$		Outperform $t(\alpha) > 1.96$	Insignificant $-1.96 > t(\alpha) > 1.96$	Underperform $t(\alpha) < -1.96$
5-year	2*	13	0	15	2*	15	0
3-year	2*	15	0	17	2*	15	0
1-year	2*	24	3	29	2*	24	3

Note: Summary of FOFs Jensen alpha when FOF monthly returns are regressed against S&P 500, best-fit benchmark, category average and simulated benchmarks on 5, 3 and 1-year horizons.
* The two outperformers are the T. Rowe Price and Vanguard FOFs, funds that are restricted to investing inside their own family.

2.4.6 FOF expense analysis

Perhaps the most interesting aspect of FOF management is their implementation of management fees. Table 2.11 presents a breakdown of the expense ratios on funds held in each FOF, the incremental FOF expense charge and the total FOF expense ratio. For purposes of appropriate cross-sectional averaging, the data includes only those FOFs with three or more years of data. All expense data was provided by Morningstar and does not include front or back end load fees (none of the FOFs included in our analysis charged either a front or deferred load). The expense ratios on the FOFs and the individual holdings of the FOF are the total percentages of fees paid for operating expenses, management fees, 12b-1 fees, administrative fees, and all other asset-based costs incurred by the fund.

Expenses on the securities held by the FOF are a weighted average based upon the FOF's percentage holding in each of its positions. We were able to track the expense ratio for 85–100 percent of the funds held in each of the FOFs. The remaining unidentified expenses were assumed to be the average expense ratio of those funds which were identified.

As mentioned previously, there are two funds (Vanguard STAR and T. Rowe Price Spectrum Growth) which do not charge an incremental FOF management fee since they restrict investment to funds in their own family. Notice that with the exception of the above mentioned funds, all FOFs charge a higher management fee than the collective average of the funds that they hold. In fact, the average expense ratio on FOFs is nearly *double* the average expense ratio on the funds that they hold at 1.81 percent vs. 0.98 percent. Furthermore, if the low-expense Vanguard and T.Rowe Price funds are excluded the overall average FOF expense ratios jumps to 3.08 percent vs. 2.79 percent with the no-charge FOFs included.

Thus, it is obvious that FOFs effectively buy lower expense mutual funds and bundle them into a higher expense fund, but are the differences economically meaningful? Table 2.12 highlights two key facts. First, the average expense ratio on the funds that FOFs hold is lower than the overall average expense ratio across every investment objective. Thus, it appears that FOFs are targeting low expense funds for their holdings. Second, FOF expense add-ons are 180 percent of the expenses of the individual funds they hold. This leads to an overall average expense ratio of 2.9 percent for FOFs that is nearly double the average non-FOF expense ratio of 1.5 percent. In sum, FOFs buy lower than average expense funds for their portfolios, but charge higher than average expense fees to manage them.

This result coupled with previous results regarding performance, selectivity and timing suggest that FOFs may be engaged in a type of expense arbitrage. Though there is mixed evidence as to the incremental benefits provided by FOFs, it is clear that whatever these benefits, they are likely, at best, to provide similar performance net of fees as that generated by the average mutual

Table 2.11 Funds of funds annual expense ratios by investment objective (distinct portfolios, inception dates prior to 12/31/96)

	Panel A: FOFs that select funds from *outside* the FOF's fund family					Panel B: FOFs that select funds from *within* the FOF's fund family					Panel C: Mutual funds excluding FOFs		
Investment objective	Number of funds	Expense ratio of funds held by FOF	Expense ratio of FOF	Total FOF expense ratio: average	Total FOF expense ratio: size W_t average	Number of funds	Expense ratio of funds held by FOF	Expense ratio of FOF	Total FOF expense ratio: average	Total FOF expense ratio: size W_t average	Number of funds	Annual expense ratio: average	Annual expense ratio: size W_t average
Asset allocation	7	1.01	1.58	2.36	1.88	19	0.73	0.13	0.84	0.58	104	1.23	0.81
Balanced	3	0.77	1.48	2.25	2.19	8	0.86	0.78	1.60	0.55	174	1.10	0.70
Growth	4	1.00	1.96	2.86	2.64	8	0.98	0.78	1.72	1.00	622	1.22	0.88
Average across objectives shown above		0.93	1.67	2.49	2.24		0.86	0.56	1.39	0.71		1.19	0.80
Average without partitioning or excluding objectives		1.03	1.54	2.41	2.16		0.79	0.42	1.19	0.62		1.21	0.81

Notes: All panels exclude funds with inception dates prior to December 31, 1996, investment objectives with fewer than three FOFs operating within the objective and multiple share classes of the same fund portfolio. Expense ratio is the annual percentage of the fund expenses divided by the net asset value of the fund. Information is based on the most recent semi-annual report during 1999. The figures for the column titled "Expense ratio of funds held by FOF" is the average FOF's position weighted expense ratio of funds held in the portfolio. Total FOF expense ratio is the sum of the FOF expense ratio and expenses of funds held by the FOF. The total expense ratio is expressed as an average across funds and as a weighted (W_t) average based upon the size (total assets managed) of the FOF. Panel A is the subset of FOFs that select funds from outside the FOF's fund family. Panel B is the subset of funds that are restricted in selecting funds from within the FOF's fund family. Panel C is the set of mutual funds excluding FOFs. The figures shown the row titled "Average without partitioning by objectives" do not exclude any FOF investment objectives.

Table 2.12 Funds of funds annual expense ratios by investment objective of distinct portfolios

	Panel A: FOFs that select funds from *outside* the FOF's fund family					Panel B: FOFs that select funds from *within* the FOF's fund family					Panel C: Mutual funds excluding FOFs		
Investment objective	**Number of funds**	**Expense ratio of funds held by FOF**	**Expense ratio of FOF**	**Total FOF expense ratio: average**	**Total FOF expense ratio: size W_t average**	**Number of funds**	**Expense ratio of funds held by FOF**	**Expense ratio of FOF**	**Total FOF expense ratio: average**	**Total FOF expense ratio: size W_t average**	**Number of funds**	**Annual expense ratio: average**	**Annual expense ratio: size W_t average**
Asset allocation	7	1.01	1.58	2.36	1.88	29	0.72	0.32	1.01	0.59	115	1.24	0.82
Balanced	3	0.77	1.48	2.25	2.19	16	0.82	0.72	1.52	0.58	191	1.11	0.70
Foreign stock	3	1.23	0.79	1.98	1.94	5	1.03	0.69	1.56	0.48	313	1.52	1.07
Growth	7	1.16	1.43	2.38	2.34	20	0.96	0.69	1.61	1.03	818	1.24	0.89
Growth and income	4	1.03	1.33	2.15	2.10	8	0.86	0.40	1.24	1.63	368	1.08	0.57
Average across objectives shown above		1.04	1.32	2.22	2.09		0.88	0.56	1.39	0.86		1.24	0.81
Average without partitioning or excluding objectives		1.07	1.40	2.31	2.10		0.84	0.57	1.37	0.66		1.22	0.82

Notes: Panels include all distinct portfolios of FOFs and mutual funds with inception dates prior to December 31, 1999. Investment objectives with fewer than three distinct FOF portfolios operating within the objective have been excluded. Expense ratio is the annual percentage of the fund expenses divided by the net asset value of the fund. Information is based on the most recent semi-annual report during 1999. The figures for the column titled "Expense ratio of funds held by FOF" is a size weighted average based upon the FOF portfolio weighting. Total expense ratio is the sum of the FOF expense ratio and expenses of funds held by the FOF. The total expense ratio is expressed as an average across funds and as a weighted (W_t) average based upon the size (total assets managed) of the FOF. Panel A is the subset of FOFs that select funds from outside the FOF's fund family. Panel B is the subset of funds that are restricted in selecting funds from within the FOF's fund family. Panel C is the set of mutual funds excluding FOFs.

fund. Thus, any incremental fund manager outperformance just compensates for the higher expense fees that FOF investors incur.

2.5 CONCLUSION

This chapter has presented an analysis of an emerging mutual fund product known as funds of funds (FOFs). We provide evidence on the risk characteristics, performance and expense characteristics on all FOFs with one, three or five years of returns history which manage in excess of $14 billion in assets. Since no FOF dissolved over our analysis period, the results are not subject to survivorship bias. For robustness, we employ a variety of benchmarking techniques including the Morningstar Best Fit index, an investment objective category index and an equally weighted simulated index constructed to best mimic the individual fund of fund objectives. We find that FOFs in general perform no better than their respective benchmarks and exhibit a propensity for statistical and economic under-performance across all investment objectives (Aggressive Growth, Asset Allocation, Balanced, Growth, Growth and Income, Multi-Asset, and World Stock). Furthermore, there is little evidence that any additional diversification obtained by FOFs exceeds its incremental cost. Thus, FOFs could be viewed merely as a specialized index type mutual fund product. Perhaps most importantly, we find that FOFs incur much higher expenses than their non-FOF counterparts. To compensate for this handicap, fee-challenged FOFs invest in lower than average expense funds. The total fee paid by a FOF investor is nevertheless nearly double that paid by an investor holding a more traditional mutual fund. Thus, FOFs may be engaging in a type of "expense arbitrage" effectively buying their holdings low and selling them high (in terms of expense ratios). Due to the inherently short time series length of the FOF dataset and the problems therein, statistical inference is inevitably weak. Nonetheless, the evidence when taken in total, points clearly to a need for future research on the benefits versus the costs of funds of funds.

APPENDIX A: FUND OF FUNDS SUMMARY STATISTICS

Fund name	3-year % rank	5-year % rank	Fund size ($ million)	Fund age (years)
AARP Diversified Growth			140.7	2.8
AARP Divr Income with Growth			92.3	2.8
AIM Global Trends A			20.5	2.3
AIM Global Trends Adv			1.0	2.3
AIM Global Trends B			29.1	2.3
American Gen Con GrLife A			1.9	1.1

→

Appendix A Continued

Fund name	3-year % rank	5-year % rank	Fund size ($ million)	Fund age (years)
American Gen Con GrLife B			6.2	1.1
American Gen Con GrLife In I			1.4	1.1
American Gen Con GrLife InII			1.6	1.1
American Gen Gr Life A			2.1	1.1
American Gen Gr Life B			5.5	1.1
American Gen Gr Life I			1.7	1.1
American Gen Gr Life II			1.6	1.1
American Gen Mod GrLife A			2.0	1.1
American Gen Mod GrLife B			6.2	1.2
American Gen Mod GrLife In I			1.5	1.1
American Gen Mod GrLife InII			1.7	1.2
API Capital Income	45	75	14.2	11.7
API Growth	39	35	75.0	14.5
Ark Intl Equity Select Instl			36.6	2.7
Barr Rosenberg Db Alp Mkt Is			8.4	1.7
BB&T Capital Mgr Cons Gr Tr			32.4	2.2
BB&T Capital Mgr Growth Tr			26.1	2.2
Delaware Foundation Bal A			18.1	2.0
Delaware Foundation Bal B			1.1	2.0
Delaware Foundation Bal C			0.8	2.0
Delaware Foundation Bal Inst			0.1	2.0
Delaware Foundation Gr A			12.1	2.0
Delaware Foundation Gr B			1.8	2.0
Delaware Foundation Gr C			0.5	2.0
Delaware Foundation Gr Inst			0.1	2.0
Delaware Foundation Inc A			17.3	2.0
Delaware Foundation Inc B			0.3	2.0
Delaware Foundation Inc C			0.2	2.0
Delaware Foundation Inc Inst			0.1	2.0
DFA Intl Small Company	100		250.9	3.3
Diversified Inv Intm Str	47		291.7	3.5
Diversified Inv Intm/Lg Str	18		339.8	3.5
Diversified Inv Short Str	13		61.8	3.5
Federated Intl Growth A			39.4	2.4
Federated Intl Growth B			12.3	2.4
Federated Intl Growth C			2.3	2.4
Fidelity Four-in-One Index			159.4	0.5
Fidelity Freedom 2000	40		675.4	3.2
Fidelity Freedom 2010	8		1492.9	3.2
Fidelity Freedom 2020	55		1384.2	3.2
Fidelity Freedom 2030	44		657.4	3.2
Fidelity Freedom Income	75		289.3	3.2

→

Appendix A Continued

Fund name	3-year % rank	5-year % rank	Fund size ($ million)	Fund age (years)
First American Strat Aggress	84		80.1	3.2
First American Strat Gr&Inc	58		218.1	3.2
First American Strat Growth	39		96.1	3.2
First American Strat Income	2		72.8	3.2
Firstar Stellar Internl Eq A			59.5	2.1
Flex-funds Muirfield	7	51	155.1	11.3
Flex-Partners Tact Ast Alc A	12		0.6	3.3
Flex-Partners Tact Ast Alc C	14		22.0	4.5
Forward Global Asset Alloc			106.9	1.7
Franklin Templeton Con Tgt A	67		15.5	3.0
Franklin Templeton Con Tgt C	70		10.8	3.0
Franklin Templeton Gr Tgt A	24		48.5	3.0
Franklin Templeton Gr Tgt C	29		24.6	3.0
Franklin Templeton Mod Tgt A	47		32.5	3.0
Franklin Templeton Mod Tgt C	55		25.3	3.0
FundManager Agg Growth A	81	80	17.1	15.1
FundManager Bond A	92	91	9.3	15.1
FundManager Growth A	11	21	17.1	15.1
FundManager Growth w/ Inc A	28	39	20.6	15.1
FundManager Mgd Tot Ret A	91	96	15.6	11.3
GMO Global Balanced AllocIII			125.5	2.5
GMO Global Equity Alc III			37.9	2.7
GMO International Eq Alc III	91		80.9	3.0
GMO U.S. Sector III	8	8	16.4	6.9
Goldman Sachs Agg Gr Str A			58.3	1.9
Goldman Sachs Agg Gr Str B			47.5	1.9
Goldman Sachs Agg Gr Str C			28.4	1.9
Goldman Sachs Agg Gr Str Is			3.7	1.9
Goldman Sachs Agg Gr Str Svc			0.1	1.9
Goldman Sachs Balanced Str A			39.8	1.9
Goldman Sachs Balanced Str B			33.0	1.9
Goldman Sachs Balanced Str C			23.3	1.9
Goldman Sachs Balanced Str I			2.2	1.9
Goldman Sachs Balanced Str S			0.4	1.9
Goldman Sachs Conserv St A			1.7	0.8
Goldman Sachs Conserv St B			10.5	0.8
Goldman Sachs Conserv St C			3.9	0.8
Goldman Sachs Conserv St Ins			0.0	0.8
Goldman Sachs Conserv St Svs			0.0	0.8
Goldman Sachs Grth & IncStrA			195.1	1.9
Goldman Sachs Grth & IncStrB			143.8	1.9
Goldman Sachs Grth & IncStrC			95.5	1.9

→

Appendix A Continued

Fund name	3-year % rank	5-year % rank	Fund size ($ million)	Fund age (years)
Goldman Sachs Grth & IncStrl			30.3	1.9
Goldman Sachs Grth & IncStrS			1.8	1.9
Goldman Sachs Grth Str A			130.6	1.9
Goldman Sachs Grth Str B			121.9	1.9
Goldman Sachs Grth Str C			70.1	1.9
Goldman Sachs Grth Str Inst			6.6	1.9
Goldman Sachs Grth Str Svc			0.7	1.9
Integrity Fund of Funds	91	97	21.7	4.9
Kobren Growth	79		69.9	3.0
Kobren Moderate Growth	23		38.9	3.0
Lord Abbett Alpha A			80.8	2.0
Lord Abbett Alpha B			57.2	2.0
Lord Abbett Alpha C			37.8	2.0
Markman Aggressive Alloc	45		126.4	4.8
Markman Conservative Alloc	22		31.7	4.8
Markman Moderate Alloc	2		93.3	4.8
Maxus Laureate Inv	19	20	26.8	6.6
Merriman Asset Allocation	68	77	10.9	10.6
Merriman Captl Appreciation	54	81	13.1	10.6
Merriman Flexible Bond	48	74	7.6	11.2
Merriman Growth & Income	89	97	9.2	11.0
Merriman Leveraged Growth	11	7	21.0	7.6
MSDW Fund of Funds DomesticA			1.2	2.1
MSDW Fund of Funds DomesticB			26.6	2.1
MSDW Fund of Funds DomesticC			1.4	2.1
MSDW Fund of Funds DomesticD			0.0	2.1
MSDW Fund of Funds Intl A			1.2	2.1
MSDW Fund of Funds Intl B			9.6	2.1
MSDW Fund of Funds Intl C			0.6	2.1
MSDW Fund of Funds Intl D			1.0	2.1
MSDW Strategic Adviser Agg A			6.2	2
MSDW Strategic Adviser Agg B			0.7	2
MSDW Strategic Adviser ConsA			4.4	2
MSDW Strategic Adviser ConsB			0.6	2
MSDW Strategic Adviser Mod A			5.7	2
MSDW Strategic Adviser Mod B			0.7	2
Munder Life All-Ssn Agg Y			60.1	2.7
Nations LifeGoal Bal Gr InvA	57		2.2	3.1
Nations LifeGoal Bal Gr InvC	61		2.0	3.2
Nations LifeGoal Bal Gr PriB	58		0.3	3.2
Nations LifeGoal Grth Inv A	85		4.2	3.2
Nations LifeGoal Inc&Gr InvA	89		0.8	3.2

→

Appendix A Continued

Fund name	3-year % rank	5-year % rank	Fund size ($ million)	Fund age (years)
New Century Balanced	21	34	64.5	10.9
New Century Capital	70	80	113.6	10.9
One Group Inv Bal A	44		213.9	3.0
One Group Inv Bal B	50		279.4	3.0
One Group Inv Bal C			18.5	2.4
One Group Inv Bal I	42		86.1	3.0
One Group Inv Cons Grow A	81		34.4	3.0
One Group Inv Cons Grow I	77		36.2	3.0
One Group Inv Grow A	69		118.6	3.0
One Group Inv Grow B	71		220.9	3.0
One Group Inv Grow C			17.5	2.4
One Group Inv Grow I	67		106.3	3.0
One Group Inv Grth & Inc A	84		271.5	3.0
One Group Inv Grth & Inc B	87		283.2	3.0
One Group Inv Grth & Inc C			16.0	2.4
One Group Inv Grth & Inc I	84		210.1	3.0
OPTI-flex Dynamic	8		18.7	3.2
Rightime	76	85	111.4	14.3
Schwab MarketManager Bal	11		121.0	3.1
Schwab MarketManager Growth	54		180.0	3.1
Schwab MarketManager Intl	11		103.0	3.2
Schwab MarketManager Sm Cap			123.0	2.3
Schwab MarketTrack All Eqty			202.0	1.6
Scudder Pathway Balanced	53		270.2	3.1
Scudder Pathway Conservative	91		29.9	3.1
Scudder Pathway Growth	73		125.6	3.1
SEI Asset All Div Cons Inc A	82		29.4	3.5
SEI Asset All Div Cons Inc D	62		8.9	3.5
SEI Asset All Div Conserv A	51		47.0	3.5
SEI Asset All Div Conserv D	83		16.1	3.4
SEI Asset All Div Glob Gr A	55		107.7	3.5
SEI Asset All Div Glob Gr D	62		26.0	3.6
SEI Asset All Div Mod Grth A	28		187.8	3.5
SEI Asset All Div Mod Grth D	35		38.6	3.6
SEI Asset All Div US Stock A	19		88.1	3.6
SEI Asset All Div US Stock D	22		44.5	3.4
Smith Barney Conc Alc Bal A	78		229.1	3.8
Smith Barney Conc Alc Bal B	85		246.4	3.8
Smith Barney Conc Alc Bal L	85		35.3	3.8
Smith Barney Conc Alc Cons A	93		72.6	3.8
Smith Barney Conc Alc Cons B	94		68.5	3.8
Smith Barney Conc Alc Cons L	94		7.3	3.8

→

Appendix A Continued

Fund name	3-year % rank	5-year % rank	Fund size ($ million)	Fund age (years)
Smith Barney Conc Alc Grth A	31		446.8	3.8
Smith Barney Conc Alc Grth B	39		503.9	3.8
Smith Barney Conc Alc Grth L	39		59.4	3.8
Smith Barney Conc Alc HiGr A	36		454.4	3.8
Smith Barney Conc Alc HiGr B	44		388.7	3.8
Smith Barney Conc Alc HiGr L	44		47.5	3.8
Smith Barney Conc Alc Inc A	31		32.6	3.8
Smith Barney Conc Alc Inc B	54		30.3	3.8
Smith Barney Conc Alc Inc L	58		3.8	3.8
SSgA Life Solutions Balanced			119.6	2.4
SSgA Life Solutions Growth			67.2	2.4
SSgA Life Solutions Inc & Gr			24.5	2.4
STAAR Alternative Categories	76		0.5	3.7
STAAR Larger Company Stock	92		2.3	3.7
STAAR Smaller Company Stock	50		2.0	3.7
STI Classic Balanced Port Tr			93.0	2.5
STI Classic Gr and I Port Tr			20.3	2.5
STI Classic Maximum Gr Tr			20.1	2.5
T. Rowe Price Spectrum Grth	83	82	2835.5	9.5
T. Rowe Price Spectrum Inc	11	18	2589.0	9.5
T. Rowe Price Spectrum Intl	18		71.7	3.0
TIAA-CREF Managed Alloc			185.8	2.3
Vanguard LifeStrat Cons Grth	46	59	1713.6	5.3
Vanguard LifeStrat Growth	69	79	2938.3	5.3
Vanguard LifeStrat Income	73	88	559.7	5.3
Vanguard LifeStrat Mod Grth	20	23	3300.4	5.3
Vanguard STAR	46	35	8056.9	14.8
Vanguard Total Intl Stk Idx	73		2264.9	3.7
Victory LifeChoice Cons Inv	59		6.9	3.0
Victory LifeChoice Grow Inv	66		16.6	3.0
Victory LifeChoice Mod Inv	61		23.3	3.0
Wells Fargo Aggr Bal-Eq I			71.9	2.0
Wells Fargo Growth Bal I	19	28	974.1	5.1
Wells Fargo Mod Bal I	44	76	540.0	5.1
Wells Fargo Strat Inc I	74	97	264.6	5.1
WM Str Asset Mgmt Balanced A	16		114.0	3.4
WM Str Asset Mgmt Balanced B	22		161.5	3.4
WM Str Asset Mgmt Cons GrowA	61		124.3	3.4
WM Str Asset Mgmt Str Grow A	33		34.7	3.4
WM Str Asset Mgmt Str Grow B	40		92.8	3.4
Average	51.9	59.8	202.1	3.6
Median	54.0	75.0	32.1	3.0
Standard dev.	27.0	30.5	711.0	2.9

APPENDIX B: BEST-FIT INDEX AND OUTSIDE-FUND SELECTION STATUS

Fund name	Prospectus objective	Best fit index	Selects funds outside own fund family
API Capital Income	Multi-Asset Global	S&P 500	Yes
API Growth	World Stock	S&P 400	Yes
DFA Intl Small Company	Foreign Stock	MSCI PACIFIC	No
Diversified Inv Intm Str	Asset Allocation	S&P 500	No
Diversified Inv Intm/Lg Str	Asset Allocation	S&P 500	No
Diversified Inv Short Str	Asset Allocation	LB Corporate	No
Fidelity Freedom 2000	Asset Allocation	S&P 500	No
Fidelity Freedom 2010	Asset Allocation	S&P 500	No
Fidelity Freedom 2020	Asset Allocation	S&P 500	No
Fidelity Freedom 2030	Asset Allocation	S&P 500	No
Fidelity Freedom Income	Asset Allocation	S&P 500	No
First American Strat Aggress	Aggressive Growth	Wilshire 4500	No
First American Strat Gr&Inc	Balanced	Wilshire 4500	No
First American Strat Growth	Growth	Wilshire 4500	No
First American Strat Income	Corp Bond–General	LB Corporate	No
Flex-funds Muirfield	Asset Allocation	S&P 500	Yes
Flex-Partners Tact Ast Alc C	Asset Allocation	S&P 500	Yes
FundManager Agg Growth A	Aggressive Growth	Wilshire 4500	Yes
FundManager Bond A	Corp Bond–General	LB Corporate	Yes
FundManager Growth A	Growth	S&P 500	Yes
FundManager Growth w/Inc A	Growth and Income	S&P 500	Yes
FundManager Mgd Tot Ret A	Balanced	S&P 500	Yes
GMO U.S. Sector III	Growth and Income	S&P 500	No
Integrity Fund of Funds	Growth	S&P 500	Yes
Markman Aggressive Alloc	Aggressive Growth	Wilshire 4500	Yes
Markman Conservative Alloc	Balanced	Wilshire 4500	Yes
Markman Moderate Alloc	Growth and Income	Wilshire 4500	Yes
Maxus Laureate Inv	World Stock	MSCI AC World	Yes
Merriman Asset Allocation	Multi-Asset Global	MSCI AC World	Yes
Merriman Captl Appreciation	Asset Allocation	MSCI AC World	Yes
Merriman Flexible Bond	Multi-Sector Bond	LB Corporate	Yes
Merriman Growth & Income	Growth and Income	MSCI AC World	Yes
Merriman Leveraged Growth	Growth	MSCI AC World	Yes
Nations LifeGoal Bal Gr InvC	Balanced	MSCI AC World	No
Nations LifeGoal Grth Inv A	Growth	MSCI AC World	No
Nations LifeGoal Inc&Gr InvA	Equity Income	S&P 500	No
New Century Balanced	Balanced	Wilshire 4500	Yes
New Century Capital	Growth	MSCI AC World	Yes

→

Appendix B Continued

Fund name	Prospectus objective	Best fit index	Selects funds outside own fund family
OPTI-flex Dynamic	Asset Allocation	Wilshire 4500	Yes
Rightime	Asset Allocation	MSCI EASEA ND	Yes
Schwab MarketManager Bal	Asset Allocation	Wilshire 4500	Yes
Schwab MarketManager Growth	Asset Allocation	Wilshire 4500	Yes
Schwab MarketManager Intl	Foreign Stock	MSCI WdxUS	Yes
Scudder Pathway Balanced	Balanced	MSCI AC World	No
Scudder Pathway Conservative	Asset Allocation	S&P 500	No
Scudder Pathway Growth	Asset Allocation	MSCI AC World	No
SEI Asset All Div Cons Inc A	Asset Allocation	S&P 500	No
SEI Asset All Div Conserv A	Asset Allocation	S&P 500	No
SEI Asset All Div Glob Gr A	Asset Allocation	MSCI AC World	No
SEI Asset All Div Mod Grth A	Asset Allocation	S&P 500	No
SEI Asset All Div US Stock A	Growth	S&P 500	No
Smith Barney Conc Alc Bal L	Balanced	S&P 500	No
Smith Barney Conc Alc Cons L	Corp Bond–General	S&P 500	No
Smith Barney Conc Alc Grth L	Growth	Wilshire 4500	No
Smith Barney Conc Alc HiGr L	Growth	Wilshire 4500	No
Smith Barney Conc Alc Inc L	Corp Bond–General	LB Corporate	No
STAAR Alternative Categories	Multi-Asset Global	Wilshire 4500	Yes
STAAR Larger Company Stock	Growth and Income	S&P 500	Yes
STAAR Smaller Company Stock	Small Company	Russ 2000	Yes
T. Rowe Price Spectrum Grth	Growth	MSCI AC World	No
T. Rowe Price Spectrum Inc	Multi-Sector Bond	FB High Yield	No
Vanguard LifeStrat Cons Grth	Asset Allocation	S&P 500	No
Vanguard LifeStrat Growth	Asset Allocation	S&P 500	No
Vanguard LifeStrat Income	Asset Allocation	S&P 500	No
Vanguard LifeStrat Mod Grth	Asset Allocation	S&P 500	No
Vanguard STAR	Balanced	S&P 500	No
Vanguard Total Intl Stk Idx	Foreign Stock	MSCI WdxUS	No
Wells Fargo Growth Bal I	Asset Allocation	S&P 500	No
Wells Fargo Mod Bal I	Balanced	S&P 500	No
Wells Fargo Strat Inc I	Balanced	S&P 500	No
WM Str Asset Mgmt Balanced B	Balanced	MSCI AC World	No
WM Str Asset Mgmt Cons GrowA	Growth	Wilshire 4500	No
WM Str Asset Mgmt Str Grow B	Growth	Wilshire 4500	No

NOTES

1. Federal Reserve Statistical Release, September 21, 2005, Flow of Funds Accounts of the United States, Second Quarter 2005.
2. No load FOF share classes were used for the purpose of calculating returns net of fees.
3. Sharpe's Ratio, $SR_i = \dfrac{\frac{1}{T}\sum_{i=1}^{T} R_{it} - R_{ft}}{\sigma_{R_i - R_f}}$, Treynor's Ratio, $TR_i = \dfrac{\frac{1}{T}\sum_{i=1}^{T} R_{it} - R_{ft}}{\beta_i}$
4. For example, Carhart (1997), Elton, Gruber and Blake (1996) and Christopherson, Ferson and Glassman (1998).
5. It should be noted that the representative benchmarks for each investment category is determined by a simple majority rule. For instance, 84% of balanced MFs have the S&P 500 as the best-fit benchmark, 9% use the S&P 400, 4% use the long-term bond index, etc. The best-fit benchmark chosen for all balanced MFs is the S&P 500. Appendix B reports the distribution of funds in the same investment objective.
6. Recall that FOFs on average hold 91% of their assets in their top 10 holdings.
7. Corrected for heteroscedasticity using White's consistent estimators.
8. Work by Kothari and Warner (1998) finds that Jensen's alpha tends to detect underperformance too often when using a value-weighted equity index such as the S&P 500. We also find mostly negative or very small alphas when using this type of equity index. Using an equally weighted average and simulated benchmarks reduces this bias. The effect of using a multi-factor model such as the Carhart (1997) 4-factors or the Fama-French 3-factors is likely to shift the alpha estimates downwards.
9. This misspecification may bias the alpha estimates.
10. Once again, Kothari and Warner document a bias toward excessive rejection of the null in timing measures. However, they find that the magnitude in the alpha bias is much greater than timing skills measures and thus, it would require a massive underestimation of timing skills in order to offset the overestimated alphas. This seems quite unlikely given the very low alphas already reported.

REFERENCES

Brignoli, R. (1989) "Toward a Unified Theory of Investing", in R. Folger and D. Bayston (eds), *Improving Portfolio Performance with Quantitative Models* (Charlottesville, VA: Institute of Chartered Financial Analysts).

Brown, S., Goetzmann, W., Ibbotson, R. and Ross, S. (1992) "Survivorship Bias in Performance Studies", *Review of Financial Studies*, 5(4): 553–80.

Campbell, J., Lo, A. and MacKinlay, A. (1997) *The Econometrics of Financial Markets* (Princeton, NJ: Princeton University Press).

Capriles, A., de la Torre, J., Fujiwara, M., Lopez-Soriano, F., Wang, S. and Youn, S. (1995) "A Systematic Approach to Error-Correction and Revision in Intertemporal Portfolio Optimization: The Funds of Funds Problem", *Proseminar in Financial Engineering, Morgan Stanley Presentation*, Spring 1995.

Carhart, M.M. (1997) "On Persistence in Mutual Fund Performance", *Journal of Finance*, 52(1): 57–82.

Christopherson, J., Ferson, W. and Glassman, D. (1994) "Conditioning Manager Alphas on Economic Information: Another Look at the Persistence of Performance", Working Paper, October 1994.

Constantinides, G. and Malliaris, A. (1995) "Portfolio Theory", in R. Jarrow, V. Maksimovic and W. Ziemba (eds), *Handbook in Operations Research and Management Science*, Vol. 9, pp. 1–27 (North-Holland: Elsevier Science, B.V.).

Cowles, A. (1933) "Can Stock Market Forecasters Forecast", *Econometrica*, 1(3): 309–25.

Fama, E. (1972) "Components of Investment Performance", *Journal of Finance*, 27(3): 551–67.

Ferson, W. and Schadt, R. (1996) "Measuring Fund Strategy and Performance in Changing Economic Conditions", *Journal of Finance*, 51(2): 425–61.

Goetzmann, W. and Ibbotson, R. (1994) "Do Winners Repeat?", *Journal of Portfolio Management*, Winter 1994: 9–18.

Grinblatt, M. and Titman, S. (1989) "Portfolio Performance Evaluation: Old Issues and New Insights", *Review of Financial Studies*, 2(3): 393–421.

Grinblatt, M. and Titman, S. (1992) "The Persistence of Mutual Fund Performance", *Journal of Finance*, 47(5): 1977–84.

Grinblatt, M. and Titman, S. (1995) "Performance Evaluation", in R. Jarrow, V. Maksimovic and W. Ziemba (eds), *Handbook in Operations Research and Management Science*, Vol. 9, pp. 581–609 (North-Holland: Elsevier Science, B.V.).

Hendricks, D., Patel, J. and Zeckhauser, R. (1993) "Hot Hands in Mutual Funds: Short Run Persistence of Relative Performance, 1974–1988", *Journal of Finance*, 48(1): 93–130.

Henriksson, R. and Merton, R. (1981) "On Market Timing and Investment Performance, II. Statistical Procedures for Evaluating Forecasting Skills", *Journal of Business*, 54(4): 513–34.

Hensley, S. (1996) "U.S. Bancorp Seeks SEC Nod to Create 4 'Funds of Funds' ", *American Banker*, April 12: 1.

Ippolito, R. (1989) "Efficiency with Costly Information: A Study of Mutual Fund Performance: 1965–1984", *Quarterly Journal of Economics*, 43(2): 1–23.

Jaffe, J. (1995) "SEC Relaxes Limits on Funds of Funds", *Institutional Investor*, October 2, I(8): 1.

Jensen, M. (1968) "The Performance of Mutual Funds in the Period 1945–1964", *Journal of Finance*, 23(2): 389–416.

Kothari, S. and Warner, J. (1998) "Evaluating Mutual Fund Performance", Working Paper, Sloan School of Management, MIT and William E. Simon Graduate School of Business Administration, University of Rochester.

Lehmann, B. and Modest, D. (1987) "Mutual Fund Performance Evaluation: A Comparison of Benchmarks and Benchmark Comparisons", *Journal of Finance*, 42(2): 233–65.

Lehmann, B. and Modest, D. (1989) "Empirical Foundations of the Arbitrage Pricing Theory", *Journal of Financial Economics*, 21(2): 213–54.

Malkiel, B. (1995) "Returns from Investing in Equity Mutual Funds 1971–1991", *Journal of Finance*, 50(2): 549–72.

Middleton, T. (1997). "Mutual Funds: A.A.R.P. Is Adding Some Spice to Its Menu", *New York Times*, February 2, Section 3, Page 7, Column 1.

Treynor, J. and Mazuy, K. (1966) "Can Mutual Funds Outguess the Market?", *Harvard, Business Review*, 44(2): 131–6.

Volkman, D. and Wohar, M. (1995) "Determinants of Persistence in Relative Performance of Mutual Funds", *Journal of Financial Research*, 18(4): 415–30.

Williamson, C. (1997) "Fund of Funds Boom Possible", *Crain Communications*, 6(1): 2.

Willis, C. (1997) "New T. Rowe Price Fund Offers Simple Way To Invest", *Reuter Business Report*, February 13.

CHAPTER 3

Are Investors Home Biased? Evidence from Germany

*Andreas Oehler, Marco Rummer, Thomas Walker and Stefan Wendt**

3.1 INTRODUCTION AND RELATED WORK

In most if not all countries the proportion of portfolio assets that investors allocate to foreign securities is clearly less than mean-variance analysis predicts. In Germany, for example, mutual funds hold only 66 percent of their investments in non-German securities while the latter represent almost 85 percent of the worldwide market value for bonds and 95 percent for equities. Even greater discrepancies exist for other financial intermediaries such as insurance companies or pension funds. Finally, the poorest portfolio diversification is exhibited by private German investors whose direct investments abroad only amount to 37 percent and 19 percent of their stock and bond holdings, respectively (for the year 2001: see Deutsche Bundesbank, 2001, 2004c).

* This chapter benefited from discussions with Gerrit Klages and Tilo Wannow. We also thank seminar participants at Bamberg University and participants at the workshop Economics Meets Psychology 2005 held by the German Central Bank (Deutsche Bundesbank). The authors are grateful to Ralf Borger, Peter Thomas, and Kerstin Voeller for technical support. The usual disclaimer applies. The authors are grateful to the mutual funds for providing us with their reports and to Morgan Stanley for their support on MSCI All-Country Index data.

The phenomenon that professional and individual investors hold too little of their wealth in foreign assets has been noted in the finance literature at least since the 1970s (Levy and Sarnat, 1970; Lessard, 1973, 1976; Solnik, 1974) and has been called "home (asset) bias" or "domestic (asset) bias" since the early 1990s. In studies that focus only on stocks, the phenomenon is often referred to as an "equity home bias".[1] This preference for domestic over foreign assets has been documented for investors in several countries by many authors (including French and Poterba, 1990, 1991; Tesar and Werner, 1992, 1994, 1995; and Cooper and Kaplanis, 1994). Investors who engage in such biased allocation strategies suffer from a sub-optimal degree of international diversification through both, a lower rate of return and higher risk (Lewis, 1999; Jeske, 2001; French and Poterba, 1990, 1991). For Germany, these effects have been calculated more recently by Maurer and Mertz (2000). Later replications that focus only on the equity market can be found in von Nitzsch and Stotz (2005) and Gerke, Mager, and Röhrs (2005).

Many explanations have been proposed in the finance literature since the first studies were conducted. Most of these theories relate the home bias to one of three factors: (1) transaction costs, (2) hedging possibilities and omitted assets, or (3) information asymmetries.

From a theoretical standpoint, it can be argued that if the costs of acquiring and holding foreign equities are sufficiently higher than they are for domestic securities, investors may be induced to keep their wealth at home. Direct transaction costs and other costs associated with international diversification, such as foreign taxes, information gathering costs, and costs resulting from institutional barriers to trade assets, reduce the gains from diversifying abroad because the expected returns on foreign assets are reduced relative to domestic assets which makes the latter more attractive. Yet, despite its theoretical footing, empirical findings in this area are generally poor (see French and Poterba, 1990, 1991; Tesar and Werner, 1992, 1994, 1995; Cooper and Kaplanis, 1994; Lewis, 1999; Coen, 2001; and Glassman and Riddick, 2001). Moreover, in recent years asset markets have been deregulated and liberalized – a trend which will likely diminish the domestic bias. However, differences in legal frameworks as they pertain to accounting systems, corporate governance, restrictive investment regulations, or investor protection simply exist and can likely explain at least part of the home bias (see Rowland, 1999; Dahlquist *et al.*, 2003; Giannetti and Koskinen, 2003; and Chan, Covrig and Ng, 2004).[2]

Another set of explanations for the international diversification puzzle stems from the argument that domestic assets provide a better hedge for risks that are home country specific. First, hedging possibilities arise when the purchasing power parity – which implies equal inflation rates across countries – does not hold. Stulz (1981) and Adler and Dumas (1983) present models incorporating deviations from the purchasing power parity and inflation risk against which investors demand assets to hedge domestic inflation. However, Cooper and Kaplanis (1994) show that very low levels of risk-aversion would be necessary to account for inflation hedging as a plausible explanation (see Lewis, 1999, for an additional analysis).

Second, hedging possibilities arise from the country-specific risks of non-traded wealth, such as human capital or other omitted assets like real estate, and of traded wealth like bonds. Generally, the extent of the error introduced by an omitted asset is primarily a function of whether or not it provides a significant additional source of diversification, as captured in terms of correlation measures. In fact, the majority of empirical work on the home bias has only looked at international equity holdings and thus at the equity home bias. Very few papers also include bonds and mutual fund shares (for example, Tesar and Werner, 1992, and our own study on the German market in this chapter). A few other studies investigate whether incorporating human capital in the international portfolio generates a home bias (see Brainard and Tobin, 1992; Bottazzi, Pesenti, and van Wincoop, 1996; Baxter and Jerman, 1997; Coen, 2001). If investors have exogenously fixed human capital holdings whose returns vary with shocks to labor income, they can use equities to hedge the risk from their human capital. Thus, the size of human capital holdings and the size and the sign of the correlation with equity returns are crucial to the analysis in these studies. Most of the studies show that the returns on human capital and the returns on domestic financial capital are highly positively correlated. This makes the home bias even worse. As a consequence, investors' optimal portfolios should have a short position in domestic equity in favor of foreign equity. There is only one exception, the paper of Bottazzi, Pesenti, and van Wincoop (1996), which observes negative correlations between the returns on human capital and equity, thus supporting the home bias. However, Lewis (1999) concludes more generally that "the desire to hedge non-tradables risk may even imply that domestic investors should increase their holdings of foreign equities, thus deepening the puzzle".

A third source for hedging possibilities emanates from domestic, but internationally operating companies. In principle, their business allows investors to benefit from international diversification. However, since the movement of stock returns of multinationals is closely related to their national markets, multinationals provide only slightly better diversification than the domestic market (for example, Jacquillat and Solnik, 1978; Heston and Roewenhorst, 1994; Lewis, 1999). Lewis (1999) argues that many multinationals are important components of the domestic stock market index and, therefore, gains from international diversification "require holdings of foreign assets that are not a part of the domestic index".

The remaining stream of explanations is based on asymmetric information and its consequences such as adjustments to perceived risk and asymmetric expectations. Some theoretical models assume that domestic investors have access to superior information about payoffs in the domestic market which result in a higher demand for domestic assets (Gehrig, 1993; Brennan and Cao, 1997; Kang and Stulz, 1997). While asymmetric information may explain a considerable portion of the home asset bias, Jeske (2001) argues that it would theoretically require an unrealistically large reduction of domestic risk. However, empirical findings such as those by Kang and Stulz (1997) support the notion that asymmetric information of this type drives the home bias. Kang and Stulz (1997) find that foreign investors in Japan do not hold the Japanese market portfolio, but prefer large and well-known companies. One reason for this is the difference between the theoretically correctly adjusted figures and the perceived risk in reality.

This deviation from adjusting the perceived risk of foreign assets upwards or of domestic assets downwards is mirrored in the results of other studies. Shiller, Kon-Ya and Tsutsui (1991) report survey data that indicate that domestic investors tend to be more optimistic about domestic market returns than foreign investors are. French and Poterba (1991) reach a similar conclusion, and, more recently, Lütje and Menkhoff (2004) report a relative return optimism for German fund managers. From their research on learning management, van Nieuwerburgh and Veldkamp (2004a) contribute to this discussion by pointing out that the assumption of information being tradable and easy to acquire is flawed. They argue that if investors have asymmetric prior beliefs and a limited learning capacity that they allocate before making investment decisions, they will not necessarily acquire foreign information. In a second study, van Nieuwerburgh and Veldkamp (2004b) show more generally that increasing returns to scale in learning (by exploiting increasing returns to specialization) drives underdiversification. As an investor holds more of an asset (for example, a domestic asset), the value of learning about it increases. At the same time, as she learns more about the asset, it becomes less risky and more desirable to hold. As a result, the investor tends to invest relatively more in such (domestic) assets (see also Gehrig, 1993).

Overall, theories based on an adjustment to perceived risk constitute the more behavioral explanations for the home bias. As such, they assume implicitly or explicitly bounded rationality. Heath and Tversky (1991) show empirically that when having to choose between two identical games, with the same probability, economic agents perceive the game they know less as being riskier. These results correspond to the research on ambiguity aversion which shows that there is not only a risk premium, but also an ambiguity premium (for example, Kahn and Sarin, 1988; Weber, 1990). Extending the approach of Heath and Tversky, Kilka (1998) suggests that investors' home bias is driven by the perception of competence, meaning that their perception of knowledge or familiarity might influence probability estimations and, perhaps, their (illusionary) control (a summary can be found in Kilka and Weber, 2000). The competence effect means that investors feel skillful or knowledgeable about domestic assets (see also Graham, Harvey, and Huang, 2005).

Such explanations emanating from a behavioral finance view are also considered to be the driving force of observed investments in firms which are geographically proximate to the investor. Recent empirical studies show that the home bias is not only international, but also regional and could be called a "home bias at home" (for example, Coval and Moskowitz, 1999; Grinblatt and Keloharju, 2001; Kumar, 2004; Goetzmann and Kumar, 2004). The regional bias was first explained by Fellner and Maciejovsky (2003) who show that social identity and social forces, triggered by group affiliations, drive underdiversified and domestically biased portfolios. Lauterbach and Reisman (2004) argue consistently that investors prefer domestic assets because they also serve the objective of mimicking the economic fortunes and welfare of the investor's neighbors, countrymen, and social reference group. In addition, this approach also explains the patriotism in portfolio allocation, reported from the USA by Morse and Shive (2003). Familiarity and perceived competence also cause investors to invest in stocks closely related to their non-financial income (Massa and Simonov, 2004). This issue is well-known from Germany where employees show a strong tendency to buy stocks from their own company (see also the above mentioned problems with hedging the human capital risk).

Our discussion of the different streams of research that aim to explain the home bias shows that the most convincing and empirically supported set of explanations encompasses models that are based on asymmetric information. In contrast, theories based on transaction costs and hedging possibilities have found little empirical support to date. Behavioral approaches based on bounded rationality and perceived risk adjustments are particularly appealing as they illustrate the competence effect and the issue of social identity. As the above mentioned literature shows, both factors have been shown to influence the behavior of individual and institutional investors.

Most of the empirical studies in this area were conducted in the 1990s. Given the speed of technological advancement in today's society, it is likely that the demand for international diversification has increased as the development of cheaper and more efficient information and communication technologies has reduced information asymmetries in terms of perceived costs in recent years (for example, Amadi, 2004) who explicitly points out the advent of the Internet). Concerning potential legal framework barriers, Pesenti and van Wincoop (2002) expect that the diffusion of a core set of international accounting standards and a more liberal regulatory environment worldwide are likely to contribute to this process as well. In addition, there is a worldwide industrialization in the mutual funds sector which could have caused investors to indirectly diversify internationally through their mutual funds' increasing foreign portfolio allocation. These trends and developments inspire us to take a more recent look at the home bias.

While the home bias effect has been identified and documented for a number of countries, in-depth research on this phenomenon in Germany is still scarce. We fill this gap by providing a detailed analysis of the home bias displayed by individual and institutional German investors. We employ a data-set that is based on official statistical reports of the German Central Bank (Deutsche Bundesbank). Our sample covers information about the composition of mutual fund assets and of securities accounts of private investors held at financial intermediaries such as investment companies, mutual funds and banks, including the German Central Bank and the Federal Securities Administration, for the period from 1990 to 2005.

In a second part of our study, we take a closer look at the home bias effect in Germany's mutual fund industry. Here, we employ data extracted from the annual reports of German mutual funds for the years 2000 to 2003. Our sample covers more than 100 mutual funds and represents over 75 percent of Germany's mutual fund landscape (in value terms) over the period from 2000 to 2003.

We find strong evidence for the home bias effect over the whole period. The extent of this bias, however, is significantly lower than the reported levels from the 1990s would have suggested. Mutual fund managers seem to extend their investment focus by putting less weight on German stocks, but more on stocks from other European countries. This behavior indicates increasing financial market integration within Europe.

The chapter is organized as follows. Section 3.2 describes the data-sets used for our analysis. The empirical analysis and its results are presented and discussed in section 3.3, and section 3.4 summarizes the key aspects and concludes our analysis.

3.2 DATA

3.2.1 Data from the German Central Bank (Deutsche Bundesbank)

In order to give an overview of whether or not individual and institutional investors in Germany are biased towards domestic securities when making their investment decision, the first part of our data-set is constructed from data contained in the official statistical reports of the German Central Bank. On a monthly basis, the German Central Bank publishes data about the situation and development of the financial market in Germany (see Deutsche Bundesbank, *Monthly Report* no. 2 on financial markets, 1991a–2005a). From the data provided in these reports, we extract information about the composition of mutual fund assets and of securities accounts of private investors held at financial intermediaries such as investment companies, mutual funds and banks, including the German Central Bank and the Federal Securities Administration (for the latter see Deutsche Bundesbank, *Yearly Report* no. 9 on securities accounts, 1991b–2005b). The resulting data-set comprises the respective figures in five-year intervals from 1990 through 2005 (the data for private securities accounts deviates from these intervals as it was only available for 2004 but not yet for 2005 at the time of our data collection). With this data-set we are able to calculate the proportion of mutual fund investments and of private security accounts invested in foreign equities, bonds, and mutual funds.

3.2.2 Data from mutual fund accounting reports

The second part of our data-set is constructed from information contained in the annual reports of German mutual funds for the years 2000 through 2003. In this part of our study, we only include funds in our analysis that invest more than 50 percent of their total assets in equities. This equity focus is applied for two reasons. First, it allows us to construct a meaningful benchmark (see our discussion below). Second, it allows for a comparison of our results to prior findings in the literature which – as mentioned earlier – generally focuses on equities. Due to the multitude of German mutual fund companies, we limit our analysis to the five largest ones. A further limitation is undertaken by including only mutual funds whose assets exceed €100 million in each year of our sample period. The reason for applying this threshold is the existence of a large number of relatively small funds (in terms of assets) that only represent a tiny share of the mutual fund market, and hence, will not significantly change our results. We are well-aware of the fact that by excluding funds that fall below the threshold in one or more of the years of the period investigated but otherwise lie above the limit we introduce a small bias in our sample selection process. The driving force behind the procedure of strictly applying this threshold, however, is to exclude funds that might – due to smaller amounts of assets – be limited in their opportunities to diversify internationally (for example, due to costly information acquisition), and hence, are not able to reach a composition of their equity portfolio reflecting the diversification in the world stockmarket portfolio.

When applying these criteria we get a data sample that contains 408 annual reports (102 mutual funds over the entire period of four years). From these reports we hand-collect the market value of the equity securities of every company included in the fund. In addition, every company that these funds invested in is assigned to the country in which it is incorporated – a procedure that creates some difficulties. Some companies emanate from mergers on an international level or have expanded their activities to a number of countries (see the remarks on multinational firms in the introduction). Hence, it is difficult to identify a criterion that unambiguously defines which country each of the companies has to be assigned to. In order not to be caught in this trap, we use the country of incorporation or – in case this country could not be identified – the country in which the company is headquartered. Furthermore, we have to face the problem that not all of the funds follow the same fiscal year, meaning that reporting dates are spread over nearly all months in a given year. To make the mutual fund data comparable with our benchmark we ignore different reporting dates and center all mutual fund data around the same point in time of each year.

To round our data-set off, we hand-collect data on total investments, bank deposits, and total net assets for each fund. Despite the restrictions we place on the necessary amount of assets for a fund to be included in our sample, our data-set covers more than 75 percent of total assets in the German mutual fund market when compared to statistics provided by the German Central Bank (Deutsche Bundesbank, 2004a).

We calculate the share of each country invested in by the funds as follows. The market value of the equities that a fund invested in is added up according to the country the respective company has been assigned to. As we do not want to investigate individual funds but the German mutual fund universe as a whole, we add up the fund-specific results for each country across all funds. The procedure is repeated for every year of the investigation period. Consequently, we calculate the country shares by dividing the respective sum of the market values of the single stocks of companies from one country by the sum of the market values of all equities of the respective year.

3.2.3 Benchmark composition

A good benchmark portfolio is crucial to identify deviations from the diversification represented by the world stockmarket portfolio. We are very thankful to Morgan Stanley Capital International Inc. (henceforth MSCI) for providing us with quarterly data on the market shares of countries included in the MSCI All-Country Index. Based on the composition of the index, our benchmark world market portfolio includes the market shares of 49 countries. This benchmark portfolio is used for the analysis of the hand-collected mutual fund data in section 3.3.2.

In order to guarantee a meaningful benchmark we have to account for the mismatch in the timing of the MSCI All-Country Index compared to the fiscal year of the mutual funds (see above). Therefore, we adjust the MSCI All-Country Index as follows to create our benchmark. For each quarter of the year, we add up the equities – meaning the sum of the market value of all stocks in a fund – of the mutual funds whose annual report was published in the respective quarter. By doing so, we get the percentage of the equities of one year covered by the mutual funds of the respective quarter. The four values we get over the year are used as weights for the country shares given by the quarterly MSCI All-Country Index. The result is a weighted average of each country share over one calendar year. Combining these weighted country shares gives the benchmark portfolio.

3.3 EMPIRICAL ANALYSIS

3.3.1 Analysis of the portfolios of mutual funds and private investors

Following the suggestions of the German Central Bank, we use the share of German and non-German securities of the world portfolio as a benchmark for diversification results (see Deutsche Bundesbank, 2001).

The German share of equities is calculated by dividing the market capitalization of German-listed firms by the market capitalization of all listed companies around the world. The benchmark amounts to a proportion of 5 percent for German equities for the last few years. A similar calculation is done for bonds. We divide the market value of listed bonds issued by the German government and German companies by the market value of all listed bonds worldwide. This results in a German share of 15 percent for bonds for the last few years. Alternative calculations which only use the major countries and/or assume a specific level of risk aversion provide an overall benchmark for equities and bonds of approximately 20 percent to 30 percent (Tesar and Werner, 1992; Statman, 1999; Amadi, 2004).

In the first part of our study, we analyse mutual fund portfolios. In the second part, we look at private investor behavior. German mutual funds are divided into two different groups: funds for private investors and funds for financial institutions and companies such as insurance firms, smaller banks, and pension funds. We analyse data for the last 15 years.

Table 3.1 shows the proportion of foreign investments for mutual funds which are sold to private investors. In the first column mutual funds are reported which mainly invest in equities.[3] The second column shows the same results for funds that mainly invest in bonds, while column 3 reports combined results for all mutual funds of this type.

The figures strongly support the expected home bias for mutual funds. The bias appears particularly strong in the 1990s and seems to be most prevalent for equities. While our data suggest that in recent years the funds begin to optimize their portfolios, in 2005 they are still far away from their respective benchmarks. The difference amounts to approximately 30 percentage points for equities and 25 points for bonds.

When we consider the second type of mutual funds (funds which are primarily bought by financial institutions) the figures in Table 3.2 paint a much grimmer picture for the 1990s. Yet, these mutual funds appear to optimize their portfolios more consistently in recent years. Thus, while they still remain below the benchmark, the difference amounts to only 10 percentage points for equities and about 20 points for bonds.

Overall, we observe a strong optimization rally, probably forced by the integration process of the European monetary union. Yet, much work remains to be done in future portfolio diversification.

Table 3.1 Foreign portfolio proportions of mutual funds for private investors

Year	Foreign portfolio proportion for *equities* and equity mutual funds sold to private investors	Foreign portfolio proportion for *bonds* and bond mutual funds sold to private investors	Foreign portfolio proportion for *equities and bonds* and all mutual funds sold to private investors
1990	22%*	72%	64%
1995	29%	48%	41%
2000	70%	59%	67%
2005 (June)	65%	58%	63%

Notes: We analyse the proportion of foreign investments for mutual funds which are sold to private investors. Column 1 shows the foreign share for mutual funds which mainly invest in equities (more than 50% of the fund's assets). Column 2 provides results for funds that mainly invest in bonds and column 3 reports the overall results for the foreign share of all mutual funds bought by private investors. The benchmark amounts to 5% for equities, 15% for bonds, and (when using major countries and/or assuming a specific level of risk aversion) 20% to 30% for both kinds of securities.

* Including mixed funds (where equities comprise more than 50% of total fund assets).

Table 3.2 Foreign portfolio proportions of mutual funds for (financial) institutions and firms

Year	Foreign portfolio proportion for *equities* and equity mutual funds sold to institutional investors	Foreign portfolio proportion for *bonds* and bond mutual funds sold to institutional investors	Foreign portfolio proportion for *equities and bonds* and all mutual funds sold to institutional investors
1990	n. a.*	n. a.*	18%
1995	21%	12%	17%
2000	76%	35%	53%
2005 (June)	84%	62%	65%

Notes: We analyse the proportion of foreign investments for mutual funds which are sold to institutional investors. Column 1 shows the foreign share for mutual funds which mainly invest in equities (more than 50% of the fund's assets). Column 2 provides results for funds that mainly invest in bonds and Column 3 reports the overall results for the foreign share of all mutual funds bought by institutional investors. The benchmark amounts to 5% for equities, 15% for bonds, and (when using major countries and/or assuming a specific level of risk aversion) 20% to 30% for both kinds of securities.

* Data not available from the official statistical report.

The second part of our analysis focuses on private investor behavior. We use data on direct investments of private investors, counted in their securities accounts at financial intermediaries (including the Central Bank). Again, we employ Central Bank data for the last 15 years.

Table 3.3 shows our results for the foreign share in private investors' portfolios, separated by equities (column 1), bonds (column 2), and mutual funds (column 3). Column 4 presents combined results for equities and bonds, while the figures in column 5 incorporate all three types of securities. Please note that for the years 1990, 1995 and 2000 some data are not available from the statistical reports and that the last available year is 2004.

At first glance, the figures in Table 3.3 suggest a very strong home bias of private investors for all types of securities. The portfolio diversification in equities and bonds appears to be very poor. We observe only a slight tendency for private investors to more optimally diversify in recent years.

At second glance, we have to take into consideration that at the same time private investors also buy mutual fund shares. As mentioned above, these funds display a much better diversification in their holdings than

Table 3.3 Foreign portfolio proportions of private investors' direct investments

Year	Foreign portfolio proportion for *equities* (direct investment of private investors)	Foreign portfolio proportion for *bonds* (direct investment of private investors)	Foreign portfolio proportion for *mutual fund shares* (direct investment of private investors)	Foreign portfolio proportion for *equities and bonds* (direct investment of private investors)	Foreign portfolio proportion for *all securities* (direct investment of private investors)
1990	n. a.*	19%	n. a.*	n. a.*	16%
1995	n. a.*	8%	n. a.*	n. a.*	15%
2000	n. a.*	11%	n. a.*	n. a.*	25%
2004	20%	18%	36%	19%	27%

Notes: We analyse the proportion of foreign investments for private investors' direct investments, held in their securities accounts at financial intermediaries (including the Central Bank). Column 1 shows the foreign share for equities. Columns 2 and 3 report the same results for bonds and mutual fund shares, respectively. Column 4 presents combined results for equities and bonds, while the figures in Column 5 incorporate all three types of securities. Please note that for the years 1990, 1995, and 2000 some data are not available from the statistical reports and that the last available year is 2004. The benchmark amounts to 5% for equities, 15% for bonds, and (when using major countries and/or assuming a specific level of risk aversion) 20% to 30% for both kinds of securities.

* Data not available from the official statistical report.

private investors. The overall investment in such mutual funds amounts to €173 billion and the direct investments only amount to €115 billion. Thus, we can conclude that the diversification of private investors is still very poor, but not hopeless.

In the next section we analyse mutual funds which are sold to private investors in detail. Following the extant literature we focus on the *equity* home bias and therefore discuss funds which mainly invest in equities (>50% of assets).

3.3.2 Analysis of the collected mutual fund data

The variables in this section are defined below. Please note that several countries are combined into groups. These combinations do not represent any political opinion or statement but are made purely for analytical purposes.

Descriptive statistics

Table 3.4 provides descriptive statistics for our data-set. Out of the average total net assets, security investments and bank deposits (cash holdings) range from 93.4 to 94.7 percent and 4.9 to 6.4 percent, respectively. In years in which the sum of security investments and bank deposits lies above 100 percent, there are – on average – short-term liabilities of the funds to be deducted to get the 100 percent in total net assets. If this sum lies below 100 percent, there are minor other assets, such as interest or dividend claims, that are not taken into consideration in our analysis.

The following empirical analysis is based on the share of equities in the securities investments of the funds. Over the whole period, this share lies at 99.0 percent or above, indicating that only a minimal share of the invested capital of the 102 funds is invested in bonds.

Table 3.4 Composition of the mutual funds' total net assets

	2000	2001	2002	2003
Share of total net assets				
security investments	94.4	93.4	94.5	94.7
bank deposits (cash)	5.8	6.4	5.5	4.9
Share of security investments				
equities	99.1	99.4	99.0	99.5

Notes: We analyse the proportion of securities investments and bank deposits (cash) in total net assets across all funds for the years 2000 to 2003. Furthermore the share of equities in security investments is documented over the same period. All values are in percent.

Results

After we documented a strong bias towards domestic equities in the mutual fund industry based on German Central bank data, the analysis of hand-collected data from the annual reports is intended to show where the excess weight relative to the benchmark comes from. For analytical purposes, we compare the share of German equities to that of equities from other major countries. In this analysis we apply the benchmark presented in section 3.2.3. As a selection criterion we use a threshold share of one percent in the benchmark index. The shares of countries with a weight of less than 1 percent are grouped under a separate category entitled "rest of the world" (ROW). The results are summarized in Table 3.5. The first outcome of this analysis is – not surprisingly – the confirmation of the home bias effect in Germany's mutual fund industry. While, according to the benchmark, the proportion of German equities in the portfolio should be around 4 to 5 percent, the actual share ranges from 18.8 percent in 2000 to 21.6 percent in 2003, hence a positive difference of 14.7 to 17.7 percentage points. Considerable excess weights can also be observed for France with about 4 to 5 percentage points above the benchmark, for Great Britain (about +2 to +4 points), and for the Netherlands (about +3 points). This investment behavior has to be balanced out by putting too little weight on other countries compared to the benchmark index. These countries are mainly the United States of America (about −12.2 to −23.2 points compared to the benchmark), Japan (about −4.1 to −7.7 points), and Canada (about −2 points).

Two effects deserve a closer examination: first, the strong decrease in mutual funds' US equity holdings despite an increase in the proportion of US equities in the benchmark portfolio, and second, the development of the share of the ROW during the period investigated. While this latter share represents a big deviation from the benchmark in 2000 (−5.8 percentage points), the divergence becomes comparatively small (−1.6 points) in the years 2002 and 2003. Some of the strong increase in the difference of equities from the US can be explained by a considerable increase of the US share in the benchmark from 2000 to 2001 (about 6 points). The biggest part of this increase appears to stem from the decrease in the share of Japan in the same period. This development is by no means reflected in US investments by the fund industry. The sharp decline in the actual proportion invested in stocks from US companies from 29 percent in 2001 to 25 percent in 2002, however, may be due to investors fearing a further deterioration of the US dollar value relative to the euro. Between the end of 2001 (€1 = $0.886) and the end of 2002 (€1 = $1.0481), the value of one US dollar had already fallen by about 15 percent compared to the euro. In order not to accrue further losses because of changes in the euro–dollar exchange rate, German investors might have significantly reduced their exchange rate exposure with regard to the US dollar by putting less money in funds that invested in US stocks.

Table 3.5 Proportion of equities invested in the largest countries

Country	2000			2001			2002			2003		
	ACT	BM	Diff.	ACT	BM	Diff.	ACT	BM	Diff.	ACT	BM	Diff.
AU	0.71	1.33	−0.62	0.48	1.14	−0.66	0.73	1.21	−0.48	0.58	1.18	−0.60
CA	0.59	2.29	−1.70	0.42	2.05	−1.62	0.35	1.87	−1.52	0.46	2.45	−1.98
CH	3.96	3.06	0.90	4.07	3.51	0.56	5.41	3.01	2.40	4.55	2.54	2.01
DE	18.83	4.16	14.67	19.83	5.02	14.71	19.86	4.29	15.58	21.55	3.83	17.73
ES	2.02	1.15	0.87	2.74	1.46	1.27	2.08	1.29	0.78	2.81	1.24	1.57
FR	8.92	3.27	5.64	9.54	4.26	5.28	9.34	4.22	5.12	9.59	4.97	4.62
GB	10.62	9.04	1.58	12.55	10.18	2.37	13.27	9.57	3.70	11.34	8.87	2.48
IT	2.79	1.54	1.25	2.71	2.13	0.58	3.28	1.94	1.34	2.65	1.92	0.73
JP	7.09	14.83	−7.74	5.35	9.40	−4.05	5.84	11.17	−5.32	7.18	11.88	−4.70
NL	5.57	2.43	3.13	5.86	2.59	3.27	5.78	2.50	3.28	5.00	2.38	2.62
US	29.99	42.17	−12.18	29.08	47.98	−18.90	24.96	48.20	−23.24	24.43	47.26	−22.83
ROW	8.92	14.73	−5.80	7.47	10.28	−2.81	9.11	10.74	−1.63	9.85	11.48	−1.63

Note: We analyse the proportion of mutual fund assets invested in equities from the eleven largest countries and the rest of the world. The determination of the size of the countries is based on their share of total market capitalization in the benchmark portfolio. For each year (2000 to 2003) the actual share of equities from the respective country is reported in the first column, denoted by ACT. The second column in the respective year provides the weight of the country in the benchmark (BM). The third column reports the difference (Diff.) between the actual weight and the benchmark weight, calculated as ACT-BM. Countries are abbreviated as follows: AU = Australia, CA = Canada, CH = Switzerland, DE = Germany, ES = Spain, FR = France, GB = Great Britain, IT = Italy, JP = Japan, NL = Netherlands, US = United States of America, ROW = Rest of the world. All values are in percent.

Another factor that may explain at least some of the decrease of the proportion of US equities in the mutual funds appears to lie in the development of the ROW.

In order to examine the above described development of the USA and the ROW and to take the excess weight of the mentioned European countries into account, we regroup our data as follows: the share of Germany remains separate and, hence, unchanged. The countries of the EU15 without Germany – Austria, Belgium, Denmark, Finland, France, Great Britain, Greece, Ireland, Italy, Luxemburg, the Netherlands, Portugal, Spain and Sweden, plus Liechtenstein, Norway and Switzerland – are combined to form the category Western Europe, whereas Eastern Europe comprises all remaining European countries provided that they are included in our data-set – Croatia, the Czech Republic, Estonia, Lithuania, Poland, Russia, Slovakia, Slovenia and Ukraine. Any European country that is not covered by one of the above variables is neither included in the MSCI All-Country Index nor were any of the mutual funds invested in that country. All other countries, meaning all non-European countries, are aggregated under the "rest of the world" category.

The illustrated procedure provides the results presented in Table 3.6. In addition to the already described home bias that causes investors to overinvest in German equities, we document that mutual fund managers invest a significantly higher share in Western European equities than would be appropriate according to the benchmark index. This positive divergence ranges between 13.1 and 16.7 percentage points without any clear upward or downward trend. We argue that these excess weights arise from a shift of the strong bias towards Germany (as reported for the 1990s in section 3.3.1) to a stronger focus on Western European countries at the end of the 1990s when the euro was introduced and stockmarkets became increasingly integrated. Even more remarkable, however, is the increase in the share of equities from Eastern Europe. While the benchmark weight of these equities decreased from 2000 to 2001 by nearly 50 percent and stayed at this low level through 2003, the share of the total investments in equities from Eastern Europe approximately doubled over the same period, leading to a proportion of these equities that is four times as high as the respective share in the benchmark index. Obviously, this result can be explained by strong economic growth prospects and by the development of the stock markets in Eastern European countries. These were driven – at least in some countries, for example, Poland or the Czech Republic – by the anticipated enlargement of the European Union that created overly optimistic investors throughout Europe. Investor over-optimism was particularly high in Germany – an economy that connects the "old" EU with the new member states. The share of the rest of the world in the examined funds fluctuates minimally around 30 percent, indicating that the changes in the shares of non-European countries, for example, the USA and Japan, offset each other nearly perfectly. The latter result

Table 3.6 Proportion of equities invested in Europe

	2000			2001			2002			2003		
	ACT	BM	Diff.	ACT	BM	Diff.	ACT	BM	Diff.	ACT	BM	Diff.
DE	18.83	4.16	14.67	19.73	5.02	14.71	19.86	4.29	15.58	21.55	3.83	17.73
W.Eur.	39.48	24.00	15.48	41.86	28.40	13.46	43.09	26.38	16.70	39.36	26.25	13.11
E.Eur.	0.64	0.48	0.15	0.72	0.26	0.46	1.30	0.24	1.07	1.20	0.28	0.92
ROW	41.06	71.35	−30.29	37.69	66.32	−28.63	35.75	69.09	−33.35	37.88	69.64	−31.76

Notes: We analyse the proportion of mutual fund assets invested in equities from Germany, Eastern and Western Europe, and the rest of the world. For each year (2000 to 2003) the actual share of equities from the respective country/group of countries is reported in the first column, denoted by ACT. The second column in the respective year provides the weight of the country/group of countries in the benchmark (BM). The third column reports the difference (Diff.) between the actual weight and the benchmark weight, calculated as ACT-BM. The countries/groups of countries are abbreviated as follows: DE = Germany, W.Eur. = Western Europe, E.Eur. = Eastern Europe, ROW = Rest of the world. All values are in percent.

supports our explanation given in the analysis of the major countries. Combining the above results, one has to conclude that there exists a strong – as we call it – "Europe bias" in the German mutual fund industry. The proportion of assets that is invested in European equities (including Germany) is approximately 70 percent, while investments in the rest of the world, including the two largest economies (the USA and Japan), account for the remaining 30 percent. According to the benchmark index, these distributions should be reversed. The strong focus on European equity, however, indicates that there is clear capital market integration across Europe, not surprising with regard to Western Europe, but in its extent somewhat unexpected for Eastern Europe. The extent of the home bias and of the Europe bias, however, is too high as that it could be explained by actively managed asset allocation as previously proposed in the literature.

3.4 CONCLUSION

The home bias of investors has caught the attention of academics since the 1970s. We have contributed to the extant research by examining the portfolio composition of private and institutional investors in Germany. The finance literature provides three alternative theories aimed to explain the bias of investors towards holding a greater proportion of domestic assets in their portfolio than would be adequate under traditional mean-variance analysis. Proponents of the first theory argue that direct transaction costs and other costs of international diversification are the driving forces behind the home-bias phenomenon. The second theory proposes that domestic assets provide a better hedge against home-country specific risks from non-traded wealth. As empirical support for these theories has been weak to date, we follow the third strand of research, which argues that the home bias is a result of investors being confronted with asymmetrically distributed information. This information asymmetry results in adjustments to perceived risk and asymmetric expectations. Within this framework, we analyze a data-set that incorporates official statistics of the German Central Bank and hand-collected data from the annual accounting reports of mutual funds.

Our results can be summarized as follows: both private and professional investors show a significant home bias; the extent of this anomaly, however, has substantially declined during the 1990s. In particular, mutual funds sold to institutional investors have taken the biggest strides towards international diversification. The extent of the bias in the portfolio allocation of private investors' direct investments is highest among all groups. Furthermore, the phenomenon of home-biased investors can be found for investments in both bonds and equities. By taking a closer look at the investment behavior of mutual funds in Germany, we could identify another phenomenon: these funds do not only show a home bias with regard to Germany, but also exhibit a "Europe bias", meaning that they invest a higher proportion of their assets than that predicted by our benchmark portfolio in companies from Eastern and Western Europe, whereas non-European countries, in particular Canada, Japan and the USA, are – compared to the benchmark – strongly underrepresented in the composition of the mutual funds' net assets.

We argue that the decline in the home bias is a result of improved (and cheaper) access to information, driven by the development of the Internet and other communication technologies. The Europe bias can be explained by forces coming from outside Germany, namely increasing capital market integration in Europe due to the European Monetary System as well as strong growth prospects in Eastern Europe. Although the extent of the home bias at the end of the investigation period becomes smaller, it is still far too great as that it could be explained by an actively managed allocation of the funds' assets. We argue that information remains asymmetrically distributed, although to a reduced degree, and that information asymmetry continues to be the primary reason for the irrational behavior of German investors.

NOTES

1. A related phenomenon is known in the macroeconomics literature. The observation that consumption growth rates do not move together across countries as much as international risk-sharing would suggest is referred to as "consumption home bias" (Lewis, 1999, and, more recently, Sorensen *et al.*, 2005). Real economy models which take consumer preferences into account show how consumers in different countries with different but uncertain production possibilities and different consumption preferences, can maximize utility by buying the equity of each producer of the separate commodities, of which there are two in each country in a simple example. If individuals in each country share risk from their country-specific production processes, then they hold securities that pay out claims against each other's production processes. Consumers in different countries should optimally diversify their domestic output risk by purchasing claims on the output of other countries. Due to space constraints we do not address this issue here in more detail.
2. Another issue related to adjusting returns is to account for estimation risk because returns cannot be precisely measured. However, Jorion (1985) as well as Glassman and Riddick (1994) have found that estimation risk can explain only a small part of the home bias.
3. We include mixed funds as long as the funds allocate more than 50 percent of their total assets to equities, measured in terms of market value.

REFERENCES

Adler, M. and Dumas, B. (1983) "International Portfolio Choice and Corporate Finance: A Synthesis", *Journal of Finance*, 38(3): 925–84.

Amadi, A. (2004) "Equity Home Bias: A Disappearing Phenomenon?", Working Paper, University of California at Davis.

Baxter, M. and Jermann, U.J. (1997) "The International Diversification Puzzle Is Worse than You Think", *American Economic Review*, 87(1): 170–80.

Bottazzi, L., Pesenti, P. and van Wincoop, E. (1996) "Wages, Profits, and the International Portfolio Puzzle", *European Economic Review*, 40(2): 219–54.

Brainard, W.C. and Tobin, J. (1992) "On the Internationalization of Portfolios", *Oxford Economic Papers*, 44(4): 533–65.

Brennan, M. and Cao, H. (1997) "International Portfolio Investment Flows", *Journal of Finance*, 52(5): 1851–80.

Chan, K., Covrig, V. and Ng, L. (2004) "What Determines the Domestic Bias and Foreign Bias? Evidence from Mutual Fund Equity Allocations Worldwide", Working Paper, Hong Kong University.

Coen, A. (2001) "Home Bias and International Capital Asset Pricing Model with Human Capital", *Journal of Multinational Financial Management*, 11(4–5): 497–513.

Cooper, I.A. and Kaplanis, E. (1994) "Home Bias in Equity Portfolios, Inflation Hedging, and International Capital Market Equilibrium", *Review of Financial Studies*, 7(1): 45–60.

Coval, J. and Moskowitz, T. (1999) "Home Bias at Home: Local Equity Preference in Domestic Portfolios", *Journal of Finance*, 54(6): 2045–73.

Dahlquist, M., Pinkowitz, L., Stulz, R.M. and Williamson, R. (2003) "Corporate Governance and the Home Bias", *Journal of Financial and Quantitative Analysis*, 38(1): 87–110.

Deutsche Bundesbank (1991a–2005a) *Monthly Report No. 2 on Financial Markets* (Frankfurt: Deutsche Bundesbank).

Deutsche Bundesbank (1991b–2005b) *Yearly Report No. 9 on Securities Accounts* (Frankfurt: Deutsche Bundesbank).

Deutsche Bundesbank (2001) *Monthly Report December* (Frankfurt: Deutsche Bundesbank).

Deutsche Bundesbank (2004c) *Monthly Report July* (Frankfurt: Deutsche Bundesbank).

Fellner, G. and Maciejovsky, B. (2003) "The Equity Home Bias: Contrasting an Institutional with a Behavioral Explanation", Working Paper, Max Planck Institute for Research into Economic Systems, Jena.

French, K.R. and Poterba, J.M. (1990) "Japanese and US Cross-border Common Stock Investments", *Journal of the Japanese and International Economies*, 4(4): 476–93.

French, K.R. and Poterba, J.M. (1991) "Investor Diversification and International Equity Markets", *American Economic Review*, 81(2): 222–6.

Gehrig, T. (1993) "An Information Based Explanation of the Domestic Bias in International Equity Investment", *Scandinavian Journal of Economics*, 95(1): 97–109.

Gerke, W., Mager, F. and Röhrs, A. (2005) "Twenty Years of International Diversification from a German Perspective", *Schmalenbach Business Review*, 57(April): 86–102.

Giannetti, M. and Koskinen, Y. (2003). "Investor Protection and Equity-Holdings: An Explanation of Two Puzzles?", SSE/EFI Working Paper No. 526, Stockholm.

Glassmann, D.A. and Riddick, L.A. (1994) "International Diversification: New Evidence on Market Segmentation", *International Review of Economics and Finance*, 3(1): 73–92.

Glassmann, D.A. and Riddick, L.A. (2001) "What Causes Home Asset Bias and How Should It Be Measured?", *Journal of Empirical Finance*, 8(1): 35–54.

Goetzmann, W.N. and Kumar, A. (2004) "Why Do Individual Investors Hold Under-Diversified Portfolios?", Working Paper, Yale University, New Haven.

Graham, J.R., Harvey, C.R. and Huang, H. (2005)."Investor Competence, Trading Frequency, and Home Bias", Working Paper, Duke University, Durham.

Grinblatt, M. and Keloharju, M. (2001) "How Distance, Language, and Culture Influence Stockholdings and Trades", *Journal of Finance*, 56(3): 1053–73.

Heath, C. and Tversky, A. (1991) "Preference and Belief: Ambiguity and Competence in Choice Under Uncertainty", *Journal of Risk and Uncertainty*, 4(1): 5–28.

Heston, S.L. and Roewenhorst, K.G. (1994) "Does Industrial Structure Explain the Benefits of International Diversification?", *Journal of Financial Economics*, 36(1): 3–27.

Jacquillat, B. and Solnik, B.H. (1978) "Multinationals Are Poor Tools for Diversification", *Journal of Portfolio Management*, 4(2): 8–12.

Jeske, K. (2001) "Equity Home Bias: Can Information Cost Explain the Puzzle?", *Federal Reserve Bank of Atlanta Economic Review*, 86(3): 31–42.

Jorion, P. (1985) "International Portfolio Diversification with Estimation Risk", *Journal of Business*, 58(3): 259–78.

Kahn, B.E. and Sarin, R.K. (1988) "Modeling Ambiguity in Decisions Under Uncertainty", *Journal of Consumer Research*, 15(2): 265–72.

Kang, J.-K. and Stulz, R.M. (1997) "Why Is There a Home Bias? An Analysis of Foreign Portfolio Equity Ownership in Japan", *Journal of Financial Economics*, 46(1): 3–28.

Kilka, M. (1998) *Internationale Diversifikation von Aktienportfolios* (Frankfurt: Lang).

Kilka, M. and Weber, M. (2000) "Home Bias in International Stock Return Expectations", *Journal of Psychology and Financial Markets*, 1(3): 176–92.

Kumar, A. (2004) "Is the Local Bias of Individual Investors Induced by Familiarity or Information-Asymmetry?", Working Paper, University of Notre Dame.

Lauterbach, B. and Reisman, H. (2004) "Keeping Up with the Joneses and the Home Bias", *European Financial Management*, 10(2): 225–34.

Lessard, D.R. (1973) "International Portfolio Diversification: A Multivariate Analysis for a Group of Latin American Countries", *Journal of Finance*, 28(3): 619–33.

Lessard, D.R. (1976) "World, Country, and Industry Relationships in Equity Returns: Implications for Risk Reduction through International Diversification", *Financial Analysts Journal*, 32(1): 32–8.

Levy, H. and Sarnat, M. (1970) "International Diversification of Investment Portfolios", *American Economic Review*, 60(4): 668–75.

Lewis, K.K. (1999) "Trying to Explain Home Bias in Equities and Consumption", *Journal of Economic Literature*, 37(2): 571–608.

Lütje, T. and Menkhoff, L. (2004) "What Drives Home Bias? Evidence from Fund Managers' View", Working Paper, University of Hannover.

Massa, M. and Simonov, A. (2004) "Hedging, Familiarity and Portfolio Choice", CEPR Discussion Paper 4789.

Maurer, R. and Mertz, A. (2000) "Internationale Diversifikation von Aktien- und Anleiheportfolios aus der Perspektive deutscher Investoren", *Die Betriebswirtschaft*, 60(4): 423–40.

Morse, A. and Shive, S. (2003) "Patriotism in Your Portfolio", Working Paper, University of Michigan at Ann Arbor.

Pesenti, P. and van Wincoop, E. (2002) "Can Nontradables Generate Substantial Home Bias?", *Journal of Money, Credit, and Banking*, 34(1): 25–49.

Rowland, P.F. (1999) "Transaction Costs and International Portfolio Diversification", *Journal of International Economics*, 49(1): 145–70.

Shiller, R.J., Kon-Ya, F. and Tsutsui, Y. (1991) "Speculative Behavior in the Stock Markets", NBER Working Paper 3613.

Solnik, B.H. (1974) "Why not Diversify Internationally Rather than Domestically?", *Financial Analysts Journal*, 30(4): 48–54.

Sorensen, B.E., Wu, Y.-T., Yosha, O. and Zhu, Y. (2005) "Home Bias and International Risk Sharing: Twin Puzzles Separated at Birth", Working Paper, University of Houston.

Statman, M. (1999) "Foreign Stocks in Behavioral Portfolios", *Financial Analysts Journal*, 55(2): 12–6.

Stulz, R.M. (1981) "On the Effects of Barriers to International Investment", *Journal of Finance*, 36(4): 923–34.

Tesar, L. and Werner, I.M. (1992) "Home Bias and the Globalization of Securities Markets", NBER Working Paper 4218.

Tesar, L. and Werner, I.M. (1994) "International Equity Transactions and US Portfolio Choice", in Frankel, J.A. (ed.), *The Internationalization of Equity Markets*, pp. 185–227 (Chicago, IL: University of Chicago Press).

Tesar, L. and Werner, I.M. (1995) "Home Bias and High Turnover", *Journal of International Money and Finance*, 14(4): 467–92.

Van Nieuwerburgh, S. and Veldkamp, L. (2004a) "Information Immobility and the Home Bias", Working Paper, Stern School of Business, New York University.

Van Nieuwerburgh, S. and Veldkamp, L. (2004b) "Information Acquisition and Portfolio Under-Diversification", Working Paper, Stern School of Business, New York University.

Von Nitzsch, R. and Stotz, O. (2005) "Zu welchen Renditeeinbußen führt der Home Bias?" *Forschungsbericht* 04/05, Aachen.

Weber, M. (1990) *Risikoentscheidungskalküle in der Finanzierungstheorie*, Stuttgart, Poeschel.

CHAPTER 4

International Mutual Fund Efficiency and Monetary Policy Sensitivity

Giampaolo Gabbi

4.1 INTRODUCTION

The financial literature demonstrates that mutual funds offer an efficient solution to diversify capital investments. If possible, this diversification is the highest when all the markets can be allocated in portfolios. This makes it obvious that international funds should be the most efficient to choose. The benefits of portfolio diversification across international investments have been considered by several researchers (Lessard, 1973; Errunza, 1983; Bailey and Stulz, 1990; Bailey and Lin, 1992; Eun, Kolodney and Resnick, 1991). On one hand, is it possible to measure the market efficiency of funds? On the flip side, shared funds' performance depend only upon managers' ability to forecast the timing and selection of stock and bonds? This study attempts to answer these questions, considering, above all, the sensitivity of funds' efficiency to monetary policy.

It is common knowledge that markets are influenced by macroeconomics events. Jensen and Johnson (1995) study the impact on the US equity market and Johnson, Buetow and Jensen (1999) examine the impact on international equity indices. Parallel to our study are authors that analyse how interest rates affect stock prices (Chen, Roll and Ross, 1986; Chang and Pinegar, 1990; Gangopadhyay, 1994; Ahmed and Lockwood, 1998).

The main thrust of this chapter is to examine whether there exists a strong relation between efficiency and monetary policy style. The plan of our study is as follows. In section 4.2 we present a model to estimate efficiency in the international mutual funds market and apply the model to international funds distributed in Italy. In section 4.3 we investigate how markets change their correlations when monetary policy alters their regime, while section 4.4 is devoted to demonstrating how international funds change their efficiency in different monetary environment.

4.2 THE EFFICIENCY MODEL AND ESTIMATES

Our theoretical approach to measure market efficiency is based on an asset management industry equilibrium environment with heterogeneous portfolio managers, along the lines suggested by Gomes (2001). We firstly analyse the behavior of three kinds of international funds operating in Italy:

(a) equity funds ($N = 205$);

(b) funds balanced between equity and bonds ($N = 100$);

(c) bond funds ($N = 135$).

These will be evaluated in terms of efficiency compared with their benchmark along five different holding periods. Efficiency is defined by the degree of losing or inefficient funds from the universe. We could say that the market will be inefficient if all the portfolio managers were able to beat the benchmark (1st and 2nd quadrants of Figure 4.1).

The benchmarks compared with fund performance and volatility are the MSCI AC Free World for equity, 50 percent JPM global and 50 percent MSCI AC World for balanced, and JPM Government Global for bond categories. The analysis has been carried out for five years, from September 1999 to September 2004. Five holding periods are computed backward from the final date (see Figure 4.2).

The first efficiency ratio ($ER1$) is simply computed as follows:

$$ER1 = \frac{\sum_{1}^{j} l_i}{n} \tag{4.1}$$

where l_i are all the funds that, independently from their volatility spread, are either in the third or in the fourth quadrant, and n is the number of the funds of the category.

What emerges from the analysis is that for shorter periods, the efficiency ratio is quite different from equity bond and balanced international

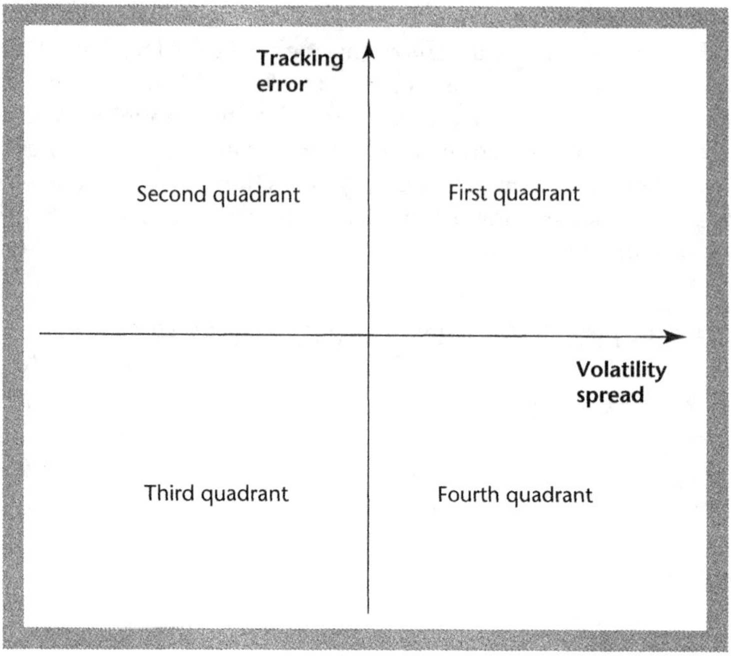

Figure 4.1 Dimensions of portfolio managers' efficiency
Notes: The figure is generated on the x-axis by the difference of funds and index standard deviations, and on the y-axis by the tracking error, that is the difference between the fund's performance and the index return. The best portfolio manager is placed in the second quadrant; the worst manager is placed in the fourth quadrant. When all the funds are located in the 3rd and/or in the 4th quadrant, it means that nobody is able to beat the market. In this case the market is considered efficient.

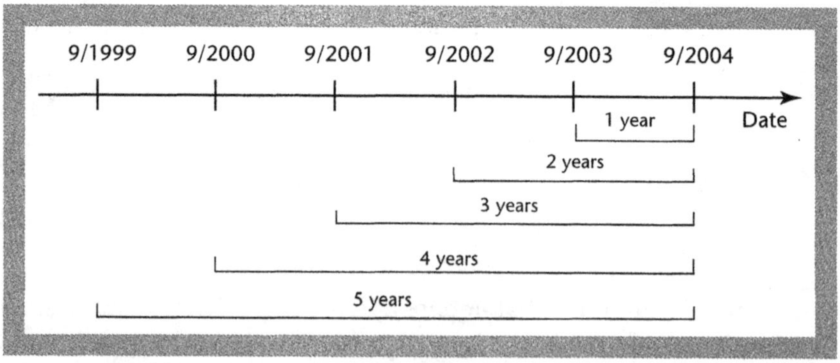

Figure 4.2 Holding periods, September 1999 to September 2004
Note: The figure shows how holding periods are computed to estimate the efficiency ratio as described in equation (4.1).

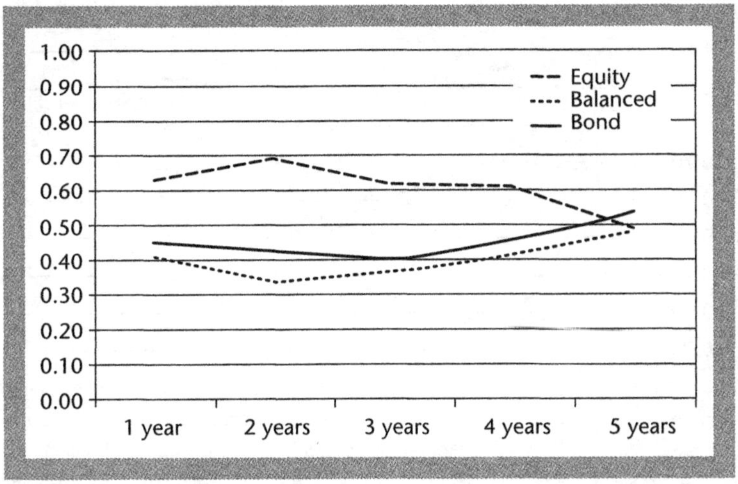

Figure 4.3 First efficiency ratio for international funds, September 1999 to September 2004

Note: The figure illustrates the dynamics of the first efficiency ratio according to equation (4.1) over five holding periods for three categories of international funds managed in the Italian market.

funds (Figure 4.3). In fact, for two years of time horizon the efficiency ratio reaches the 69.1 percent level in the equity class, and 34 percent for balanced funds. For five years, equity and balanced become almost equivalent (49 percent) and bond funds reach an efficiency ratio of 54 percent.

The efficiency ratio does not consider the volatility component but only the tracking error; what might usefully be reexamined is the nature of the odd quadrants. The third quadrant should be excluded by the computation because the volatility spread is negative, so performance is comprehensibly lower than the benchmark. On the opposing side, the first quadrant includes funds whose positive tracking error is justified by the positive volatility spread.

Therefore, the second efficiency ratio (*ER*2) is computed as follows:

$$ER2 = \frac{\sum_{1}^{m} Q_y^4}{\sum_{1}^{h} Q_k^2 + \sum_{1}^{m} Q_y^4} \tag{4.2}$$

where Q_y^4 are the *m* funds with higher volatility than their benchmark but with a lower performance (quadrant 4); and Q_k^2 are the *h* funds with lower volatility than their benchmark and, nevertheless, higher performance (quadrant 2).

As shown in Figure 4.4, the pattern of the second efficiency ratio is not considerably different from the first (Figure 4.3), except for balanced funds which appear to be in between equity and bond classes in four periods out

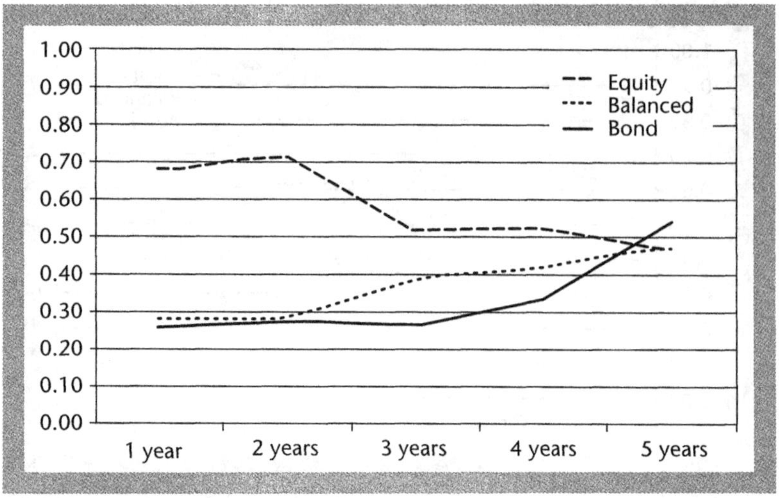

Figure 4.4 Second efficiency ratio for international funds, September 1999 to September 2004

Note: The figure illustrates the dynamics of the second efficiency ratio according to equation (4.1) over five holding periods for three categories of international funds managed in the Italian market.

of five. The reasons that explain the phenomenon described by the two ratios are as follows:

(a) active equity international funds, in general terms, are more weighted in European markets than US and Japanese funds;

(b) in the short-run the equity class of funds appears more efficient than the bond class: this is due to the ability of portfolio managers to forecast interest rate dynamics, while stock selection appears to be more problematical;

(c) finally, for point (b), balanced funds are more bond than equity-oriented: this is due to their close similarity.

Estimation of the two efficiency ratios reveals that the three principal equity markets behave differently from each other. Figures 4.5 and 4.6 show that the curves for Japan and North American equity funds are in the upside area, indicating a higher level of efficiency than Europe; additionally, the longer the holding period the higher the efficiency in Japan and North America.

On the other hand, the European equity funds hover around the 50 per cent value, with a negative slope for longer periods. The same slope, even though with different values, is displayed by the second efficient ratio for the three markets (Figure 4.6). If portfolio managers followed the weights of the three markets in the MSCI World they would have a larger component of efficient funds which implies unprofitable stocks. Table 4.1 contains

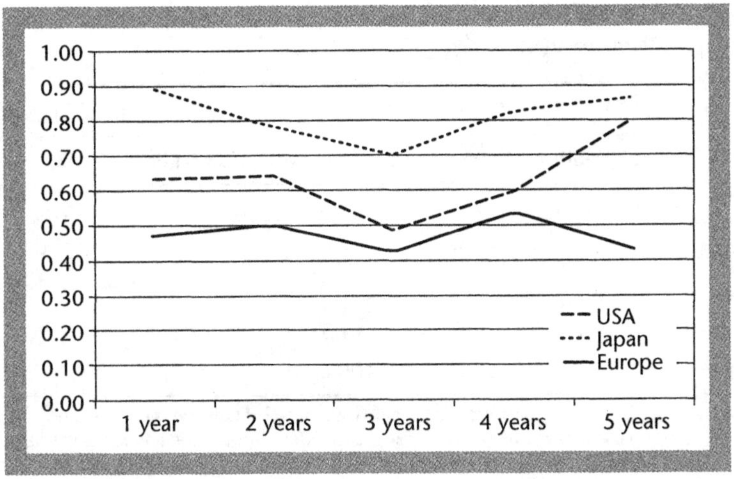

Figure 4.5 First efficiency ratio for international funds, September 1999 to September 2004

Note: The figure illustrates the dynamics of the first efficiency ratio according to equation (4.1) over five holding periods for three categories of geographical (North America, Japan and Europe) funds managed in the Italian market.

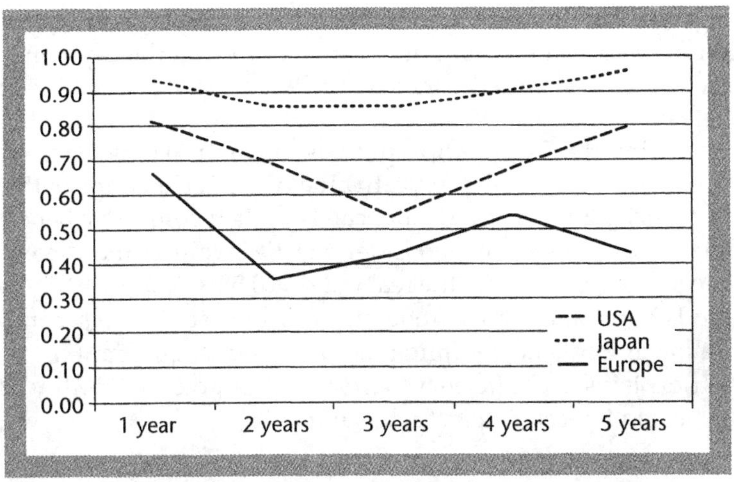

Figure 4.6 Second efficiency ratio for international funds, September 1999 to September 2004

Note: The figure illustrates the dynamics of the second efficiency ratio according to equation (4.2) over five holding periods for three categories of geographical (North America, Japan and Europe) funds managed in the Italian market.

Table 4.1 Total market capitalization of the MSCI Global Capital Markets Index, 31 March 2005

	Equity			Fixed income		
	US$ trillion	**%**	**% in equity**	**US$ trillion**	**%**	**% in bond**
USA	11.19	27.7	53.0	8.00	19.8	41.5
Europe	6.30	15.6	29.8	6.18	15.3	32.1
Japan	2.46	6.1	11.7	2.83	7	14.7
Other	1.17	2.9	5.5	2.26	5.6	11.7
Total	**21.13**	**52.3**	**100.0**	**19.27**	**47.7**	**100.0**

Notes: The table shows how financial wealth is shared, firstly between equities and bonds, and secondly among the three primary economic areas. *Other* contains the emerging markets and high yield bonds. In *High Yield* bonds are globally considered and not shared by geographical area. The *US* row includes, for the fixed income data, not only sovereign and investment grade issues, but also mortgages. *Japan* contains investments in the Pacific area too. The second column illustrates the global weights of equities in the world, while in the third column we compute how the four areas become part of the MSCI Equity World. The fifth column illustrates the global weights of fixed income in the world, while in the sixth column we compute the breakdown of the World Bond Index.
Source: MSCI Global Capital Markets Index™.

the weights according to the MSCI Global Capital Markets Index™. We computed the theoretical efficient ratios generated under the hypothesis for every international fund with the weights illustrated in Table 4.1.

Figure 4.7 shows a rational behavior of portfolio managers in international funds distributed in Italy. In fact, following the capitalization of the index, the average and theoretical efficient ratio would be higher than the actual one.

Averaging the five holding periods, our indexes display a real *ER1* of 0.61 compared with a theoretical value of 0.67. This implies that there are more than 6 percent of funds that can beat their respective benchmark. The difference is higher if we consider the *ER2* values: the theoretical index would suggest 0.74, while the real index is 0.58. In this case, the lower value depends both on a higher frequency of funds set in the second quadrant, and a lower frequency of funds set in the fourth quadrant. A second point which explains the efficiency pattern is the potential ability of portfolio managers to forecast interest rates dynamics.

4.3 MONETARY POLICY SENSITIVITY OF INTERNATIONAL INDICES

The financial literature has examined the relation between fund returns and monetary policy, displaying how correlations between benchmarks change

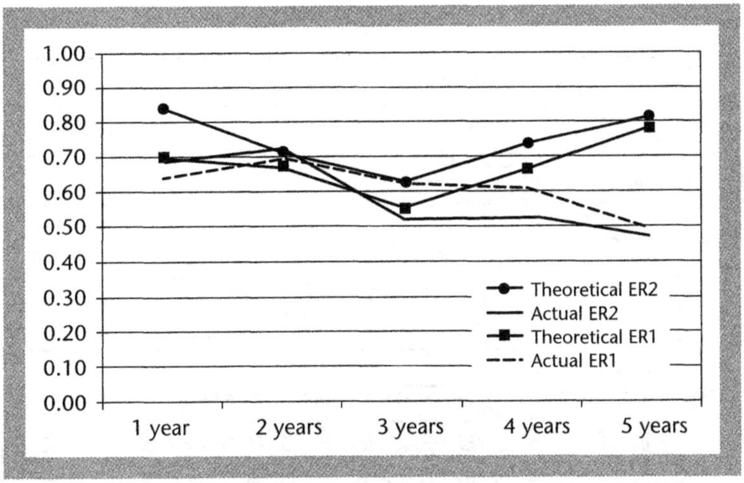

Figure 4.7 Actual and theoretical efficiency ratios for equity funds, September 1999 to September 2004

Notes: The figure illustrates the dynamics of the two efficiency ratios according to equations (4.1) and (4.2) periods for equity funds compared with the theoretical ratios. Theoretical efficient ratios are generated under the hypothesis that every international fund has the weights of the total market capitalization of the MSCI Global Capital Markets Index shown in Table 4.1.

in different periods for interest rates trends. Figure 4.8 is the evidence for the dynamics of official rates in the three primary markets where international funds invest money.

During the period under examination, the Japanese economy experienced a long deflationary phase, and the Bank of Japan tried to tackle the problem through a zero rate monetary policy. However, we do not comment on this policy, but believe that deflation is quite costly and is a key element in both preventing and escaping deflation. This is viewed as the management of expectations, using either price level or inflation targeting, because the zero lower bound on interest rates means that the overnight interest rate can no longer be used as the instrument of monetary policy. This way, portfolio managers investing in Japanese markets are quite sure of the future pattern of interest rates. The level and trend of Japanese rates is probably ineffective in terms of portfolio choice. On the flip side, the US rate followed two important phases which significantly altered the volatility of interest rates and the relative performance of funds.

Until the end of 2000, American monetary policy

focused on promoting price stability over the long run ... pre-emptive policymaking is equally applicable in both directions, as has been evident over the years both in our inclination to raise interest rates when the potential for inflationary pressures

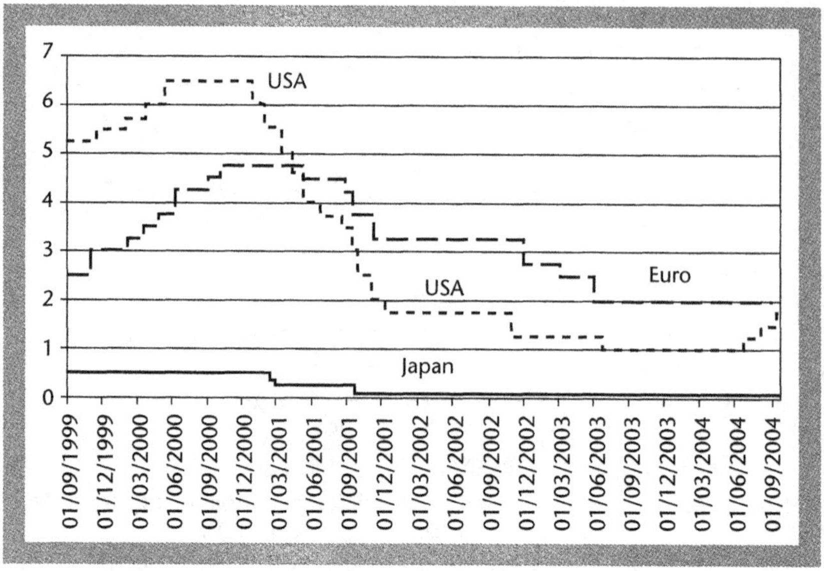

Figure 4.8 Pattern of official rates in the USA, Euro area and Japan, September 1999 to September 2004

emerged, as in the spring of 1994, or to lower rates when the more palpable risk was economic weakness, as in the fall of last year … Stable prices allow households and firms to concentrate their efforts on what they do best: consuming, producing, saving, and investing. A rapidly rising or a falling general price level would confound market signals and place strains on the system that ultimately may throttle economic expansion.

(Greenspan, 1999)

The policy from the beginning of 2001 changed into a development-orientation, by decreasing interest rates from 6.5 to 1.0 percent. But, since July 2004 the policy has changed to become anti-inflationary.

The European Central Bank is generally known to target its monetary policy towards a stability of interest rates; nevertheless, during the period 1999–2003 the direction and cyclical phases of Fed and ECB interventions were not very different. This is the reason why there is an impact of the Fed rate changes over the efficiency of international-oriented funds in Italy.

The first element we investigate is the correlation coefficient among benchmarks in different monetary policy phases. This factor is crucial since diversification benefits are usually quoted as the reason to invest in portfolios (or funds) internationally oriented, both in equity and in fixed-income securities. Sometimes, correlations are supposed to increase in bear periods, especially when characterized by negative shocks; the domino effect moves into global crisis making covariance coefficients higher than in normal times; however, on some occasions correlations are linked to monetary policy

Table 4.2 Correlations among the MSCI Indexes and the Fed rate

	MSCI AC Europe	MSCI AC Free World	MSCI Japan	MSCI USA
Panel A: Entire sample period, Sept. 1999–Sept. 2004				
MSCI AC Europe	1	0.95	0.38	0.91
MSCI AC Free World	0.95	1	0.53	0.98
MSCI Japan	0.38	0.53	1	0.44
MSCI USA	0.91	0.98	0.44	1
	MSCI AC Europe	**MSCI AC Free World**	**MSCI Japan**	**MSCI USA**
Panel B: Following increases in the FED Discount Rate (9/1999–12/2000)				
MSCI AC Europe	1	0.87	0.54	0.77
MSCI AC Free World	0.87	1	0.82	0.97
MSCI Japan	0.54	0.82	1	0.78
MSCI USA	0.77	0.97	0.78	1
	MSCI AC Europe	**MSCI AC Free World**	**MSCI Japan**	**MSCI USA**
Panel C: Following decreases in the FED Discount Rate (1/2001–6/2004)				
MSCI AC Europe	1	0.95	0.47	0.9
MSCI AC Free World	0.95	1	0.61	0.98
MSCI Japan	0.47	0.61	1	0.53
MSCI USA	0.9	0.98	0.53	1
	MSCI AC Europe	**MSCI AC Free World**	**MSCI Japan**	**MSCI USA**
Panel D: Following increases in the FED Discount Rate (6/2004–9/2004)				
MSCI AC Europe	1	0.89	0.34	0.87
MSCI AC Free World	0.89	1	0.69	0.98
MSCI Japan	0.34	0.69	1	0.62
MSCI USA	0.87	0.98	0.62	1

Notes: In this table we provide the correlations among monthly index returns for MSCI AC Europe, MSCI AC Free World, MSCI Japan and MSCI USA. Correlations are shown for the entire sample period and also over sub-periods of increasing and decreasing US Federal Reserve discount rate.

styles. Johnson, Buetow and Jensen (1999), investigating the behavior of US balanced mutual funds and different international indexes, find that correlation matrices do not change significantly between the two monetary regimes.

Ahmed, Gangopadhyay and Nanda (2001) study the dynamics of correlation coefficient for funds investing in emerging markets. One of their purposes is to find out whether there is an effect generated by the US monetary policy change. In their study, correlations among emerging markets are higher in expansionary monetary periods than in restrictive ones. They substantiate this conclusion because "diversification benefits of investing in emerging market funds are greater in restrictive monetary environments, which are precisely when an American investor might look towards investing outside their domestic market".

Our study is focused in rich markets, and the "flight to quality" rationalization cannot be applied. In fact, our outcomes (Table 4.2) show that correlations increase in restrictive monetary policy periods. On average, correlations for the entire period of our study are 0.6983. When Fed rates increase, correlations increase to 0.7917.

The results are not different if we consider the European Central Bank policy, where the correlations increase to 0.79 (Table 4.3).

These findings show a difference between our results and those of previous studies. Our empirical evidence is consistent with the hypothesis that

Table 4.3 Correlations among the MSCI Indexes and the ECB rate

	MSCI AC Europe	MSCI AC Free World	MSCI Japan	MSCI USA
Panel A: Entire sample period (9/1999–9/2004)				
MSCI AC Europe	1	0.95	0.38	0.91
MSCI AC Free World	0.95	1	0.53	0.98
MSCI Japan	0.38	0.53	1	0.44
MSCI USA	0.91	0.98	0.44	1
	MSCI AC Europe	**MSCI AC Free World**	**MSCI Japan**	**MSCI USA**
Panel B: Following increases in the ECB Refinancing Rate (9/1999–5/2001)				
MSCI AC Europe	1	0.88	0.54	0.78
MSCI AC Free World	0.88	1	0.8	0.97
MSCI Japan	0.54	0.8	1	0.77
MSCI USA	0.78	0.97	0.77	1
	MSCI AC Europe	**MSCI AC Free World**	**MSCI Japan**	**MSCI USA**
Panel C: Following increases in the ECB Refinancing Rate (5/2001–9/2004)				
MSCI AC Europe	1	0.94	0.44	0.89
MSCI AC Free World	0.94	1	0.59	0.98
MSCI Japan	0.44	0.59	1	0.51
MSCI USA	0.89	0.98	0.51	1

Notes: In this table we provide the correlations among monthly index returns for MSCI AC Europe, MSCI AC Free World, MSCI Japan, MSCI USA. Correlations are shown for the entire sample period and also over sub-periods of increasing and decreasing European Central Bank (ECB) discount rate.

official interest rates rise more frequently in phases of high development, at least in the US market during recent years, and not the opposing direction as suggested by Ahmed, Gangopadhyay and Nanda (2001).

4.4 INTERNATIONAL MUTUAL FUNDS EFFICIENCY AND MONETARY POLICY

The last section of our study analyses the impact of monetary policy on efficiency in international mutual funds. We demonstrate how the different monetary environments can affect the behavior of portfolio managers, using both the plot of Figure 4.1 and the efficiency ratios (*ER*1 and *ER*2). In the case of equity funds, when interest rates trend upwards, the preponderance of managers tends to increase the volatility spread (Figure 4.9).

As expected, the function that describes the interpolated values is positively sloped, with a coefficient of 0.45, even though *R*-squared is quite low (approximately 12 percent). Everything changes in the expansive phase when Fed interest rates dropped from 6.5 to 1.0 percent and the expectations were clearly managed by the central bank towards a negative direction for approximately three years.

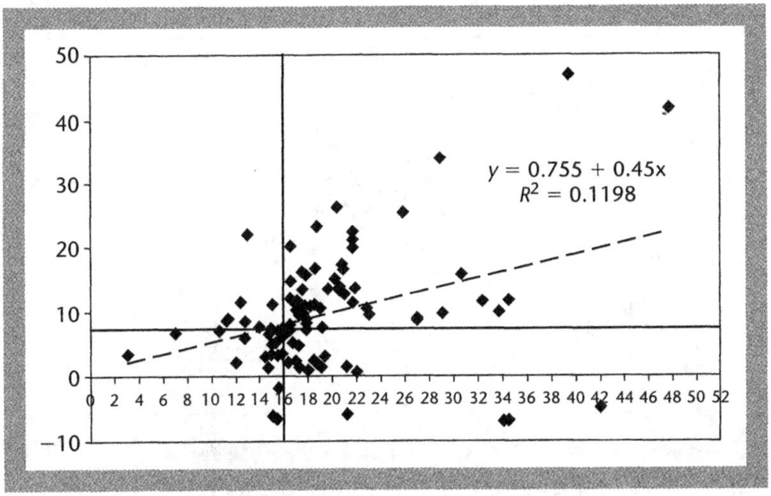

Figure 4.9 Equity international funds in a restrictive environment, September 1999 to December 2000

Notes: The figure illustrates the scattering graph of the equity international funds in the Fed restrictive environment. The x-axis dimension is the standard deviation, the y-axis dimension is the tracking error. The intersection of the two lines is the benchmark (MSCI AC Free World) origin, which generates the four quadrants described in Figure 4.1. The dotted line is the linear interpolated regression model and the *R*-squared value is displayed.

Figure 4.10 shows that funds are generally more concentrated around the benchmark, but, above all, the interpolation is negatively-sloped (coefficient −0.87), with a higher *R*-squared (51.2 percent).

The same behavior is shown by bond mutual funds. During the restrictive period (Figure 4.11), the funds are distributed more widely around the index (JPM Global): the value of *R*-squared, in fact, reflects this, being only 34.4 percent. In the expansive phase (Figure 4.12), it becomes 67.8 percent. Almost all the funds appear close to the interpolating function. But, like the phenomenon already described for the equity class of funds, fixed income funds also distribute more in the first and third quadrant in the restrictive period and more in the second and fourth quadrant in the expansive environment.

Our findings depend on the fact that when interest rates increase, both equity and bond portfolio managers tend to heterogeneous behaviors, at least in term of volatility. The performance gives on average a premium to portfolios with betas higher than 1 (first quadrant). The opposite occurs in the case of expansive monetary policy. The case we studied was probably sufficiently long (3.5 years) that some active managers were able to generate returns higher than the benchmark even with lower volatility. That was the case for the bond market, where long positions generated good performance coherently with the expectations of interest rate cuts (Table 4.4).

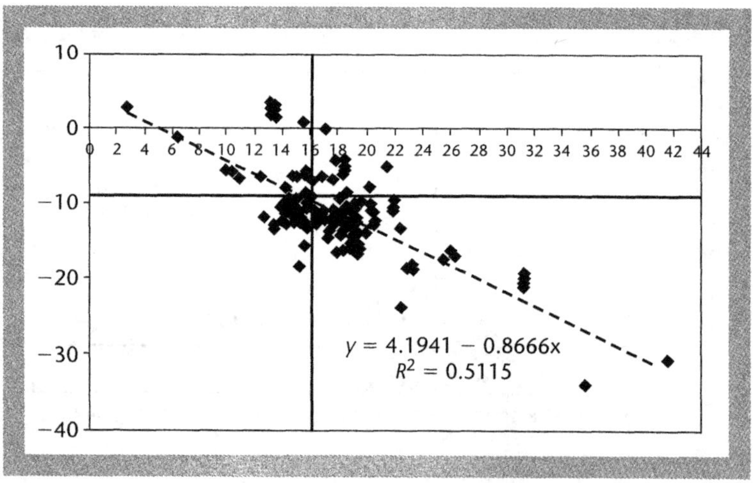

Figure 4.10 Equity international funds in expansive environment, January 2001 to June 2004

Notes: The figure illustrates the scattering graph of the equity international funds in the Fed expansive environment. The x-axis dimension is the standard deviation; the y-axis dimension is the tracking error. The intersection of the two lines is the benchmark (MSCI AC Free World) origin, which generates the four quadrants described in Figure 4.1. The grey line is the linear interpolated regression model and the *R*-squared value is displayed.

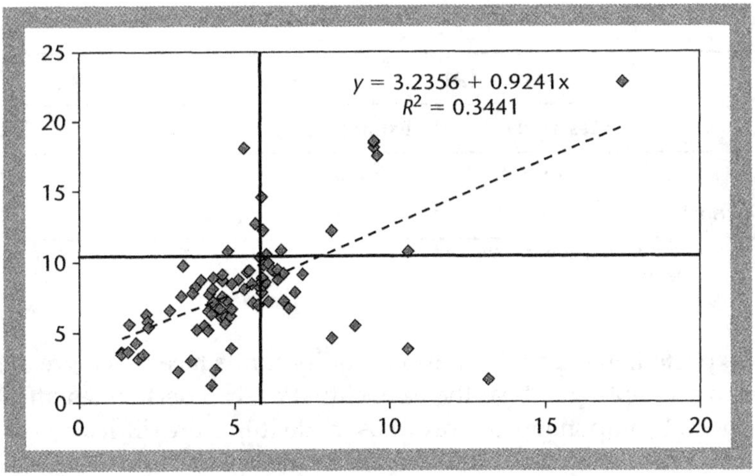

Figure 4.11 Fixed income international funds in restrictive environment, September 1999 to December 2000

Notes: The figure illustrates the scattering graph of the fixed income international funds in the Fed restrictive environment. The x-axis dimension is the standard deviation; the y-axis dimension is the tracking error. The intersection of the two lines is the benchmark (JPM Global) origin, which generates the four quadrants described in Figure 4.1. The dotted line is the linear interpolated regression model and the *R*-squared value is displayed.

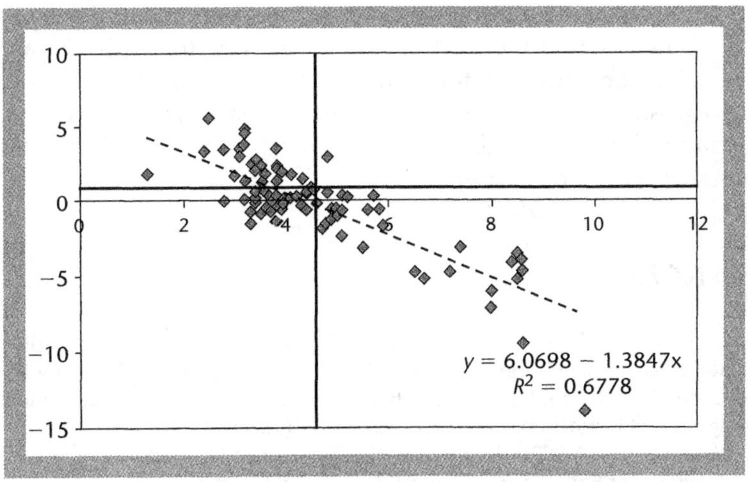

Figure 4.12 Fixed income international funds in expansive environment, January 2001 to June 2004

Table 4.4 Efficient ratios in restrictive and expansive environments

	*ER*1		*ER*2	
	Restrictive	**Expansive**	**Restrictive**	**Expansive**
Equity	42,7	78,9	76,67	79,51
Fixed income	80,7	65,8	83,33	44,12

Note: In this table we provide the efficient ratios (*ER*1 and *ER*2) for equity and bond mutual funds computed in the two monetary regimes.

As expected, in expansive periods equity funds face much greater difficulties in attempting to beat their benchmark. The crisis which affected all the principal components of portfolios made this more difficult.

4.5 CONCLUSION

In this study we have developed a model to estimate efficiency in international mutual funds. We interpret returns and volatility spreads with benchmarks and construct a four-diagram plot to calculate two efficiency ratios. We have studied international funds (distributed in Italy) investing in equities and bonds. We have showed that in the short run portfolio managers prefer fixed incomes for their ability to forecast the interest rate direction. In the long run (4–5 years) this ability lessens and efficiency increases.

The capability to understand the interest rate trend depends on monetary policy style, which tries to affect markets, even before official interventions. We demonstrate there is an asymmetry in terms of portfolio decisions and performances when the central bank (in our case the Federal Reserve) moves the official interest rate. Our outcomes can be useful for portfolio managers, for asset allocators and investors. All of them can decide to take an active or a positive position (in terms of tracking-error volatility), not only evaluating timing and stock/bond picking ability, but also the sensitivity of the mark to the monetary policy regime.

REFERENCES

Ahmed, P., Gangopadhyay, P. and Nanda, S. (2001) "Performance of Emerging Market Mutual Funds and U.S. Monetary Policy", Penn State Harrisburg Working Paper.

Ahmed, P. and Lockwood, L.J. (1998) "Changes in Factor Beta and Risk Premiums Over Varying Market Conditions", *Financial Review*, 33(2): 149–68.

Bailey, W. and Lin, J. (1992) "Evaluating the Diversification Benefits of New Country Funds", *Journal of Portfolio Management*, 18(1): 74–80.

Bailey, W. and Stulz, R.M. (1990) "Benefits of International Diversification: The Case of Pacific Basin Stock Markets", *Journal of Portfolio Management*, 16(1): 57–61.

Chang, E.C. and Pinegar, J.M. (1990) "Stock Market Seasonals and Prespecified Multifactor Pricing Relations", *Journal of Financial and Quantitative Analysis*, 25(4): 517–32.

Chen, N.F., Roll, R. and Ross, S.A. (1986) "Economic Forces and the Stock Market", *Journal of Business*, 59(3): 383–403.

Errunza, V.R. (1983) "Emerging Markets: A New Opportunity for Improving Global Portfolio Performance", *Financial Analysts Journal*, 39(1): 51–8.

Eun, C.S., Kolodny, R. and Resnick, B.G. (1991) "U.S. Based International Mutual Funds: A Performance Evaluation", *Journal of Portfolio Management*, 19(1): 88–94.

Gangopadhyay, P. (1994) "Risk-Return Seasonality and Macroeconomic Variables", *Journal of Financial Research*, 17(3): 347–61.

Gomes, J. (2001) "Financing Investment", *American Economic Review*, 91(3–4): 1263–85.

Greenspan, A. (1999). *Testimony of Chairman Alan Greenspan. The Federal Reserve's Semi-annual Report on Monetary Policy Before the Committee on Banking and Financial Services,* U.S. House of Representatives, July 22.

Jensen, G.R. and Johnson, R.R. (1995) "Discount Rate Changes and Security Returns in the U.S., 1962–1991", *Journal of Banking and Finance*, 19(1): 79–95.

Johnson, R.R., Buetow, G.W. and Jensen, G.R. (1999) "International Mutual Fund Returns and Federal Reserve Policy", *Financial Services Review*, 8(2): 199–210.

Lessard, D.R. (1973) "International Portfolio Diversification: A Multivariate Analysis for a Group of Latin American Countries", *Journal of Finance*, 28(4): 619–33.

Takatoshi, I. and Mishkin, F.S. (2004) "Two Decades of Japanese Monetary Policy and the Deflation Problem", NBER Working Paper. www.nber.org/papers/w10878.pdf

CHAPTER 5

Equity Portfolio Construction: A Comparative Analysis

Raffaele Zenti, Massimiliano Pallotta, Claudio Marsala and Stefano Ricci

5.1 INTRODUCTION

Alpha generation and portfolio construction are key parts of the investment process, together with portfolio implementation. The purpose of portfolio construction is to create and maintain, through a logical sequence of steps, optimal combinations of investment vehicles to achieve stated goals, starting from a set of forecasted asset returns. In other words, it is the process by which individual assets are combined together to create a portfolio which meets given objectives in terms of return and risk.

Portfolio construction starts after the alpha generation process is completed, that is, after performing proper market analysis and generating forecasts for asset returns.[1] A portfolio manager's "investment philosophy" can lead to a variety of methods for forecasting asset returns: style rotation, momentum strategies, fundamental analysis, macroeconometric modelling, time series analysis, and so on. A survey of methods to extract alpha can be found, among others, in Oberuc (2003) and in Cochrane (2001).

Analysing the alpha generation process is beyond the scope of this work; we prefer instead to focus on portfolio construction issues for several reasons. First, forecasting returns is a difficult task, if not impossible. Hence, any method for successfully forecasting returns is so valuable that it would be unrealistic and ingenuous to publish it. Secondly, many investment managers, especially traditional stock-pickers, often believe that their portfolios of attractive stocks must form attractive portfolios: portfolio managers' fascination with security valuation tends to obscure critical issues of portfolio construction. These issues can eventually determine whether a portfolio is attractive or not in terms of actual returns. Scherer (2004) shows that investment success for a given level of skill is significantly higher when a portfolio construction process is in place. This is especially true for low levels of investment skill, which (unfortunately for us asset managers) are also the most realistic. Hence, in our opinion it is well worth looking at portfolio construction techniques.

It is worth noting that portfolio management does not end with alpha generation and portfolio construction. There is another key phase that starts after portfolio construction: portfolio implementation. Portfolio implementation is about transforming a model portfolio into a real-world portfolio; that is, creating and executing orders in an efficient way: the point is that defining a portfolio is one thing, delivering it to clients is another. A good portfolio implementation includes benefiting from the greater efficiency provided by electronic communications networks. Thanks to advances in technology, opportunities have arisen for investors to change the way orders are routed, secure lower trading costs, and eventually enhance investment returns. Those investors who are willing to invest in order to exploit the use of new electronic trading technologies can really minimize the difference between "model" and "actual" portfolios. Neglecting the portfolio implementation phase can easily lead to destroy any value added so far by the investment process.

The portfolio construction process begins by defining the portfolio's goals. We assume the perspective of a professional investor that manages a portfolio whose goals are well-defined, that is, she or he knows the desired return and risk profile and the main investment constraints. In particular, in this work we assume that the goal is to construct a minimum-variance, benchmark-relative, equity portfolio, using a subset of the available stocks; for example, benchmark constituents. Hence we are talking of minimum Tracking Error Volatility (TEV) portfolios defined using a subset of constituents. Our interest in this kind of portfolio arises from the fact that it may be crucial to define such portfolios in order to track indices with a relatively small amount of money (small passive portfolios), or excluding certain assets that are not actively traded, for example, not liquid enough. In addition, these tracking portfolios are central in core-satellite investing. Core-satellite investing is a relatively new paradigm that advocates the clear distinction of investments into a passive part (the core) and an active part (one or more satellites). The main reason for core-satellite investing is to rationalize the allocation of alpha and beta bets: exposure to the stockmarket, for example beta exposure, is managed through the passive sub-portfolio and some cash or futures, while market-neutral stock bets, for example alpha bets, are distinctly managed using satellite sub-portfolios that should exhibit low correlation with the rest of the portfolio. Minimum TEV portfolios are also valuable as building blocks for tactical asset allocation strategies, when the use of futures or ETFs is impracticable or more expensive. Anyway, minimum TEV portfolios allow us to bypass the problem of predicting returns.

The goal of this chapter is to compare different ways to deal with constructing benchmark-relative, low TEV, portfolios of stocks.

The rest of the chapter is organized as follows. We describe the main steps of portfolio construction, discussing various alternatives that a practitioner has to choose from, in section 5.2. Our methodology for comparing the outcome of each alternative that we examine is described in section 5.3, alongside the characteristics of the data-sets we use for back-testing. The results are listed in section 5.4, and we summarize and conclude in section 5.5.

5.2 PORTFOLIO CONSTRUCTION: THE MAIN STEPS

Having completed our market analysis and generated forecasts (alpha signals, that can be absent for a pure passive portfolio) we employ a structured process to turn them into portfolio decisions. This process involves several steps, and in what follows we discuss the main steps. We also describe the choices we make (and subsequently test) for each step. We examine several combinations of these elements, where each alternative is called a "specification".

5.2.1 Use of constraints

Restrictions on the investment universe

There are several types of constraints. Some clients or mandates specify the assets in which a portfolio manager may not invest or, instead, specify concentration limits. Typically, these constraints origin from unique preferences and needs, or specific risk aversion, or from tax issues, and they may concern single securities or asset classes. Constraints may relate to countries, sectors/industries, and so on. Similarly, there are regulatory constraints on how much or how little may be invested in a particular asset class, or financial instrument, or issuer.

Restrictions are usually expressed in terms of linear constraints on portfolio weights, and can be expressed in absolute terms or as deviations from the benchmark portfolio. Introducing constraints generally reduces the efficiency of the solution. Thinking in terms of mathematical programming, a constrained solution is less optimal than an unconstrained solution, if constraints are binding (if not, there is no difference).

Imposing constraints is a simple way to cope with the unstable and extreme weights that arise from the application of standard optimal allocation policies based on Markowitz's basic (1952, 1959) model. Jagannathan and Ma (2003) show that the use of constraints can be interpreted as a Bayesian shrinkage of the covariance matrix. We will discuss Bayesian shrinkage estimators of the covariance matrix in section 5.2.3.

In all the specifications we impose the standard constraints that the portfolio has to be long-only (short-sales are not allowed) and that weights sum up to 1.

We also impose constraints derived from concentration limits of the UCITS rules, binding for most portfolios in the European Union. Basically, they say that the maximum weight allowed, for each security held, is 10 percent, and that the sum of all the securities' weights that exhibit weight greater than 5 percent has to be bounded to 40 percent. There are other limits imposed by law, but these two are the most relevant from our practical perspective.

From a formal point of view, this means that we impose the following constraints:

$$w_i \in [0,\ 0.1], \qquad i = 1, 2, 3, \ldots, n \tag{5.1}$$

$$\sum_{i:w_i \geq 0.05} w_i \leq 0.4 \tag{5.2}$$

$$\sum_i w_i = 1 \tag{5.3}$$

where w_i is the weight of asset i in our portfolio, and n is the number of securities in the investment universe.

As our aim is to replicate an index with a limited number of securities, we also put a constraint on the maximum number of assets held, *Max_n*, that is:

$$n \leqslant Max\_n. \tag{5.4}$$

For our base case we set *Max_n* equal to 250 (out of more than 500 stocks), even if we also attempt to optimize with 100 securities in order to check the robustness of the process.

In order to impose a similar structure to both portfolio and benchmark in some specifications we also constrain sectors' weights, that is:

$$\sum_{i \in Sector_j} w_i \in [L_j, U_j], \qquad j = 1, 2, 3, \ldots, S \tag{5.5}$$

where S is the number of sectors considered, and L_j and U_j are, respectively, the lower and upper bound on the cumulative weight of assets belonging to a particular sector j. We take into consideration the 10 main MSCI sectors, according to the MSCI Global Industrial Classification (World Developed Markets), that is, Sector Level 1.

For similar reasons we try to constrain the minimum weight of small cap stocks. Small cap stocks represent a classic financial driver, see Fama and French (1993): the firm-size effect is one of the oldest and most studied market anomalies. The effect is the empirical observation that the stocks of small firms have higher beta-adjusted expected returns than the stocks of large firms. As the portfolio construction process that we adopt tends to privilege stocks with a corresponding high weight in the benchmark index, we want to avoid this negative bias toward small cap stocks. Therefore, we try forcing the optimization algorithm to include at least a given amount of the smallest stocks that belong to the benchmark. More precisely, we set:

$$\sum_{i:w_i^{BMK} \leq \Xi} w_i \geq \sum_{i:w_i^{BMK} \leq \Xi} w_i^{BMK} - \tau \tag{5.6}$$

where w_i^{BMK} is the weight of asset i in the benchmark, Ξ is the size threshold, for example, if a given stock exhibits a weight below Ξ, then is considered "small cap", while τ is a tolerance. After some explorative analysis we set Ξ equal to 0.005, and τ equal to 0.02.

Restriction on financial factors exposures

Other constraints are related to portfolio exposure to financial factors. The concept of factor is well-known and widespread in the finance community: factors range from exogenous variables, such as fundamental or macroeconomic variables, to more intangible factors formed as linear (or non-linear) combinations of returns or prices, as a result of some statistical analysis. Factors can be the expression of a financial theory or the result of a statistical process aimed to reduce the dimensionality of the problem. The simplest factor models are based on a single factor: the Capital Asset Pricing Model of Sharpe (1964) and Lintner (1965) can indeed be expressed as a single factor; hence this is an archetypal example of this class of models.

Anyway, many practitioners prefer multifactor models, as they tend to exhibit better fit to reality. The typical example of this class of models is the APT model, see Ross (1976). An excellent review of factor models can be found in Focardi and Fabozzi (2004). We focus on the most commonly used models, that is, linear factor models applied to returns. They can be expressed in matrix notation as follows:

$$\mathbf{r} = \boldsymbol{\alpha} + \boldsymbol{\beta} \cdot \mathbf{f} + \boldsymbol{\varepsilon} \tag{5.7}$$

where $\mathbf{r}$ is the $n \times 1$ vector of assets' returns, $\boldsymbol{\alpha}$ is a $n \times 1$ vector of constants, $\boldsymbol{\beta}$ is a $n \times K$ matrix of sensitivities to K factors ("factor loadings"), $\mathbf{f}$ is a $K \times 1$ vector of factors' returns, and $\boldsymbol{\varepsilon}$ is a $n \times 1$ vector of disturbances. Basically, we express a multivariate process (for example, returns) as a linear function of another multivariate process with smaller dimensionality (for example, factors).

The use of statistical techniques, mainly principal component analysis (PCA) or factor analysis, to examine the existence of common movements in stock returns is quite extensive in finance; see for instance Alexander and Dimitriu (2004). We extract principal components (PC) using the following spectral decomposition of the covariance matrix Σ, see Johnson and Wichern (1998):

$$\Sigma = \mathrm{E} \cdot \Lambda \cdot \mathrm{E}' \tag{5.8}$$

where Λ is the diagonal matrix of eigenvalues (conventionally in descending order, so that $\lambda_1 > \lambda_2 > \lambda_3 > \ldots > \lambda_K > 0$) and E is the orthogonal matrix of the corresponding eigenvectors. That is, we have the eigenvalues-eigenvectors pairs $(\mathbf{e}_j,\lambda_j)$, $j = 1,2,3, \ldots K$, where $\mathbf{e}_j$ is the jth column of E.

The factor loadings on the jth factor are $\sqrt{\lambda_j} \cdot \mathbf{e}_j$. Hence the factor loading on the jth factor for the generic asset i is $\beta_{ij} = \sqrt{\lambda_j} \cdot e_{ij}$. Portfolio and benchmark sensitivities to the j th factor are respectively:

$$\beta_j^{PTF} = \sum_i \beta_{ij} \cdot w_i, \qquad \beta_j^{BMK} = \sum_i \beta_{ij} \cdot w_i^{BMK} \tag{5.9}$$

where w_i^{BMK} is the weight of asset i in the benchmark.

As the first few PCs account for a large part of the total variability of the investment universe, it is possible to reduce the dimensionality in a substantial way, filtering out some noise. In order to give an example, consider the daily returns, from the beginning of April, 1996 to the end of February 2005, of the stocks included in the Dow Jones Eurostoxx index as of February 2005. The first three PCs explain more than 30 percent of the total variability of returns, as shown in Figure 5.1. The first PC alone accounts for more than 25 percent and it is apparent that the marginal contribution of each successive PC decreases rapidly.

In principle, it seems meaningful to avoid sensible differences between portfolio and benchmark sensitivities to the first PCs. From the financial point of view, this would ensure that the portfolio does not show undesired exposure to financial drivers that could introduce some "phantom drift" in excess returns. From the statistical point of view, we impose a somewhat common structure to portfolio and benchmark. Therefore we test the following constraints:

$$(1 - \xi_i) \cdot \beta_j^{BMK} \leq \beta_j^{PTF} \leq (1 + \xi_i) \cdot \beta_j^{BMK}, \qquad j = 1, 2, 3 \tag{5.10}$$

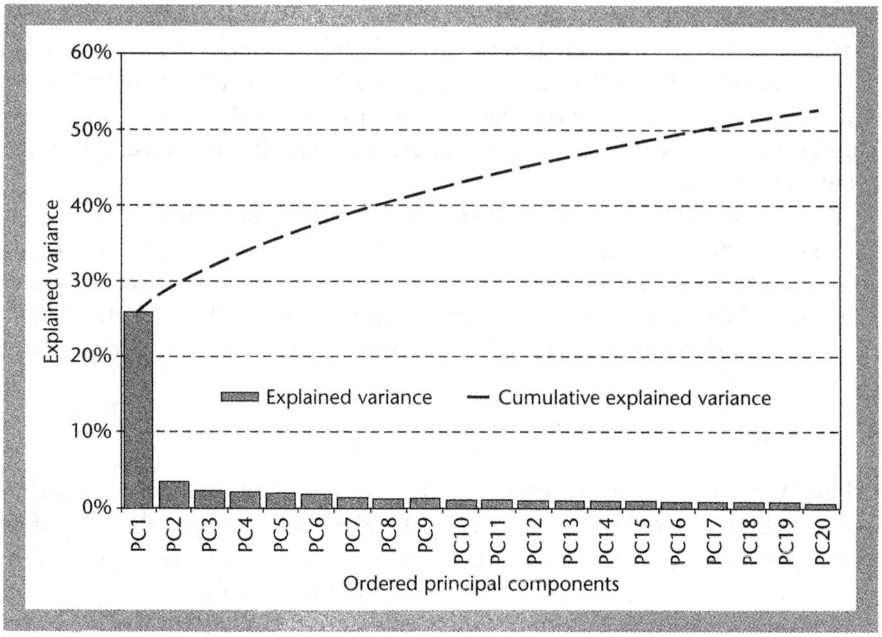

Figure 5.1 Percentage of variance explained by each principal component on European stocks belonging to Dow Jones Eurostoxx as of February 2005

For ξ_1, ξ_2 and ξ_3 we adopt, respectively, the following values: 0.01, 0.08, and 0.15.

We also try the simpler specification with $j = 1$, for example, we consider just the first PC, basically estimating a single factor model through PCA. If the second and the third PCs are relatively unstable (for example, eigenvectors $\mathbf{e}_j$ and eigenvectors λ_j change significantly over time) then the associated constraints might introduce noise in the portfolio construction process. In different specifications, we also try constraining just a single factor, where the single factor is not extracted through PCA, but using instead the benchmark return. Every time we constrain the single factor, we make use of ξ_1 equal to 0.01.

Another well-known approach in the literature is the Fama and French (1993) methodology for determining the common risk factors in the return of stocks. They proposed a three-factor model to explain the sources of excess return: the "market" factor (the market return), a "size" factor (the return of small less large cap stocks) and a "value" factor (the return of high book/market minus low book/market value stocks). For the sake of brevity, we do not consider this kind of constraints on financial factors, because we have tested that the results are comparable (but never superior) to the ones obtained using the factors estimated using PCA.[2] Nevertheless, we analyse *ex post* the exposure of the different specifications to these factors, as they are easily checked and, above all, easily interpreted by the finance community.

Beta estimation

If we focus on constraints on a single market factor, a key question arises: how to estimate beta, for example, the factor loading? As this could be eventually crucial in order to obtain good performances of some specifications, we try two different methods.

The first method we use to estimate beta is based on robust linear regression, see Huber (1981). The robust regression uses an iteratively re-weighted least-squares algorithm, with the weights at each iteration calculated by applying the bi-square function to the residuals from the previous iteration. This algorithm gives lower weight to points that do not fit well. Thus, the results are less sensitive to outliers in the data as compared with ordinary-least-squares (OLS) regression.

The second estimator of beta is based on the Bayesian adjustment proposed by Vasicek (1973) that shrinks the OLS estimate towards the overall average beta of all the stocks of the investment universe. The idea behind this estimator is that individual stock betas follow a kind of mean-reverting stochastic process: a very high individual beta tends to overestimate the true beta, while a very low beta tends to be an underestimation. Vasicek's beta is expressed as:

$$\begin{aligned} \beta_V &= \theta\beta_{OLS} + (1-\theta)\bar{\beta}_{OLS} \\ \theta &= \frac{\sigma_\beta^2}{(\sigma_\beta^2 + \sigma_{OLS}^2)} \end{aligned} \tag{5.11}$$

where β_{OLS} is the OLS estimate; $\bar{\beta}_{OLS}$ is the average OLS beta of all stock in the investment universe; σ_{OLS} is the standard error of the OLS estimate of beta; and σ_β is the cross-sectional standard deviation of all the estimated beta.

It can be easily seen that when the spread across the betas is large, then an OLS beta estimator is more likely. Otherwise, when the standard error of the OLS beta is large relative to the cross-sectional standard error, then the Bayesian estimate will be shrunk to the overall average beta.

Third, we use an exponentially weighted moving average estimator (EWMA) to forecast variances and covariances, see J.P.Morgan Bank (1995). Formally, the estimator is:

$$\beta_{EWMA(\lambda)} = \frac{Cov_{EWMA(\lambda)}(PTF, BMK)}{Var_{EWMA(\lambda)}(BMK)} \tag{5.12}$$

where $Cov_{EWMA(\lambda)}$ (PTF, BMK) and $Var_{EWMA(\lambda)}(BMK)$ are, respectively, the covariance of benchmark and portfolio returns and the variance of benchmark returns using an EWMA estimator with decay factor λ equal to 0.97. The underlying idea is to capture the dynamic features of volatility and covariances using an exponential moving average of historical observations, where the latest observations carry the highest weight in the beta estimate. This means that beta reacts faster to shocks in the market, as recent data carry more weight than data in the distant past. Second, following a shock (a large return) the beta changes exponentially as the weight of the shock observation falls. In principle, this should help to capture the time-varying nature of financial metrics like betas.

5.2.2 Estimating risk

It is well-known that a basic application of the Markowitz optimization procedure produces portfolios with poor out-of-sample performance. This is due to the fact that quadratic optimization procedures are very powerful tools: these algorithms give solutions that are very precise, but extremely sensible to the inputs (for example, expected returns and covariances), that are assumed to be known with certainty.

In reality, we obviously do not know the true parameters, but we make estimates that are prone to errors, as we can observe only few realizations of the real data generation process. This estimation error, if not managed properly, is amplified through the optimization procedure. Securities with extreme values for returns and variances will be overweighted or underweighted in the portfolio. Securities with large returns and low variances will be overweighted; securities with low returns and high variances will be underweighted.

This problem affects all the inputs, even if, as pointed out by Chopra and Ziemba (1993) and Best and Grauer (1991), the error is about 10 times more relevant for the expected returns than for the covariance matrix. The main consequences of estimation error are that the optimized portfolios are very concentrated, with unstable weights through time and with poor out-of-sample performance. To reduce these problems, various covariance estimation techniques have been suggested. In the following paragraphs we briefly describe the covariance estimators used in this chapter.

Sample covariance

The historical covariance matrix is the base estimator for quadratic optimization problems. It is the maximum likelihood estimator and this means that, under the normality assumption, it is the best unbiased estimator. This appealing property may become a drawback, as in small samples we are exposed to the problem of data overfitting. This means that the matrix, which is the best in sample estimator, may have very poor performance out of sample. Furthermore, the sample matrix may be very unstable through time, and can generate concentrated portfolios with a high turnover. Another problem with sample covariance may arise when the ratio T/n becomes small (T is the number of observations in the sample). If $T/n < 1$ the matrix is not-invertible. Even if these properties are well-known, we use this matrix as a base case. Throughout the rest of the chapter we will refer to this technique as the Historical covariance matrix.

Exponential weighted moving average covariance

The exponential weighted moving average proposed by J.P.Morgan Bank (1995), is a conditional estimator of the covariance matrix. As previously noted, it gives different weights to recent and old returns, according through an exponential weighting. We use a decay factor equal to 0.97. This estimator has the advantage of rapidly taking into consideration new information, but this property also represents its drawback, as the matrix may change rapidly in successive periods, yielding unstable portfolios. There is not any guarantee that this matrix is invertible. All over the rest of the paper, this technique is named EWMA lambda 0.97.

Shrinkage estimators

The idea of shrinkage statistics dates back to Stein (1956) and it aims to reduce estimation error by using an average of alternative estimators as in the general expression below:

$$\hat{\Sigma} = (1-\alpha)\cdot\hat{\Sigma}^{A} + \alpha\cdot\hat{\Sigma}^{B} \tag{5.13}$$

where, $\hat{\Sigma}^{A}$ and $\hat{\Sigma}^{B}$ are two different estimators (in our case of the covariance matrix) and α is a weight that is usually determined through the application of optimality criteria.

The advantage of this kind of estimator is that extreme observations may be shrinked to the center. For example, extreme positive or negative covariances may be due only to the sample under analysis, and may be not reliable out of sample, as they are due to measurement error. Through this optimal averaging we can exclude extreme statistics, thus limiting estimation error and portfolio instability.

Obviously, we can include in (5.13) several estimators, averaging an unstructured estimator with a structured one in order to trade off measurement error with specification error. For the unstructured one, the typical choice is the sample covariance, which is a maximum likelihood estimator, it is unbiased, and it relies only on the data. As a rule, a shrinking target is a highly structured matrix. This kind of estimator is often misspecified and biased, but contains less sampling error. The alpha coefficient will determine the optimal weighting scheme. A key point is that a covariance matrix estimated through appropriate shrinkage methods is guaranteed by construction to be invertible, even when the number of assets is greater than the number of observations. This property is quite appealing in application to financial markets.

A lot of alternative shrinking statistics have been proposed in the recent literature. We will take into analysis only few relevant examples:

(a) **Ledoit and Wolf Covariance.** This estimator has been proposed by Ledoit and Wolf (2004). After showing how an optimal shrinking coefficient may be determined in Ledoit and Wolf (2003), they suggest adopting the constant correlation matrix as a target. The idea is that extreme positive or negative covariances may contain more estimation error: hence they should be shrinked to a more central value. Through the rest of the paper, we will refer to this technique as the LEDOIT-WOLF covariance matrix.

(b) **Shrinking to RMT Covariance.** Ledoit and Wolf (2003) suggest using as a shrinking target the covariance matrix implied by a factor model, and in particular they suggest using a standard CAPM model. Bengtsson and Holst (2004) extend this approach to multi-factor models, where the number of factors is decided according to the Random Matrix Theory approach (RMT). RMT is a technique widely used in physics that has been recently applied in finance by Plerou, Gopikrishnan, Rosenow, Amaral, Guhr and Stanley (2002) or by Laloux, Cizeau, Potters and Bouchaud (2000).

    RMT studies the properties and the distribution of the eigenvalues of randomly generated correlation matrices. These results may be used to make inference on the sample correlation matrices and to decide how much information is contained in the estimator. In particular, the separation between noise and signal is possible through the analysis of the eigenvalues spectrum of the correlation matrix. Eigenvalues that are outside the bound predicted by RMT may be considered genuinely non-random and may be used for forecasting purposes.

    The approach of Bengtsson and Holst (2004), combines the sample covariance matrix with a structured estimator derived from a multi-factor model with a dynamic number of statistical factors. As in Ledoit and Wolf (2003), the alpha coefficient optimally weights the two estimators. Through the rest of this chapter, we will refer to this technique as the Shrink-RMT covariance matrix.

(c) **Jagannathan and Ma Covariance.** Jagannathan and Ma (2003) propose an approach similar to that of Ledoit and Wolf (2003). They estimate the covariance matrix through the use of an equally weighted average of three estimators: the sample covariance (the "full" K factors model), the CAPM matrix (the one factor model) and the diagonal part of the sample matrix (the zero factors model).

Through the rest of the chapter we will refer to this technique as the COV-MIX covariance matrix.

5.2.3 Assessing portfolio weightings

Asset weights can be defined without optimizing: in order to minimize TEV, a portfolio manager can use a stratified replication method, that is, she purchases only a certain a number of the largest capitalization stocks of each country and/or sector, and any country/sector is held in the same proportion as the benchmark. Many financial practitioners believe that optimizing is not optimal at all, as it can lead to extreme active weights which fluctuate considerably over time. Other practitioners, anyway, think to portfolio construction as synonymous of optimization.

We believe that in order to trade-off risk and return in a rigorous manner, the use of optimization technology should help, even if, in practice, much of the work is done before the optimizer enters the picture. As we have already seen, the point is that the classic Markowitz algorithm performs error maximization: it amplifies measurement errors associated to inputs. Therefore, as the portfolio manager makes new estimates for risk and return and revises the portfolio, the optimal weights will be excessively unstable.

This problem can be largely avoided using "intelligent" inputs, reducing the impact of estimation errors through statistical techniques that filter-out the noise (see previous section). Nevertheless, a portfolio manager can also adopt optimization algorithms that lead to more diversified portfolio weights and provide stable portfolios that change allocations slowly over time. A notable example is portfolio resampling, see Michaud (1989). Setting constraints on optimal weights also helps to mitigate the problem.

Our aim is to minimize tracking error volatility with respect to a predefined benchmark, with several constraints (C).[3] Formally, the model is:

$$\min_{w_{PTF}}(w - w^{BMK})' \cdot \Sigma \cdot (w - w^{BMK}) \tag{5.14}$$

Subject to

$$w_i \in [0,\ 0.1], \qquad i = 1, 2, 3, \ldots, n \tag{C1}$$

$$\sum_{i:w_i \geq 0.05} w_i \leq 0.4 \tag{C2}$$

$$\sum_i w_i = 1 \tag{C3}$$

$$n \leqslant Max\_n \tag{C4}$$

$$\sum_{i \in Sector_j} w_i \in [L_j, U_j], \qquad j = 1, 2, 3, \dots, S \tag{C5}$$

$$(1 - \xi_i) \cdot \beta_j^{BMK} \leq \beta_j^{PTF} \leq (1 + \xi_i) \cdot \beta_j^{BMK}, \qquad j = 1, 2, 3 \tag{C6}$$

$$\sum_{i: w_i^{BMK} \leq \Xi} w_i \geq \sum_{i: w_i^{BMK} \leq \Xi} w_i^{BMK} - \tau \tag{C7}$$

where Max_n is an integer and L_j, U_j, ξ_j, Ξ, and τ are real numbers.

In certain specifications some constraints are activated, and other not: the formulation above include all the specifications we consider. Note that constraint (C2) is rather tough: it is a conditional constraint not easily managed by a standard optimizer. It is not easy to deal with the cardinality constraint (C4), too, as it involves the following "count-function":

$$\sum_i \delta_i \leq Max\_n, \quad \text{where} \quad \delta_i(w_i) = \begin{cases} 0 & \text{if } w_i = 0 \\ 1 & \text{otherwise} \end{cases} \tag{5.15}$$

The typical dimension of the problem is in the range 100–700 securities: most indices that portfolio managers aim to track are in that range. Bigger problems pose serious challenges to optimizers. Smaller problems can be reasonably tackled with full replication, for example, simply creating a portfolio which includes all the shares in the index at their relevant weights.[4]

In order to test our specifications and to solve problem (5.14) we use an optimization heuristic based on an algorithm named Differential Evolution, a numerical optimization approach that is very efficient and reliable on a variety of real-world problems (see Paterlini and Krink, 2004, 2005; and Krink, Filipic, Fogel and Thomsen, 2004). We use a proprietary version of the algorithm, called Differential Evolution Benchmark Replication (DEBR), a single-objective population-based search heuristic developed by Krink. The reason for using a search heuristic is that problem (5.14) is a quadratic programming problem with continuous variables and both linear and nonlinear, discontinuous cardinality constraints. Branch and bound and quadratic programming are not applicable to problem (5.14) in its original form. Instead, the implemented program DEBR is a specialized algorithm aimed to explore asset position selection, and to handle complex constraints.

We do not test other optimization algorithms as this is not the goal of this article. Our aim is to test several specifications of problem (5.14).

There are several standard algorithms, available on the marketplace, that are able to solve this kind of problem. For instance, a simple alternative is represented by the standard QP algorithm provided by the Matlab®'s Optimization Toolbox, that is the *quadprog* function. In order to deal with constraint (C2) and (C4) it is possible to use a simple two-steps procedure:

1 Select the first *Max_n* stocks based on their market capitalization;
2 Solve problem (5.14) using the selected *Max_n* stocks, where the maximum individual weight is bounded to 4.5 percent, altering constraint (C1) so that constraint (C2) is never active.

This method is *a priori* suboptimal, as it excludes a portion of the solutions' space, but it delivers reasonable solutions.

5.2.4 Rebalancing strategically

To maintain a portfolio's tracking capability, periodic rebalancing must be done. This ensures that the portfolio continues to reflect a low level of relative risk, for example, low TEV. How often should a portfolio manager rebalance her tracking portfolio? There is a clear trade-off. Of course, the downside of frequent rebalancing is represented by the transactions costs that investors are subject to. Nevertheless, a low rebalancing frequency exposes portfolio managers to the risk that the statistical estimates used during the portfolio construction process are changed: volatilities, correlations, and factor loadings tend to vary over time. This means that *ex post* performance might differ substantially from *ex ante* estimates.

We test different rebalancing periods: 21, 50 and 100 business days. Based on our experience, we believe that the base frequency is 21 business days: not a very low frequency, but neither a high frequency. In addition, it often corresponds to formal portfolio assessments (for example, investment committees). Hence the other frequencies are mostly control-cases. Table 5.1 describe all the specifications we back-test.

We also check the robustness of our findings:

- altering the investment universe, trying to solve the problem using US stocks;
- changing the maximum number of stocks held, *Max_n*;
- changing the rebalancing frequency from 21 business days to 50 and 100.

In Table 5.2 we report the main attributes of these additional tests.

Table 5.1 Back-testing specifications

Specification number	Beta constraints	Beta specification	Factors constraints	Factors specification	Sector constraints	Small cap constraint	COV matrix	Number of assets	Reb. horizon
1	NO		NO		NO	NO	HISTORICAL	250	21
2	NO		NO		NO	NO	EWMA lambda 0.97	250	21
3	NO		NO		NO	NO	COV-MIX	250	21
4	NO		NO		NO	NO	Shrink-RMT	250	21
5	NO		NO		NO	NO	LEDOIT-WOLF	250	21
6	YES	Robust Regression on 1000 returns	NO		NO	NO	LEDOIT-WOLF	250	21
7	YES	Robust regression on 125 returns	NO		NO	NO	LEDOIT-WOLF	250	21
8	NO		YES	3 PCA Factors on 1000 returns	NO	NO	LEDOIT-WOLF	250	21
9	NO		YES	1 PCA Factors on 1000 returns	NO	NO	LEDOIT-WOLF	250	21
10	YES	EWMA Beta (lambda 0.97) on 125 returns	NO		NO	NO	LEDOIT-WOLF	250	21
11	YES	Beta VASICEK on 125 returns	NO		NO	NO	LEDOIT-WOLF	250	21
12	NO		NO		YES	NO	LEDOIT-WOLF	250	21
13	YES	Beta VASICEK on 125 returns	NO		YES	NO	LEDOIT-WOLF	250	21
14	YES	Beta VASICEK on 125 returns	NO		NO	NO	COV-MIX	250	21
15	YES	Beta VASICEK on 125 returns	NO		NO	NO	Shrink-RMT	250	21
16	NO		NO		NO	YES	LEDOIT-WOLF	250	21

Table 5.2 Main attributes of back testing specifications

Specification number	Beta constraints	Beta specification	COV matrix	Number of assets	Reb. horizon	Dataset
17	YES	Beta VASICEK on 125 returns	LEDOIT-WOLF	100	21	Europe
18	YES	Beta VASICEK on 125 returns	LEDOIT-WOLF	250	50	Europe
19	YES	Beta VASICEK on 125 returns	LEDOIT-WOLF	250	100	Europe
20	NO		LEDOIT-WOLF	250	21	America
21	YES	Beta VASICEK on 125 returns	LEDOIT-WOLF	250	21	America

5.3 BACK-TESTING METHODOLOGY AND DATASETS FEATURES

First, we explain our methodology for comparing the performance of the various portfolio construction specifications. Secondly, we describe the various metrics and analysis used to evaluate and compare the performance of the different specifications.

5.3.1 Back-testing methodology

The analysis of each specification consists of the following steps:

1 At the rebalancing date, we define the investment universe as the set of assets belonging to the benchmark at that date. All the assets that have a number of missing data per year greater than a certain target are excluded from the investment universe, even if they contribute to benchmark's performance. The number of stocks excluded in this way ranges from 38 to 81 (out of 500 and more shares), and the sum of the corresponding weights in the benchmark is never greater than 4.94 percent.

2 We choose a sample window to estimate the parameters. We try estimation windows of $T = 125$, and $T = 1000$ data points; for daily datasets, this corresponds approximately to six months and four years, respectively. These values can be considered as the extremes of the axis representing the estimation window: six months leads to short-history estimates, while four years leads to long-history estimates. Different parameters can be estimated using different estimation window. In particular we estimate covariances using 1,000 data points, while we estimate betas using both

1,000 and 125 data points. We do not attempt using halfway estimation windows because our purpose is to understand if a short history is better than a long history, but we want to avoid data overfitting.

3 We estimate the parameters of interest over the chosen estimation windows.

4 Using these estimated parameters, we solve the model for the optimal portfolio weights.

5 We measure the return from holding the portfolio with these weights over the next period, that is, out-of-sample. In this study, the out-of-sample holding period is 21 days in the base case, leaving 50 and 100 days to the robustness check.

6 Finally, we compare portfolio and benchmark performance.

In order to make the back-testing procedure realistic and to avoid any survival bias problem, we take into consideration the evolution of the benchmark's composition. That is, at the end of each month we update the list of the benchmark's constituents: some assets that were in the index the previous month become out of benchmark (and cannot be bought as long as they remain out of the benchmark investment universe), and vice versa. During the following month, for the sake of simplicity, we adopt the hypothesis that the investment universe does not show any further modification in its composition. This means that we rule out changes in constituents due to corporate actions (for example, mergers) during that month. The only possible variation concerns assets weights, that during the month under consideration evolve according to a constant-share strategy.

5.3.2 Data

The investment universe used in this chapter is the European equity market in the period 1 January 1999 to 8 March 2005. We use daily returns in euro terms and the market is represented by the MSCI Europe Index (source Datastream International).

Following these rules, our investment universe is a dynamic set: it varies from month to month and it includes a number of stocks ranging from 502 to 569. For each asset we store the time series of prices, the weight in the benchmark (at each date in which it belongs to the index) and the Datastream sector classification, which is used to set constraints (C5).

This dynamic set of assets is also used to construct a capitalization weighted index that is updated monthly. This index will be the benchmark index for all the investment models we will present in the rest of the chapter. Obviously, it must be noticed that the performance of this index will differ (slightly) from that of the MSCI Europe Index, that is potentially updated daily. In any case, the use of this reconstructed index ensures a fair comparison between portfolio and benchmark results. Furthermore, to keep all the comparisons homogenous, we do not take into consideration dividends, neither in the portfolio, nor in the benchmark.

The out-of-sample period, when the sample period is 1,000 days, ranges from February 2003 to August 2005. In order to analyse how tracking portfolios are exposed to size and to styles, we also include in the database the MSCI Europe Value, Growth and Small Cap indexes. All these indices are price index (no dividend reinvested) and are in Euro terms. They are used to calculate the daily returns of the size factor (SML), calculated as the difference between MSCI Europe and MSCI Europe Small Cap, and the "value" factor (HML), that is the difference between MSCI Europe Value and MSCI Europe Growth.

In order to check the robustness of our results, we use also an alternative investment universe, namely the set of constituents of the MSCI USA Index (source Datastream International), considering, as in the previous case, daily returns in euro terms spanning from 1 January 1999 to 8 March 2005. In terms of number of constituents, this index is comparable to MSCI Europe.

To summarize, we stress that:

- the test is genuinely out of sample;
- there is no survivor bias;
- there is a fair comparison between portfolio and benchmark;
- the test mimics the real-world process.

5.3.3 Valuation

In this section we describe each of the out-of-sample summary statistics reported for each portfolio construction specification and explain how this quantity is computed. We use the following performance and risk metrics:

- Annualized excess return.
- Annualized tracking error volatility, that is the standard deviation (per annum) of excess return over the whole back-testing period.
- *Ex post* information ratio (IR), the ratio of annualized excess return to annualized TEV.
- Maximum draw-down, that is the largest drop from a peak to a bottom over a given period (the back-testing period, in our case). Being the minimum cumulated return from any beginning points over a certain time period, it is a good "worst scenario" metric.

Formally, following Magdon-Ismail, Atiya, Pratap, and Abu-Mostafa (2004), we define Maximum Draw-Down (MDD) as:

$$MDD(\mathrm{T}) = -\sup_{t\in[0,\mathrm{T}]}\left[\sup_{s\in[0,t]} Cer(s) - Cer(t)\right] \tag{5.16}$$

where $Cer(t)$ is the cumulative excess return over the period $[0,t]$, that is $(V^{PTF}(t) - V^{PTF}(0)) - (V^{BMK}(t) - V^{BMK}(0))$, while $V^{PTF}(h)$ and $V^{BMK}(h)$ are, respectively, portfolio and benchmark value at time h.

- Average turnover (AT), calculated as $Turnover = \sum_i |\Delta w_i|/2$ on each rebalancing date. This means that if we rebalance each month, this number is a monthly statistic and in order to get the approximate annual statistic it must be multiplied by 12. Average Turnover is a good proxy for transaction costs: the higher the turnover, the higher the transaction and execution costs.
- *Ex post* factor exposures, using the three classic Fama and French factors, for example, market, SML, and HML. We estimate those betas using a robust regression (see section 5.2.1), using a sample period of 100 days, so that the estimates are rather sensitive to changing market conditions. The idea is that a good tracking portfolio should not exhibit any evident bias: it would be undesirable to discover that excess returns are driven by factors that are not under control.
- We estimate the probability density function of quarterly excess return. We use a block-bootstrap procedure, see Efron and Tibshirani (1998). Basically, from the time series of realized daily excess returns of each specification, $\{e_t\}_j, j = 1,2,n\_spec$, where *n_spec* is the number of specifications we analyse, we randomly extract 1,000 "strips" of $21 \times 3 = 63$ days, for example, approximately two months. We compound each strip, so that at the end of the process we get 1,000 cumulative quarterly returns. Their frequency distribution is considered a non-parametric estimate of the probability density function.

Please note that all returns are calculated without taking into account any hedging of foreign exchange exposures of non-euro stocks.

5.4 MAIN RESULTS

Table 5.3 reports the main results of the back-testing experiment for all the specifications considered. Figure 5.2, Figure 5.3 and Figure 5.4 show, respectively, the cumulative excess returns over time, the estimate of the

Table 5.3 Results of back-testing for all specifications

Specification number	Annualized tracking error	Annualized excess return	Information ratio	Maximum drawdown	Average turnover (on rebalancing frequency)	Beta	Beta vs. SML	Beta vs. HML
1	0.64%	**−0.18%**	**−0.28**	−0.9%	13%	0.989	−0.016	−0.001
2	0.78%	**−0.46%**	**−0.59**	−1.3%	28%	0.997	−0.014	0.006
3	0.62%	**−0.51%**	**−0.83**	−1.2%	5%	0.986	−0.022	−0.002
4	0.63%	**−0.41%**	**−0.65**	−1.0%	9%	0.989	−0.018	−0.011
5	0.63%	**−0.33%**	**−0.53**	−1.1%	10%	0.989	−0.018	−0.006
6	1.08%	**−0.43%**	**−0.40**	−2.2%	20%	1.021	−0.042	−0.007
7	0.63%	**−0.29%**	**−0.46**	−1.0%	11%	0.992	−0.018	−0.002
8	2.55%	**0.74%**	**0.29**	−2.7%	52%	1.049	0.121	−0.003
9	0.66%	**−0.47%**	**−0.71**	−1.3%	18%	0.991	−0.014	−0.012
10	0.64%	**−0.36%**	**−0.56**	−1.0%	12%	0.988	−0.017	−0.006
11	0.64%	**−0.03%**	**−0.05**	−0.6%	12%	0.998	−0.016	−0.013
12	0.64%	**−0.21%**	**−0.32**	−0.9%	11%	0.989	−0.016	−0.008
13	0.65%	**−0.27%**	**−0.41**	−1.0%	12%	0.998	−0.016	−0.012
14	0.63%	**−0.46%**	**−0.72**	−1.5%	7%	0.996	−0.024	−0.007
15	0.66%	**−0.23%**	**−0.35**	−1.0%	11%	0.998	−0.015	−0.005
16	7.14%	**6.32%**	**0.89**	−6.0%	50%	0.992	−0.009	0.042

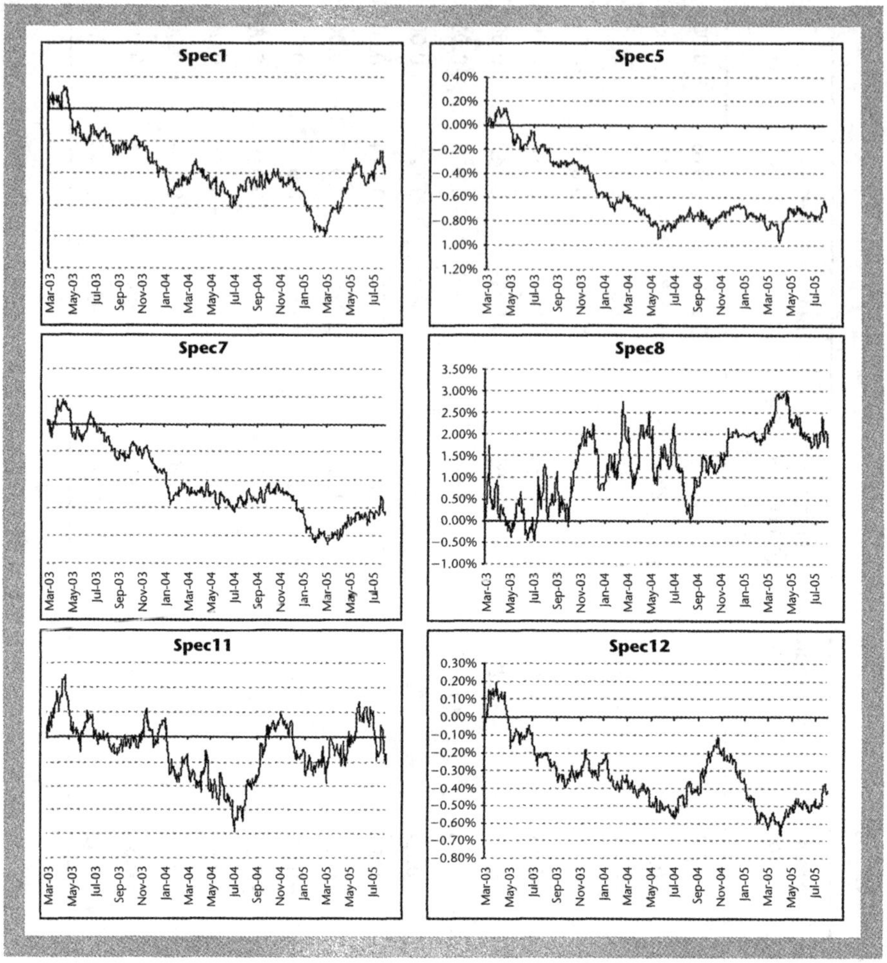

Figure 5.2 Cumulative excess returns of some specifications of particular interest

probability density function for quarterly excess returns, and the exposures to market, size and value factor for a selection of specifications.

We start with the worst results. From Table 5.3 we see that Spec8 exhibits a high TEV (2.55 percent) and a stellar AT (52 percent on a monthly basis). MDD is also disappointing (−2.7 percent). From Figure 5.2 we see that the out-of-sample path of excess returns is positively biased (up to 3.0 percent). This is not a nice empirical property, as a tracking portfolio is supposed to display excess returns close to zero. Figure 5.3 shows the distribution of quarterly excess returns of several specifications: it is apparent that Spec8 displays a wider distribution if compared with other specifications. The key element of this specification is given by constraint (C6) on the first three statistical

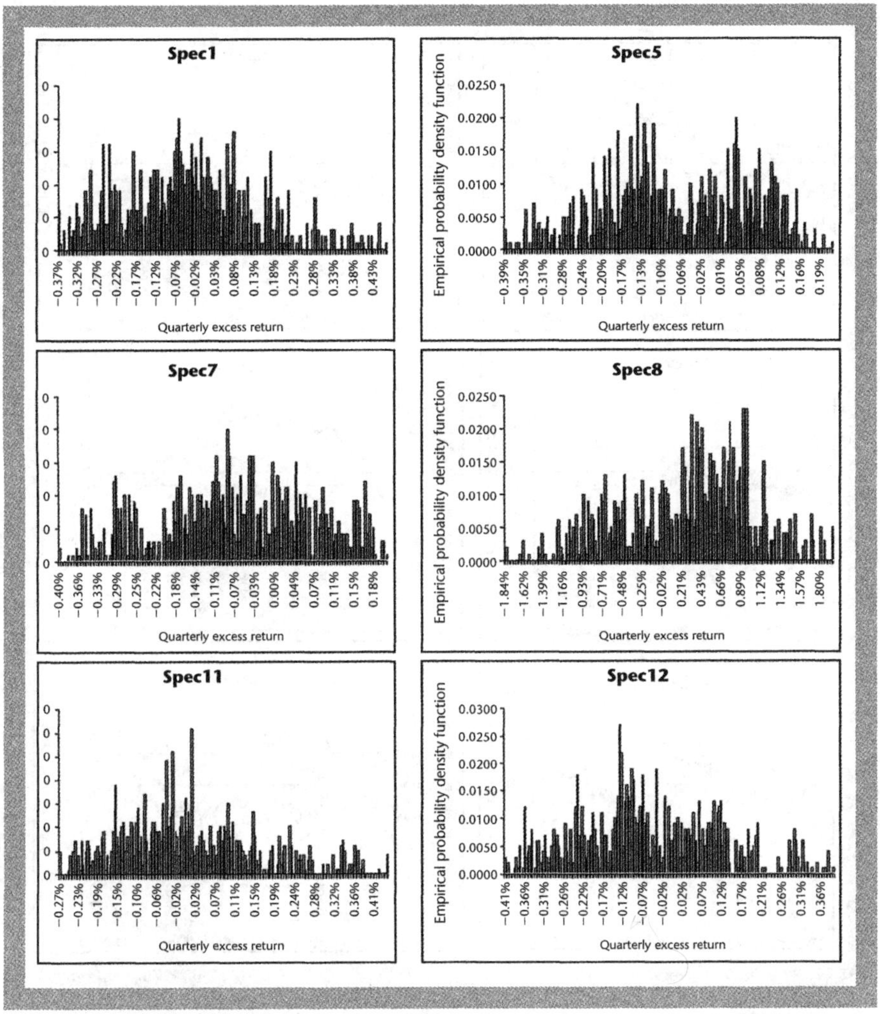

Figure 5.3 Estimates of the probability density function of quarterly excess returns obtained using a block-bootstrap procedure, for some specifications of particular interest

factors, which is active. Hence, even if keeping under control the first three statistical drivers seems a good idea, the out of sample performance is poor. In other words, using these factors induces some data over-fitting that does not pay out of sample, mainly because of factors instability, as confirmed by the high Turnover. Using the Fama and French 3-factor model (market, SML, and HML), instead of statistical factors, does not lead to better results; we do not report these results, for the sake of brevity, but they are available on request. Market, SML and HML exposures, measured by means of the corresponding betas are also far from neutrality, as shown in Figure 5.4.

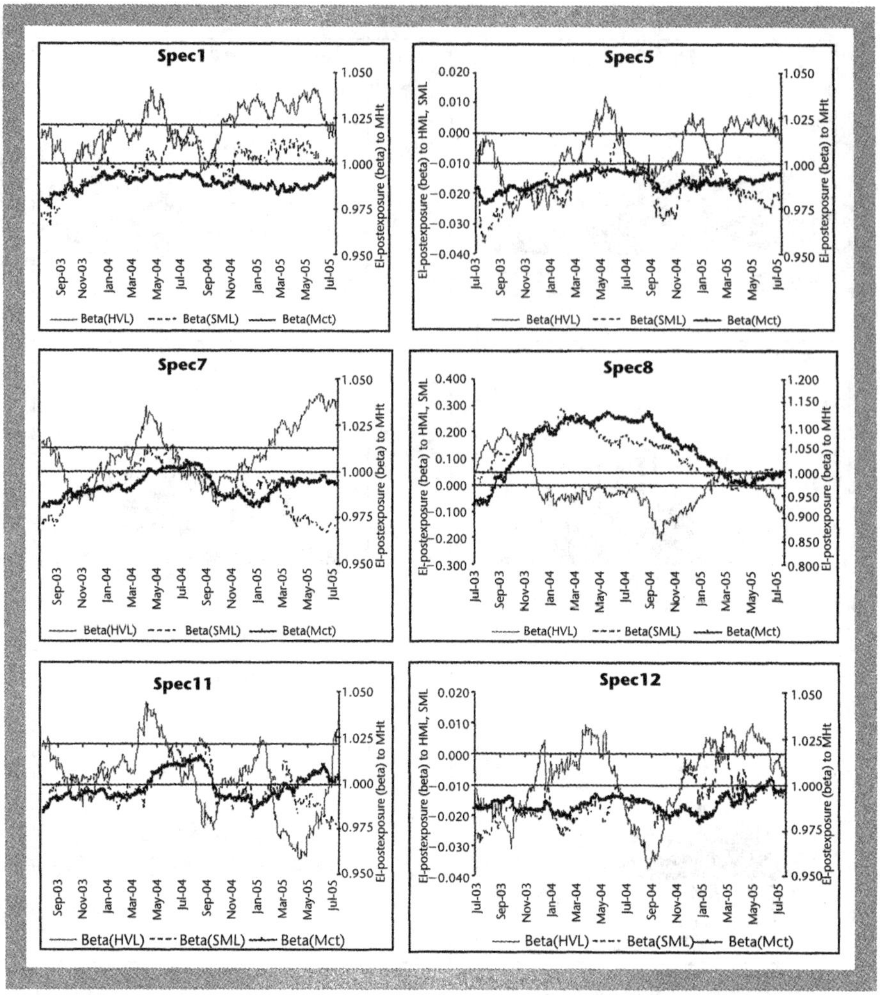

Figure 5.4 *Ex post* factor exposures, using the Fama and French 3-factor model

From Table 5.3 we see that Spec16 shows the highest reported TEV and an average turnover of 50 percent, with MDD equal to a unacceptable −6.0 percent. This means that setting a constraint on the minimum portfolio weight of the small caps is, again, good in principle and bad in practice. The smallest shares are prone to go into the benchmark and then, maybe just one month later, to go out of the index, generating skyscraping turnover and TEV. Hence, controlling for several factors does not work well in a realistic passive portfolio construction process.

We try to use just the constraints on the first factor. Spec9 uses a single statistical factor (PC1), while Spec6 makes use of the benchmark index and robust regression. In both cases the sample used to estimate the factor loadings has length equal to 1,000 days, for example, we use a long history. Results are roughly comparable and there is a clear improvement with respect to previously discussed specifications: the more interesting statistics are TEV and MDD, which are significantly lower, as well Turnover, which is around 20 percent.

Thus, it seems that using constraints on a single factor is useful. With Spec7 we try robust regression using a short sample, for example, 125 data points. We do not use statistical factors because, with such a small sample, it happens that $T/n < 1$, and this would mean using a singular covariance matrix. Spec7 exhibits good results, as TEV is 0.63 percent, Turnover is 11 percent, MDD is -1.0 percent, without any huge factor bias.

At this point we see that (i) using constraints on a single factor does work; and (ii) a short sample is probably better than a long sample. We make an effort to exploit the use of beta, testing the other estimators considered in this work. Spec10 and Spec11 focus on beta estimation using respectively, an EWMA an the Bayesian adjustment proposed by Vasicek. Results are roughly comparable, even if Vasicek's beta is probably slightly better, as it leads to lower MDD. In addition, the cumulative excess return is relatively stable around zero (see Figure 5.2), while exposures to financial factors, for example, market, SML and HML, are almost neutral (see Figure 5.4).

Up to now we have used the Ledoit–Wolf estimator of covariances. We can verify how other methods perform out-of-sample. Spec1, Spec2, Spec3 and Spec4 focus on testing, respectively, sample covariance, EWMA, COV-MIX, Shrink-RMT and Ledoit–Wolf estimators. The results in Table 5.3 show mainly that the EWMA estimate generate a significantly higher Turnover, with slightly larger TEV. The other results are approximately equivalent. Without restriction on beta, financial factors exposures tend to diverge from neutrality in a consistent way: as an example, Figure 5.4 shows the exposures for Spec1 and Spec5.

Spec12 and Spec13 test the impact of constraining sectors' weights, respectively without and with beta constraint. They can be compared with Spec11. From Table 5.3 it is apparent that the main difference is that Spec11 has a lower (in absolute value) MDD. From Figure 5.2 it is apparent that without beta constraint the cumulative excess return of Spec12 drifts away from zero. Hence it seems that constraining the single factor beta makes the difference, not constraining sectors.

Spec14 and Spec15 test if, constraining the single factor beta, using COV-MIX or Shrink-RMT respectively, instead of Ledoit–Wolf (see Spec11), might lead to significantly different results. The main difference is that, like Spec3, Spec14 exhibits low Turnover and larger (in absolute value) MDD.

The main results of the additional test we perform to check the robustness of our findings is presented in Table 5.4. We perform these tests on one of the most successful specifications, that is we use a beta constraint (except

Table 5.4 Robustness of findings

Specification number	Annualized tracking error	Annualized excess return	Information ratio	Maximum drawdown	Average turnover (on rebalancing frequency)
17	1.07%	**−2.00%**	**−1.88**	−4.2%	25%
18	0.66%	**−0.23%**	**−0.35**	−1.4%	13%
19	0.64%	**−0.23%**	**−0.37**	−0.5%	13%
20	1.36%	**−0.41%**	**−0.30**	−1.2%	12%
21	1.36%	**−0.64%**	**−0.47**	−1.7%	14%

in one case, Spec20), estimating beta using the Vasicek's model and estimating the covariance matrix with Ledoit–Wolf.

With a small number of assets (Spec17), that is 100 out of more than 500, we find that TEV is slightly higher, but extreme excess returns are more likely, as MDD is −4.2 percent. Turnover, as one can expect with such a small number of stocks, is large.

A longer rebalancing horizon (Spec18 and Spec19) does not significantly affect our results. Finally, changing the investment universe (from European to US stocks), with or without the constraint on beta (respectively, Spec20 and Spec21), increases out-of-sample TEV, which becomes slightly larger than 1 percent. Other statistics remain similar.

5.5 CONCLUSION

The goal of this chapter has been to evaluate, from a practitioner perspective, different ways to construct benchmark-relative portfolios of stocks with a limited number of assets and with small tracking error volatility. We have considered various alternatives, back-testing the associated portfolios, comparing results according to several metrics.

The main findings of our out-of-sample, real-world test are summarized below:

- Setting constraints on several factors disturbs index tracking. Instead, putting constraints on a single factor does help.
- Applying Bayesian shrinkage techniques to beta estimation improves tracking performance, and a short sample (less than 1 year) is better than a very long sample (4 years or more). The mean reason is that portfolio metrics, like beta, are time-varying.

- Portfolio managers using covariance estimates that take into account measurement error, like Bayesian shrinkage estimators, are likely to experience better results. Anyway, among Bayesian shrinkage estimators, there is little gain in picking a particular estimator.
- Setting constraints on sectors' weights has a negligible impact on out-of-sample results.
- The smaller the maximum number of stocks allowed (for example, the stronger the cardinality constraint), the higher the Tracking Error Volatility and the Turnover (and hence associated trading costs).
- Results do not vary noticeably when rebalancing frequency decreases from 21 days to 100 days.
- Changing the investment universe worsens Tracking Error Volatility. This probably means that, in this case, some kind of fine-tuning could be useful.

A final note: it is realistic to think that these results should hold when expected returns are introduced in the optimization process, for example when the goal is not index-tracking.

NOTES

1. Passive portfolio managers can in principle avoid this step.
2. Results are available from authors on request.
3. Of course, instead of using a quadratic goal function, one could use a different distance measure, for example, Mean Absolute Deviation, or Expected Shortfall.
4. Anyway, even a small index (for example, the Dow Jones Stoxx 50) might pose some problems, as the biggest constituents' weights could exceed the maximum weight allowed by current rules. In this case, optimization is, again, a critical tool.

REFERENCES

Alexander, C. and Dimitriu, A. (2004) "Sources of Over-Performance in Equity Markets: Common Trends, Mean Reversion and Herding", *Journal of Portfolio Management*, 58(4): 70–185.

Bengtsson, C. and Holst, J. (2004) "On Portfolio Selection: Improved Covariance Matrix Estimation for Swedish Asset Returns", Working Paper, Lund University, Lund, Sweden.

Best, M.J. and Grauer, R.R. (1991) "On the Sensitive of Mean–Variance Efficient Portfolios to Changes in Asset Means: Some Analytical and Computational Results", *Review of Financial Studies*, 4(2): 315–42.

Chopra, V. and Ziemba, W. (1993) "The Effects of Errors in Means, Variances and Covariances on Optimal Portfolio Choice", *Journal of Portfolio Management*, 19(2): 6–11.

Cochrane, J.H. (2001) *Asset Pricing* (Princeton, NJ: Princeton University Press).

Efron, B. and Tibshirani, R. (1998) *An Introduction to the Bootstrap*, 2nd edn (New York, NY: Chapman & Hall).

Fama, E. and French, K. (1993) "Common Risk Factors in the Returns on Stocks and Bonds", *Journal of Financial Economics*, 33(1): 3–56.

Focardi, S. and Fabozzi, F.J. (2004) *The Mathematics of Financial Modeling and Investment Management* (Hoboken, NJ: John Wiley & Sons).

Huber, P.J. (1981) *Robust Statistics* (New York, NY: John Wiley & Sons).

Jagannathan, R. and Ma, T. (2003) "Risk Reduction in Large Portfolios: Why Imposing the Wrong Constraints Helps", *Journal of Finance*, 58(1): 1651–84.

Johnson, R.A. and Wichern, D.W. (1998) *Applied Multivariate Statistical Analysis* (Upper Saddle River, NJ: Prentice-Hall).

J.P. Morgan Bank (1995) *RiskMetrics Technical Manual* (New York, NY: J.P. Morgan Bank).

Krink, T., Filipic, B., Fogel, G.B. and Thomsen, R. (2004) "Noisy Optimization Problems – A Particular Challenge for Differential Evolution?" *Proceedings of the Sixth Congress on Evolutionary Computation (CEC-2004)* (Piscataway, NJ: IEEE Press).

Laloux, L., Cizeau, P., Potters, M. and Bouchaud, J.-P. (2000) "Random Matrix Theory and Financial Correlations", *International Journal of Theoretical and Applied Finance*, 3(3): 391–7.

Ledoit, O. and Wolf, M. (2003) "Improved Estimation of the Covariance Matrix of Stock Returns with an Application to Portfolio Selection", *Journal of Empirical Finance*, 10(5): 603–21.

Ledoit, O. and Wolf, M. (2004) "Honey, I Shrunk the Covariance Matrix", *Journal of Portfolio Management*, 31(4): 110–19.

Lintner, J. (1965) "The Valuation of Risk Assets and the Selection of Risky Investments in Stock Portfolios and Capital Budgets", *Review of Economics and Statistics*, 47(1): 13–37.

Magdon-Ismail, M., Atiya, A.F., Pratap, A. and Abu-Mostafa, Y.S. (2004) "On the Maximum Drawdown of a Brownian Motion", *Journal of Applied Probability*, 41(1): 1250–4.

Markowitz, H.M. (1952) "Portfolio Selection", *Journal of Finance*, 7(1): 77–91.

Markowitz, H.M. (1959) *Portfolio Selection: Efficient Diversification of Investments* (New Haven, CT: Yale University Press).

Michaud, R. (1989) "The Markowitz Optimization Enigma: Is Optimized Optimal?" *Financial Analyst Journal*, 45(1): 31–42.

Oberuc, R.E. (2003) *Dynamic Portfolio Theory and Management* (New York: Irwin Library of Investment and Finance, McGraw-Hill).

Paterlini, S. and Krink, T. (2004) "High Performance Clustering with Differential Evolution", *Proceedings of the Sixth Congress on Evolutionary Computation (CEC-2004)*, Vol. 2, pp. 2004-11 (Piscataway, NJ: IEEE Press).

Paterlini, S. and Krink, T. (2005) "Differential Evolution and Particle Swarm Optimization in Partitional Clustering", *Computational Statistics and Data Analysis*, 50: 1220–47.

Plerou, V., Gopikrishnan, P., Rosenow, B., Amaral, L.A.N., Guhr, T., Stanley, H.E. (2002) "A Random Matrix Approach to Cross-Correlations in Financial Data", *Physical Review*, E 65: 1–17.

Ross, S.A. (1976) "The Arbitrage Theory of Capital Asset Pricing", *Journal of Economic Theory*, 13: 343–62.

Scherer, B. (2004) *Portfolio Construction and Risk Budgeting*, 2nd edn (London, UK: Risk Books).

Sharpe, W. (1964) "Capital Asset Prices: A Theory of Market Equilibrium Under Conditions of Risk", *Journal of Finance*, 19(5): 425–42.

Stein, C. (1956) "Inadmissibility of the Usual Estimator for the Mean of a Multivariate Normal Distribution", in J. Neyman, (ed.), *Proceedings of the Third Berkeley Symposium on Mathematical and Statistical Probability* (University of California Press), pp. 197–206.

Vasicek, O.A. (1973) "A Note on Using Cross-Sectional Information in Bayesian Estimation of Betas", *Journal of Finance*, 28(5): 1233–9.

CHAPTER 6

Improvements and Limitations of the Revised Morningstar Fund Rating Methodology

Roman Kräussl

"The brand that has emerged as dominant in the 1990s is not Fidelity, Putnam, or even Merrill Lynch – but instead is Morningstar."

Robert C. Pozen (1998, p. 75) in *The Mutual Fund Business*

6.1 INTRODUCTION

Households increasingly use mutual funds as their main long-term investment vehicles. Today, the number of mutual funds available exceeds 17,000 in the United States alone.[1] Market participants are therefore in need of valid, unbiased and straightforward information in order to select mutual funds with the best future prospects. But how does the average investor distinguish a superior mutual fund from another?

This need for information has led to an increased demand for services that rate mutual funds. The best-known and widely used rating system is provided by Morningstar, Inc. Introduced in 1985, the 5-star rating system enables a fund's characteristics to be summarized in a comprehensive way, easily understood by the average investor: the star rating. Similar to ratings given to hotels, restaurants and movies, Morningstar rates mutual funds on a scale from one star (lowest) to five stars (highest) according to past investment performance. The star rating is a useful tool for investors, as it gives them a risk-adjusted measure of the fund returns which also takes expenses into account.

Morningstar clearly states that star ratings are achievement marks rather than predictors of future mutual fund performance. Nonetheless, the heavy use of Morningstar ratings in mutual fund advertising suggests that fund companies assume that investors use Morningstar ratings also for deciding on their investments. It is likely that investors will avoid funds with the lowest ratings and choose funds with the highest ratings in the expectation that they will increase the future returns received on their investments. Indeed, Del Guercio and Tkac (2002) provide empirical evidence that the Morningstar rating itself has a significant effect on fund flows.

Back in 1985, most investors were not sure whether to invest value- or growth-oriented, whether they should choose a small-cap fund or one that bought into large caps. Instead, they preferred a mutual fund that would perform well in a variety of market conditions. The original 5-star rating system allowed investors to evaluate a fund's past performance within four broad asset classes: domestic stock, international stock, taxable bonds and municipal bonds. In the past twenty years, however, mutual funds have become more specialized. Over time, asset-allocation concepts have been introduced and funds have moved from a "stand-alone" investment to being part of a larger portfolio.

Numerous studies have indicated the importance of investment style when explaining stock returns. In their seminal paper, Fama and French (1992) showed that stock returns vary systematically across two dimensions: size and value-growth. However, the original 5-star rating system compared large-capitalization with small-capitalization funds. This had the unfortunate side effect that when a particular style of investing was hot, a disproportionate share of funds within that style received four or five stars. Because of such a style bias, the original star rating was very sensitive to market movements rather than to whether the fund manager had superior management skills.

In mid-2002 Morningstar revised its 5-star rating methodology to assign ratings based on comparisons of funds within a specific investment category. Instead of four broad asset classes, there are now 64 categories within which mutual funds will be sorted and ranked. In addition, Morningstar enhanced its rating approach with a new measure of risk-adjusted return by explicitly considering the upside volatility of mutual funds.

The purpose of this chapter is to present a comprehensive analysis of the new fund rating methodology and to illustrate its improvements and its shortcomings. It will be shown that while the Morningstar rating system has many attractive features, such as the ability to incorporate risk-adjusted returns and different types of funds all within the simple framework of a single star rating, the approach is not without limitations.

The remainder of this chapter is organized as follows. Section 6.2 explores the new Morningstar fund-rating approach. In a first step, the principles of the Morningstar star rating will be discussed. Then, the 64 mutual fund categories will be presented and the enhanced Morningstar risk-adjusted return will be analysed. Finally, the attribution of the overall star ratings will be examined. Section 6.3 discusses improvements and limitations of the new rating methodology such as the still-existing age bias. Moreover, it will be analysed as to whether star ratings help in predicting future mutual fund performance. Section 6.4 concludes and summarizes the findings.

6.2 THE NEW MORNINGSTAR FUND-RATING APPROACH

6.2.1 Principles

Morningstar is an independent mutual fund rating agency. Founded in 1984, the Chicago investment-research firm went public in May 2005. Today, more than 100 research analysts ensure that mutual funds are properly categorized. Morningstar serves more than 4 million investors, 140,000 professional financial advisors, and 500 institutional clients around the world. As of 31 December 2004, the company covered more than 17,000 mutual fund share classes in the United States, 38,000 mutual funds and similar vehicles in international markets, 5,800 stocks, 4,700 separable accounts, 700 closed-end funds 42,000 variable annuity/life sub-accounts, 190 exchange-traded funds, 1,200 hedge funds, and more than 80,000 college savings plans.

Morningstar does not charge or accept payment from portfolio managers to rate their funds. They do sell their other products and services to fund managers without influence on how they allocate their star ratings. If a fund manager wants to use their star ratings in their promotions, Morningstar charges an intellectual property licensing fee.

Star ratings assess a mutual fund's historical risk and return as compared to other funds with similar investment objectives. The rating is not determined by an analyst's review, and Morningstar cannot change a star rating because it likes or dislikes the fund's manager, portfolio holdings, investment strategy, or because Morningstar is convinced the fund will exhibit superior future performance. Instead of reflecting an analyst's subjective opinion, the star rating is based solely on the statistical measure of past performance.

Morningstar calculates past performance based on the returns a fund earns after the ongoing annual management expense ratio is taken into account. However, star ratings do not consider transaction entry or exit fees because these vary from investor to investor. A number of situations preclude a star rating. For instance, funds with a track record of less than three years or funds where too little information is available to properly categorize them will not be rated.

Morningstar (2003) clearly states that star ratings are achievement marks rather than predictors of future mutual fund performance. A star rating is intended as the starting point in the fund selection process. Therefore, a high rating alone should not be the one and only reason for investing in a particular mutual fund. The 5-star rating system can be a useful tool for narrowing down the mutual fund universe to a more manageable number. It can help investors to screen similar investments which may offer the return characteristics they seek within the risk parameters they feel most comfortable with.

The revised Morningstar star rating system was implemented for US mutual funds in July 2002, beginning with the performance period ending 30 June 2002. Historical star ratings remain unchanged.

6.2.2 Mutual fund categories

Within the original rating methodology, Morningstar classified mutual funds into one of four broad asset classes: domestic equity, international equity, taxable bond, and municipal bond. In order to calculate the star rating, Morningstar compared the fund's performance with the risk-adjusted returns of the other funds in the same peer group. However, diverse investment styles often have different levels of risk and lead to variations in returns. For example, a US large-cap fund performs quite differently than a US small-cap fund and, thus, the two funds should not be scored relative to each other.

Morningstar's decision to change its original rating methodology reflected a decade of studies on the importance of investment style in explaining stock returns. In their seminal study, Fama and French (1992) concluded that stock returns can best be explained when stocks are separated into portfolios based on size as measured by market capitalization and value-growth as measured by book-to-market ratios.

In the United States, the revised Morningstar star rating methodology distinguishes between 64 mutual fund categories (see Table A1 in the Appendix) rather than simply using four broad peer groups.[2] Morningstar developed this separate rating category already in 1996, but it was not integrated into its star-rating methodology until mid-2002. This category classification was introduced to help investors make meaningful comparisons between mutual funds and to better build well-diversified portfolios. Morningstar (2003) argues that funds within a category invest in similar types of securities and therefore share the same risk factors. Thus, funds in the same category can be considered as reasonable substitutes for purposes of portfolio construction.

Morningstar itself conducts the determination of a mutual fund's classification. Funds are placed in a given category by the type of investments that are predominant in their underlying portfolio holdings over the past three years. In general, category membership is based on a fund's long-term or normal style profile. When necessary, Morningstar may change a category assignment based on recent changes to the portfolio.

6.2.3 Morningstar risk-adjusted return (MRAR)

One of the most notable changes in the revised star-rating methodology is how the MRAR is calculated. In the original approach, Morningstar assessed a mutual fund's riskiness by looking at the degree to which its monthly returns had underperformed those of the 90-day Treasury-bill rate. They then calculated an average monthly underperformance statistic, which they compared with those of other funds in the same broad asset class to assign the risk scores. This resultant risk score expressed how risky the fund was relative to the average fund in its category.

The setback with this approach, however, was that it failed to identify mutual funds whose enormous returns indicated they were engaging in risky behavior. For example, the star rating failed to adequately penalize many growth- and tech-stock-laden funds in the late 1990s. Since their returns outperformed the Treasury-bill benchmark for many successive months, the funds were considered to be riskless and received very high star ratings.

The new rating methodology is still based on risk-adjusted returns but motivated by expected utility theory.[3] Morningstar (2003) assumes that investors are more concerned about a possible poor outcome than an unexpectedly good outcome. Further, the utility function models that investors are risk averse. They are willing to give up some portion of their expected return in exchange for greater certainty of return. The new star rating rewards consistent performance and considers that higher return is good and higher risk is bad under all circumstances.

6.2.4 Attribution of stars

For calculating the overall star rating, Morningstar determines in a first step time-specific ratings. To assign the three-year ratings, Morningstar calculates the load-adjusted MRAR of total returns for all mutual funds that have at least 36 continuous months of total return data. In the next step, each fund is placed in the category indicated in the most recent monthly record. Finally, all mutual funds in a peer group are ranked in descending order according to their MRAR.

The three-year time-specific is then attributed to each fund according to its position in the distribution of MRAR values. Figure 6.1 illustrates that funds with the highest 10 percent of risk- and load-adjusted returns within each category are assigned the highest rating of five stars. The mutual funds in the following 22.5 percent of the MRAR distribution obtain four stars, those in

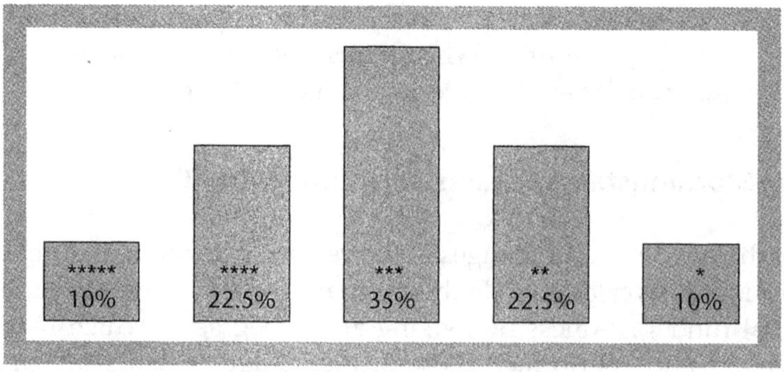

Figure 6.1 Morningstar's rating classes

Table 6.1 Weighing scheme for the overall star rating

Age of fund	Overall star rating
At least three years, but less than five years	100% three-year rating
At least five years, but less than ten years	60% five-year rating
	40% three-year rating
At least ten years	50% 10-year rating
	30% five-year rating
	20% three-year rating

the following 35 percent of their fund category receive three stars, and funds in the ensuing 22.5 percent obtain two stars. Finally, those mutual funds in the bottom 10 percent of the MRAR distribution of each category receive the lowest rating of one star. Morningstar updates these rankings every month.

For mutual funds aged enough to have sufficient historical return data, this process is repeated using the most recent five and ten years of fund performance data. Thus, young funds have only a three-year time-specific rating, middle-aged funds have three- and five-year time-specific ratings, and seasoned funds have three-, five and ten-year time-specific ratings.

Once these category- and time-specific star ratings are assigned, Morningstar determines the overall star rating for each mutual fund using a weighted average of its time-specific ratings. The way this overall star rating is calculated varies in an important way by the age of the mutual fund being rated, as the weighting scheme in Table 6.1 displays.

For a young fund the overall star rating is equal to its three-year time-specific rating. For a middle-aged fund, the overall star rating is based on 40 percent of its three-year rating and on 60 percent of its five-year rating. For a seasoned fund, the overall star rating results from the average of 20 percent of its three-year rating, 30 percent of its five-year rating and

Table 6.2 Similarity matrix of mutual fund categories

Category	LV	LB	LG	MV	MB	MG	SV	SB	SG
Large value (LV)	1.00								
Large blend (LB)	0.50	1.00							
Large growth (LG)	0.00	0.50	1.00						
Mid-cap value (MV)	0.50	0.25	0.00	1.00					
Mid-cap blend (MB)	0.25	0.50	0.25	0.50	1.00				
Mid-cap growth (MG)	0.00	0.25	0.50	0.00	0.50	1.00			
Small value (SV)	0.00	0.00	0.00	0.50	0.25	0.00	1.00		
Small blend (SB)	0.00	0.00	0.00	0.25	0.50	0.25	0.50	1.00	
Small growth (SG)	0.00	0.00	0.00	0.00	0.25	0.50	0.00	0.50	1.00

50 percent of its ten-year rating. The resultant number, rounded to the nearest integer, is the number of overall stars for the fund.[4]

Further changes in the rating methodology concern the way how Morningstar deals with funds that have switched investment categories. For example, if a fund built its early record as a large-growth fund but the (new) portfolio manager switched over to a small-value style, the star rating should attribute more weight to how the fund has performed as a small-value fund and less weight to its earlier performance record. Morningstar (2003) argues that this ensures the fairest comparison and minimizes the incentive for fund companies to change a fund's style in an attempt to receive a better star rating.

Table 6.2 shows the matrix that Morningstar (2003) utilizes to measure the similarity between the fund's current category and its previous category if the fund has changed its investment style over time.

For example, Table 6.2 indicates that for a mutual fund that had shifted from its mid-cap-value category to a large-value investment style, Morningstar would still place a fair amount of weight on its record as a mid-value fund, because the two style boxes are contiguous. A fund that shifted from large-growth to small-value, however, would see its performance history as a large-growth fund entirely discounted.

6.3 IMPROVEMENTS AND LIMITATIONS

6.3.1 Measurement of risk

In mid-2002 Morningstar realized the shortcomings of the MRAR measure used to calculate its stars for 17 years. The problem of the original fund rating system was primarily that it did not evaluate mutual fund risk accurately. It failed to point out funds whose huge returns indicated they were engaging in risky investments. Therefore, in the revised version of the star rating the MRAR calculation was modified.

For the new methodology, Morningstar adopts methods more similar to those that have been standard in the investment literature for many years. While maintaining a traditional emphasis on downside risk, the enhanced MRAR measure does not take only downside volatility but also upside volatility into account. Funds with highly volatile returns are penalized, whether the volatility is on the up- or on the downside. Risks that have not yet surfaced will be apparent in funds that have extraordinary upside volatility. Consistent performance is in the new framework more highly rewarded.

The advantages of these conceptual improvements can be best understood by looking at the experience with Internet funds. In the late 1990s, Morningstar considered these funds as not risky – as they only exhibited upside volatility – and assigned the majority of these tech-stock-laden funds the highest rating of five stars. As it appeared, their fabulous gains indicated serious potential for extreme losses: they lost on average 14 percent in 2000. One-star rated value-oriented mutual funds gained on average during the same time 6 percent.[5]

The revised star-rating methodology accounts for all variations in a fund's month-to-month performance. As a result, the possibility of strong short-term performance masking the inherent risk of a fund has now been reduced and it is more difficult for high-risk funds to earn high star ratings. Re-adjusting for beginning of the year 2000 shows that the enhanced risk measure would have qualified those funds with a higher risk level and, thus, a significantly lower star rating than the previous MRAR measure did.

Despite these improvements, it seems that Morningstar has not learned all the lessons from the stock market crash in 2000 and from recent research in empirical finance. Morningstar does not perform and, thus, does not include in the fund's overall star rating, the calculation of the extreme loss potential (VaR) to which mutual funds are exposed. This is quite problematic since funds are increasingly invested in assets that present non-normal distributions, which makes the use of volatility as the only risk measure highly illusory.

6.3.2 Categories

The original star-rating system was too heavily influenced by cyclical market trends. It was sensitive to the popularity of investment styles. When a particular style of investing was hot, a disproportionate share of funds within that style received four or five stars. This style bias implied that the stars were rewarding the asset class favored by the market more than the portfolio manager's management skills.

To make the fund-rating system less vulnerable to the changing popularity of investment styles, Morningstar expanded the number of fund categories from four broad groups to 64 specialized investment styles, putting each fund in a more narrowly defined peer group. For example, Morningstar placed in the original star rating system all US stock funds into just one group. This implies that a fund's star rating no longer depends on the relative strength or weakness of the fund's investment style. In theory, this revised rating methodology will make it less likely that lower-rated mutual funds will outperform the five stars.

The revised Morningstar fund rating methodology is designed to better measure the value added by fund managers. Because the new system gives funds in every category an equal opportunity for receiving a five-star rating, it does on one hand a much better job of identifying winning funds whose styles are simply out of favor. On the other hand, it punishes weak funds that are only taking advantage of being member of a hot asset class. The switch to smaller groups will more effectively measure whether a fund manager has added value, helping investors to better distinguish among funds that share a similar investment style.

While the expansion to 64 categories certainly improved Morningstar's fund rating system, it does not completely solve the previous discussed difficulties. The rating system uses a relative ranking of fund performance so that the attributed star ratings are totally dependent on the definition of the categories. However, Morningstar is not able to verify and monitor the composition of portfolios and, thus, has to rely on the portfolio holdings that are proclaimed by the fund managers.[6] Moreover, the increasing number of complex financial products prevents Morningstar from being sure that all the funds in the category are alike. Star ratings are thus compiled for funds that may not share the same risk profile.

Narrow groups take style management better into account. However, some categories had to be defined broadly to incorporate enough funds for a meaningful comparison group. It is apparent that there are larger style differences among funds in some categories. This implies that funds can have very different risk levels within a specific category.

Another difficulty is related to the fact that the style of a fund may not be stable over time, so the category in which the fund is classified may differ from its current style category. For instance, Kim, Shukla and Tomas (2000) show that more than half of the mutual funds were misclassified; that is, their investment attributes were not consistent with the Morningstar category. Since the rated funds have an allocation that differs from the initial allocation, they have not been exposed to the same risks during the whole period. This would imply that a large number of the stars attributed by Morningstar in reference to a predefined category are wrongly attributed.

6.3.3 Attribution of stars

Morningstar rewards mutual funds' risk-adjusted past performance by employing its original five-star rating system. Its revised rating methodology compares a large-cap growth fund's performance with the performance of other large-cap growth funds. In addition, it is style neutral since a fund's rating is independent on whether the fund's style has been hot or cold. At all times, 10 percent of large-cap growth funds will receive five stars and 22.5 percent will receive four stars.

One major problem with the revised star rating methodology is that depending on the market climate, the quality of funds that receive five stars may differ. Since Morningstar uses a predefined percentile distribution to attribute their stars, even the weakest investment style is guaranteed its share of five-star funds. This implies that some mutual funds whose investors have taken massive losses can still earn five stars.

To overcome this difficulty, Morningstar should define its stars as an absolute rating that relies on comparable arithmetic values such as the fund' alpha, which are totally free of a specific choice of categories. The percentile number of funds that will receive the maximum number of stars should not be pre-determined, so that the quality of funds receiving five stars remains equal all the time. There would be no chance for a poorly performing fund to obtain a high star rating, only because it was less bad than others in its category. Thus, considering the number of stars a fund has received, investors would know exactly how the mutual fund has performed with regard to its benchmark.

Another difficulty lies in the fact that Morningstar's star ratings follow the mutual fund, not the fund manager. Therefore, a fund's rating might be based almost entirely on the success of a manager who is no longer with the fund.

6.3.4 Age bias

There are numerous empirical studies indicating a potential age bias in Morningstar's original 5-star fund-rating methodology. Blume (1998) was among the first to investigate the relationship between a fund's age and its star rating. He found that fewer seasoned funds received five stars. Morey (2002) concludes that the overall star ratings of older funds are higher than of younger funds. Although their findings differ in the results, both authors attributed this age bias phenomenon to Morningstar's return weighting system.

Despite the improvements of the methodology, a potential age bias still exists in the star ratings. Adkisson and Fraser (2004) show that this bias is made up of three components. The first is due to Morningstar's return-weighting system. The second component is related to market conditions throughout the evaluation period. The third constituent stems from the relationship between a fund' age and its size.

Morningstar's return-weighting system places the greatest emphasis on a fund's most recent 36 monthly returns. It seems that the ten-year time-specific rating is given the most weight in determining the overall star rating for seasoned funds. However, the most recent 36 months of performance data are triple-counted in the calculation of the three-year, five-year and ten-year time-specific star ratings. The months 37 to 60 are double-counted in the five-year and ten-year star ratings. Therefore, in the overall star rating the actual data weighting for the most recent 36 months is 42 percent, the weighting for the prior months 37 to 60 is 23 percent and the weighting for the prior months 61 to 120 is 35 percent.[7]

On the other hand, it is important to understand that a five-year time-specific rating basically means that two more years of historical performance data are used. An investor needs to decide whether this additional information is helpful. Superior performance data from the more distant past could mask poorer recent performance. For example, a mutual fund with a ten-year performance history and with a three-year one-star rating, a five-year three-star rating and a ten-year five-star rating would receive an overall four-star rating.[8] If the same fund had had just a history of three (five) years, Morningstar would have assigned an overall star rating of one (two) stars. This case illustrates why investors should be careful when interpreting the overall star ratings as signals of past performance. Indeed, funds may be rated differently not because of past performance, but rather because of the length of the history of the mutual fund.

The second component of Morningstar's star rating methodology which is responsible for the age bias is related to the market climate during the evaluation period. The equity risk-premium is likely to vary depending on market conditions. Adkisson and Fraser (2004) mention that star ratings of young funds are based firmly on returns drawn from a bear market. However, slightly more than half of the returns that make up the overall star ratings of the middle-aged funds were earned under much more favorable business conditions during the bull market of the 1990s.

Therefore, the changing state of the market may affect the apparent relationship between the age of a fund and its overall star rating. The star ratings of funds of different ages are affected in different ways because the funds have passed through different patterns of the market cycle. Different market conditions and cycles over the evaluation period cause a change in the relative rankings of funds, even within 64 investment categories. This makes it difficult to compare funds that are evaluated over different periods.

Finally, fund size also contributes to the age bias in the Morningstar ratings. Compensation to the fund management company is typically a percentage of assets under management. Because there are some economies of scale that make larger funds less expensive to run, there is a strong incentive to increase fund size as quickly as possible.[9]

Younger funds tend to be smaller than older funds and are consequently more sensitive to skillful stock-picking. When the fund' portfolio is small, a few big winning positions can make a noticeable difference in the fund's total return. This increases the fund's ability to compete for new investment dollars and discourage investors from selling. As a result, as funds grow older, they tend to become larger.

Because larger funds usually have a greater number of holdings, they begin to resemble the overall market as they age. This size effect implies that older funds become progressively less likely to exhibit extreme performance. This explains why seasoned funds tend to evolve towards the market mean and receive often an overall three-star rating. Adkisson and Fraser (2004) prove that older funds have higher (lower) overall star ratings when the three-year time-specific rating is low (high). On the other hand, young funds generally receive both higher time-specific ratings and, thus, also higher overall star ratings than "middle-aged" and "seasoned" funds. This age bias is not due to a survivorship bias, but rather to the methodology that Morningstar uses to calculate its star ratings.

Understanding the nature of the age bias and its sources is important because it means that the star rating for funds of different ages and/or from different time periods are not perfectly comparable. Adjusting the star ratings for fund size could possibly reduce the age bias.

6.3.5 Performance persistence

Morningstar does not claim that its rating system can predict future mutual fund performance; they rather regard the star ratings as achievement scores that investors should use to narrow down their search for the best suitable mutual fund. While such advice is obviously sound, many people still use the star ratings as indicators of future performance. In fact, knowing the relative rankings of mutual funds is of little interest if it is not possible to use the results for future investment decisions. Thus, it is highly likely that those investors using the star system will avoid funds with the lowest ratings and choose funds with the highest ratings precisely in the expectation that they will increase the future returns received on their investments.

Several empirical studies have underlined the fact that investors tend to rely greatly on Morningstar's star ratings to select their mutual funds. For example, Del Guercio and Tkac (2002) find that the star rating itself has a significant effect on fund flows. They conclude that a fund's initial five-star rating produced an abnormal inflow of 53 percent above the normal expected inflow for about six months. In another study, Reichenstein (2004) shows that in 1999, mutual funds with four or five stars had net inflows of $234 billion, while lower rated funds had net outflows of $132 billion.

Blake and Morey (2000) were the first to analyse the performance persistence of Morningstar's fund ratings. They find that low ratings indicate relatively poor future performance, while high star ratings were not predictors of future top performance. Five-star rated funds did not outperform the four stars or even median-ranked funds.

In a more recent study, Kräussl (2005) examines the performance persistence of Morningstar's revised rating methodology. Since this empirical analysis is based on only three years of historical performance data, it is far too early to draw strong conclusions on Morningstar's out-of-sample forecasting qualities. Early indications show that the revised star rating system has some predictive abilities. For nearly half of the 64 asset classes, five-star funds outperform lower-rated funds from the same category from 1 July 2002, to 30 June 2005. Likewise, one-star funds underperform higher-rated mutual funds. Funds with less than three stars generally have much worse future performance than higher-rated ones. These results are relatively robust over different categories, ages of funds, styles of funds, and time periods.

These empirical results are broadly consistent with much of the mutual fund performance persistence literature. Researchers have found that while it is relatively easy to predict poor performance, it is much more difficult to consistently predict superior performance.[10] Some have argued according to the size-effect: when mutual funds perform well, their assets increase so significantly that it makes them unmanageable. Others have suggested that if markets are efficient, high outperformance is more a matter of luck than management skill and, thus, over time, fund performance will tend to revert towards the mean.

6.4 CONCLUSION

In June 2002, Morningstar revised its original 5-star rating methodology and changed the comparison groups from four broad asset classes to 64 specific categories. This was done to ensure that funds would earn high star ratings only when their portfolio managers added value, rather than when their investment style performed well. Nowadays, comparisons are made between funds that are managed according to the same investment style. After the experiences with many high-rated growth- and tech-stock-laden mutual funds during the stockmarket crash in 2000, Morningstar also aimed at a better reflection of a fund's risk level. Therefore, Morningstar adopted for its new MRAR measure an expected utility framework which penalizes a fund's volatility in either direction.

Aside from the switch to category-based peer groups and its enhanced MRAR, the basic framework for the original star rating methodology remains intact. This study of the revised Morningstar 5-star rating system has shown that despite all the improvements, not all previously encountered problems in the original approach have been solved.

Morningstar's practice of assigning a weight to a fund's most recent performance according to its age, with different age groups receiving different weights, is still at the root of the age bias in its star ratings. A more general problem is that the star rating measures past performance and therefore does not immediately reflect fundamental changes in a mutual fund's asset allocation strategy. For example, a leave of the portfolio manager may alter a fund's long-term prospects but the star rating would not reflect the change.

This chapter is not stating that there is no need for Morningstar or similar mutual fund rating services. These services are great sources of information. Morningstar provides a simple and easy-to-understand 5-star rating system for the average investor, incorporating risk-adjusted returns for different types of mutual funds. It gives investors the ability to quickly identify funds that may be valuable for additional research.

However, investors should be aware that the star ratings are somewhat dependent upon the age and the asset class of the fund. The results of this article suggest that investors should compare funds of the same age and evaluated over the same time period. If a mutual fund receives a five-star overall rating as well as high time-specific ratings, an investor can be quite sure that the fund has been a winning fund. Nevertheless, high performance in the past is not a sign of future high performance.

While it would be nice to have a simple, universal system to identify lucrative investments, there is just no substitute for thorough research, thoughtful consideration, and an individual's own evaluation of his personal investment goals. Morningstar can provide some help with an individual's financial decision-making, but its star ratings are only part of what is required to make an informed choice. The 5-star rating system will work best as a screen for narrowing a crowded mutual fund field down to a more manageable size. It provides an efficient solution in identifying the weakest funds. With more than 17,000 mutual funds available, it might be a good starting point to screen out the one- and two-stars. After that, however, an investor has to do his own investigative work on a fund's fundamentals to find his winning mutual fund.

APPENDIX

Table A1 Mutual Fund Categories

US Stock	International Stock	Taxable Bond	Municipal Bond
Large Value	Foreign Large Value	Long Government	Muni National Long
Large Blend	Foreign Large Blend	Intermediate Government	Muni National Interm
Large Growth	Foreign Large Growth	Short Government	Muni National Short
Mid-Cap Value	Foreign Small/ Mid Value	Long-Term Bond	High Yield Muni
Mid-Cap Blend	Foreign Small/ Mid Growth	Intermediate-Term Bond	Muni Single State Long
Mid-Cap Growth	World Stock	Short-Term Bond	Muni Single State Interm
Small Value	Diversified Emerging Markets	Ultrashort Bond	Muni Single State Short
Small Blend	Latin America Stock	Bank Loan	Muni California Long
Small Growth	Europe Stock	High Yield Bond	Muni California Int/Sh
Specialty Communications	Japan Stock	Multisector Bond	Muni Florida
Specialty Financial	Pacific/Asia ex-Japan Stock	World Bond	Muni Massachusetts
Specialty Health	Diversified Pacific/Asia	Emerging Markets Bond	Muni Minnesota
Specialty Natural Resources	Specialty Precious Metals	Stable Value	Muni New Jersey
Specialty Real Estate	World Allocation		Muni New York Long
Specialty Technology			Muni New York Int/Sh
Specialty Utilities			Muni Ohio
Bear Market			Muni Pennsylvania
Convertibles			
Conservative Allocation			
Moderate Allocation			

NOTES

1. This chapter concentrates on Morningstar's 5-star fund rating system for the US market. However, the main findings are also applicable to its rating methodology in other geographical regions.
2. The list of fund categories depends on the area of the world in which the star rating system is used. For instance, in Europe, Morningstar has created a single set of fund categories for the entire European mutual fund universe.

3. In order to establish a mutual fund ranking, Morningstar has to make the assumption that all investors use the same utility function.
4. For instance, a seasoned fund that had a four-star rating for the three-year time horizon, a four-star rating for the five-year time horizon and a three-star rating for the ten-year time horizon would receive a 3.5, so that Morningstar would assign this fund a four-star overall rating.
5. The problem of Morningstar's risk evaluation was also brought to light for bond funds when two Heartland Group Inc. high-yield municipal bond funds lost 70 percent and 44 percent of their value in just one day. Both funds had five-star ratings and were among the best-performing municipal funds, but it appeared that they were strongly invested in illiquid and distressed securities.
6. The difficulty of *a priori* classification of securities according to their characteristics has also been highlighted by numerous empirical studies. For example, diBartolemeo and Witkowski (1997) showed that the category declared is not always the true category of the fund. They performed a style analysis on 748 funds and found that 40 percent were actually following an investment style other than the one declared.
7. For the overall star calculation for "middle-aged" mutual funds the most recent 36 months are involved in the calculation of both the three-year and the five-year time-specific rating. This implies that the actual data weighting for the most recent 36 months is 71 percent and the weighting for the months 37–60 is 29 percent.
8. The overall star rating would be calculated as $0.2 * 1 + 0.3 * 3 + 0.5 * 5 = 3.6$, which is rounded up to the nearest integer of 4, thus, resulting in a four-star rating.
9. Wermers (2000) argues that economies of scale benefits the fund's management. A decline in trading costs gives the fund room to increase management fees without changing the total cost to investors.
10. See, for example, the empirical studies by Brown and Goetzmann (1995), Carhart (1997), Elton, Gruber and Blake (1996), and Grinblatt and Titman (1992).

REFERENCES

Adkisson, J.A. and Fraser, R.D. (2004) "Is There Still an Age Bias in the Morningstar Ratings?", Working Paper, A&M University, Texas.

Blake, C.R. and Morey, M.R. (2000) "Morningstar Ratings and Mutual Fund Performance", *Journal of Financial and Quantitative Analysis*, 35(3): 451–83.

Blume, M. (1998) "An Anatomy of Morningstar Ratings", *Financial Analysts Journal*, 54(2): 19–27.

Brown, S.J. and Goetzmann, W.N. (1995) "Performance Persistence", *Journal of Finance*, 50(2): 679–98.

Carhart, M.M. (1997) "On Persistence in Mutual Fund Performance", *Journal of Finance*, 52(1): 57–82.

Del Guercio, D. and Tkac, P.A. (2002) "The Effect of Morningstar Ratings on Mutual Fund Flows", Working Paper, University of Oregon.

diBartolomeo, D. and Witkowski, E. (1997) "Mutual Fund Misclassification: Evidence Based on Style Analysis", *Financial Analysts Journal*, 53(5): 32–43.

Elton, E.J., Gruber, M.J. and Blake, C.R. (1996) "The Persistence of Risk-Adjusted Mutual Fund Performance", *Journal of Business*, 69(2): 133–57.

Fama, E. and French, K. (1992) "The Cross-Section of Expected Stock Returns", *Journal of Finance*, 47(2): 427–65.

Grinblatt, M. and Titman, S. (1992) "The Persistence of Mutual Fund Performance", *Journal of Finance*, 47(5): 1977–84.

Kim, M., Shukla, R. and Tomas, M. (2000) "Mutual Fund Objective Misclassification", *Journal of Economics and Business*, 52(4): 309–23.

Kräussl, R. (2005) "Do 5-Star Ratings Predict Future Performance of Mutual Funds? An Empirical Analysis of the Revised Morningstar Fund Rating Methodology", Working Paper, Vrije Universiteit, Amsterdam.

Morey, M.R. (2002) "Mutual Fund Age and Morningstar Ratings", *Financial Analysts Journal*, 58(2): 56–63.

Morningstar (2003) *The Morningstar Rating Methodology* (Chicago, IL: Morningstar Publications).

Pozen, R.C. (1998) *The Mutual Fund Business* (Cambridge, MA: MIT Press).

Reichenstein, W. (2004) "Morningstar's New Star Rating System: Advances and Innovations", *Journal of Financial Planning*, 17(3): 40–7.

Wermers, R. (2000) "Mutual Fund Performance: An Empirical Decomposition into Stock-Picking Talent, Style, Transaction Costs and Expenses", *Journal of Finance*, 55(4): 1655–95.

CHAPTER 7

Mutual Fund Flows and Expected Stock Returns in Germany: The Role of the Benchmark and of Expectation Biases

Wolfgang Breuer and Olaf Stotz

7.1 INTRODUCTION

The growth in mutual fund investment has been substantial in the past decades. As a result, mutual funds are now one of the largest owners of equities. For example, in 2003 mutual funds owned almost 30 percent of outstanding equities in the USA and 15 percent in Europe (Fefsi, 2003). A growing body of research is investigating how mutual fund flows and stock prices are related (for example, Warther, 1995; Choe, Ko and Stulz, 1999; Fant, 1999; Edelen and Warner, 2001; Froot, O'Connel and Seasholes, 2001; Bekaert, Harvey and Lumsdaine, 2002). These studies document in general that there is a positive relationship between fund flows and stock prices. For the US market, for example, Warther (1995) reports that an unexpected flow into mutual funds of 1 percent of total stock fund assets corresponds to a 5.7 percent increase in the stock price index.

There are two reasons why rational investors delegate their wealth management to mutual fund managers. First, economies of scale, exploited by the mutual fund manager, lead to decreasing wealth management costs. Second, private investors might suspect that professional mutual fund managers have superior management skills, leading to positive risk-adjusted excess returns. If professional fund managers did have superior investment skills, private investors would achieve better returns via portfolio delegation. However, Jensen (1968) and others have shown that mutual funds do not on average achieve a superior return compared to a benchmark index. Thus, only economies of scale remain as a main reason for wealth delegation. Additionally, there are also behavioral explanations for fund flows. In contrast to the rational arguments above, Woerheide (1982), as well as Jain and Wu (2000), demonstrates that an important factor for mutual fund flows is the marketing effort of the fund company. Fund flows are closely related to fund advertising: an increase in advertising leads to increasing inflows. However, it is shown that advertising is not informative on future fund performance. In the following, we want to develop an analytical framework for gaining additional insights into the causes and consequences of monetary flows from private investors to mutual funds.

Applying portfolio optimization models with exogenously given expected returns (which is the common approach) cannot model a positive relationship between the demand of a stock and its price. With exogenously given expected returns, investors are assumed to be price-takers and the supply of assets to be infinitely elastic. Thus, investors can buy (or sell short) as much of an asset at a given price as they demand. To relate stock demand to resulting stock prices within a portfolio optimization model, expected returns have to be made endogenous. In this chapter, a solution is proposed that relates expected returns to demand by applying the dividend growth model as an estimator for expected returns. An equilibrium condition ensures that the demand for assets equals their supply. This approach allows us to investigate how fund flows may impact prices. In particular, the possibly different consequences for prices of benchmark stocks and non-benchmark stocks can be analyzed.

In order to do so, we allow for different portfolio selection behaviors of private investors and professional fund managers. While the former are assumed to follow traditional mean-variance optimization, as proposed by Markowitz (1952, 1959), the latter will typically choose portfolios in line with a tracking-error optimization, particularly analysed by Roll (1992). Tracking-error optimization captures today's professional practice: fund managers are typically evaluated and compensated relative to a pre-specified benchmark portfolio. The portfolios selected by fund managers might differ from optimal portfolios identified by the classical mean-variance approach. The question arises as to whether tracking-error optimization helps to explain the empirical observation of a positive relationship between flows and prices. To see the intuition behind this supposition, consider a mutual fund manager who gets additional money from private investors. If he does not invest the money immediately, he faces the risk of underperforming the benchmark.

Thus, sufficiently risk averse fund managers tend to invest (part of) new liquidity (that is, inflow) immediately, regardless of whether prices are high or low. If investors demand their funds back (that is, outflow), fund managers are forced to sell stocks, irrespective of their price level, in order to meet the obligation to pay back investors. Therefore, the buying and selling behavior of mutual fund managers is, to some extent, unrelated to either the price level or the fundamental data. This investment behavior might temporarily drive prices away from their long-run equilibrium value. As a result, expected returns will become time varying. These patterns can be indeed observed in many international stockmarkets (for example, Fama and French, 1988). Moreover, on this basis we will expect a different price behavior of benchmark stocks and non-benchmark stocks, since fund managers' activities will in particular be geared towards the purchase and sale of benchmark stocks. The impact of the benchmark on stock prices can also be observed in another context, for example when the benchmark changes its composition. On average, stocks included in the benchmark earn a positive excess return and stocks excluded from the benchmark earn a negative excess return after the index composition has been altered (for example, Harris and Gurel, 1986; Shleifer, 1986; Dhillon and Johnson, 1991; Beneish and Whaley, 1996; Lynch and Mendenhall, 1997).

This study contributes to the fund flows literature in two ways. First, an equilibrium framework is proposed that allows us to discuss numerically the relationship between prices, expected returns and flows. Our analysis is thereby based on *ceteris paribus* variations of several exogenous parameters such as initial investors' wealth or dividend expectations. A central feature of this framework is that expected returns are not exogenously given. Expected returns and prices are determined in equilibrium on the basis of fundamental data. Second, the implications of our model are empirically investigated. The empirical results for the German stockmarket provide evidence that fund flows are related differently to benchmark stocks and non-benchmark stocks. Moreover, we find that our numerical and empirical results are consistent with each other only if we assume mean-reverting expectation biases with respect to future fund returns. Since such biases in particular may be caused by marketing efforts of fund companies, this outcome can be considered a reasonable addition to the findings by Woerheide (1982) as well as by Jain and Wu (2000).

The chapter is organized as follows: portfolio selection with exogenously given expected returns is reviewed in section 7.2, while portfolio selection with endogenously determined expected returns and our equilibrium framework are developed in section 7.3. Section 7.4 investigates the model numerically, and in section 7.5 hypotheses are derived which are empirically tested in section 7.6. Moreover, possible explanations of our results are discussed in this section. Section 7.7 concludes.

7.2 PORTFOLIO SELECTION AND EXOGENOUS RETURNS

7.2.1 Tracking-error optimization of portfolio manager *P*

Even nowadays the concept of mean-variance optimization, as introduced by Markowitz (1952, 1959) describes the most important decision model for portfolio selection. Some years ago, this concept was extended by Roll (1992) to include tracking-error optimization. In this case, a professional portfolio manager is considered who is judged by his total return performance relative to a benchmark portfolio, typically a broadly diversified index of assets. To be precise, consider a (representative) portfolio manager P who can choose between a riskless asset and N risky ones. A risky asset i yields a one-period return from t to $t+1$ of $R_{i,t+1}$, unknown at t. The one-period return of the riskless asset is known at t and denoted by $R_{f,t+1}$.

Portfolio manager P's total return performance is measured relative to a pre-specified benchmark portfolio. A benchmark portfolio is a subset of the N risky assets, consisting of M ($M < N$) securities. Thus, the benchmark portfolio has $N - M$ zero weights of risky assets. If, for example, the benchmark is the S&P 500, while the market consists of the 5,000 stocks listed on US stock-markets (for example, NASDAQ), there would be $5{,}000 - 500 = 4{,}500$ zero weights of risky assets.

Let $R_{t+1}^{(P)}$ denote the uncertain return of P's portfolio as held from t to $t+1$ and let $R_{t+1}^{(B)}$ be the corresponding uncertain return of the benchmark portfolio B. We assume that P's salary amounts to $\alpha \cdot (R_{t+1}^{(P)} - R_{t+1}^{(B)}) + \beta$ and is thus a linear function of his relative return performance $R_{t+1}^{(P)} - R_{t+1}^{(B)}$. Portfolio manager P is assumed to maximize $E[\alpha \cdot (R_{t+1}^{(P)} - R_{t+1}^{(B)}) + \beta] - 0.5 \cdot k^{(P)} \cdot \mathrm{Var}[\alpha \cdot (R_{t+1}^{(P)} - R_{t+1}^{(B)}) + \beta]$ so that he is a mean-variance optimizer with respect to his personal payoff. From this, we immediately get that P is only interested in a high expected return $E(R_{t+1}^{(P)})$ of his portfolio and a low corresponding tracking-error $\omega_{t+1}^{(P)2} := \mathrm{Var}(R_{t+1}^{(P)} - R_{t+1}^{(B)})$ according to an objective function $E(R_{t+1}^{(P)}) - 0.5 \cdot k^{(P)+} \cdot \omega_t^{(P)2}$ with $k^{(P)+} := \alpha \cdot k^{(P)}$.

Roll (1992) has solved such a portfolio optimization problem for the case that P is not allowed to invest in the riskless asset. In contrast to the situation in Roll (1992), our portfolio manager has additional access to the risk free asset. However, it is worth noting that an investment in the risk free asset increases the tracking error, as the risk free asset is not included in the benchmark. The optimal portfolio which consists of a relative amount $x_{0,t}^{(P)}$ of the riskless asset and of relative amounts $x_{i,t}^{(P)}$ of the N risky assets $i = 1, \ldots, N$ is (see the Appendix for details):

$$x_{i,t}^{(P)} = x_{i,t}^{(B)} + \frac{1}{\alpha \cdot k^{(P)}} \cdot \sum_{j=0}^{N} \left[\sigma_{ij,t+1}^{(P)|1}\right]^{-1} \cdot \left[E_t(R_{j,t+1}) - R_{f,t+1}\right], \qquad i = 0, \ldots, N \tag{7.1}$$

with $[\sigma_{ij,t+1}^{(P)|1}]^{-1}$ being an element (i, j) of the inverse of an extended variance-covariance matrix $\sigma_{t+1}^{(P)|1}$(as defined in the Appendix) and $x_{i,t}^{(B)}$denoting the relative monetary weight of asset i in benchmark portfolio B at time t. If the portfolio manager P is infinitely risk averse (that is, $k^{(P)} = \infty$), he places 100 percent weight on the benchmark portfolio, that is, $x_t^{(P)} = x_t^{(B)}$, since this leads to a tracking error of 0. Thus, the benchmark portfolio B acts as some kind of riskless asset for P.

7.2.2 Traditional mean-variance optimization of investor I

As pointed out in the introduction, transaction costs considerations seem to be a main reason for delegated wealth management. According to this, we assume that a (representative) investor I hands over the amount $W_t^{(P)}$of his total wealth W_t to our (representative) portfolio manager P. Moreover, in the case of positive transaction costs we must generally distinguish between gross returns, that is returns before subtraction of transaction costs, and net returns, that is returns after subtraction of transaction costs. This distinction is not relevant for the derivation of (7.1), as long as we assume the portfolio manager to be acting without incurring (significant) transaction costs and, thus moreover, to be evaluated according to gross returns (equalling in this special case net returns as well), but it becomes important for investor I's portfolio selection problem. Since the investor's portfolio optimization is mainly driven by transaction costs differences between him and the professional portfolio manager, it indeed suffices to explicitly consider transaction costs solely with respect to the investor's optimization problem. (For selected scenarios, we repeated our numerical analysis (section 7.4 below) with positive transaction costs for portfolio managers, but this did not lead to new insights regarding comparative statistics.)

Let, therefore, $P_{i,t}$ be the price of security i at time t as well as $R_{i,t+1}$ be the gross return of security i from t to $t + 1$ and assume fixed relative transaction costs $c_i^{(I)}$ for selling security i at time $t + 1$ for an investor I. As a result, net revenues only amount to $(1 - c_i^{(I)}) \cdot P_{i,t+1}$. Then net return $\hat{R}_{i,t+1}^{(I)}$ of security i from t to $t + 1$ for investor I results as $R_{i,t+1} \cdot (1 - c_i^{(I)}) - c_i^{(I)}$.

With $\hat{R}_{i,t+1}^{(I)}$ as the net return of investor I's portfolio and $(1 + \hat{R}_{i,t+1}^{(I)}) \cdot W_t$ as the uncertain terminal wealth of investor I at time $t + 1$ he is assumed to maximize his objective function $E[(1 + \hat{R}_{i,t+1}^{(I)}) \cdot W_t] - 0.5 \cdot k^{(I)} \cdot \text{Var}[(1 + \hat{R}_{i,t+1}^{(I)}) \cdot W_t]$. This problem can be simplified to the maximization of $E(\hat{R}_{i,t+1}^{(I)}) - 0.5 \cdot k_t^{(I)+}$ $\text{Var} \cdot (\hat{R}_{t+1}^{(I)})$ with $k_t^{(I)+} := W_t \cdot k^{(I)}$. As a consequence of possible wealth delegation from investor I to portfolio manager P, the former can select from among $N + 1$ risky securities, where security $N + 1$ is the (optimal) portfolio of portfolio manager P (that is, a mutual fund). Hence, we have

$$\hat{R}^{(I)}_{N+1,t+1} = \left[x^{(P)}_{0,t} \cdot R_{f,t+1} + \sum_{j=1}^{N} x^{(P)}_{j,t} \cdot R^{(P)}_{j,t+1} \right] \cdot \left(1 - c^{(I)}_{N+1}\right) - c^{(I)}_{N+1} \tag{7.2}$$

Once again, we must look at net returns, but this time the management fee $c^{(I)}_{N+1}$ has to be considered. This fee need not be identical with the private investor's corresponding transaction costs parameters $c^{(I)}_{j}$ ($j = 1, \ldots, N$). It is just a compensation of the mutual fund company for its services and it is computed as a certain percentage of total fund wealth at time $t = 1$, hence including riskless lending (and borrowing). Moreover, formula (7.2) implicitly assumes that the portfolio manager's salary is paid by the mutual fund corporation and not directly by the investor.

Investor I can borrow or lend money at a certain interest rate $R_{f,t+1}$, too. The solution to his maximization problem is well-known as (for example, Campbell and Viceira, 2002):

$$x^{(I)}_{i,t} = \frac{1}{W_t \cdot k^{(I)}} \cdot \sum_{j=1}^{N+1} \sigma^{-1}_{ij,t+1} \cdot (E_t(\hat{R}^{(I)}_{j,t+1}) - R_{f,t+1}), \quad i = 1, \ldots, N+1 \tag{7.3}$$

with $\sigma^{(-1)}_{ij,t+1}$ being an element (i, j) of the inverse of the variance-covariance matrix of the net returns of the $N + 1$ risky assets. $x^{(I)}_{0,t} = 1 - \sum_{j=1}^{N+1} x^{(1)}_{j,t}$ denotes the relative engagement in the risk-free asset. Investor I's preference parameter $k^{(I)}$, as well as his initial wealth W_t, enter the optimal portfolio only through the scalar term $1/(W_t \cdot k^{(I)})$. Thus, the structure of the risky portfolio is independent of this preference parameter and the level of initial wealth. This is the well-known mutual fund theorem by Tobin (1958), whereby within (7.1) and (7.3) the size of wealth delegation (that is, fund flows from investors to mutual fund managers), reflected by $x^{(I)}_{N+1,t} \cdot W_t =: W^{(P)}_t$, is endogenously determined mainly by the transaction cost parameters $c^{(I)}_j$.

7.3 PORTFOLIO SELECTION AND ENDOGENOUS RETURNS

Optimal portfolios according to (7.1) and (7.3) are selected for exogenously given expected returns. This implies that market participants can buy as much stock as they demand at given prices. As a consequence, expected returns and prices are not influenced by demand variations. For example, in this case, fund flows will have no impact on prices. This implication contradicts the empirical evidence of many studies. For example, Warther (1995) shows that fund flows significantly influence prices. Scholes (1972) and Shleifer (1986) demonstrate that the prices of stocks depend on overall demand. The assumption that expected returns are exogenously given is now relaxed. To make expected returns endogenous, we first specify the relation between prices and expected returns and then consider the effects of that specification in market equilibrium.

Expected returns are related to prices by the assumption that market participants form their return expectations according to the Gordon (1962) dividend discount model:

$$\mu_{j,t+1} = \frac{E_t(D_{j,t+1})}{P_{j,t}} + g_{j,t+1} \tag{7.4}$$

with $\mu_{j,t+1}$ as the estimation for expected (gross) return of security j from t to $t+1$, $E_t(D_{j,t+1})$ as the expected dividend for $t+1$ for holder of security j as seen from t, and $g_{j,t+1}$ as the constant expected one-period dividend growth rate of security j from $t+1$ to ∞ as seen from t.

Expected dividends and growth rates are given exogenously. Since (representative) investor I's total wealth W_t (which is identical to total market capitalization of all stocks and the riskless asset) is divided into the amount of wealth delegation $W_t^{(P)}$ to (representative) portfolio manager P and remaining wealth $W_t^{(I)} = W_t - W_t^{(P)}$ invested directly by I himself, capital market equilibrium requires:

$$\begin{aligned} x_{j,t}^{(M)} &= \frac{1}{W_t} \cdot (x_{j,t}^{(I)} \cdot W_t^{(I)} + x_{j,t}^{(P)} \cdot W_t^{(P)}) \\ \Rightarrow x_{j,t}^{(M)} \cdot W_t &= x_{j,t}^{(I)} \cdot W_t^{(I)} + x_{j,t}^{(P)} \cdot W_t^{(P)} \end{aligned} \tag{7.5}$$

where $x_{j,t}^{(M)}$ denotes the market weight of asset j (including the market capitalization of the riskless asset). We assume (without loss of generality) that for each stock the total number of shares issued is one, so that $P_{j,t} = x_{j,t}^{(M)} \cdot W_t$. However, this single share is perfectly divisible. Then the price of a share in stock j is:

$$P_{j,t} = x_{j,t}^{(I)} \cdot W_t^{(I)} + x_{j,t}^{(P)} \cdot W_t^{(P)} \tag{7.6}$$

This allows us to replace the price $P_{j,t}$ in (7.4) with (7.6) and the resulting estimator for the expected return in (7.1) and (7.3). Explicitly taking transaction costs into account finally yields:

$$\begin{aligned} x_{i,t}^{(I)} = \frac{1}{W_t \cdot k^{(I)}} \cdot \sum_{j=1}^{N+1} [\sigma_{ij,t+1}]^{-1} \cdot \Bigg[\Bigg(& \frac{E_t(D_{j,t+1})}{x_{j,t}^{(I)} \cdot W_t^{(I)} + x_{j,t}^{(I)} \cdot W_t^{(I)}} + g_{j,t+1} \Bigg) \\ & \cdot (1 - c_{j,t}^{(I)}) - c_{j,t}^{(I)} - R_{f,t+1} \Bigg], \qquad i = 1, \ldots, N+1 \end{aligned} \tag{7.7}$$

$$x_{i,t}^{(P)} = x_{i,t}^{(B)} + \frac{1}{\alpha \cdot k^{(P)}} \cdot \sum_{j=0}^{N} \left[\sigma_{ij,t+1}^{(P)|1}\right]^{-1} \cdot \left[\left(\frac{E_t(D_{j,t+1})}{x_{j,t}^{(I)} \cdot W_t^{(I)} + x_{j,t}^{(P)} \cdot W_t^{(P)}} + g_{j,t+1}\right) - R_{f,t+1}\right], \quad i = 0, \ldots, N \quad (7.8)$$

In contrast to (7.1) and (7.3), changes in wealth now have an impact on the composition of optimal portfolios in equilibrium. An increase in wealth will *ceteris paribus* increase prices through (7.6) and decrease expected returns through (7.4). Note, that we still assume investor I and portfolio manager P to be price-takers but allow for price effects as a consequence of variations of (aggregate) security demand. This implies that they should both, in fact, be considered representative market participants.

Unfortunately, (7.7) and (7.8) cannot be simplified further in such a way as to isolate portfolio weights $x_{i,t}^{(I)}$ and $x_{i,t}^{(P)}$. We therefore have to rely upon numerical analyses in order to find out the relevance of different parameters for optimal portfolio composition in equilibrium and, thus, for prices, expected returns and wealth delegation. Besides such variables as total wealth or the investor's risk-aversion we are even able to allow for "biased" investor's expectations regarding the expected return of the mutual fund, that is, asset $N+1$. We call expectations biased with respect to asset $N+1$, if investor I deviates from (7.2) when estimating $E_t(\hat{R}_{N+1,t+1}^{(I)})$. A bias in return expectations can be justified in particular as a consequence of the marketing effort of a fund company. We will return to this issue later on. The following section discusses the consequences of such a situation (and others) in detail.

7.4 NUMERICAL ANALYSIS

This section presents a numerical analysis of the model implications of (7.1) and (7.3) as well as (7.7) and (7.8). We investigate the German stockmarket situation at the end of 2002. The annual risk-free rate, proxied by the average yield of government bonds, equals 3.78 percent and is assumed to be exogenously given. The combined wealth of domestic private households amounted up to €591.579 billion, of which €142.07 billion were invested in risk-free assets (proxied by investments in bonds), €169.346 billion were invested in equities and €280.163 billion in mutual funds (see Table 7.1). Among mutual funds, Deutsche Bundesbank (2003) does not distinguish between bond funds and equity funds. However, a survey of BVI (2003) shows that mutual funds approximately invest 40 percent of their funds in equities. The rest is invested in cash and bonds. Based on this observation,

Table 7.1 Overview of wealth distribution of private households in Germany as of December 2002 (in billion euros), Deutsche Bundesbank (2003)

	Direct investment	Mutual funds	Total
Risk free assets	142.070	168.098	310.168
Equity	169.346	112.065	281.411
Total	311.416	280.163	591.579

we assume that the wealth invested in mutual funds consists of €112.065 billion equity and €168.098 billion risk free assets. Overall, private households invested (directly or indirectly) €310.168 billion in risk-free assets and €281.411 billion in equities.

We consider two risky assets ($N = 2$). Asset $j = 1$ consists of stocks included in the major German equity index (that is, the benchmark index), the DAX 30, since many of the German mutual fund managers are evaluated in comparison to this benchmark. Asset $j = 2$ combines the stocks of the MDAX index (that is, a non-benchmark index). The MDAX index contains 70 (on 24 March 2003 the number was reduced to 50) large companies after DAX 30 stocks. Both indexes had a combined market value of €465.035 billion in December 2002, of which €400.698 billion can be attributed to DAX 30 companies and €64.337 billion to MDAX companies. Their combined market value exceeds the overall (direct and indirect) investment of domestic private households in stocks. Therefore, remaining stocks are held by other institutional and foreign investors. For convenience reasons we will refrain from explicitly modeling this group of individuals in our numerical analysis and just restrict ourselves to the examination of a capital market with only two participants: a representative private investor I and a representative portfolio manager P. For such a situation, the resulting relevant model parameters can be summarized as follows: $E_t(D_{1,t+1}) = €12{,}316$ bn; $E_t(D_{2,t+1}) = €2{,}054$ bn; $g_1 = 7.10\%$; $g_2 = 6.78\%$; $W_t = €591$ bn; $\sigma_1 = 22.26\%$, $\sigma_2 = 16.73\%$; $\sigma_{12} = 84.06\%$; $k^{(I)+} := W_t \cdot k^{(I)} = k^{(P)+} := \alpha \cdot k^{(P)} = 1.66$; $c_1^{(I)} = c_2^{(I)} = 1\%$; $c_3^{(I)} = 0.9768\%$. This setting must now be explained in detail.

Expected dividends $E_t(D_{1,t+1})$ and $E_t(D_{2,t+1})$ equal dividends that have been paid out in the year 2003. Thus, we implicitly assume that investors forecast dividends correctly. Risk parameters σ_1 and σ_{12} have been estimated with monthly stock return data from 1973 to 2003, dividend growth rates g_1 and g_2 have been set to 7.10 percent and 6.78 percent respectively. This approximately equals the realized dividend growth rates in the period 1973 to 2003. Transaction cost parameters for stocks $c_1^{(I)}$ and $c_2^{(I)}$ are set to 1 percent. These parameters will reflect our base scenario. The risk-aversion parameter $k^{(I)+}$ now determines the size of stockmarket valuation. Within (7.7) and

(7.8), a risk-aversion parameter $k^{(I)+} = 1.66$ leads to a stockmarket valuation of €465.04 billion close to the observed value of €465.035 billion. Assuming an exponential utility function and normally distributed returns, the parameter $k^{(I)+}$ expresses relative risk-aversion. Arrow (1971) argues that the relative risk-aversion parameter should equal 1. Friend and Blume (1975) derive from the allocation of household portfolios in the USA that the relative risk-aversion parameter is about 2. Thus, the empirical findings with respect to the amount of relative risk-aversion correspond fairly well with our numerical calibration. The market value of €465.04 billion can be split into €400.787 billion (DAX companies) and €64.253 billion (MDAX companies). These market valuations proxy the observed ones very accurately (DAX: €400.698 bn, MDX: €64.337 bn). In order to arrive at the empirically observable relation between the market valuation of DAX and MDAX companies, it turns out to be necessary to adjust risk parameter σ_2 in an adequate way. In fact, instead of applying a historical estimator for σ_2, this parameter is implicitly defined by the condition of assuring the right relationship between both index market values. This leads to the assumption of a standard deviation σ_2, which exceeds the historical volume by about 30 percent. Note that the results of the numerical analysis do not change significantly if σ_2 is estimated in the same (historical) way as σ_1 and σ_{12}. Moreover, the investor's (relative) risk-aversion would only have to be slightly changed to approximately 1.8 in order to guarantee an overall market valuation of stocks (as well as wealth delegation) according to empirical findings. The only other consequence would be that the relation between the market values of benchmark and non-benchmark stocks in our base scenario would not coincide with real-life evidence.

Furthermore, a management fee $c_3^{(I)}$ of 0.9768 percent implies an optimal portfolio delegation of €111.983 billion which approximates quite well the actual amount (=€112.065 bn). Portfolio manager P's risk-attitude parameter has almost no influence on prices, since investor I knows P's risk-aversion parameter and takes it into account when selecting his portfolio and determining the amount of wealth delegation. To be precise, (at least in our base scenario) investor I correctly anticipates the return properties of the investment fund, and that is all that matters.

In the following we investigate numerically how prices, expected security returns and wealth delegation are related to changes of various parameters (that is, transaction costs, wealth, risk-aversion parameters, dividend expectations and expected fund returns).

Panel A of Table 7.2 displays the effects of a variation in portfolio manager P's management fee, as incurred by investor I. A lower (higher) management fee $c_3^{(I)}$ for trading in risky assets increases (decreases) the size of wealth delegation significantly. A small modification in transaction costs results in a considerable shift in wealth delegation. For example, when the management fee is increased from 0.9768 percent (base scenario) to 0.99

percent, the size of delegated wealth is more than halved, from €112 billion to €48 billion. However, the effect on prices is negligible. Equilibrium prices and expected returns do not change with a variation in transaction costs. These results confirm the supposition that investor I implicitly undertakes some kind of cost arbitrage while economies of scale are exploited. When transaction costs and management fee are the same ($c_i^{(I)} = 1\%$, $i = 1, 2, 3$), wealth delegation from I to P does not take place. In this case, I directly invests 68 percent of his wealth in DAX 30 stocks and 11 percent of his wealth in MDAX stocks. For a management fee of $c_3^{(I)} = 0.95\%$, I directly invests none of his wealth in DAX 30 stocks and only 6 percent in MDAX stocks. Lowering the management fee further results in a short position of investor I in the DAX 30 stocks. Thus, the direct investment in benchmark stocks reacts very sensitively to changes in transaction costs. To sum up, in equilibrium, transaction costs have no significant impact on prices. However, they do have a significant impact on the size of wealth delegation.

Panel B of Table 7.2 presents the results of changing initial wealth holding $k^{(I)+} = k^{(P)+}$ constant. An increase in wealth leads to an increase in prices and a decrease in expected returns. For example, if wealth is €800 billion, the equilibrium price of benchmark stocks increases by about 22 percent to €487 billion, and the price of non-benchmark stocks increases by approximately 20 percent to €77 billion. With an increase in wealth, the size of wealth delegation also increases. However, the proportion of wealth delegation to total wealth remains nearly the same. The proportion varies between 18 percent (W_t = €400 bn) and 20 percent (W_t = €800 bn). By changing wealth, the impact on endogenous expected returns becomes obvious. Applying (7.1) and (7.3) instead of (7.7) and (7.8) would imply no changes in prices.

The reaction of price levels, wealth delegation, and expected returns subject to a variation of risk-aversion parameters are shown in Panel C of Table 7.2. A lower risk-aversion leads to an increase in prices of risky assets, since risky assets become *ceteris paribus* more attractive in relation to the riskless one. For example, when (for given wealth) risk-aversion parameters $k^{(I)+} = k^{(P)+}$ are set to 1, the market price of benchmark stocks (non-benchmark stocks) rises by 39 percent to €559 billion (by 36% to €87 bn). In general, the prices of benchmark stocks as well as non-benchmark stocks are relatively altered almost in the same way. Corresponding to this result the size of wealth delegation changes nearly in the same proportion as the market value of stocks. A variation of aggregate risk-aversion, thus, does not imply a fundamental change in the allocation of riskily invested wealth.

Panel D of Table 7.2 shows the effects of a variation in dividend expectations. Higher dividend expectations make stocks more attractive and, therefore, lead to growing prices and, in general, to increasing expected returns. In Panel D1, a change in dividend expectations of benchmark stocks is displayed. Non-benchmark stocks become relatively more attractive for lower

Table 7.2 Prices and expected returns for different scenarios

Scenario	Benchmark stock: $P_{1,t}$ (change relative to base scenario)	Non-benchmark stock: $P_{2,t}$ (change relative to base scenario)	$x_{3,t} \cdot W_t =$ wealth delegation (change relative to base scenario)	$E(R_{1,t})$	$E(R_{2,t})$
Base scenario	400.787	64.253	111.983	10.17%	9.98%
Panel A: variation of transaction costs					
$c_3^{(I)} = 0.96\%$	401 (≈0%)	64 (≈0%)	196 (75.03%)	10.17%	9.98%
$c_3^{(I)} = 0.97\%$	401 (≈0%)	64 (≈0%)	146 (30.38%)	10.17%	9.98%
$c_3^{(I)} = 0.98\%$	401 (≈0%)	64 (≈0%)	96 (−14.27%)	10.17%	9.98%
$c_3^{(I)} = 0.99\%$	401 (≈0%)	64 (≈0%)	48 (−57.14%)	10.17%	9.98%
$c_3^{(I)} = 1.00\%$	401 (≈0%)	64 (≈0%)	0 (−100%)	10.17%	9.98%
Panel B: variation of wealth					
$W_t = 400$	314 (−21.74%)	51 (−20.54%)	71 (−36.6%)	11.03%	10.80%
$W_t = 500$	360 (−10.10%)	58 (−9.47%)	92 (−17.84%)	10.52%	10.31%
$W_t = 600$	404 (0.91%)	65 (0.84%)	114 (1.8%)	10.15%	9.95%
$W_t = 700$	447 (11.45%)	71 (10.58%)	136 (21.45%)	9.86%	9.67%
$W_t = 800$	487 (21.63%)	77 (19.85%)	158 (41.09%)	9.63%	9.45%
Panel C: variation of risk-aversion parameters					
$k^{(I)+} = k^{(P)+} = 1$	559 (39.46%)	87 (35.79%)	153 (36.63%)	9.30%	9.13%
$k^{(I)+} = k^{(P)+} = 1.5$	428 (6.72%)	68 (6.23%)	120 (7.16%)	9.98%	9.79%
$k^{(I)+} = k^{(P)+} = 2$	356 (−11.12%)	58 (−10.43%)	99 (−11.59%)	10.56%	10.35%
$k^{(I)+} = k^{(P)+} = 2.5$	310 (−22.61%)	51 (−21.37%)	84 (−24.99%)	11.07%	10.85%
Panel D: variation of dividend expectations					
Panel D1: benchmark stocks					
$E_t(D_{1,t+1}) = 5$	269 (−32.76%)	93 (45.27%)	123 (9.84%)	8.96%	8.98%
$E_t(D_{1,t+1}) = 10$	365 (−8.72%)	70 (9.79%)	115 (2.69%)	9.83%	9.69%

Continued

Table 7.2 Continued

Scenario	Benchmark stock: $P_{1,t}$ (change relative to base scenario)	Non-benchmark stock: $P_{2,t}$ (change relative to base scenario)	$x_{3,t} \cdot W_t =$ wealth delegation (change relative to base scenario)	$E(R_{1,t})$	$E(R_{2,t})$
$E_t(D_{1,t+1}) = 15$	437 (9.01%)	59 (−8.76%)	109 (−2.66%)	10.53%	10.28%
$E_t(D_{1,t+1}) = 20$	496 (23.66%)	51 (−20.55%)	104 (−7.13%)	11.14%	10.80%
Panel D2: non-benchmark stocks					
$E_t(D_{2,t+1}) = 1$	418 (4.26%)	34 (−47.40%)	112 (≈0%)	10.05%	9.74%
$E_t(D_{2,t+1}) = 1.5$	409 (2.15%)	49 (−24.08%)	112 (≈0%)	10.11%	9.86%
$E_t(D_{2,t+1}) = 2$	402 (0.20%)	63 (−2.28%)	112 (≈0%)	10.17%	9.97%
$E_t(D_{2,t+1}) = 2.5$	394 (−1.60%)	76 (18.27%)	112 (≈0%)	10.22%	10.07%
$E_t(D_{2,t+1}) = 3$	388 (−23.66%)	88 (20.55%)	111 (≈0%)	10.28%	10.17%
Panel D3: benchmark stocks and non benchmark stocks: $E_t(D_{i,t+1}) \cdot F\ (i = 1, 2)$					
$F = 0.5$	318 (−20.81%)	49 (−23.94%)	122 (8.95%)	9.04%	8.88%
$F = 0.8$	370 (−7.59%)	59 (−8.57%)	116 (3.59%)	9.76%	9.58%
$F = 1.5$	466 (16.38%)	76 (18.22%)	105 (−6.24)	11.06%	10.84%
$F = 2.0$	522 (30.33%)	86 (33.57%)	100 (−10.7%)	11.82%	11.57%
Panel E: expectation bias					
Bias = 0.01%-pt.	425 (6.09%)	68 (5.29%)	136 (21.45%)	10.00%	9.82%
Bias = 0.02%-pt.	450 (12.29%)	71 (10.61%)	160 (42.88%)	9.84%	9.67%
Bias = 0.03%-pt.	474 (18.35%)	74 (15.72%)	183 (63.42%)	9.70%	9.54%
Bias = 0.04%-pt.	500 (24.79%)	78 (21.07%)	207 (84.85%)	9.56%	9.42%

Notes: W_t denotes the investor's wealth at time t, $k^{(I)+}$ and $k^{(P)+}$ stand for the investor's and the portfolio manager's risk-aversion parameters, respectively, $D_{i,t}$ characterizes dividends for benchmark stocks ($i = 1$) and non-benchmark stocks ($i = 2$) at time t, and "Bias" represents the investor's expectation bias when estimating expected returns of a fund engagement.

expected dividends of benchmark stocks and, as a result, their prices rise. The opposite can be observed when dividend expectations of non-benchmark stocks are changed (Panel D2). If dividend expectations of benchmark and of non-benchmark stocks are increased, all prices rise simultaneously (Panel D3). Moreover, in Panel D1, the amount of wealth delegation is increasing with lower expected dividend expectation regarding benchmark stocks, and in Panel D2 almost unaffected by expectation variations regarding future dividends of non-benchmark stocks. As both effects are at work in Panel D3, there are higher expected dividends combined with a reduced amount of wealth delegation. This relationship between expected dividends of benchmark stocks and the intensity of wealth delegation may be caused by a relatively higher relevance of transaction cost considerations for lower expected dividend levels of benchmark stocks.

Panel E of Table 7.2 summarizes the influence of a bias in the investor's return expectations of the mutual fund (for example, caused by an overoptimistic marketing campaign). This bias is an example for the effect of wealth delegation, which is not determined in a rational expectations equilibrium. In contrast to the results of Panel A regarding transaction cost changes, a variation of expectation bias has a very strong effect not only on the amount of wealth delegation but also on stock prices. For example, if investors have a bias of just 0.04 percentage points in return expectations of the mutual fund, they almost double their size of wealth delegation to €207 billion. Prices of benchmark stocks rise by 25 percent. The price increase of non-benchmark stocks is slightly lower. As a byproduct, one can just imagine the high relevance of marketing effort by fund companies in order to positively influence investors' return expectation for their respective funds. This numerical finding fits rather well the results of empirical studies by Woerheide (1982), as well as by Jain and Wu (2000), who point out the important role of marketing activities as a determinant of fund flows.

Summarizing, there are several variables which influence the amount of wealth delegation chosen by the investor and which lead to specific consequences for expected asset returns in equilibrium as well. In the following section, we present our basic empirical setting, by which we try to find out more about the relationship between wealth delegation and expected security returns. Here, we will attempt to utilize the numerical results of section 7.4 in order to investigate the driving forces behind empirical changes in wealth delegation.

7.5 IMPLICATIONS AND HYPOTHESES

The relationship between returns and wealth delegation can be investigated by two different approaches. First, realized returns can be directly related to changes in wealth delegation (=fund flows). Most fund flows studies (for example, Warther, 1995; Breuer and Stotz, 2006) follow this approach. From Panel D of the last section, we know that changes in current dividend expectations impact prices and thus realized security returns. Therefore, the relation between realized returns and fund flows may be influenced by changes in dividend expectations. The second approach which we follow relates fund flows directly to expected returns. This approach has the advantage that because of offsetting stock price movements, expected returns already reflect current dividend expectations and, therefore, changes in dividend expectations do not distort expected returns. With $P_{1,t}$ and $P_{2,t}$ as total market capitalization of benchmark stocks and non benchmark stocks respectively, expected returns for these indexes can be calculated by (7.4). Since we do not have access to better information, we assume (as in section 7.4) that investors forecast dividends perfectly, that is, $E_t(D_{j,t+1}) = D_{j,t+1}$.

We first consider the role of wealth delegation on returns by running the regression:

$$E_t(R_{j,t+1}) = a_j + b_j \cdot L_{t-\tau,t} + \varepsilon_t, \quad j = 1, 2, \qquad (7.9)$$

with $E_t(R_{j,t+1})$ computed according to (7.4) for $E_t(D_{j,t+1}) = D_{j,t+1}$ and $L_{t-\tau,t}$ as the normalized money flow from investors to fund managers from $t - \tau$ to t. With $L^{(bn)}_{t-\tau,t}$ as fund flow before normalization we have:

$$L_{t-\tau,t} = \frac{L^{(bn)}_{t-\tau,t}}{W^{(r)}_{t-\tau}} \qquad (7.10)$$

This division by total market capitalization $W^{(r)}_{t-\tau}$ of risky assets, analogously to other studies (for example, Warther (1995)), takes into consideration that the impact of €1 of fund flows is not expected to be constant over time. In our numerical analysis, fund flows are not directly observable, but must be derived from the level of wealth delegation WD_t at different points in time t. In fact, we approximate $L^{(bn)}_{t-\tau,t}$ by the difference

$$WD_t - WD_{t-\tau} \cdot \frac{W^{(r)}_t}{W^{(r)}_{t-\tau}}$$

Obviously, we thus apply a second normalization which is necessary because the total change $WD_t - WD_{t-\tau}$ in wealth delegation will be partly caused by changes in stock prices from $t - \tau$ to t and not by real additional flows to mutual funds. To isolate the latter, we use the factor $W^{(r)}_t / W^{(r)}_{t-\tau}$ as a correction term.

If fund flows do not impact returns as implied by (7.1) and (7.3) or by a change in transaction costs in (7.7) and (7.8), the estimation of parameter b_j should be equal to zero. If, however, fund flows were related to expected returns according to Panel B to E of the numerical analysis of (7.7) and

(7.8), b_j should be different from zero. Thus, the return impact hypothesis (RIH) (sometimes also called price pressure hypothesis) will be tested as follows:

$$H_0\text{: } b_j = 0 \text{ (RIH)} \tag{7.11}$$

In fact, our numerical considerations in section 7.4 may help us to find out possible causes for a positive or a negative sign of b_j. To this end, we use the numerical results of Table 7.2 in order to artificially create a short time series of stock returns and fund flows, which can be used as the basis for linear regression approaches as described above. Here, as a consequence of the specific measure of normalized fund flows applied in our empirical study, the signs of regression coefficients will be varying even for given parameters under consideration with a changing sequence of a given set of different parameter realizations over time. Therefore, for each parameter, we allow for three scenarios: positive trend, negative trend, and mean-reversion development. Regression (7.9) is run for all these three artificial scenarios, each with *ceteris paribus* time-varying total wealth, dividend expectations with respect to benchmark stocks or all stocks, risk-aversion, and expectation bias. Changing dividend expectations regarding non-benchmark stocks are not part of the analysis since, from Table 7.2, it is known that the impact of such variations on fund flows is negligible. Variations of transaction costs $c_3^{(I)}$ are excluded from calculations as well because of their missing influence on expected returns. For example, increasing total wealth is characterized by a time series of total wealth at times $t = 0, 1, 2, 3, 4$ of €400 billion, €500 billion, €600 billion, €700 billion, and €800 billion. Accordingly, the time series of decreasing total wealth consists of wealth levels of €800 billion, €700 billion, €600 billion, €500 billion, and €400 billion, and finally mean-reverting variations of total wealth are described by the time series €400 billion, €700 billion, €400 billion, €500 billion, and €400 billion. In the same way, time series of about four or five components each (based on the results of Table 7.2) are assumed for other parameters under consideration.

Table 7.3 presents resulting signs of the regression coefficients b_1 and b_2 as well as differences $b_1 - b_2$ for all regressions under consideration according to (7.9). We do not deem all possible scenarios to be equally plausible. In fact, we believe wealth and dividend expectations to be growing over time while market risk-aversion and expectation biases will certainly be mean-reverting. Those practically most important scenarios are shaded in Table 7.3. In the table, W denotes the investor's wealth, $k^{(I)+}$ and $k^{(P)+}$ stand for the investor's and the portfolio manager's risk-aversion parameters, respectively, D_{BM} and D_{all} characterize dividend expectations for benchmark stocks and all stocks, and *Bias* represents the investor's expectation bias when estimating expected returns from a fund engagement.

Table 7.3 Regression coefficients of (7.9) for artificially created time series

		b_1	b_2	$b_1 - b_2$
W	I	> 0	> 0	< 0
	D	$<$	$<$	$>$
	M	$<$	$<$	$<$
$k^{(I)+} = k^{(P)+}$	I	$<$	$<$	$>$
	D	$>$	$>$	$<$
	M	$<$	$<$	$<$
D_{BM}	I	$>$	$>$	$<$
	D	$<$	$<$	$>$
	M	$<$	$<$	$<$
D_{all}	I	$>$	$>$	$<$
	D	$<$	$<$	$>$
	M	$<$	$<$	$<$
Bias	I	$>$	$>$	$<$
	D	$<$	$<$	$>$
	M	$<$	$<$	$<$

Notes: "*I*" stands for increasing levels, "*D*" for decreasing levels and "*M*" for mean-reverting development. Shaded rows are the most plausible scenarios.

For differences $b_1 - b_2$, which are not equal to zero, returns of benchmark stocks and non benchmark stocks are influenced differently by fund flows. Considering the trading behavior of fund managers, these effects are obvious. Fund managers, whose performance is compared to the benchmark return, are more concerned with benchmark stocks than with non benchmark stocks. Holding the benchmark portfolio is riskless for them, while investing in non benchmark stocks would increase their risk, that is, tracking error. We test whether benchmark stocks and non-benchmark stocks are affected differently by fund flows using the return difference hypothesis (RDH):

$$H_0\colon b_1 - b_2 = 0 \text{ (RDH)} \tag{7.12}$$

In particular, if causes for fund flows are not characterized by a certain trend but exhibit mean-reverting properties, as will be the case for expectation biases, the same will certainly hold true for effects on prices and expected returns. Hence, there are good reasons to expect both expected returns (and prices) and the differences in expected returns (and prices) to be mean-reverting. The distinction between mean-reverting and permanent changes in expected returns (and prices) or their differences, respectively, will be tested by two additional hypotheses.

The permanent spread impact hypothesis (PSIH) postulates that changes in differences in expected returns (=spreads) will be permanent. To test this hypothesis, the following regression will be calculated:

$$E_t(R_{1,t+1}) - E_t(R_{2,t+1}) = a + b \cdot [E_{t-\tau}(R_{1,t+1}) - E_{t-\tau}(R_{2,t+1})] + \varepsilon_t \quad (7.13)$$

If the change in the expected return spread is permanent, parameter b should be equal to one. Temporary changes in spreads should coincide with a parameter b smaller than one (for example, Johnston, 1991). Accordingly, the permanent spread impact hypothesis will be tested as follows:

$$H_0: b = 1 \text{ (PSIH)} \quad (7.14)$$

If b is significantly smaller than one, the permanent spread impact hypothesis would be rejected.

The permanent return impact hypothesis (PRIH) requires expected returns of each segment to be mean-reverting. Therefore, the following regression will be separately calculated for benchmark stocks and non benchmark stocks:

$$E_t(R_{j,t+1}) = a_j + b_j \cdot E_{t-\tau}(R_{j,t+1}) + \varepsilon_t, \quad j = 1, 2 \quad (7.15)$$

If changes in expected returns are permanent, parameter b should equal one. For temporary changes in expected returns, parameter b should be smaller than one. Therefore, the permanent return impact hypothesis would restrict parameter b_j to one:

$$H_0: b_j = 1 \text{ (PRIH).} \quad (7.16)$$

7.6 EMPIRICAL ANALYSIS

7.6.1 Data

To test our hypotheses, we investigate German equities over the period from January 1973 to June 2002. As the benchmark index, DAX 30, was introduced on 1 July 1988, we divide our sample into two periods. The first period covers the years of monthly data from January 1973 to December 1985, that is, before the benchmark index has been introduced, the second period covers the time interval January 1991 to June 2002, that is, the months after the DAX 30 index has already been established. We allow fund managers to get used to the new benchmark index by ending the first period in 1985 and starting the second period in 1991. However, an extension of both periods to 1988 does not change the conclusions of this section decisively. Splitting the whole period into two sub-periods allows us to investigate whether the benchmark has become a more important factor.

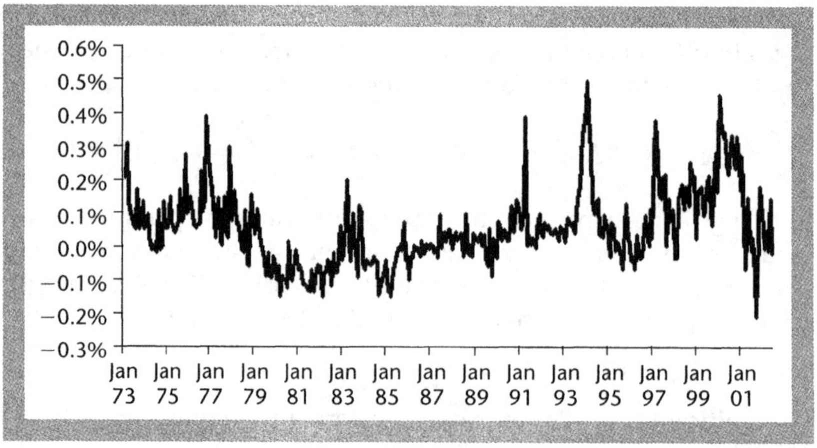

Figure 7.1 Normalized fund flows

Aggregate flow data are obtained from Deutsche Bundesbank. Therefore, normalized fund flows can – in principle – be calculated directly as described in (7.10). Over the entire period, normalized monthly fund flows averaged to 0.055 percent of stockmarket capitalization with a standard deviation of 0.115 percent. This is approximately the same as Warther (1995) and Fant (1999) obtain for the US market. For example, for the period from 1984 to 1992, Warther (1995) calculates a mean of 0.052 percent and a standard deviation of 0.077 percent. Figure 7.1 displays the normalized monthly flow.

7.6.2 Results

Table 7.4 presents the results with respect to the return impact hypothesis (RIH). Diagnostic tests of regression (7.9) indicate, that resulting residuals are autocorrelated (that is, the Durbin–Watson statistic is less than 1). Therefore, we include a lag of the expected return in the regression equation to remove autocorrelation and (7.9′) changes to:

$$E_t(R_{j,t+1}) = a_j + b_j \cdot L_{t-\tau,t} + c_j \cdot E_{t-\tau}(R_{j,t+1}) + \varepsilon_t, \quad j = 1, 2 \tag{7.9'}$$

We use two time intervals – one month ($\tau = 1$) and three months ($\tau = 3$) – to check if our results are robust across different horizons. In general, this is the case for all tested hypotheses. For both indexes, the DAX 30 index ($j = 1$) and the MDAX index ($j = 2$), and for each time interval, the estimated parameter b is smaller than zero. Standard errors of estimated parameters b are rather large in the period from 1973 to 1985. However, they decrease substantially in the period from 1991 to 2002, that is, after the introduction of the benchmark index. Therefore, we can reject the RIH (7.11) in the recent period at the conventional significance level of

Table 7.4 Results for the return impact hypothesis (RIH)

		$E_t(R_{j,t+1}) = a_j + b_j \cdot L_{t-\tau,t} + c_j \cdot E_{t-\tau}(R_{j,t+1}) + \varepsilon_t$ (7.9′)			
		$\tau = 1$ month		$\tau = 3$ months	
		DAX	MDAX	DAX	MDAX
01/1973	a	0.003	0.007	0.010	0.024
to 12/1985[b]	b	−0.127	−0.039	−0.104	−0.259
	(t-value)	(−0.798)	(−0.350)	(−0.196)	(−0.668)
	c	0.970	0.930	0.910	0.748
	adjusted R^2	90.4%	84.4%	75.0%	51.9%
	DW[a]	2.087	1.770	1.606	1.559
	KS[a]	1.055	1.001	0.944	0.616
01/1991[b]	a	0.007	0.007	0.021	0.030
to 06/2002	b	−0.152	−0.091	−0.609	−0.385
	(t-value)	(−1.767)	(−1.501)	(−1.960)	(−1.751)
	c	0.928	0.917	0.773	0.653
	adjusted R^2	91.4%	89.7%	73.4%	40.8%
	DW	1.972	1.719	2.381	1.902
	KS	0.766	0.725	0.714	0.617

Notes: [a] DW = Durbin–Watson statistics (test for autocorrelation), KS = Kolmogorov–Smirnov Z-statistics (test for normality), t-value for parameter = 0. The DW-test indicates that residuals of the regression are not autocorrelated, the KS-test suggests that residuals are normally distributed.
[b] The first time period ends before the DAX 30 index has been introduced, the second period starts after the DAX 30 index has been introduced to allow fund managers to adapt to the new index. However, the length of this intermediate period does not influence the results decisively. For example, extending the first period and the second period to the month of introduction of the DAX 30 index in July 1988 and, therefore, allowing for no adaptation time, leads to almost the same parameter estimations.

5 percent. This increase in significance levels of the estimated parameter b is a first indication that the benchmark index DAX 30 has become a more important factor since its introduction. In general, the results suggest that fund flows are related to expected returns and, therefore, prices as expected from our numerical analysis. Thus, equations (7.7) and (7.8) describe the determination of optimal portfolios and expected returns better than equations (7.1) and (7.3) do. For example, over the recent time period with a quarterly time interval, an inflow of 0.1 percent of market capitalization is translated into a decrease in expected returns of DAX 30 companies approximately of 0.0609 percentage points. This coincides with an increase in prices. For the MDAX index, the impact is considerably smaller. An inflow of 0.1 percent is translated into a decrease of 0.0385 percentage points in expected returns and an increase in prices. To sum up, the empirical result shows that expected returns are influenced by fund flows according to (7.7) and (7.8).

Table 7.5 Results for return difference hypothesis (RDH)

	$\tau = 1$ month		$\tau = 3$ months	
	01/1973 to 12/1985	01/1991 to 06/2002	01/1973 to 12/1985	01/1991 to 06/2002
$b_1 - b_2$	−0.088	−0.061	0.155	−0.224

A look at the differences $b_1 - b_2$, displayed in Table 7.5, sheds some more light on the role of the benchmark. Over the period from 1973 to 1985, differences of $b_1 - b_2$ are negative for $\tau = 1$ and positive for $\tau = 3$. Thus, before the introduction of the benchmark index, the sign of the difference is not clear. However, over the later time period, when the benchmark index DAX 30 has been introduced, differences become negative for both time horizons. For example, for $\tau = 3$, the difference $b_1 - b_2$ decreases from 0.155 in the earlier period to −0.224 in the recent period. This indicates that expected returns of DAX 30 stocks react stronger to fund flows than MDAX stocks since the benchmark index has been introduced. Therefore, expected returns of benchmark stocks seem to be driven by fund flows more intensively than non-benchmark stocks. This result is a second indication that the introduction of the benchmark index DAX 30 has changed the behavior of stocks.

Within our numerical analysis, the results of Tables 7.4 and 7.5 can solely be obtained for a mean-reverting development of the exogenously varied parameter. Since we only deem mean-reverting behavior of risk-aversion and expectation biases to be plausible, it seems reasonable to elaborate somewhat further on the relevance of these scenarios. In particular, up to now, we have not allowed for short sales restrictions for market participants. As is well-known, it is not possible to derive analytical closed-form solutions for such a portfolio selection problem, even in the case of exogenous market prices. Nevertheless, it is not difficult to solve such decision problems numerically. Based on the plausible scenarios of Table 7.3, we find that in a situation with short-sales restrictions, only mean-reverting expectation biases are compatible with our empirical results from Tables 7.4 and 7.5.

Since increasing wealth and dividend expectations over the past years seem to be very plausible, we finally combined this scenario with the assumption of mean-reverting expectation biases. For the time period 1991 to 2003, we assumed growth rates of total wealth as well as dividend expectations according to the (nominal) growth of the German gross national product, while simultaneously allowing for mean-reverting expectation biases. In fact, this mean-reverting effect overcompensates the consequences of wealth and dividend expectations growth; this means that even this combined scenario is compatible with the empirical results of Tables 7.4 and 7.5.

Finally, the empirical results do not support the RDH (7.12) and we conjecture that mean-reverting expectation biases are the main cause for our

Table 7.6 Results for permanent spread impact hypothesis (PSIH)

		$E_t(R_{1,t+1} - R_{2,t+1}) = a + b \cdot E_{t-\tau}(R_{1,t+1} - R_{2,t+1}) + \varepsilon_t$	(7.13)
		τ = 1 month	τ = 3 months
01/1973	a	0.000	0.001
to 12/1985[b]	b	0.956	0.939
	(t-value)	(−1.692)	(−1.034)
	adjusted R^2	89.5%	83.3%
	DW[a]	2.356	1.676
	KS[a]	1.097	0.771
01/1991[b]	a	0.000	0.000
to 06/2002	b	0.967	0.917
	(t-value)	(−1.737)	(−1.731)
	adjusted R^2	94.8%	84.9%
	DW	2.112	2.519
	KS	0.885	0.504

Notes: [a] DW = Durbin-Watson statistics (test for autocorrelation), KS = Kolmogorov–Smirnov Z-statistics (test for normality), t-value for parameter = 1. The DW-test indicates that residuals of the regression are not autocorrelated, the KS-test suggests that residuals are normally distributed.
[b] The first time period ends before the DAX 30 index has been introduced, the second period starts after the DAX 30 index has been introduced to allow fund managers the adaptation of the new index. However, the length of this intermediate period does not influence the results decisively. For example, extending the first period and the second period to the month of introduction of the DAX 30 index in July 1988 and therefore, allowing for no adaptation time, leads almost to the same parameter estimations.

empirical findings. This further implies that differences of expected returns should be mean-reverting. The mean-reversion feature will be tested by the PSIH. Results according to (7.13) are displayed in Table 7.6 and are compatible with mean-reversion in return differentials. Within the sample from 1973 to 1985, for a time horizon of three months, parameter b equals 0.939 which indicates that, after three months, about 6 percent of changes in return expectations differentials are reversed. Estimated standard errors of b are rather large, so that we can reject the PSIH in the first period only at significance levels of about 10 percent. However, within the recent period 1991 to 2002, the mean-reversion effect becomes stronger. Parameter b equals 0.917 which means that more than 8 percent of changes in return expectations differentials are reduced after a year. This parameter is significantly smaller than one and the PSIH can be rejected at a conventional significance level of 5 percent. Therefore, the introduction of the benchmark index seems to have strengthened the mean-reverting property of return differentials which can also be interpreted as a third indication that the benchmark index has changed the return behavior of stocks.

The results above are consistent with mean-reverting expected return differentials. This assessment is further confirmed when looking at the mean-reversion property of expected returns of benchmark stocks and non-benchmark stocks alone as displayed in Table 7.7. These results can also be found in Table 7.4 looking at parameter c which is similar to b in Table 7.7. Over the last period, for example, for DAX 30 stocks, changes in expected returns are reversed by approximately as much as 18 percent after three months. The estimated parameter b is significantly smaller than one. Changes in expected returns for MDAX stocks are even more reversed. Therefore, changes in expected returns have a significant temporary component. Our results, thus, indirectly support the assertion that mean-reverting expectation biases could be a central factor for the determination of fund flows. Moreover, for DAX 30 and MDAX stocks, the estimated parameter b is smaller in the period from 1991 to 2002 than in the period from 1973 to 1985. Additionally, parameter b differs more significantly from one in the recent period than in the first period. These results are a fourth indication that the introduction of the benchmark index has changed the return behavior of stocks.

Table 7.7 Results for permanent return impact hypothesis (PRIH)

		$E_t(R_{j,t+1}) = a_j + b_j \cdot E_{t-\tau}(R_{j,t+1}) + \varepsilon_t$ (7.15)			
		$\tau = 1$ month		$\tau = 3$ months	
		DAX	MDAX	DAX	MDAX
01/1973	a	0.003	0.007	0.010	0.024
to 12/1985[b]	b	0.969	0.931	0.905	0.753
	(t-value)	(−1.280)	(−2.156)	(−1.301)	(−2.470)
	adjusted R^2	90.4%	84.5%	75.5%	52.4%
	DW[a]	2.089	1.764	1.675	1.571
	KS[a]	0.998	0.561	0. 893	0. 681
01/1991[b]	a	0.005	0.007	0.016	0.029
to 06/2002	b	0.942	0.920	0.820	0.656
	(t-value)	(−2.320)	(−2.051)	(−2.368)	(−2.797)
	adjusted R^2	91.3%	80.5%	71.7%	38.0%
	DW	1.950	1.693	2.467	1.913
	KS	0.781	0.908	0.835	0.911

Notes: [a]DW = Durbin–Watson statistics (test for autocorrelation), KS = Kolmogorov–Smirnov Z-statistics (test for normality), t-value for parameter = 1.
The DW-test indicates that residuals of the regression are not autocorrelated, the KS-test suggests that residuals are normally distributed.
[b]The first time period ends before the DAX 30 index has been introduced, the second period starts after the DAX 30 index has been introduced to allow fund managers the adaptation of the new index. However, the length of this intermediate period does not influence the results decisively. For example, extending the first period and the second period to the month of introduction of the DAX 30 index in 07/1988 and therefore, allowing for no adaptation time, leads almost to the same parameter estimations.

7.7 CONCLUSION

This chapter has examined the relation between fund flows and expected returns. We have investigated this issue within a model that captures two kinds of investors: mean-variance investors and tracking-error investors. The numerical analysis of our portfolio selection model in section 7.4 suggests that fund flows can be related to transaction costs, risk-aversion, wealth, expectations on fundamental data, and biases in return expectations. The empirical results of section 7.6 are based on the analysis of the German capital market from 1973 to 2002 and can be summarized as follows:

- Fund flows impact expected returns. This is consistent with the assumption that the demand and supply of institutional investors drive asset prices.
- Fund flows impact expected returns of benchmark stocks and non-benchmark stock differently. This is consistent with the presumption that institutional investors act as tracking-error investors. The demand of institutional investors is different for benchmark stocks and non-benchmark stocks.
- Expected returns and differences in expected returns are mean-reverting. This is consistent with the supposition that the impact of fund flows on expected returns is temporary.

The presented results support a portfolio selection model with endogenous returns (equations (7.7) and (7.8)) and reject one with exogenous returns (equations (7.1) and (7.3)), because positive flows coincide with greater prices and smaller expected returns, while negative flows are connected with smaller prices and greater expected returns. Thus, fund managers buy stocks at higher prices and sell stocks at lower prices. The popular press also recognizes the "buy high, sell low" practice of mutual fund investors (for example, Boyle, 2004). An investor in mutual funds would be well-advised not to invest money in funds at times when many other investors are doing so. In the long term, the "buy high, sell low" practice of investors would lead to a below-average performance. Instead, an investor should buy mutual funds when the average investor is a seller, and thus avoid any kind of herding.

Relating the empirical results to the numerical results in section 7.4 suggests that a mean-reverting expectation bias seems to be a plausible argument for fund flows. A mean-reverting expectation bias and short sales constraints produce the same signs in the regression coefficients, as can be observed in the German stockmarket. This expectation bias could be caused, for example, by the aggregate marketing effort of the fund companies. Fund advertising might cause investors to form irrational return expectations because mostly funds are advertised that have experienced above-average returns in the past.

However, fund advertising is not informative on future fund performance, as documented by Jain and Wu (2000). Correspondingly, the empirical relationship between past and future fund performance is mixed. Carhart (1997) finds no positive relationship between past and future risk adjusted performance, while Elton, Gruber and Blake (1996) report a positive relationship. As a result, a higher marketing effort can lead to biased expectations and, according to our portfolio selection model as described by equations (7.7) and (7.8), to a higher fund inflow. On an individual fund level, the irrational causes for fund flows have been documented by Woerheide (1982) and Jain and Wu (2000) and Elton, Gruber and Busse (2004). On an aggregate level, as investigated in this chapter, these causes should also be relevant. Unfortunately, we cannot give direct evidence on this issue as we lack data on aggregate fund marketing.

Furthermore, our results suggest that benchmark stocks and non-benchmark stocks are influenced differently by fund flows. This observation can be explained by the behavior of institutional investors. They are most likely to behave like tracking-error investors and not like mean-variance investors, as they are evaluated and compensated in comparison to a prespecified benchmark index. Thus, fund flows influence the demand and supply of institutional investors for benchmark stocks and non-benchmark stocks differently. This generates institutional trading which is (partly) not related to the price level and the expected return of a stock. In the short run (observation periods of only a few days), the impact of institutional trading has been reported, for example, by Edelen and Warner (2001). In the long run (of one or three months), as presented in this chapter, the influence of fund flows on expected returns is higher for benchmark stocks than it is for non-benchmark stocks.

In general, the different impact of the benchmark index on prices could be reduced if the benchmark were to be defined as broadly as possible. Thus, the relevant benchmark for fund managers' performance evaluation should not only include the largest and most liquid stocks (as is the current practice), but, in fact, all risky assets. Such advice, also given by the prominent capital asset pricing model (CAPM), ensures that mutual fund managers choose portfolios which are also efficient for individual investors (for example, Roll, 1992). In this case, there would be no distinction between benchmark stocks and non-benchmark stocks and, therefore, mutual fund managers would generate no institutional trading that impacts stocks differently. However, looking at the practice of the fund manager of today, one has to remain sceptical that such a benchmark definition could become common practice in the near future.

APPENDIX: OPTIMAL PORTFOLIOS FOR TRACKING-ERROR INVESTORS

The tracking-error investor's objective is to maximize:

$$\max_{x_t^{(P)}} \left[E_t(R_{t+1}^{(P)}) - 0.5 \cdot k^{(P)+} \cdot \omega_t^{(P)2} \right]$$

subject to the full investment constraint, that is, $\sum_{i=0}^{N} x_{i,t}^{(P)} = 1.$

Define a (transposed) vector of benchmark deviations:

$$\delta_t^{(P)} := \left(\delta_{0,t}^{(P)}, \delta_{1,t}^{(P)}, \ldots, \delta_{N,t}^{(P)}\right)^T := \left(x_{0,t}^{(P)} - x_{0,t}^{(B)}, x_{1,t}^{(P)} - x_{1,t}^{(B)}, \ldots, x_{N,t}^{(P)} - x_{N,t}^{(B)}\right)^T$$

a (transposed) vector of (expected) returns:

$$E_t(R_{t+1}) := (R_{f,t+1}, E_t(R_{1,t+1}), \ldots, E_t(R_{N,t+1}))^T$$

and an extended variance-covariance-matrix:

$$\sigma_{t+1}^{(P)} = \begin{pmatrix} 0 & 0 & 0 & 0 \\ 0 & \sigma_{11,t+1} & \cdots & \sigma_{N1,t+1} \\ 0 & \vdots & \ddots & \vdots \\ 0 & \sigma_{1N,t+1} & \cdots & \sigma_{NN,t+1} \end{pmatrix} \quad (\sigma_{ij,t+1} := \mathrm{Cov}_t(R_{i,t+1}, R_{j,t+1}))$$

With these definitions and because of $\omega_{t+1}^{(P)2} = \sum_{i=1}^{N} (x_{i,t}^{(P)} - x_{i,t}^{(B)}) \cdot \sum_{i=1}^{N} (x_{i,t}^{(P)} - x_{i,t}^{(B)}) \cdot \sigma_{ij,t+1}$ the maximization problem can be rewritten as:

$$\max_{\delta_t^{(P)}} \left[\delta_t^{(P)T} \cdot E_t(R_{t+1}) - 0.5 \cdot k^{(P)+} \cdot \delta_t^{(P)T} \cdot \sigma_{t+1}^{(P)} \cdot \delta_t^{(P)} \right], \text{ s.t. } \sum_{i=0}^{N} \delta_{i,t}^{(P)} = 0$$

To solve this maximization problem, consider the Lagrangian function:

$$\mathrm{L} \equiv \delta_t^{(P)T} \cdot E_t(R_{t+1}) - 0.5 \cdot k^{(P)+} \cdot \delta_t^{(P)T} \cdot \sigma_{t+1}^{(P)} \cdot \delta_t^{(P)} + \lambda_t^{(P)} \cdot \sum_{i=0}^{N} \delta_{i,t}^{(P)}$$

Let $\partial L/\partial \delta_t^{(P)}$ be defined as the vector of partial derivatives of L with respect to $\delta_{i,t}^{(P)}$ ($i = 0, \ldots, N$). Then the first-order necessary and sufficient condition for the tracking-error's optimal portfolio runs:

$$\frac{\partial L}{\partial \delta_t^{(P)}} = E_t(R_{t+1}) - k^{(P)+} \cdot \sigma_{t+1}^{(P)} \cdot \delta_t^{(P)} + \lambda_t^{(P)} \cdot E = 0 \tag{A1}$$

and

$$\frac{\partial L}{\partial \lambda_t^{(P)}} = \sum_{i=0}^{N} \delta_{t,i}^{(P)} = 0 \tag{A2}$$

where E is a vector of ones. The first row of (A1) is $R_{f,t+1} + \lambda_t^{(P)} = 0$. Define the matrix:

$$\sigma_{t+1}^{(P)|1} := \begin{pmatrix} 1 & 1 & \cdots & 1 \\ 0 & \sigma_{11,t+1} & \cdots & \sigma_{N1,t+1} \\ 0 & \vdots & \ddots & \vdots \\ 0 & \sigma_{1N,t+1} & \cdots & \sigma_{NN,t+1} \end{pmatrix}$$

With $\lambda_t^{(P)} = -R_{f,t+1}$, (A1) and (A2) together can be written as:

$$E_t(R_{t+1}) - k^{(P)+} \cdot \sigma_{t+1}^{(P)|1} \cdot \delta_t^{(P)} - R_{f,t+1} \cdot E = 0 \tag{A3}$$

Solving (A3) leads to optimal benchmark deviations:

$$\delta_t^{(P)} = \frac{1}{k^{(P)+}} \cdot \left[\sigma_{t+1}^{(P)|1}\right]^{-1} \cdot \left[E_t(R_{t+1}) - R_{f,t+1} \cdot E\right] \tag{A4}$$

Thus, manager P's optimal portfolio is $x_t^{(P)} = x_t^{(B)} + \delta_t^{(P)}$, which immediately implies equation (7.1).

REFERENCES

Arrow, K.J. (1971) *Essays in the Theory of Risk Bearing* (Amsterdam: North-Holland).

Bekaert, G., Harvey, C.R. and Lumsdaine, R.L. (2002) "The Dynamics of Emerging Market Equity Flows", *Journal of International Money and Finance*, 21(3): 295–350.

Beneish, M.D. and Whaley, R.E. (1996) "An Anatomy of the 'S&P Game': the Effects of Changing the Game", *Journal of Finance*, 51(3): 1909–30.

Boyle, M. (2004) "By the Numbers: Whatever Happened to 'Buy Low, Sell High'?", *Fortune*, 4: 17.

Breuer, W. and Stotz, O. (2006) "Mutual Fund Flows, Mean Reverting Stock Prices, and Extrapolative Investors' Expectations: The German Case", Working Paper, Aachen.

BVI (2003) *Investment 2002 – Daten, Fakten, Entwicklungen, Bundesverband Deutscher Investment- und Vermögensverwaltungsgesellschaften e.V.* Frankfurt, Germany.

Campbell, J.Y. and Viceira, L.M. (2002) *Strategic Asset Allocation* (Oxford, UK: Oxford University Press).

Carhart, M.M. (1997) "On Persistence in Mutual Fund Performance", *Journal of Finance*, 52(1): 57–82.

Choe, H., Kho, B.C. and Stulz, R. (1999) "Do Foreign Investors Destabilize Stock Markets? The Korean Experience in 1997", *Journal of Financial Economics*, 54(2): 227–64.

Deutsche Bundesbank (2003) *Wertpapierdepots. Deutsche Bundesbank, September.* Frankfurt, Germany.

Dhillon, U. and Johnson, H. (1991) "Changes in the Standard and Poor's List", *Journal of Business*, 64(1): 75–85.

Edelen, R.M. and Warner, J.B. (2001) "Aggregate Price Effects of Institutional Trading: a Study of Mutual Fund Flows and Market Return", *Journal of Financial Economics*, 59(2): 195–220.

Elton, E.J., Gruber, M.J. and Blake, C.R. (1996) "The Persistence of Risk-Adjusted Mutual Fund Performance", *Journal of Business*, 69(2): 133–57.

Elton, E.J., Gruber, M.J. and Busse, J.A. (2004) "Are Investors Rational? Choices among Index Funds", *Journal of Finance*, 59(1): 261–88.

Fama, E.F. and French, K.R. (1988) "Permanent and Temporary Components of Stock Prices", *Journal of Financial Economics*, 96(2): 246–73.

Fant, L.F. (1999) "The Behaviour of Mutual Fund Shareholders: The Evidence from Aggregate Fund Flows", *Journal of Financial Markets*, 2(4): 391–402.

Fefsi (Fédération Européenne des Fonds et Sociétés d'Investissement) (2003) *Worldwide Investment Fund Assets and Flows, International Statistical Release*, October 9, Brussels.

Friend, I. and Blume, M.E. (1975) "The Demand for Risky Assets", *American Economic Review*, 65(5): 900–22.

Froot, K.A., O'Connell, P.G.J. and Seasholes, M.S. (2001) "The Portfolio Flows of International Investors", *Journal of Financial Economics*, 59(2): 151–94.

Gordon, M. (1962) *The Investment, Financing, and Valuation of the Corporation* (Homewood, IL: Irwin).

Harris, L. and Gurel, E. (1986) "Price and Volume Effects Associated with Changes in the S&P 500 List: New Evidence for the Existence of Price Pressures", *Journal of Finance*, 41(4): 815–29.

Jain, P.C. and Wu, J.S. (2000) "Truth in Mutual Fund Advertising: Evidence on Future Performance and Fund Flows", *Journal of Finance*, 55(2): 937–58.

Jensen, M.C. (1968) "The Performance of Mutual Funds in the Period 1945–1964", *Journal of Finance*, 23(2): 389–416.

Johnston, J. (1991) *Econometric Methods* (Singapore: McGraw-Hill).

Lynch, A.W. and Mendenhall, R.R. (1997) "New Evidence on Stock Price Effects Associated with Changes in the S&P 500 Index", *Journal of Business*, 70(3): 351–83.

Markowitz, H. (1952) "Portfolio Selection", *Journal of Finance*, 7(1): 77–91.

Markowitz, H. (1959) *Portfolio Selection: Efficient Diversification of Investments* (New York, NY: Yale University Press).

Roll, R. (1992) "A Mean/Variance Analysis of Tracking Error", *Journal of Portfolio Management*, Summer, 13–22.

Scholes, M.S. (1972) "The Market for Securities: Substitution versus Price Pressure and the Effects of Information on Share Prices", *Journal of Business*, 45(2): 179–211.

Shleifer, A. (1986) "Do Demand Curves for Stocks Slope Down?", *Journal of Finance*, 41(3): 579–90.

Tobin, J. (1958) "Liquidity Preference as Behaviour towards Risk", *Review of Economic Studies*, 25(2): 65–86.

Warther, V.A. (1995) "Aggregate Mutual Fund Flows and Security Returns", *Journal of Financial Economics*, 39(2–3): 209–35.

Woerheide, W. (1982) "Investor Response to Suggested Criteria for Selection of Mutual Funds", *Journal of Financial and Quantitative Analysis*, 17(1): 129–37.

CHAPTER 8

Herding Behavior: Evidence from Portuguese Mutual Funds

*Júlio Lobão and Ana Paula Serra**

8.1 INTRODUCTION

For the last two decades, the importance of mutual funds all over the world has increased enormously. In 1950, institutional investors in the USA held 6 percent of the stockmarket. Today that share represents over 50 percent of the stockmarket capitalization (around US dollars 30 trillion) and mutual funds are the more popular way to invest in the stockmarket. In Europe, the role of institutional investors is far from what it represents in the USA but it is growing at a very fast pace. By the end of the 1990s, total assets managed by mutual funds amounted to 70 percent, 60 percent, 90 percent, 60 percent and 200 percent of GNP, respectively, in Italy, Germany, France, Spain, the Netherlands and the UK.

The growth of Portuguese mutual funds, over the last decade, has also been impressive: by the end of 2001, total assets in management by mutual funds amounted to 20 billion euros, 20 percent of GNP (12 percent of the Portuguese stockmarket capitalization) against less than 5 percent in 1990.

* Acknowledgments: CEMPRE – Centro de Estudos Macroeconómicos e Previsão – is supported by the Fundação para a Ciência e a Tecnologia, Portugal, through the Programa Operacional Ciência, Tecnologia e Inovação (POCTI) of the Quadro Comunitário de Apoio III, which is financed by FEDER and Portuguese funds.

Mutual funds are thus important players in the market and their trading accounts for an increasing share of total trading.

More and more, institutional investors trading strategies impact prices. Institutional investors may have incentives to buy and sell the same stocks at the same time. This convergence in trading strategies is commonly known as herding. Herding may affect market prices by driving prices away or close from fundamental values.

There are several ways to define herding. Broadly, herding could be defined as correlation in the behavior of investors. Yet the fact that a group of investors trade the same stock, in the same direction, over a period of time does not necessarily mean that investors are influenced by others. Trading together could result because investors are independently influenced by common information or factor (spurious herding). Therefore, a more restrict definition of herding would rule out clustering, caused by some omitted factor, and would take in consideration only correlated trades originated by copying or imitation. In other words, a more restrict definition of herding focuses only on correlation in trades that results from interactions between investors.

Herding behavior – rational or irrational – may lead to errors and misvaluation of assets. Investigating and measuring the level of herding on institutional investors trading could shed light on different phenomena such as excess volatility, price momentum, systematic errors in expectations causing systematic market misvaluations, crashes, speculative bubbles, fades, and so on.[1] Evidence regarding the impact of herding on prices is therefore valuable to current debates on market efficiency and on the validity of traditional asset pricing models.

The fact that, across different investor groups, there are different problem sets and different incentives implies that, within a certain group, we should observe a more homogeneous trading behavior across investors. Evidence on herding by a particular type of investors, for example institutional investors, could thus shed light on whether there are different types or styles of investors, each type with a particular trading pattern. Furthermore it may inform us whether active portfolio management is done on the basis of superior information and expertise.

Investigating herding on securities markets could thus be valuable for researchers and could have important implications and practical value for investors, traders and regulators.

It is commonly accepted among academic researchers that investors trade together or follow similar trading strategies.[2] Why do investors herd?

There are two ways to approach the question: the first approach suggests that herding is irrational and is caused by herd instinct or by investor psychology. The second approach claims that it may be entirely rational to trade together. Several theories may help explain why rational investors trade together: informational cascades, agency reputation based models and information inefficiencies.

Informational cascades are the more common explanation for herding. The observation of prior investors' trades can be so informative that investors are better-off disregarding their private information and trading in the same direction (Bikhchandani, Hirschleifer and Welch, 1992; Banerjee, 1992). An alternative explanation for herding is reputational risk: under certain circumstances, asset managers have incentives not to act differently from other competing managers, regardless of their own signals (Scharfstein and Stein, 1990). Finally, herding could result from the way investors deal with information: investors may find attractive to use only private information shared by other investors, and disregard any other private unique information they have. Resource allocation regarding information acquisition is inefficient in this setting (see, for example, Froot, Schaferstein and Stein, 1992; Hirshleifer, Subrahmanyan and Titman, 1994).

To what extent do investors herd? Evidence on the extent of herding in securities markets is recent and most of the studies have examined herding behavior by institutional investors in the UK and in the USA.

Lakonishok, Shleifer, Thaler and Vishny (1992) studied 769 US pension funds, managed by 341 different portfolio managers, between 1985 and 1989. They found that the level of herding is not significant. Grinblatt, Titman and Wermers (1995) analysed trading data for 274 mutual funds in the USA over the period 1974 to 1984 and found evidence of trade convergence for the majority of mutual funds. Wermers (1999) investigated herding over a 20-year period using quarterly portfolio holdings for all mutual funds based in the USA from 1975 to 1994. He found a low level of herding among mutual funds, but stronger herding effects among growth-oriented mutual funds and in small and winner stocks. Wylie (2000) examined data on 268 mutual funds operating in the UK from 1986 to 1993 and found that the level of herding is similar to the herding found for US institutional investors.

In this chapter we test for herding by Portuguese mutual funds. We focus on mutual funds for several reasons. First, mutual funds are prone to exhibit herding because the different theoretical arguments referred above apply to them and, as such, may allow disentangling the causes of herding. In particular, herding driven by agency problems makes sense only for institutional investors. Second, it is important to study mutual funds given their increasing importance in the stockmarket. Third, the availability of data for Portuguese mutual funds provides a good opportunity for an out-of-sample test. Comparing the results for Portugal with the results observed for mature stockmarkets like the USA and the UK may generate insights on the validity of the different theoretical arguments that have been put forward to explain herding.[3]

We employ the measure of herding developed by Lakonishok, Schleifer, Thaler and Vishny (1992). Several studies (Lakonishok, Schleifer, Thaler and Vishny, 1992; Grinblatt, Titman and Wermers, 1995; Wermers, 1999; Wylie, 2000) have used this same measure. This measure compares the effective proportion of funds that bought stocks during a particular period, with the proportion that should be observed if there was no herding.

We use quarterly data on the portfolios of 32 Portuguese mutual funds from 1998 to 2000. We find strong evidence of herding behavior for the average fund in our sample. Furthermore, the overall level of herding is much stronger (4 to 5 times) than that found in previous studies for the UK and the USA. Portuguese mutual funds exhibit herding either when buying or when selling stocks, but the herding effect is stronger for purchases. Looking at subgroups of funds, we find higher levels of herding among medium cap funds and for funds that hold more stocks in their portfolios. Finally, the positive feedback trading seems to be much weaker when the stock market is doing well and (less significantly) when the market is more volatile. Altogether our results are consistent with an information-based explanation.

The remainder of the chapter is organized as follows. In section 8.2 we discuss the hypotheses to test and describe the methodology of our study. Section 8.3 provides a description of Portuguese mutual funds and of the data. Empirical findings are presented in section 8.4, and section 8.5 concludes.

8.2 HYPOTHESES AND METHODOLOGY

8.2.1 Hypotheses

The main objective of this study is to assess if Portuguese mutual funds exhibit herding and to what extent. In addition, we analyse the behavior of several subgroups of funds. We argue that the existence of different levels of herding behavior by subgroups of funds can enlighten the debate on the causes of herding. In addition to fund-specific characteristics (market capitalization, portfolio holdings and rebalancing frequency), we investigate the inference by market conditions (stockmarket returns and volatility).

The different theoretical arguments reviewed above may yield different predictions for the relation between the level of herding and the variables we analyse. The implications of the different rational explanations for the variation in herding are discussed below.

Market capitalization

Larger funds are more likely to have superior resources to collect and process information. If that is the case, large funds should be imitated by (smaller) funds with more difficult access to information. For large and small funds, within their group, we should expect to see lower levels of herding. Herding should occur mainly between groups with different resources or capabilities and not within groups of funds with the same size. Therefore we should expect to find higher levels of herding for the universe of funds than for subgroups of funds. Medium-cap funds should exhibit more herding than very large or very small funds.

Reputation risk may predict a different relation. On one hand, managers of funds with a similar size may have incentives to imitate their peers. On the other hand, compensation schemes may be indexed to assets in management so there may be incentives for large funds to herd, and keep their relative positions, and for small funds to deviate from others, implementing distinctive investment strategies to grow. In this setting, we should expect to find higher levels of herding for subgroups of funds than for the universe of funds, and small and medium cap funds should exhibit more herding than large funds.

Portfolio holdings

Collecting information and analysing securities is costly. If funds invest in several asset classes (bonds, stocks, derivatives), they potentially have either higher costs in processing information or less precise signals, leading to greater herding. If this explanation is true, we should observe lower levels of herding for subgroups of funds that are concentrated in one asset class than for more diversified funds.

Frequency in portfolio rebalancing

Information inefficiency models predict higher levels of herding in funds with shorter investment horizons that may find profitable (less costly) using only private information shared with other funds; because they choose to analyse the same information, they end up trading in the same direction. On the contrary, funds that implement buy and hold strategies, because they have long horizons, have fewer incentives to implement tacit manipulation strategies given that in the long run prices will be close to fundamentals. They thus have an incentive to use all the information that they have (shared or unique) and therefore herd less in trading. We should then observe higher (lower) levels of herding for subgroups of funds that have shorter (longer) horizons and these funds usually show more (less) frequency in portfolio rebalancing.[4]

Market stock returns

Informational cascades predict that when markets are doing well, investors are more confident and that may increase the likelihood of using their private signals and deviating from others. We should expect thus to find lower levels of herding when markets are doing well.[5]

Differently, agency models suggest that when the market is doing very well or very badly, the signals are more precise, it is easier to detect a good from a bad manager and therefore bad managers will try to mimic good managers more often to fool their clients. Thus we should expect higher levels of herding when markets are doing very well or very badly.

Market volatility

Most theories predict higher levels of herding when markets are more volatile. For example, higher uncertainty may result in that information becomes less precise and reliable and therefore (not necessarily) cascades are more likely to occur. Higher uncertainty in private information may result in that cascades start sooner. Therefore we should observe higher levels of herding for periods when market volatility is high.

One implication of this argument for the variation in herding across markets is the following: we should find higher levels of herding for Portuguese mutual funds than that found in the USA and the UK given that the volatility in the Portuguese stockmarket is higher.[6]

Informational cascades models may also predict a negative relation between volatility and the level of herding. The argument is that if investors are not *ex ante* identical, the arrival of an individual with deviant information or unexpected public information, can dislodge the cascade. Therefore we could also observe lower levels of herding for periods when market volatility is high.

8.2.2 Measuring herding

We use the measure of herding developed by Lakonishok, Schleifer, Thaler and Vishny (1992). This measure defines herding as the tendency of funds to trade a given stock together and in the same direction, for whatever reason, more often than would be expected if funds were trading randomly and independently. A group of funds exhibits herding behavior when there is unbalance between funds that buy and funds that sell a given stock (assuming that trades would be balanced if there was no herding). In other words, there is herding behavior when the proportion of funds that trade in a stock in the same direction (buying or selling) is above the expected proportion of funds trading in that direction under the null hypothesis of independent trading decisions by the funds.

The measure is defined as:

$$H(i,t) = \left|p(i,t) - p(t)\right| - AF(i,t)$$

where

$$p(i,t) = \frac{B(i,t)}{B(i,t) + S(i,t)}$$

and

$$p(t) = \frac{\sum_{i=1}^{n} p(i,t)}{n}$$

$B(i, t)$ [$S(i, t)$] is the number of funds that buy (sell) the stock i during quarter t, $p(i, t)$ is the proportion of funds trading stock i that were buyers and $p(t)$ is a proxy for the expected proportion of buyers under the null of independently trading by funds, $E(p(i, t))$, and is given by the proportion of all stock trades by funds that were purchases during that quarter t. $p(t)$ is constant for all stocks during a quarter but varies over time. The adjustment factor $AF(i, t)$ is given by:

$$AF(i,t) = E[|p(i,t) - E(p(i,t)|]$$

This factor allows to capture the random variation of $p(i, t)$ around its expected proportion of buyers. Under the null hypothesis of independent trading, $B(i, t)$ has a binomial distribution with parameter $p = p(t)$.[7] Yet the expected value of the absolute difference between $p(i, t)$ and $p(t)$ may be different from zero even under the hypothesis of no herding.

The null hypothesis states that if herding does not exist, the proportion of buyers (and sellers) has the same expected value for all stocks in a given period and is constant equal to $p(t)$ $[1 - p(t)]$. Under the null, $H(i, t) = 0$. Deviations from $p(t)$, above the expected $AF(i, t)$, signal herding.

As $N(i, t) = B(i, t) + S(i, t)$ becomes larger then, under the null, $AF(i, t)$ will be close to zero. The main reason for including the adjustment factor is to account for bias that would occur if stocks were illiquid and traded only by a few investors.

Positive (or negative) significant values of $H(i, t)$ can be interpreted as the percentage of funds that were buyers (sellers) in a certain stock above the expected proportion.

To evaluate herding for a given subgroup of funds, we compute the average of the measure of herding $H(i, t)$ across all stocks and quarters in that particular group. For example, we can measure the herding effect for a subgroup of funds – large-cap funds – or for a subset of quarters – when the market is positive.

The herding measure can also be computed separately for stocks that observed higher proportion of buyers (sellers) than the overall average. The averaging is done as above. These conditional measures, the buy herding measure and the sell herding measure, respectively, are defined as:

$$BH(i,t) = H(i,t) \mid p(i,t) > p(t)$$

$$SH(i,t) = H(i,t) \mid p(i,t) < p(t)$$

By analysing these conditional measures $BH(i, t)$ and $SH(i, t)$ we can assess whether herding effects are more common when funds are buying or selling.[8]

Measuring the herding behavior on the basis of Lakonishok, Schleifer, Thaler and Vishny (1992) has important limitations. First, this measure captures correlation in trades but does not, by itself, disentangle the determinants of herding. Second, this measure does not take into consideration whether the correlation trades results from imitation or merely reflects that traders use the same information. Finally, this measure is biased when there are limitations to short selling strategies. If short selling is prohibited, as it was the case for Portugal until mid 1999, or costly, the measure overestimates true herding: the measure may yield a positive value, indicating herding, when herding effectively does not occur.

Another concern regards the measurement unit to use to compute the herding measure. If we use funds as the measurement unit, the measure may be biased upward. Research buying lists are most of the times used across funds managed by the same company. As a result, a positive value of the herding measure could occur merely reflecting "spurious" herding and not positive feedback trading.

8.3 DATA

8.3.1 The mutual fund industry in Portugal

By June 2001, there were 260 investment funds in Portugal managed by 18 different companies. Total net assets under management amounted to around 21 thousand million euros.

The breakdown of the funds' assets by country was the following: 33 percent of total assets were invested in Portugal, 69 percent were invested in European Union countries (excluding Portugal) and the remaining 9 percent were invested in countries outside the EU. On aggregate, 43 percent of total assets were invested in Corporate Bonds, 6 percent in Stocks, 13 percent in Treasury Bonds, 11 percent in International Mutual Funds and the remaining were invested in cash. 90 percent of total assets were denominated in euros and 6 percent in US dollars.

The largest asset management company held 37 percent of total assets. The three largest asset management companies held 69 percent of total assets.

8.3.2 Sample

The data used in our study consists of quarterly portfolio holdings for 32 equity mutual funds based in Portugal, between 1998 and 2000. The data is from Bolsa de Valores de Lisboa e Porto. The 32 funds were selected from a total of 53 equity mutual funds operating in Portugal at the end of 1997 and for which we could trace data in any quarter starting in 1988. As in previous studies, we selected those funds that had at least 75 percent of their total assets invested in stocks (domestic or foreign) by the end of 1997. We impose no minimum survival period requirement for a fund to be included in the sample.[9]

By the end of 1997, equity mutual funds in Portugal managed around 2,000 million euros of which around 1,700 million euros were invested in domestic stocks, accounting for 5 percent of the Portuguese stockmarket capitalization. Foreign stocks accounted for less than 5 percent of total assets. By the end of 2001, total assets in management are similar. Equity holdings account, as in 1997, for over 90 percent of total assets but foreign stocks represent now over 75 percent of total stocks.The 32 funds in our sample held 1,310 million euros in domestic equities, 78 percent of the total equities held by equity mutual funds in Portugal.

The total net assets for the average fund in our sample amounted to 52 million euros.[10] The largest fund in the sample managed 230 million euros and 13 funds managed total net assets above 50 million euros. Table 8.1 shows that, for the average fund, domestic equity holdings account for 79 percent of total net assets; foreign equity holdings represent only 5 percent of total net assets. Domestic securities (mainly stocks and bonds) account for 81 percent of total assets. Nineteen funds in our sample did not invest in foreign securities.

The 32 funds in sample were managed by 12 different asset management companies, of which five accounted for more than 80 percent of total assets managed by the funds in our sample.[11]

We consider 84 distinct stocks out of the holdings of the 32 funds in our sample. We excluded those securities that were traded by only one or two funds over the sample period. Our data-set is composed of 32 different panels containing the quarterly shareholdings for each individual fund, from the last quarter of 1997 to the last quarter of 2000. The average quarter has information for 27 funds that, on average, held 27 stocks.

Table 8.1 presents statistics regarding the portfolio holdings of the funds in our sample broken down by size quintiles, using the fund market capitalization at the end of the last quarter of 1997.[12] If there is a relation

Table 8.1 Portfolio holdings for funds in sample by fund size quintiles

	Fund size (4th quarter 1997)					Total
	Quintile 1 (small)	Quintile 2	Quintile 3	Quintile 4	Quintile 5 (large)	
% Domestic stocks	75.69%	83.52%	84.44%	69.09%	81.39%	79.17%
% Foreign stocks	7.91%	0.83%	1.54%	14.52%	2.07%	5.14%
% Total stocks	83.60%	84.35%	85.98%	83.61%	83.46%	84.31%
% Domestic securities	79.52%	84.36%	86.48%	72.20%	82.72%	81.40%
% Foreign securities	7.91%	0.83%	1.54%	14.55%	2.09%	5.15%
$\frac{\text{Domestic stocks}}{\text{Domestic securities}}$	95.18%	99.00%	97.64%	95.69%	98.39%	97.26%
$\frac{\text{Foreign stocks}}{\text{Foreign securities}}$	99.99%	99.99%	99.99%	99.79%	99.04%	99.81%

Notes: The table shows the percentage of stocks (domestic and foreign) held by the 32 Portuguese mutual funds in our sample, by size quintiles at the end of the last quarter of 1997, and the proportion of domestic/foreign stocks (securities) in total holdings. The portfolio holdings are obtained from Bolsa de Valores de Lisboa e Porto. Total funds in management by the funds in sample accounted to 1,310 million euros.

between fund size and portfolio holdings, we have to be careful when interpreting the results partitioned by portfolio holdings because we may be capturing a size effect instead.

Examination of Table 8.1 shows that there seems to be no monotonic relation between fund size and portfolio holdings. The fact that portfolio holdings are similar for large and small funds could result from the fact that the mutual fund industry in Portugal is still incipient. The first equity fund was launched in 1986 but the important growth in the industry started only a few years ago.[13] On the other hand, the fact that most asset companies are held by banks, and given that the banking sector in Portugal has been through a process of reorganization over the last decade, may also explain why we observe so little variation in the funds' portfolio holdings.

Table 8.2 presents the aggregate statistics on the trades of the funds, which we infer from changes in the quarterly portfolio holdings of each fund. Because we focus on changes in holdings that result from trades (purchases and sales), we excluded all stock/quarter observations whose changes were related with shares adjustments (for example, stock issues or splits). We have a total of 31,456 changes; 51.5 percent of the changes are positive (buys), and 49.5 percent are negative (sales). When we analyse the changes, quarter by quarter, the balance between purchases and sales is also even.

Table 8.2 Buys and sells

	Quarter				1998–2000
	1st	2nd	3rd	4th	
Buys	4160 (50.52%)	4037 (50.57%)	3949 (50.55%)	3741 (50.38%)	15887 (50.50%)
Sells	4075 (49.48%)	3946 (49.43%)	3863 (49.45%)	3685 (49.62%)	15569 (49.50%)
Total	8235 (100%)	7983 (100%)	7812 (100%)	7426 (100%)	31456 (100%)

Notes: The table shows the trading data for 32 Portuguese mutual funds. Trades are inferred from changes in quarterly portfolio holdings, for the all sample period, 1998 to 2000, and by quarter. For each average quarter and for the all period, this table documents the number of purchases, sales and aggregate trades and the proportion of buys and sells. The portfolio holdings are obtained from Bolsa de Valores de Lisboa e Porto.

8.4 RESULTS

8.4.1 Overall levels of herding by mutual funds

In Table 8.3 we present the overall levels of herding exhibited by our sample, for the total period and for each of the three years, 1998, 1999 and 2000.

The herding measure of 11.38 percent shown in Table 8.3 is the Lakonishok, Schleifer, Thaler and Vishny (1992) measure of herding computed over all stock-quarters during the three-year period. We can interpret this average herding measure as meaning that, if 100 funds trade a given stock, then approximately 11 more funds trade on one side of the market than would be expected if there was no positive feedback trading between funds. In other words, if the number of changes in holdings was, *a priori*, equally balanced between positive and negative changes, 61.38 percent (50% + 11.38%) of the funds traded in one direction and the remaining 38.62 percent (50% − 11.38%) traded in the opposite direction.

The average herding measure does not vary much across the three years in sample, the lowest level being observed in 1999 (H = 9.08%). The overall level of herding we find is much higher than that reported in previous studies using UK and US mutual and pension fund data (see Table 8.4). The overall level of herding in our study is close to what has been reported by Choe, Kho and Stulz (1999) for their study on the herding behavior of foreign individual investors in the Korean stockmarket (they find no herding measure below 20%).

This higher average level of herding for less mature stockmarkets is consistent with arguments that rely on informational cascades or information inefficiencies arguments. Agency models would not predict different levels of herding across stockmarkets in different stages of maturity.

Table 8.3 Herding levels in Portuguese mutual funds

Number of funds trading in the period	1998	1999	2000	1998–2000
$n \geq 1$	11.25[a] (3018)	9.08[a] (2691)	14.25[a] (2281)	11.38[a] (7990)
$n \geq 2$	12.45[a] (3000)	9.88[a] (2676)	15.47[a] (2263)	12.44[a] (7939)
$n \geq 5$	12.42[a] (2902)	12.07[a] (2578)	16.83[a] (2154)	13.54[a] (7634)
$n \geq 10$	13.08[a] (2603)	13.13[a] (2249)	16.16[a] (1884)	13.96[a] (6736)
$n \geq 15$	12.11[a] (2132)	12.68[a] (1865)	16.63[a] (1610)	13.60[a] (5607)
$5 > n \geq 2$	10.57[b] (98)	−3.52 (98)	9.81[b] (109)	5.77[b] (305)
$10 > n \geq 5$	8.95[b] (299)	9.62[b] (329)	11.47[a] (270)	9.95[b] (898)
$15 > n \geq 10$	14.32[a] (471)	13.87[a] (384)	9.90[b] (274)	13.09[a] (1129)

Notes: The table reports the Lakonishok, Schleifer, Thaler and Vishny (1992) herding measure for a sample of 32 Portuguese mutual funds. The herding statistic for a given stock-quarter is defined as $|p(i, t) - p(t)| - E|p(i, t) - p(t)|$, where $p(i, t)$ is the proportion of funds trading stock i during quarter t that are buyers and $p(t)$ is the average of $p(i, t)$ over all stocks i in quarter t. $E|p(i, t) - p(t)|$ is the adjustment factor calculated using a binomial distribution under the hypothesis of no herding. n is the number of funds required to trade a stock in each quarter used to compute the herding measure. The herding measures are computed in each stock-quarter and then averaged over the constituents of each group. The number of stock-quarters in each subgroup is in parentheses. [a]indicates statistical significance at the 1% level; [b]indicates statistical significance at the 5% level.

Information models could predict those differences: our evidence suggests that in stockmarkets that exhibit poorer aggregation of information and where the precision of the public pool of information is lower, herds seem to form more often. One observable implication of these results should be that as stockmarkets become more mature, the level of herding decreases.

We expect to find a stronger decrease in the herding measure when we require a larger number of funds to trade a given stock-quarter, given that stocks that are traded by many funds usually have more public information and, as such, the herding effect should be lower. When we introduce restrictions on the minimum number of funds trading in a given stock-quarter, there is very little difference in the results. Table 8.3 shows that if we impose hurdles of up to ten funds (herds of 2, 5 or 10 funds) the measure of herding increases slightly ($H = 12.44, 13.54, 13.96$). For a minimum of 15 funds trading a given stock-quarter the measure slightly decreases to 13.60.

Table 8.4 Comparative results

Number of funds trading in in the period	1998–2000	Results from US and UK studies		
		US mutual funds (1975–94)	US pension funds (1985–89)	UK mutual funds (1986–93)
$n \geq 1$	11.38	–	2.7	–
	(7990)	–	(N/A.)	–
$n \geq 5$	13.54	3.4	–	2.5
	(7634)	(109486)	–	(10522)
$n \geq 15$	13.60	–	–	4.3
	(5607)	–	–	(1007)
$5 > n \geq 2$	5.77	–	–	2.6
	(305)	–	–	(16492)
$10 > n \geq 5$	9.95	–	–	2.1
	(898)	–	–	(7180)
$15 > n \geq 10$	13.09	–	–	2.8
	(1129)	–	–	(2335)

Notes: The table compares the Lakonishok, Schleifer, Thaler and Vishny (1992) herding measure for a sample of 32 Portuguese mutual funds with the results reported using US and UK fund data. The herding statistic for a given stock-quarter is defined as $|p(i, t) - p(t)| - E|p(i, t) - p(t)|$, where $p(i, t)$ is the proportion of funds trading stock i during quarter t that are buyers and $p(t)$ is the average of $p(i, t)$ over all stocks i in quarter t. $E|p(i, t) - p(t)|$ is the adjustment factor calculated using a binomial distribution under the hypothesis of no herding. n is the number of funds required to trade a stock in each quarter used to compute the herding measure.The herding measures are computed in each stock-quarter and then averaged over the constituents of each group. The number of stock-quarters in each subgroup is in parentheses. US pension funds data, US mutual fund data and UK mutual fund data are, respectively, from Lakonishok, Schleifer, Thaler and Vishny (1992), Wermers (1999) and Wylie (2000).

8.4.2 Buy-herding and sell-herding

Table 8.5 reports average buy-herding and sell-herding measures for the total period and for each individual year. As stated above, the comparison of the two measures of herding reveals whether herds tend to form more often on one side of the market.

We find higher levels of herding on the buy side.[14] Although the level of herding is significant in either side of the market, over time, the value of the statistic changes and so does the side of the market where herding is predominant. In particular, herding in sales seems to have been predominant in 1999.

The evidence in our study is similar to that reported by previous studies (Wylie, 2000, reports a stronger herding effect on the buy side while Grinblatt, Titman and Wermers (1995) reports a stronger effect on the sell side).

Table 8.5 Buy and sell herding levels

Number of funds trading in the period	1998		1999		2000		1998–2000	
	Buy	Sell	Buy	Sell	Buy	Sell	Buy	Sell
$n \geq 1$	12.40[a]	10.37[a]	8.41[a]	9.76[a]	16.59[a]	12.05[a]	12.30[a]	10.63[a]
	(1634)	(1384)	(1387)	(1304)	(1223)	(1058)	(4244)	(3746)
$n \geq 2$	12.55[a]	12.45[a]	7.65[a]	12.27[a]	15.92[a]	15.08[a]	11.93[a]	13.11[a]
	(1611)	(1389)	(1392)	(1284)	(1250)	(1013)	(4253)	(3686)
$n \geq 5$	13.28[a]	11.74[a]	13.74[a]	10.66[a]	19.09[a]	14.14[a]	15.15[a]	11.99[a]
	(1491)	(1411)	(1217)	(1361)	(1142)	(1012)	(3850)	(3784)
$n \geq 10$	13.24[a]	12.95[a]	15.18[a]	11.50[a]	14.25[a]	18.34[a]	14.14[a]	13.79[a]
	(1314)	(1289)	(1038)	(1211)	(1034)	(850)	(3386)	(3350)
$n \geq 15$	14.07[a]	10.46[a]	16.67[a]	9.62[a]	18.10[a]	15.22[a]	16.09[a]	11.49[a]
	(1015)	(1117)	(829)	(1036)	(783)	(827)	(2627)	(2980)
$5 > n \geq 2$	10.47[a]	10.81[a]	−10.60[a]	11.20[a]	12.99	10.30[a]	3.46	10.72[a]
	(41)	(57)	(51)	(43)	(45)	(62)	(137)	(162)
$10 > n \geq 5$	8.00[a]	9.75[a]	10.13[a]	9.12[a]	11.37[a]	12.42[a]	9.81[a]	10.29[a]
	(139)	(160)	(150)	(179)	(131)	(139)	(420)	(478)
$15 > n \geq 10$	14.33[a]	14.27[a]	10.42[a]	16.82[a]	11.51	8.84[a]	12.32[a]	13.76[a]
	(230)	(241)	(190)	(194)	(128)	(146)	(548)	(581)

Notes: The table reports the Lakonishok, Schleifer, Thaler and Vishny (1992) herding measure for a sample of 32 Portuguese mutual funds segregated by purchases and sales. The herding statistic for a given stock-quarter is defined as $|p(i, t) - p(t)| - E|p(i, t) - p(t)|$, where $p(i, t)$ is the proportion of funds trading stock i during quarter t that are buyers and $p(t)$ is the average of $p(i, t)$ over all stocks i in quarter t. $E|p(i, t) - p(t)|$ is the adjustment factor calculated using a binomial distribution under the hypothesis of no herding. Buy herding stock-quarters are those where $p(i, t) > p(t)$, that is, the proportion of buyers was greater than the expected proportion of buyers; sell stock-quarters are those where $p(i, t) < p(t)$ meaning the proportion of sellers was greater than the expected proportion of sellers. n is the number of funds required to trade a stock in each quarter used to compute the herding measure.The herding measures are computed in each stock-quarter and then averaged over the constituents of each group. The number of stock-quarters in each subgroup is in parentheses. [a]indicates statistical significance at the 1% level; [b] indicates statistical significance at the 5% level.

8.4.3 Herding and fund-specific characteristics

Size /market capitalization

Table 8.6 presents the herding measures averaged over stock-quarters segregated by fund size. Size quintiles are formed each year so that each quintile has the same number of funds except for the mid-quintile.

We find that the levels of herding computed for these subgroups of funds are much smaller than that observed for the overall sample. As discussed in section 8.2, we might think that funds within the same size-class would show less herding because the imitation would occur across different size groups.

Table 8.6 Herding levels segregated by fund size

Fund size	1998	1999	2000	1998–2000
Quintile 1	−1.18	0.88	3.00[b]	0.85
(small)	(399)	(358)	3.00[b]	(1089)
Quintile 2	1.44	1.04	3.65[b]	2.06
	(656)	(355)	(486)	(1497)
Quintile 3	1.27	3.14[b]	1.24	1.90
	(818)	(727)	(599)	(2144)
Quintile 4	2.65	0.15	5.91[b]	2.81[b]
	(454)	(423)	(388)	(1265)
Quintile 5	0.57	−1.45	−0.15	−0.16
(large)	(691)	(395)	(436)	(1522)

Notes: The table reports the Lakonishok, Schleifer, Thaler and Vishny (1992) herding measure for a sample of 32 Portuguese mutual funds segregated by fund size. Size is measured by total assets under management. Each quintile is formed on the basis of the size of the fund during the quarter prior to the herding measure quarter. Quintiles are recalculated every year. The herding statistic for a given stock-quarter is defined as $|p(i, t) - p(t)| - E|p(i, t) - p(t)|$, where $p(i, t)$ is the proportion of funds trading stock i during quarter t that are buyers and $p(t)$ is the average of $p(i, t)$ over all stocks i in quarter t. $E|p(i, t) - p(t)|$ is the adjustment factor calculated using a binomial distribution under the hypothesis of no herding. The herding measures $|p(i, t) - p(t)| - E|p(i, t) - p(t)|$ are averaged separately over stock-quarters belonging to different fund size quintiles. In each stock-period the funds of the sample were divided R times into 5 with a remainder of S. Then the qth quintile contains R observations, except the third quintile which contains $R + S$ observations. We impose no minimum requirement on the number of funds trading a stock in each period. The herding measures are computed in each stock-quarter and then averaged over the constituents of each group. The number of stock-quarters in each subgroup is in parentheses. [a]indicates statistical significance at the 1% level; [b]indicates statistical significance at the 5% level.

In particular, small funds would follow large, presumably more informed funds. Yet if the behavior of funds were driven by reputation concerns, funds would herd within their group to preserve their status quo. Another potential reason for low herding for size subgroups of funds might be that size is not the central characteristic when choosing the fund to imitate. Within the same size group we may have funds with completely different styles and the herds may be formed based on style, not size.

Our results suggest that size is not indeed an important factor: herds seem to be formed with funds of different sizes. Medium-cap funds exhibit the highest level of herding. The average level of herding is particularly low for the extreme quintiles (very large or very small funds). A lower level of herding among small funds is consistent with the hypothesis that these funds prefer to imitate large funds that are expected to have superior information resources and therefore more precise signals. A lower level of herding among large funds could be driven by the fact that they use their private information to trade.

Lakonishok, Schleifer, Thaler and Vishny (1992) report similar results: size subgroups of funds exhibit lower levels of herding than that observed

Table 8.7 Herding levels segregated by fund portfolio holdings

Fund portfolio holdings	1998	1999	2000	1998–2000
Quintile 1 (less stocks)	3.58 (727)	2.12 (442)	0.38 (462)	2.28 (1631)
Quintile 2	5.22[b] (500)	11.84[a] (473)	10.00[a] (391)	8.89[b] (1364)
Quintile 3	3.65 (795)	2.81 (562)	9.90[a] (593)	5.31[b] (1950)
Quintile 4	1.81 (421)	−1.42 (359)	3.25[b] (468)	1.42 (1248)
Quintile 5 (more stocks)	−2.25 (575)	−1.70 (422)	8.13[a] (367)	0.71 (1364)

Notes: The table reports the Lakonishok, Schleifer, Thaler and Vishny (1992) herding measure for a sample of 32 Portuguese mutual funds segregated by portfolio holdings. Portfolio holdings are measured by the percentage of stocks in the fund portfolio. Each quintile is formed on the basis of the holdings of the fund during the quarter prior to the herding measure quarter. Quintiles are recalculated every year. The herding statistic for a given stock-quarter is defined as $|p(i, t) - p(t)| - E|p(I, t) - p(t)|$, where $p(i, t)$ is the proportion of funds trading stock i during quarter t that are buyers and $p(t)$ is the average of $p(i, t)$ over all stocks i in quarter t. $E|p(i, t) - p(t)|$ is the adjustment factor calculated using a binomial distribution under the hypothesis of no herding. The herding measures $|p(i, t) - p(t)| - E|p(i, t) - p(t)|$ are averaged separately over stock-quarters belonging to different fund size quintiles. In each stock-period the funds of the sample were divided R times into 5 with a remainder of S. Then the qth quintile contains R observations, except the third quintile which contains $R + S$ observations. We impose no minimum requirement on the number of funds trading a stock in each period. The herding measures are computed in each stock-quarter and then averaged over the constituents of each group. The number of stock-quarters in each subgroup is in parentheses. [a] indicates statistical significance at the 1% level; [b] indicates statistical significance at the 5% level.

for the overall sample. They also find that the level of herding is lower within the subgroup of small funds.

Our results seem to be consistent with cascade or information inefficiency based explanations. The implication of the reputational explanation for the levels of herding across different subgroups is not borne out by the data.

Portfolio holdings

We next examine the levels of herding for subgroups formed by portfolio holdings. Quintiles are formed each year so that each quintile has the same number of funds except for the mid-quintile. In Table 8.7, we report these results. We find that the levels of herding computed for these subgroups of funds are also much smaller than that observed for the overall sample. As for size, portfolio holdings do not seem to be the elected factor to choose which fund to imitate.

If we exclude the first quintile, the results suggest a negative relation between the proportion of stocks held by a fund and the level of herding: funds that hold more stocks do not seem to trade together so often. This evidence is consistent with the hypothesis that higher costs in processing information on several asset classes result in that funds that are more diversified should exhibit higher levels of herding. Table 8.7 shows that funds that have less stocks – and therefore hold other assets – herd more often.

As above, results are consistent with an explanation that relies on information. The interpretation of this last result should not be taken too far given that the quintiles formed here do not yield very different groups in terms of portfolio holdings. Please recall that the funds in our sample have a minimum of 75 percent of their portfolio invested in stocks.

Frequency in portfolio rebalancing

To explore whether herding is different for funds with longer or shorter investment horizons (assuming that these correspond to funds that trade less or more frequently), we divided the sample into quintiles formed on the basis of the degree of portfolio rebalancing. To proxy the degree of rebalancing, we computed, for each fund-quarter, the average across stocks of a measure of permanence of a given stock. As before, quintiles are formed each year so that each quintile has the same number of funds except for the mid-quintile (Table 8.8).

We find that the levels of herding computed for subgroups of funds are again much smaller than that observed for the overall sample and for the three individual years, suggesting that the level of herding is lower among funds with similar trading patterns.

The results in Table 8.8 do not suggest a relation between the level of herding and the degree of rebalancing: herds seem to be formed with funds with different trading strategies. The evidence presented here does not support an informational inefficiency based explanation, that would predict that funds with higher turnover rates and, presumably lower investment horizons, exhibit higher levels of herding.

8.4.4 Herding and market conditions

Market stock returns

In Table 8.9, we segregate stock-quarters by market aggregate returns. For a particular quarter, market returns are calculated using the average daily market returns of the PSI 20.[15] We sorted the quarters and we construct three

Table 8.8 Herding levels segregated by frequency in portfolio rebalancing

Portfolio rebalancing	1998	1999	2000	1998–2000
Quintile 1 (more frequent portfolio rebalancing)	2,70[b] (462)	−2,41[b] (438)	6,32[a] (915)	3,29[b] (1815)
Quintile 2	4,97[a] (452)	−0,31 (325)	6,29[a] (494)	4,13[a] (1271)
Quintile 3	1,28 (783)	3,34[a] (561)	7,26[a] (620)	3,76[b] (1964)
Quintile 4	4,27[a] (578)	0,83 (534)	9,52[a] (484)	4,71[a] (1596)
Quintile 5 (less frequent portfolio rebalancing)	−0,64 (433)	3,56[a] (526)	3,16[b] (262)	1,98 (1221)

Notes: The table reports the Lakonishok, Schleifer, Thaler and Vishny (1992) herding measure for a sample of 32 Portuguese mutual funds segregated by portfolio rebalancing frequency. Portfolio rebalancing frequency is defined as $(X^1_{t,A} - X^1_{t-1,A})^2/[(X^1_{t,A} + X^1_{t-1,A})/2]^2$ where $X^1_{t,A}$ represents the number of company A stocks that fund 1 holds on quarter t. The rebalancing frequency is the average of the statistic calculated over the stocks held by the fund in a particular quarter. The value of the statistic increases when portfolio rebalancing is less frequent. Each quintile is formed on the basis of the frequency statistic of the fund during the quarter prior to the herding measure quarter except for the year 1998 that we used the first quarter of 1998. Quintiles are recalculated every year. The herding statistic for a given stock-quarter is defined as $|p(i, t) - p(t)| - E|p(i, t) - p(t)|$, where $p(i, t)$ is the proportion of funds trading stock i during quarter t that are buyers and $p(t)$ is the average of $p(i, t)$ over all stocks i in quarter t. $E|p(i, t) - p(t)|$ is the adjustment factor calculated using a binomial distribution under the hypothesis of no herding. The herding measures $|p(i, t) - p(t)| - E|p(i, t) - p(t)|$ are averaged separately over stock-quarters belonging to different fund size quintiles. In each stock-period the funds of the sample were divided R times into 5 with a remainder of S. Then the qth quintile contains R observations, except the third quintile which contains $R + S$ observations. We impose no minimum requirement on the number of funds trading a stock in each period. The herding measures are computed in each stock-quarter and then averaged over the constituents of each group. The number of stock-quarters in each subgroup is in parentheses. [a]indicates statistical significance at the 1% level; [b]indicates statistical significance at the 5% level.

different subgroups from our original sample. For example, the first subgroup includes the herding measures for the quarters were market returns were low. Each subgroup has the same number of funds except for the mid-group.

There seems to be a clear pattern here: the level of herding seems to decrease when market returns are higher. This negative relation is consistent with some of theoretical arguments exposed above. When markets are doing well, institutional investors feel more confident and are thus more likely to use their own signals and therefore trade independently.

Our evidence is also consistent with Cai, Kaul and Zheng (2000): they argue that mutual fund trading is highly correlated with market contemporaneous returns. Returns seem to drive trading and not the other way around.

Table 8.9 Herding levels segregated by market stock returns

Number of funds trading in the period	Sub-group 1 (lowest returns)	Sub-group 2	Sub-group 3 (highest returns)
$n \geq 1$	14.27[a] (2389)	10.75[a] (2707)	9.60[a] (2894)
$n \geq 2$	15.26[a] (2375)	12.13[a] (2687)	10.47[a] (2877)
$n \geq 5$	16.26[a] (2249)	14.15[a] (2592)	10.75[a] (2793)
$n \geq 10$	15.29[a] (1966)	15.41[a] (2272)	10.90[a] (2498)
$n \geq 15$	16.95[a] (1591)	14.15[a] (1931)	10.07[a] (2085)
$5 > n \geq 2$	10.64[a] (126)	0.08 (95)	4.42 (84)
$10 > n \geq 5$	15.68[a] (283)	7.84[b] (320)	8.06[a] (295)
$15 > n \geq 10$	12.94[a] (375)	19.98[a] (341)	11.58[a] (413)

Notes: The table reports the Lakonishok, Schleifer, Thaler and Vishny (1992) herding measure for a sample of 32 Portuguese mutual funds segregated by market stock returns. Subgroups are formed on the basis of the Portuguese Stock Index (PSI20) averaged daily returns. Sub-group 1 contains the observations for the four quarters with the lowest returns. Sub-group 3 contains observations for the four quarters with the highest returns. Sub-group 2 contains the observations for the remaining quarters. The herding statistic for a given stock-quarter is defined as $|p(i, t) - p(t)| - E|p(i, t) - p(t)|$, where $p(i, t)$ is the proportion of funds trading stock i during quarter t that are buyers and $p(t)$ is the average of $p(i, t)$ over all stocks i in quarter t. $E|p(i, t) - p(t)|$ is the adjustment factor calculated using a binomial distribution under the hypothesis of no herding. n is the number of funds required to trade a stock in each quarter used to compute the herding measure. The herding measures are computed in each stock-quarter and then averaged over the constituents of each group. The number of stock-quarters in each subgroup is in parentheses. [a] indicates statistical significance at the 1% level; [b] indicates statistical significance at the 5% level.

Market volatility

We further investigate if feedback-trading strategies occur more often in periods of high or low market volatility. Table 8.10 shows the results for subgroups formed on the basis of the level of aggregate market volatility. For example, the third subgroup includes the herding measures for the more volatile quarters.

The results suggest that the level of herding is lower when the market is more volatile. Higher volatility can be caused by more uncertainty about future values. If that is the case, then higher volatility reflecting less precise information should result in higher levels of herding. If alternatively, higher volatility proxies, new unexpected information, then higher volatility, reflecting more information, should result in lower levels of herding. Our evidence

Table 8.10 Herding levels segregated by market volatility

Number of funds trading in the period	Sub-group 1 (lowest volatility)	Sub-group 2	Sub-group (highest volatility)
$n \geq 1$	12.22[a]	10.54[a]	11.86[a]
	(2285)	(2757)	(2948)
$n \geq 2$	13.62[a]	11.14[a]	13.10[a]
	(2267)	(2744)	(2928)
$n \geq 5$	14.95[a]	13.59[a]	12.61[a]
	(2155)	(2640)	(2839)
$n \geq 10$	13.29[a]	14.97[a]	13.33[a]
	(1876)	(2332)	(2528)
$n \geq 15$	15.21[a]	13.53[a]	12.42[a]
	(1530)	(1955)	(2122)
$5 > n \geq 2$	6.26[b]	−2,52	11.39[a]
	(112)	(104)	(89)
$10 > n \geq 5$	17.85[a]	6.28[b]	7.46[b]
	(279)	(308)	(311)
$15 > n \geq 10$	11.59[a]	18.82[a]	14.10[a]
	(346)	(377)	(406)

Notes: The table reports the Lakonishok, Schleifer, Thaler and Vishny (1992) herding measure for a sample of 32 Portuguese mutual funds segregated by market volatility. Subgroups are formed on the basis of the Portuguese Stock Index (PSI20) daily returns standard deviation in each quarter. Sub-group 1 contains the observations for the four quarters with the lowest volatility. Sub-group 3 contains the observations for the four quarters with the highest volatility. Sub-group 2 contains the observations for the remaining quarters. The herding statistic for a given stock-quarter is defined as $|p(i,t) - p(t)| - E|p(i,t) - p(t)|$, where $p(i,t)$ is the proportion of funds trading stock i during quarter t that are buyers and $p(t)$ is the average of $p(i,t)$ over all stocks i in quarter t. $E|p(i,t) - p(t)|$ is the adjustment factor calculated using a binomial distribution under the hypothesis of no herding. n is the number of funds required to trade a stock in each quarter used to compute the herding measure. The herding measures are computed in each stock-quarter and then averaged over the constituents of each group. The number of stock-quarters in each subgroup is in parentheses. [a] indicates statistical significance at the 1% level; [b] indicates statistical significance at the 5% level.

supports this latter argument. This interpretation of the results is, one more time, based on information models.

8.5 CONCLUSION

This chapter provides additional evidence on the level of herding in the trades of institutional investors. We have investigated the existence and magnitude of herding for a sample of 32 Portuguese mutual funds for the period 1998 to 2000. In addition, we examined herding by subgroups of funds formed on the basis of fund specific characteristics and market conditions.

As in previous studies, we have used the measure of herding developed by Lakonishok, Schleifer, Thaler and Vishny (1992). This measure evaluates if the proportion of funds that trade in a stock in the same direction (buying or selling) is above the expected proportion of funds trading in that direction if there was no herding.

The overall level of herding is very significant. For every 100 funds that trade a given stock, approximately 11 trade on one side of the market, above what would have been expected if they were trading independently. The level of herding does not vary much over time or when we impose a minimum number of funds to trade a given stock. The level of herding is significant in either side of the market, purchases or sales.

The average level of herding for Portuguese mutual funds is four to five times higher than that found in previous studies for the USA and the UK. This result seems to suggest that herding is higher on more volatile markets.

We find that the overall level of herding is much higher than that observed within subgroups of funds. Herds seem thus to be formed with funds of different size, different portfolio holdings and different trading strategies. The low and high cap subgroups of funds exhibit lower levels of herding and funds with fewer stocks seem to herd more often. Finally, we find lower levels of herding when the market is doing well and when the market is more volatile. Altogether our results are consistent with the implications of information-based models.

Work in progress analyses a longer period (from January 1996 to September 2002) and monthly portfolios. With this larger sample, we are able to analyse herding across asset management companies instead of funds and include more explanatory variables (fund performance measures and stock characteristics). Finally we are looking at conditional probabilities to account for short selling restrictions.

APPENDIX 1: FUNDS IN SAMPLE

Fund	Asset management company
Atlântico Acções	AF – INVESTIMENTOS, Fundos Mobiliários, S.A.
Barclays FPA	BARCLAYS FUNDOS, S.A.
Barclays Premier Acções Portugal	BARCLAYS FUNDOS, S.A.
BCI Acções Portugal/ Santander Acções Portugal	BCI – Sociedade Gestora de Fundos de Investimento Mobiliário, S.A./SANTANDER – Sociedade Gestora de Fundos de Investimento Mobiliário, S.A.
BCI Iberfundo Acções/ Santander Iberfundo Acções	BCI – Sociedade Gestora de Fundos de Investimento Mobiliário,S.A./SANTANDER – Sociedade Gestora de Fundos de Investimento Mobiliário, S.A.
BCP Acções	AF – INVESTIMENTOS, Fundos Mobiliários, S.A.
BNU Acções	INVESTIL – Sociedade Gestora dos Fundos de Investimento Mobiliário, S.A.

→

Appendix 1 Continued

Fund	Asset management company
BNU PPA	INVESTIL – Sociedade Gestora dos Fundos de Investimento Mobiliário, S.A.
BPI Acções	BPI FUNDOS – Gestão de Fundos de Investimento Mobiliário, S.A.
BPI Poupança Acções	BPI FUNDOS – Gestão de Fundos de Investimento Mobiliário, S.A.
Caixagest Acções Portugal	CAIXAGEST – Técnicas de Gestão de Fundos, S.A.
Caixagest Internacional/ Caixagest Acções Europa	CAIXAGEST – Técnicas de Gestão de Fundos, S.A.
Caixagest Valorização	CAIXAGEST – Técnicas de Gestão de Fundos, S.A.
Capital Portugal	TOTTA Fundos, S.A./MC – FUNDOS - Sociedade Gestora de Fundos de Investimento Mobiliário, S.A.
DB – Investimento	DB FUNDOS – Sociedade Gestora de Fundos de Investimento Mobiliário, S.A.
ES Portugal Acções	ESAF – Espírito Santo Fundos de Investimento Mobiliário, S.A.
Eurocapital – FA	BPI FUNDOS – Gestão de Fundos de Investimento Mobiliário, S.A.
FAIMIABV Lisboa	AF – INVESTIMENTOS, Fundos Mobiliários, S.A.
Fipor Poupança Investimento	AF – INVESTIMENTOS, Fundos Mobiliários, S.A.
Luso – Acções	BCI – Sociedade Gestora de Fundos de Investimento Mobiliário, S.A./SANTANDER – Sociedade Gestora de Fundos de Investimento Mobiliário, S.A.
Luso – Capital	BCI – Sociedade Gestora de Fundos de Investimento Mobiliário, S.A./SANTANDER – Sociedade Gestora de Fundos de Investimento Mobiliário, S.A.
M Acções Portugal	M FUNDOS – Gestora de Fundos de Investimento Mobiliário, S.A./ MELLO ACTIVOS FINANCEIROS - Gestora de Fundos de Investimento Mobiliário, S.A.
M Capital	M FUNDOS – Gestora de Fundos de Investimento Mobiliário, S.A./ MELLO ACTIVOS FINANCEIROS - Gestora de Fundos de Investimento Mobiliário, S.A.
MG Acções	MG FUNDOS – Sociedade Gestora de Investimento Mobiliário, S.A.
Novo - Fundo Capital	AF – INVESTIMENTOS, Fundos Mobiliários, S.A.
Portugal Acções	DB FUNDOS – Sociedade Gestora de Fundos de Investimento Mobiliário, S.A.
PPA Atlântico	AF – INVESTIMENTOS, Fundos Mobiliários, S.A.
PPA BCP-FPA	AF – INVESTIMENTOS, Fundos Mobiliários, S.A.
PPA Grupo BFE/PPA Grupo BPI	BPI FUNDOS – Gestão de Fundos de Investimento Mobiliário, S.A.
Sotto PPA	PLURIFUNDOS – Sociedade Gestora de Fundos de Investimento Mobiliário, S.A.
Totta Acções	TOTTA Fundos, S.A.
Unicapital	TOTTA Fundos, S.A.

APPENDIX 2: QUARTER BY QUARTER HERDING

Table A2.1 Quarter by quarter herding levels

Number of funds trading in the period	1998				1999				2000			
	1st	2nd	3rd	4th	1st	2nd	3rd	4th	1st	2nd	3rd	4th
$n \geq 1$	11.14[a]	7.48[b]	15.91[a]	10.51[a]	8.67[a]	7.33[b]	13.25[a]	6.88	9.88[a]	19.13[a]	13.58[a]	14.71[a]
Number of stock-quarters	826	749	738	705	670	641	696	684	679	654	592	356
$n \geq 2$	2.44[a]	8.41[b]	17.60[a]	11.35[a]	9.72[a]	8.13[b]	14.40[a]	7.08	11.00[a]	19.34[a]	15.99[a]	15.96[a]
Number of stock-quarters	820	745	733	702	664	636	694	682	673	653	584	353
$n \geq 5$	0.05[a]	10.78[a]	17.26[a]	11.92[b]	11.60[a]	11.51[a]	15.19[a]	9.82[a]	11.19[a]	22.19[a]	19.03[a]	14.06[a]
Number of stock-quarters	800	722	707	673	633	605	679	661	659	624	558	313
$n \geq 10$	12.30[a]	11.28[a]	20.81[a]	8.21[b]	14.98[a]	9.07[b]	17.34[a]	11.06[b]	12.02[a]	22.55[a]	18.03[a]	8.73
Number of stock-quarters	753	652	603	595	564	550	562	573	577	543	494	270
$n \geq 15$	9.60[a]	12.59[a]	19.26[a]	6.76	11.46[a]	13.02[a]	16.37[a]	9.84[b]	14.06[a]	20.23[a]	16.18[a]	15.28[b]
Number of stock-quarters	637	516	527	452	469	409	497	490	506	480	449	175
$5 > n \geq 2$	26.15[a]	−7.81	19.29[b]	6.60	−3.33	−5.00	6.25	−8.59	−6.48	9.66	5.21	18.60[a]
Number of stock-quarters	20	23	26	29	31	31	15	21	14	29	26	40
$10 > n \geq 5$	−4.01	9.00	4.61	22.51[b]	1.41	19.14	11.94	7.01	6.72	7.70	9.03	31.28[b]
Number of stock-quarters	47	70	104	78	69	55	117	88	82	81	64	43
$15 > n \geq 10$	18.64[b]	8.82	24.79	10.48	23.94[a]	3.61	20.32[b]	14.71	2.49	27.79[a]	26.85[a]	−4.44
Number of stock-quarters	116	136	76	143	95	141	65	83	71	63	45	95

Notes: The table reports quarter by quarter Lakonishok, Schleifer, Thaler and Vishny (1992) herding measures for a sample of 32 Portuguese mutual funds. The herding statistic for a given stock-quarter is defined as $|p(i, t) - p(t)| - E|p(i, t) - p(t)|$, where $p(i, t)$ is the proportion of funds trading stock i during quarter t that are buyers and $p(t)$ is the average of $p(i, t)$ over all stocks i in quarter t. $E|p(i, t) - p(t)|$ is the adjustment factor calculated using a binomial distribution under the hypothesis of no herding. n is the number of funds required to trade a stock in each quarter we use to compute the herding measure. The herding measures are computed in each stock-quarter and then averaged over the constituents of each group. The number of stock-quarters in each subgroup is in parentheses. [a] indicates statistical significance at the 1% level; [b] indicates statistical significance at the 5% level.

Table A2.2 Quarter by quarter buy and sell herding levels in 1998

Number of funds trading in the period	Quarter							
	1st		2nd		3rd		4th	
	Buy	Sell	Buy	Sell	Buy	Sell	Buy	Sell
$n \geq 1$	14.15[a]	8.34[b]	5.55	9.86	22.10[a]	11.84[a]	9.18	11.92[a]
Number of stock-quarters	423	403	421	328	363	375	427	278
$n \geq 2$	15.85[a]	9.52[b]	6.32	11.27[b]	23.25[a]	13.89[a]	7.03	16.50[a]
Number of stock-quarters	379	441	444	301	361	372	427	275
$n \geq 5$	13.35[a]	7.17	10.32[b]	11.32	20.22[a]	15.20[a]	9.63	14.31[a]
Number of stock-quarters	386	414	391	331	353	354	361	312
$n \geq 10$	15.52[a]	9.40[b]	11.81[b]	10.68	26.78[a]	16.60[a]	2.14	16.44[a]
Number of stock-quarters	355	398	347	305	263	340	349	246
$n \geq 15$	12.48[b]	7.10	10.78	14.93[b]	28.19[a]	13.51[b]	6.45	7.04
Number of stock-quarters	302	335	291	225	214	313	208	244
$5 > n \geq 2$	18.97[b]	35.71	−15.63	0.00	41.44[b]	8.22	6.67	6.55
Number of stock-quarters	10	10	11	12	8	18	12	17
$10 > n \geq 5$	−6.11	−2.43	5.80	13.78	−0.12	6.97	23.96	21.06
Number of stock-quarters	20	27	44	26	34	70	41	37
$15 > n \geq 10$	15.41	23.49	15.11	3.58	39.25	17.55	3.43	17.52
Number of stock-quarters	70	46	60	76	27	49	73	70

Notes: The table reports quarter by quarter Lakonishok, Schleifer, Thaler and Vishny (1992) herding measures for a sample of Portuguese mutual funds in 1998 segregated by purchases and sales. The herding statistic for a given stock-quarter is defined as $|p(i, t) - p(t)| - E|p(i, t) - p(t)|$, where $p(i, t)$ is the proportion of funds trading stock i during quarter t that are buyers and $p(t)$ is the average of $p(i, t)$ over all stocks i in quarter t. $E|p(i, t) - p(t)|$ is the adjustment factor calculated using a binomial distribution under the hypothesis of no herding. Buy herding stock-quarters are those where $p(i, t) > p(t)$, that is, the proportion of buyers was greater than the expected proportion of buyers and likewise sell stock-quarters are those where $p(i, t) < p(t)$ meaning the proportion of sellers was greater than the expected proportion of sellers. n is the number of funds required to trade a stock in each quarter we use to compute the herding measure. The herding measures are computed in each stock-quarter and then averaged over the constituents of each group. The number of stock-quarters in each subgroup is in parentheses. [a] indicates statistical significance at the 1% level; [b] indicates statistical significance at the 5% level.

Table A2.3 Quarter by quarter buy and sell herding levels in 1999

Number of funds trading in the period	Quarter							
	1st		2nd		3rd		4th	
	Buy	Sell	Buy	Sell	Buy	Sell	Buy	Sell
$n \geq 1$	8.78	8.56[b]	4.46	10.42[b]	12.61[b]	13.78[a]	7.56	6.31
Number of stock-quarters.	395	275	336	305	344	352	312	372
$n \geq 2$	9.80	9.63[b]	3.89	12.92[b]	12.14	16.25[a]	4.57	9.50[b]
Number of stock-quarters	392	272	334	302	326	368	340	342
$n \geq 5$	19.52[a]	5.74	10.39	12.58[b]	14.41[b]	15.79[a]	11.64[a]	8.23
Number of stock-quarters	268	365	302	303	295	384	352	309
$n \geq 10$	21.90[a]	9.69	4.68	14.09[b]	21.55[b]	14.62[a]	15.14[b]	8.00
Number of stock-quarters	242	322	297	253	236	326	263	310
$n \geq 15$	16.88[b]	6.94	16.00	10.64	18.87	14.63[a]	14.96	6.00
Number of stock-quarters	207	262	181	228	213	284	228	262
$5 > n \geq 2$	−13.33	6.67	−12.50	6.25	0.00	10.42	−9.38	34.38
Number of stock-quarters	15	16	19	12	6	9	11	6
$10 > n \geq 5$	11.72	−5.47	15.35	23.88	5.11	18.78[a]	12.99	3.02
Number of stock-quarters	26	43	29	26	59	58	36	52
$15 > n \geq 10$	37.68[b]	15.70	−6.59	24.03[b]	32.70	14.12	15.68	13.98
Number of stock-quarters	35	60	97	44	23	42	35	48

Notes: The table reports quarter by quarter Lakonishok, Schleifer, Thaler and Vishny (1992) herding measures for a sample of Portuguese mutual funds in 1999 segregated by purchases and sales. The herding statistic for a given stock-quarter is defined as $|p(i, t) - p(t)| - E|p(i, t) - p(t)|$, where $p(i, t)$ is the proportion of funds trading stock i during quarter t that are buyers and $p(t)$ is the average of $p(i, t)$ over all stocks i in quarter t. $E|p(i, t) - p(t)|$ is the adjustment factor calculated using a binomial distribution under the hypothesis of no herding. Buy herding stock-quarters are those where $p(i, t) > p(t)$, that is, the proportion of buyers was greater than the expected proportion of buyers and likewise sell stock-quarters are those where $p(i, t) < p(t)$ meaning the proportion of sellers was greater than the expected proportion of sellers. n is the number of funds required to trade a stock in each quarter we use to compute the herding measure. The herding measures are computed in each stock-quarter and then averaged over the constituents of each group. The number of stock-quarters in each subgroup is in parentheses. [a] indicates statistical significance at the 1% level; [b] indicates statistical significance at the 5% level.

Table A2.4 Quarter by quarter buy and sell herding levels in 2000

Number of funds trading in the period	Quarter							
	1st		2nd		3rd		4th	
	Buy	Sell	Buy	Sell	Buy	Sell	Buy	Sell
$n \geq 1$	12.11[b]	8.17[b]	20.89[b]	17.56[a]	17.27[b]	10.29	14.23[b]	15.24[a]
Number of stock-quarters	298	381	379	275	326	266	220	136
$n \geq 2$	11.62	10.51[a]	22.69[a]	16.47[a]	14.41[b]	17.79[a]	12.44[b]	20.06[a]
Number of stock-quarters	300	373	378	275	365	219	207	146
$n \geq 5$	16.19[b]	7.99	20.93[a]	23.51[a]	22.90[a]	15.38[b]	12.34[b]	16.26
Number of stock-quarters	235	424	407	217	313	245	187	126
$n \geq 10$	9.72	13.89[a]	19.81[a]	25.97[a]	16.51[a]	20.32[b]	6.28	12.09
Number of stock-quarters	252	325	317	226	301	193	164	106
$n \geq 15$	11.96	15.68[b]	23.12[a]	17.35	22.02[a]	10.87	11.73[a]	21.50
Number of stock-quarters	218	288	244[b]	236	210	239	111	64
$5 > n \geq 2$	18.06	−11.39[a]	31.25	5.21	−1.67	12.08	11.90	25.30[a]
Number of stock-quarters	3	11	10	17	12	14	20	20
$10 > n \geq 5$	13.16	0.27	8.38	7.36	−3.46	27.77[a]	34.86	27.70[b]
Number of stock-quarters	46	36	25	56	37	27	23	20
$15 > n \geq 10$	15.23	−3.88	31.45[b]	25.36[b]	26.43	27.28	−7.73	−1.16
Number of stock-quarters	27	44	27	36	23	22	51	44

Notes: The table reports quarter by quarter Lakonishok, Schleifer, Thaler and Vishny (1992) herding measures for a sample of Portuguese mutual funds in 2000 segregated by purchases and sales. The herding statistic for a given stock-quarter is defined as $|p(i, t) - p(t)| - E|p(i, t) - p(t)|$, where $p(i, t)$ is the proportion of funds trading stock i during quarter t that are buyers and $p(t)$ is the average of $p(i, t)$ over all stocks i in quarter t. $E|p(i, t) - p(t)|$ is the adjustment factor calculated using a binomial distribution under the hypothesis of no herding. Buy herding stock-quarters are those where $p(i, t) > p(t)$, that is, the proportion of buyers was greater than the expected proportion of buyers and likewise sell stock-quarters are those where $p(i, t) < p(t)$ meaning the proportion of sellers was greater than the expected proportion of sellers. n is the number of funds required to trade a stock in each quarter we use to compute the herding measure. The herding measures are computed in each stock-quarter and then averaged over the constituents of each group. The number of stock-quarters in each subgroup is in parentheses. [a] indicates statistical significance at the 1% level; [b] indicates statistical significance at the 5% level.

Table A2.5 Quarter by quarter herding levels segregated by fund size

Fund size	1998				1999				2000			
	1st	2nd	3rd	4th	1st	2nd	3rd	4th	1st	2nd	3rd	4th
Quintile 1 (small)	1.00	3.48	−1.43	−11.36	2.82	1.68	−0.93	0.04	−0.61	2.82	9.34[a]	0.91
Number of stock-quarters	142	102	80	75	95	77	92	94	120	97	92	63
Quintile 2	−3.91	0.14	5.80[b]	4.77	−1.47	1.17	5.81	−1.06	−2.11	9.84[a]	1.95	5.41
Number of stock-quarters	171	184	147	154	94	80	88	93	136	134	123	93
Quintile 3	0.43	−1.36	2.20	3.09	1.58	4.97	2.17	4.32	−4.27	5.18	3.85	1.01
Number of stock-quarters	177	183	226	232	216	172	175	164	188	174	142	95
Quintile 4	7.63[b]	3.07	0.98	−2.92	−0.11	−2.76	4.26[b]	−0.69	1.32	14.62[b]	4.44	−1.19
Number of stock-quarters	140	97	121	96	113	99	100	111	116	113	120	39
Quintile 5 (large)	0.96	−5.01	3.80	3.37	−1.08	0.00	−1.57	−3.20	−2.82	4.81	−2.59	−1.31
Number of stock-quarters	196	183	164	148	100	96	105	94	119	136	115	66

Notes: The table reports quarter by quarter Lakonishok, Schleifer, Thaler and Vishny (1992) herding measures for a sample of Portuguese mutual funds segregated by fund size. Size is measured by total assets under management. Each quintile is formed on the basis of the size of the fund during the quarter prior to the herding measure quarter. Quintiles are recalculated every year. The herding statistic for a given stock-quarter is defined as $|p(i, t) - p(t)| - E|p(i, t) - p(t)|$, where $p(i, t)$ is the proportion of funds trading stock i during quarter t that are buyers and $p(t)$ is the average of $p(i, t)$ over all stocks i in quarter t. $E|p(i, t) - p(t)|$ is the adjustment factor calculated using a binomial distribution under the hypothesis of no herding. The herding measures $|p(i, t) - p(t)| - E|p(i, t) - p(t)|$ are averaged separately over stock-quarters belonging to different fund size quintiles. In each stock-period the funds of the sample were divided R times into 5 with a remainder of S. Then the qth quintile contains R observations, except the third quintile which contains $R + S$ observations. We impose no minimum requirement on the number of funds trading a stock in each period. The herding measures are computed in each stock-quarter and then averaged over the constituents of each group. The number of stock-quarters in each subgroup is in parentheses. [a] indicates statistical significance at the 1% level; [b] indicates statistical significance at the 5% level.

Table A2.6 Quarter by quarter herding levels segregated by fund portfolio holdings

Fund portfolio holdings	1998				1999				2000			
	1st	2nd	3rd	4th	1st	2nd	3rd	4th	1st	2nd	3rd	4th
Quintile 1 (less stocks)	5.28[b]	6.81[b]	2.83	−0.66	−3.05	5.11	2.54	4.48	−2.61	6.12[b]	−4.31	3.49
Number of stock-quarters	196	177	172	182	120	107	106	109	118	110	129	105
Quintile 2	2.62	7.12[b]	9.12[a]	0.70	15.94[a]	9.07[a]	10.78[a]	11.15[a]	11.89[a]	10.61[a]	10.63[a]	−0.77
Number of stock-quarters	144	145	125	86	127	116	116	114	133	124	98	36
Quintile 3	−0.77	6.85[b]	7.53[b]	1.31	7.05[b]	2.73	1.21	−0.52	7.14[b]	15.54[a]	9.81[a]	1.41
Number of stock-quarters	198	190	196	211	167	113	138	144	199	184	154	56
Quintile 4	0.74	5.21[b]	3.33	−0.46	−1.38	−1.19	−5.38[b]	2.22	1.02	5.05	4.46	1.61
Number of stock-quarters	137	77	94	113	92	81	92	94	122	139	127	80
Quintile 5 (more stocks)	−0.37	−7.00	1.09	−2.51	−0.97	−4.31	0.46	−2.07	7.40[a]	6.86[b]	12.04[a]	6.52[a]
Number of stock-quarters	151	160	151	113	112	107	108	95	107	97	84	79

Notes: The table reports quarter by quarter Lakonishok, Schleifer, Thaler and Vishny (1992) herding measures for a sample of Portuguese mutual funds segregated by fund portfolio holdings. Portfolio holdings are measured by the percentage of stocks in the fund portfolio. Each quintile is formed on the basis of the holdings of the fund during the quarter prior to the herding measure quarter. Quintiles are recalculated every year. The herding statistic for a given stock-quarter is defined as $|p(i, t) - p(t)| - E|p(i, t) - p(t)|$, where $p(i, t)$ is the proportion of funds trading stock i during quarter t that are buyers and $p(t)$ is the average of $p(i, t)$ over all stocks i in quarter t. $E|p(i, t) - p(t)|$ is the adjustment factor calculated using a binomial distribution under the hypothesis of no herding. The herding measures $|p(i, t) - p(t)| - E|p(i, t) - p(t)|$ are averaged separately over stock-quarters belonging to different fund size quintiles. In each stock-period the funds of the sample were divided R times into 5 with a remainder of S. Then the qth quintile contains R observations, except the third quintile which contains $R + S$ observations. We impose no minimum requirement on the number of funds trading a stock in each period. The herding measures are computed in each stock-quarter and then averaged over the constituents of each group. The number of stock-quarters in each subgroup is in parentheses. [a] indicates statistical significance at the 1% level; [b] indicates statistical significance at the 5% level.

Table A2.7 Quarter by quarter herding levels segregated by frequency in portfolio rebalancing

Portfolio rebalancing	1998				1999				2000			
	1st	2nd	3rd	4th	1st	2nd	3rd	4th	1st	2nd	3rd	4th
Quintile 1 (more frequent portfolio rebalancing)	2.84	5.71[b]	0.65	0.88	0.18	−5.80[b]	−4.00	−0.41	2.97	7.58[b]	9.09[a]	5.88
Number of stock-quarters	131	127	118	86	114	99	114	111	245	239	220	211
Quintile 2	1.63	8.04[a]	6.98[b]	3.17	3.21	−4.12[b]	−5.14[a]	2.47	1.18	8.16[a]	10.60[a]	5.22
Number of stock-quarters	142	141	90	79	111	63	75	76	126	132	121	115
Quintile 3	1.11	1.49	2.66	−0.01	4.74	−0.94	2.12	7.31[b]	1.80	8.98[a]	10.91[a]	9.56[a]
Number of stock-quarters	245	181	174	183	144	134	145	138	199	172	163	86
Quintile 4	8.24[a]	2.17	7.27[b]	−0.12	1.09	−0.34	3.41	−1.02	4.72	20.80[a]	6.85[b]	−5.19[b]
Number of stock-quarters	150	158	125	145	137	133	138	126	153	148	146	37
Quintile 5 (less frequent portfolio rebalancing)	1.34	−3.50	−2.41	1.61	2.47	7.23[b]	2.14	2.65	3.13	5.13	1.14	0.60
Number of stock-quarters	125	108	96	104	143	124	125	134	82	95	63	22

Notes: The table reports quarter by quarter Lakonishok, Schleifer, Thaler and Vishny (1992) herding measures for a sample of 32 Portuguese mutual funds segregated by portfolio rebalancing frequency. Portfolio rebalancing frequency is defined as $(X^1_{t,A} - X^1_{t-1,A})^2/[(X^1_{t,A} + X^1_{t-1,A})/2]^2$ where $X^1_{t,A}$ represents the number of company A stocks that fund 1 holds on quarter t. The rebalancing frequency is the average of the statistic calculated over the stocks held by the fund in a particular quarter. The value of the statistic increases when portfolio rebalancing is less frequent. Each quintile is formed on the basis of the frequency statistic of the fund during the quarter prior to the herding measure quarter except for the year 1998 that we used the first quarter of 1998. Quintiles are recalculated every year. The herding statistic for a given stock-quarter is defined as $|p(i,t) - p(t)| - E|p(i,t) - p(t)|$, where $p(i,t)$ is the proportion of funds trading stock i during quarter t that are buyers and $p(t)$ is the average of $p(i,t)$ over all stocks i in quarter t. $E|p(i,t) - p(t)|$ is the adjustment factor calculated using a binomial distribution under the hypothesis of no herding. The herding measures $|p(i,t) - p(t)| - E|p(i,t) - p(t)|$ are averaged separately over stock-quarters belonging to different fund size quintiles. In each stock-period the funds of the sample were divided R times into 5 with a remainder of S. Then the qth quintile contains R observations, except the third quintile which contains $R + S$ observations. We impose no minimum requirement on the number of funds trading a stock in each period. The herding measures are computed in each stock-quarter and then averaged over the constituents of each group. The number of stock-quarters in each subgroup is in parentheses. [a] indicates statistical significance at the 1% level; [b] indicates statistical significance at the 5% level.

NOTES

1. Lakonishok *et al.* (1992) note that empirical evidence that shows that herding by institutional investors impacts prices, does not imply necessarily that herding causes volatility. If, for example, institutional investors are better informed than individual investors, their trading could drive market prices close to the assets' intrinsic values (see, for example, Froot, Scharfstein and Stein, 1992; Bikhchandani, Hirshleifer and Welch, 1992; Hirshleifer, Subrahmanyam and Titman, 1994; Wermers, 1999).
2. The notion that managers and investors are influenced by others has interested economists for some time. Keynes (1936) suggested that investors behave as judges in beauty contests: instead of truly judging the beauty of each contestant, they decide upon their expectation of how the other members of the jury will vote.
3. For example, one possible implication of informational cascades models is that, in stockmarkets that exhibit poorer aggregation of information and where the precision of the public pool of information is lower, the likelihood of departing from a pool should be higher (see, for example, Bikhchandani, Hirshleifer and Welch, 1992; Cao and Hirshleifer, 1997).
4. Grinblatt and Titman (1989) and Grinblatt, Titman and Wermers (1995) show that there is a strong relation between the frequency of portfolio rebalancing and momentum strategies. Funds with higher frequency in rebalancing may thus exhibit correlation in trades (spurious herding).
5. Additionally, if mutual funds share higher aversion to stocks with high risk than other investors, then when the market is down, they should trade together reflecting their willingness to lower the risk in their portfolio.
6. During the period from 1997 to 2001, the standard deviation of the Portuguese stockmarket was 24 percent against 18 percent in the USA and the UK (based on monthly returns of the MSCI country indices).
7. The probability density function of the binomial distribution is given by $b[N(i, t), B(i, t), p(t)] = \binom{N(i,t)}{B(i,t)} p(t)^{B(i,t)}[1 - p(t)]^{[N(i,t)-B(i,t)]}$, where $N(i, t)$ is the number of funds trading the stock i during quarter t. $B(i, t)$ and $p(t)$ are defined above.
8. The adjustment factor $AF(i, t)$ and $p(t)$ are computed accordingly, for that subset of stock-quarters.
9. See, for example, Grinblatt and Titman (1995) and Wermers (1999). Previous research has shown that the impact of survival bias on performance (Grinblatt and Titman, 1989; Brown and Goetzmann, 1995) and herding (Wermers, 1999; Wylie, 2000) is trivial.
10. Around that date, the average fund in the UK and in the USA managed, respectively, 175 and 475 million euros.
11. Given that the Portuguese mutual fund industry is concentrated in the hands of a few companies, the upward bias referred above may be severe. To avoid that bias, we could compute the herding measures looking at the aggregate holdings of funds within the same asset management company and measure herding across different management companies. We do not compute those statistics here because of the limited number of asset management companies in our sample.
12. Each quintile has the same number of observations, R, except for the third quintile that has $R + S$ observations.
13. In 1990, 1995 and 1998, total net assets in management accounted for, respectively, 1,897, 10,639 and 24,087 million euros.

14. The difference between herding on purchase and herding on sales is significant at a 1 percent significance level except when the hurdle of the number of funds is set above ten funds.
15. PSI20 stands for the Portuguese Stock Market Index that includes the 20 largest (and more liquid) stocks listed on the Portuguese Stock Exchange.

REFERENCES

Banerjee, A. (1992) "A Simple Model of Herd Behavior", *Quarterly Journal of Economics*, 107: 797–818.

Bikhchandani, S., Hirshleifer, D. and Welch, I. (1992) "A Theory of Fads, Fashion, Custom, and Cultural Change as Informational Cascades", *Journal of Political Economy*, 100: 992–1026.

Brown, S.J. and Goetzmann, W.N. (1995) "Performance Persistence", *Journal of Finance*, 50: 679–98.

Cai, F., Kaul, G. and Zheng, L. (2000) "Institutional Trading and Stock Returns", SSRN Working Paper.

Cao, H. and Hirshleifer, D. (1997) "Limited Observability, Reporting Biases and Informational Cascades", Working Paper, Ohio Sate University.

Choe, H., Kho, B. and Stulz, R.M. (1999) "Do Foreign Investors Destabilize Stock Markets? The Korean Experience in 1997", *Journal of Financial Economics*, 54: 227–64.

Froot, K., Scharfstein, D. and Stein, J. (1992) "Herd on the Street: Informational Inefficiencies in a Market with Short-Term Speculation", *Journal of Finance*, 47: 1461–84.

Grinblatt, M. and Titman, S. (1989) "Mutual Fund Performance: An Analysis of Quarterly Portfolio Holdings", *Journal of Business*, 62: 394–415.

Grinblatt, M., Titman, S. and Wermers, R. (1995) "Momentum Investment Strategies, Portfolio Performance, and Herding: A Study of Mutual Fund Behavior", *American Economic Review*, 85: 1088–105.

Hirshleifer, D., Subrahmanyam, A. and Titman, S. (1994) "Security Analysis and Trading Patterns When Some Investors Receive Information Before Others", *Journal of Finance*, 49: 1665–98.

Keynes, J.M. (1936) *The General Theory of Employment, Interest and Money* (London: Macmillan).

Lakonishok, J., Shleifer, A., Thaler, R.H. and Vishny, R.W. (1992) "The Impact of Institutional Trading on Stock Prices", *Journal of Financial Economics*, 20: 23–43.

Scharfstein, D. and Stein, J. (1990) "Herd Behavior and Investment", *American Economic Review*, 80: 465–79.

Wermers, R. (1999) "Mutual Fund Herding and the Impact on Stock Prices", *Journal of Finance*, 54: 581–622.

Wylie, S. (2000) "Fund Manager Herding: Tests of the Accuracy of Measures of Herding Using UK Data", Working Paper, Dartmouth University.

CHAPTER 9

The "Best of Both Worlds" Fund: Exchange Traded Funds in Australia

*Paul U. Ali**

9.1 INTRODUCTION

Exchange Traded Funds (ETFs) are amongst the most popular mutual funds worldwide for both institutional and retail investors. In general, they offer lower fees and greater pricing transparency and liquidity than other mutual funds following the same investment strategies (Bansal and Somani, 2002; Ciccotello, Edelen, Greene and Hodges, 2002; Russel, Shekhar and Malhotra, 2004). ETFs come in a wide range of flavours but, by far, the dominant type of ETF is the passively-managed or index-tracking ETF.

The Australian ETF market remains relatively small compared to more mature North America, European and Japanese markets. Nonetheless, the Australian market displays a similar product diversity to those other markets. The ETFs on offer to Australian investors comprise ETFs that track the two major Australian equity indices, an ETF that tracks the major Australian listed property index and, unique to the Australian and UK markets, an ETF that tracks the gold price. There are, as yet, no bond ETFs in Australia and the listed funds in Australia that have been promoted as actively-managed ETFs are not, in fact, ETFs. As will be seen below, the defining characteristic

* This research was supported by a grant from the Australian Research Council (DP0557673).

Table 9.1 Australian ETFs

Fund	Benchmark	Listing	Manager
streetTRACKS S&P/ ASX 50 Fund	S&P/ASX 50 Index	Australian Stock Exchange (ASX)	State Street Global Advisors (SSGA)
streetTRACKS S&P/ ASX 200 Fund	S&P/ASX 200 Index	ASX	SSGA
streetTRACKS S&P/ ASX 200 Listed Property Fund	S&P/ASX 200 Listed Property Trust Index	ASX	SSGA
Gold Bullion Securities	Gold price (as fixed by the London bullion market)	ASX	World Gold Council Investor Resources Holdings

of the ETF (other than the obvious fact of it being listed on an official exchange) is its dual trading facility. In the absence of that characteristic, one is left with a mutual fund that is no different to other mutual funds that happen to be listed.

ETFs originated in Canada. In 1989, Toronto Index Participations were listed on the Toronto Stock Exchange. However, it was not until ETFs were introduced to the US market did they attract global attention. The first US ETF, known as Spiders or SPDRS (Standard & Poor's Depositary Receipts), was listed on the American Stock Exchange in 1993 and is, today, still the largest ETF by market capitalization. The first Asian ETF was the Tracker Fund of Hong Kong, which was listed on the Hong Kong Stock Exchange in 1999 while, in Australia, the first ETFs, called "streetTRACKS" were listed on the Australian Stock Exchange in 2001 (Ali, Stapledon and Gold, 2003). Table (9.1) summarizes the ETFs currently available to investors in Australia.

This chapter explains the legal structure of ETFs, and also considers the potential application of the anti-delegation rule to index-tracking ETFs under Australian law. This concerns the risk that the selection of portfolio constituents based solely on the composition of an index may be viewed by an Australian court as being inconsistent with the duty of fund trustees and other fiduciary investors to exercise their investment powers personally.

9.2 ETF STRUCTURE

The structural uniqueness of ETFs can be summarized as follows: an ETF is a hybrid mutual fund that features both the in-kind redemption mechanism of the investment trust and the tradability of the listed investment management company. This dual trading structure under which large blocks of interests in an ETF can be created or redeemed and small blocks of those interests can be bought or sold on a stock exchange provides pricing transparency. It also creates significant arbitrage opportunities and means that ETFs, unlike other listed mutual funds, do not generally trade at sustained discounts or premiums to their net asset values. Exchange-listing provides liquidity benefits (Hedge and McDermott, 2004) and, moreover, index-tracking ETFs levy lower fees than other mutual funds that track the same index.

ETFs combine the best structural features of open-end investment trusts and closed-end listed investment companies while also avoiding the key defects of those two common mutual fund structures (Gastineau and Weber, 2000; Fuher, 2001; Gastineau, 2001; Gastineau, 2002b; Ali, Stapledon and Gold, 2003). One may readily characterize an ETF as a best of both worlds fund.

In the case of mutual funds that have been structured as investment trusts, investor entry occurs through the subscription by investors for interests or units in the fund. New units are issued by the trustee of the fund in exchange for a cash contribution by the investor reflecting the then net asset value of the fund. The trustee usually has the discretion to accept investment assets from institutional investors in place of cash, where the investor exchanges securities that fall within the fund's investment mandate for units. Investors exit their positions, not through the sale of their units in a secondary market, but, instead, by having the fund trustee buy back or redeem their units for the then net asset value of the fund.

There are two key defects (Ali, Stapledon and Gold, 2003). First, in contrast to listed investment companies, the units in an unlisted investment trust do not enjoy continuous pricing. Instead, there is only a single, daily price at which investors can enter and exit the investment trust. This is because the net asset value of the trust is typically calculated at the end of each trading day. The second defect concerns the cash management issue. When new units are created, the cash contributions of the investors must be invested by the trustee, leading to transaction costs being incurred. Likewise, when investors exit the trust, the trustee will normally have to realize portfolio securities to finance the redemption of the units (if the mutual fund is either fully invested or its cash buffer is inadequate to cover the redemption), also leading to transaction costs being incurred. In addition, the realization of securities may crystallize a taxable gain that will have to be borne by the remaining investors in the fund.

These two defects are avoided by closed-end investment companies (Ali, Stapledon and Gold, 2003). Shares in the company are listed and, accordingly, the investors have the benefit of continuous pricing. In addition, after the subscription period for shares in the company has closed, investor entry can only be effected via the purchase of shares in the secondary market. Equally, investor exit is effected through the sale of shares, not via the redemption of shares. However, as is the case with other listed securities, the shares in the investment company may trade at significant discounts or premia to their net asset value and the sale and purchase of shares, particularly large parcels of shares, in the company will also be hindered by poor market liquidity.

The dual trading structure common to all true ETFs is designed to overcome these problems (Wiandt and McClatchy, 2002; Ali, Stapledon and Gold, 2003). Interests in an ETF, which typically takes the form of an open-end investment trust, can be bought and sold in the secondary market, in equivalent fashion to the shares in a listed investment company and other listed securities. However, investor entry and exit is not limited to the secondary market. Investors can participate in an ETF by either buying interests in the ETF on-market or by subscribing for new interests. Equally, investors can exit an ETF by selling their interests on-market or by redeeming those interests.

Interests in an ETF can, however, only be created and redeemed in large parcels (effectively limiting this option to institutional investors and high net-worth investors). In addition, the cash option is absent. The creation and redemption of interests are effected through the transfer in and out respectively of securities. An institutional investor can, instead of purchasing interests in an ETF on-market, subscribe for new interests in the ETF by depositing with the trustee of the ETF securities whose composition closely resembles the ETF portfolio and of a value equal to the then net asset value of the ETF. Investors can exit an ETF by selling their interests on-market or by redeeming those interests. In the latter instance, the interests will be cancelled with the investor receiving a pool of securities with a value equal to the then net asset value of the ETF and representing the investor's proportionate interest in the assets of the ETF. Investors cannot redeem their interests for cash. Nor, once the initial subscription period has closed, can investors subscribe for interests in an ETF for cash.

The in-kind redemption of ETF interests means that the ETF avoids incurring a taxable gain on the exit of investors. Further, the alternative to the secondary market offered by ETFs, enables the acquisition and disposal of large parcels of interests in an ETF without being constrained by how liquid the secondary market for those interests is.

This dual trading structure, when combined with the continuous pricing of both interests in the ETF and the ETF's portfolio constituents (typically, listed equity securities, debt securities, LPTs (Listed Property Trusts) or REITs (Real Estate Investment Trusts)), presents significant arbitrage opportunities. This ensures that, unlike the shares in listed investment companies, the listed interests in an ETF will trade close to their net asset value (Ali, Stapledon and Gold, 2003). Spreads between the market price of the listed interests in an ETF and the ETF's net asset value will tend to be eliminated by institutional investors exchanging portfolio constituents for interests in the ETF and selling those interests in the secondary market (where interests in the ETF are trading at a premium to net asset value) or redeeming interests in the ETF for portfolio constituents and selling those constituents (where interests in the ETF are trading at a discount to net asset value).

Most ETFs, as noted above, follow index-tracking strategies. The portfolios of these ETFs are constructed in the same way as the portfolios of other index-tracking mutual funds, namely through the use of sampling or replication techniques (Ali, Stapledon and Gold, 2003). Index-tracking ETFs, due to the factors discussed above, are a more efficient passive investment mechanism than other index-tracking mutual funds (Dellva, 2001; Gastineau, 2002a; Kostovetsky, 2003; Gastineau, 2004). However, irrespective of how the index-tracking objective is achieved, the key attribute of index-tracking funds (whether they track equity, bond or property indices) is that the composition of the portfolio is transparent. That is also the case with commodity-linked ETFs, such as the ASX-listed Gold Bullion Securities that invests only in gold traded in the London bullion market. The lack of portfolio transparency (or rather the disclosure of portfolio constituents) is a major hurdle to the creation of actively-managed ETFs (Securities and Exchange Commission, 2001). To date, actively-managed ETFs have not been implemented in Australia.

9.3 THE ANTI-DELEGATION RULE

It is trite law to state that institutional investors, such as trustees of pension funds and other investment funds, are fiduciaries (Ali, Stapledon and Gold, 2003). This status is attributable to the entrustment to such parties of the investment of assets for the benefit of third parties (for example, the members of a pension fund or the investors in an investment fund). The allocation of assets by an institutional investor to an ETF (or other passively-managed fund) raises the fundamental legal issue of whether that allocation is consistent with the legal requirement imposed upon fiduciaries to exercise their investment powers personally. That requirement is known as the anti-delegation rule.

The issue of compliance with the anti-delegation rule arises each time a party entrusted with the power to invest appoints another party to exercise that power (Ali, Stapledon and Gold, 2003). The delegation can take place directly through the appointment of a fund manager by the institutional investor or indirectly through the allocation of assets to an investment fund (where the investment of the assets is undertaken by the trustee of that fund) or the adoption of an index-tracking strategy (where the institutional investor mimicks the selection of investments by an index compiler). This issue is particularly acute in the context of investments in passively-managed funds such as ETFs and index-tracking strategies. In both instances, it can be contended that the exercise of investment powers has been delegated to the index compiler as the institutional investor is unable to intercede in the selection of index constituents.

As a general principle of Australian trust law, an institutional investor or other fiduciary possessing investment powers cannot delegate the selection of investments to other parties except in two limited circumstances: first, where it is not commercially prudent for the fiduciary, as opposed to its delegate, to exercise the relevant investment power; and, second, where the delegate becomes a co-fiduciary provided that that appointment does not entail a relinquishment of control over the selection of investments by the original fiduciary (Ali, Stapledon and Gold, 2003). The delegation of an investment power outside of these two circumstances is void and the fiduciary will be personally liable to its investors, for any losses incurred as a result of the selection of investments by its delegate.

It is obvious that this constraint on the delegation of investment powers is fundamentally inconsistent with the way in which institutional investors manage their assets. Indeed, the UK Law Commission has gone so far as to state that "[far] from promoting the more conscientious discharge of the obligation of trusteeship, the rule may therefore force trustees to commit breaches of trust in order to achieve the most effective administration of the trust" (Law Commission, 1999).

The anti-delegation rule has been substantially modified by the Australian companies legislation, in the case of trustees and managers of mutual funds, through the introduction of a statutory power of delegation. This statutory power is expressed in sufficiently wide terms (to do anything that the trustee or manager has been authorized to do in connection with the fund) so as to permit a fiduciary to delegate its investment powers through the allocation of assets to an ETF or the adoption of an index-tracking strategy (Ali, Stapledon and Gold, 2003). This legislative updating of the anti-delegation rule which makes it unnecessary to rely upon the two exceptions detailed above is, however, available only in the case of mutual funds. It does not apply to other institutional investors such as the trustees of pension funds.

The legislation that governs pension funds in Australia also includes a statutory power of delegation but there is considerable uncertainty as to the scope of that power (Ali, Stapledon and Gold, 2003). The power, unlike the corresponding power in the Australian companies legislation, simply permits the trustee of a pension fund to engage or appoint other parties to act on its behalf. A narrow reading of this power suggests that it is only competent for the trustee to appoint a delegate to implement investment decisions which have been made by the trustee. The allocation of assets to an ETF or index-tracking strategy would, on this view, fall outside this statutory delegation power. It is questionable even whether a wider reading of the power would assist the trustee, as the delegate must still exercise the investment powers for the trustee, rather than in place of the trustee. That implies, at the very least, the retention by the trustee of some form of supervisory power in relation to the delegate and thus also in relation to the selection of investments by the delegate. In contrast, the more broadly expressed power in the Australian companies legislation, permits the delegate to act in place of the fiduciary. The adoption of an index-tracking strategy necessarily involves the trustee giving up control over the investment of the assets allocated to that strategy. Once assets have been allocated to such a strategy, either via an ETF or otherwise, there is no scope for further involvement by the trustee in the investment process.

9.4 CONCLUSION

ETFs combine the best features of unlisted investment trusts and listed investment companies. Their dual trading structure carries with it significant pricing transparency and liquidity benefits for investors. In addition, ETFs, in general, are less expensive for investors, in terms of management fees, than other mutual funds following the same strategy. Accordingly, it is not surprising that ETFs, since their introduction in Canada in 1989, have evolved into one of the most popular types of mutual fund for both institutional and retail investors.

The majority of ETFs both in Australia and worldwide adopt passive or index-tracking strategies, designed to replicate the returns of equity, bond or listed property indices. These strategies, despite their broad acceptance in the investor community, are not wholly free from legal risk. There is, under Australian law, an element of uncertainty as to whether the adoption of an index-tracking strategy is consistent with the legal duty of pension fund trustees and other non-mutual fund fiduciary investors to exercise their investment powers personally.

REFERENCES

Ali, P.U., Stapledon, G. and Gold, M. (2003) *Corporate Governance and Investment Fiduciaries* (Sydney, Australia: Thomson Legal & Regulatory).

Bansal, V.K. and Somani, A. (2002) "Exchange Traded Funds: Challenge to Traditional Mutual Funds", *Review of Business*, 23(3): 40–3.

Ciccotello, C.S., Edelen, R.M., Greene, J.T. and Hodges, C.W. (2002) "Trading at Stale Prices with Modern Technology: Policy Options for Mutual Funds in the Internet Age", *Virginia Journal of Law and Technology*, 7: 6–98.

Dellva, W. (2001) "Exchange-Traded Funds Not for Everyone", *Journal of Financial Planning*, 14(4): 110–24.

Fuhr, D. (2001) "Exchange-Traded Funds: A Primer", *Journal of Asset Management*, 2(3): 260–73.

Gastineau, G.L. (2001) "Exchange-Traded Funds: An Introduction", *Journal of Portfolio Management*, 27(3): 88–96.

Gastineau, G.L. (2002a) "Equity Index Funds Have Lost Their Way", *Journal of Portfolio Management*, 28(2): 55–64.

Gastineau, G.L. (2002b) *The Exchange-Traded Funds Manual* (Hoboken, NJ: John Wiley & Sons).

Gastineau, G.L. (2004) "The Benchmark Index ETF Performance Problem", *Journal of Portfolio Management*, 30(2): 96–104.

Gastineau, G.L. and Weber, C.J. (2000) "Exchange-Traded Equity Funds – Genesis, Growth and Outlook", in J.C. Francis, W.W. Toy and J.G. Whittaker (eds), *The Handbook of Equity Derivatives* (New York, NY: Revised edition, John Wiley & Sons).

Hedge, S.P. and McDermott, J.B. (2004) "The Market Liquidity of DIAMONDS, Q's and Their Underlying Stocks", *Journal of Banking and Finance*, 28(5): 1043–66.

Kostovetsky, L. (2003) "Index Mutual Funds and Exchange-Traded Funds: A Comparison of Two Methods of Passive Investment", *Journal of Portfolio Management*, 29(4): 80–92.

Law Commission (1999) *Trustees' Powers and Duties* (London: Law Commission).

Russel, P., Shekhar, C. and Malhotra, D. (2004) "Exchange-Traded Funds: Poised to Challenge Index Funds", *Journal of the Securities Institute of Australia*, 3: 27–30.

Securities and Exchange Commission (2001) "Actively Managed Exchange-Traded Funds", *Concept Release*, 17 CFR Part 270, Release No. IC-25258, November 8.

Wiandt, J. and McClatchy, W. (2002). *Exchange Traded Funds: An Insider's Guide to Buying the Market* (Hoboken, NJ: John Wiley & Sons).

CHAPTER 10

The Relative Impact of Different Classification Schemes on Mutual Fund Flows

*Alexei P. Goriaev**

10.1 INTRODUCTION

The US mutual fund industry experienced tremendous growth during the past two decades. In November 2001 there were 8,282 mutual funds controlling over US$6.9 trillion dollars in assets, which by far exceeds 665 funds with US$241.4 billion in assets in 1981 (Investment Company Institute, 2001). With so many funds around, investors face a difficult task of selecting a fund with the desired risk and performance profile. Mutual fund categories composed of funds with a similar investment approach help investors to simplify their decision problem. Investors often first choose the category that suits their preferences and then select the best fund in that category, based on fund performance and/or other fund characteristics (see, for example, Kim, Shukla and Tomas, 2000). This investor behavior results in a specific structure of mutual fund flows, which depends on a fund's relative performance within its category. As a consequence, the classification system

*I would like to thank Theo Nijman, Bas Werker and participants in presentations at the CSEF (University of Salerno), New Economic School, Tilburg University, Vrije Universiteit (Amsterdam), the 2002 ENTER Jamboree conference, and conference on distribution and pricing of delegated portfolio management at the Wharton School, 2002, for their helpful comments and suggestions. The usual disclaimer applies.

also influences the incentives of fund managers, whose compensation is usually based on a percentage of fund assets (see, for example, Khorana, 1996). Given that top performers in a category attract most of the inflows, fund managers have an incentive to maximize their performance relative to other funds in the same category. This may not be consistent with their shareholders' interests.

Currently, there are several coexisting categorization schemes of mutual funds. Traditionally, funds have been classified according to the investment objective declared in their prospectus, such as aggressive growth or growth and income. Along with the increase in the number of funds in 1990s, there appeared evidence that many funds exhibit investment behavior that cannot be characterized by their stated objective (see, for example, Brown and Goetzmann, 1997; diBartolomeo and Witkowski, 1997). In the early 1990s, several mutual fund data vendors such as Morningstar and Lipper introduced a new classification scheme, which was supposed to reflect funds' actual investment style. For example, Morningstar's equity style box is a three-by-three matrix with the division based on the market capitalization and book value of a fund's latest portfolio. As witnessed in a recent Barra Strategic Consulting Group report (2001), "these style-based ranking systems have become well entrenched and highly influential" (p. 6). As one of the examples of this new trend, *Business Week*'s Mutual Fund Scoreboard replaced in 1997 the stated objective classification system with a new one based on Morningstar's style box. Besides the stated objective and style categories, funds are often evaluated within broad investment classes such as diversified stock and international stock. Such an approach is used to compute the widely publicized Morningstar star ratings. The class return rankings are often referred to in the financial press. For instance, the *Wallstreet Journal Europe*'s Fund Scorecard regularly reports 15 leading and 10 lagging performers in the US equity, US bond, and other classes of funds.

Despite the wide use of these classification schemes, little is known about their relative impact on mutual fund flows. In the existing literature on the determinants of fund flows, two types of performance definitions are typically used: (1) in terms of raw or risk-adjusted returns (see, for example, Gruber, 1996), and (2) in terms of rankings within a stated objective category (see, for example, Sirri and Tufano, 1998). All these studies find a clear positive relationship between fund flows and their past performance. Moreover, this relationship appears to be convex, for example, the flow-performance sensitivity is higher for well-performing funds than for poorly performing funds (see, for example, Chevalier and Ellison, 1997; Sirri and Tufano, 1998). The lag structure of the flow–performance relationship is also nonlinear, with performance from six to eight months ago having the highest impact on current flows (see Goriaev, Nijman and Werker, 2001). Obviously, the use of raw or risk-adjusted returns ignores the effects of relative performance on fund flows. An alternative approach considers only the rankings based on the stated objective categorization scheme, assuming that investors only compare funds with the same investment objective. I would like to argue that ignoring the impact of alternative classification schemes on mutual fund flows, we are potentially missing important insights about investor behavior and the resulting incentives of fund managers.

In this chapter I analyse the relationship between fund flows and their past relative performance with respect to different classification schemes. Specifically, I define a fund's relative performance as the (normalized) performance rank within three types of categories: funds with the same stated objective, funds with the same Morningstar style, and funds within the same asset class. My primary goal is to disentangle the impact of fund relative performance on flows into the components corresponding to these stated objective, Morningstar style, and asset class. This will allow us to learn which mutual fund classification schemes are more important for investors. This information will be relevant for managers who would like to know with which funds they should compete for investors' money. In addition, I investigate the relative impact of cardinal and ordinal performance measures on fund flows. This is important for determining whether fund managers are more interested in maximizing fund return or return rankings.

A related strand of literature analyses the relationship between flows and performance on the level of fund family. It has been demonstrated that consumers invest more money in fund families with a star performer and fund families with higher average performance (see, for example, Ivkovic, 2000). Moreover, Nanda, Wang and Zheng (2000) find that top performance helps to boost flows not only to a star fund, but also to the other funds in the family. In this chapter I study the star spillover effect in more detail. In particular, I investigate whether this effect differs across the family funds depending on their category (for example, stated objective, Morningstar style, or asset class) and category of a star fund. The disentangling of the star spillover effect is important, since top performance of a star fund could actually "cannibalize" flows to the other funds in its family that have a similar investment approach, while boosting flows to the remaining funds in the family. In my analysis, I disentangle the flow spillover effect from a star fund to the other funds in the family into components corresponding to funds with the same stated objective, funds with the same Morningstar style, and funds in the same asset class as the star fund.

My empirical results are based on the sample of US mutual funds belonging to one of four asset classes (domestic stock, international stock, taxable bond, and municipal bond) during the period from January 1993 (January 1994 for bond funds) to March 1999. In my main model, I analyse how monthly flows are influenced by the funds' normalized rankings based on the raw return over the last three years within the stated objective, Morningstar style, and asset class categories. I strongly reject the traditional specification, where relative performance is defined only with respect to the stated objective category. In all four fund classes, the Morningstar style and asset class rankings have both economically and statistically significant impact on fund flows on top of the impact of the stated objective rankings. With the only exception for international stock funds, the asset class ranking appears to be the most important relative performance measure for investors. It accounts for 58 percent of the total impact of relative performance on fund flows in the domestic stock class, and about 80 percent and 86 percent in the taxable bond and municipal bond classes. Apparently, investors of these funds most often consider the asset class as a peer group for performance evaluation. Flows to domestic stock funds are also significantly related to their stated objective and Morningstar style rankings, which account for 28 percent and 14 percent of the total impact, respectively. The importance of the Morningstar style ranking is increasing over time, which reflects the growing interest to the Morningstar classification in the media as well as in the academic and applied literature (see, for example, Bogle, 1998; Davis, 2001). The stated objective and Morningstar style classification systems are especially important for institutional investors of domestic stock funds, who pay hardly any attention to the fund asset class rankings. In contrast, the differences between funds' objectives and styles do not play a large role for investors of taxable bond and municipal bond funds. The Morningstar style ranking accounts for about 10 percent of the total impact of relative performance on flows into bond funds, while the impact of the stated objective ranking is even smaller. Investors of international stock funds have a different hierarchy of the classification schemes, with 57 percent of the total impact of relative performance on flows due to the stated objective ranking and most of the remaining impact due to the asset class ranking. In contrast to the other asset classes, international stock funds are designed primarily for foreign investment and their region-based objectives are clearly defined. This may explain why the stated objective rankings of international stock funds appear reliable to their investors.

In a joint model of ordinal and cardinal performance measures, the impact of total return on fund flows never exceeds the combined impact of performance rankings. The ordinal measures of performance are especially important for investors of stock funds. In the domestic stock and international stock classes, the total impact of performance rankings on flows is approximately five times larger than the impact of raw returns. This implies that investors prefer to select funds that not only have good performance, but also outperform their competitors. Such investor behavior creates strong incentives for fund managers to maximize their category rankings, which however may be inconsistent with the interests of fund shareholders.

The main model specification is extended to examine the star spillover effect in detail. I find that strong performance of a star fund (fund with the return over the last three years belonging to top 5 percent within its asset class) usually has a positive spillover effect on flows to the other funds in its family. For example, domestic stock nonstar funds from star families attract about 3.6 percent additional expected flows per year. In the municipal bond class, the flow spillover effect seems to be limited to funds with a similar investment approach (same Morningstar style or stated objective) as the star fund, which enjoy extra flows ranging from 2 percent to 5 percent per year. In the taxable bond class, the presence of a star fund is beneficial for flows to funds with the same stated objective as the star fund and detrimental for flows to funds with the same Morningstar style as the star fund, leading to the inflows of 6 percent and outflows of 4.5 percent per year, respectively. Naturally, star funds benefit the most from their stellar performance attracting as much as 18 percent extra flows in the domestic stock and municipal bond classes and about 9 percent extra flows in the taxable bond class. In the international stock class, I find no significant star spillover effect.

The structure of the chapter is as follows. Sections 10.2 and 10.3 describe the data-set and the methodology, respectively. Section 10.4 presents the results concerning the relationship between fund flows and relative performance defined only with respect to the stated objective category. The results on the dependence of fund flows on performance rankings based on different classification schemes are discussed in section 10.5. In section 10.6, I investigate the relative impact of cardinal and ordinal measures of performance on fund flows. Section 10.7 is devoted to the category-specific analysis of the star spillover effect. In section 10.8, I conclude and discuss the implications of my research.

10.2 DATA DESCRIPTION

In my empirical analysis, I use a merged data-set taken from two sources: Micropal and Morningstar (April 1999 Principia Pro Data Disk). The former data set contains monthly total net asset values of US mutual funds in January 1991 – March 1999, while the latter provides fund monthly returns in January 1970 – March 1999, inception date, annual equity and fixed-income style box classifications in 1992–99, annual expense ratio and turnover rate in 1970–99, and various fund characteristics (for example, family indicator, front and deferred loads, 12b1 fees, manager tenure, minimum investment requirements, etc.) as of April 1999. (12b1 fees are extra fees mutual funds charge to cover marketing, advertising, and promotional expenses.) The merged data-set contains 9,277 funds, which constitute approximately 87 percent funds covered by Morningstar in April 1999.

Currently, Morningstar classifies mutual funds into four investment classes: domestic stock, international stock, taxable bond, and municipal bond (money market funds are not included in the Morningstar's database). As the flow-performance relationship is potentially different in the four classes, I estimate each model separately in the four samples corresponding to the fund classes. Since the domestic stock class is the largest and the most studied so far, it receives most of the attention in the discussion of the results. Since Morningstar started its style-box classification in 1992, I take January 1993 – March 1999 as the sample period for domestic stock and international stock funds.[1] However, only a few bond funds have fixed-income style data in 1992. Therefore, the sample period for taxable bond and municipal bond funds is from January 1994 to March 1999. Since I use a three-year period to evaluate fund performance, my analysis is restricted to the funds with at least three years of returns history. In order to reduce the impact of the typos and mergers, I exclude from my sample 1 percent of the outliers based on net relative flows (0.5 percent of the outliers with the largest positive flows and 0.5 percent of the outliers with the largest negative flows). The funds closed to the public and funds without Morningstar style data[2] are also excluded from the sample. In all regressions, flows are annualized to make my results comparable with the existing evidence.

It should be noted that my data-set contains only the funds that survived till April 1999 and is survivorship-biased. However, it is straightforward to show that this does not affect the consistency of OLS or WLS estimates, if past flows do not influence the probability of fund survival in a joint regression with returns. This assumption is in accordance with the empirical findings in Brown and Goetzmann (1995). Not surprisingly, Chevalier and Ellison (1997), Goetzmann and Peles (1997) and Sirri and Tufano (1998) find the same results in survivorship-biased and unbiased samples.

In order to illustrate the relation between the stated objective and Morningstar-style classification schemes, Table 10.1 presents the composition of the respective categories in the domestic stock class. It shows the number of fund-month observations with a given stated objective and Morningstar equity style accumulated over the sample period. Domestic stock funds fall into one of five diversified stock objective categories (aggressive growth, growth, growth and income, equity-income, and small company), eight specialty stock objective categories (health, financial, natural resources, precious metals, technology, utility, real estate, and communications), and four hybrid objective categories (asset allocation, balanced, convertibles, and multi-asset global). These funds also belong to one of nine Morningstar equity-style categories, which group funds on the basis of the market capitalization and growth potential of their portfolios (see the Appendix for the definition of the Morningstar styles).

Table 10.1 demonstrates that the objective and style classifications are not independent. For instance, about 75 percent of aggressive growth funds follow small and medium growth styles, while most of the funds with more conservative objectives (such as, balanced and equity-income) are concentrated in the large value and large blend style categories. However, the dispersion in styles among the funds from the same objective category is quite high, which is consistent with the existing evidence on misclassification of

Table 10.1 Composition of the stated objective and Morningstar style categories of US domestic stock funds

Objective/Style	Large value	Large blend	Large growth	Medium value	Medium blend	Medium growth	Small value	Small blend	Small growth
Aggressive growth	52	84	420	19	289	1,959	84	268	1,004
Growth	3,200	7,131	6,854	2,054	4,680	5,854	845	979	668
Growth & income	5,858	9,125	1,234	1,855	1,161	169	35	88	24
Equity-income	3,123	1,427	80	939	283	36	45	0	0
Small company	0	0	0	218	516	1,511	3,444	3,411	4,590
Health	0	0	377	0	60	351	0	2	253
Financial	289	0	0	501	60	12	141	0	0
Natural resources	194	88	84	236	465	320	54	117	148
Precious metals	0	0	121	24	15	1,182	51	56	376
Technology	36	48	297	48	72	795	0	24	103
Utility	1,047	24	12	1,764	15	0	3	0	0
Real estate	0	0	0	122	74	8	243	610	24
Communications	12	81	139	0	29	254	0	0	12
Asset allocation	901	2,390	439	362	487	127	258	36	69
Balanced	3,112	3,465	1,547	1,340	780	493	175	16	58
Multi-asset global	492	699	86	325	327	238	116	121	48
Convertibles	451	147	120	136	290	90	75	107	20

Note: The table reports the number of fund-month observations with a given stated objective and Morningstar equity style accumulated within the domestic stock fund class over the period January 1993–March 1999.

funds in the objective categories (see, for example, Brown and Goetzmann, 1997). Only in case of a few specialty stock objectives, there is a style containing more than 60 percent of the funds in a given objective category. In fact, eight from 17 objective categories have funds spanning all nine cells in a style box. Similar levels of dispersion across styles are also observed in the other fund classes. As a result, there is sufficient variation between fund rankings relative to the stated objective and Morningstar style categories, which allows me to identify their separate effects on fund flows.

Table 10.2 presents the summary statistics of the funds belonging to the four classes under consideration, calculated throughout the sample period. During the sample period, an average domestic stock fund had a 13-year performance record, $766 million in total net assets and a 1.3 percent expense ratio and experienced approximately 8 percent net flow per year. In contrast, funds from the other classes were smaller (from $289 million to $544 million in total net assets for an average municipal bond and international stock fund, respectively) and younger (7–9 years) and attracted lower net flows

Table 10.2 Summary statistics of U.S. mutual funds

Fund characteristics	Dom. stock		Int. stock		Tax. bond		Mun. bond	
	Mean	Standard deviation	Mean	Standard deviation	Mean	Standard deviation	Mean	Standard deviation
Net relative flow, %	7.96	55.59	1.07	69.4	1.62	60.51	0.91	38.57
Total net assets, $mln	766.37	2,294.32	544.43	1,648.07	431.06	987.59	288.82	798.49
Age, years	12.52	13.65	6.94	5.92	8.83	8.06	7.39	4.06
Expense ratio, %	1.32	0.57	1.73	0.62	1.02	0.48	0.94	0.42
Total risk, %	3.51	1.18	4.17	1.29	1.19	0.62	1.34	0.3
# funds in the family	13.35	26.58	14.08	28.3	13.83	27.74	13.91	27.92
Family TNA, $bln	4.47	20.30	4.76	22.11	4.58	20.99	4.63	21.28
Family age, years	15.11	17.68	15.07	17.58	15.06	17.62	15.06	17.6
Objective flow, %	6.04	15.11	3.14	14.28	−0.98	13.76	−1.97	3.36
Style flow, %	6.23	10.01	1.81	15.63	−0.22	11.87	−2.58	6.45
Total return, %	16.47	5.49	8.45	7.79	7.22	2.3	6.45	0.93

Notes: The table presents summary statistics of the domestic stock, international stock, taxable bond, and municipal bond classes of US mutual funds. For each fund class, the table reports the mean and standard deviation of the respective fund characteristics over the sample period (January 1993–March 1999 for stock funds and January 1994–March 1999 for bond funds). Note that total return and flows are annualized.

(about 1% per year) during the sample period. Since most families include different types of funds, the family characteristics are similar across the classes. An average fund family includes about 14 funds and controls approximately $4.5 billion of assets.

10.3 METHODOLOGY

In this chapter I analyse the relationship between fund flows and their past relative performance with respect to three types of categories: stated objective, Morningstar style and asset class. For a given fund, these categories consist of funds with the same stated objective, funds with the same Morningstar style (equity style for stock funds and fixed-income style for bond funds), and funds within the same Morningstar asset class (domestic stock, international stock, taxable bond or municipal bond), respectively. Note that the stated objective and Morningstar style categories include only the funds within the respective asset class, since I do not consider performance relative to funds from the other asset classes. Estimating the flow-performance relationship, I would like to control for the other determinants of flows previously identified in the literature, such as size, age, fees and risk of a given fund, size, age and number of funds in the fund's family, and category-specific flows (see, for example, Sirri and Tufano, 1998; Nanda, Wang and Zheng, 2000). Since some of these factors were also found to affect the sensitivity of flows with respect to performance (see, for example, Chevalier and Ellison, 1997; Sirri and Tufano, 1998), I model both the performance-unrelated part of flows and flow-performance sensitivity as linear functions of the control variables. Specifically, my basic model (10.1) is as follows:

$$f_{i,t} = x'_{i,t-1}a + (x'_{i,t-1}b) * (c_1 RP^{obj}_{i,t-1} + c_2 RP^{style}_{i,t-1} + c_3 RP^{class}_{i,t-1}) + e_{i,t} \quad (10.1)$$

where $RP^{obj}_{i,t-1}$, $RP^{style}_{i,t-1}$, and $RP^{class}_{i,t-1}$ denote fund i's relative performance with respect to the stated objective, Morningstar style, and asset class categories and $x'_{i,t-1}$ is a vector of fund i's control variables at month $t-1$. In order to identify the parameters in the model, I impose the restriction that the sum of the performance coefficients c_k be equal to one.

The dependent variable in the model is fund i's net relative flow. In line with the previous studies (see, for example, Gruber, 1996), it is defined as the growth in the fund assets net of reinvested dividends:

$$f_i^t = \frac{TNA_{i,t} - (1 + R_{i,t})TNA_{i,t-1}}{TNA_{i,t-1}} \quad (10.2)$$

where $TNA_{i,t}$ denotes fund i's total net assets at the end of month t and $R_{i,t}$ is return of fund i over month t. Here, I assume that all earnings are automatically reinvested in the fund and that flows occur at the end of the month.

Fund i's performance relative to a given category RP_i^{cat} is measured as a *normalized category ranking*:

$$RP^{cat}_{i,t} = \left[\rho^{cat}_{i,t} - \frac{1}{2}\right] \frac{p\,(.95)^{class}_{i,t} - p(.05)^{class}_{i,t}}{p\,(.95)^{cat}_{i,t} - p(.05)^{cat}_{i,t}} \quad (10.3)$$

where $\rho^{cat}_{i,t}$ is fund i's fractional rank in a given category based on its total return over the past 36 months[3] and $p(x)^{cat}$ is the xth percentile of three-year returns of funds belonging to a given category. Defining fund ranking as a fractional rank (a fraction of funds from the category with lower return than fund i) ranging from 0 to 1 is traditional in the literature (see for example, Sirri and Tufano, 1998). I adjust the fractional rank by 0.5 to assign zero ranking to a median fund in the category. This allows me to interpret the performance-unrelated part $x'_{i,t-1}\,a$ of the model as expected flows of a fund with neutral performance. The original category rankings are normalized to make sure that they change by the same amount in response to a given change in fund's return.[4] For a given category, the normalization coefficient is equal to the return dispersion in the asset class divided by the return dispersion in this category.[5] Thus, the assets-class rankings do not change with normalization, while the normalized stated objective and Morningstar style rankings become equivalent to the asset-class rankings. After normalization, the total impact of a unit change in fund's relative performance on its flows is equal to the flow-performance sensitivity times the sum of the performance coefficients. Because of the identifying restriction that the sum of the performance coefficients be equal to one, each performance coefficient c_k can be interpreted as a percentage of the total impact of relative performance on the fund's flow due to the change in rankings in the respective category.

Both the performance-unrelated flows and flow-performance sensitivity are modelled as linear functions of the control variables: $x'_{i,t-1}a$ and $x'_{i,t-1}b$, respectively. By construction, a parameters measure the impact of the control variables on expected flows of a fund with median category rankings, while b parameters show how the sensitivity of flows to performance varies with fund characteristics. The vector of fund i's control variables $x'_{i,t-1}$ includes a constant, four fund-specific factors (log size, log age, expense ratio, and total risk of a fund), three family-specific factors (log of the number of funds in the family; log size and log age of the family), and two category-specific factors (stated objective and Morningstar style category flows).

The effects of fund size and age on flows were identified, for example, in Chevalier and Ellison (1997) and Goriaev, Nijman and Werker (2001), who find that smaller and younger funds enjoy larger performance-unrelated flows as well as higher flow-performance sensitivity. These findings could be caused by more active advertising by young funds, who have not yet acquired the long-term reputation of the old funds. I include log fund size and log fund age to the model to control for these effects. The impact of the expense ratio on flows can be twofold. On the one hand, higher expense ratio may lead to lower flows, as investors would like to maximize net-of-fee earnings. On the other hand, a higher expense ratio is associated with larger advertising expenditures and may increase fund flows. The existing evidence does not give a clear answer which effect prevails. Most studies document a negative impact of fund expense ratios on flows (see, for example, Nanda, Wang and Zheng, 2000), while Barber, Odean and Zheng (2001) find a positive relation between expenses and flows in a sample of large diversified equity funds. If investors prefer less risk, flows should be negatively related to fund total risk measured as the standard deviation of total returns during the last 36 months. Indeed, several studies find a negative relation between fund flows and total risk (see, for example, Nanda, Wang and Zheng, 2000; Barber, Odean and Zheng, 2001).

The dependence of individual fund flows on family characteristics has received much attention in the recent literature (see, for example, Nanda, Wang and Zheng, 2000). It has been documented that funds belonging to larger families attract higher flows (see Ivkovic, 2000), while older families achieve larger market share (see Khorana and Servaes, 2000). These findings are probably due to the greater visibility and better distribution networks available to the funds from large and old families. I measure family size by log of the number of funds in the family and log of the family total net assets. Family age is measured as log of the age of the oldest fund in the family.

The existing studies document a strong dependence of individual fund flows on flows to fund's objective category (see, for example, Sirri and Tufano, 1998). In my model, I include both stated objective and Morningstar style category flows as the control variables. They should control for the temporal changes in the individual fund flows due to movement in the category-specific flows. The objective and style flows are measured as the TNA-weighted average net relative flows of funds within the respective categories.

Throughout the chapter I run panel regressions with fixed time effects and compute weighted least-squares estimates with the variance of the residuals $e_{i,t}$ modelled as:

$$Var(e_{i,t}) = \exp(x^{'}_{i,t-1}w) \tag{10.4}$$

where $x^{'}_{i,t-1}$ is the vector of fund i's control variables defined as before. The w coefficients are estimated on the basis of the OLS residuals. The model parameters in (10.1) are estimated by means of a concentrated least-squares approach. For the pre-specified values of b parameters, the model (10.1) is linear in the remaining parameters. Therefore, one can easily calculate the least-squares estimates of the remaining parameters and the corresponding sum of the squared residuals. By numerically maximizing the concentrated sum of squares over the b parameters, I obtain the least-squares estimates of the b parameters and, consequently, of the remaining parameters in the model.

10.4 RELATIONSHIP BETWEEN FLOWS AND PERFORMANCE RELATIVE TO THE STATED OBJECTIVE CATEGORY

In previous studies of the flow-performance relationship, a fund's relative performance is typically measured with respect to its stated objective category (see, for example, Sirri and Tufano, 1998). Therefore, I use the normalized stated objective rankings RP^{obj} as the only performance measure in my first model specification, which is equivalent to model (10.1) with the additional restriction $c_2 = c_3 = 0$.

Table 10.3 reports the results based on samples of domestic stock, international stock, taxable bond, and municipal bond funds. During the sample period, an average domestic stock, international stock, or municipal bond fund with median performance relative to its objective category attracted between 5 percent and 7 percent net flows per year. Flows to taxable bond funds were much lower, about 1.3 percent per year. Consistent with the existing evidence, I find a clear positive relation between the stated objective ranking of a fund and its flows. A 10 percentile move in the stated objective ranking leads to about 3 percent additional flows for an average domestic or international stock fund. Flows to taxable bond and municipal bond funds would change by approximately 1.3 percent and 1.6 percent, respectively.

Most of the control variables prove to have both economically and statistically significant impacts on expected fund flows. Confirming the presence of the size effect, I find that a twofold increase in fund size is associated with a flow decrease from about 0.9 percent for a municipal bond fund to about 1.8 percent for a domestic or international stock fund. The sensitivity of fund flows to performance is only marginally (and in most classes insignificantly) affected by fund size. As expected, younger funds enjoy larger flows as well as higher flow-performance sensitivity. All other things being equal, a two-time difference in age implies approximately 4 percent difference in flows of a fund with median performance and 0.3 percent difference in the sensitivity of fund flows with respect to 10 percentile change in the objective rankings.

The effect of the expense ratio on flows differs across the asset classes. In response to a 1 percent increase in the expense ratio, flows to a domestic stock fund will increase by about 3.2 percent, while flows to an international stock fund will decrease by approximately 3.7 percent. In the case of bond funds, the expense ratio also has a negative although insignificant impact on flows. My finding of a positive relation between expenses and flows of domestic stock funds is similar to that of Barber, Odean and Zheng (2001), who explain it by greater marketing efforts of funds with higher expense ratios. It appears that this effect does not outweigh the costs associated with higher fees for investors of the other fund classes. Probably, larger advertising expenditures of domestic stock and taxable bond funds with higher expense ratios make their flows more sensitive to past performance. In these classes, a 1 percent increase in the expense ratio is associated with an approximately 0.7 percent rise in sensitivity of flows to a 10 percentile move in the stated objective rankings.

In line with the expectations, I find a negative relation between fund flows and total risk, which is significant in the domestic stock and municipal bond classes. In these classes, a 1 percent increase in the fund's total risk leads on average to about 1.5 percent and 2.2 percent decrease in the subsequent flows. The effect of total risk on the flow-performance sensitivity is more ambiguous, being significantly positive for domestic stock funds and significantly negative for international stock and municipal bond funds.

Table 10.3 Relationship between flows and relative performance with respect to the stated objective category

Panel A: performance-unrelated flows

	Dom. stock		Int. stock		Tax. bond		Mun. bond	
Const	11.32	(2.91)	25.51	(6.22)	3.28	(4.17)	10.45	(3.26)
log $FundTNA_{i,t-1}$	−2.42	(0.15)	−2.62	(0.55)	−2.15	(0.35)	−1.25	(0.19)
log $FundAge_{i,t-1}$	−4.63	(0.31)	−6.37	(0.97)	−4.59	(0.84)	−6.50	(0.79)
$FundExpenseRatio_{i,t-1}$	3.21	(0.61)	−3.66	(1.04)	−0.79	(0.84)	−0.81	(1.04)
$FundRisk_{i,t-1}$	−1.51	(0.29)	−0.35	(0.50)	−0.19	(0.90)	−2.24	(0.87)
log $Family\ \#\ funds_{i,t-1}$	−3.46	(0.28)	−3.33	(0.75)	−4.34	(0.46)	−5.14	(0.32)
Log $FamilyTNA_{i,t-1}$	2.88	(0.24)	2.96	(0.64)	3.97	(0.54)	3.38	(0.24)
Log $FamilyAge_{i,t-1}$	2.75	(0.35)	−1.01	(0.67)	−0.92	(0.75)	−0.73	(0.31)
$ObjectiveFlow_{i,t-1}$	0.42	(0.10)	0.88	(0.03)	0.53	(0.09)	0.35	(0.05)
$StyleFlow_{i,t-1}$	0.36	(0.04)	0.29	(0.04)	0.16	(0.05)	0.42	(0.06)

Panel B: flow-performance sensitivity

	Dom. stock		Int. stock		Tax. bond		Mun. bond	
Const	−5.77	(3.61)	65.13	(9.30)	1.22	(3.96)	34.14	(6.72)
log $FundTNA_{i,t-1}$	−0.16	(0.42)	1.94	(0.76)	0.50	(0.38)	0.13	(0.53)
log $FundAge_{i,t-1}$	−4.35	(0.58)	−3.17	(1.64)	−3.93	(1.33)	−5.13	(2.09)
$FundExpenseRatio_{i,t-1}$	7.65	(1.09)	−0.80	(1.66)	7.80	(1.28)	−2.69	(3.42)
$FundRisk_{i,t-1}$	6.54	(0.94)	−5.81	(1.02)	1.81	(1.00)	−7.62	(1.96)
log $Family\ \#\ funds_{i,t-1}$	−4.79	(0.67)	8.18	(1.17)	−2.74	(0.60)	6.72	(1.08)
log $FamilyTNA_{i,t-1}$	1.87	(0.66)	−4.67	(1.00)	3.06	(0.72)	−1.77	(0.63)
log $FamilyAge_{i,t-1}$	3.98	(0.67)	−2.54	(1.40)	−3.25	(1.17)	−2.46	(1.17)
$ObjectiveFlow_{i,t-1}$	0.15	(0.14)	0.13	(0.08)	0.13	(0.06)	0.00	(0.11)
$StyleFlow_{i,t-1}$	0.04	(0.06)	−0.20	(0.05)	−0.06	(0.03)	−0.04	(0.14)

Notes: The table documents the relationship between fund flows and stated objective rankings in the domestic stock, international stock, taxable bond, and municipal bond classes of US mutual funds. For each fund class, the table reports the estimated coefficients and standard errors (in the parentheses) based on the model (10.1) with the restriction $c_2 = c_3 = 0$. The identifying restriction is that the coefficient on the stated objective ranking c_1 is equal to one. The dependent variable is fund's annualized net relative flow. The control variables include a constant, logs of fund size and age, fund expense ratio and risk, log of number of funds in the family, logs of fund family size and age, objective and style category flows. Both the performance-unrelated flows and flow-performance sensitivity are linear functions of the control variables. The sample period is January 1993–March 1999 for stock funds and January 1994–March 1999 for bond funds.

Consistent with the previous studies (see, for example, Nanda, Wang and Zheng, 2000), I find a significant impact of the family-specific variables on individual fund flows. In all four classes, funds belonging to families with larger total net assets attract significantly higher flows. At the same time, the growth of fund families may have a cost, since the number of funds in a family appears to have a significantly negative impact on flows. This is probably explained by investors' preferences to invest in more focused families (see Siggelkow, 1998). On average, a twofold increase in family size or a twofold decrease in the number of funds in the family yields about 2–3 percent additional flows. The impact of the age of the fund family on flows is significantly positive in the domestic stock class and significantly negative in the municipal bond class (in the other classes, it is also negative, but insignificant). A two-time difference in fund family age implies about 2 percent and 0.5 percent difference in flows to funds belonging to these classes, respectively. The effects of the family-specific variables on the flow-performance sensitivity differ across the fund classes. Flows to an average domestic stock fund are more sensitive to its past performance, if it belongs to a larger or older family or family with the lower number of funds.

Finally, I find that fund flows are strongly related to the category-specific flows. A domestic stock fund with a median stated objective ranking is expected to attract about 42 percent of its objective flow and 36 percent of its style flow. Flows to international stock and taxable bond funds seem to be even more related to the objective flows, while flows to municipal bond funds are more sensitive to the style flows. These results provide preliminary evidence of the impact of the Morningstar style classification scheme on fund flows, which appear to be related not only to the objective-specific, but also to the style-specific flows. Further analysis of the category-specific factors driving fund flows is carried out in the next section.

10.5 RELATIONSHIP BETWEEN FLOWS AND PERFORMANCE RELATIVE TO THE STATED OBJECTIVE, MORNINGSTAR STYLE, AND ASSET CLASS CATEGORIES

The main goal of the chapter is to examine the dependence of fund flows on relative performance measures based on the alternative classification schemes. Therefore, in this section I relax the assumption that fund flows are driven only by the stated objective rankings and analyse the relationship between fund flows and their normalized performance rankings within the stated objective, Morningstar style, and asset class categories.

Table 10.4 presents the results based on model (10.1). The coefficients on the control variables are hardly affected by the introduction of the additional performance measures and are omitted from the table. Panel A of Table 10.4 reports the performance coefficients and the corresponding standard errors, while Panel B presents *p* values of the pairwise tests of equality between the performance coefficients.

First of all, I find that the Morningstar style and asset-class rankings have a strong positive impact on fund flows on top of the impact of the stated

Table 10.4 Relationship between flows and relative performance with respect to the stated objective, Morningstar style, and asset class categories

Panel A: performance coefficients

	Dom. stock	Int. stock	Tax. bond	Mun. bond
Relative performance measures				
RP^{obj}	0.28 (0.04)	0.57 (0.06)	0.09 (0.04)	0.04 (0.18)
RP^{style}	0.14 (0.03)	0.09 (0.07)	0.12 (0.03)	0.10 (0.05)
RP^{class}	0.58 (0.05)	0.34 (0.11)	0.80 (0.05)	0.86 (0.21)

Panel B: *p*-values of the pairwise tests

	Dom. stock	Int. stock	Tax. bond	Mun. bond
$H_0{:}c_1 = c_2$ (RP^{obj} vs. RP^{obj})	0.013	0.000	0.456	0.725
$H_0{:}c_1 = c_3$ (RP^{obj} vs. RP^{class})	0.000	0.171	0.000	0.038
$H_0{:}c_2 = c_3$ (RP^{style} vs. RP^{class})	0.000	0.147	0.000	0.002

Notes: The table documents the relationship between fund flows and stated objective, Morningstar style, and asset-class rankings (RP^{obj}, RP^{style}, and RP^{class} respectively) in the domestic stock, international stock, taxable bond, and municipal bond classes of US mutual funds. For each fund class, the table presents the results based on the model (10.1). The identifying restriction is that the sum of the performance coefficients is equal to one. The dependent variable is fund's annualized net relative flow. The control variables include a constant, logs of fund size and age, fund expense ratio and risk, log of number of funds in the family, logs of fund family size and age, objective and style category flows. Both the performance-unrelated flows and flow-performance sensitivity are linear functions of the control variables. The sample period is January 1993–March 1999 for stock funds and January 1994–March 1999 for bond funds. Since the coefficients of the control variables stay approximately the same as in the previous model (see Table 10.3), Panel A of the table only reports the estimated coefficients and standard errors (in the parentheses) of the performance variables. Panel B presents *p*-values of the pairwise tests for the equality of the respective performance coefficients.

objective rankings. In all four asset classes, I strongly reject the traditional specification, where relative performance is defined only with respect to the objective category. In fact, the asset class ranking appears to be the most important relative performance measure for investors of domestic stock as well as investors of taxable and municipal bond funds. In these asset classes, the difference between the coefficients on the asset-class ranking and the other two types of rankings is significant at the 1 percent level (see Table 10.4, Panel B). Only in the international stock class, fund flows are most sensitive to the stated objective ranking, although the difference between its coefficient and coefficient on the asset class ranking is not significant.

By construction, each performance coefficient can be interpreted as the percentage of the total impact of relative performance on fund flows attributed to the respective category. Alternatively, one can also interpret the performance coefficients as the percentage of investors, who use categories based on the respective classification schemes as peer groups for the evaluation of fund performance. The relative impact of the stated objective, Morningstar style, and asset-class rankings on fund flows in different fund classes is illustrated

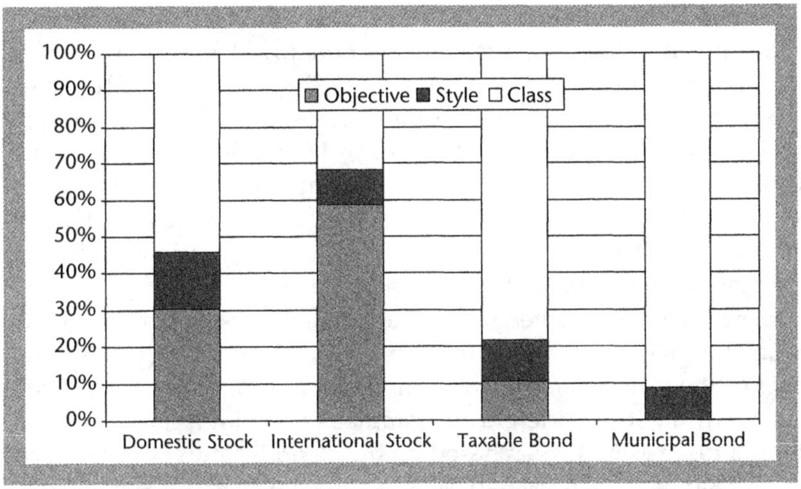

Figure 10.1 Relative impact of different classification schemes on flows to US mutual funds

Notes: The graph presents the coefficients of the stated objective, Morningstar style, and asset class rankings on flows to domestic stock, international stock, taxable bond, and municipal bond funds, based on model (10.1). Each performance coefficient is interpreted as a percentage of the total impact of fund relative performance on flows, which is due to the respective classification scheme. The sample period is January 1993–March 1999 for stock funds and January 1994–March 1999 for bond funds.

graphically in Figure 10.1. In the domestic stock class, 58 percent of the total impact is attributed to the asset-class ranking, while about 28 percent and 14 percent of the total impact are due to the stated objective and Morningstar style rankings, respectively. Thus, there is a clear hierarchy of the different classification schemes with respect to their importance for investors. Apparently, investors of domestic stock funds (or their financial advisors) most often consider the asset class as a peer group for performance evaluation, followed by the stated objective category and Morningstar style category.

This is consistent with Carhart *et al.* (2002), who find that marking up at the last trading day of the year to improve a calendar-year performance is stronger among equity funds with top universe-relative performance than among equity funds with top category-relative performance (in my terminology, funds with top asset class rankings and funds with top stated objective rankings, respectively).

Investors of taxable bond and municipal bond funds use a similar hierarchy, in which the asset-class ranking is even more important, accounting for 80 percent and 86 percent of the total impact of relative performance on flows, respectively. The differences in fund investment policies do not seem to play a large role for these investors, which may explain the marginal impact of the stated objective and Morningstar style rankings on flows to bond funds. Investors of international stock funds appear to have a different hierarchy of the classification schemes; with 57 percent of the total impact of relative performance on flows due to the stated objective ranking and 34 percent due to the asset-class ranking (the Morningstar style ranking has a positive but insignificant impact on flows). In contrast to the other fund classes, international stock funds are designed primarily for foreign investment. Typically, their objective is to invest in stocks from a certain geographical region such as Latin America or Japan. Since these region-based objectives are more clearly defined and also appear more distinct from each other than, say, growth-and-income and equity-income objectives in the domestic stock class, the stated objective rankings of international stock funds may seem reliable to their investors.

The hierarchy of the different classification schemes for investors of domestic stock funds is further illustrated in Figure 10.2. It presents the relative impact of the stated objective, Morningstar style, and asset class rankings on fund flows within different subsamples of the domestic stock class.

First, I discuss the results based on the periods January 1993–December 1996 and January 1997–March 1999. I observe that the stated objectives as well as Morningstar style rankings have become somewhat more

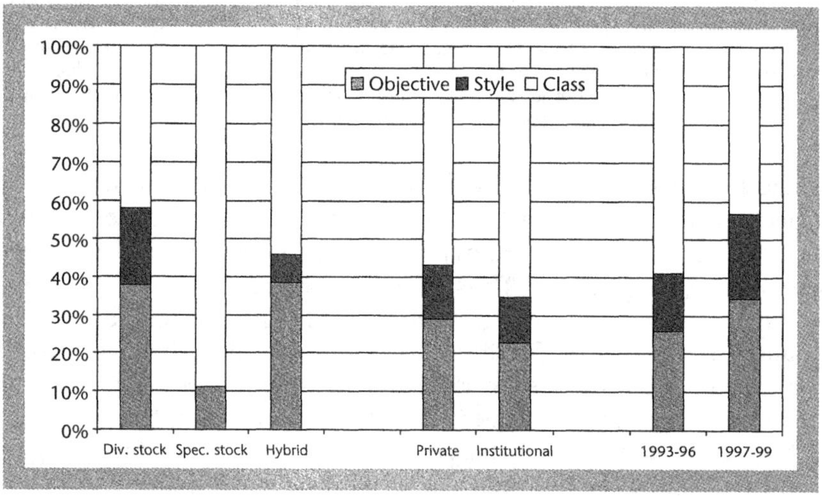

Figure 10.2 Relative impact of different classification schemes on flows to domestic stock funds

Notes: The graph presents the coefficients of the stated objective, Morningstar style, and asset class rankings on flows to the different subsamples of the domestic stock class, based on model (10.1). Each performance coefficient is interpreted as a percentage of the total impact of fund relative performance on flows, which is due to the respective classification scheme. Unless otherwise specified, the sample period is January 1993–March 1999. The first two columns in the graph present results based on the periods January 1993–December 1996 and January 1997–March 1999. The second division of the domestic stock class into subsamples (see columns three to five) is based on fund stated objectives. Diversified stock funds have an aggressive growth, growth, growth and income, equity-income, or small company objective, specialty stock funds have a health, financial, natural resources, precious metals, technology, utility, real estate, or communications objective, while hybrid funds have an asset allocation, balanced, convertibles, or multi-asset global objective. The last two columns in the graph are based on the subsamples of primarily private and primarily institutional funds, defined as funds with a minimum initial purchase of less than $25,000 and at least $25,000, respectively.

important over time. Probably, the latter tendency is due to the fact that in 1997 Morningstar started to use its equity and fixed-income style boxes to categorize funds. Note that Morningstar category does not always coincide with Morningstar style. The former is based on fund's investment policy over the past three years, while the latter is based on fund's latest portfolio holdings. In addition, Morningstar keeps using the stated objective categories for specialty funds and classifies most hybrid funds into the domestic hybrid or international hybrid categories. The highest correlation between Morningstar styles and categories is for the diversified stock funds, which constitute the majority of the domestic stock class. Indeed, the concept of Morningstar equity styles is most applicable to this type of funds, since hybrid funds invest a large part of their portfolios in bonds and specialty stock funds invest in narrow market segments. This may explain why the impact of the Morningstar style ranking is higher for diversified stock funds than for specialty stock and hybrid funds. In general, the hierarchy of the classification schemes for diversified stock, specialty stock, and hybrid funds is similar to that of all domestic stock funds, with the asset-class ranking having the largest impact on flows. The asset-class ranking is especially important for investors of specialty stock funds, who seem to attach only marginal importance to funds' stated objective rankings that are based on a relatively small number of funds specializing in the same market sector.

There are remarkable differences between the hierarchies of the classification schemes in the subsamples of primarily private and primarily institutional funds (defined in line with Chevalier and Ellison (1997), as funds with a minimum initial purchase of less than $25,000 and at least $25,000, respectively). Most private investors compare the return of a given fund with that of other domestic stock funds. This indicates that they are style-timers, choosing funds with larger holdings of recent winners. In contrast, institutional investors use only the categories grouping funds with a similar investment approach for performance evaluation, attaching approximately equal weights to the stated objective and Morningstar style classifications. This finding is similar to that of Del Guercio and Tkac (2002) who document that pension fund clients (primarily institutional investors) use more quantitatively sophisticated performance measures than mutual fund customers (primarily private investors).

A number of existing studies (see, for example, Sirri and Tufano, 1998) have demonstrated the non-linearity of the flow-performance relationship. To adjust for this, I extended the basic model specification (10.1) to allow the coefficients on the stated objective, Morningstar style, and asset class rankings to differ across the respective performance quintiles. In all four asset classes, the average impact of the different relative performance measures based on the extended model remained practically the same as in the basic model (10.1). These results are not reported here, but are available upon request.

10.6 RELATIONSHIP BETWEEN FLOWS AND ORDINAL AS WELL AS CARDINAL MEASURES OF PERFORMANCE

So far, the analysis has been limited to the ordinal measures of performance based on the three classification schemes under consideration. All these measures are based on a fund's total return, which is a cardinal performance measure. It is an interesting question which type of performance measure, cardinal or ordinal, is more important for investors. To formulate this differently, do investors pay more attention to fund returns or return ranks? To answer this question, I extend the basic model (10.1) by adding a cardinal performance measure to the regressors:

$$f_{i,t} = x'_{i,t-1}a + (x'_{i,t-1}b) * (c_1 RP^{obj}_{i,t-1} + c_2 RP^{style}_{i,t-1} + c_3 RP^{class}_{i,t-1} + c_4 return_{i,t-1}) + e_{i,t} \quad (10.5)$$

where $return_{i,t-1}$ is fund i's total return over the last 36 months (from $t-1$ to $t-36$). As before, the identifying restriction is that the sum of c_1, c_2 and c_3 be equal to one.

Table 10.5 reports the estimation results (as in Table 10.4, I omit the coefficients on the control variables, since they stay approximately the same). In a joint model, both ordinal and cardinal performance measures prove to be significant. In all asset classes except for the international stock class, fund's return has a significantly positive impact on flows. For instance, in the domestic stock class a 1 percent change in return keeping all performance rankings unchanged is associated with a 0.4 percent change in fund flows. The inclusion of the cardinal performance measure hardly changes the category-specific composition of the total impact of ordinal performance measures on flows. In the domestic stock, taxable bond, and municipal bond classes, the asset class ranking remains the most important relative performance measure, although its weight has slightly decreased. In order to compare the relative impact of ordinal and cardinal performance measures on fund flows, I normalize the return coefficient by multiplying it by the average return dispersion (the difference between the maximum and minimum returns) in the respective asset class (see the last row of Table 10.5).

For the domestic stock and international stock funds, the normalized return coefficient is about 0.18, which implies that the impact of total return on fund flows is about 18 percent of the combined impact of relative performance measures. The total return is relatively more important for investors of municipal bond and especially taxable bond funds, accounting for about

Table 10.5 Relationship between flows and relative performance with respect to the stated objective, Morningstar style, and asset-class categories

	Dom. stock	Int. stock	Tax. bond	Mun. bond
Relative performance measures				
RP^{obj}	0.31 (0.05)	0.64 (0.08)	0.15 (0.07)	0.16 (0.25)
RP^{style}	0.15 (0.03)	0.08 (0.08)	0.19 (0.05)	0.15 (0.05)
RP^{class}	0.54 (0.06)	0.27 (0.12)	0.66 (0.10)	0.69 (0.27)
Ordinal performance measure				
Return	0.010 (0.002)	0.008 (0.007)	0.097 (0.028)	0.146 (0.054)
*Return * dispersion*	0.182	0.189	0.951	0.507

Notes: The table documents the relationship between fund flows and ordinal as well as cardinal performance measures in the domestic stock, international stock, taxable bond, and municipal bond classes of US mutual funds. The ordinal performance measures are fund's stated objective, Morningstar style, and asset-class rankings (RP^{obj}, RP^{style}, and RP^{class} respectively), while the cardinal performance measure is fund's total return over the last 36 months. For each fund class, the table presents the results based on the model (10.5). The identifying restriction is that the sum of the coefficients on the ordinal performance measures is equal to one. The dependent variable is fund's annualized net relative flow. The control variables include a constant, logs of fund size and age, fund expense ratio and risk, log of number of funds in the family, logs of fund family size and age, objective and style category flows. Both the performance-unrelated flows and flow-performance sensitivity are linear functions of the control variables. The sample period is January 1993–March 1999 for stock funds and January 1994–March 1999 for bond funds. Since the coefficients of the control variables stay approximately the same as in the previous model (see Table 10.3), the table only reports the estimated coefficients and standard errors (in parentheses) of the performance variables. The last row of the table presents the normalized coefficient on total return, which is equal to the original coefficient on total return times the average return dispersion (the difference between the maximum and minimum returns) in a given class. The normalized return coefficient is directly comparable with the coefficients on the performance rankings.

51 percent and 95 percent of the total impact of relative performance, respectively. These results suggest that ordinal performance measures are at least as important for investors as cardinal performance measures. In other words, investors (especially those of stock funds) prefer to select funds that not only have a good performance but also outperform the others.

10.7 CATEGORY-SPECIFIC FLOW SPILLOVER EFFECT FROM A STAR FUND TO THE OTHER FUNDS IN THE FAMILY

In this section I examine whether the star spillover effect, identified for example in Nanda, Wang and Zheng (2000), differs across the funds from star families depending on their category (for example, stated objective, Morningstar style or asset class) and category of a star fund. Specifically, I disentangle the flow spillover effect from a star fund to the other funds in the family into components corresponding to funds with the same stated objective, funds with the same Morningstar style, and funds within the same asset class as the star fund. In line with the previous studies (see, for example, Ivkovic, 2000), I define a star fund as a fund with performance (the total return over the past 36 months) in the top 5 percent within its asset class. The basic model (10.1) is extended as follows:

$$f_{i,t} = x'_{i,t-1}a + (x'_{i,t-1}b) * (c_1 RP^{obj}_{i,t-1} + c_2 RP^{style}_{i,t-1} + c_3 RP^{class}_{i,t-1} + d_1 D^{star}_{i,t} + d_2 D^{obj}_{i,t} + d_3 D^{style}_{i,t} + d_4 D^{class}_{i,t}) + e_{i,t} \quad (10.6)$$

where $D^{star}_{i,t}$ is a dummy equal to one if fund i is a star fund, and $D^{obj}_{i,t}$ ($D^{style}_{i,t}$, $D^{class}_{i,t}$) is a dummy equal to one if fund i belongs to the same stated objective (Morningstar style, asset class) category as one of the star funds in its family. Since within each asset class $D^{class}_{i,t}$ is equal to one for all funds in a star family (family with at least one star fund), d_4 shows the difference between expected flows to funds from star families and other funds. For funds from star families, the coefficients d_1, d_2, and d_3, show the additional expected flows of a star fund, funds with the same stated objective as one of the star funds, and funds with the same Morningstar style as one of the star funds, respectively. As before, I impose the identifying restriction that the sum of c_1, c_2, and c_3 be equal to one.

The estimation results are presented in Table 10.6 (as before, the coefficients on the control variables are omitted). Consistent with Ivkovic (2000), I find a presence of the statistically and economically significant flow spillover effect from a star fund to the other funds in the family in all asset classes

Table 10.6 Category-specific flow spillover effect from a star to the other funds in the family

	Dom. stock	Int. stock	Tax. bond	Mun.bond
Relative performance measures				
RP^{obj}	0.30 (0.04)	0.59 (0.07)	0.11 (0.04)	0.11 (0.24)
RP^{style}	0.14 (0.03)	0.08 (0.07)	0.12 (0.03)	0.10 (0.07)
RP^{class}	0.56 (0.05)	0.34 (0.11)	0.77 (0.05)	0.78 (0.28)
Category dummies				
D^{star}	0.39 (0.04)	0.01 (0.08)	0.30 (0.07)	1.51 (0.28)
D^{obj}	−0.03 (0.02)	−0.08 (0.07)	−0.14 (0.06)	0.14 (0.06)
D^{style}	−0.04 (0.02)	0.01 (0.07)	0.20 (0.08)	0.44 (0.08)
D^{class}	0.07 (0.01)	0.04 (0.05)	0.02 (0.02)	−0.09 (0.08)

Notes: The table documents the flow spillover effect from a star fund to the other funds in the family, including funds with the same stated objective, funds with the same Morningstar style, and funds within the same asset class (see the coefficients on D^{obj}, D^{style} and D^{class} respectively). The coefficient on D^{star} captures the difference between flows to a star fund and flows to the other funds in the star family. The corresponding results are based on the model (10.6) and samples of domestic stock, international stock, taxable bond, and municipal bond funds. Standard errors are in parentheses. The identifying restriction is that the sum of the performance coefficients is equal to one. The dependent variable is fund's annualized net relative flow. The control variables include a constant, logs of fund size and age, fund expense ratio and risk, log of number of funds in the family, logs of fund family size and age, objective and style category flows. Both the performance-unrelated flows and flow-performance sensitivity are linear functions of the control variables. The sample period is January 1993–March 1999 for stock funds and January 1994–March 1999 for bond funds. Since the coefficients of the control variables stay approximately the same as in the previous models (see Table 10.3), they are omitted from the table.

except for the international stock class. The flow spillover effect is typically positive, as the presence a star fund helps to boost flows to the other funds in the family. In the domestic stock class, the magnitude of the flow spillover effect does not differ significantly across different types of nonstar funds in star families that attract about 3.6 percent additional expected flows per year. In the municipal bond class, the flow spillover effect seems to be limited to funds with the same Morningstar style and funds with the same stated objective as one of the star funds in their families, which enjoy about 5 percent and 2 percent extra flows, respectively. In the taxable bond class, the presence of a star fund is beneficial for flows to funds with the same stated objective as the star fund and detrimental for flows to funds with the same Morningstar style as the star fund, leading to the inflows of 6 percent and outflows of 4.5 percent per year, respectively. Naturally, star funds benefit the most from their stellar performance attracting as much as 18 percent extra flows in the domestic stock and municipal bond classes and about 9 percent extra flows in the taxable bond class.

10.8 CONCLUSION

Classification systems are designed to facilitate the performance evaluation of mutual funds by their investors. A classification scheme divides the fund universe into a number of categories that group funds with a similar investment philosophy. This allows investors to compare fund's performance to performance of its peers, the other funds in the category. However, there is no ideal classification scheme, which would categorize funds in truly homogenous groups. As noted by Brown and Goetzmann (1997), "there is a fundamental question whether any classification system (which, after all, is only a multinomial statistic) is sufficient to characterize differences in fund management" (p. 375). As a result, there exist several classification schemes, which categorize funds, for example, according to their stated objective or actual investment style.

This chapter has documented that performance rankings based on different classification systems are an important determinant of fund flows. The fund ranking within the asset class appears to be the most important relative performance measure for private investors of domestic stock and especially for investors of taxable bond and municipal bond funds. Less than half of the total impact of relative performance on flows to domestic stock funds is due to the stated objective and Morningstar style rankings (28% and 14 %, respectively). However, institutional investors of domestic stock funds pay hardly any attention to the fund asset class rankings, using only the Morningstar style and stated objective classification systems to evaluate fund performance. In the taxable bond and municipal bond classes, the stated objective and Morningstar style rankings have a marginal impact on flows. Only in the international stock class, fund flows are most sensitive to the stated objective rankings. In a joint model of ordinal and cardinal performance measures, the impact of total return on fund flows never exceeds the combined impact of performance rankings. This implies that investors (especially those of stock funds) prefer to select funds that not only have a good performance but also outperform the others. In addition, I find that the presence of a star fund is typically beneficial for flows to the other funds in the family. Only in case of taxable bond funds, top performance of a star fund cannibalizes flows to funds with the same stated objective as the star fund.

The observed hierarchy of the classification schemes with respect to their importance for investors has clear implications for mutual funds and their regulators. Managers of domestic stock as well as taxable and municipal bond funds have a strong incentive to maximize their relative performance within the respective asset class, since it is used as a peer group for performance evaluation by most of their investors. However, maximizing the asset class rankings may not be consistent with the interests of fund shareholders, who are interested in maximizing the fund's risk-adjusted performance.

This divergence of interests may be especially large in the domestic stock class, in which there are large differences between the risk profiles of different types of funds (say, growth funds and income funds). In particular, funds with more conservative investment styles have an incentive to take more risk to maximize the chance of outperforming their competitors, which have a riskier investment approach. Thus, classification systems on the one hand facilitate fund performance evaluation, while on the other hand they may create adverse incentives for fund managers.

APPENDIX: DESCRIPTION OF THE MORNINGSTAR EQUITY AND FIXED-INCOME STYLE BOXES

In 1992, Morningstar introduced a style-box scheme for classifying mutual funds on the basis of their actual investment style rather than declared objective. Using the latest data on fund portfolio composition, Morningstar assigns equity and fixed-income styles to a fund, provided that a sufficiently large part of the portfolio is invested in stocks and bonds, respectively. A style box is a three-by-three matrix based on two classification criterions: market capitalization and book value for equity funds; credit quality and duration for bond funds. An equity fund is classified large, medium or small, if the weighted-average market capitalization of the middle size quintile of its stocks falls into the top 5 percent, the next 15 percent or the remaining 80 percent of the 5,000 largest US companies, respectively. A similar procedure is applied to determine whether value or growth stocks prevail in a fund's portfolio. Each fund is assigned price-to-earnings (P/E) and price-to-book (P/B) scores computed as weighted averages of P/E and P/B ratios in the respective middle quintiles. The fund is considered growth, value or blend, if the sum of P/E and P/B scores exceeds 2.25, is below 1.75 or falls between 1.75 and 2.25, respectively. The combination of the two criterions yields nine style categories: large value, large blend, large growth, medium value, medium blend, medium growth, small value, small blend, and small growth. The first criterion for a fixed-income style box is credit quality of the bonds in the fund portfolio. A fund is classified as high or low quality, if it has an average credit rating of AAA or AA, or lower than BBB, respectively. Medium-quality funds fall between these two extremes. The second criterion is the interest rate sensitivity of the fund portfolio, measured as the average duration of bonds in the portfolio. Funds with an average duration less than 3.5 years, between 3.5 and 6 years, and longer than 6 years are considered as short, intermediate and long, respectively. Thus, a fixed-income style box comprises high short, high intermediate, high long, medium short, medium intermediate, medium long, low short, low intermediate, and low long styles.

See Morningstar's website (www.morningstar.com) for a more detailed definition of the styles.

NOTES

1. Since Morningstar annual style classifications are as of the end of the year, I use fund style of year $t - 1$ in the regressions of monthly flows realized in year t, assuming that the fund style did not change during the year. The results stay qualitatively the same, if fund style of year t is used in the regressions of that year.

2. During the sample period, more than 94 percent of domestic and international stock funds had Morningstar equity style data, while about 67 percent of taxable and municipal bond funds had Morningstar fixed-income style data. The main results do not change if I assign median-style rankings to funds with missing style data and keep them in the sample.
3. The three-year performance horizon should be long enough, since Goriaev, Nijman and Werker (2001) find that past three years account for approximately 90 percent of the total performance impact on flows. I use total returns to construct rankings, since fund rankings published in the mass media are typically based on raw rather than risk-adjusted returns. I account for the effect of fund risk on flows by including a measure of a fund's total risk as one of the control variables.
4. A simple example illustrates that a direct comparison of the original category ranking coefficients can be misleading. Suppose that a 1 percent change in return is equivalent to a 0.1 change in the objective category rankings and 0.3 change in the style category rankings and that the estimated ranking coefficients are 10 and 5, respectively. However, the fact that the first coefficient is larger than the second does not imply that flows are more sensitive to the objective category rankings. A 1 percent change in fund return would lead to 10*0.1 = 1 percent change in flows due to the objective category rankings and 5*0.3 = 1.5 percent change in flows due to the style category rankings.
5. A return dispersion in a given category is defined as the difference between 95 percent and 5 percent return percentiles in the category rather than the difference between the maximum and minimum returns in the category, since it is more robust against the outliers.

REFERENCES

Barber, B.M., Odean, T. and Zheng, L. (2001) "Out of Sight, Out of Mind. The Effect of Expenses on Mutual Fund Flows", Working Paper, Graduate School of Management, UC Davis and School of Business Administration, University of Michigan.

Barra Strategic Consulting Group (2001) "Style is Dead. Long Live Style!", August, Research Report.

Bogle, J.C. (1998) "The Implications of Style Analysis for Mutual Fund Performance", *Journal of Portfolio Management*, 24(4): 34–42.

Brown, S.J. and Goetzmann, W.N. (1995) "Performance Persistence", *Journal of Finance*, 50(2): 679–98.

Brown, S.J. and Goetzmann, W.N. (1997) "Mutual Fund Styles" *Journal of Financial Economics*, 43(3): 373–99.

Capon, N., Fitzsimons, G.J. and Prince, R.A. (1996) "An Individual Level Analysis of Mutual Fund Investment Decisions", *Journal of Financial Services Research*, 10: 59–82.

Carhart, M., Kaniel, R., Musto, D.K. and Reed, A.V. (2002) "Leaning for the Tape: Evidence of Gaming Behavior in Equity Mutual Funds", *Journal of Finance*, 57(2): 661–93.

Chevalier, J. and Ellison, G. (1997) "Risk Taking by Mutual Funds as a Response to Incentives", *Journal of Political Economy*, 105(6): 1167–200.

Davis, J.L. (2001) "Mutual Fund Performance and Manager Style", *Financial Analysts Journal*, 57(1): 19–27.

Del Guercio, D. and Tkac, P.A. (2002) "The Determinants of the Flow of Funds of Managed Portfolios: Mutual Funds versus Pension Funds", *Journal of Financial and Quantitative Analysis*, 37: 523–57.

diBartolomeo, D. and Witkowski, E. (1997) "Mutual Fund Misclassification", *Financial Analysts Journal*, 53(5): 32–43.

Goetzmann, W.N. and Peles, N. (1997) "Cognitive Dissonance and Mutual Fund Investors", *Journal of Financial Research*, 20(2): 145–58.

Goriaev, A.P., Nijman, T.E. and Werker, B.A.J. (2001) "The Dynamics of the Impact of Past Performance on Mutual Fund Flows", Working Paper, Tilburg University.

Gruber, M.J. (1996) "Another Puzzle: The Growth in Actively Managed Mutual Funds", *Journal of Finance*, 51(3): 783–810.

Investment Company Institute (2001) "Trends in Mutual Fund Investing", December, Statistical Release.

Ivkovic, Z. (2000) "Is Blood Thicker than Water? Spillovers in Mutual Fund Families", Working Paper, Yale School of Management.

Khorana, A. (1996) "Top Management Turnover. An Empirical Investigation of Mutual Fund Managers", *Journal of Financial Economics*, 40(3): 403–27.

Khorana, A. and Servaes, H. (2000) "What Drives Market Share in the Mutual Fund industry?", Working Paper, DuPree College of Management, Georgia Institute of Technology, and London Business School.

Kim, M., Shukla, R. and Tomas, M. (2000) "Mutual Fund Objective Misclassification", *Journal of Economics and Business*, 52(4): 309–23.

Nanda, V., Wang, Z. and Zheng, L. (2000) "Family Values and the Star Phenomenon", Working Paper, University of Michigan Business School.

Siggelkow, N. (1998) "Why Focus? A Study of Intra-industry Focus Effects", Working Paper, Wharton School, University of Pennsylvania.

Sirri, E.R. and Tufano, P. (1998) "Costly Search and Mutual Fund Flows", *Journal of Finance*,53(5): 1589–622.

CHAPTER 11

Exploiting Industry Momentum with Sector Funds: The Case of the European Market

Radu Burlacu, Patrice Fontaine and Sonia Jimenez-Garces

11.1 INTRODUCTION

Academics and practitioners show a tremendous interest in the trending behavior of stock prices. A wide empirical literature establishes that common stocks exhibiting high returns on a period of 3–12 months (past winners) will overperform on subsequent periods. Moreover, past losers continue to be losers on future periods. This phenomenon, called momentum, represents one of the most important challenges for the concept of market efficiency. In practice, financial planners argue that momentum is one of the most effective investment vehicles.

The academic literature on the serial correlation between stock returns is rich and concerns mainly the American stock market. For example, Jegadeesh and Titman (1993, 2001) have studied intermediate-term serial correlations for American-listed common stocks in the 1965–89 period. An investor identifying common stocks that have overperformed during a 6-month period (lag period) and holding these stocks during a subsequent period of six months (hold period) is shown to realize a yearly abnormal return of approximately 12 percent. Similar results have been obtained by other researchers, such as Chan, Jegadeesh and Lakonishok (1996, 1999) on the American market, and Rouwenhorst (1998, 1999), Schiereck, De Bondt and

Weber (1999), Nijman, Swinkels and Verbeek (2004) on the European market and on emerging markets.[1]

How to reconcile the profitability of momentum strategies with the market efficiency hypothesis? Why is the positive performance realized with momentum strategies persistent in time? Some researchers (see for example, Conrad and Kaul, 1998) provide a rational explanation to this phenomenon: momentum abnormal returns are simply the compensation that investors ask for (still) unobserved common factors of risk. Easley, Hvidkjaer and O'Hara (2002) suggest that momentum may be related to information risk, an argument that is consistent with rational expectations equilibrium models considering asymmetrically informed investors (see, for example, Wang, 1993). Other authors put forward arguments based on behavioral finance (Barberis, Schleifer and Vishny, 1998; Daniel, Hirshleifer and Subrahmanyam, 1998; Hong and Stein, 1999). Behavioral arguments seem more in line with the empirical results obtained on the American market (Jegadeesh and Titman, 2001) and on the European market (Van Dijk and Huibers, 2002). The empirical literature suggests indeed that momentum profits are driven by delayed investors' overreactions that reverse in time.

From the practical point of view, profiting from stock return patterns with momentum strategies may be difficult, since investors incur transaction costs and must manage a high number of different common stocks. Moreover, most strategies put forward in the literature are based on shorting stocks, which may also be problematic. More importantly, in a paper entitled "The Illusory Nature of Momentum Profits", Lesmond, Schill and Zhou (2004) find that momentum strategies require frequent trading in securities with high trading costs. Stocks generating higher momentum returns incur higher trading costs as well. This prevents profitable realisation of momentum strategies. Earning profits with individual common stocks seems to be an illusion.

One way to circumvent these problems is to invest in mutual funds exhibiting strong performance persistence. Sector funds are a relevant investigation field for momentum since the latter is particularly strong at the industry level (see, for example, Moskowitz and Grinblatt, 1999). From the practical point of view, trading on sector funds is more convenient than trading with common stocks for individual investors. Moreover, transaction costs are fully known, making it easier to assess the profitability of momentum strategies. O'Neal (2000) has investigated the profitability of momentum strategies with industry-sector mutual funds. He argues that the main problem with constructing a momentum strategy with sector funds is that they are actively managed. Thus, momentum strategies may be ineffective due to poor active sector fund management, and not because of low momentum profitability with common stocks. If momentum strategies are profitable with sector funds, momentum becomes a real challenge for the market efficiency hypothesis since this would imply that investors are able to put in practice such strategies.

Using a sample of 31 Fidelity sector mutual funds with return data on a 10-year period, O'Neal (2000) finds that trading strategies of buying intermediate-term top-performing sector funds provide better returns than the market index (approached by the S&P 500 index). But these strategies do not appear to provide positive abnormal risk-adjusted returns since they entail higher total and systematic risk. Sector-fund momentum portfolios provide, however, better performance than actively managed equity mutual funds. The results obtained by Eakins and Stansell (2004) are more optimistic. Based on a sample of 19 sector funds with return data between 1995 and 2001, they find that momentum provides a higher level of return per unit of risk than investments in the Dow, the S&P 500, and the Wilshire 500 indexes. It is not clear, however, what momentum strategies are best-performing: the best strategies in the past are not necessarily those that should be used in the future. Moreover, their sample fund and analysis period are quite small, making the inferences lowly reliable from a statistical point of view.

This chapter contributes to the literature by investigating the profitability of momentum strategies with sector mutual funds on the European market. While momentum is clearly established for European common stocks, the effectiveness of momentum strategies for individual investors has not yet been analysed for this market. On a practical ground, our main objective is to assess the possibility of a European investor to earn substantial gains by trading on momentum with sector funds. We enrich the existing literature by controlling momentum for size and book-to-market effects. Existing studies analyse only market risk adjusted performance. Moreover, our study provides additional evidence on the importance of industry effects for explaining momentum. On the American market, momentum seems to be almost exclusively engendered by industry effects (see, for example, Moskowitz and Grinblatt, 1999). What distinguishes the European market is that industry effects are less pervasive relative to the American market. For example, Nijman, Swinkels and Verbeek (2004) find that industries account for about 30 percent of momentum effects, while individual stock-specific factors account for almost 60 percent (the remaining 10% being driven by country effects). This result is intriguing to the extent that the European Economic and Monetary Union (EMU) has increased the opportunity of diversification across industries to the detriment of country diversification. Industry effects are thus expected to be more important nowadays.

From a statistical point of view, this chapter contributes to the literature by considering a larger sample with a longer period relative to existing studies. We analyse 195 European sector funds for the 20-year period from March 1983 to March 2003. A problem that we solve, at least partially, is survivorship bias. While existing studies consider only surviving funds, we are able to collect data on dead funds by considering several Micropal S&P Mutual Fund Database disks available from 1998. It is well known that the survivorship bias tends to increase fund performance and, more importantly, induces artificial performance persistence. These problems are particularly stringent for sector funds. These funds have indeed higher probability of disappearance since they are concentrated in specific industries, incurring thus more risk. Since sector fund momentum may be partly driven by survivorship bias effects, we give special consideration to controlling for such effects.

Our chapter is structured as follows. The next section provides an overview of sector mutual funds in Europe. Then we present our sample and some descriptive statistics. The fourth section analyses the returns obtained by momentum portfolios while the fifth section deals rather with risk-adjusted returns. The sixth section presents some additional investigations on the profitability of momentum strategies by considering the returns consistency in time and some benchmark issues. The last section concludes.

11.2 INDUSTRY-SECTOR MUTUAL FUNDS

Sector funds, also called industry-specific funds, are actively managed equity mutual funds that specialize in firms belonging to a given industry or to a limited number of industries. Sector investing is thus an intermediate investment between placing in individual common stocks and in diversified equity portfolios.[2] This kind of placement is ideal for investors having a certain vision about economic sectors and seeking some diversification inside them.[3] When index funds were bringing high returns, sector funds were considered as unnecessarily volatile. From some years, investors turn toward sector investing for two main reasons. The first is that, in a world of increasing globalization, the industry may outperform the geography as a performance driver. The second is that sector placement may be used in order to counter bad market conditions. These two conditions undoubtedly meet for some years.

Sector funds' popularity has strongly increased during recent years in Europe; the number of sector funds created each year in Europe has almost doubled from 1997 to 2001. Professionals argue that industries are a better vehicle of portfolio diversification than countries after the EMU and the euro creation. According to a survey by Merrill Lynch and Gallup (*Les Echos*, February 2001), the percentage of European mutual fund assets managed by country/industry was respectively 48%/23% in 1997, and 8%/68% in 2001. During 2001, European sector mutual funds accounted for 5 percent (4.5%) of the number (total net assets) of actively managed equity funds. Moreover, the rise of the European market volatility these last years has incontestably provided strong opportunities for industry-based active management, explaining the rapid growth of industry-sector mutual funds. Industry factors make active management effective (see, for example,

Kacperczyk, Sialm and Zheng, 2005) since these factors are known to have private information content.[4]

Despite the popularity of sector funds and their rapid increase over recent years, the financial literature in this field is poor. The popular press states that the role of sector funds is to improve the performance of an already diversified portfolio but they should occupy only a small part of a client's portfolio. The arguments explaining their role are often conflicting, undoubtedly because sector funds are among the best but also among the worst performers.

The academic literature says little about sector funds and concentrates almost exclusively on performance issues. Sector funds do not appear to earn positive risk-adjusted abnormal returns on the American and European markets.[5] The evidence on momentum is mixed. While some authors document momentum effects for sector funds (O'Neal, 2000; Eakins and Stansell, 2004), others do not detect performance persistence for these funds (Khorana and Nelling, 1997; Tiwari and Vijh, 2001). Performance persistence for European sector funds has not already been studied as far as we know. Our paper tries to fill this gap by proposing a study of momentum profitability with sector funds on this market.

11.3 SAMPLE AND DESCRIPTIVE STATISTICS

The sample consists of 195 European sector funds[6] with at least five years of complete monthly return data between 1 March 1983 and 1 March 2003. The data has been extracted from various versions of the Micropal S&P Mutual Fund Database beginning in 1998 and from the Datastream Database. In our sample, 156 sector funds have return data on 10 years, while 31 funds have return data on 20 years. From previous versions of the Micropal database and Datastream, we have obtained data on 39 sector funds that disappeared before March 2003. All funds in our sample have at least five years of uninterrupted return data. The choice of a minimum five-year return period per fund is a compromise between the number of observations needed for robust performance estimation and the necessity to have a sufficient number of dead funds in order to mitigate survivorship bias issues. Returns are adjusted for capital gains and dividend distributions. We calculate returns based on funds' net asset values (NAV). The NAVs are net of expenses, transaction costs and management fees. Any front- or back-end load fees will be accounted for when we construct the momentum strategies.

The investment objective is provided by the Micropal's "Detailed Category" data-type. We consider sector funds with the following investment objectives: Biotechnology (3 funds), Distribution (1 fund), Energy (10 funds), Finance (27 funds), Food & Beverage (4 funds), Gold & Precious Metals (30 funds), Healthcare/Pharmaceuticals (37 funds), Information technology (1 fund), Leisure (3 funds), Multimedia (4 funds), Technology

Table 11.1 European sector mutual funds, 1983–2003

Type of fund	Number of funds		
	1983	1993	2003
Portuguese Mutual Funds	–	–	1
Austrian Mutual Funds	–	2	2
Belgian Mutual Funds	–	–	2
German Mutual Funds	4	4	3
Luxembourg Mutual Funds	3	9	8
Swedish reg. Funds	–	2	11
Italian Mutual Funds	–	10	11
Netherlands Mutual Funds	–	1	11
Norwegian Mutual Funds	–	–	15
Spanish Mutual Funds	2	6	20
Swiss Mutual Funds	2	9	25
French FCP and SICAV	5	23	32
UK Unit Trusts	15	38	54
Total	31	104	195

(61 funds), Telecommunications (14 funds) and Utilities (1 fund). Information on the type of fund (that is the country where the fund is managed) is provided in Table 11.1.

Most sector funds in our sample are UK unit trusts and French SICAV (Société d'Investissement à Capital Variable) and FCP (Fonds Communs de Placement), followed by Spanish and Swiss Mutual Funds. The management characteristics of our sample funds are provided in Table 11.2. Expenses represent about 1.5 percent of the total investment each year, front loads represent about 3.7 percent of the initial investment, while redemption fees are quite low, 0.25 percent of the ending investment value.

Expenses are automatically taken into account when we calculate the performance of the momentum portfolio since returns are net of expenses. Front loads intervene in our momentum performance calculations since they affect the initial investment. For example, for an initial investment of €1,000, the mean amount that is capitalized (in order to calculate the ending investment value) is 1,000 * (1 – 3.7%) = €963. For each momentum strategy, we deduce from the initial investment a front load which is the equally-weighted mean of the front loads of the sector funds in the portfolio (all momentum portfolios are equally weighted). Redemption fees will be accounted for each time when the portfolio will be rebalanced and at the date when the portfolio is completely liquidated (31 March 2003).

Table 11.2 Management characteristics for sector mutual funds

	TNA	Expenses	Front Loads	Redemption fees
Biotechnology	569.06	1.76	3.26	0.38
Energy	53.66	1.44	2.63	0.14
Finance	154.48	1.23	3.74	0.04
Food & Beverage	56.30	1.20	3.75	0.00
Healthcare	319.98	1.38	3.78	0.41
Technologies Information	120.54	1.75	3.00	0.00
Leisure	123.45	1.50	4.46	0.00
Multimedia	52.91	1.50	3.71	0.00
Gold & Precious Metals	54.21	1.66	3.09	0.23
Technology	249.02	1.40	4.35	0.35
Telecommunications	394.92	1.23	2.92	0.08
Utilities	106.02	1.50	5.25	–
All Funds	226.35	1.45	3.71	0.25

Notes: This table presents management characteristics for 195 European sector funds (1983–2003). The statistics provided are equally-weighted means. "TNA" (total net assets) is the closing market value of securities owned, plus all assets, minus all liabilities. TNA are reported in millions of €. "Expenses" (over the calendar year) refer to the percentage of the total investment that shareholders pay for the mutual fund's operating expenses. "Front loads" are the charges applied at the initial purchase. "Redemption fees" are fees charged to shareholders who sell fund shares. Expenses, front loads and redemption fees are all expressed as a percentage of the initial investment.

The IIA Europe is used as the proxy for the European market. Monthly index time series have been obtained from Independence International Associates (IIA). The IIA Europe Small Cap and Large Cap are the proxies for size indices, while the IIA Europe Value and Growth indexes are the proxies for the corresponding style segments. The return of the Small Minus Big size portfolio (SMB) is estimated by the difference in returns between the Small Cap and Large Cap indices. The return of the High Minus Low book-to-market portfolio (HML) is estimated by the difference in returns between the Value and Growth indices. EONIA (Euro Interbank Offered Rate) is taken as the risk-free rate of return.

As a preliminary analysis, we first construct an equally weighted portfolio of all sample sector funds during the analysis period 1983–2003. Figure 11.1 presents the value of a one-euro investment in the European market portfolio (the IIA European Index) and the equally weighted portfolio of all sample sector funds. Panel A presents the value of this investment for the entire analysis period (1983–2003), while Panel B presents the results on the more recent 10-year period 1993–2003. We have distinguished these two periods since the

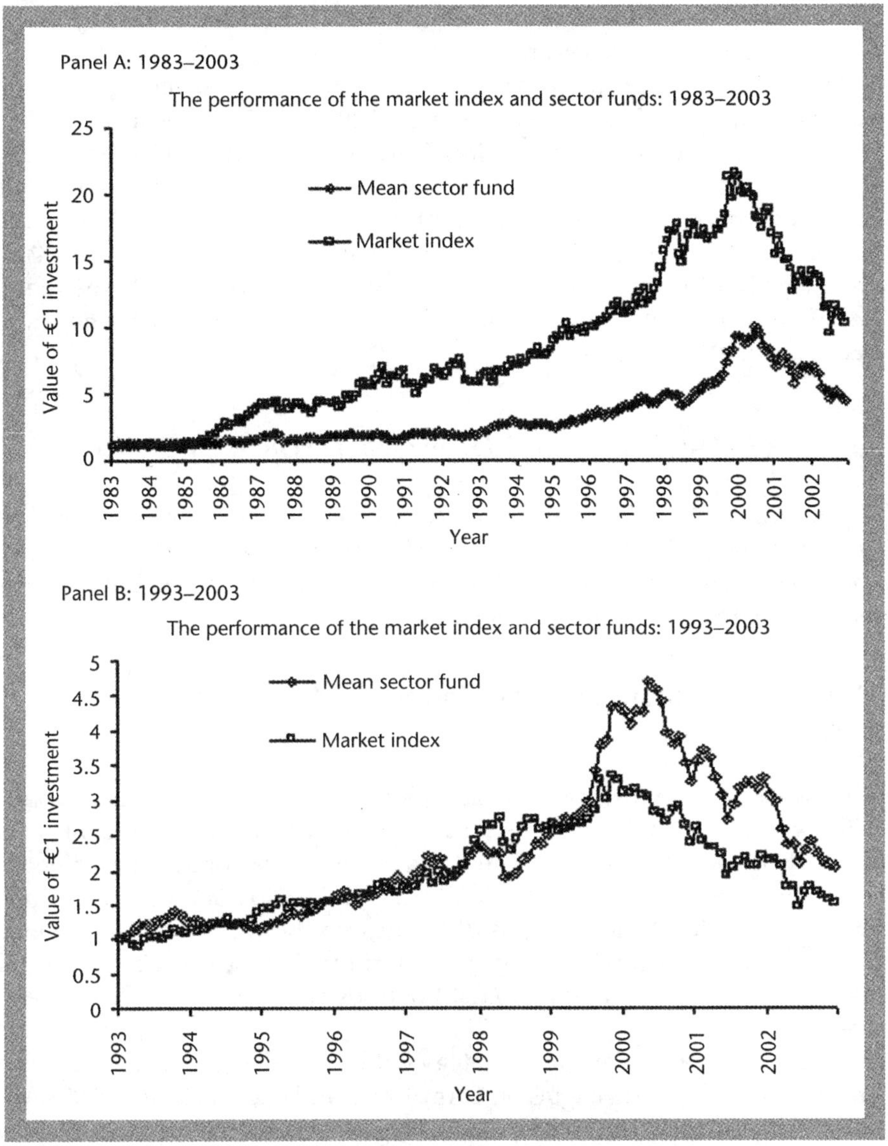

Figure 11.1 The performance of the market index and the equally weighted portfolio of sector funds

Notes: The figure presents the value of €1 investment in the market portfolio, approached by the IIA European Market Index, and an equally weighted portfolio of all sector funds in our sample. Panel A considers the entire analysis period, 1983–2003, while Panel B considers the more recent period, 1993–2003.

European market has experienced a significant bull market followed by a bear market during the last ten years.

The sector-fund portfolio has obtained a lower mean return than the European market index for the entire period 1983–2003. The picture is different for the more recent 10-year period. During the bull market in this period, the sector-fund portfolio seems to perform as well as the market index, but clearly overperforms in the more recent period during which the European market has experienced a strong decrease. Over the 5-year period 1998–2003, the sector-fund portfolio exhibits a positive mean return while the mean return of the market portfolio (and of the other style portfolios) is negative (see also Table 11.3).

11.4 AVERAGE RETURNS OF MOMENTUM PORTFOLIOS

This section presents the performance and risk of momentum portfolios. We first provide a preliminary analysis by considering momentum portfolios investing in a single rank position. We then consider momentum portfolios investing in several rank positions.

11.4.1 Momentum portfolios formed with a single ranked sector fund

We first verify the industry momentum effect by considering momentum portfolios based on a single rank position of the lag period. Since momentum is generally detected on intermediate-term periods, most of our strategies are based on 3, 6 and 12 months lag/hold periods. We do not report the results obtained with lag period lengths different from hold period lengths since they do not fundamentally change our interpretations. Most of our reported results consider on 6-month lag/hold periods since they provide the best-performing strategies.

We illustrate our momentum strategy with 3-month lag/hold periods. The first lag 3-month period begins on 1 April 1983 and ends on 31 June 1983. We have compounded the three corresponding monthly adjusted returns of all sample sector funds and then we have ranked them based on the resulting quarterly return. The momentum strategy one considers the best fund on each lag period (for example, the one that has obtained the highest return). Precisely, on 1 July 1983 we buy the fund exhibiting the best return on the lag period and then we hold this fund during the subsequent 3-month hold period (01/07/1983–30/09/1983). We then repeat this procedure on each consecutive 3-month non-overlapping period. The hold period for a given trading round represents the lag period for the next trading round and so on until the end of the analysis period. The momentum strategy two is

Table 11.3 Index and mutual fund return data

Benchmark	Return (%/year)	Standard deviation (%/year)
Panel A: 1983–2003		
IIA European Market Index	15.07	23.00
IIA Large Cap Index	15.60	23.56
IIA Small Cap Index	11.46	18.08
IIA Value Index	15.25	22.98
IIA Growth Index	12.22	19.05
Portfolio of sector funds	9.41	17.87
Portfolio of equity funds	10.26	15.59

Benchmark	Return (%/year)	Standard deviation (%/year)
Panel B: 1993–2003		
IIA European Market Index	6.72%	19.83%
IIA Large Cap Index	7.78%	19.83%
IIA Small Cap Index	4.58%	17.83%
IIA Value Index	5.61%	19.70%
IIA Growth Index	7.66%	20.25%
Portfolio of sector funds	9.76%	19.51%
Portfolio of equity funds	7.23%	16.11%

Benchmark	Return (%/year)	Standard deviation (%/year)
Panel C: 1998–2003		
IIA European Market Index	−1.57%	22.38%
IIA Large Cap Index	−0.60%	22.38%
IIA Small Cap Index	−4.33%	21.61%
IIA Value Index	−4.23%	21.46%
IIA Growth Index	−0.27%	24.89%
Portfolio of sector funds	3.42%	22.61%
Portfolio of equity funds	−1.14%	18.47%

Note: The table reports the mean annualized return and the annualized standard deviation of returns for market and style indices, for the equally weighted portfolio of European sector funds (195 funds) and for the equally weighted portfolio of European equity funds (2,319 funds).

identical to the momentum strategy one, the only difference being that we buy the second best fund of each lag period. The momentum strategy 195 consists of buying the sector fund exhibiting the lowest return on the lag period. We thus construct 195 strategies based on our 195 sample funds.

Since the number of funds at each lag period is not necessarily equal to the total number of strategies (195), several momentum portfolios may contain the same fund during some holding periods. For example, there are 31 funds with available data on the first lag period (01/03/1983 to 30/06/1983) while the number of strategies amounts to 195. For the lag periods with $n \leqslant 195$ available funds, we have ranked the available funds and then we have normalized the ranks by placing them uniformly in the interval [0; 1]. The fractional rank-interval corresponding to the least performing fund is thus $[0;1/n]$, while the fractional rank-interval of the best performing fund is $[(n-1)/n;1]$. The momentum strategy "i", where $i \in [1,2,\ldots,195]$, consists of buying the fund which fractional rank-interval includes $i/195$. Figure 11.2 reports the mean return and return standard deviation for these single-rank strategies.

Momentum strategies based on funds with high past returns (past winners) provide better future returns than strategies based on funds with mid or poor past returns (past losers). Nevertheless, high past winners incur more total risk. We also note that the link between risk and return is not linear. Past losers and past winners seem to exhibit similar levels of risk. This represents a pessimistic picture for momentum strategies based on poor past performers. Another conclusion that we draw is that strategies based on single rank positions present quite inconsistent correlations between ranks and returns since the dispersion of return–rank points around the least-squares line is quite high. Similar results have been obtained on the American market by O'Neal (2000) and Eakins and Stansell (2004). Forming momentum strategies with several ranked sector funds may be a solution to this problem.

11.4.2 Momentum portfolios formed with several ranked funds

We construct several strategies depending on the number of funds forming the momentum portfolios. The most diversified momentum portfolios are based on three percentile groupings. With such groupings, the "High" portfolio is formed with sector funds for which lag-period compounded returns are superior to the 66th return percentile. The "Low" portfolio is formed with sector funds for which lag-period returns are inferior to the 33th return percentile. Finally, the "Mid" portfolio includes sector funds for which lag-period returns are inferior to the 66th return percentile and superior to the 33th return percentile. All these portfolios are equally weighted. Front loads and redemption fees are assessed whenever investors face such costs by pursuing the corresponding strategy. We also form more narrowly

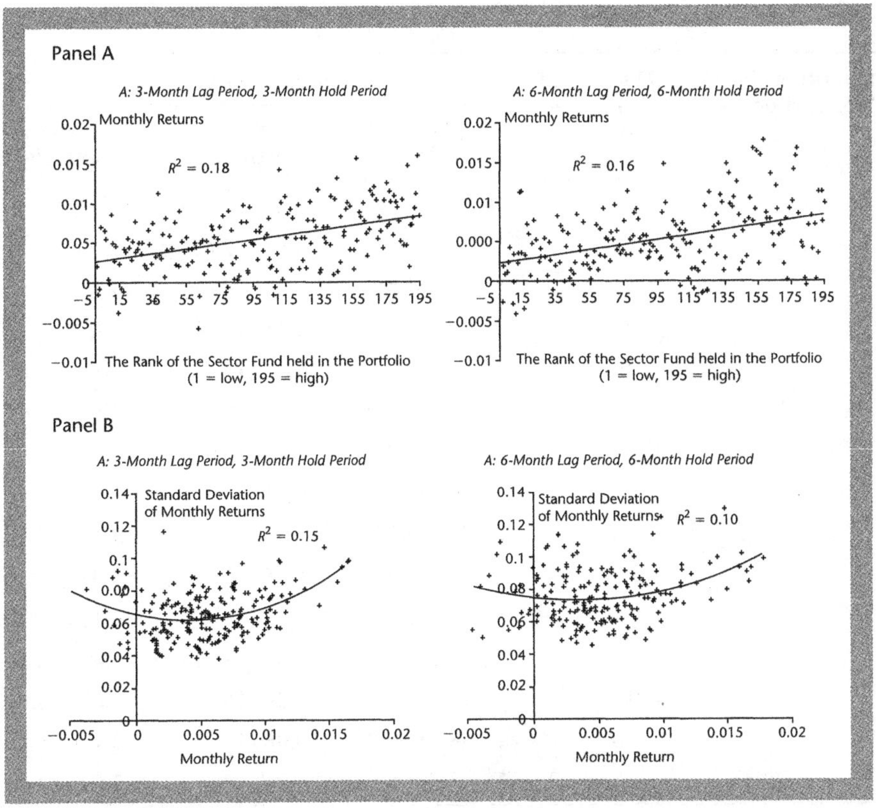

Figure 11.2 Monthly returns and standard deviations of single-fund momentum strategies

Notes: Panel A presents the mean monthly return obtained by each single-fund momentum portfolios on the analysis period, 1983–2003. Panel B presents the standard deviation of momentum portfolios' monthly returns plotted against mean monthly returns.

defined portfolios, based on 5, 10, 20 and 30 percentile groupings. With 30 percentile groupings, the three (High, Mid and Low) portfolios are formed with about six sector funds. In order to mitigate problems related to the non-adequacy between the number of available funds in each lag period and the number of funds needed for each portfolio, we use fractional ranks, as explained previously, rather than absolute ranks. Table 11.4 reports average returns for all combinations of (1) lag/hold period lengths, and (2) percentile groupings based on which the portfolios are formed.

Clearly, there is evidence of industry momentum for "High" portfolios (past winners). Momentum effects attain the highest level for narrowly defined portfolios (20 and 30 percentile groupings) constructed with 6-month lag/hold periods.[7] For example, with 20 percentile groupings (meaning

Table 11.4 Returns of momentum strategies, 1983–2003

Length of the lag/hold period	Number of percentile groups	Return (%/year)		
		High portfolio	Mid portfolio	Low portfolio
3 Months	3	10.73 (20.74)	11.86 (19.46)	6.97 (21.55)
	5	12.31 (22.61)	10.61 (17.65)	5.88 (24.5)
	10	12.76 (24.85)	9.33 (17.42)	5.71 (26.55)
	20	15.89 (27.27)	8.43 (17.3)	5.43 (27.94)
	30	14.34 (27.27)	8.14 (17.21)	5.26 (29.27)
6 Months	3	14.6 (20.17)	17.33 (21.43)	4.67 (21.57)
	5	17.24 (21.29)	13.96 (19.14)	3.94 (23.88)
	10	18.14 (23.79)	8.21 (18.47)	2.35 (26.4)
	20	22.85 (25.33)	7.85 (17.76)	2.19 (27.98)
	30	22.39 (27.8)	8.74 (18.11)	0.47 (28.75)
12 Months	3	10.73 (21.55)	7.42 (18.43)	6.19 (21.32)
	5	12.56 (22.9)	7.33 (16.42)	5.4 (23.74)
	10	14.97 (25.49)	8.56 (16.61)	5.83 (25.05)
	20	17.58 (26.99)	10.88 (17.06)	3.79 (25.16)
	30	18.67 (27.6)	10.94 (17.3)	1.91 (24.14)

Notes: This table presents annualized percentage returns and annualized standard deviations (between parentheses) for momentum portfolios constructed with 195 European sector funds on the period between 1983 and 2003. The "High" portfolio is formed with funds for which lag-period returns belong to the highest return percentile. The "Low" portfolio considers funds with lag-period returns in the lowest percentile. The "Mid" portfolio includes sector funds for which lag-period returns are in the middle return percentile. We form the momentum portfolios with various numbers of percentile groupings (3, 5, 10, 20 and 30 groupings). All momentum portfolios are equally weighted.

that the momentum portfolio is formed with approximately 10 funds), the "High" momentum strategy based on 6-month lag/hold periods provides an annualized return of 22.85 percent with a standard deviation of 25.33 percent. For comparison, the annualized return of the European market index on the same period is about 15.07 percent with a standard deviation of 23 percent, while the return of the equally weighted portfolio of all sample sector funds is 9.41 percent with a standard deviation of 17.87 percent (see Table 11.3). Momentum is less evident for diversified portfolios based on 6-month lag/hold periods: 3 and 5 percentile groupings indeed provide the lowest returns. Table 11.4 shows that momentum strategies produce similar levels of returns and risk for the more recent period 1993–2003, while the market index exhibits low returns for this period.

The picture for "Mid" portfolios and "Low" ones is pessimistic. Both categories produce noticeably lower returns than "High" portfolios. "Mid" portfolios provide better returns and lower risk than "Low" portfolios. The best "Mid" and "Low" portfolios are those based on a lower number of percentile groupings, contrary to "High" portfolios. Finally, we note that the total risk of "Low" portfolios is quite large, similar to the level of risk of "High" portfolios. This suggests that the risk-adjusted performance of "Low" portfolios is poor.

11.5 THE PERFORMANCE OF MOMENTUM PORTFOLIOS

Momentum strategies provide high level of returns but incur high levels of risk as well, making it necessary to analyze risk-adjusted returns. We adjust momentum portfolio returns for market-wide risk with Jensen's (1968) model, and for size and book-to-market risk with the Fama and French (1993) model. Jensen's (1968) model assumes that the realized excess return on a portfolio is a linear function of its systematic risk. In this context, a portfolio provides positive performance if its mean excess return is superior to the risk-premium corresponding to the portfolios' exposure to the market factor. The portfolio's performance is captured by the intercept α_i from the following equation:

$$r_{it} - r_{ft} = \alpha_i + \beta_{1i}(r_{mt} - r_{ft}) + \varepsilon_{it} \tag{11.1}$$

where r_{it} is the return on the portfolio i over the period t, r_{ft} is the risk-free rate of return, r_{mt} is the return on the market portfolio, α_i is the regression's intercept, β_{1i} is the portfolio's beta and ε_{it} is the error term. If the portfolio over-performs the market, then α_i is positive and vice versa.

Jensen's (1968) model may have little relevance for sector funds because they have specific characteristics in terms of investment style: they are known to overinvest in small, low-value firms. The Fama and French (1993) three-factor model is expected to be more relevant for sector funds since this model controls additionally for size and book-to-market risk. Fama and French (1993) suggest adding the returns of the SMB and HML portfolios as additional explanatory variables to equation (11.1):

$$r_{it} - r_{ft} = \alpha_i + \beta_{1i}(r_{mt} - r_{ft}) + \beta_{2i}SMB_t + \beta_{3i}HML_t + \varepsilon_{it} \tag{11.2}$$

where SMB_t is the difference in returns between small and large capitalization stocks and HML_t is the difference in returns between high and low book-to-market stocks over the period t. A positive α_i indicates that the portfolio's mean excess return is higher than the sum between the market, size, and book-to-market risk premiums.

Table 11.5 provides Jensen's (1968) and Fama and French's (1993) alphas of various momentum portfolios, depending on the length of the lag/lead period and percentile groupings based on which the portfolios are formed.

Table 11.5 Performance of momentum strategies, 1983–2003

Length of lag/hold period	Number of percentile groups	Jensen's (1968) alpha (%/year)		Fama and French's (1993) alpha (%/year)	
		High portfolio	Low portfolio	High portfolio	Low portfolio
3 Months	3	2.06 (0.14)	−1.63 (0.10)	2.12 (0.23)	−2.15 (0.24)
	5	3.67 (0.4)	−2.64 (0.21)	3.75 (0.59)	−3.18 (0.39)
	10	4.15 (0.44)	−2.82 (0.2)	4.47 (0.64)	−3.21 (0.3)
	20	6.68 (0.91)	−2.74 (0.17)	7.23 (1.32)	−3.01 (0.23)
	30	5.11 (0.51)	−3.16 (0.21)	5.51 (0.74)	−3.60 (0.3)
6 Months	3	5.48 (1.13)	−3.69 (0.47)	5.40 (1.78)	−4.03 (0.79)
	5	8.06 (2.16)	−4.25 (0.49)	8.07 (3.13)*	−4.62 (0.77)
	10	8.91 (1.95)	−5.65 (0.74)	9.04 (2.72)*	−5.93 (1.07)
	20	12.99 (3.5)*	−6.06 (0.82)	13.27 (4.59)**	−6.20 (1.04)
	30	12.40 (2.69)	−7.49 (1.22)	12.89 (3.7)*	−7.60 (1.53)
12 Months	3	1.63 (0.08)	−2.03 (0.15)	1.6 (0.15)	−2.57 (0.31)
	5	3.31 (0.3)	−2.45 (0.18)	3.27 (0.51)	−2.76 (0.29)
	10	5.63 (0.69)	−2.22 (0.14)	5.57 (1.10)	−2.40 (0.2)
	20	8.14 (1.26)	−4.36 (0.52)	7.96 (1.83)	−4.39 (0.63)
	30	9.03 (1.49)	−5.79 (0.99)	8.79 (2.12)	−5.94 (1.19)

Notes: This table presents annualized percentage alphas and, between parentheses, *t*-statistics for momentum portfolios constructed with 195 European sector funds (1983–2003). The "High" portfolio is formed with funds for which lag-period returns are in the highest return percentile. The "Low" portfolio considers funds with lag-period returns in the lowest percentile. The "Mid" portfolio includes sector funds for which lag-period returns are in the middle return percentile. We form the momentum portfolios with various percentile groupings (3, 5, 10, 20 and 30 groupings). All momentum portfolios are equally weighted.

The results reported in this table strengthen our previous conclusions. The best strategies are those formed with 6-month lag/lead periods and with narrowly defined percentile groupings. For example, with 20 percentile groupings, the momentum portfolio overperformed the market, on a risk-adjusted basis, by a significant 12.99 percent. The results obtained with Fama and French's (1993) model are even more optimistic and have higher significance levels. "Low" portfolios exhibit negative alphas, but these alphas are not significant. Portfolios formed with 3 and 12 months lag/lead periods obtain lower risk-adjusted returns.

Table 11.6 presents the rough returns and risk-adjusted returns for momentum portfolios for the more recent period between 1993 and 2003. Momentum portfolios based on 6-month lag/lead periods continue to provide the best

Table 11.6 Performance of momentum strategies, 1993–2003

Length of lag/hold period	Number of percentile groups	Returns (%/year)		Jensen's (1968) alpha (%/year)		Fama and French's (1993) alpha (%/year)	
		High portfolio	Low portfolio	High portfolio	Low portfolio	High portfolio	Low portfolio
3 Months	3	10.73 (20.74)	6.97 (21.55)	10.60 (1.81)	−1.87 (0.07)	8.63 (1.56)	−3.67 (0.28)
	5	12.31 (22.61)	5.88 (24.5)	15.22 (2.99)*	−3.52 (0.19)	13.21 (2.75)*	−5.33 (0.48)
	10	12.76 (24.85)	5.71 (26.55)	16.85 (2.98)*	−6.46 (0.59)	15.31 (2.72)*	−7.97 (0.95)
	20	15.89 (27.27)	5.43 (27.94)	21.18 (3.37)*	−5.07 (0.32)	19.58 (3.44)*	−6.49 (0.54)
	30	14.34 (27.27)	5.26 (29.27)	20.51 (2.99)*	−6.40 (0.46)	18.64 (2.89)*	−7.98 (0.71)
6 Months	3	14.49 (20.05)	4.67 (21.57)	13.26 (3.24)*	−2.29 (0.1)	11.14 (3.09)*	−3.99 (0.35)
	5	17.01 (21.23)	3.94 (23.88)	17.01 (4.31)**	−5.68 (0.5)	15.15 (4.15)**	−7.25 (0.94)
	10	17.91 (23.70)	2.35 (26.40)	20.77 (4.06)**	−6.37 (0.53)	18.87 (4.01)**	−8.01 (0.97)
	20	22.68 (25.21)	2.19 (27.98)	25.49 (4.68)**	−6.97 (0.55)	23.73 (4.74)**	−8.52 (0.93)
	30	22.22 (27.66)	0.47 (28.75)	26.46 (3.86)**	−7.73 (0.59)	24.62 (4.24)**	−9.37 (0.99)
12 Months	3	10.46 (21.25)	6.19 (21.32)	6.88 (0.66)	−0.3 (0.01)	4.58 (0.47)	−1.74 (0.07)
	5	12.14 (22.62)	5.40 (23.74)	8.64 (0.89)	−1.74 (0.05)	6.39 (0.72)	−2.89 (0.15)
	10	14.33 (25.16)	5.83 (25.05)	12.48 (1.46)	−2.16 (0.07)	10.02 (1.30)	−3.19 (0.16)
	20	16.89 (26.72)	3.79 (25.16)	14.7 (1.77)	−2.72 (0.10)	12.12 (1.57)	−3.74 (0.21)
	30	17.92 (27.30)	1.91 (24.14)	17.03 (2.15)	−4.86 (0.36)	14.24 (1.95)	−5.72 (0.52)

Notes: This table presents annualized percentage alphas and, between parentheses, *t*-statistics for momentum portfolios constructed with 195 European sector funds (1993–2003). The "High" portfolio is formed with funds for which lag-period returns are in the highest return percentile. The "Low" portfolio considers funds with lag-period returns in the lowest percentile. We form the momentum portfolios with various percentile groupings (3, 5, 10, 20 and 30 groupings). All momentum portfolios are equally weighted.
* 0.10 significance level; ** 0.05 significance level.

results, with alphas exceeding 20 percent for portfolios based on narrowly defined percentile groupings. Such increased outperformance is not unexpected: the market portfolio has earned low returns on this period and its volatility has attained high levels. Even 3-month lag/lead momentum portfolios provide significant positive alphas for such groupings, while 12-month lag/lead portfolios exhibit non-significant performance. "Low" momentum portfolios exhibit poor mean returns and negative alphas, strengthening the previous finding that momentum is driven mainly by past winners.

11.6 ADDITIONAL INVESTIGATIONS

We provide additional insights on the profitability of momentum strategies with sector funds by comparing them with alternative benchmarks, such as diversified equity mutual funds and style benchmarks. We also check performance consistency by studying the sign of momentum portfolios' abnormal returns. Finally, we check the robustness of our results with alternative (industry-based) benchmarks.

11.6.1 Comparison with equity funds and market/style indices

For the entire analysis period 1983–2003, we have computed various performance measures, such as Sharpe's ratio, Treynor's ratio, and Jensen's (1968) and Fama and French's (1993) alphas for momentum portfolios, equity funds and market/style indices. The Sharpe ratio is calculated by dividing the excess average annualized return of the portfolio by the portfolio's standard deviation. Treynor's ratio is obtained by dividing the excess average annualized return by the portfolio's (or benchmark's) beta. While the Treynor reward-to-volatility measure is adapted for diversified portfolios, the Sharpe measure may be relevant for sector funds since these funds are concentrated in specific market segments. The results are provided in Table 11.7. Since 6-month lag/lead portfolios have systematically obtained the best performances, we do not include 3 and 12-month lag/lead momentum in our presentation.

All "High" momentum portfolios obtained with 6-month lag/lead periods outstripped the mean European equity fund and the market/style indices over the analysis period 1983–2003. At the other extreme, all "Low" momentum portfolios are dominated by the mean equity fund and market/style indices. The Sharpe and Treynor ratios of "Low" momentum portfolios are all negative, indicating that these portfolios have obtained lower returns than the risk-free asset over the analysis period.

Table 11.7 Performance of momentum strategies, 1983–2003

Portfolio	Number of percentile groups	Sharpe ratio (%)	Treynor ratio (%)	Jensen's (1968) alpha (%/year)	Fama and French's (1993) alpha (%/year)
"High" momentum	3	27.08	24.63	5.48 (1.13)	5.40 (1.78)
	5	36.67	38.14	8.06 (2.16)	8.07 (3.13)*
	10	34.06	39.79	8.91 (1.95)	9.04 (2.72)*
	20	48.59	51.97	12.99 (3.5)*	13.27 (4.59)**
	30	40.28	43.75	12.40 (2.69)	12.89 (3.7)*
"Low" momentum	3	−21.38	−21.29	−3.69 (0.47)	−4.03 (0.79)
	5	−24.46	−28.85	−4.25 (0.49)	−4.62 (0.77)
	10	−30.28	−41.73	−5.65 (0.74)	−5.93 (1.07)
	20	−30.61	−37.82	−6.06 (0.82)	−6.20 (1.04)
	30	−36.17	−50.82	−7.49 (1.22)	−7.60 (1.53)
Equity funds		12.88	6.48	0.82 (0.25)	0.21 (0.07)
Large Cap IIA Index		23.75	5.61	0.49 (0.39)	0.24 (0.18)
Small Cap IIA Index		15.21	4.13	−0.73 (−0.33)	−0.09 (−0.04)
Value IIA Index		23.47	5.65	0.51 (0.33)	−0.14 (−0.1)
Growth IIA Index		18.77	4.46	−0.52 (−0.38)	−0.22 (−0.15)

Notes: This table presents annualized percentage Sharpe ratios, Treynor ratios and Jensen's (1968) and Fama and French's (1993) alphas for momentum portfolios constructed with 195 European sector funds (the analysis period is 1983–2003). We provide the same performance measures for equity funds and market/style indices. Alpha's *t*-statistics are provided between parentheses. The "High" momentum portfolio is formed with funds for which lag-period returns are in the highest return percentile. The "Low" momentum portfolio considers funds with lag-period returns in the lowest percentile. We form the momentum portfolios with various percentile groupings (3, 5, 10, 20 and 30 groupings). All momentum portfolios are equally weighted.

11.6.2 Consistency of abnormal returns

Sector-fund investors are known to be highly speculative, implying that they are sensitive to the change in abnormal returns. It is even stated that the high uncertainty of cash-flows from sector-fund investors is the main reason for the disappearance of many sector funds. We adopt the perspective of sector-fund investors and check the consistency of momentum strategies over time by analysing the number of months with positive abnormal returns. The abnormal return is the difference between the realized return and the expected (normal) return. The latter is approached in several ways: by (1) the market return, (2) the expected return from the market model (Jensen, 1968) and (3) the expected return from a model considering the market, size, and book-to-market factors (Fama and French, 1993). The abnormal return specifications are respectively:

$$AR^1_{it} = r_{it} - r_{ft} - (r_{mt} - r_{ft}) = r_{it} - r_{mt} \tag{11.3}$$

$$AR^2_{it} = r_{it} - r_{ft} - \beta^M_i (r_{mt} - r_{ft}) \tag{11.4}$$

$$AR^3_{it} = r_{it} - r_{ft} - \beta^M_i (r_{mt} - r_{ft}) - \beta^{SMB}_i SMB_t - \beta^{HML}_i HML_t \tag{11.5}$$

where the notations are as follows: r_{it} is the return of the portfolio i over the period t; r_{ft} is the risk-free rate of return; r_{mt} is the return on the market portfolio; SMB_t is the difference in returns between small and large capitalization stocks t; HML_t is the difference in returns between high and low book-to-market stocks; β^M_i is the funds' beta with respect to the market factor; β^{SMB}_i is the funds' beta with respect to the SMB factor; and β^{HML}_i is the funds' beta with respect to the HML factor. Table 11.8 reports the number of months in percentage of the total number of months that momentum portfolios exhibited positive abnormal returns. The analysis in performed on the period 1983–2003, and then on the more recent period, 1993–2003. For expositional convenience, we provide only the results obtained for 6-month lag/lead momentum portfolios.

The various "High" momentum portfolios have provided positive abnormal returns in more than 50 percent of all months. On the more recent 10-year period, the percentage of "High" momentum portfolios that provided positive abnormal returns was close to 60 percent. The higher percentages are found, without surprise, for narrowly defined portfolios, that is portfolios based on a high number of percentile groupings. "Low" portfolios provided positive abnormal returns in less than 50 percent of all months during the 20-year analysis period and during the more recent 10-year period. Similar (unexposed) results have been found when we have aggregated abnormal returns on quarterly and yearly periods.

Table 11.8 Percentage of months with positive abnormal returns

Portfolio	Number of percentile groups	Period: 1983–2003			Period: 1993–2003		
		Market	Jensen (1968)	Fama and French (1993)	Market	Jensen (1968)	Fama and French (1993)
"High"	3	49.6	51.7	50.0	54.2	57.9	53.7
	5	51.3	51.7	50.9	56.7	57.9	56.2
	10	51.7	51.3	50.9	56.7	56.2	57.0
	20	53.4	54.3	53.0	59.2	60.3	57.9
	30	53.4	56.0	54.7	58.3	62.0	59.5
"Low"	3	48.3	50.6	47.3	50.0	52.1	45.5
	5	46.2	50.2	48.5	47.5	48.8	45.5
	10	45.3	49.4	47.3	45.0	47.9	46.3
	20	45.7	46.4	45.6	44.2	46.3	43.8
	30	44.4	45.6	46.0	45.0	45.5	47.1

Notes: This table presents the number of months with positive abnormal returns divided by the total number of months during the corresponding analysis period (in percentage). The momentum portfolios are constructed with 195 European sector funds. The "High" momentum portfolio is formed with funds for which lag-period returns are in the highest return percentile. The "Low" momentum portfolio considers funds with lag-period returns in the lowest percentile. Momentum portfolios are formed with various percentile groupings (3, 5, 10, 20 and 30 groupings). All momentum portfolios are equally weighted.

11.6.3 Benchmark specification

Do momentum strategies perform better than the corresponding industry indexes? In other words, is the performance of momentum portfolios simply the consequence of the good performance of the corresponding industry indexes? To answer this question, one needs to consider industry benchmarks. Moreover, the existing literature suggests that a relevant benchmark should reflect common factors of returns that are representative of the fund's investment universe (Lehmann and Modest, 1987; Rennie and Cowhey, 1990; Elton, Gruber, Sanjiv and Hlavka, 1993). Following this line of theory, industry indices may be more appropriated for determining the performance of sector-fund managers, and consequently for our momentum strategy, since these funds are concentrated in specific industry market segments.

We have calculated Jensen's (1968) and Fama and French (1993) alphas with respect to industry indexes for various momentum portfolios. For expositional convenience, only the results are presented here. In one approach, we have used the S&P Europe Industrial Index as a common industry index for all sector funds. In a second approach, we have considered Dow Jones Euro Stoxx indices that we have matched to our sample sector funds depending on their investment objective. Then, for each momentum portfolio and during each given month, we have formed an industry benchmark as an equally weighted average of the Dow Jones Euro Stoxx indices matched to the sector funds in the momentum portfolio. Whatever the approach, our results do not change fundamentally: 6-month lag/lead "High" momentum portfolios still exhibit significantly positive alphas, and vice versa for "Low" momentum portfolios. Once again, we find that 3-month and 12-month lag/lead portfolios exhibit poor performance. Nevertheless, our results have lower significance levels, suggesting that the performance of momentum portfolio is partly due to the momentum in industry indices. Controlling for the latter makes the momentum effect in our portfolios less pervasive.

11.7 CONCLUSION

The literature is skeptical about the possibility to earn, in practice, abnormal returns with momentum strategies based on individual common stocks (Lesmond, Schill and Zhou, 2004). Sector funds may be of interest for individual investors in order to put in practice strategies exploiting industry momentum effects. We have attempted to study the profitability of such strategies using a large sample of European sector funds aver a 20-year analysis period. Relative to the existing literature, we alleviate survivorship-bias issues and we use more sophisticated performance measures in order to account for the profitability of momentum strategies.

While momentum strategies seem to provide non-significant performance over the entire 20-year analysis period, we find significant performance with 6-month lag/lead strategies formed with past winners on the 10-year period between 1993 and 2003. These strategies are particularly profitable if the momentum portfolios are formed with a small number of sector funds. Our results are robust to market, size, and book-to-market effects. Moreover, abnormal returns are consistent in time, which may present an interest for sector fund investors which are known to be highly speculative. Our results seem not to be simply the outcome of momentum industry effects. Indeed, we find that momentum portfolios provide significant abnormal returns even when the performance is controlled for industry effects with Dow Jones Euro Stoxx indices.

One explanation for the good performance of sector fund momentum strategies is that the bad economic conditions of recent years may have provided strong opportunities for active management. Such opportunities may have been accelerated by the EMU, especially after 1992, a year that paved the way to the single European currency and diminished the advantage of passive management on the European market. Moreover, active management opportunities may have been boosted by the strong market volatility experienced by the European market during recent years. Informational asymmetries between investors are known to be stronger under such circumstances. The academic research suggests that private information effects induce momentum in stock returns (Wang, 1993, 1994), a topic that is expected to receive special attention in the empirical literature (Easley, Hvidkjaer and O'Hara, 2002). We leave this intriguing research issue for future research.

NOTES

1. For additional evidence on momentum with common stocks on the European market, see also Bird and Whitaker (2003, 2004), Becker and Ochman (2004) and Forner and Marhuenda (2003). All these studies show that there is a significant momentum effect for European common stocks.
2. For example, "technology" sector funds are funds investing a large part of their assets in global technology equities or related instruments. Some of the sub-sectors include multimedia, semiconductors or networking.
3. In the same category, we find global sector funds including portfolios specializing in several lowly correlated industries for diversification purposes. A more general group is called specialty funds or theme-funds including funds that specialize indirectly in certain economic sectors. This category includes environment and ethical funds, which are funds that concentrate their assets in economic sectors or firms that show consideration for contemporaneous social values. We do not consider such funds in our sample since they are rather diversified across industries, making industry effects less evident.
4. For example, Foster (1980) finds significant intra-industry reactions to the timing and content of information releases by firms. Foster (1980, 1981) documents significant firm stock price reactions to earnings announcements of other firms in the same industry. Szewczyk (1992) finds that informational effects associated with the announcement of common stock and convertible debt offerings by a firm have significant impact on the share prices of other firms in the same industry.
5. Khorana and Nelling (1997) analyse the performance of 147 American sector funds to the period 1976–92. Sector funds perform better than sector indexes but less well than diversified indexes. Dellva, DeMaskey and Smith (2001) find positive stock-picking and negative market timing performance for a sample of 35 Fidelity sector funds over the period 1989–98. Tiwari and Vijh (2001) find non-significant performance for a survivorship-bias-free sample of 607 American sector funds.
6. These funds are domiciled and invest most of their assets in European equity securities.
7. This result is different from that found by O'Neal (2000) for the American market. For the American market, momentum is strongest for 12-month holding periods.

REFERENCES

Barberis, N., Schleifer, A. and Vishny, R. (1998) "A Model of Investor Sentiment", *Journal of Financial Economics*, 49(3): 307–43.

Becker, Y. and Ochman, R. (2004) "Predicting Extreme Performers in European Equities", *Journal of Asset Management*, 4(6): 367–91.

Bird, R. and Whitaker, J. (2003) "The Performance of Value and Momentum Investment Portfolios: Recent Experience in the Major European Markets", *Journal of Asset Management*, 4(4): 221–46.

Bird, R. and Whitaker, J. (2004) "The Performance of Value and Momentum Investment Portfolios: Recent Experience in the Major European Markets Part 2", *Journal of Asset Management*, 5(3): 157–75.

Chan, L.K.C., Jegadeesh, N. and Lakonishok, J. (1996) "Momentum Strategies", *Journal of Finance*, 51(5): 1681–713.

Chan, L.N., Jegadeesh, N. and Lakonishok, J. (1999) "The Profitability of Momentum Strategies", *Financial Analysts Journal*, 55(6): 80–90.

Conrad, J. and Kaul, G. (1998) "An Anatomy of Trading Strategies", *Review of Financial Studies*, 11(3): 489–519.

Daniel, K., Hirshleifer, D. and Subrahmanyam, A. (1998) "A Theory of Over-Confidence, Self-Attribution, and Security Market Under- and Over-Reactions", *Journal of Finance*, 53(6): 1839–86.

Dellva, W.L., DeMaskey, A.L. and Smith, C.A. (2001) "Selectivity and Market Timing Performance of Fidelity Sector Mutual Funds", *The Financial Review*, 36(1): 39–54.

Eakins, S. and Stansell, S. (2004) "Do Momentum Strategies Work?", *Journal of Investing*, 13(3): 65–71.

Easley, D., Hvidkjaer, S. and O'Hara, M. (2002) "Is Information Risk a Determinant of Asset Returns", *The Journal of Finance*, 52(5): 2185–221.

Elton, E.J., Gruber, M.J., Sanjiv, D. and Hlavka, M. (1993) "Efficiency with Costly Information: A Reinterpretation of Evidence from Managed Portfolios", *Review of Financial Studies*, 6(1): 1–22.

Fama, E.F. and French, K.R. (1993) "Common Risk Factors in the Return of Bonds and Stocks", *Journal of Financial Economics*, 33(1): 3–53.

Forner, C. and Marhuenda, J. (2003) "Contrarian and Momentum Strategies in the Spanish Stock Market", *European Financial Management*, 9(1): 67–88.

Foster, G. (1980) "Externalities and Financial Reporting", *Journal of Finance*, 35(2): 521–33.

Foster, G. (1981) "Intra-Industry Information Transfers Associated with Earnings Releases", *Journal of Accounting and Economics*, 24(3): 201–32.

Hong, H. and Stein, J.C. (1999) "A Unified Theory of Underreaction, Momentum Trading, and Overreaction in Asset Markets", *Journal of Finance*, 54(6): 2143–84.

Jegadeesh, N. and Titman, S. (1993) "Returns to Buying Winners and Selling Losers: Implications for Stock Market Efficiency", *Journal of Finance*, 48(1): 65–91.

Jegadeesh, N. and Titman, S. (2001) "Profitability of Momentum Strategies: An Evaluation of Alternative Explanations", *Journal of Finance*, 51(2): 699–720.

Jensen, M. (1968) "The Performance of Mutual Funds in the Period 1945–1964", *The Journal of Finance*, 23(2): 389–416.

Kacperczyk, M., Sialm, C. and Zheng, L. (2005) "On the Industry Concentration of Actively Managed Equity Mutual Funds", *Journal of Finance*, 60(4): 1983–2011.

Khorana, A. and Nelling, E. (1997) "The Performance, Risk and Diversification of Sector Funds", *Financial Analysts Journal*, 53(3): 62–74.

Lehmann, B.N. and Modest, D.M. (1987) "Mutual Fund Performance Evaluation: A Comparison of Benchmarks and Benchmark Comparisons", *Journal of Finance*, 42(2): 233–65.

Lesmond, D., Schill, M. and Zhou, C. (2004) "The Illusory Nature of Momentum Profits", *Journal of Financial Economics*, 71(2): 349–81.

Moskowitz, T.J. and Grinblatt, M. (1999) "Do Industries Explain Momentum?", *Journal of Finance*, 54(4): 1249–90.

Nijman, T., Swinkels, L. and Verbeek, M. (2004) "Do Countries or Industries Explain Momentum in Europe?", *Journal of Empirical Finance*, 11(4): 461–81.

O'Neal, E. (2000) "Industry Momentum and Sector Mutual Funds", *Financial Analysts Journal*, 56(4): 37–49.

Rennie, E. and Cowhey, T. (1990) "The Successful Use of Benchmark Portfolios: A Case Study", *Financial Analysts Journal*, 46(5): 18–26.

Rouwenhorst, G.K. (1998) "International Momentum Strategies", *Journal of Finance*, 53(1): 267–84.

Rouwenhorst, G.K. (1999) "Local Return Factors and Turnover in Emerging Stock Markets", *Journal of Finance*, 54(4): 1439–64.

Schiereck, D., De Bondt, W. and Weber, M. (1999) "Contrarian and Momentum Strategies in Germany", *Financial Analysts Journal*, 55(6): 104–16.

Szewczyk, S. (1992) "The Intra-Industry Transfer of Information Inferred from Announcements of Corporate Security Offerings", *Journal of Finance*, 17(5): 1935–45.

Tiwari, A. and Vijh, A. (2001) "Sector Fund Performance", Working Paper, University of Iowa, Henry B. Tippie College of Business, p. 39.

Van Dijk, R. and Huibers, F. (March/April 2002) "European Price Momentum and Analyst Behavior", *Financial Analysts Journal*, 58(2): 96–105.

Wang, J. (1993) "A Model of Intertemporal Asset Prices Under Asymmetric Information", *Review of Economic Studies*, 60(2): 249–82.

Wang, J. (1994) "A Model of Competitive Stock Trading Volume", *Journal of Political Economy*, 102(1): 127–68.

CHAPTER 12

US and Chinese Mutual Fund Regulation

*Mercer Bullard, Guangxi Jia, Jin Meng and Ji Qi**

12.1 INTRODUCTION

During the last quarter century, mutual funds have become the investment vehicle of choice for most American investors. Six percent of US households had $135 billion invested in mutual funds in 1980, and by the end of 2004, 48 percent of households had $8.1 trillion invested in mutual funds (Investment Company Institute, 2005). There are now more than 8,000 US mutual funds, compared with only 564 in 1980 (*ibid.*).

The popularity of mutual funds in the USA has been attributable to their operational structure and, in no small part, to the regulatory regime under which they operate. Mutual funds generally offer the benefits of diversification and professional management at substantially lower cost than individual brokerage accounts. Buying and selling mutual fund shares is a simple process, and fund shares, even shares of funds that invest in less liquid asset classes, are highly liquid, because US law requires that funds value their shares at their market value, honor redemption requests at the same-day closing price of the fund, and pay the proceeds shortly thereafter. Fund fees and investment performance are standardized and relatively transparent, thereby facilitating comparisons among different funds. In contrast, the rules governing the operation of unregistered funds, known as hedge funds, vary substantially by fund.

In comparison to the US mutual fund industry, mutual funds in China are a nascent industry – only $52 billion in assets – with a nascent regulatory structure (Hamlin, 2005). In the last few years, China has adopted a

* The authors thank Martin Chen, Taylor Hui, Ya-ping Lee and Qiumei Yang for their helpful comments and suggestions.

slew of statutes and rules for mutual funds. If the US experience is any guide, the success of the Chinese mutual fund industry will depend greatly on the efficacy of the regulatory system under which it operates. This chapter surveys key aspects of the current state of Chinese mutual fund regulation and compares these aspects to regulation in the USA. The ensuing discussion addresses the following topics: fund offerings; fund governance; disclosure requirements; fund fees; distribution compensation; pricing, sales and redemptions; affiliated transactions; and money market funds.

12.2 BACKGROUND

The primary regulator of US mutual funds is the Securities and Exchange Commission (SEC), which is responsible for administering and promulgating rules under the Investment Company Act of 1940 and other federal securities laws. The primary regulator of Chinese mutual funds is the Chinese Securities Regulatory Commission (CSRC), which is responsible for administering and promulgating rules under the Law of the People's Republic of China on Securities Investment Fund (Investment Fund Law) and other national statutes. Both the SEC and CSRC are independent agencies with primary authority over securities regulation. Neither agency has the authority to bring criminal cases, but both may refer securities cases to the relevant prosecutorial authority and provide support in criminal proceedings brought by criminal prosecutors.

In both the USA and China, mutual funds are primarily regulated under a statute that specifically governs the operation of investment companies, including mutual funds: the Investment Company Act in the USA, and the Investment Fund Law in China. Mutual funds may also be directly or indirectly regulated under other securities laws, including particularly statutes relating to the offer and sales of securities, the regulation of brokers and investment advisers, and the operation and structure of companies.

One significant difference between US and Chinese mutual fund regulation is that the SEC's authority is not exclusive. The SEC shares authority over certain aspects of securities regulation with the legislatures and securities regulators of the states. The states generally have the authority to enact securities legislation, adjudicate civil claims, and bring enforcement cases related to securities activities within their jurisdictions unless there is a direct conflict with federal law. During the last ten years, the US Congress has enacted legislation substantially limiting states' securities regulatory authority, but states continue to have the ability to substantially influence securities regulation in the USA. In contrast, Chinese securities regulation finds its exclusive source in national law. There are no Chinese legislative bodies or securities regulators that can operate independent of the oversight of the Standing Committee of the National People's Congress and the CSRC under the State Council.

12.3 FUND OFFERINGS

The USA and China take fundamentally different regulatory approaches to the public offering of mutual funds. The public offering of mutual funds in the USA is regulated directly through rules that apply to the fund itself. This reflects the customary organization of mutual funds as independent business entities, such as corporations or business trusts, that issue interests that constitute securities under the securities laws. Mutual funds are overseen by a board of directors and have all of the essential characteristics of other types of business entities, including the right to enter into contracts, sue and be sued, and hire and fire fund managers. Mutual funds are generally organized under state corporate and business trust laws that have been modified to make them especially attractive to mutual funds. For example, these states' laws generally do not require mutual funds to hold annual shareholder meetings.

In contrast, Chinese mutual funds are not organized as independent business entities, but as a nexus of contracts, and much of the regulation of mutual funds is accomplished through the regulation of the fund's manager as opposed to the fund. Fund managers for Chinese mutual funds must be approved by the CSRC as fund managers and comply with a number of substantive restrictions under Chinese law. Chinese fund managers must currently be organized as limited liability companies under the Company Law of the People's Republic of China, have at least two but no more than 50 shareholders, and not be publicly traded. CSRC rules require that fund managers employ no fewer than 15 qualified personnel, and the rules place significant restrictions on foreign ownership and foreign owners of fund managers. A fund manager's largest shareholders are subject to specific rules touching on, among other things, their registered capital (minimum RMB300 million), operating and compliance record, and public credit standing, and they may not have been subjected to administrative or criminal sanctions in the preceding three years. Chinese fund managers are also subject to certain provisions of the Investment Fund Law, which requires, for example, that a fund manager have paid-in capital of at least RMB100 million, effective compliance, supervision and risk control systems, and personnel that meet minimum qualifications.

In contrast, US fund managers do not need regulatory approval in order to manage a mutual fund, and they are subject to far less substantive regulation than Chinese fund managers. A US fund manager must register with the SEC, but there are no capital or other professional qualifications, and they generally must only disclose prior administrative or criminal sanctions. States do not regulate mutual fund managers as such, but many do impose minimum bonding, testing and other requirements on investment advisers that have clients other than mutual funds. Many mutual fund managers have such clients, so they may be indirectly subject to certain qualification tests under state law, but neither US nor state law requires prior regulatory approval for investment advisers. Although the Investment Company Act automatically bars fund managers that have been subject to certain administrative or criminal sanctions from managing a mutual fund, the SEC routinely grants exemptions from this prohibition.

In both the USA and China, the fund itself must be reviewed by regulators before it can sell shares to the public. In the USA, a mutual fund must file a registration statement with the SEC, part of which comprises the fund's prospectus. The registration statement must include detailed information required by SEC rules. In order to prevent a fund from being sold, the SEC would have to institute a legal action against the fund, without which the fund's registration statement could become automatically effective. As a practical matter, however, funds virtually always obtain SEC approval before offering their shares.

A Chinese mutual fund cannot be sold without the prior, affirmative approval of the CSRC. The fund must submit to the CSRC an: application report, fund contract, fund prospectus, fund custody agreement, documentation of the fund manager's and custodian's qualifications and their audited financial statements, and a legal opinion. The CSRC can delay its final decision on the application for six months, at which time it can deny the application without the necessity of bringing any legal action.

12.4 FUND GOVERNANCE

The differences between US and Chinese fund governance rules are similar to the differences described above. US fund governance is regulated through rules that apply directly to the fund itself, whereas Chinese fund governance is regulated through rules that apply the fund manager.

US mutual funds are subject to the ultimate authority of the fund's board of directors, which is elected by the fund's shareholders. US rules effectively require that the fund's board have a majority of independent directors, and recently proposed rules would raise that minimum to 75 percent and require that the fund's chairman be independent. A person is "independent" in as much as he or she is not an "interested person" of the fund under the Investment Company Act. The term "interested person" is defined to include close relatives of fund manager executives, shareholders of the fund manager, and other persons whose judgment, by reason of a personal, familial or professional relationship with the fund manager, might be unduly subject to the fund manager's influence. There are significant gaps in this definition, however, that allow conflicted persons to qualify as independent directors, such as for former executives of the fund manager.

A Chinese mutual fund does not have a board of directors, but a fund custodian, and the custodian's role is essentially limited to ensuring compliance with the term's of the fund contract and applicable laws. Although Chinese mutual fund regulation in many instances refers to a fund's "trust agreement" and to "trust fees", existing Chinese mutual funds were formed prior to the enactment of the Trust Law of the People's Republic of China and continue to operate within a contractual, rather than trust, framework. Chinese law looks to the overseers of the fund manager, rather than the fund, for independent oversight of the fund.

CSRC rules require that a fund manager have at least three independent directors that comprise at least one-third of the board. CSRC rules enacted in 2004 require that independent fund manager directors: (1) have never held a position with the fund manager, any shareholder of the fund manager, any entity having business relations with the fund manager, or any interested person of the fund manager; (2) not be an interested person of certain senior officials of the fund manager, and (3) not have certain familial relationships with persons who hold positions with the fund manager. In addition to satisfying these independence standards, an independent director also must have at least five years certified experience in banking, law or financial affairs, and have "adequate time to perform his duties".

The independent directors of a US mutual fund technically have absolute authority over the operation of the fund because they constitute a controlling majority of the board, whereas the independent directors of a Chinese fund manager have unconditional authority only over certain enumerated areas of the fund manager's operations. CSRC rules provide that the approval by at least two-thirds of the independent directors is expressly necessary only for: "major connected transactions" between the fund and the fund manager; fund audits and the hiring and firing of the fund's accounting firm; and the fund's semi-annual and annual reports. The scope of the term "major connected transactions" has not been established, but if interpreted broadly it gives the independent fund manager directors a degree of authority over Chinese mutual funds that is comparable to the authority of independent directors of US mutual funds.

Of course, there is a real question as to whether true independence can ever be legislated. US independent fund directors only "technically" control the fund because many are selected because of their close personal and/or professional ties with the fund manager and may in practice be inclined to do the fund manager's bidding. This may be equally true for Chinese independent fund manager directors. US fund directors have a fiduciary duty to act solely in the best interests of fund shareholders, and CSRC rules require that independent fund manager directors attend all board meetings and provide an independent voice for the interests of fund shareholders, but these standards are difficult to measure and enforce.

One potential weakness of the Chinese approach to fund governance is that it creates a conflict of interest for the independent directors of the fund manager. Under Chinese law, independent fund manager directors generally have a duty to safeguard both the interests of the fund manager and its shareholders and the interests of the fund's shareholders. These duties will conflict when the interests of fund manger's shareholders and the fund's shareholders diverge. This is a significant concern because it is precisely when the interests of fund manager's shareholders and the fund's shareholders diverge that an effective, independent advocate for fund shareholders is most needed. Under US law, the independent directors of US mutual funds owe their allegiance exclusively to fund shareholders, which means that when the interests of the fund manager and the fund diverge, the independent fund directors have a duty to act solely in the best interests of the fund.

There is also a potential advantage for Chinese fund shareholders in that a government-owned entity may be a substantial shareholder of some fund managers. A government-owned entity arguably may be more inclined than private shareholders of the fund manager to protect the interests of retail shareholders because the fund manager's shareholders' primary motivation is to maximize their own profits. A governmental shareholder's interests as shareholder to generate profits may trump its interests as public representative, however, especially if shares of the fund are widely sold outside of the governmental shareholder's jurisdiction.

12.5 DISCLOSURE REQUIREMENTS

As discussed above, the capacity of fund governance rules to regulate conflicts of interest between funds and their managers is inherently limited. Disclosure requirements provide one way to mitigate these limitations by enlisting market forces as a disciplining influence on fund managers. Public disclosure of information about fund fees, investment performance, investment objectives and policies, and fund personnel enables investors, rather than fund directors, to make their own decisions about what practices and policies best serve investors' interests. As Justice Brandeis famously said in his classic work, *Other People's Money*, "sunlight is said to be the best of disinfectants".

As noted above, a US mutual fund may not sell its shares unless it has filed a registration statement with the SEC and the registration statement has been declared effective. The registration statement comprises three parts: the prospectus, statement of additional information, and exhibits. The prospectus provides essential information about a fund's fees, investment risks, portfolio, investment performance, investment objectives and style, management team, and distribution arrangements. The prospectus also provides a table of financial highlights and certain shareholder information regarding the pricing, purchase, and redemption of fund shares. The statement of additional information, as its name implies, generally provides more detailed information about the topics addressed in the prospectus. The third part of the registration statement includes exhibits, such as a list of certain fund affiliates, additional information about the fund manager and the fund's underwriter, and certain other technical information.

The only part of the US registration statement used directly by shareholders is the prospectus. The prospectus must be delivered to shareholders at or before the completion of the purchase of fund shares, which typically means that it is mailed to the shareholder with a written confirmation of the transaction. In contrast, the statement of additional information is required to be provided only upon request. The exhibits are available on the SEC's website, but are very difficult to find for average investors.

As a practical matter, the US fund prospectus does not play a significant role in most investors' investment decisions. Most fund shares are sold through intermediaries who are not required to deliver a prospectus before an investor makes an investment decision. For example, an investor can purchase shares through his broker during a telephone call without ever having been provided with or seen a prospectus. The prospectus would not be delivered until the transaction confirmation was sent, days after the investor made the investment decision. The SEC has proposed a new rule that would require that brokers deliver, before the investor makes the investment decision, a document that includes extensive information about fund fees but not other information about the fund. In other contexts, such as when an investor purchases a mutual fund through an employer-sponsored retirement plan, the prospectus delivery requirement does not even apply, although some employers provide fund prospectuses to their employees.

The only situation in which investors routinely will have had access to a prospectus before making an investment decision is when the fund is "direct-sold", that is, sold directly by the fund and not through an intermediary. It is ironic that investors in direct-sold funds, who are often relatively well-informed and self-directed, are more likely to have had access to a prospectus than investors who use intermediaries, although one might argue that the latter group uses intermediaries precisely because they wish to delegate investment decisions to someone else and accordingly would not read the prospectus even if it were provided.

One mitigating factor regarding the foregoing is that while the prospectus may not be used directly by US investors, it is the source of much of the information used by brokers, employers, financial press and third-party information providers that investors do receive and use when making investment decisions. These parties routinely extract information about fund expense ratios, investment performance, investment objectives and risks, portfolio managers, for example, and repackage that information for investors in a variety of formats. Disclosure not only ensures that this information is publicly available, but also that, in many cases such as investment performance, expense ratios, and distribution fees, the information is standardized and accordingly can be used to make comparisons between different funds.

Because mutual funds are continuously selling their shares, the registration statement must be kept current. It is industry practice to send every shareholder an updated prospectus each year, and funds are required to provide promptly information about important changes. Mutual funds are also required to send annual and semi-annual reports to their shareholders that include financial information and information about, among other things, the funds' investment performance, fees and proxy votes.

Chinese mutual fund disclosure is somewhat similar to US disclosure, with most differences being attributable to the contractual nature of the fund shareholder's investment. For example, under US law the fund itself is primarily responsible for its registration statement, although as a practical matter the fund manager plays a significant supporting role in its drafting and submission. In China, the fund manager and custodian are directly responsible for compliance with fund disclosure requirements.

The fund manager must file the following documents with the CSRC: application report; fund manager and trustee qualifying certificates; audited financial statements for the fund manager and fund custodian; legal opinions; and drafts of the fund prospectus, shareholder contract, and fund trust agreement. Fund shares cannot be sold until the CSRC has approved these documents. When purchasing fund shares, the investor receives two of these documents: the prospectus and the shareholder contract. The prospectus is intended to serve as the primary disclosure document, while the contract constitutes the agreement between the investor and the fund.

The prospectus must include, among other things, the following information: a summary of the shareholder contract and fund trust agreement, basic information about the fund's manager and custodian, the manner and amount of compensation paid to the fund manager and custodian; warnings regarding the investment risks of the fund; the manner of distribution of fund shares and the name of distributor; and the names and domiciles of the fund's law firm and accountant. An updated prospectus must be filed with the CSRC semiannually within 30 days of the end of the period, and if one of the major events listed in the applicable CSRC rule occurs, the event must be reported to the CSRC within two days and posted at the fund manager's main office.

The shareholder contract must include, among other things: the fund's name and objective; the names and domiciles of the fund manager and custodian; minimum shares to be sold; method of determining fund share prices and fund expenses; shareholder meeting procedures; timing and method of purchases and redemptions of fund shares and distribution of fund proceeds; the manner and amounts of compensation paid to the fund manager and custodian; investment style and restrictions; the method of publicly dissemination of fund net asset value; and dispute resolution methods.

While the content of US and Chinese mutual fund disclosure is somewhat similar, the information dissemination process is quite different. One difference is that Chinese rules require two documents, a prospectus and contract, the first of which provides a summary of important information, and the latter of which provides more detailed information. Although US law permits the use of a short-form prospectus, this is neither required nor practiced. In addition, under Chinese law, the fund manager must "publicize" the prospectus, shareholder contract and other fund documents three days prior to the offering of fund shares, and the semiannual updates to those documents within 45 days of the end of the period. The term "publicize" refers to the publishing of the information in national newspapers and periodicals designated by the CSRC and on the web sites for the fund manager and custodian. The closest US equivalent is the required filing of fund registration statements on the SEC's website, but this database is virtually impenetrable to the average investor. Finally, Chinese mutual fund materials effectively must be provided to the investor before the investment decision has been made because a purchase occurs only upon execution by the investor of the shareholder contract itself. Most fund purchases in the USA occur without the shareholder being provided with a prospectus before the purchase.

12.6 FUND FEES

The fee structure for US and Chinese mutual funds is generally similar. In both countries, mutual funds generally charge an asset-based management fee that covers the cost of portfolio management, trading personnel, fund administration and accounting, shareholder services and other aspects of core fund operations. In both jurisdictions, there are no express limits on fees with the exception of distribution fees (as discussed further in the next section), and fund assets can be used to pay for virtually any type of services related to the management and operation of the fund.

One important difference is that the fee charged by a US fund manager can be increased after the investor has purchased shares, although the express approval of the fund's shareholders is required. This rule does not apply to fees paid to third parties, such as the fund's custodian, because the law assumes that such fees are negotiated at arms-length. These fees can be changed at any time by the fund's board, without approval of or notice to shareholders. US law requires shareholder approval of fee increases for fees paid to the fund manager because the fund manager has an incentive to use its influence over the fund and the fund's board to negotiate a higher fee. The shareholder approval requirement is designed to ameliorate this conflict.

It is not clear that a Chinese fund manager has the ability to increase its fee. Fund fees are established by the shareholder contract, and Chinese securities law does not provide for the means by which the shareholder contract may be amended to increase the fee. The CSRC has provided that fees may be paid out of fund assets for certain enumerated purposes and for purposes set forth in the shareholder contract. The rules nowhere address fee increases, however, except for distribution fees.

Nor does Chinese law provide for performance fees. In contrast, US mutual funds are expressly authorized to charge performance fees, provided that they are structured as fulcrum fees. A fulcrum fee is a performance fee according to which the amount of any fee increase that is based on the fund's outperformance of a specified benchmark is matched by a fee reduction that is based the fund's underperformance of the benchmark.

12.7 DISTRIBUTION COMPENSATION

The regulation of distribution compensation (distribution here refers to the selling activities of fund distributors and underwriters) in the USA and China, like the regulation of other types of fund fees, is generally similar. Both US and Chinese laws impose limits on the maximum amount of distribution compensation. In the USA, limits on distribution compensation are imposed by the National Association of Securities Dealers (NASD), a self-regulatory organization operated by US broker-dealers that is subject to SEC oversight. The NASD rules generally limit one-time commissions on purchases of fund shares to 8.5 percent of the purchase amount, which generally is reduced to 6.25 percent of the purchase amount when asset-based distribution fees are also charged. Such asset-based fees, which are deducted from a shareholder's account on an ongoing basis, may not exceed 1.00 percent. The one-time commission also can be collected at the time of redemption, in which case the amount owed typically declines with the length of the holding period.

CSRC rules also limit distribution fees. Subscription, purchase and redemption fees may not exceed 5 percent of the amount of the purchase price. Subscription, purchase and redemption fees may be discounted based on the amount of the investment; such discounts are referred to in the USA as breakpoints. Redemption fees, like deferred commissions on US mutual fund purchases, also may be reduced based on the investor's holding period. Unlike the US deferred commission, at least 25 percent of the Chinese redemption fee must be paid into the fund. US funds treat these payments separately, with a fee paid to the fund upon redemption generally being called a redemption fee, and a commission paid by the shareholder upon redemption generally being called a "contingent deferred sales load" or "CDSL". The redemption fee and CDSL are disclosed separately in a US fund's prospectus, whereas it appears that in a Chinese prospectus they are combined.

One important difference between US and Chinese regulation of distribution compensation is that China appears not to permit deductions from fund assets for distribution fees. A Chinese fund manager is permitted to collect subscription and purchase fees from an investor at the time of purchase or on an installment basis during the holding period, but there is no provision that expressly permits the deduction of an asset-based fee from fund assets for the purpose of financing distribution activities.

In contrast, US law permits deductions from fund assets to finance payments to distributors that are measured as a percentage of assets (for example, are asset-based), and these deductions do not directly correlate to the amount of the commission that the shareholder would otherwise have paid. These asset-based fees are referred to as 12b-1 fees after the SEC rule that permits them. The payment of 12b-1 fees is not as transparent to the marketplace as the payment of commissions, which is one aspect of 12b-1 fees that has generated controversy about whether the SEC should continue to permit their use, as opposed to permitting deductions from assets only on an account-by-account basis and only as a direct alternative to the payment of a commission by the investor.

Another controversial practice in the USA is the payment of additional compensation by the fund manager to the distributor without disclosing the arrangement to investors. These payments are generally referred to as revenue sharing or shelf space payments, and are they not expressly prohibited under US law. The SEC and state regulators have brought a number of enforcement actions relating to revenue sharing arrangements. It is likely that this will be an area of regulatory reform in the near future.

The status of revenue sharing payments under Chinese law also is somewhat uncertain. Chinese law does not expressly permit revenue sharing payments. Chinese law permits, for example, fund assets to be used to pay for the fund manager's overhead expenses, but revenue sharing payments would not seem to qualify as overhead expenses. Chinese law is silent regarding whether a fund manager may use its own assets to pay for distribution – a common practice in the USA – or whether such payments would be considered a use of fund fees that was not permitted under applicable law.

12.8 PRICING, SALES AND REDEMPTIONS

Both US and Chinese law set forth specific requirements regarding the pricing, sale and redemption of mutual fund shares. In the USA, fund shares must generally be priced at least once each business day, and most do so as of 4:00 p.m. eastern standard time. US law requires that fund prices be based on the market value of the fund's securities as of the time that they are priced. If market prices are not readily available, such as when a fund holds a restricted security or the exchanges on which the fund's securities are traded are closed, the securities must be valued based on their fair value as determined by the board of directors.

Transactions in US mutual fund shares generally must be effected at the fund's next-calculated price. Thus, if a shareholder enters an order to purchase or redeem fund shares at 3:00 p.m., he will receive the price calculated as of 4:00 p.m. Any orders received after 4:00 p.m. must be assigned the next day's price. The recent mutual fund scandal primarily involved violations these rules (Bullard, 2006). To ensure that funds have sufficient cash to honor redemptions, the SEC informally requires that no more than 15 percent of a mutual fund's portfolio (10% for a money market fund) represent securities that could not be sold within seven days at their carrying value.

Chinese pricing rules generally are similar to US rules. Chinese fund shares must be priced based on the per share net asset value of the fund, and purchases must be effected at the price next calculated by the fund. A Chinese fund's prospectus and shareholder contract must state the dates on which it will effect purchases and redemptions. CSRC rules require that funds price their shares after the market close each day, although it is not clear whether this means that funds must stand ready to sell and redeem shares on each day the market is open. CSRC rules require that funds maintain at least 5 percent of their assets in cash to meet redemptions.

US and Chinese fund managers appear to have very different degrees of flexibility to restrict the sale of fund shares. The only limit on a US fund manager's ability to restrict the sale of fund shares generally is that the fund's practices be consistent with its disclosure documents. In contrast, although Chinese law expressly permits the fund manger to suspend sales because of the size of the fund or restrict holdings of fund shares by a single shareholder, these provisions suggest that these may be the only circumstances when sales may be restricted.

Ironically, whereas Chinese law seems to be more restrictive of a fund manager's ability to refuse to sell fund shares, it is less restrictive of a fund manager's ability to refuse to redeem fund shares. Under US law, the unconditional right of redemption is considered by many to be the single most important feature offered by mutual funds, and only in extraordinary situations are funds permitted to suspend the right of redemption. In addition, US law requires funds to pay redemption proceeds within seven days of tender of the shares, and SEC policies and rules have, as a practical matter, shortened that period to three days in most cases.

Chinese law permits restrictions on and the suspension of redemptions under a range of circumstances. For example, a Chinese fund can refuse redemption requests for the first three months of a fund's life, whereas a US fund must honor redemption requests from the date of the first sale of fund shares. Chinese fund managers are also permitted to delay honoring redemptions in excess of 10 percent of the fund's assets for up to 20 days. Although a Chinese fund manager must pay redemption proceeds within seven days of receiving a redemption application, the fund may take up to an additional three days to confirm the validity of the redemption request.

12.9 AFFILIATED TRANSACTIONS

Perhaps the most significant difference between US and Chinese mutual fund regulation is the treatment of affiliated transactions. The US Investment Company Act's affiliated transaction prohibitions generally are considered to be the heart of the statute. The Act generally prohibits a broad range of transactions between mutual funds and their affiliates, and the term "affiliated person" is broadly defined. In contrast, Chinese law generally relies on fiduciary principles to protect funds from abusive self-dealing by fund affiliates.

US law expressly prohibits fund affiliates from purchasing securities or other property from, or selling securities or other property to, the fund. Fund affiliates that control or are under common control with the fund are prohibited from borrowing money or other property from the fund. Fund affiliates also are prohibited from engaging in joint transactions with the fund, or acting as agent for the fund except when acting as broker, and then only in accordance with compensation restrictions. Finally, a fund may not purchase securities in an underwriting in which certain fund affiliates are participating.

The Investment Company Act defines "affiliated person" to include, among others: the fund manager; persons controlling, controlled by, and under common control with the fund; holders of 5 percent of the fund's voting shares; entities of which the fund owns 5 percent of the voting shares; and the fund's officers, directors, partners and employees. This definition is not so broad standing alone, but it is substantially expanded by the fact that the affiliated transaction prohibitions that restrict principal, agency, joint and lending transactions apply to affiliated persons of the fund and affiliated persons of such persons.

Thus, the affiliated transaction prohibitions create two tiers of affiliates. For example, a 5 percent owner of shares of the fund manager is not an affiliated person of the fund, but he would be an affiliated person of the fund manager, which is an affiliated person of the fund. A 5 percent owner of the shares of a fund portfolio company would not be an affiliated person of the fund, but if the fund owned 5 percent of the portfolio company's shares, then the portfolio company would be an affiliated person, and the 5 percent owner of the company would be an affiliated person of an affiliate person. As these illustrations suggest, the affiliated transaction prohibitions have a long reach, and US mutual fund lawyers and compliance personnel spend much of their time sorting through the complexities of these rules. The SEC has the authority to exempt transactions from these prohibitions, however, and it has often used this authority to substantially mitigate the burdens of compliance. The SEC also has frequently used its enforcement authority against fund affiliates who have violated the affiliated transaction prohibitions.

Chinese mutual fund law contains no such broad prohibitions against affiliated transactions or a detailed definition of affiliated persons, but it does prohibit certain transactions that could be interpreted to cover much, if not all, of the territory covered by US rules. For example, a fund manager may not use fund assets in joint investments with the fund manager or others, use fund property to seek benefits for any third parties, or treat different funds unfairly. Chinese law also expressly imposes on fund managers the duties of good faith and loyalty and a responsibility to use fund assets for the benefit of the fund's shareholders. Only time will tell whether the combination of these provisions and others will evolve into a system of regulating affiliated transactions that is comparable the very restrictive system in the USA.

12.10 MONEY MARKET FUNDS

Money market funds have been especially successful in the USA, where they comprise approximately 25 percent of all mutual fund assets, and are worthy of special mention. They also are subject to special regulation under both US and Chinese law. Both jurisdictions have found that money market funds create an expectation of safety that necessitates detailed rules relating to the maturity, creditworthiness and diversification of their portfolios. These rules generally apply to funds that are held out as cash equivalents, such as by using the terms "cash" or "money" in their names.

Under US law, money market funds are subject to detailed restrictions on their portfolio securities that relate primarily to: (1) the creditworthiness of the issuers, (2) the maturity of the fixed income instruments, and (3) the diversification of the portfolio. For example, a US money market fund may generally invest only in fixed income instruments that have received a rating from a bond rating organization in one of the two highest applicable categories and have a remaining maturity of no more than 397 days. Money market fund portfolios must generally maintain an average weighted maturity of 90 days or less, and they generally cannot hold more than 5 percent of their assets in the securities of a single issuer.

Chinese law imposes similar restrictions. A money market fund may invest only in fixed income instruments that have maturity of no more than 397 days, and a fund portfolio's average weighted maturity portfolio shall not exceed 180 days. Money market funds may not invest in privately-issued bonds that have a credit rating below AAA or in privately-issued bonds of a single issuer if they exceed 10 percent of the fund's assets. Other investment restrictions apply for deposits in commercial banks and bonds that trade in the national inter-bank market.

One unique aspect of China's money market fund rules is that they provide for the joint regulation of the rules by the CSRC and the People's Bank of China. In contrast, the SEC has exclusive jurisdiction over US money market funds. In the infancy of the US money market fund industry, US banks attempted to extinguish money market funds because they presented a major competitive threat to bank deposit accounts. This attempt failed, and assets in US money market funds have since surpassed total assets in bank deposit accounts. The joint jurisdiction of Chinese securities and banking regulators over money market funds may create special frictions if Chinese money market funds are as successful at challenging banks' dominance as they have been in the USA.

12.11 CONCLUSION

As the foregoing discussion suggests, the Chinese regulatory system for mutual funds bears a strong resemblance to the system in the USA. The structure of a regulatory system, however, may reveal little about its actual operation. The understanding of US law set forth above is based on the confirmation of decades of SEC enforcement actions, rulemakings and interpretations, and private litigation, within the American social, political and economic context. How Chinese law, thus far set forth only on paper, will unfold in actual experience will similarly depend on a milieu as varied and wide-ranging as Chinese culture itself.

REFERENCES

Bullard, M. (2006) "The Mutual Fund as a Firm: Fund Arbitrage, Frequent Trading and the SEC's Response to the Mutual Fund Scandal", *Houston Law Review*, 42: 1271.
Hamlin, K. (2005) "The Feeling's Mutual", *Institutional Investor*, October: 58–60.
Investment Company Institute (2005) *Investment Company Fact Book* (Washington, DC: ICI).

The following provides a partial list of sources of mutual fund law in the USA and China:

US law

Investment Company Act, 15 U.S.C. §§ 80a-1–80a-59.
Rules under the Investment Company Act, 17 C.F.R. §§ 270.0-1–.60a-1.

Chinese law

Company Law of the People's Republic of China (27 Oct. 2005).
Law of the People's Republic of China on Securities Investments Funds (28 Oct. 2003).
Securities Law of the People's Republic of China (27 Oct. 2005).
Trust Law of the People's Republic of China (28 Apr. 2001).
Announcement of the People's Bank of China, the China Banking Regulatory Commission and the China Securities Regulatory Commission (20 Feb. 2005).

Circular of China Securities Regulatory Commission on Issuing the Provisions on Strengthening the Protection of the Rights and Interests of the General Public Shareholders (4 Dec. 2004).
Circular to Fund Management Companies and Fund Custodian Banks on Issues relating to the Investment by Money Market Fund in Short-Term Financing Bond (30 Sep. 2005).
Circular on Issues Concerning Bank Deposit Investment by Money Market Funds (21 Nov. 2005).
Circular on Issues Concerning Further Improving the Review Procedures for Capital-Raising Application for Establishment of Securities Investment Funds (16 June 2005).
Circular on Issues Concerning Warrant Investment by Securities Investment Funds in the Split Share Structure Reform (15 Aug. 2003).
Circular of the State Administration of Foreign Exchange Concerning the Relevant Issues of the Foreign Exchange Administration of Fund Management Companies with Foreign Shares (29 Mar. 2003).
Measures for the Administration of Information Disclosure of Securities Investment Fund (8 June 2004).
Measures for the Administration of Operation of Securities Investment Fund (29 June 2004).
Measures for the Administration of Post-holding of Senior Officers of Securities Investment Fund Management Companies (29 June 2004).
Measures for the Administration of Sale of Securities Investment Fund (25 June 2004).
Measures for the Administration of Securities Investment Fund Management Companies (16 Sep. 2004).
Notice of the China Securities Regulatory Commission on the Issue Concerning the Use of Self-Owned Capital of Fund Management Companies for Fund Investment (8 June 2005).
Notice of the China Securities Regulatory Commission and the People's Bank of China About Promulgating the Interim Provisions on the Management of Monetary Market Funds (16 Aug. 2004).
Notice of China Securities Regulatory Commission on the Relevant Issues Concerning Major Alterations of Fund Management Companies (21 Mar. 2002).
Rules on the Establishment of Foreign-Shared Fund Management Companies (1 June 2002).

CHAPTER 13

Some Insights on the Behavior of the Mutual Fund Industry in Spain

*Manuel Moreno and Gonzalo Rubio**

13.1 INTRODUCTION

Performance evaluation of professionally managed portfolios is a key topic of financial economics. Hence, most of the papers on mutual funds have examined whether portfolio managers are able to present superior performance in some sense previously defined.

Generally speaking and somehow surprisingly, the traditional results are disappointing. On average, mutual funds do not seem to be able to generate enough returns to compensate their risks, expenses and transaction costs. Traditional measures like Jensen's alpha are estimated to be negative more often than positive across an enormous amount of studies.[1] For example, in a celebrated paper, Gruber (1996) shows that, using an unconditional CAPM, the risk-adjusted return of US mutual funds is −1.56 percent per year. His results also show that a 4-factor model which includes the Fama–French risk factors plus a long-term government debt excess return underperformed by 65 basis points per year. The most recent studies, however, tend to show non-statistically significant results. This is of course comforting. Mutual fund returns are measured net of all fees and trading costs. Superior management ability should be interpreted as an increment to these costs. A manager with a zero (non-significant) alpha has enough

*Gonzalo Rubio acknowledges the financial support provided by Ministerio de Educación y Ciencia grant SEJ2005-08931-CD2-01/ECON.

ability to cover his risk, costs and fees. This non-significant (and even positive) performance has been reported by Carhart (1997) using his 4-factor model, which includes the three well-known Fama–French factors plus a momentum factor, and by Ferson and Qian (2004) using a simple CAPM unconditional model with a long history of data from January 1973 to December 2000 and a very large number of funds which ranges from 146 to 27,289 at the end of sample. Similarly, using a performance evaluation technique based on portfolio holdings, Daniel, Grinblatt, Titman and Wermers (1997) report mostly neutral performance results, although they even find that high-risk funds do show a positive and significant performance.

All of these studies employ unconditional risk-adjusted measures of performance in the sense that expected returns and betas are unconditional moments since they are estimated as simple past averages. The empirical evidence of modern asset pricing shows that a number of variables forecast aggregate stock and bond excess returns. Thus, expected excess returns and risk are time-varying. As pointed out by Ferson and Schadt (1996), if the risk exposure of a mutual fund varies predictably with the business cycle, but the manager does not really have superior skills, the traditional unconditional evaluation may confuse the observed common variation in fund risk and expected market return with abnormal performance. In other words, if the risk strategy of the fund follows the aggregate dividend yield which has been shown to forecast returns, we should not judge the manager as having superior performance. Conditional performance evaluation accounts for the changes of risk with the state of the economy, and therefore controlling for a potential common variation. Interestingly, Ferson and Schadt (1996), Ferson and Qian (2004) and Lynch, Wachter and Boudry (2004) among others show that performance and market timing ability of mutual funds look better compared with the traditional unconditional approach.

Recently, however, literature on investment companies have realized than we can actually learn more from analysing this industry than whether managers are able to obtain risk-adjusted excess returns. In particular, Brown, Harlow and Starks (1996) and Chevalier and Ellison (1997) study how incentives influence the behavior of mutual funds managers, Tufano and Sevick (1997) analyse the determinants of costs and fees in the fund industry, and Warther (1995) and Sirri and Tufano (1998) study the flows of funds into and out equity mutual funds in order to understand the behavior and reaction of investors to relative past performance of the funds. In related papers, Gruber (1996) and Zheng (1999) have also analysed the relationship between performance and flows to learn whether individual investors can earn excess returns by actively selecting mutual funds.

A seemingly accepted result is that past relative performance of the mutual fund industry is positively related to the so called net flow as the difference between inflows and outflows of the funds. However, as first pointed out by Gruber (1996), the flow of new money into the best-performing funds is much larger than the flow of money out of the poorest performing funds. This positive but convex relationship has been confirmed by Sirri and Tufano (1998) by measuring net flows as the growth rate in the total assets of the fund adjusted by the its return during the same period. It is very important to point out that performance in these studies is always measured as past total returns rather than risk-adjusted returns. There are basically two explanations of these results. Gruber (1996) argues that there exist two very different clienteles investing in mutual funds: the sophisticated clientele who direct their money to funds based on past performance, and the disadvantaged clientele who are unable to change their money within funds.[2] On the other hand, Lynch and Musto (2003) argue that the convex relationship may be explained by rational investors who either direct money into the best performing funds or maintain their money in the funds because they expect a change in the management and risk strategy of the fund in the case of a poor performance record. Consequently, past performance in the later funds is not signalling their investment and performance future behavior.

Finally, previous US evidence provided by Elton, Gruber, Das and Hlavka (1993) and Carhart (1997) shows that higher-fee funds do not perform as well as lower-fee funds. Moreover, Sirri and Tufano (1998) find that high-fee funds present a much stronger performance-flow relationship than do the rest of funds. Fees are probably the key variable in the performing behavior of mutual funds. In this regard, a number of papers have analysed the determinants of fees and ownership costs; Tufano and Sevick (1997), Christoffersen (2001), Berkowitz and Kotowitz (2002) and Luo (2002) are some relevant examples.

The Spanish evidence shows very negative performance results. Rubio (1995) reports significant negative alphas for alternative unconditional models and for the positive period weighting of Grinblatt and Titman (1989). He shows that this negative record is very much related to the portfolio turnover of the funds and their fee-setting strategy. In an excellent paper, Martínez (2003) shows that the negative performance found in Spanish mutual funds cannot be explained by the legal constraints faced by the funds. At the same time, fee-setting does not seem to be consistent with a competitive industry. The legal framework in the Spanish mutual fund sector and the dominance of the industry by commercial and savings banks seem to favor a surprising and continuous abuse in fee-setting by most funds.

As in the US market, the recent evidence provided by Moreno and Rodríguez (2005), using weekly data from 1998 to 2003 and a new co-skewness factor associated with market timing, shows non-significant alphas for Spanish funds investing in equity stocks. Moreover, Ciriaco and Santamaría (2005) report that the Spanish funds present significant persistence of performance when investing in fixed income securities. However, this persistence becomes much weaker when moving into funds with mostly risky stocks in their portfolios. This suggests that persistence, as pointed out by Carhart (1997), may be explained by fees charged by mutual funds given the relatively high and stable fees characterizing the Spanish fixed-income funds. Unfortunately, they do not report evidence on this conjecture. Moreover, Ciriaco and Santamaría (2005) also show a positive and convex relationship between past relative performance and the growth rate of flows as measured by the adjusted change on total net assets of the funds. They report some weak evidence in favor of the explanation provided by Lynch and Musto (2003). As in the previous US literature, past performance is measured by total returns.

A key paper regarding the determinants of fee-setting in the Spanish mutual fund industry is Gil-Bazo and Martínez (2004). In a cross-sectional study on December 2001 and using a comprehensive sample of 743 non-guaranteed and 257 guaranteed mutual funds, they find that investors in older and lower average investment non-guaranteed funds tend to pay higher management fees. Moreover, they report that some mutual funds enjoy better conditions from custodial institutions than others. Once again, the effect of the banking sector on mutual fund behavior is disturbing. Finally, in contrast to evidence from the US market, larger funds are not associated with lower fees.

Most of the papers regarding the behavior of mutual funds tend to aggregate data on the risk supported by them. This chapter presents empirical evidence on various aspects of performance and fee-setting at a more disaggregated level than previous papers. This is our key objective and the most novel aspect of our study. We want to show performance and understand some issues of fee-setting, analysing the industry by management companies. Hence, we report our evidence simultaneously in terms of management companies and the investment objectives of funds. We argue that this is very important; there are a lot of performance differences between individual funds and management companies. If we tend to aggregate the results simply by some measure of average risk, a lot of key information is lost. From the investors' point of view, it is not clear what the relevance of showing results by aggregating performance across mutual funds is. Unfortunately, however, we employ a very limited-in-time data-set. Therefore, the evidence shown should be taken as a discussion on some potential new insights that should be investigated much more carefully and with longer time-series data. In any case, fees are a key determinant of performance, although not all management companies use them in the same way and with the same intensity. Funds which belong to banks, savings banks or independent management companies present some striking differences in behavior and performance that should be reported independently.

The rest of the chapter is organized as follows: section 13.2 briefly discusses the fund industry in Spain, while section 13.3 explains the data and the variables employed in the analysis. Section 13.4 discusses the performance evaluation models used in the research; section 13.5 reports the results; and, finally, section 13.6 concludes.

13.2 THE MUTUAL FUND INDUSTRY IN SPAIN

In 1986, two years after the approval of a new legislation which clarified the framework of institutional investments in Spain, the number of funds and the value of assets experienced a tremendous increase. Since then, the industry of mutual funds in Spain has presented a steady growth. By year-end 2002, the Spanish mutual fund sector ranked 6th in the world in number of funds and 12th in terms of assets under management.

As pointed out by Gil-Bazo and Martínez (2004), the Spanish mutual fund industry has two distinct features that make it interesting relative to other more mature industries in Europe and in the USA. First, credit institutions heavily dominate the Spanish funds. In 2002, 91 percent of mutual funds are distributed through banks and savings banks. Similarly, 91 percent of mutual fund assets are managed by companies belonging to either banks or savings banks. It seems clear that the traditional universal banking model characterizing the financing system in Spain explains this dominance. Credit institutions have a very large base of clients for their mutual funds. Moreover, revenues from their mutual funds are a non-negligible portion of Spanish banks' revenues. Gil-Bazo and Martínez (2004) note that the sales revenues of the three largest management companies which belong to credit institutions represent 1.71, 2.15 and 3.22 percent of their respective group's total ordinary revenues. This gives rise to a number of potential conflicts of interest. For instance, bank customers are more vulnerable to marketing or advice from their bank. In fact, the average investor maintains a long-term relationship with the management company and this loyalty has clearly been transmitted from the management company to the fund itself. Moreover, until recently tax legislation has not facilitated the movement of money within funds. Fund managers could also be biased towards investing in financial assets issued by companies belonging to their own financial group. Finally, the fact that only credit institutions can become custodial institutions of the assets held by the mutual funds, gives banks and savings banks an unfair advantage over independent management companies.

The second characteristic we want to notice is that Spanish mutual funds charge the highest average expenses to investors in a sample of countries that includes Austria, Belgium, France, Germany, Ireland, Italy, Luxembourg, Sweden, Switzerland and UK. In particular, the average total expense ratio (which includes management, custody and audit expenses) amounts to 2.09 percent of fund assets. The average total expense ratio across the rest of countries is only 1.57 percent.[3] It should be made clear that, as in most countries, Spanish mutual fund participants face four different types of fees. Investors sometimes pay a sales charge on purchases, or front load, as a fraction of the total amount invested. When investors redeem fund shares, they may have to pay a deferred sales charge, or redemption fee, which is computed as a percentage of the shares' net asset value. Apart from one-time loads, which are basically concentrated in guaranteed funds, investors also pay annual management (to the management company) and custody fees (to the custodial bank).[4] These fees are calculated as a fraction of the mutual fund's assets and paid by the mutual fund on a daily basis. These are the key fees affecting the net asset value of non-guaranteed funds which will be the only type of funds in our database. Their maximum annual fee is 2.25 percent of assets under management, while the annual custodial fees may not exceed 0.40 percent of a fund's assets.

13.3 DATA

Monthly data on 1,000 Spanish non-money-market open-end mutual fund characteristics were obtained by Javier Gil-Bazo and Miguel Martínez from the Spanish regulatory and supervisory authority covering the June 1999–December 2001 period. From their large sample of funds, we only use three types of funds classified according to their objective which are very much representative of the Spanish industry as a whole.[5] The first group (Spanish equities), must invest over 75 percent in equities listed on Spanish markets (including assets of Spanish issuers listed on other markets) and a maximum of 30 percent in non-euro currencies; the second group (mixed equities) must hold between 30 and 75 percent in equities and a maximum of 30 percent in non-euro currencies; finally, the third group (mixed fixed-income) must invest a maximum of 30 percent in equities and 5 percent in non-euro currencies. Our sample includes 113 funds in the first group; 199 in the second and 241 in the third final group.

Table 13.1 summarizes the statistics for the final sample. Our sample is very representative in terms of the total number of funds and it has slightly lower numbers than the average figures for the whole sample except for the case of management fees which are higher than the fee charged by the average fund. This is expected since our data cover funds investing mainly in risky stocks and pure fixed-income funds tend to charge lower management fees.[6]

Besides the number of participants and the total value of assets for each fund, we also have the total value of inflows and outflows for each fund. This is an important piece of information since we are then able to calculate

Table 13.1 Descriptive statistics

Type of funds	Number of funds	Average assets	Average number of participants	Average age	Management fee	Custody fee	Front load	Redemption fee
Spanish equities	113	48,737	2,454	6.60	1.84 (0.45)	0.13 (0.06)	0.00 (0.00)	0.45 (0.62)
Mixed equities	199	53,614	2,410	6.39	1.58 (0.53)	0.13 (0.06)	0.06 (0.46)	0.38 (0.61)
Mixed fixed-income	241	52,345	2,396	6.49	1.48 (0.36)	0.14 (0.06)	0.00 (0.00)	0.27 (0.47)
Total industry	1,000	64,867	2,769	6.46	1.42 (0.52)	0.13 (0.07)	0.85 (1.69)	0.89 (1.41)

Notes: This table shows the number of funds, the average assets per fund (in thousands of euros), the average number of participants per fund, the average fund's age, and the average fees and standard deviation of fees (in parentheses) for each fund category according to investment objectives. The period goes from June 1999 to December 2001.

Table 13.2 Number of funds for each management company and their investment objective

Management company	Spanish equities	Mixed equities	Mixed fixed income
BBVA	11	6	14
SCH	11	10	33
Other Banks	38	67	58
Banks	60	83	105
Saving Banks	25	51	57
Independents	28	65	79
Total	113	199	241

the net flow of each fund as the difference between inflows and outflows. To the best of our knowledge, this net flow has not been used before when studying the relationship between past relative performance and the flow of money going into and out of each fund. It should be recalled than in previous studies net flow was approximated by the growth rate of assets adjusted by the total return of the fund. Finally, we have management and custody fees for each fund, and their monthly returns.

Table 13.2 reports the number of funds in each category and for each management company. Our numbers also distinguish between the funds which belong to the banking sector as a whole from the funds of the two largest Spanish banks, namely Banco Bilbao Vizcaya Argentaria (BBVA) and Santander Central Hispano (SCH). It is interesting to notice that banks invest a higher percentage than other management companies in Spanish Equities (the riskier funds), while independent management companies invest the lowest percentage in the same riskier funds among all management companies. It may suggest a relatively conservative strategy from independent companies. Of course, it may be recalled that independent management companies do not enjoy the vast base of clients that credit institutions have in Spain.

Finally, we employ several well-known risk factors that will be used in our alternative evaluation asset-pricing models. Table 13.3 reports summary statistics on the benchmark returns.[7] It is important to note that our sample period is characterized by a strong overall market decline; the annualized market portfolio return, as represented by the Ibex 35 Stock Index, has a negative 7 percent annual average return during the sampling period and a volatility of 23 percent. It should be noted, however, that two clear distinct sub-periods characterize the whole period. From June 1999 to February 2000, the annualized mean market return was 29 percent, while from March 2000 to December 2001 it was a negative 22 percent. On the other hand, it should also be noticed that the one-month lagged spread

Table 13.3 Risk factors and benchmarks summary statistics June 1999 to December 2001

Mean and volatility			**Cross-correlations**							
Index	**Annual mean**	**Annual volatility**	**T- bill**	**YTM GBond**	**F.I. index**	**SMB**	**HML**	**MOM**	**Spread**
Market Ibex35	−7.04	23.05	−0.172	−0.065	0.009	−0.347	0.373	−0.023	0.245
T. bill	3.91	0.24		0.831	0.305	−0.179	0.021	−0.217	−0.524
YTM GBond	4.68	0.20			0.093	−0.183	0.226	−0.178	−0.043
F.I. Index	3.88	3.58				−0.111	0.028	−0.157	−0.288
SMB	3.67	3.54					−0.046	−0.164	−0.092
HML	−0.28	5.75						0.310	0.382
MOM	−1.62	21.04							0.264
Spread	0.77	0.13							

Notes: The market portfolio return is the Ibex 35 Spanish Stock Index; YTM GBond is the yield to maturity of the 5-year government bond; F.I. Index is the total return index of Spanish medium and long-term government bonds; SMB and HML are the size and book-to-market Fama–French factors; MOM is the 6-month momentum factor; Spread is the (one-month lagged) yield differential between the 5-year government bond and the 3-month Treasury bill rate. Mean returns and volatility are given in annualized terms.

between the yield of the 5-year government bond and the 3-month Treasury bill has a positive correlation of 0.25 with the market return. This is consistent with the well-known evidence of the yield spread being a good predictor of future economic activity. In this chapter we employ the yield spread as the instrument in the conditional models of performance evaluation. Ferreira, Martínez, Navarro and Rubio (2005) present empirical evidence showing that the yield spread is an excellent predictor of future economic activity in several European countries including Spain. Moreover, Ferson and Qian (2004), among others, show that the slope of the term structure is a powerful predictor, not just for fixed income but also for equity returns. In particular, they find that high levels of short-term interest rates predict relatively high and volatile short-term bond returns and low stock returns.

13.4 MODELS OF PERFORMANCE EVALUATION

Modern asset pricing theory establishes that any gross return, R_{jt+1}, that is correctly priced by the stochastic discount factor, M_{t+1}, satisfies:

$$E_t[M_{t+1}R_{jt+1}] = 1 \tag{13.1}$$

Under the conditional CAPM framework, the stochastic discount factor is linear in the return on the market with time-varying coefficients which are elements of the time-t information set:

$$M_{t+1} = a_t + b_t R_{mt+1} \tag{13.2}$$

If we make the further assumption that the coefficients are linear functions of an information variable, Z_t, which summarizes all relevant information available for the investor:

$$\begin{aligned} a_t &= a_0 + a_1 Z_t \\ b_t &= b_0 + b_1 Z_t \end{aligned} \tag{13.3}$$

we obtain a conditional CAPM performance evaluation framework in which we have a dynamic or time-varying conditional performance measure:

$$r_{jt+1} = \alpha_{jc0} + \alpha_{jc1} Z_t + \beta_{jm} r_{mt+1} + \beta_{jzm}(Z_t r_{mt+1}) + \varepsilon_{jt+1} \tag{13.4}$$

where $r_{jt+1} \equiv R_{jt+1} - R_{ft+1}$ is the excess return of fund j, R_{ft+1} is the return on the Treasury bill, $r_{mt+1} \equiv R_{mt+1} - R_{ft+1}$ is the market excess return, and Z_t is the yield spread between the 5-year Government bond and the 3-month Treasury bill. Finally, $\alpha_{jc0} + \alpha_{jc1} Z_t$ measures the time-varying conditional alpha. It is also interesting to point out that the coefficient α_{jc1} measures the extent to which conditional performance moves with the state variable Z_t. Alternatively, it indicates how a particular fund performs along the business cycle. As usual, with conditional performance evaluation models, the cross-product term, $Z_t r_{mt+1}$, may be interpreted as the return to a dynamic strategy, which holds Z_t units of the market portfolio, financed by borrowing Z_t in Treasury bills.

Alternatively, if in expression (13.3) only the slope coefficient is allowed to change with the economic conditions, we obtain the model proposed by Ferson and Schadt (1996):

$$r_{jt+1} = \alpha_{jc} + \beta_{jm} r_{mt+1} + \beta_{jzm}(Z_t r_{mt+1}) + \varepsilon_{jt+1} \tag{13.5}$$

We also employ the more traditional unconditional performance evaluation framework. In particular, we use the unconditional CAPM, a 2-factor model with a government bond index total return, and the Carhart 4-factor model.[8] They are given by the following expressions respectively:

$$r_{jt+1} = \alpha_{jm} + \beta_{jm} r_{mt+1} + \varepsilon_{jt+1} \tag{13.6}$$

$$r_{jt+1} = \alpha_{jmd} + \beta_{jm} r_{mt+1} + \beta_{jd} r_{dt+1} + \varepsilon_{jt+1} \tag{13.7}$$

where $r_{dt+1} \equiv R_{dt+1} - R_{ft+1}$ is the medium-long-term government bond excess return, and

$$\begin{aligned} r_{jt+1} = \alpha_{j4} &+ \beta_{jm} r_{mt+1} + \beta_{jsmb} r_{smbt+1} \\ &+ \beta_{jhml} r_{hmlt+1} + \beta_{jmom} r_{momt+1} + \varepsilon_{jt+1} \end{aligned} \tag{13.8}$$

where we use the three Fama–French factor portfolios and the momentum factor proposed by Carhart (1997).

13.5 EMPIRICAL RESULTS

This section discusses the empirical results on performance, fees, determinants of fees, and the relationship between flows and performance. We separate the results by management companies and the investment objective of the funds.

13.5.1 The performance of Spanish mutual funds

In this sub-section we employ models (13.5) to (13.8) to report the performance of managed portfolios in Spain. It must be recalled that our sampling period is very short to draw general conclusions on the ability of managers in the Spanish fund industry. However, this is the first time that we observe results by management companies. We argue that this is the proper aggregation when presenting performance of mutual funds. Further research along these lines with a much longer time period is required. As in the rest of the chapter, we separate the evidence on performance for Spanish equities, mixed equities and mixed fixed income. The results are reported in Tables 13.4, 13.5 and 13.6 for each category respectively.

Despite the fact that the average market portfolio return is negative during the period, funds investing in Spanish equities present the best overall performance independently of the management company. Interestingly, funds with mixed fixed income assets clearly have the worst performance. This is even true for the model in which a government bond index return is included as an additional risk factor.

As mentioned above, our sampling period is characterized by two very different economic states. The bull market of the beginning of the period is followed by a bear market starting on March 2000. We employ the dynamic conditional performance evaluation model to estimate the α_{jc1} coefficient of regression (13.4). This is the coefficient that indicates how performance moves with the business cycle. It must be noted that our conditioning variable, the yield spread, is a pro-cyclical variable in the sense that inverted zero-coupon curves tend to anticipate recessions, while upward-sloping curves tend to forecast expansions. Hence, if the estimate of α_{jc1} is positive, it indicates that the fund has a pro-cyclical performance. The average estimates of α_{jc1} are reported in Table 13.7 by management companies and by the three categories of funds we use in this research. It turns out that all mutual funds in Spain have on average a pro-cyclical performance, but it is important to notice that the performance of funds which belong to banks are certainly more cyclical than the performance of savings banks and independent companies. In two out of the three categories of funds, independent companies have the less cyclical performance. Moreover, funds with mixed fixed income assets have the lowest cyclical performance independently of the management company.[9] This suggests that these types of funds may not take advantage of timing the market as other funds with alternative more aggressive objectives. In our specific sampling period this seems to be important. Similarly, funds which belong to independent companies also present the worst performance record among all management companies in all types of funds except mixed fixed income. Once again, they have the less cyclical performance relative to other management companies. Also, along this line of reasoning, it turns out that the mixed fixed income funds of savings banks present not only the worst performance but also the less cyclical performance among all categories. As before, further research on conditional performance evaluation with a longer time series would be welcome.

Generally speaking, banks have the best performance behavior among all management companies independently of the category of the funds. In particular, mutual funds from both BBVA and SCH have a surprising positive performance, especially in Spanish equities. However, it is interesting to note that, when focusing on mixed equity funds, saving banks slightly outperform banks.

Finally, as the empirical evidence reported by Ferson and Qian (2004) and others, we find a better performance when using the conditional evaluation model. The conditional alpha of model (13.5) tends to be the highest among the alternative models employed in this chapter.[10] As discussed by Ferson and Qian (2004), this result may be attributed to predictable patterns of new money flows in and out of mutual funds. Managers (particularly those in SCH) seem to respond passively to new money flows, so their market exposures are lower when more new money flows enter the fund. Moreover, it is probably the case that more money comes in for mutual funds when high expected returns are predicted. The combined effect lowers the unconditional performance, but not the conditional performance. On the other hand, the poorest performance results are associated with the Carhart 4-factor model. It suggests that mutual funds tend to find serious difficulties when trying to earn risk-adjusted returns from strategies which are not based on size, book-to-market or momentum.

Table 13.4 The performance of Spanish mutual funds by management companies: Spanish equities

Panel A: CAPM

Management companies	Very poor $t \leqslant -1.96$	Poor $-1.96 < t \leqslant -1.64$	Neutral (−) $-1.64 < t \leqslant 0.00$	Neutral (+) $0.00 < t \leqslant 1.64$	Good $1.64 < t \leqslant 1.96$	Very good $1.96 < t$
BBVA	–	–	1	2	3	5
SCH	–	–	2	7	1	1
Other banks	–	–	6	21	1	10
Banks	–	–	9 (15.0)	30 (50.0)	5 (8.3)	16 (26.7)
Savings banks	–	–	4 (16.0)	14 (56.0)	–	7 (28.0)
Independents	–	2 (7.1)	7 (25.0)	16 (57.1)	2 (7.1)	1 (3.6)

Panel B: CAPM + government bonds

Management companies	Very poor $t \leqslant -1.96$	Poor $-1.96 < t \leqslant -1.64$	Neutral (−) $-1.64 < t \leqslant 0.00$	Neutral (+) $0.00 < t \leqslant 1.64$	Good $1.64 < t \leqslant 1.96$	Very good $1.96 < t$
BBVA	–	–	1	3	2	5
SCH	–	–	2	7	1	1
Other banks	–	–	6	21	1	10
Banks	–	–	9 (15.0)	31 (51.7)	4 (6.7)	16 (26.7)
Savings banks	–	–	4 (16.0)	14 (56.0)	1 (4.0)	6 (24.0)
Independents	–	1 (3.6)	8 (28.6)	15 (53.6)	3 (10.7)	1 (3.6)

Panel C: Carhart 4-factor model

Management companies	Very poor $t \leqslant -1.96$	Poor $-1.96 < t \leqslant -1.64$	Neutral (−) $-1.64 < t \leqslant 0.00$	Neutral (+) $0.00 < t \leqslant 1.64$	Good $1.64 < t \leqslant 1.96$	Very good $1.96 < t$
BBVA	–	–	2	4	1	4
SCH	–	–	3	7	–	1
Other banks	1	–	7	20	2	8
Banks	1 (1.7)	–	12 (20.0)	31 (51.7)	3 (5.0)	13 (21.7)
Savings banks	1 (4.0)	–	8 (32.0)	12 (48.0)	2 (8.0)	3 (12.0)
Independents	2 (7.1)	1 (3.6)	6 (21.4)	17 (60.7)	2 (7.1)	–

Panel D: Conditional CAPM with bond yield spreads as instrument

Management companies	Very poor $t \leqslant -1.96$	Poor $-1.96 < t \leqslant -1.64$	Neutral (−) $-1.64 < t \leqslant 0.00$	Neutral (+) $0.00 < t \leqslant 1.64$	Good $1.64 < t \leqslant 1.96$	Very good $1.96 < t$
BBVA	–	–	–	3	5	3
SCH	–	–	–	3	2	6
Other banks	–	–	9	16	2	11
Banks	–	–	9 (15.0)	22 (36.7)	9 (15.0)	20 (33.3)
Savings banks	–	–	3 (12.0)	12 (48.0)	3 (12.0)	7 (28.0)
Independents	1 (3.6)	–	6 (21.4)	17 (60.7)	2 (7.1)	2 (7.1)

Note: This table reports the number of funds with a t-statistic on alpha lying in the given interval for a particular asset pricing model (percentage of funds for a given category in parentheses).

Table 13.5 The performance of Spanish mutual funds by management companies: mixed equity funds

Panel A: CAPM

Management companies	Very poor $t \leq -1.96$	Poor $-1.96 < t \leq -1.64$	Neutral (−) $-1.64 < t \leq 0.00$	Neutral (+) $0.00 < t \leq 1.64$	Good $1.64 < t \leq 1.96$	Very good $1.96 < t$
BBVA	–	–	4	2	–	–
SCH	–	–	9	1	–	–
Other banks	4	1	33	27	2	–
Banks	4 (4.8)	1 (1.2)	46 (55.4)	30 (36.1)	2 (2.4)	–
Savings banks	1 (2.0)	1 (2.0)	26 (51.0)	22 (43.1)	1 (2.0)	–
Independents	6 (9.2)	4 (6.2)	32 (49.2)	23 (35.4)	–	–

Panel B: CAPM + government bonds

Management companies	Very poor $t \leq -1.96$	Poor $-1.96 < t \leq -1.64$	Neutral (−) $-1.64 < t \leq 0.00$	Neutral (+) $0.00 < t \leq 1.64$	Good $1.64 < t \leq 1.96$	Very good $1.96 < t$
BBVA	–	–	4	2	–	
SCH	–	–	9	1	–	–
Other banks	3	2	32	27	2	1
Banks	3 (3.6)	2 (2.4)	45 (54.2)	30 (36.1)	2 (2.4)	1 (1.2)
Savings banks	1 (2.0)	1 (2.0)	24 (47.1)	24 (47.1)	1 (2.0)	–
Independents	4 (6.2)	5 (7.7)	32 (49.2)	24 (36.9)	–	–

Panel C: Carhart 4-factor model

Management companies	Very poor $t \leqslant -1.96$	Poor $-1.96 < t \leqslant -1.64$	Neutral (−) $-1.64 < t \leqslant 0.00$	Neutral (+) $0.00 < t \leqslant 1.64$	Good $1.64 < t \leqslant 1.96$	Very good $1.96 < t$
BBVA	–	–	4	2	–	–
SCH	–	–	8	2	–	–
Other banks	6	2	36	23	–	–
Banks	6 (7.2)	2 (2.4)	48 (57.8)	27 (32.5)	–	–
Savings banks	1 (2.0)	3 (5.9)	29 (56.9)	18 (35.3)	–	–
Independents	6 (9.2)	5 (7.7)	33 (50.8)	20 (30.8)	1 (1.5)	–

Panel D: Conditional CAPM with bond yield spreads as instrument

Management companies	Very poor $t \leqslant -1.96$	Poor $-1.96 < t \leqslant -1.64$	Neutral (−) $-1.64 < t \leqslant 0.00$	Neutral (+) $0.00 < t \leqslant 1.64$	Good $1.64 < t \leqslant 1.96$	Very good $1.96 < t$
BBVA	–	–	4	2	–	–
SCH	–	–	8	2	–	–
Other banks	1	1	39	24	2	–
Banks	1 (1.2)	1 (1.2)	51 (61.4)	28 (33.7)	2 (2.4)	–
Savings banks	–	1 (2.0)	21 (41.2)	28 (54.9)	–	1 (2.0)
Independents	4 (6.2)	3 (4.6)	25 (38.5)	30 (46.2)	2 (3.1)	1 (1.5)

Note: This table reports the number of funds with a *t*-statistic on alpha lying in the given interval for a particular asset pricing model (percentage of funds for a given category in parentheses).

Table 13.6 The performance of Spanish mutual funds by management companies: mixed fixed income funds

Panel A: CAPM

Management companies	Very poor $t \leqslant -1.96$	Poor $-1.96 < t \leqslant -1.64$	Neutral (−) $-1.64 < t \leqslant 0.00$	Neutral (+) $0.00 < t \leqslant 1.64$	Good $1.64 < t \leqslant 1.96$	Very good $1.96 < t$
BBVA	3	1	8	2	–	–
SCH	–	1	23	9	–	–
Other banks	7	1	29	18	3	–
Banks	10 (9.5)	3 (2.9)	60 (57.1)	29 (27.6)	3 (2.9)	–
Savings banks	7 (12.3)	5 (8.8)	37 (64.9)	6 (10.5)	1 (1.8)	1 (1.8)
Independents	12 (15.2)	12 (15.2)	36 (45.6)	17 (21.5)	1 (1.3)	1 (1.3)

Panel B: CAPM + government bonds

Management companies	Very poor $t \leqslant -1.96$	Poor $-1.96 < t \leqslant -1.64$	Neutral (−) $-1.64 < t \leqslant 0.00$	Neutral (+) $0.00 < t \leqslant 1.64$	Good $1.64 < t \leqslant 1.96$	Very good $1.96 < t$
BBVA	3	1	8	2	–	–
SCH	–	2	25	6	–	–
Other banks	7	1	30	17	3	–
Banks	10 (9.5)	4 (3.8)	63 (60.0)	25 (23.8)	3 (2.9)	–
Savings banks	6 (10.5)	9 (15.8)	35 (61.4)	4 (7.0)	2 (3.5)	1 (1.8)
Independents	16 (20.3)	5 (6.3)	40 (50.6)	16 (20.3)	1 (1.3)	1 (1.3)

Panel C: Carhart 4-factor model

Management companies	Very poor $t \leqslant -1.96$	Poor $-1.96 < t \leqslant -1.64$	Neutral (−) $-1.64 < t \leqslant 0.00$	Neutral (+) $0.00 < t \leqslant 1.64$	Good $1.64 < t \leqslant 1.96$	Very good $1.96 < t$
BBVA	5	1	6	2	–	–
SCH	–	4	23	6	–	–
Other banks	9	3	27	18	1	–
Banks	14 (13.3)	8 (7.6)	56 (53.3)	26 (24.7)	1 (1.0)	–
Savings banks	18 (31.6)	8 (14)	26 (45.6)	3 (5.3)	1 (1.8)	1 (1.8)
Independents	15 (19)	6 (7.6)	42 (53.2)	13 (16.5)	1 (1.3)	2 (2.5)

Panel D: Conditional CAPM with bond yield spreads as instrument

Management companies	Very poor $t \leqslant -1.96$	Poor $-1.96 < t \leqslant -1.64$	Neutral (−) $-1.64 < t \leqslant 0.00$	Neutral (+) $0.00 < t \leqslant 1.64$	Good $1.64 < t \leqslant 1.96$	Very good $1.96 < t$
BBVA	3	1	8	2	–	–
SCH	1	2	23	7	–	–
Other banks	8	2	26	20	1	1
Banks	12 (11.4)	5 (4.7)	57 (54.2)	29 (27.6)	1 (1.0)	1 (1.0)
Savings banks	9 (15.8)	3 (5.3)	38 (66.7)	6 (10.5)	1 (1.8)	–
Independents	16 (20.3)	4 (5.1)	36 (45.6)	21 (26.6)	–	2 (2.5)

Note: This table reports the number of funds with a *t*-statistic on alpha lying in the given interval for a particular asset pricing model (percentage of funds for a given category in parentheses).

Table 13.7 Time-varying performance over the business cycle

Management company	Spanish equities	Mixed equities	Mixed fixed income
Banks	6.33	14.21	3.23
Savings banks	5.55	6.55	1.11
Independents	3.29	5.08	2.04

Notes: This table shows the average coefficients α_{jc1} for each class of management company and category of funds estimated from the following regression:

$$r_{jt+1} = \alpha_{jc0} + \alpha_{jc1} Z_t + \beta_{jm} r_{mt+1} + \beta_{jzm}(Z_t r_{mt+1}) + \varepsilon_{jt+1}$$

where the conditional time-varying alpha is given by $\hat{\alpha}_{jc0} + \hat{\alpha}_{jc1} Z_t$, and Z_t is the bond yield spread. The α_{jc1} coefficient reflects the extent to which conditional performance moves with the state of the economy as described by the bond yield spread.

13.5.2 The relationship between fees and performance

Rational frictionless behavior implies that mutual funds charging higher management and custody fees should compensate investors with higher returns. Managed portfolios with superior effort and ability justify higher fees. Given that net asset values are obtained after subtracting expenses and management fees, difference in performance across mutual funds with different fees should not be observed.

In this sub-section we analyse whether mutual funds with higher fees (management plus custody fees) obtain higher average returns. To test this relationship we perform cross-sectional regressions of estimated alphas with models (13.4) to (13.8) on fees:

$$\alpha_j = a + bFees_j + u_j \tag{13.9}$$

Our reasoning implies that the estimate of the slope should not be statistically different from zero. Even if higher fees are reducing returns, these funds should also be able to generate higher returns before fees, so that the net effect should be zero.[11]

The results across management companies and categories of funds are reported in Tables 13.8, 13.9 and 13.10. Overall, our results indicate a strong negative relationship between risk-adjusted performance and fees. Funds charging higher fees do not obtain enough returns to compensate higher costs to investors. On the contrary, mutual funds with higher fees present the worst performance. This is a very disturbing result.

When observing the results by categories of funds, it is clear that mutual funds investing in Spanish equities (the riskiest funds in our sample) have the stronger negative relationship with mostly negative and significant slope coefficients and relatively high R^2. All management companies have

Table 13.8 The relationship between alphas and fees: Spanish equities

Panel A: CAPM

Management companies	$\hat{a}$	$\hat{b}$	R^2 (%)
BBVA	0.0161 (1.66)	−0.5298 (−1.21)	11.65
SCH	0.0049 (4.09)	−0.1903 (−3.42)	68.29
Other banks	0.0071 (4.84)	−0.2172 (−3.43)	11.09
Banks	0.0072 (5.18)	−0.2088 (−3.43)	8.18
Savings banks	0.0076 (5.76)	−0.2747 (−4.37)	32.84
Independents	0.0111 (2.22)	−0.4584 (−1.99)	11.78

Panel B: CAPM + government bonds

Management companies	$\hat{a}$	$\hat{b}$	R^2 (%)
BBVA	0.0167 (1.43)	−0.5382 (−1.04)	8.90
SCH	0.0053 (4.05)	−0.2077 (−3.42)	69.79
Other banks	0.0072 (4.72)	−0.2163 (−3.15)	9.55
Banks	0.0074 (4.92)	−0.2125 (−3.26)	6.91
Savings banks	0.0074 (5.50)	−0.2623 (−4.07)	29.43
Independents	0.0110 (2.24)	−0.4466 (−1.98)	11.20

Panel C: Carhart 4-factor model

Management companies	$\hat{a}$	$\hat{b}$	R^2 (%)
BBVA	0.0125 (1.19)	−0.4184 (−0.89)	6.93
SCH	0.0049 (3.16)	−0.2202 (−3.03)	61.59
Other banks	0.0048 (2.35)	−0.1477 (−1.69)	3.85
Banks	0.0055 (3.47)	−0.1713 (−2.55)	3.12
Savings banks	0.0059 (4.02)	−0.2338 (−3.27)	25.71
Independents	0.0120 (2.14)	−0.5168 (−2.05)	10.16

Panel D: conditional CAPM with bond yield spreads as instrument

Management companies	$\hat{a}$	$\hat{b}$	R^2 (%)
BBVA	0.0177 (3.08)	−0.6008 (−2.26)	26.12
SCH	0.0059 (7.80)	−0.1363 (−4.09)	68.00
Other banks	0.0059 (3.74)	−0.1581 (−3.25)	5.91
Banks	0.0070 (5.66)	−0.1791 (−3.25)	7.49
Savings banks	0.0078 (5.44)	−0.2464 (−3.46)	22.49
Independents	0.0098 (2.15)	−0.3513 (−1.67)	10.03

Continued

Table 13.8 Continued

Panel E: conditional CAPM with bond yield spreads as instrument and dynamic alphas

Management companies	$\hat{a}$	$\hat{b}$	R^2 (%)
BBVA	0.0174 (3.00)	−0.5933 (−2.17)	26.40
SCH	0.0062 (7.47)	−0.1488 (−4.07)	68.91
Other banks	0.0064 (4.11)	−0.1854 (−2.75)	8.20
Banks	0.0073 (6.05)	−0.2005 (−3.75)	9.60
Savings banks	0.0078 (5.45)	−0.2451 (−3.50)	23.51
Independents	0.0097 (2.13)	−0.3447 (−1.65)	9.70

Note: This table reports the results from the following regression by management companies:

$$\alpha_j = a + bFees_j + u_j$$

where fees includes both deposit and management fees, and performance is measured relative to five alternative asset pricing models (*t*-statistic in parentheses based on heteroskedasticity-consistent White standard errors).

Table 13.9 The relationship between alphas and fees: mixed equity funds

Panel A: CAPM

Management companies	$\hat{a}$	$\hat{b}$	R^2 (%)
BBVA	0.00432 (1.55)	−0.24724 (−1.79)	44.45
SCH	−0.00585 (−2.85)	0.26204 (2.03)	33.99
Other banks	0.00180 (1.61)	−0.16050 (−2.59)	9.33
Banks	0.00076 (0.77)	−0.10529 (−1.91)	4.32
Savings banks	0.00018 (0.12)	−0.02754 (−0.36)	0.27
Independents	0.00006 (0.05)	−0.03382 (−0.62)	0.61

Panel B: CAPM + government bonds

Management companies	$\hat{a}$	$\hat{b}$	R^2 (%)
BBVA	0.00453 (1.51)	−0.25469 (−1.71)	42.12
SCH	−0.00504 (−2.78)	0.22559 (1.98)	32.83
Other banks	0.00182 (1.61)	−0.15372 (−2.45)	8.43
Banks	0.00091 (0.93)	−0.10554 (−1.93)	4.38
Savings banks	0.00058 (0.42)	−0.04579 (−0.64)	0.84
Independents	0.00016 (0.14)	−0.03451 (−0.65)	0.67

Panel C: Carhart 4-factor model

Management companies	$\hat{a}$	$\hat{b}$	R^2 (%)
BBVA	0.00377 (1.38)	−0.27818 (−2.05)	51.25
SCH	−0.00561 (−3.73)	0.24162 (2.55)	44.89

Continued

Table 13.9 Continued

Management companies	$\hat{a}$	$\hat{b}$	R^2 (%)
Other banks	0.00116 (0.97)	−0.17802 (−2.68)	9.94
Banks	0.00033 (0.32)	−0.12973 (−2.28)	6.01
Savings banks	−0.00031 (−0.24)	−0.03252 (−0.49)	0.50
Independents	−0.00142 (−1.26)	−0.01128 (−0.22)	0.07

Panel D: conditional CAPM with bond yield spreads as instrument

Management companies	$\hat{a}$	$\hat{b}$	R^2 (%)
BBVA	0.00186 (0.99)	−0.13224 (−1.43)	33.72
SCH	−0.00540 (−1.73)	0.21667 (1.10)	13.16
Other banks	0.00304 (2.76)	−0.21777 (−3.54)	16.20
Banks	0.00168 (1.64)	−0.14901 (−2.62)	7.79
Savings banks	0.00062 (0.43)	−0.03899 (−0.53)	0.56
Independents	0.00111 (0.96)	−0.05371 (−0.99)	1.54

Panel E: conditional CAPM with bond yield spreads as instrument and dynamic alphas

Management companies	$\hat{a}$	$\hat{b}$	R^2 (%)
BBVA	0.00167 (0.99)	−0.12114 (−1.44)	34.20
SCH	−0.00585 (−1.74)	0.24243 (1.15)	14.12
Other banks	0.00281 (2.80)	−0.19911 (−3.56)	16.31
Banks	0.00141 (1.46)	−0.12971 (−2.40)	6.66
Savings banks	0.00059 (0.41)	−0.03805 (−0.51)	0.53
Independents	0.00216 (2.00)	−0.09123 (−1.81)	4.95

Notes: This table reports the results from the following regression by management companies:

$$\alpha_j = a + bFees_j + u_j$$

where fees includes both deposit and management fees, and performance is measured relative to five alternative asset pricing models (t-statistic in parentheses based on heteroskedasticity-consistent White standard errors).

a negative relationship between performance and fees. However, this is especially true for savings banks and SCH. The coefficient associated with BBVA is also negative, but it is statistically significant only when alphas are estimated with conditional models. When moving to mixed equities, we also find an overall negative relationship. However, it is only significant in the case of banks. The R^2 coefficient is quite high for BBVA, although in this case the slope coefficient is not statistically different from zero when using conditional alphas. The R^2 coefficient is also high for SCH, although surprisingly it is the

Table 13.10 The relationship between alphas and fees: mixed fixed income funds

Panel A: CAPM

Management companies	$\hat{a}$	$\hat{b}$	R^2 (%)
BBVA	−0.00172 (−0.83)	0.03891 (0.29)	0.67
SCH	0.00894 (0.30)	−0.04460 (−0.02)	0.00
Other banks	−0.00083 (−0.62)	0.01754 (0.22)	0.09
Banks	0.00281 (0.40)	−0.04600 (−0.10)	0.01
Savings banks	0.00102 (1.46)	−0.11280 (−2.74)	12.02
Independents	0.00123 (1.46)	−0.15702 (−3.00)	10.46

Panel B: CAPM + government bonds

Management companies	$\hat{a}$	$\hat{b}$	R^2 (%)
BBVA	−0.00141 (−0.69)	0.02074 (0.15)	0.20
SCH	0.00803 (0.30)	−0.038 (−0.02)	0.00
Other banks	−0.00084 (−0.62)	0.01335 (0.17)	0.05
Banks	0.00252 (0.39)	−0.04583 (−0.11)	0.01
Savings banks	0.00096 (1.39)	−0.11330 (−2.77)	12.23
Independents	0.00121 (1.41)	−0.15807 (−2.96)	10.25

Panel C: Carhart 4-factor model

Management companies	$\hat{a}$	$\hat{b}$	R^2 (%)
BBVA	−0.00145 (−≤0.84)	0.01413 (0.12)	0.13
SCH	0.00743 (0.30)	−0.05599 (−0.03)	0.00
Other banks	−0.00210 (−1.18)	0.06253 (0.59)	0.62
Banks	0.00148 (0.25)	−0.01666 (−0.04)	0.00
Savings banks	0.00104 (1.46)	−0.13635 (−3.23)	15.98
Independents	0.00089 (1.06)	−0.15512 (−2.95)	10.13

Panel D: conditional CAPM with bond yield spreads as instrument

Management companies	$\hat{a}$	$\hat{b}$	R^2 (%)
BBVA	−0.00268 (−1.20)	0.10718 (0.73)	4.24
SCH	0.01232 (0.32)	−0.06397 (−0.02)	0.00
Other banks	0.00293 (3.29)	−0.17889 (−3.37)	16.84
Banks	0.00631 (0.68)	−0.19072 (−0.32)	0.10
Savings banks	0.00067 (0.96)	−0.09096 (−2.20)	8.06
Independents	0.00141 (1.58)	−0.14781 (−2.65)	8.38

Continued

Table 13.10 Continued

Panel E: conditional CAPM with bond yield spreads as instrument and dynamic alphas			
Management companies	$\hat{a}$	$\hat{b}$	R^2 (%)
BBVA	−0.00267 (−1.22)	0.10679 (0.74)	4.38
SCH	0.01300 (0.32)	−0.06393 (−0.02)	0.00
Other banks	0.00281 (3.13)	−0.17100 (−3.19)	15.37
Banks	0.00651 (0.66)	−0.18971 (−0.30)	0.09
Savings banks	0.00068 (0.96)	−0.09111 (−2.19)	8.04
Independents	0.00142 (1.57)	−0.14989 (−2.66)	8.39

Note: This table reports the results from the following regression by management companies:

$$\alpha_j = a + bFees_j + u_j$$

where fees includes both deposit and management fees, and performance is measured relative to five alternative asset pricing models (*t*-statistic in parentheses based on heteroskedasticity-consistent White standard errors).

only case with a positive slope coefficient. However, once again, it becomes non-significant when we employ conditional alphas. Savings banks and independents companies do not have significant estimates of the slope. Finally, for the less risky funds, mixed fixed income funds, we observe a weak relationship between performance and fees for banks, but negative and significant in the cases of savings banks and independent companies.

To summarize, banks present a stronger negative relationship between performance and fees for risky funds than for less risky investments. Although during our sampling period, banks (and particularly large banks) obtain an overall good performance record, it seems that the success lies on the cheapest high risk funds. On the other hand, savings banks and independent companies have a similar behavior. They have a significant negative relationship between performance and fees for both high and low risk funds. The declining monotonic pattern between the negative relationship and the risk level of the fund which we reported for banks does not seem to be so clear in the case of savings banks and independent companies.

13.5.3 Some evidence on the determinants of fees

As mentioned in the introduction, Gil-Bazo and Martínez (2004) have recently studied in detail the determinants of fees in the Spanish mutual fund industry. We do not pretend to replicate their findings, but just complement the key result of their paper. It turns out that, for a given investment objective, the average investment (measured by the natural logarithm of the fund's assets minus the natural logarithm of the fund's number of participants) and age are the two most important variables explaining fees.

In this research, for a given management company and a given investment objective, we analyse the total value of assets, the number of participants, the net flow (which we define as inflows minus outflows) and past returns as potential variables in explaining fees. In non-reported results we were not able to find any significant result except for the number of participants. Hence, we report the results of the following cross-sectional regression performed with funds that belong to a particular management company within a given investment objective:

$$Fees_j = a + b\ln Part_j + u_j \tag{13.10}$$

where $ln\ Part_j$ is the natural logarithm of the number of investors in each fund j. The results reported in Tables 13.11, 13.12 and 13.13 are striking. Overall, there is a very strong positive and significant relationship between fees and number of participants. This explains the strong negative result reported by Gil-Bazo and Martínez (2004) between average investment *per* number of participants and fees. It seems that the number of participants is the variable behind their significant results.

Our results show that, independently of the investment objective of the fund, large banks have a very strong positive relationship between fees and number of participants. The average R^2 is in between 32.1 percent for SCH in the case of mixed fixed income funds and 76.9 percent for BBVA when investing in Spanish equity funds. In fact, BBVA has a strikingly large R^2 for

Table 13.11 The relationship between fees and number of participants: Spanish equities

Management companies	$\hat{a}$	$\hat{b}$	R^2 (%)
BBVA	−0.0045 (−0.93)	0.0029 (5.12)	76.95
SCH	−0.0134 (−1.94)	0.0040 (5.09)	58.59
Other banks	0.0109 (3.11)	0.0011 (2.32)	7.16
Banks	0.0066 (2.11)	0.0016 (4.19)	18.05
Savings banks	0.0126 (2.04)	0.00099 (1.26)	5.88
Independents	0.0061 (1.68)	0.0022 (4.09)	27.96

Note: This table reports the results from the following regression by management companies:

$$Fees_j = a + b\ ln\ Part_j + u_j$$

where fees includes both deposit and management fees, and participants is the average number of investors in the fund during the sample period (t-statistic in parentheses based on heteroskedasticity-consistent White standard errors).

all categories with a declining monotonic relationship between the positive coefficient and the risk supported by the funds. On the average, the number of participants explains 61.7 percent of the variability of fees in the case of BBVA, and 41.8 percent for SCH. These are amazing numbers. They suggest that large banking management companies, with their stable base of clients, charge high fees once they have consolidated the fund with a large base of participants. This is especially the case for Spanish equities, although it remains highly significant for less risky funds. BBVA and SCH simply

Table 13.12 The relationship between fees and number of participants: mixed equity funds

Management companies	$\hat{a}$	$\hat{b}$	R^2 (%)
BBVA	−0.00163 (−0.19)	0.00266 (2.53)	61.50
SCH	−0.00421 (−0.68)	0.00264 (3.14)	55.23
Other banks	0.01196 (4.48)	0.00075 (1.88)	5.18
Banks	0.00988 (4.13)	0.00103 (2.97)	9.80
Savings banks	0.01267 (4.23)	0.00084 (2.10)	8.25
Independents	0.01380 (2.46)	0.00076 (0.78)	0.96

Note: This table reports the results from the following regression by management companies:

$$Fees_j = a + b \ln Part_j + u_j$$

where fees includes both deposit and management fees, and participants is the average number of investors in the fund during the sample period (*t*-statistic in parentheses based on heteroskedasticity-consistent White standard errors).

Table 13.13 The relationship between fees and number of participants: mixed fixed income funds

Management companies	$\hat{a}$	$\hat{b}$	R^2 (%)
BBVA	0.00486 (1.68)	0.00165 (3.46)	49.88
SCH	0.00577 (2.71)	0.00109 (3.83)	32.14
Other banks	0.01419 (3.93)	0.00013 (0.25)	0.11
Banks	0.00935 (4.86)	0.00077 (2.77)	6.93
Savings banks	0.00869 (4.62)	0.00111 (4.24)	24.65
Independents	0.01254 (6.08)	0.00052 (1.48)	2.77

Note: This table reports the results from the following regression by management companies:

$$Fees_j = a + b \ln Part_j + u_j$$

where fees includes both deposit and management fees, and participants is the average number of investors in the fund during the sample period (*t*-statistic in parentheses based on heteroskedasticity-consistent White standard errors).

take advantage that they have a lot of clients with lack of mobility within funds and management companies to increase their fees.

On the other hand, for small banks and independent companies, this significant and positive relationship between fees and number of participants is only found for Spanish equity funds. For these types of companies, it seems that in mutual funds where the risk strategy is probably more similar among funds and management companies (mixed equities and mixed fixed income), it is more difficult to justify high fees among funds with a large number of participants.

Finally, savings banks follow the opposite strategy than commercial banks. They have a significant positive relationship between fees and number of participants in less risky funds. The relationship is not significantly different from zero in Spanish equity funds. This is interesting since savings banks are owned and managed by local or regional governments, and they are (in principle) not-for-profit and therefore tax-exempt organizations. The loyalty of their clients is a very important characteristic of these organizations. To relate fees with the number of participants in funds with less-demanding investment strategies (mixed equities and mixed fixed income) is a particularly good and safe business for them. Lack of real competition in the Spanish mutual fund industry is a very disturbing feature that should be studied using more recent data to see whether recent legal changes have increased the desired competition among management companies.

13.5.4 The relationship between past performance and net flow

One of the most popular topics in the recently available research on mutual funds is the relationship between relative past performance and net flow. In this sub-section we provide a preliminary analysis for the Spanish mutual fund industry using the proper definition of net flow as the difference between inflows and outflows.

First of all, for each mutual fund we perform a time-series regression of the monthly percentage variation of the number of participants on the time-varying conditional alpha from model (13.4), where the monthly conditional alpha, $Calpha_t$, is given by $\hat{\alpha}_{jc0} + \hat{\alpha}_{jc1}Z_t$:

$$\Delta Part_{t+1} = a + bCalpha_t + \varepsilon_{t+1} \qquad (13.11)$$

If investors are highly rational and sophisticated, we would expect to find positive and significant slope coefficients for most mutual funds. Good past conditional risk-adjusted performance would be received as a good signal and we should observe an increase in the number of participants. A similarly reasoning may be done using net flow as the dependent variable:

$$NetFlow_{t+1} = c + dCalpha_t + \varepsilon_{t+1} \quad (13.12)$$

The results are reported in Tables 13.14, 13.15 and 13.16. Unfortunately, we do not observe a clean positive pattern dominating the results. It is true, however, that we tend to observe more mutual funds having a positive relationship between past performance and either changes of participants or net flow than having a negative one. This is comforting, although we do not provide formal statistical analysis of the results. This pattern is especially clear in mixed equities and mixed fixed income and less-pronounced in Spanish equities. Also, the results are slightly more positive using the variation in the number of participants than net flow. At the same time, it does not seem to be a very different pattern among management companies, except for banks in the case of Spanish equities when using net flow. In this case, there are more funds having a negative relationship than a positive one. Finally, it should be mentioned the case of other banks (all banks except BBVA and SCH). They tend to have a much larger number of funds with a positive relationship independently of using participants or net flow.

It is clear than the previous one-lagged monthly regressions are very demanding in terms of a rational response to performance. As a final exercise, for a given management company and an investment objective, we classify all funds in four portfolios (rankings) by their average conditional dynamic alpha, $\hat{\alpha}_{jc0} + \hat{\alpha}_{jc1}Z_t$, from June 1999 to June 2001. Then, we calculate their average net flow from July 2001 to December 2001. This exercise is similar to the empirical analysis of Sirri and Tufano (1998), who find a positive but convex relationship between relative past performance and net flow. However, they use the growth rate of asset values adjusted by the return of each fund, and past total return to classify funds into a given ranked portfolio. On the contrary, we use conditional risk-adjusted returns as a measure of performance and the actual net flow of each fund. However, we just report a graphical representation of the results given the limited time-series data available in the research.

The results are shown in Figures 13.1, 13.2 and 13.3. The best-performing funds are situated in rank-sorted portfolio four, while the worst fund are located in rank-sorted portfolio one. In the case of Spanish equities, all management companies have an increase in the net flow for their best-performing funds. The effect is especially stronger for independent management companies. However, it is also true that the worst performing funds also experienced a relatively high net flow. This pattern seems to be consistent with Lynch and Musto (2003). Surprisingly, this convex relationship no longer holds for mixed equity funds except for independent management companies. The behavior of banks and savings banks is quite disappointing. Once again, it seems that investors using funds of independent companies closely follow their best performing funds. Finally, a positive relationship is again found in the case of mixed fixed income funds for banks and independent companies. However, once again this result does not hold for savings banks.

Table 13.14 The relationship between flows and performance: Spanish equities

Panel A: Changes in the number of participants and past conditional performance

Management companies	Very negative $t \leqslant -1.96$	Negative $-1.96 < t \leqslant 1.64$	Neutral(−) $-1.64 < t \leqslant 0.00$	Neutral (+) $0.00 < t \leqslant 1.64$	Positive $1.64 < t \leqslant 1.96$	Very positive $1.96 < t$
BBVA [Avg. R^2 = 16.88]	6 [28.09]	–	3 [3.05]	2 [4.02]	–	–
SCH [Avg. R^2 = 5.43]	–	–	4 [1.30]	4 [3.58]	–	3 [13.42]
Other banks [Avg. R^2 = 11.28]	3 [31.70]	3 [10.72]	16 [4.63]	9 [4.24]	2 [10.47]	5 [32.82]
Banks [Avg. R^2 = 11.24]	9 (15.0) [29.29]	3 (5.0) [10.72]	23 (38.3) [3.84]	15 (25.0) [4.03]	2 (3.3) [10.47]	8 (13.3) [25.55]
Savings banks [Avg. R^2 = 11.58]	5 (20.0) [17.14]	2 (8.0) [13.31]	9 (36.0) [3.33]	3 (12.0) [7.40]	1 (4.0) [11.29]	5 (20.0) [22.73]
Independents [Avg. R^2 = 10.94]	3 (10.7) [17.75]	2 (7.1) [11.15]	6 (21.4) [0.46]	8 (28.6) [1.56]	1 (3.6) [11.15]	8 (28.6) [25.54]

Panel B: Net flows and past conditional performance

Management companies	Very negative $t \leqslant -1.96$	Negative $-1.96 < t \leqslant 1.64$	Neutral(−) $-1.64 < t \leqslant 0.00$	Neutral (+) $0.00 < t \leqslant 1.64$	Positive $1.64 < t \leqslant 1.96$	Very positive $1.96 < t$
BBVA [Avg. R^2 = 18.70]	5 [33.13]	–	3 [6.25]	3 [7.09]	–	–
SCH [Avg. R^2 = 10.99]	2 [20.59]	2 [10.63]	1 [2.74]	3 [3.09]	1 [18.34]	2 [14.06]

Other banks [Avg. $R^2 = 11.09$]	7 [22.67]	3 [13.53]	13 [3.80]	10 [2.24]	2 [10.47]	3 [44.37]
Banks [Avg. $R^2 = 12.47$]	14 (23.3) [26.11]	5 (8.3) [12.37]	17 (28.3) [4.17]	16 (26.7) [3.31]	3 (5.0) [13.09]	5 (8.3) [32.25]
Savings banks [Avg. $R^2 = 3.90$]	1 (4.0) [14.45]	2 (8.0) [8.62]	14 (56.0) [1.54]	7 (28.0) [3.63]	–	1 (4.0) [18.81]
Independents [Avg. $R^2 = 10.29$]	5 (17.9) [19.93]	1 (3.6) [11.94]	8 (28.6) [3.48]	9 (32.1) [1.80]	–	5 (17.9) [26.50]

Notes: To test the relationship between flows and performance, this table reports the results from two alternative regressions for each mutual fund:

Panel A: $\Delta Part_{t+1} = a + bCalpha_t + \varepsilon_{t+1}$
Panel B: $NetFlow_{t+1} = c + dCalpha_t + \varepsilon_{t+1}$

where *ΔPart* in the percentage monthly variation in the number of participants in each of the mutual funds in the sample, *NetFlow* is the inflow minus outflow for each fund during each month, and the dynamic conditional alpha is given by the following regression:

$$r_{jt+1} = \alpha_{jc0} + \alpha_{jc1}Z_t + \beta_{jm}r_{mt+1} + \beta_{jzm}(Z_t r_{mt+1}) + \varepsilon_{jt+1}$$

where $Calpha_{t+1} = \hat{\alpha}_{jc0} + \hat{\alpha}_{jc1}Z_t$, and Z_t is the bond yield spread.

The table shows the number of funds with a *t*-statistic on alpha lying in the given interval. In brackets we report the R^2 of each category and in parenthesis the percentage of funds within a given *t*-statistic interval.

Table 13.15 The relationship between flows and performance: mixed equity funds

Panel A: Changes in the number of participants and past conditional performance

Management companies	Very negative $t \leqslant -1.96$	Negative $-1.96 < t \leqslant 1.64$	Neutral (−) $-1.64 < t \leqslant 0.00$	Neutral (+) $0.00 < t \leqslant 1.64$	Positive $1.64 < t \leqslant 1.96$	Very positive $1.96 < t$
BBVA [Avg. $R^2 = 16.86$]	–	–	1 [0.45]	2 [1.21]	1 [11.97]	2 [43.15]
SCH [Avg. $R^2 = 16.77$]	–	–	1 [0.03]	2 [1.23]	1 [11.90]	6 [25.56]
Other banks [Avg. $R^2 = 11.72$]	–	5 [11.91]	18 [3.37]	23 [4.30]	6 [10.69]	15 [33.46]
Banks [Avg. $R^2 = 12.70$]	–	5 (6.02) [11.91]	20 (24.10) [3.05]	27 (32.53) [3.85]	8 (9.64) [11.00]	23 (27.71) [32.24]
Savings banks [Avg. $R^2 = 13.29$]	3 (5.88) [36.64]	3 (5.88) [10.92]	8 (15.69) [2.87]	20 (39.22) [3.04]	–	17 (33.33) [26.54]
Independents [Avg. $R^2 = 12.00$]	6 (9.23) [26.10]	3 (4.62) [11.56]	17 (26.15) [2.90]	25 (38.46) [3.37]	4 (6.15) [9.62]	10 (15.38) [41.66]

Panel B: Net flows and past conditional performance

Management companies	Very negative $t \leqslant -1.96$	Negative $-1.96 < t \leqslant 1.64$	Neutral (−) $-1.64 < t \leqslant 0.00$	Neutral (+) $0.00 < t \leqslant 1.64$	Positive $1.64 < t \leqslant 1.96$	Very positive $1.96 < t$
BBVA [Avg. $R^2 = 17.04$]	–	–	2 [1.05]	2 [4.25]	–	2 [45.84]
SCH [Avg. $R^2 = 15.26$]	–	–	2 [0.16]	2 [5.05]	1 [11.17]	5 [26.21]

Other banks [Avg. $R^2 = 12.19$]	4 [24.27]	3 [15.03]	17 [2.93]	26 [4.20]	1 [12.41]	16 [31.46]
Banks [Avg. $R^2 = 12.91$]	4 (4.82) [24.27]	3 (3.61) [15.03]	21 (25.30) [2.49]	30 (36.14) [4.26]	2 (2.41) [11.79]	23 (27.71) [31.57]
Savings banks [Avg. $R^2 = 13.18$]	10 (19.61) [21.67]	–	10 (19.61) [2.17]	18 (35.29) [3.38]	3 (5.88) [10.58]	10 (19.61) [34.11]
Independents [Avg. $R^2 = 11.59$]	5 (7.69) [37.08]	4 (6.15) [16.70]	23 (35.38) [3.62]	19 (29.23) [3.18]	4 (6.15) [12.48]	10 (15.38) [30.73]

Notes: To test the relationship between flows and performance, this table reports the results from two alternative regressions for each mutual fund:

Panel A: $\Delta Part_{t+1} = a + bCalpha_t + \varepsilon_{t+1}$
Panel B: $NetFlow_{t+1} = c + dCalpha_t + \varepsilon_{t+1}$

where $\Delta Part$ in the percentage monthly variation in the number of participants in each of the mutual funds in the sample, *NetFlow* is the inflow minus outflow for each fund during each month, and the dynamic conditional alpha is given by the following regression:

$r_{jt+1} = \alpha_{jc0} + \alpha_{jc1}Z_t + \beta_{jm}r_{mt+1} + \beta_{jzm}(Z_t r_{mt+1}) + \varepsilon_{jt+1}$

where $Calpha_{t+1} = \hat{\alpha}_{jc0} + \hat{\alpha}_{jc1}Z_t$, and Z_t is the bond yield spread.

The table shows the number of funds with a t-statistic on alpha lying in the given interval. In brackets we report the R^2 of each category and in parenthesis the percentage of funds within a given t-statistic interval.

Table 13.16 The relationship between flows and performance: mixed fixed income funds

Panel A: Changes in the number of participants and past conditional performance

Management companies	Very negative $t \leqslant -1.96$	Negative $-1.96 < t \leqslant 1.64$	Neutral (−) $-1.64 < t \leqslant 0.00$	Neutral (+) $0.00 < t \leqslant 1.64$	Positive $1.64 < t \leqslant 1.96$	Very positive $1.96 < t$
BBVA [Avg. $R^2 = 6.26$]	1 [14.06]	–	4 [3.26]	8 [3.57]	–	1 [31.90]
SCH [Avg. $R^2 = 14.16$]	1 [29.50]	2 [11.81]	12 [3.99]	10 [4.63]	1 [11.35]	7 [44.06]
Other banks [Avg. $R^2 = 11.48$]	5 [26.23]	–	17 [3.36]	18 [3.61]	7 [11.32]	11 [30.30]
Banks [Avg. $R^2 = 11.62$]	7 (6.67) [24.96]	2 (1.90) [11.81]	33 (31.43) [3.58]	36 (34.29) [3.88]	8 (7.62) [11.33]	19 (18.10) [35.45]
Savings banks [Avg. $R^2 = 11.84$]	7 (12.28) [28.23]	–	12 (21.05) [2.27]	23 (40.35) [3.65]	–	15 (26.32) [24.42]
Independents [Avg. $R^2 = 10.32$]	5 (6.33) [28.96]	–	18 (22.78) [2.00]	38 (48.10) [3.39]	2 (2.53) [15.06]	16 (20.25) [29.74]

Panel B: Net flows and past conditional performance

Management companies	Very negative $t \leqslant -1.96$	Negative $-1.96 < t \leqslant 1.64$	Neutral (−) $-1.64 < t \leqslant 0.00$	Neutral (+) $0.00 < t \leqslant 1.64$	Positive $1.64 < t \leqslant 1.96$	Very positive $1.96 < t$
BBVA [Avg. $R^2 = 7.94$]	1 [48.50]	1 [9.86]	4 [1.62]	7 [4.90]	1 [11.99]	–
SCH [Avg. $R^2 = 19.32$]	7 [34.18]	3 [10.99]	8 [2.96]	6 [5.50]	1 [13.53]	8 [36.87]

Other banks [Avg. $R^2 = 10.81$]	6 [26.47]	1 [10.36]	10 [3.36]	24 [3.58]	6 [11.39]	11 [24.55]
Banks [Avg. $R^2 = 13.10$]	14 (13.33) [31.90]	5 (4.76) [10.64]	22 (20.95) [2.90]	37 (35.24) [4.14]	8 (7.62) [11.73]	19 (18.10) [29.74]
Savings banks [Avg. $R^2 = 14.66$]	11 (19.30) [32.68]	–	11 (19.30) [3.70]	21 (36.84) [2.29]	2 (3.51) [9.18]	12 (21.05) [30.76]
Independents [Avg. $R^2 = 11.07$]	11 (13.92) [22.05]	3 (3.80) [15.03]	23 (29.11) [3.08]	26 (32.91) [2.85]	3 (3.80) [12.12]	13 (16.46) [31.18]

Notes: To test the relationship between flows and performance, this table reports the results from two alternative regressions for each mutual fund:

Panel A: $\Delta Part_{t+1} = a + bCalpha_t + \varepsilon_{t+1}$
Panel B: $NetFlow_{t+1} = c + dCalpha_t + \varepsilon_{t+1}$

where $\Delta Part$ in the percentage monthly variation in the number of participants in each of the mutual funds in the sample, *NetFlow* is the inflow minus outflow for each fund during each month, and the dynamic conditional alpha is given by the following regression:

$r_{jt+1} = \alpha_{jc0} + \alpha_{jc1} Z_t + \beta_{jm} r_{mt+1} + \beta_{jzm}(Z_t r_{mt+1}) + \varepsilon_{jt+1}$

where $Calpha_{t+1} = \hat{\alpha}_{jc0} + \hat{\alpha}_{jc1} Z_t$, and Z_t is the bond yield spread.

The table shows the number of funds with a *t*-statistic on alpha lying in the given interval. In brackets we report the R^2 of each category and in parenthesis the percentage of funds within a given *t*-statistic interval.

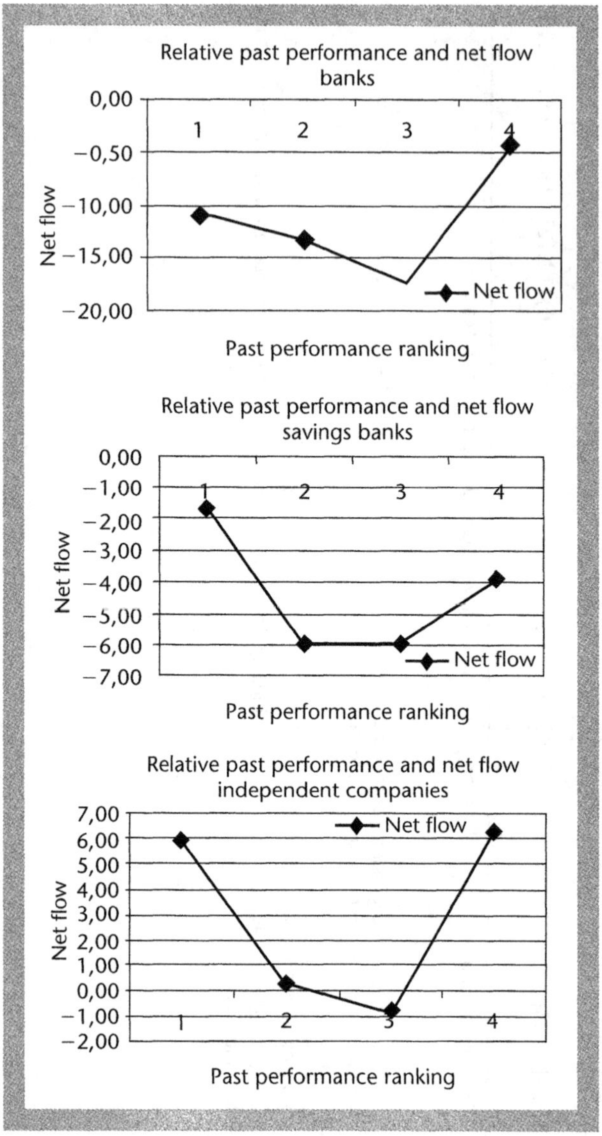

Figure 13.1 The mean net flow (inflows minus outflows) of Spanish Equity funds as a function of their relative risk-adjusted performance as measured by a dynamic conditional alpha

From our point of view, the aggregate results previously reported in the literature should be taken with care. The relationship between past performance and flow may be very different if we separate observations by management companies. Similarly, the results may potentially be different

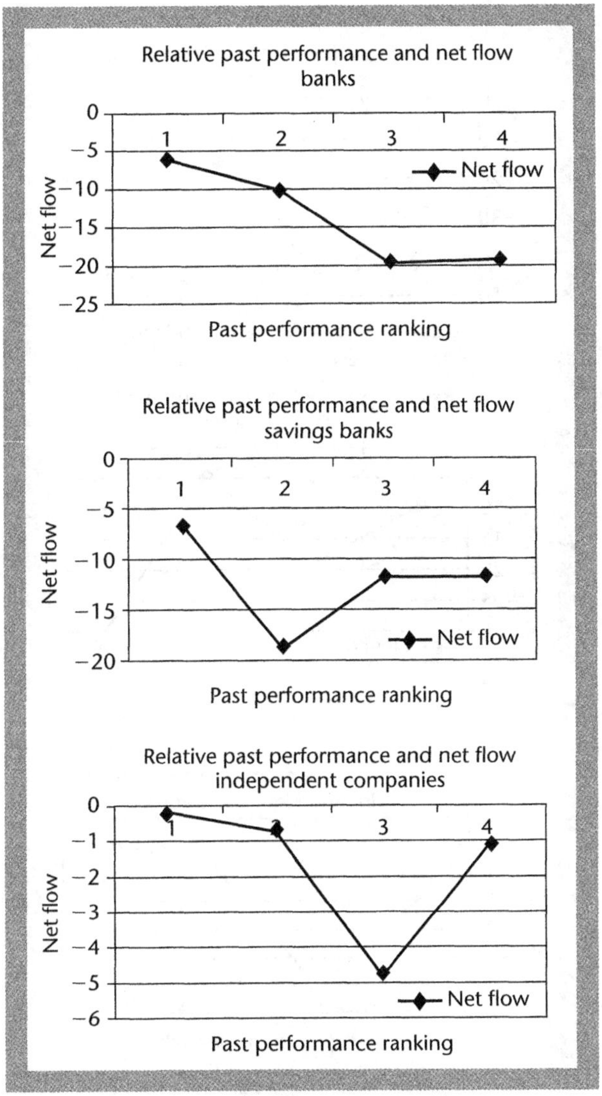

Figure 13.2 The mean net flow (inflows minus outflows) of Mixed Equity funds as a function of their relative risk-adjusted performance as measured by a dynamic conditional alpha

depending upon the objective of the fund. In general, we may conclude that investors from independent management companies monitor closely the past performance of their best performing funds and strongly respond to good past risk-adjusted performance. On the other hand, investors from savings banks do not seem to properly react to past risk-adjusted performance.

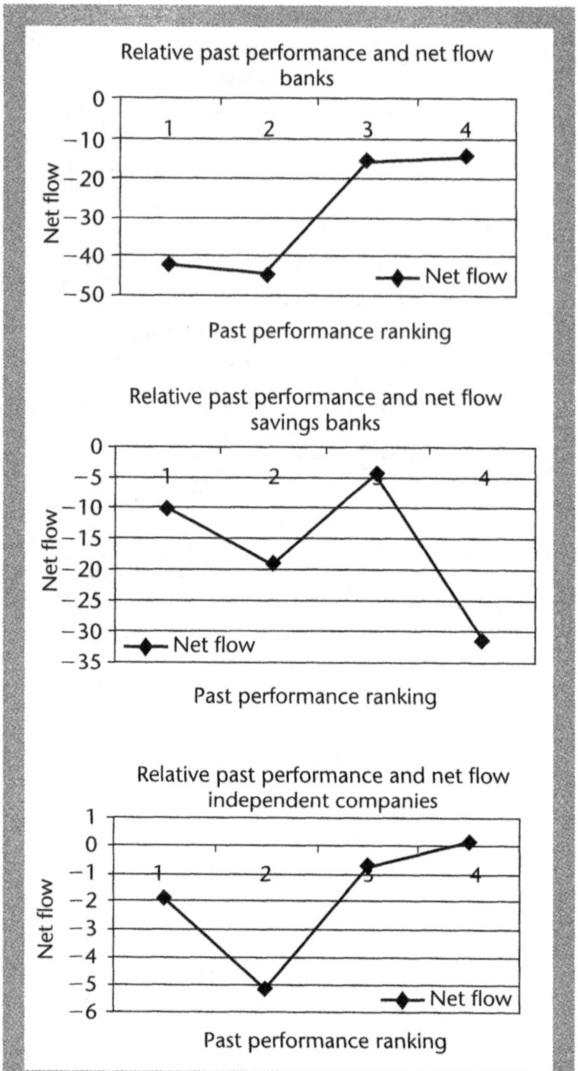

Figure 13.3 The mean net flow (inflows minus outflows) of mixed fixed Income funds as a function of their relative risk-adjusted performance as measured by a dynamic conditional alpha

13.6 CONCLUSION

This chapter has presented preliminary evidence on the behavior of Spanish mutual funds regarding performance, its relation with management and custody fees, the importance of the number of participants and the temporal relationship between past relative risk-adjusted performance and net flows. The novel aspect of our study is in reporting the evidence on the basis of management companies and the investment objective of the funds. Previous research has ignored the importance of presenting results according to management companies. However, we show that this way of aggregating the behavior of mutual funds is probably the most informative about the nature of their investment strategies.

There are striking differences between the results obtained for our alternative management companies. Mutual funds from banks have a strong pro-cyclical performance. In particular, large banks have a good risk-adjusted performance, while mutual funds from independent companies tend to have the worst performance. It turns out that they also have the less cyclical performance which seems to be very important in our sampling period.

Banks and savings banks exploit their large and loyal base of clients to charge high fees to funds with a large number of participants. It turns out that they present a significant negative relationship between risk-adjusted performance and the level of fees. It suggests that positive performance comes from new mutual funds of banks with a relatively low number of participants and low fees. On the other hand, mutual funds from independent companies seem to find more difficult to combine fees, number of participants and cyclical performance to obtain competitive results. Interestingly, however, it is also the case that investors in mutual funds of independent companies closely follow their best performing funds. In these types of funds, they strongly invest according to the recent past risk-adjusted performance. Overall, this evidence is less clear for banks and savings banks. Finally, the previous well-known positive and convex evidence reported between flows and past relative performance for the mutual fund industry as a whole, may be quite different if research would be based on competing management companies using risk-adjusted conditional performance and the actual net flow instead the traditional approximation employed in most papers.

To conclude, it seems clear that further research with a longer time-series data and a more formal statistical analysis of the Spanish mutual fund industry would be welcomed. Lack of competition has been the key characteristic of the industry for many years. We certainly hope that the recently approved new legal framework for institutional investment companies will make the industry more competitive.

NOTES

1. It should be pointed out, that most of the available evidence (at least discussed in literature) is related to US mutual funds.
2. They can be uninformed investors, institutional investors restricted by pension accounts, and tax disadvantaged investors.
3. See Gil-Bazo and Martínez (2004).

4. Among all non-guaranteed registered funds, only 1.5 percent of funds have a front-load fee, while only 34.8 percent charge a redemption fee.
5. We thank Javier Gil-Bazo and Miguel Martínez for allowing us to use their data.
6. Other funds include international and guaranteed funds.
7. We thank David Moreno and Rosa Rodríguez for facilitating these data to us.
8. These are obtained as specializations of the stochastic discount factor in which M depends linearly on one or more risk factors but always with constant parameters.
9. These are average coefficients from individual regressions. We do not report formal statistical significance tests; however, most of the significant coefficients are in Spanish equities and mixed equities.
10. The difference between the alphas from model (13.5) and the average (over time) dynamic conditional alphas from model (13.4) are negligible.
11. Similar results are obtained when estimating alphas using gross returns.

REFERENCES

Berkowitz, M. and Kotowitz, Y. (2002) "Managerial Quality and the Structure of Management Expenses in the US Mutual Fund Industry", *International Review of Economics and Finance*, 11(3): 315–30.

Brown, K., Harlow, V. and Starks, L. (1996) "Of Tournaments and Temptations: An Analysis of Managerial Incentives in the Mutual Fund Industry", *Journal of Finance*, 51(1): 85–110.

Carhart, M. (1997) "On the Persistence of Mutual Fund Performance", *Journal of Finance*, 52(1): 57–82.

Chevalier, J. and Ellison, G. (1997) "Risk Taking by Mutual Funds as a Response to Incentives", *Journal of Political Economy*, 105(6): 1167–200.

Christoffersen, S. (2001) "Why Do Money Fund Managers Voluntarily Waive Their Fees?", *Journal of Finance*, 56(3): 1117–40.

Ciriaco, A. and Santamaría, R. (2005) "Persistencia de Resultados en los Fondos de Inversión Españoles", Documento de Trabajo, Facultad de Ciencias Económicas y Empresariales, Universidad Pública de Navarra.

Daniel, K., Grinblatt, M., Titman, S. and Wermers, R. (1997) "Measuring Mutual Fund Performance with Characteristic-Based Benchmarks", *Journal of Finance*, 52(3): 1035–58.

Elton, E., Gruber, M., Das, S. and Hlavka, M. (1993) "Efficiency with Costly Information. A Reinterpretation of Evidence from Managed Portfolios", *Review of Financial Studies*, 6(1): 1–22.

Ferreira, E., Martínez, I., Navarro, E. and Rubio, G. (2005) "Economic Sentiment and Yield Spreads in Europe", *European Financial Management Journal*, forthcoming.

Ferson, W. and Qian, M. (2004) "Conditional Performance Evaluation, Revisited", Working Paper, The Research Foundation of the Association for Investment Management and Research and Blackwell Series in Finance.

Ferson, W. and Schadt, R. (1996) "Measuring Fund Strategy and Performance in Changing Economic Conditions", *Journal of Finance*, 51(2): 425–62.

Ferson, W., Farnsworth, H., Jackson, D. and Todd, S. (2002) "Performance Evaluation with Stochastic Discount Factors", *Journal of Business*, 75(3): 473–504.

Gil-Bazo, J. and Martínez, M. (2004) "The Black Box of Mutual Fund Fees", *Revista de Economía Financiera*, 4: 54–82.

Grinblatt, M. and Titman, S. (1989) "Portfolio Performance Evaluation: Old Issues and New Insights", *Review of Financial Studies*, 2(3): 393–421.

Gruber, M. (1996) "Another Puzzle: The Growth in Actively Managed Mutual Funds", *Journal of Finance*, 51(3): 783–810.

Luo, G. (2002) "Mutual Fund Fee-Setting, Market Structure and Mark-Ups", *Economica*, 69(274): 245–71.

Lynch, A. and Musto, D. (2003) "How Investors Interpret Past Fund Returns", *Journal of Finance*, 58(5): 2033–58.

Lynch, A., Wachter, J. and Boudry, W. (2004) "Does Mutual Fund Performance Vary Over the Business Cycle?", Working Paper, Stern School of Business, New York University.

Martínez, M. (2003) "Legal Constraints, Transaction Costs and the Evaluation of Mutual Funds", *European Journal of Finance*, 9(3): 199–218.

Moreno, D. and Rodríguez, R. (2005) "The Coskewness Factor: Implications for Performance Evaluation", Working Paper, Facultad de Ciencias Sociales y Jurídicas, Universidad Carlos III, Madrid.

Rubio, G. (1995) "Further Evidence on Performance Evaluation: Portfolio Holdings, Recommendations and Turnover Costs", *Review of Quantitative Finance and Accounting*, 5(2): 127–53.

Sirri, E. and Tufano, P. (1998) "Costly Search and Mutual Fund Flows", *Journal of Finance*, 53 (5): 1589–622.

Tufano, P. and Sevick, M. (1997) "Board Structure and Fee-Setting in the U.S. Mutual Fund Industry", *Journal of Financial Economics*, 46(3): 321–55.

Warther, V. (1995) "Aggregate Mutual Fund Flows and Security Returns", *Journal of Financial Economics*, 39(2–3): 209–35.

Zheng, L. (1999) "Is Money Smart? A Study of Mutual Fund Investors' Fund Selection Ability", *Journal of Finance*, 54(3): 901–33.

CHAPTER 14

On the Supposed Foreign Superiority: The Italian Tax Puzzle

Roberto Savona

14.1 INTRODUCTION

The increase in the number of assets under management by mutual funds over the last two decades represents one of the most significant changes in the structure of household portfolios that has attracted much attention in the financial and economic literature. The mechanism through which investors select mutual funds involves economic as well as psychological factors, which makes the optimal selection problem difficult. This is especially true for global markets, where consumers can choose between local and foreign funds. The rapid expansion of the mutual fund industry around the world has in fact stimulated major players to look beyond national borders, distributing their products in markets that offer significant growth opportunities. Italy is one of these. In the period 1998–2002 alone, the assets managed by funds rose from €395,102 to €502,418 million, and the role of foreign firms has grown significantly in terms of market share reaching, at the end of 2002, about one-third of the total assets under management (AUM). Why such a foreign fund preference?

Intuitively, some factors contribute to the success of these financial vehicles. First, aggressive marketing strategies have spread the opinion that foreign managers achieve much higher performance than domestic firms. Second, funds offered by Italian firms are perceived as passive portfolios tracking their own benchmarks, whereas active strategies are often thought to be the prerogative of foreign operators. Finally, a third possibility comes from the tax treatment of the mutual funds. Italian funds are in fact penalized by requiring payment of taxes on a daily basis even if the capital gains are unrealized, while foreign funds are taxed when the capital gains are collected. This curious anomaly leads one to suppose that taxation could translate into performance producing a sort of clientele effect which acquires a critical function in capital allocation, as we learned from the work of Elton and Gruber (1970).

Our chapter investigates this supposed foreign superiority, to verify whether the performance of domestic funds is significantly different from that of foreign funds.

Using data on 4,178 open-ended mutual funds over the period 10 July 1998 to 27 December 2002, our empirical analyses lead us to conclude that the reason underlying the popular perception that foreign managers are more skillful than domestic managers is due to the tax distortion between domestic and non-domestic funds. The different return patterns between funds can be attributed to the taxation system. Indeed, after removing the tax asymmetry, domestic and foreign funds exhibit similar performance patterns.

The structure of the chapter is as follows. Section 14.2 discusses the economic framework in which the issue is explored; section 14.3 illustrates the taxation asymmetry between domestic and foreign funds; section 14.4 describes the data-set; section 14.5 reports empirical results; and section 14.6 concludes.

14.2 ECONOMIC FRAMEWORK

The hypothesis of foreign superiority is based on the assumption that managers have different informational endowments. As argued by Coval and Moskowitz (1999), due to problems of distance, language and communications, domestic mutual funds are geographically biased towards the home of the fund, information on the local economy being virtually costless. If we generalize this intuition, it is plausible to suppose that some groups of funds will be better informed than others about the payoffs on pre-specified asset classes. This conjecture, which appears consistent with Merton's investor-recognition hypothesis (1987), for which "…investor uses security k in constructing his optimal portfolio only if the investor knows about security k", implies that sophisticated investors would revise their portfolio positions gainfully, according to their market expectations. Within this context, a perfect timer will tend to modify his exposure towards the benchmark anticipating future market trends. As noted by Fung and Hsieh (2001), in the presence of short sales constraints the convexity of a portfolio return pattern is substantially limited to upward movements, while without such restrictions the performance profile is similar to the payout of a straddle on the underlying asset (Merton, 1981). It is self-evident that, in the case of mutual funds, the possibility of delivering the embedded option on the market is seriously prejudiced by the impossibility of taking on short positions. For these reasons, we expect portfolio rebalancing to exhibit a market-timing component as an adding time-varying parameter to the systematic risk exposure towards the benchmark (the CAPM-based beta of the fund). In particular, the portfolio return-generating process is technologically specified according to the following equation:

$$R_t^i = \beta_t^i z_t^i + w_t^i \tag{14.1}$$

where R_t^i is the i-th portfolio return at time t, z_t^i is the benchmark return followed by the fund, β_t^i is the time-varying benchmark-related performance, and w_t^i is the idiosyncratic return component.

The specified structure of returns assumes that the risk sensitivity parameter β_t^i shifts dynamically as a result of the manager's forecasts for the factor $z^i{}_t$. Thus, if managers have timing abilities, that is they act as sophisticated investors, then the covariance between the beta at time t and the benchmark return at time $t+1$ will be positive in upward and downward market moves, indicating that managers successfully time the market.

In the estimation of time varying coefficients we have used the Kalman filter (1960), which is commonly applied to make inferences on the changing regression coefficients and proves to be extremely useful giving insights into how a rational economic agent would revise his estimates of the coefficients when new information is available (Kim and Nelson, 1999).

14.3 THE TAX PUZZLE

The Italian tax treatment of mutual fund investment requires domestic funds to pay a 12.5 percent rate on capital appreciation and income every day, although actual payment is made once a year, in February. Computationally, the levy is applied to the difference between the NAV at time t and the NAV at time $t-1$: if the difference is negative a tax credit results. Fund shares are quoted net of taxation and holders are not required to include any gains in their tax returns, since the manager has already paid the tax on a full-settlement basis. On the other hand, foreign funds are taxed at the same 12.5 percent levy but when incomes are collected. As is evident, there is an asymmetry between Italian and foreign fund returns due almost entirely to the different timing of taxation: on a day-to-day basis for the former and when the income is collected for the latter.

This curious asymmetric mechanism gives us a unique case study in which it is possible to investigate how taxation impacts on return pattern and performance of mutual funds operating in Italy.

This unique tax regulation leads us to suppose that the fiscal factor could explain some of the dissimilarities between domestic and foreign fund return patterns. To explore this possibility, we analysed the fiscal impact on the performance achieved by managers, verifying whether the tax bias could induce differences between domestic and foreign funds in terms of risk-adjusted returns and timing abilities.

14.4 THE DATABASE

14.4.1 Mutual funds

The mutual fund dataset used in this study comes from Morningstar. In the period starting from 10 July 1998 to 27 December 2002, 234 weekly holding period rates of returns were constructed using the NAV computed at the end of each week for all the funds having at least 12 weeks of data available at the end of 2002. All the data were converted into euros, or into ECUs before the introduction of the European currency.

Our sample consisted of 4,178 open-ended mutual funds, which were grouped into three sub-samples on the basis of management firm domicile. Namely:

1 Foreign Funds (Pure), owned by purely foreign firms (2,762 funds);

2 Foreign Funds (Italy), which are foreign funds owned by Italian groups but regulated like pure foreign funds (676 funds);

3 Italian Funds, owned by pure Italian firms and domiciled in Italy (740 funds).

We classified funds according to Morningstar's scheme, which uses the traditional self-reported investment objective of the mutual fund. The original classification was slightly modified, merging categories with similar objectives. A total of 12 classes were formed, that is:

- Equity-type funds: (1) Hi-Tech and Other spec.; (2) Europe; (3) Asia incl. Japan; (4) International; (5) North America; (6) Latin America and EM;
- (7) Balanced;
- Bond-type funds: (8) Liquidity and Short-Term; (9) Europe; (10) US Dollar; (11) International; (12) EM.

The database created by Morningstar is, in a sense, unique, since it includes pre- and after tax valuations of Italian funds, enabling us to test directly the influence of the taxation system on the performance of domestic funds. To obtain pre-tax NAV, Morningstar used the institutional model proposed in May 2001 by Assogestioni (the Italian Investment Trusts Association), with which the gross share prices were calculated by considering the outstanding number of shares and the accrued tax liabilities (for further details see the website http://www.assogestioni.it).

14.4.2 Benchmarks

As first described by Roll (1977) in his famous critique, it is well-known that the performance-measurement based benchmark is prone to selection bias. However, in this study this is not a major concern, since under Italian regulations domestic funds must declare their own benchmarks for performance-evaluation purposes. Based on the self-reported information of Italian firms, we selected the indices most used by managers in each fund category, reported below in Table 14.1. We used these benchmarks to explore whether timing abilities were statistically different between domestic and foreign fund groups. This in the spirit of the economic framework we introduced in section 14.2, which supposes that risk exposure may shift dynamically as a result of the manager's forecasts for the future benchmark return.

Table 14.1 Market benchmarks

Fund group	Market benchmark
Equity	
Hi-Tech and Other spec.	MSCI World Free
Europe	MSCI Europe
Asia incl-Japan	MSCI Pacific
International	MSCI World Free
North America	MSCI US
Latin America and EM	MSCI Emerging Markets
Balanced	0.5 JPM Global Broad Index +0.5 MSCI World Free
Bond	
Liquidity and Short-Term	0.5 JPM Global Broad Index + 0.5 Euribor 3 m (Libor 3 m in ECUs before January 1998)
Europe	JPM Europe Government Bond Index
US Dollar	JPM US
International	JPM Global Broad Index
EM	SB Emerging Markets Mutual Funds Index

Note: The table reports the self-reported benchmarks of Italian funds as of the end of 2002.

14.5 EMPIRICAL RESULTS

14.5.1 Foreign superiority

In our economic framework, we classify managers as sophisticated if they correctly modify the risk exposure towards their own benchmarks, anticipating the future payoffs of the market. Based on Graham and Harvey's Merton-style market-timing regression (1996), we conducted similar directional tests based on indicator functions for the sign of future returns. Graham and Harvey's original test explored the ability to time the market by regressing the change in net equity position on two dummy variables, that take on the value of unity when market returns are positive (first indicator function) or negative (second indicator function). Based on this approach, we conducted a similar test by replacing the dependent variable by the time-varying betas generated via the Kalman filter. Hence, we estimated the ability to increase (decrease) benchmark risk exposure when the market rises (falls). Let $I_{(z^j_{t+1}\geq 0)}$ be an indicator variable that takes on a value of one when the future return of benchmark j is positive or zero, and $I_{(z^j_{t+1}<0)}$ be an indicator for situations of future negative returns. The regression to be estimated is:

$$\beta_t^{jk} = b_{1jk} I_{(z^j_{t+1}\geq 0)} + b_{2jk} I_{(z^j_{t+1}<0)} + \varepsilon_t^{jk} \tag{14.2}$$

where j denotes the fund category of the fund group k, k being Foreign (Pure), Foreign (Italy) or Italian Funds. The unconditional measure of market-timing skills is whether $b_{1jk} > 0$ and $b_{2jk} < 0$, indicating that benchmark sensitivity is increasing (decreasing) before the future market return is positive (negative), respectively. We first estimated the time-varying beta of equation (14.1) for each of the equally weighted portfolios of funds grouped by fund objective. After generating the time-varying betas via the Kalman filter, we estimated equation (14.2) for all fund categories belonging to each group of managers.

Table 14.2 show the results. Panel A shows that the estimates of coefficients b_1 and b_2 are positive for all the k fund groups and significantly different from zero, except for the first indicator function coefficient of International Equity funds. The positive estimate of b_2 indicates that beta coefficients increase before the future benchmark return is negative. At first sight, this suggests that the ability of managers in anticipating future positive returns, which translates into positive estimates of b_1, is completely canceled out when the market falls.

To verify this possibility we relied on Wald statistics to test the hypothesis of coefficient equality. For each k fund group, the p-values of the Wald test indicated, for almost all fund categories, that we could not reject the null hypothesis of coefficient equality. It could only be rejected in a few cases, namely Equity Hi-Tech, Balanced and, for Foreign Funds (Pure) only, International Equity funds. For these categories we observed that $b_2 > b_1$, which reflected anomalous negative market timing. We also compared the distribution of coefficient estimates across groups. Panel B shows the results of the t-test, which confirmed that, for the two coefficients b_1 and b_2, the differences across fund groups are indistinguishable from zero.

As a whole, the results provided convincing evidence of a lack of timing ability for both Italian and foreign funds. Risk exposure towards the benchmark increased in both of the two states of the economy, indicating that managers did not exhibit the ability to forecast market-direction turning points. This was probably due to the fact that in the period inspected all managers implemented long-term strategies.

To conclude, the hypothesis about the foreign superiority is not supported by sufficient evidence. After controlling for the taxation factor, since the performance is calculated on pre-tax NAVs, Italian fund returns behaved similarly to their foreign counterparts, that is they timed the market only in upward movements. When the market fell, on the other hand, the risk exposure amplified the bearish trends, nullifying profits from market-timing activities.

14.5.2 The shrinking effect of taxation

The analyses on pre-tax returns are of fundamental importance, since we proved that by removing the taxation asymmetry, namely by comparing the true performance of domestic funds with the returns of foreign funds, we reject the hypothesis about foreign superiority. To explore in more depth how taxation impacts on dynamics of funds, we turned once again to the Graham and Harvey model. In detail, we ran regression (14.2) by using time-varying betas estimated on after-tax returns, comparing the results with those obtained previously for pre-tax returns. Panel A of Table 14.3 shows the estimated indicator function coefficients, indicating that taxation does not affect the signs of b_1 and b_2. More interestingly, by comparing both the coefficient distributions relative to those of foreign counterparts, and also with the pre-tax domestic funds, we found differences across groups which appeared significant from a statistical viewpoint.

To be more precise, consider the results of the t-test carried out on the mean coefficient differences, reported in Panel B. For all the fund groups, we could not accept the null coefficient distribution equivalence hypothesis for

Table 14.2 Dynamics of fund groups

Fund group	Foreign funds (pure)			Foreign funds (Italy)			Italian		
	b_1	b_2	Wald test	b_1	b_2	Wald test	b_1	b_2	Wald test
Panel A: coefficient									
Equity									
Hi-Tech and Other spec.	0.9792***	1.089***	3.6939*	1.0089***	1.0978***	3.4239*	0.9653***	1.0202***	3.4682*
Europe	0.8474***	0.8465***	0.0005	0.8508***	0.8588***	0.0522	0.9145***	0.9172***	0.0188
Asia incl-Japan	0.8159***	0.8318***	0.1584	0.8415***	0.8442***	0.0059	0.8985***	0.9063***	0.0967
International	0.0906	0.8351***	3.2372*	0.1314	0.7233***	2.4735	0.1876	0.7891***	2.0044
North America	0.4137***	0.6736***	1.2726	0.4294***	0.6388***	0.8644	0.464***	0.6432***	0.6357
Latin America and EM	0.503***	0.6455***	0.3445	0.4842***	0.649***	0.4952	0.5149***	0.6577***	0.3339
Balanced	0.7197***	0.7633***	3.7743*	0.5484***	0.5896***	5.451**	0.6466***	0.6808***	3.5642*
Bond									
Liquidity and Short-Term	1.063***	1.0631***	0.0000	0.5661***	0.5555***	1.6375	0.1104***	0.1091***	0.6018
Europe	0.398***	0.2473***	1.1993	0.4886***	0.3048***	1.1834	0.4435***	0.2905***	0.9703

Continued

Table 14.2 Continued

Fund group	Foreign funds (pure)			Foreign funds (Italy)			Italian		
	b_1	b_2	Wald test	b_1	b_2	Wald test	b_1	b_2	Wald test
US Dollar	0.5046***	0.3885***	0.2868	0.5167***	0.3967***	0.2918	0.5518***	0.4388***	0.2299
International	0.3327**	0.512***	0.5070	0.305**	0.4964***	0.6324	0.3466**	0.5776***	0.6883
EM	0.5266***	0.5466***	0.2027	0.5677***	0.5835***	0.1729	0.4975***	0.5211***	0.6246

Panel B: equivalence in mean

Mean of coefficient differences between groups	Italian *minus* foreign funds (pure)			Italian *minus* foreign funds (Italy)			Foreign funds (Italy) *minus* foreign funds (pure)		
	value	*t*-stat	*p*-value	value	*t*-stat	*p*-value	value	*t*-stat	*p*-value
b_1	−0.0544	−0.6570	0.5247	−0.0165	−0.3872	0.7060	−0.0380	−0.8342	0.4219
b_2	−0.0742	−0.9100	0.3823	−0.0156	−0.3694	0.7188	−0.0587	−1.3076	0.2177

Notes: Panel A tests whether equally-weighted portfolios of funds grouped by fund objective increase (decrease) benchmark sensitivity, expressed by the time-varying betas estimated via Kalman filter, before the future market return is positive (negative). The table also shows the Wald test to verify the coefficient equality hypothesis. Panel B shows the results of the *t*-test computed across coefficient distributions of the *k* fund groups. *, **, *** denote significance at 0.1, 0.05 and 0.001 levels, respectively.

Table 14.3 Tax impact and portfolio dynamics

Fund group	Italian funds (after-tax)		
	b_1	b_2	Wald test
Panel A: Coefficient			
Equity			
Hi-Tech and Other spec.	0.8129***	0.866***	3.4702*
Europe	0.7782***	0.7846***	0.1206
Asia incl-Japan	0.7813***	0.7857***	0.0591
International	0.1568	0.6812***	2.0821
North America	0.3916***	0.5523***	0.7235
Latin America and EM	0.4455***	0.5696***	0.3377
Balanced	0.5558***	0.5932***	4.0567**
Bond			
Liquidity and Short-Term	0.1194***	0.12***	0.2131
Europe	0.3919***	0.2537***	1.0177
US Dollar	0.4762***	0.3859***	0.1953
International	0.3078**	0.5083***	0.6657
EM	0.4675***	0.4891***	0.7779

Panel B: Equivalence in Mean

Mean of coefficient differences between groups	Italian funds (after-tax) *minus*:								
	Foreign funds (pure)			Foreign funds (Italy)			Italian (pre-tax)		
	value	*t*- stat	*p*-value	value	*t*-stat	*p*-value	value	*t*-stat	*p*-value
b_1	−0.1258	−1.6421	0.1288	−0.0878	−2.3838	0.0363	−0.0713	−5.2299	0.0003
b_2	−0.1543	−2.0676	0.0630	−0.0957	−2.6686	0.0218	−0.0801	−5.9137	0.0001

Note: *, ** and *** denote significance at 0.1, 0.05 and 0.01 levels respectively.

both the indicator functions. Except for the b_1 distribution as compared with Foreign Funds (Pure), we found that both coefficients were significantly below the values exhibited by Pure and by Italian Funds. The same conclusions held on comparing after-tax with pre-tax domestic funds. This signifies that the fiscal mechanism acts as a smoother of portfolio dynamics by reducing the magnitude of positive as well as negative returns of Italian Funds.

14.5.3 The relative performance of Italian and foreign mutual funds

In the previous section we obtained substantial evidence that taxation affects pervasively the behavior of Italian fund managers, since the levy symmetrically reduce positive as well as negative performance. In fact, using pre-tax returns our analyses indicate that domestic funds did not differ from foreign funds in terms of timing ability. This conclusion leads us to reject the hypothesis about foreign superiority. To complete our inspection of this issue, it is now tempting to explore the relative performance of funds by comparing domestic with foreign funds. To this end we measured the risk-adjusted performance of each fund of the overall sample, given 10 style benchmarks extracted from the same fund sample using cluster analysis. This procedure, which is quite similar to that of Brown and Goetzmann (1997), agglomerates funds into homogeneous groups, (a) minimizing variability within clusters, and (b) maximizing variability between clusters. We followed this approach because, if managers having the same style generate correlated returns (Fung and Hsieh, 2002), then, a good proxy of the style benchmarks can be obtained by observing how the funds behave together.

A last word is on the number of clusters, which was chosen equal to 10 for two reasons. It is firstly clear that this number was consistent with the 12 institutional categories. Secondly, we estimated that the first 10 principal components explained about 70 percent of the total variance, which appeared sufficient to describe the common investment styles followed by the managers.

Computationally, to measure the relative performance of funds we proceeded as follows. First, we split the time period into 12 non-overlapping weekly observations, computing the style benchmarks by considering only those funds with all twelve returns for that interval. This allows for shifts in style within each non-overlapping 12-week estimation period; and, second, the adoption by managers of dynamic trading strategies leading the expected returns and the factor weights to vary across the estimation period.

Second, for each sub-period, we regressed funds featuring all 12 weekly returns on the 10 style benchmarks constraining the sum of loadings to one and coefficients greater than zero, also allowing an unconstrained intercept. Indeed, we used Sharpe's technique (1992), by which weights on passive portfolios are forced to be positive and to sum to one in order to describe the styles followed by mutual funds. As is evident, our interest is on the intercept of the regression, which is a generalization of the Jensen's alpha. Mathematically:

$$\begin{aligned} R_t^i &= \alpha^i + \sum_{k=1}^{10} w_k^i K_t^k + \varepsilon_t^i \\ \text{s.t.} \ & \sum_{k=1}^{10} w_k^i = 1; \ w_k^i \geq 0 \ \ \forall k \end{aligned} \tag{14.3}$$

where R_t^i is the i-th portfolio return at time t, K_t^k denotes the style benchmarks at time t with $k = 1, 2, \ldots, 10$, w_k^i the factor loadings, α^i is the intercept and ε_t^i the error term.

Third, we calculated the equally weighted average of the intercept in (14.3) for all funds in each of the 12 investment objective category, then running the t-test on the alpha differences as obtained by comparing the fund groups two at time.

On the basis of the previous findings against the supposed foreign superiority, we expect that the performance of domestic and foreign funds will be statistically indistinguishable. Furthermore, since we proved that tax treatment affects the Italian fund returns dramatically, it is a matter of interest to explore the pervasiveness of this bias on performance. Hence, the relative performance analysis was carried out in two steps. In the first, we examined performance after controlling for the taxation of domestic funds, while in the second we compared pre-tax returns of Italian funds with their after-tax returns, to test the supposed significant underperformance induced by the taxation factor.

Let us consider initially the first step of the analysis. The results in Table 14.4 and 14.5 show the equally weighted average of the annualized alpha differences for specific and general categories, respectively. Inspection of the data suggests that the results should be interpreted relative to the ownership category. To be more precise, although we could conclude that Italian funds were substantially indistinguishable from their foreign counterparts in general, as is clear by observing the "Overall" column of Table 14.5, some significant differences arise by comparing the fund categories:

- Italian Funds vs. Foreign Funds (Pure): domestic funds outperformed in the Bond category, specifically in the Short Term, US Dollar and Emerging Markets categories;
- Italian Funds vs. Foreign Funds (Italy): domestic funds outperformed in the Bond category, specifically in the Short Term, Europe and Emerging Markets;
- Foreign Funds (Italy) vs. Foreign Funds (Pure): the extra performance of the first was significantly below that of Foreign Funds (Pure) in the Balanced category. Furthermore, it could be seen that they underperformed significantly also for Equity Asia, Equity International and Bond Europe.

Consider now the second step of the analysis. As discussed above, to test whether taxation affects Italian fund returns we measured the performance of pre-tax returns relative to after-tax returns. Results are in Table 14.6. Note firstly how taxation impacts on specific investment categories (Panel A). This is clearly visible for all bond categories excluding International Bonds, for Balanced, Equity Other Spec. and Equity North America. For all these categories, pre-tax returns were significantly higher than after-tax returns, obviously in terms of alpha. Secondly, to see whether tax-induced differences in extra performance arise also on a general basis let we consider Panel B. The empirical results indicate that, over the entire period, the overall mean alphas of the gross returns exceeded those of the net returns by 0.54 percent, which appeared significant at an acceptance level of 0.1. The Equity segment was the category in which the difference in extra performance was highest, although the *t*-stat suggested that this figure should be interpreted with caution (the *p*-value was around 19 percent).

To conclude, the analyses provided convincing evidence that Italian funds were constantly and significantly undervalued because of the negative impact of tax treatment on their returns. And this is curiously due to the Italian regulation, which obliges domestic funds to quote shares net of taxation obscuring the "true" pre-tax returns and, consequently, giving rise to biased performance measures. The popular perception in Italy about foreign superiority might, therefore, be explained by the fact that the fair added value of Italian money managers is partially offset when using after-tax returns.

14.6 CONCLUSION

The worldwide escalation of the mutual funds industry over the last two decades has stimulated major players to offer their products beyond national borders, accelerating the globalization of financial markets. In this demanding context, it is important to question whether money managers differ from one country to another, and to investigate the factors explaining any such differences.

This chapter has focused on the Italian open-ended mutual funds market, which is of particular interest from two points of view. First, it experienced a dramatic increase in foreign funds over the period 1998–2002; second, the taxation asymmetry between domestic and non-domestic funds penalizes the first by imposing payment of taxes on a daily basis.

In this framework, we tested whether foreigners are more skilful than domestic managers. Our analyses proved that tax treatment pervasively affects the dynamics of domestic fund returns. In fact, after removing the tax asymmetry, Italian and foreign funds exhibit similar performance patterns over time.

On the Japanese open-end fund puzzle Brown, Goetzmann, Hiraki, Otsuki and Shiraishi (2001) wrote:

> Our results shed some light on crucial tax and investment policy issues. In Japan, the tax effects appear dramatic enough to explain a significant component of excess return … the Japanese experience provides a framework for policy makers around the world who are considering the potential consequences of simplifying their tax code.

Table 14.4 Relative performance of the investment fund categories

From	To	Fund category											
		E_Ot	E_Eu	E_As	E_In	E_NA	E_EM	Ba	B_Sh	B_Eu	B_US	B_In	B_EM
Panel A: Italian minus foreign (pure)													
08/21/98	11/06/98	−0.0116	−0.0870	0.3979	−0.0236	0.2916	−0.1910	0.0297	0.0878	−0.0042	0.0066	0.0830	0.0818
11/13/98	01/29/99	0.0609	0.1950	−0.1487	−0.1284	−0.1534	−0.3166	0.0683	0.0996	0.0284	−0.0164	0.0494	0.0182
02/05/99	04/23/99	0.0164	−0.0712	−0.0623	0.0452	0.2051	0.0158	−0.0297	0.0422	0.0357	0.1777	−0.0143	−0.0422
04/30/99	07/16/99	0.0270	−0.0544	−0.0530	0.0768	−0.1331	−0.1098	0.0242	−0.0178	0.0090	0.1548	0.0265	−0.0361
07/23/99	10/08/99	0.1098	0.0495	−0.1002	0.0873	0.0681	−0.1657	0.0316	0.0018	−0.0050	−0.0007	0.0155	0.0467
10/15/99	12/31/99	−0.0333	0.0188	0.2140	0.1925	−0.1293	0.1153	0.0123	0.0275	0.0297	−0.0730	0.0610	−0.0362
01/07/00	03/24/00	0.0624	−0.0649	−0.3227	−0.1911	0.0427	0.0073	−0.0470	−0.0264	−0.0240	0.1336	−0.0319	−0.0336
03/31/00	06/16/00	0.0051	0.0328	−0.1738	−0.1686	0.1546	−0.2066	−0.0569	0.0032	−0.0096	0.0622	0.0116	0.0113
06/23/00	09/08/00	−0.0621	0.0224	−0.1207	−0.1363	0.1866	−0.0177	0.0161	0.0346	0.0226	0.1465	0.0271	0.0107
09/15/00	12/01/00	−0.1159	0.1323	−0.1777	−0.3092	−0.0560	−0.1397	−0.0748	−0.0282	−0.0414	0.1820	−0.0424	0.0078
12/08/00	02/23/01	−0.0901	−0.0922	−0.0625	−0.1394	−0.0755	0.3940	−0.0207	0.0287	−0.0149	−0.0501	0.0177	−0.0082
03/02/01	05/18/01	0.0443	0.0219	−0.1332	−0.1008	0.0532	−0.0206	−0.0238	−0.0067	−0.0186	0.0874	−0.0298	0.0032
05/25/01	08/10/01	0.0518	−0.0251	−0.0277	−0.0167	−0.0059	−0.0772	−0.0018	−0.0182	−0.0270	0.1023	−0.0040	0.0341
08/17/01	11/02/01	0.1108	−0.0116	−0.1466	−0.0688	−0.0459	−0.1152	0.0014	−0.0119	−0.0046	0.1037	−0.0260	0.0097
11/09/01	01/25/02	0.0078	−0.1457	0.1549	−0.0475	0.0604	0.0660	0.0176	−0.0128	−0.0096	0.0991	0.0078	0.0610
02/01/02	04/19/02	−0.2689	0.1151	−0.0507	0.0051	−0.1541	0.5293	0.0186	0.0182	0.0206	−0.0170	−0.0095	0.1149
04/26/02	07/12/02	0.3200	0.0182	0.1006	0.1860	0.1910	0.2210	0.0408	0.0156	0.0021	0.0698	0.0402	0.0849

Continued

Table 14.4 Continued

From	To	Fund category											
		E_Ot	E_Eu	E_As	E_In	E_NA	E_EM	Ba	B_Sh	B_Eu	B_US	B_In	B_EM
07/19/02	10/04/02	0.1534	0.0256	0.0940	−0.2222	0.1204	−0.0638	−0.0303	0.0298	0.0008	0.1556	0.0049	0.1010
10/11/02	12/27/02	0.0194	0.0866	0.0341	−0.0205	−0.1280	−0.0840	0.0323	0.0390	0.0191	−0.1598	−0.0135	0.1411
Mean		0.0214	0.0087	−0.0307	−0.0516	0.0259	−0.0084	0.0004	0.0161	0.0005	0.0613	0.0091	0.0300
t-stat		0.7859	0.4467	−0.8073	−1.6881	0.8149	−0.1766	0.0481	1.9755*	0.0987	2.8137**	1.1868	2.3989**
Panel B: Italian minus foreign (Italy)													
08/21/98	11/06/98	−0.0185	0.0136	na	0.0225	−0.0925	−0.0889	0.0162	0.0320	0.0060	na	0.0453	na
11/13/98	01/29/99	0.1023	0.1805	0.0139	0.2962	−0.1134	0.0887	0.1324	0.0488	0.0261	na	0.0549	0.0263
02/05/99	04/23/99	−0.2210	−0.1167	0.0110	−0.1027	−0.1211	0.0132	0.0656	0.0219	0.0564	0.2612	−0.0807	0.0365
04/30/99	07/16/99	0.0467	0.0257	0.1000	0.0390	−0.0229	−0.0498	0.0923	−0.0148	0.0453	0.0895	0.0254	0.0346
07/23/99	10/08/99	0.0352	−0.0337	−0.1028	0.0275	0.2951	0.0366	0.0048	0.0136	0.0233	0.0384	−0.0278	0.0237
10/15/99	12/31/99	−0.2195	0.0790	0.4573	0.0397	0.2035	0.2147	−0.0185	0.0125	0.0094	0.0184	−0.0151	−0.0346
01/07/00	03/24/00	−0.1857	−0.0720	−0.0418	−0.0771	0.0593	−0.0600	−0.0342	−0.0081	0.0039	−0.0502	0.0009	0.0168
03/31/00	06/16/00	0.2435	−0.0174	−0.2120	−0.0421	0.0231	−0.1467	−0.0153	−0.0020	0.0069	0.0194	0.0224	−0.0109
06/23/00	09/08/00	0.0612	0.0490	−0.0137	0.0718	0.0043	−0.1466	0.0163	0.0076	0.0206	0.0513	−0.0121	0.0695
09/15/00	12/01/00	0.0213	0.0244	−0.1419	−0.2258	−0.2584	0.1303	−0.0836	0.0031	−0.0096	−0.0449	−0.0038	−0.0092
12/08/00	02/23/01	0.1791	−0.0299	0.0095	−0.0132	0.0939	0.0045	−0.0197	0.0135	−0.0028	0.0514	0.0171	0.0371

03/02/01	05/18/01	−0.0195	−0.0160	−0.0523	−0.0311	−0.0738	0.0836	0.0009	−0.0075	0.0139	−0.0466	−0.0157	−0.0016
05/25/01	08/10/01	0.0211	−0.0034	−0.0362	0.0368	0.0564	0.0033	−0.0095	0.0013	−0.0161	0.0028	−0.0002	0.0325
08/17/01	11/02/01	0.0385	−0.0498	0.0068	0.0473	−0.0273	0.0621	0.0450	0.0028	−0.0147	−0.0137	0.0255	0.0608
11/09/01	01/25/02	0.0629	−0.1060	0.1802	0.0036	0.0393	−0.1749	0.0506	−0.0161	0.0038	0.0750	0.0684	0.1019
02/01/02	04/19/02	−0.0537	0.0904	−0.0645	−0.0719	−0.0807	−0.1159	0.0176	0.0177	0.0028	−0.0210	0.0109	0.0693
04/26/02	07/12/02	0.2918	0.1328	−0.0448	0.1765	0.2069	0.3030	0.0460	0.0267	−0.0030	0.0537	0.0048	0.1324
07/19/02	10/04/02	−0.1264	−0.0524	0.1188	−0.0507	−0.0128	0.0352	−0.0179	0.0155	0.0288	−0.0019	0.0376	0.1239
10/11/02	12/27/02	−0.0187	0.0084	0.0109	−0.0525	−0.0227	−0.1463	0.0391	0.0028	0.0239	−0.0281	−0.0026	0.0053
Mean		0.0127	0.0056	0.0110	0.0049	0.0082	0.0024	0.0173	0.0090	0.0118	0.0267	0.0082	0.0397
t-stat		0.3964	0.3186	0.3250	0.1982	0.2757	0.0819	1.5339	2.4026**	2.6921**	1.4850	1.0665	3.6486***
Panel C: foreign (Italy) minus foreign (Pure)													
08/21/98	11/06/98	0.0070	−0.0992	na	−0.0451	0.4223	−0.1119	0.0132	0.0541	−0.0101	na	0.0361	na
11/13/98	01/29/99	−0.0376	0.0123	−0.1604	−0.3289	−0.0450	−0.3728	−0.0567	0.0486	0.0023	na	−0.0052	−0.0079
02/05/99	04/23/99	0.3031	0.0514	−0.0725	0.1645	0.3700	0.0026	−0.0895	0.0199	−0.0196	−0.0665	0.0722	−0.0760
04/30/99	07/16/99	−0.0188	−0.0782	−0.1393	0.0364	−0.1128	−0.0631	−0.0625	−0.0030	−0.0348	0.0601	0.0011	−0.0684
07/23/99	10/08/99	0.0720	0.0860	0.0029	0.0582	−0.1761	−0.1953	0.0267	−0.0117	−0.0277	−0.0377	0.0445	0.0224
10/15/99	12/31/99	0.2373	−0.0559	−0.1680	0.1471	−0.2774	−0.0821	0.0314	0.0148	0.0202	−0.0897	0.0773	−0.0016
01/07/00	03/24/00	0.3034	0.0076	−0.2930	−0.1233	−0.0157	0.0715	−0.0133	−0.0185	−0.0278	0.1932	−0.0328	−0.0496
03/31/00	06/16/00	−0.1925	0.0511	0.0482	−0.1320	0.1286	−0.0700	−0.0422	0.0052	−0.0164	0.0420	−0.0106	0.0225

Continued

Table 14.4 Continued

From	To	Fund category											
		E_Ot	E_Eu	E_As	E_In	E_NA	E_EM	Ba	B_Sh	B_Eu	B_US	B_In	B_EM
06/23/00	09/08/00	−0.1163	−0.0254	−0.1084	−0.1945	0.1816	0.1505	−0.0002	0.0269	0.0019	0.0906	0.0397	−0.0550
09/15/00	12/01/00	−0.1344	0.1054	−0.0415	−0.1073	0.2711	−0.2393	0.0096	−0.0313	−0.0321	0.2374	−0.0387	0.0172
12/08/00	02/23/01	−0.2289	−0.0641	−0.0714	−0.1278	−0.1550	0.3878	−0.0010	0.0150	−0.0122	−0.0966	0.0006	−0.0436
03/02/01	05/18/01	0.0650	0.0385	−0.0852	−0.0719	0.1369	−0.0963	−0.0247	0.0008	−0.0320	0.1405	−0.0144	0.0048
05/25/01	08/10/01	0.0300	−0.0218	0.0088	−0.0517	−0.0590	−0.0802	0.0078	−0.0194	−0.0110	0.0992	−0.0038	0.0015
08/17/01	11/02/01	0.0697	0.0401	−0.1523	−0.1110	−0.0192	−0.1670	−0.0418	−0.0146	0.0102	0.1191	−0.0502	−0.0483
11/09/01	01/25/02	−0.0519	−0.0442	−0.0215	−0.0510	0.0203	0.2908	−0.0314	0.0033	−0.0134	0.0225	−0.0568	−0.0372
02/01/02	04/19/02	−0.2272	0.0227	0.0147	0.0829	−0.0797	0.7275	0.0010	0.0005	0.0178	0.0041	−0.0203	0.0427
04/26/02	07/12/02	0.0219	−0.1014	0.1521	0.0080	−0.0132	−0.0632	−0.0051	−0.0107	0.0052	0.0153	0.0352	−0.0421
07/19/02	10/04/02	0.3194	0.0822	−0.0223	−0.1805	0.1349	−0.0957	−0.0127	0.0141	−0.0273	0.1577	−0.0316	−0.0204
10/11/02	12/27/02	0.0389	0.0775	0.0229	0.0337	−0.1077	0.0728	−0.0065	0.0360	−0.0047	−0.1355	−0.0109	0.1352
Mean		0.0242	0.0045	−0.0603	−0.0523	0.0318	0.0035	−0.0157	0.0068	−0.0111	0.0445	0.0016	−0.0113
t-stat		0.6177	0.2979	−2.522**	−1.8505*	0.7446	0.0611	−2.1585**	1.2873	−2.8312**	1.7060	0.1839	−0.9564

Notes: Equally weighted average of annualized alpha differences computed by means of the Sharpe equation (1992). The results are shown for specific categories of funds over the period from 8/21/98 to 27/12/02. *, **, *** denote significance at 0.1, 0.05, and 0.001 levels, respectively.

Table 14.5 Relative performance of general fund categories

From	To	Italian minus foreign (Pure)				Italian minus foreign (Italy)				Foreign (Italy) minus foreign (Pure)			
		Equity	Balanced	Bond	overall	Equity	Balanced	Bond	overall	Equity	Balanced	Bond	overall
08/21/98	11/06/98	0.0152	0.0297	0.0901	0.0367	0.0334	0.0162	0.0164	0.0245	−0.0177	0.0132	0.0726	0.0119
11/13/98	01/29/99	0.0155	0.0683	0.0461	0.0100	0.1195	0.1324	0.0407	0.0887	−0.0931	−0.0567	0.0052	−0.0724
02/05/99	04/23/99	−0.0043	−0.0297	0.0159	0.0077	−0.1027	0.0656	0.0214	−0.0293	0.1094	−0.0895	−0.0054	0.0380
04/30/99	07/16/99	−0.0345	0.0242	0.0273	−0.0063	0.0301	0.0923	0.0278	0.0384	−0.0628	−0.0625	−0.0005	−0.0431
07/23/99	10/08/99	0.0322	0.0316	0.0022	0.0188	0.0367	0.0048	0.0066	0.0197	−0.0043	0.0267	−0.0044	−0.0009
10/15/99	12/31/99	0.0500	0.0123	0.0145	0.0326	0.1502	−0.0185	−0.0041	0.0645	−0.0873	0.0314	0.0187	−0.0300
01/07/00	03/24/00	−0.0758	−0.0470	−0.0251	−0.0438	−0.0451	−0.0342	−0.0124	−0.0270	−0.0321	−0.0133	−0.0128	−0.0172
03/31/00	06/16/00	−0.0334	−0.0569	0.0061	−0.0208	−0.0310	−0.0153	0.0051	−0.0147	−0.0025	−0.0422	0.0010	−0.0061
06/23/00	09/08/00	−0.0172	0.0161	0.0278	0.0057	0.0102	0.016	0.0088	0.0117	−0.0271	−0.0002	0.0189	−0.0059
09/15/00	12/01/00	−0.0623	−0.0748	−0.0094	−0.0494	−0.0690	−0.0836	−0.0099	−0.0504	0.0072	0.0096	0.0005	0.0011
12/08/00	02/23/01	−0.0777	−0.0207	−0.0152	−0.0554	0.0027	−0.0197	−0.0002	−0.0009	−0.0802	−0.0010	−0.0149	−0.0545
03/02/01	05/18/01	−0.0103	−0.0238	−0.0024	−0.0108	−0.0144	0.0009	−0.0044	−0.0095	0.0041	−0.0247	0.0020	−0.0013
05/25/01	08/10/01	−0.0160	−0.0018	−0.0136	−0.0136	0.0040	−0.0095	−0.0140	−0.0036	−0.0199	0.0078	0.0004	−0.0100
08/17/01	11/02/01	−0.0217	0.0014	0.0009	−0.0093	0.0053	0.0450	0.0019	0.0111	−0.0269	−0.0418	−0.0011	−0.0203
11/09/01	01/25/02	−0.0343	0.0176	−0.0082	−0.0171	−0.0218	0.0506	0.0094	0.0005	−0.0128	−0.0314	−0.0174	−0.0176
02/01/02	04/19/02	−0.0143	0.0186	0.0140	−0.0060	−0.0098	0.0176	0.0062	−0.0026	−0.0045	0.0010	0.0077	−0.0034
04/26/02	07/12/02	0.1397	0.0408	0.0324	0.0793	0.1588	0.0460	0.0279	0.0893	−0.0165	−0.0051	0.0044	−0.0092
07/19/02	10/04/02	0.0164	−0.0303	0.0154	0.0174	−0.0449	−0.0179	0.0175	−0.0197	0.0642	−0.0127	−0.0020	0.0379
10/11/02	12/27/02	0.0086	0.0323	0.0005	0.0060	−0.0246	0.0391	−0.0014	−0.0110	0.0340	−0.0065	0.0019	0.0172
Mean		−0.0065	0.0004	0.0115	−0.0010	0.0099	0.0173	0.0075	0.0095	−0.0142	−0.0157	0.0039	−0.0098
t-stat		−0.5798	0.0481	1.9156*	−0.1315	0.6250	1.5339	2.2232**	1.0847	−1.2502	−2.1585**	0.9001	−1.5415

Note: * and ** denote significance at 0.1 and 0.05 levels respectively.

Table 14.6 Tax and performance of Italian funds

From	To	Fund category											
		E_Ot	E_Eu	E_As	E_In	E_NA	E_EM	Ba	B_Sh	B_Eu	B_US	B_In	B_EM
Panel A: Specific Category													
08/21/98	11/06/98	0.0106	0.0190	0.0502	0.0237	0.0113	−0.0538	0.0185	0.0188	0.0106	0.0074	0.0228	−0.0272
11/13/98	01/29/99	0.0546	0.1492	0.0221	0.0895	0.0340	0.1148	0.0278	0.0031	0.0096	0.0209	0.0130	0.0318
02/05/99	04/23/99	−0.0035	−0.0155	0.0316	0.0121	0.0173	0.0516	0.0002	−0.0001	−0.0025	0.0129	−0.0197	0.0217
04/30/99	07/16/99	−0.0058	−0.0015	0.0016	0.0043	−0.0138	0.0043	−0.0051	−0.0017	−0.0056	−0.0017	−0.0173	−0.0282
07/23/99	10/08/99	0.0253	0.0135	−0.0186	0.0237	0.0072	−0.0068	0.0044	0.0025	0.0015	0.0083	0.0005	0.0172
10/15/99	12/31/99	0.0068	−0.0027	0.0236	0.0317	−0.0122	0.0356	−0.0096	0.0015	−0.0119	−0.0150	−0.0036	0.0059
01/07/00	03/24/00	0.0041	−0.0086	−0.0508	−0.0116	0.0295	0.0096	0.0011	0.0005	0.0050	0.0219	0.0103	0.0231
03/31/00	06/16/00	0.0178	0.0043	−0.0192	0.0028	0.0293	−0.0480	−0.0004	0.0016	0.0021	0.0091	0.0059	−0.0014
06/23/00	09/08/00	−0.0036	−0.0055	0.0047	0.0125	0.0184	−0.0047	0.0028	0.0034	0.0018	0.0240	0.0028	0.0116
09/15/00	12/01/00	−0.0051	0.0092	−0.0070	0.0052	0.0023	−0.0180	0.0037	0.0037	0.0037	0.0292	0.0020	−0.0121
12/08/00	02/23/01	0.0140	−0.0117	0.0063	−0.0230	−0.0025	0.0328	−0.0038	0.0035	−0.0059	0.0141	0.0084	−0.0023
03/02/01	05/18/01	0.0151	0.0014	0.0001	0.0132	0.0204	−0.0026	0.0043	0.0028	−0.0022	0.0070	0.0007	0.0008
05/25/01	08/10/01	0.0046	−0.0055	−0.0311	−0.0077	0.0066	−0.0314	0.0042	0.0043	0.0025	0.0158	0.0122	0.0162
08/17/01	11/02/01	0.0311	0.0271	−0.0060	0.0125	0.0072	−0.0065	0.0143	0.0035	0.0101	0.0248	0.0061	0.0130
11/09/01	01/25/02	0.0036	−0.0377	−0.0064	−0.0107	0.0094	−0.0261	0.0006	0.0013	0.0049	0.0050	−0.0051	0.0219
02/01/02	04/19/02	−0.0421	0.0335	0.0142	−0.0162	−0.0327	0.0209	0.0011	0.0030	0.0041	−0.0102	0.0007	0.0183

04/26/02	07/12/02	0.0391	0.0002	−0.0211	0.0014	0.0170	0.0348	0.0077	0.0039	0.0068	0.0015	0.0074	0.0120
07/19/02	10/04/02	−0.0068	0.0068	0.0014	−0.0219	0.0136	−0.0271	0.0100	0.0032	0.0056	0.0219	0.0140	0.0397
10/11/02	12/27/02	0.0162	0.0062	−0.0092	−0.0208	−0.0096	0.0050	0.0084	0.0021	0.0056	−0.0044	0.0011	0.0367
Mean		0.0093	0.0096	−0.0007	0.0064	0.0080	0.0044	0.0048	0.0032	0.0024	0.0101	0.0033	0.0105
t-stat		1.9639*	1.1167	−0.1365	1.0701	2.0901*	0.4946	2.4067**	3.4201***	1.7809*	3.5762***	1.4013	2.4151**

Panel B: General Category

From	To	Equity	Balanced	Bond	Overall
08/21/98	11/06/98	0.0175	0.0185	0.0153	0.0167
11/13/98	01/29/99	0.0991	0.0278	0.0090	0.0507
02/05/99	04/23/99	0.0036	0.0002	−0.0037	0.0001
04/30/99	07/16/99	−0.0015	−0.0051	−0.0073	−0.0045
07/23/99	10/08/99	0.0113	0.0044	0.0027	0.0068
10/15/99	12/31/99	0.0090	−0.0096	−0.0047	0.0007
01/07/00	03/24/00	−0.0068	0.0011	0.0061	−0.0005
03/31/00	06/16/00	0.0027	−0.0004	0.0029	0.0023
06/23/00	09/08/00	0.0017	0.0028	0.0042	0.0028

Continued

Table 14.6 Continued

From	To	Equity	Balanced	Bond	Overall
09/15/00	12/01/00	0.0019	0.0037	0.0040	0.0030
12/08/00	02/23/01	−0.0041	−0.0038	0.0016	−0.0018
03/02/01	05/18/01	0.0076	0.0043	0.0008	0.0045
05/25/01	08/10/01	−0.0072	0.0042	0.0065	−0.0001
08/17/01	11/02/01	0.0177	0.0143	0.0079	0.0134
11/09/01	01/25/02	−0.0166	0.0006	0.0023	−0.0067
02/01/02	04/19/02	0.0003	0.0011	0.0029	0.0014
04/26/02	07/12/02	0.0086	0.0077	0.0059	0.0074
07/19/02	10/04/02	−0.0037	0.0100	0.0090	0.0033
10/11/02	12/27/02	−0.0009	0.0084	0.0044	0.0026
Mean		0.0074	0.0048	0.0037	0.0054
t-stat		1.3508	2.4067**	3.0658***	1.9095*

Note: *, ** and *** denote significance at 0.1, 0.05 and 0.01 levels respectively.

Although tax treatment in Italy is very different from that of the Japanese market, our results appear to be surprisingly similar to those of Brown, Goetzmann, Hiraki, Otsuki and Shiraishi (2001).

Our findings may contribute to accelerating the fiscal reform of mutual funds, recently discussed by regulators, removing this strange taxation asymmetry.

REFERENCES

Brown, S. and Goetzmann, W. (1997) "Mutual Fund Styles", *Journal of Financial Economics*, 43(3): 373–99.

Brown, S., Goetzmann, W., Hiraki, T., Otsuki, T. and Shiraishi, N. (2001) "The Japanese Open-End Fund Puzzle", *Journal of Business*, 74(1): 59–77.

Coval, J. and Moskowitz, T. (1999) "Home Bias at Home: Local Equity Preference in Domestic Portfolios", *Journal of Finance*, 54(6): 2045–73.

Elton, E. and Gruber, M. (1970) "Marginal Stockholder Tax Rates and the Clientele Effect", *Review of Economics and Statistics*, 52(1): 68–74.

Fung, W. and Hsieh, D. (2001) "The Risk in Hedge Fund Strategies: Theory and Evidence from Trend Followers", *Review of Financial Studies*, 14(2): 313–41.

Fung, W. and Hsieh, D. (2002) "Asset-Based Style Factors for Hedge Funds", *Financial Analyst Journal*, 58(5): 16–27.

Graham, J. and Harvey, C. (1996) "Market Timing Ability and Volatility Implied in Investment Newsletters' Asset Allocation Recommendations", *Journal of Financial Economics*, 42(3): 397–421.

Kalman, R. (1960) "A New Approach to Linear Filtering and Prediction Problems", *Transactions ASME Journal of Basic Engineering*, 82(1): 35–45.

Kim, C. and Nelson, C. (1999) *State-Space Models with Regime Switching* (Cambridge, MA: MIT Press).

Merton, R. (1981) "On Market Timing and Investment Performance I: An Equilibrium Theory of Value for Market Forecasts", *Journal of Business*, 54(3): 363–407.

Merton, R. (1987) "A Simple Model of Capital Market Equilibrium with Incomplete Information", *Journal of Finance*, 42(3): 483–510.

Roll, R. (1977) "A Critique of the Asset Pricing Theory Tests: On Past and Potential Testability of the Theory", *Journal of Financial Economics*, 4(2): 129–76.

Sharpe, W. (1992) "Asset Allocation: Management Style and Performance Measurement", *Journal of Portfolio Management*, 18(1): 7–19.

CHAPTER 15

Corporate Governance of Mutual Funds in Pakistan

Muhammad Akbar Saeed and Nadeem A. Syed

15.1 INTRODUCTION

15.1.1 Origin of best practices

Codes of best practice originated in the early 1990s in the United Kingdom, the United States and Canada on account of a perceived lack of board oversight on effective corporate performance of leading companies. The Cadbury Report in the UK, the General Motors Board of Directors Guidelines in the USA, and the Dey Report in Canada have each proved influential sources for other guideline and code efforts.

Corporate governance has assumed immense importance in recent years because of the stunning corporate failures in Western well-developed market economies. Such breakdowns have severely affected the lives of not only the thousands of shareholders and employees of the failed companies, but also damaged the businesses of creditors, customers and suppliers.

In the developing world, including emerging markets and transition economies, national economies are dominated by large family-owned, state-owned and foreign-owned companies. Moreover, a significant proportion of the national employment and output is provided by the non-corporate form of business enterprises. Thus a truly public company with shares widely traded on the domestic stockmarket is exceptional. Is corporate governance of any significance in such countries?

The fundamental issue for everyone involved in financial markets, regardless of company or country, must be to maintain high standards that foster trust and confidence. Investors can – and do – move capital around the globe with a few keystrokes on a computer. Capital will flee environments that are unstable or unpredictable – whether that's a function of lax corporate governance, ineffective accounting standards, or a lack of transparency. Investors must be able to see for themselves that companies are living up to their obligations and embracing the spirit of good governance. Multiple benefits emanate from dynamic markets and enlightened corporate governance. These benefits help to provide a more stable platform for attracting domestic and foreign investment for long term economic growth and prosperity.

Companies that stress corporate governance and transparency will, over time, generate improved returns and economic performance and lower their cost of capital. The opposite is also true: companies weak in corporate governance and transparency represent increased investment risks and result in a higher cost of capital. Events of the last few years, including those at Enron, Worldcom and others, support this thesis, as does a growing body of academic research and financial market surveys. And while the spotlight started with US companies, this is not just a US problem. Similar corporate debacles have occurred recently in Canada, Germany, Italy, Sweden, Switzerland, South Korea and The Netherlands, to mention a few.

15.1.2 Corporate governance defined

"Corporate Governance" refers to the rules that guide the behavior of corporations, shareholders, and managers, as well as to government actions to promote and enforce those rules. Corporate governance provides the basis for a stable and productive business environment. It can be especially important in emerging markets and to firms that seek to distinguish themselves in the global economy.

15.1.3 Global codes of corporate governance

In 1999, the Organization for Economic Cooperation and Development (OECD) published its Principles of Corporate Governance, the first such international code of good corporate governance. The revised version of these principles was approved by the OECD member governments in 2004. Today, regulators, lawmakers, stock exchanges, central banks, international institutions like the World Bank, International Chambers of Commerce (ICC), the OECD, USAID, associations such as the AIMR (now the CFA Institute) and the association of corporate directors, the Investment Company Institute in USA, audit firms, management consultants, specialized research institutes such as the European Corporate Governance Institute and the Pakistan Corporate Governance Institute, universities, private corporate reformer groups and individuals, and many more are actively working to improve corporate governance. More than 55 countries in the world, including

Pakistan, have developed their own codes of corporate governance. At the same time numerous self-regulatory "codes" and governance "indices" are being enacted by bodies of all kinds – some acting on behalf of governments or established interest groups, others simply implementing advertising efforts by consultants eager to sell their corporate governance services (see Gerard Hertig). It is understandable that one-fit-all solution is not possible. However there is convergence on major issues such as increasing the number of independent directors of the board, the tests of director independence, compensation of the directors, and the role of the audit committee of the board, to mention a few.

15.1.4 Corporate governance in the USA

Past Research

In the United States, the board of directors is responsible for taking care of the shareholder's interest. It is therefore the first line of defense against managers acting against the interest of the shareholders. The effectiveness with which US corporate boards protect shareholders' interests has been researched considerably. The size of the board and the proportion of outside directors are the main characteristics studied in this context. The US evidence can be summarized as follows: (1) Higher proportions of outside directors are not associated with superior firm performance, but are associated with better decisions concerning such issues as acquisitions, executive compensation and CEO turnover. (2) Board size is negatively related to both general firm performance and the quality of decision-making. (3) Poor firm performance, CEO turnover and changes in ownership structure are often associated with changes in the membership of the board.

The compensation issue that is of greatest interest from a corporate governance perspective is the degree to which executive compensation aligns top executives' interests with those of their shareholders; that is, the sensitivity of executive pay to performance. US research supports several broad conclusions. First, the sensitivity of pay to performance in the USA has increased over time. Second, the vast majority of this sensitivity comes through executive ownership of common stock and of options on common stock. Finally, stock options are the fastest growing component of CEO compensation in the USA.

Sarbanes–Oxley Act

The Sarbanes–Oxley Act (SOX) was signed into law in 2002. It is aimed at restoring the trust of investors in the capital markets. For this purpose, the law expands the disclosure obligations of corporations and formalizes the processes that precede corporate reporting. Companies are obliged to establish internal control systems that must be maintained and reexamined on a regular basis. By way of certification, certain corporate officers must personally attest to the exactitude and completeness of reporting. Management must also certify that certain requirements concerning the internal control systems have been met. In addition, the law raises the requirements for the independence of auditors and contains detailed rules concerning the Audit Committee (see Sarbanes–Oxley Act 2002).

Roberta Romano (2004) evaluated SOX and concluded that SOX was enacted as emergency legislation amidst a free-falling stock market and media frenzy over corporate scandals shortly before the midterm congressional elections. The governance provisions, included toward the end of the legislative process in the Senate, were not a focus of any considered attention. Their inclusion stemmed from the interaction between election year politics and the Senate banking committee chairman's response to suggestions of policy entrepreneurs. The scholarly literature at odds with those individuals" recommendations was ignored, while the interest groups whose position was more consistent with the literature – the business community and accounting profession – had lost their credibility and become politically radioactive. Roberta Romano (RR) concludes that SOX's corporate governance provisions should be stripped of their mandatory force and rendered optional. RR suggests that other nations, such as the members of the European Union who have been revising their corporation codes, would be well advised to avoid Congress' policy blunder. The SOX, although not yet opposed by the US corporate world, is being largely lamented for high cost of compliance estimated at around $7.8 million per company (see the survey referred to in the *New York Times* report of 17 April 2005).

15.1.5 Corporate governance in United Kingdom

As stated earlier, corporate governance initiatives started in the UK also in early 1990s. The Combined Code of Corporate Governance was issued by the regulators in July 2003, and later the London Stock Exchange issued its Practical Guide on Corporate Governance in July 2004. Both of the documents are being increasingly referred to as model codes and guides in the harmonization of codes and best practices at international levels. Equity ownership in the UK has historically been much like that in the USA: large numbers of publicly-traded firms, most of which are relatively widely-held.

15.1.6 Corporate governance in Germany

Equity ownership in Germany has historically been more concentrated than in the USA. In addition, banks play more important governance roles.

In Germany the management and supervision of a corporation is carried out by two separate bodies: the Board of Management is solely responsible for the management of the company, while the Supervisory Board has a supervisory function. The supervisory board is directly involved in decisions of fundamental importance to the company. However it does not assume any executive tasks. One of its key responsibilities is the appointment and dismissal of members of the Board of Management. According to the German law on codetermination, the Supervisory Board has to be made up of representatives of shareholders and employees on a basis of parity. The chairman of the Supervisory Board coordinates the work of the Supervisory Board. The chairman of the Supervisory Board, who for all practical purposes, is a representative of the shareholders, has the casting vote in the case of split resolutions. The representatives elected by the shareholders and the representatives elected by the employees are equally obliged to act in the enterprise's best interest. The German dual board system and the US/UK single board system converge because of the intensive interaction of the Management Board and the Supervisory Board in Germany. The two-tier board is mandatory in Austria and optional in France and Finland (see Denis and McConnell, 2003).

Until recently there have been few published papers that study the effectiveness of European boards of directors. Despite this lack of evidence, and despite the fact that the US evidence is somewhat open-ended regarding the effect of board characteristics on firm value, various European commissions have embraced the idea that appropriate board composition is important to good corporate governance (see Denis and McConnell, 2003).

15.2 IMPORTANCE OF CORPORATE GOVERNANCE FOR MUTUAL FUNDS

An important feature of modern financial markets is the increased weight of institutional investors. Some, such as mutual funds and pension funds, act in a fiduciary capacity on behalf of individual investors. Others, including insurance companies and investment banks, act in their own right. The importance of institutional investors as owners of corporate equity has grown enormously over the past few years, to the point where they have become the principal players in many markets. Institutions acting in a fiduciary capacity, such as pension funds, mutual funds and other collective investment schemes, own shares on behalf of millions of investors. Institutional investors can play an important role in monitoring company performance and in conveying their concerns to the board of an investee company. They can challenge or support the board through voting at the general meetings of shareholders and they are well-placed to take their concerns directly to the board and to propose a course of action. An increasing number of institutional investors are actively exercising their ownership roles in this way.

However, the exercise of informed ownership through monitoring is costly and institutional investors are also subject to possible conflicts of interest, for example in cases where other commercial relations with the firm in question may take precedence over what might be a desirable course of action from an ownership perspective. Nor do all institutional investors have the same incentive for exercising ownership rights. Such institutions, either for prudential or other regulatory reasons or as a result of their investment strategy, may hold only small stakes in individual companies and so have little incentive to monitor these firms closely. In such cases, these institutional investors' role as owner could be enhanced by exchanging information and plans with other shareholders, leading to coordinated action. This is now happening in some countries, with institutional shareholders pooling their shares in order to attain the thresholds needed for them to be able to take specific action.

The other facet of corporate governance for mutual funds is the adherence to good governance in their own operations. The mutual funds manage public money. As such the management and employees of the fund have to demonstrate supreme standards of trust, business ethics and governance. The fund managers need to exhibit good governance practices and transparency in all their areas of operations, in particular, roles and responsibilities of the board of directors and the committees of the board, code of ethics and best practices for the employees, trading procedures and practices, brokerage commission, portfolio management, management fee and other expenses, performance measurement of the fund, and performance evaluation of the manager. These twin aspects of corporate governance for mutual funds are crucial for the pulsating capital markets.

15.3 HISTORY OF MUTUAL FUNDS IN PAKISTAN

Mutual funds were introduced in Pakistan in the 1960s. The National Investment Trust (NIT) was the first to be set up in 1962 followed by the Investment Corporation of Pakistan (ICP) in 1966. Both the institutions were under government control. NIT concentrated on open-ended schemes and ICP concentrated on closed-ended schemes and floated a series of 26 closed-ended funds up to the early 1990s. Both NIT and ICP were unable to maintain their growth during the later part of the 1990s because of the prolonged recession. As a result their net asset values dropped considerably.

15.3.1 Privatization of mutual funds

Privatization of the two state-owned funds – ICP and NIT – was initiated by the government in 2002. The 25 closed funds of ICP were split into two lots. After competitive bidding, management rights for Lot A comprising 12 funds were acquired by ABAMCO Ltd. After approval of the Securities & Exchange Commission of Pakistan (SECP) the first nine were merged into a single closed-end fund named "ABAMCO Capital Fund". The latter three funds were merged and named as the "ABAMCO Stock Market Fund".

For Lot B, comprising 13 ICP funds, management rights were acquired by PICIC Asset Management Company Ltd. In 2004–05 all of the funds in Lot B were merged to create a single closed-end fund named "PICIC Investment Fund" with a paid-up capital of Rs 2.84 billion. Afterwards, management rights of ICP-SEMF were also acquired by PICIC Asset Management Company Ltd. The fund has been renamed as the "PICIC Growth Fund" with a paid-up capital of Rs 1.28 billion. Privatization of NIT is expected to be completed during 2005.

15.3.2 Entry of the private sector into mutual funds

Private-sector participation in mutual funds started in the early 1990s with the setting-up of the first open-ended fund by ABAMCO Ltd. However, due to the prolonged recession of the later 1990s, the private sector was also unable to make any major contribution to the overall performance of the fund industry. From 2000 onwards Pakistan's economy gradually started improving and later the stockmarket also grew significantly attracting a number of new private-sector participants to the mutual fund industry. As of 31 March 2005 there were 35 mutual funds in Pakistan, 14 open-ended and 21 closed-ended. In the recent past, these funds have launched a number of new products such as Balanced Funds, Equity Funds, Money Market Funds, and Islamic Funds. Other innovative products are in the pipeline, which include Annuity Funds, Pension Funds, Infrastructure Funds, Real Estate Funds, Capital Guarantee Funds, Offshore Funds, and so on.

The past three years have seen the revival of the mutual fund industry in Pakistan. The net assets of the industry improved from Rs 25 billion in 2001 to Rs 124 billion as of 31 March 2005. The future of the industry appears to be promising and is poised for growth, and the sector will be the focus of growing public attention because of the improved investment scenario. It will also require a more effective regulatory regime. Optional adoption of international best practices and transparency in their operations by the mutual funds, rather than an obligatory implementation, could help them in strengthening their growth prospects. On the basis of "practice what you preach", the fund industry can assume the status of a role model for corporate governance in Pakistan and then infuse the same best practices through proxies into the corporate sector.

15.3.3 The regulatory framework for mutual funds

Mutual funds in Pakistan are regulated by the Non-Banking Finance Companies (Establishment & Regulation) Rules, 2003 of the Securities and Exchange Commission of Pakistan (SECP). Asset management companies set up to undertake fund management business have to comply with the listing regulations of the stock exchanges and the code of corporate governance.

15.4 CODE OF CORPORATE GOVERNANCE IN PAKISTAN AND INTERNATIONAL BEST PRACTICES

The code of corporate governance issued by the Securities & Exchange Commission of Pakistan (SECP) in 2002 is also applicable to asset management companies which manage mutual funds in Pakistan. The following part of the chapter describes important sections of the SECP code and then presents the international best practices in general and best practices in particular for mutual funds.

15.4.1 Board of directors

Independent non-executive directors

The SECP code specifies:

> That all listed companies shall encourage effective representation of independent non-executive directors, including those representing minority interests, on their Boards of Directors so that the Board as a group includes core competencies considered relevant in the context of each listed company. For the purpose, listed companies may take necessary steps such that minority shareholders as a class are facilitated to contest election of directors by proxy solicitation.

Best practices suggest that the board should have a nomination committee, which should evaluate the balance of skills, knowledge and experience of the board and, in light of this, prepare a description of the role, experience and skills required for a particular new appointment. This should be done as part of a routine succession planning process, designed to ensure that plans are in place for orderly succession to the board and other senior management positions. The role of chairman of the board and that of CEO should be split with division of responsibility between them clearly set-up in writing. Majority of the members of the nominating committee should be independent directors.

Director independence

Director independence is crucial in successful mutual fund management because of the twin facets of corporate governance as explained in the earlier section on the importance of corporate governance for mutual funds. An independent director is someone whose only connection to the company is his or her board seat. Any other relationship clouds the independence. Tests of director independence have been developed by many organizations worldwide. Best practices in this context require that, except for the chairman and the CEO, the rest of the directors are usually independent. Moreover, companies are now confirming in their annual reports as well as on their websites that the independent directors are actually independent in terms of the applicable code of corporate governance.

Number of other directorships

There is increased deliberation as to how many directorships any one person should hold, and best practices are tightening the number of directorships on other companies. It is being suggested that a full-time executive director, a CEO, or chairman should preferably not take more than one non-executive directorship of another listed company. The argument is that a full-time executive, particularly a chief executive, should not be distracted from his/her main duties by taking non-executive positions in other companies. The SECP-code has specified the maximum limit of directorship in other companies to be 10.

The Deloitte survey in the UK reports that most corporate chairmen are now non-executive and only 10 percent of executive directors hold an external directorship, and in most cases no more than one (see Deloitte & Touche survey report dated 24 October 2002).

Classified boards

In a classified or staggered board, directors are typically elected in two or more classes, serving terms greater than one year. Using an example of a three-year staggered board, at each annual meeting, one-third of the board members or nominees would be eligible for shareholder ratification for a three-year period. Proponents of classified boards argue that by staggering the election of directors, a certain level of continuity and skill is maintained. It is worth noting that this continuity can also be maintained with a policy of annual elections, if the directors are careful to address the issues of competence and succession. Staggered terms for board members make it more difficult for shareholders to make fundamental changes to the composition and behavior of boards, by making it extremely difficult for any challenge to, or change in, board control. In circumstances of deteriorating corporate performance, this difficulty could result in a permanent impairment of long-term shareholder value.

Classified boards are popular in the USA, and the technique prevents a hostile bidder from seizing control of a target's board of directors in a single shareholder election. However, staggered boards reduce shareholder value (see Robin Sidel, 2002). The proxy guidelines of the US mutual fund management companies support the single-tier board over the staggered board.

Maximum tenure for independent directors

Best practices in this context are not uniform. The UK code suggests that independent or non-executive directors preferably serve no more than three 3-year terms.

Performance evaluation of the board

The board should undertake a formal and rigorous annual evaluation of its own performance and that of its committees and individual directors. Individual evaluation should aim to show whether each director continues to contribute effectively and to demonstrate commitment to the role (including commitment of time for board and committee meetings and any other duties). The chairman should act on the results of the performance evaluation by recognizing the strengths and addressing the weaknesses of the board and, where appropriate, proposing new members be appointed to the board or seeking the resignation of directors. The board should state in the annual report how performance evaluation of the board, its committees and its individual directors has been conducted. The non-executive directors, led by the senior independent director, should be responsible for performance evaluation of the board and its chairman, taking into account the views of executive directors.

15.4.2 Board committees

Nomination committee

The nomination committee has the responsibility for leading the process for board appointments and making recommendations to the board accordingly. Best practices specify that a majority of its members should be independent non-executive directors. One of those independent non-executive directors or the chairman of the board should chair the nomination committee. An important point to note in the latter case is that the board chairman should not lead the search for his or her own successor.

Audit committee of the board

The SECP code of corporate governance has adequately covered the Audit Committee's composition and its terms of reference. The code specifies that "The board of directors of every listed company shall establish an Audit Committee, which shall comprise of not less than three members, including the chairman. Majority of the members of the committee shall be from the non-executive directors, and the chairman of the audit committee shall preferably be a non-executive director."

Best practices stress that all members of the committee be independent and, in view of the complexities involved in their roles, the board should satisfy itself that at least one member of the audit committee is an "audit committee financial expert" and the chairman of the audit committee preferably has strong financial skills. Best practices also recognize the importance of continuing education for directors to improve both board and committee performance. It is considered to be the responsibility of the board to advise the independent directors about their continuing education, including leading-edge corporate governance issues. Directors are encouraged to participate in continuing director education programs. In view of the growing complexities of the financial markets, directors of the mutual fund management companies would need to persistently update their skills.

The board should ensure that directors, especially non-executive directors, have access to independent professional advice at the company's expense where they judge it necessary to discharge their responsibilities as directors. Committees should be provided with sufficient resources to undertake their duties.

Compensation committee of the board

Remuneration of the executive and non-executive directors is the subject of widespread contemporary deliberations. Best practices indicate that the board of directors set up a three-member compensation committee, entirely from amongst the non-executive directors, responsible for determining the remuneration for all executive directors and the chairman on behalf of the whole board. The committee should preferably also determine the remuneration of the first layer of senior management below the board. The board itself should normally determine the non-executive directors' compensation. The German code of corporate governance has recommended that remuneration of all of the members of the supervisory board as well as the management board be provided in the notes to the annual accounts of the companies. Compliance of these instructions has been started by the German companies (see *Annual Report 2004* of Allianz AG, Germany).

15.4.3 Annual accounts

SECP's Code of Corporate Governance has a separate section titled "Corporate and Financial Reporting Framework" which covers vital issues about accounting and financial reporting policies and procedures of the company. These are also to be followed by the asset management companies while preparing the accounts of the different mutual funds that it is managing. However, there is no mention of the accounts of the asset management company itself. This may prove to be a critical factor in future, especially after privatization of the open-ended mutual funds. In order to improve transparency, fund management companies may consider giving out the details of their own accounts along with the accounts of the respective mutual fund. Or the same can be made available on the corporate website of the company. This would increase transparency, add to public confidence, and lead to an increase in the popularity of the fund management company. After all, the fund shareholders have the right to know about the financial health of the management company; the fund management company could encounter tribulations and hence not remain a going concern.

15.4.4 Investment management

The CFA Institute (formerly known as the Association for Investment Management and Research or AIMR), in November 2004 issued a draft of its "Asset Manager Code of Professional Conduct". This code outlines the ethical and professional responsibilities of asset management firms. The code recognizes that in the highly regulated and complex business of investment management, a code is not sufficient by itself. To be implemented effectively, the principles and standards embodied in the code must be supported by appropriate compliance procedures. The specific compliance procedures that translate principle into practice will vary based on a variety of factors, including the specific business of the manager, the type of clients, size of the firm in terms of assets under management and number of employees, the regulatory regime with which the manager must comply, as well as many other factors. For example, how should the manager exercise diligence, independence and thoroughness in analysing investments, making investment recommendations, and taking investment actions. How would the manager have a reasonable and adequate basis, supported by appropriate research and investigation, for any investment analysis, recommendation, and action. How would the manager evaluate third party research before using it, especially evaluation of the objectivity and independence of recommendations. The code provides a universal set of principles and standards relevant to all asset managers.

15.4.5 Measurement of investment performance

Investment practices, regulation, performance measurement, and reporting of performance results in the mutual fund industry have historically varied considerably from country to country. Some countries have established performance calculation and presentation guidelines that are domestically accepted, and others have few standards for presenting investment performance. These practices have limited the comparability of performance results between firms within and outside different countries and have hindered the ability of firms to penetrate markets on a global basis.

As a result of its dedicated efforts spread over ten years, the CFA Institute in February 2005 issued the Global Investment Performance Standards (GIPS®). Although the CFA Institute is funding and administering the activities of the GIPS standards, the success of the Standards is the result of an alliance among experts from a variety of fields within the global investment industry.

Investment firms from all countries are expected to comply with one standard, the GIPS standards, with effect from 1 January 2006.

15.4.6 Code of ethics

Mutual funds deal with public money. Their management and employees need to understand the importance of demonstrating trust and integrity to their customers. To this end, developing a comprehensive code of ethics is vital. Moreover the fund company needs to have an ethics office to ensure continuous evolution of the ethics code as well as its compliance. The code would need to address and develop policies on: inside information; resolution of conflicts of interest; personal investing by the fund employees especially portfolio managers, research analysts, and traders; receiving gifts, violation of the code and penalties thereof.

Some of the best practices in this context are as follows. Upon hire, employees are briefed on the Code of Ethics, provided with a copy of it, and required to acknowledge that they have read it and will abide by it. Employees are required to review the Code of Ethics annually and to acknowledge in writing that their personal investing has been conducted in compliance with it. Employees obtain pre-clearance from the Ethics Office before making a personal transaction in securities available for trading by the funds, disclose personal transactions in covered securities in any account in which they have a beneficial interest, comply with the Code's rules for buying and selling securities and conduct their personal brokerage trading through the fund company's brokerage account for employees. Employees who may be in a position to influence fund recommendations, fund investment decisions, or fund management are subject to even stricter rules. Among other requirements, these employees must: recommend suitable securities for the benefit of the funds prior to personally transacting in them; and surrender profits made from transactions in the same or equivalent securities if the transactions are made within 60 calendar days of each other. Research analysts must wait two business days following the issuance of a research note on a company before trading in securities of that company for their own accounts. Employees who are portfolio managers may not buy or sell a security that a fund they manage has traded within seven calendar days on either side of the fund's trade date. In case of violation of the code, the Ethics Office investigates the matter. Depending on the circumstances, any of the following actions may be taken: a warning; a fine; a personal trading ban; termination of employment; or referral to civil or criminal authorities.

Fund managers usually specify in their annual reports that a board-approved code of ethics has been signed to, and is being followed by all board members and employees. Some of the world's largest mutual fund companies have already posted the key features of their codes of ethics on their websites. It is being suggested that in order to improve transparency, the text of the full code be made available to shareholders on request.

15.4.7 Disclosures

Management fees and other expenses

Investors are entitled to full and fair disclosures of costs associated with the investment management services provided. This includes information on any fees paid to their managers on an ongoing basis as well as periodic costs that are known to their managers and that will affect investors' overall investment expenses. At a minimum, fund managers should provide clients with gross and net-of-fees returns and disclose any unusual expenses.

Investment performance

Fund managers should provide to their clients on a regular basis the investment performance of the portfolio, determined in accordance with the GIPS standards, as discussed above.

Valuation methods

Clients deserve to know if the assets in their portfolios are valued based on closing market values, third-party valuations, internal valuation models, or other methods. This type of disclosure allows clients to compare performance and determine whether different valuation sources and methods may explain differences in performance results.

Conflicts of interest

Conflicts of interest often arise in investment management profession and can take many forms. Best practice is to avoid such conflicts if possible. When fund managers cannot reasonably avoid conflicts, they must carefully manage them and disclose them to clients. Disclosure of conflicts protects investors by providing them with the information they need to evaluate the objectivity of their managers' investment advice or actions taken on their behalf and by giving them the information to judge the circumstances, motives, or possible manager bias for themselves. Examples of some of the types of activities that can constitute actual or potential conflicts of interest include the use of soft commissions, referral and placement fees, trailing commissions, sales incentives, directed brokerage arrangements, allocation of investment opportunities among similar portfolios, and use of affiliated brokers.

Investment process

Managers must disclose to fund shareholders the manner in which investment decisions are made and implemented. Such disclosures should address the overall investment strategy and should include a discussion of the specific risk factors inherent in such a strategy.

Proxy voting policies

It is a fiduciary duty of mutual fund companies to vote proxies in annual and special company meetings. Proxies need to be voted in a manner that best serves the interests of fund shareholders. Voting decisions need to be based on guidelines approved by the fund directors, and to promote transparency the guidelines are made available on the website of the fund company and the past voting record is also presented. The guidelines usually cover the following areas; compensation for the top executives and the board members, increase in authorized capital, election of the board especially independent board members, approval of appointment of independent auditors, approval of annual accounts.

Mutual fund managers encounter potential conflicts of interest in proxy voting, which could be referred to a proxy voting committee of senior executives for amicable resolution. Moreover, the fund company may, depending on the situation, use a full block proxy, or a partial proxy of the particular fund only.

Net asset values

Mutual fund companies should disclose to their fund holders the time of the day at which the NAVs are calculated. The SECP code has specified that the net asset value shall be provided for publication on a monthly basis to the stock exchange. Best practices indicate that fund management companies supply the latest NAVs on a daily basis on their websites. A few asset managers in Pakistan presently follow this practice.

Brokerage commission

For improved corporate governance of mutual funds, the board of directors should frame policies for payment of brokerage commission on sale and purchase of securities for the mutual fund portfolios. Such commission, fee or other remuneration should be reasonable and fair compared to the commission, fee or other remuneration received by other brokers in connection with comparable transactions involving similar securities being purchased or sold on a securities exchange during a comparable period of time. The board of directors should make and approve such changes in the policies and procedures as the board deems necessary and also determine, preferable on a quarterly basis that all such transactions effected during the preceding quarter were effected in compliance with such procedures.

Corporate website

An effective way to maintain high levels of disclosure is to make all such material available on the corporate website of the company. Listed companies as well as mutual fund companies are increasingly making use of the technology.

15.4.8 Control of companies

The SECP's Code of Corporate Governance contains the following two clauses in this context:

(i) A listed company shall endeavour that no person is elected or nominated as a director if he or his spouse is engaged in the business of stock brokerage (unless specifically exempted by the Securities and Exchange Commission of Pakistan).
(ii) The Board of Directors of each listed company includes at least one independent director representing institutional equity interest of a banking

company, Development Financial Institution, Non-Banking Financial Institution (including a modaraba, leasing company or investment bank), mutual fund or insurance company.

As per international best practices, fund managers are usually not involved in management of a company. When they buy shares of a company, it is not for acquisition of control; they buy stocks of a company believing that it will increase in value. Asset management companies generally leave the management of the company to the company's management. The LSE guide contains useful material on a company's relationship with institutional shareholders like mutual funds.

15.4.9 Governance ratings

Corporations are now being rated on their good governance, and rating services are being provided independently of, and without cost to, the rated company. The potential conflicts of interest are thus automatically averted for the firm providing governance rating. This is unlike the situation for the conventional rating agencies such as S&P and Moody's or like external auditors who take a fee from the client company for their services and possess a potential conflict of interest. The governance ratings range from 1 to 10, with stocks receiving a 10 typically having truly independent boards of directors, influential and independent audit committees, and other good governance characteristics. Mutual funds with large holdings of well-governed companies have outperformed the average fund in both three and five-year holding periods and tend to do better than funds with a large number of poorly governed companies in their portfolios over the same period (see Lipper, GMI 2004). Mutual fund investors will soon be asking their managers to disclose the governance profile of their funds; it is an investment risk they should be made aware of.

15.4.10 Disaster recovery plans

Market disruptions are possible because of national, regional and local emergencies. Fund managers' best practices for maintaining business continuity suggest the following: off-site back-up; alternative plans for monitoring, analysing and trading investments if primary systems become unavailable; procedures for communicating with critical vendors and suppliers; and plans for communicating with clients during periods of extended disruptions.

15.5 CONCLUSION

Corporate governance guidelines and codes of best practice arise in the context of, and are affected by, differing national frameworks of law, regulation and stock exchange listing rules, and differing societal values. Although boards of directors provide an important internal mechanism for holding management accountable, effective corporate governance is supported by and dependent on the market for corporate control, securities regulation, company law, accounting and auditing standards, bankruptcy laws, and judicial enforcement. Therefore, to understand one nation's corporate governance practices in relation to another's, one must understand not only the best practice documents, but also the underlying legal and enforcement framework. Some governance codes are linked to listing or legally mandated disclosure requirements. Others are purely voluntary in nature, but may be designed to help forestall further government or listing body regulation. However, in both developed and developing nations, codes focus on boards of directors and attempt to describe ways in which boards can be positioned to provide some form of guidance and oversight to management, and accountability to shareholders and society at large.

The mutual fund companies in Pakistan are presently in a distinctive position. They can assume a leadership position in corporate governance by voluntarily adopting best practices; they do not have to wait for the regulators to evolve and come up with best practice codes. In fact we do not have to reinvent the wheel, we just have to follow the good examples. A large number of best practices are already being practiced in the world, and by following these mutual fund companies would become role models for others to follow. Mutual fund companies would then be in a more imposing position to inculcate corporate governance in their investee companies by practicing what they preach. This action is likely to improve the investor base of mutual funds and also improve investor confidence in our capital markets.

APPENDIX: CORPORATE GOVERNANCE CODES AND BEST-PRACTICES GUIDES

Asset Manager Code of Professional Conduct (2004), CFA Institute, USA

Best Practices of Fund Directors (1999), Investment Company Institute, USA

Beyond Compliance: Building a Governance Culture (2001), Chartered Accountants of Canada

Global Investment Performance Standards (2005), CFA Institute, USA

Corporate Governance – A guide to good disclosure, Toronto Stock Exchange

Code of Corporate Governance (2002), Securities and Exchange Commission of Pakistan

German Code of Corporate Governance (2003), Germany

Combined Code on Corporate Governance (2003), UK

Corporate Governance – A practical Guide (2004), London Stock Exchange, UK

How Financial Institutions Are Responding to Sarbanes-Oxley, A guide by Deloitte & Touche LLP

REFERENCES

Adams, R.B., Almeida, H. and Ferreira, D. (2003) "Understanding the Relationship Between Founder-CEOs and Firm Performance", ECGI Finance Working Paper.

Anderson, G. (January 12, 2004) "Corporate Governance as a Factor in Mutual Funds Holdings", a Joint Research by Governance Metrics International – A Governance Rating Agency, and LIPPER – A Leading Global Provider of Research on Mutual Funds, New York.

Denis, D.K. and McConnell, J.J. (2003) "International Corporate Governance", ECGI Finance Working Paper No.05/2003.

Franks, J., Mayer, C. and Rossi, S. (2003) "Ownership: Evolution and Regulation", ECGI Finance Working Paper No.09/2003.

Glater, J.D. (April 17, 2005) "Here it Comes: The Sarbanes–Oxley Backlash, a Report on Survey of 90 Clients of Big Four Accounting Firms – Deloitte", E & Y, KPMG, and PWH Coopers (The New York Times).

Gregory, H.J. (2000) "International Comparison of Corporate Governance Guidelines and Codes of Best Practices – Developing and Emerging Markets".

Hertig, G. (2005) "On-Going Board Reforms: One-Size-Fits-All and Regulatory Capture", ECGI-Law Working Paper No. 25/2005.

Mueller, H.M. and Panunzi, F. (2003) "Tender Offers and Leverage", ECGI – Finance, Working Paper No. 22/2003.

Romano, R. (2004) "The Sarbanes–Oxley Act and the Making of Quack Corporate Governance", Yale Law & Econ Research Paper 297.

Sidel, R. (April 1, 2002) "Staggered Terms for Boards Erode Shareholder Value", *The Wall Street Journal.*

CHAPTER 16

Determinants of Pension Funds Underwriting and Implications for Portfolio Management: Evidence from Italy

Carlo Fiorio and Marco Percoco

16.1 INTRODUCTION

Public spending for pensions is one of the most relevant items in government budgets. Such expenditure is considered to be a necessary intervention of the State in order to provide retired workers with a given level of income and consumption during old age. According to the simple, though effective life-cycle model, individuals smooths their consumption over their lives, so that during old age the saving rate becomes negative, that is consumption is sustained by a decrease in wealth. However, very often individuals are myopic and tend to save less money than they need during old age, and because of this there seems to be scope for public intervention.

From a theoretic viewpoint, three causes are at the base of government actions in providing Social Security or pensions systems (Banks and Emmerson, 2000):

(a) financial markets are incomplete and fail in supplying instruments free of risk and miming the characteristics of real annuities (Diamond, 1977);

(b) people do not provide enough for their retirement; that is, State intervention is driven by a sort of "paternalism" meant to force individuals to undertake retirement saving (Duesenberry, 1949; Hall, 1978);

(c) social security or pensions systems can be used to redistribute resources within and across generations (Diamond, 1977).

The pension system design is characterized according to the funding and contribution schemes, and the degree of funding of a social security system is at the base of the contemporary economic policy debate. An entirely funded system collects contributions of a given cohort (or individual) and invests them, accumulating returns to be used to pay pensions of the generation when they retire. In an unfunded system, such as the pay-as-you-go system (PAYGO), the contributions of the present working generation are used to pay pensions of the generations currently in retirement.

Concerning the contribution scheme, there are two ways in which contributions in a funded scheme result in future benefits. In the defined benefit scheme (DB), the benefit formula defines future pensions on the basis of the history of earnings covered by the plan. In the defined contribution scheme (DC), contributions are channelled into individual accounts and successively invested. Capital gains and returns as well as portfolio value are converted into an annuity when the contributor retires.[1]

Public spending on pensions has become a source of concern for policymakers as, given the PAYGO system in use in most countries, the ageing of a population as measured by the percentage of individuals in working age is declining and is expected to decline even more. As a consequence, public spending for old-age pensions is likely to increase over the next 50 years. Table 16.1 reports the current and projected values to 2050 of the dependency ratio for selected countries. This index is the ratio of the population aged 65 to the working-age population; whereby the table shows a projected dramatic increase in Germany, Italy and Japan.

Obviously, as populations are ageing, the pensions item becomes increasingly relevant for economic systems. Table 16.2 reports OECD simulations over the period 2000–50 assuming unchanged policy parameters. A substantial increase of pension spending as a percentage of GDP is expected in Belgium, the Netherlands, Switzerland and the USA.[2]

The unsustainability of the current path of public spending for pensions has driven the actual need for policy reform. The reform proposal on the tables of governments all around the world is to promote private actions through specialized operators in the financial sector, namely the pension funds (Feldstein, 2005; Hines and Taylor, 2005).[3] According to this proposal, individuals are supposed to choose their pension fund on the basis of its asset allocation policy. Ideally, market efficiency would result from

Table 16.1 Trends in dependency ratios in selected countries

	1960	1990	2030
Canada	13.0	16.7	39.1
France	18.8	20.8	39.1
Germany	16.0	21.7	49.2
Italy	13.3	21.6	48.3
Japan	9.5	17.1	44.5
Sweden	17.8	27.6	39.4
UK	17.9	24.0	38.7
USA	15.4	19.1	36.8

Note: The dependency ratio is the ratio of the population aged over 65 to the working-age population.
Source: UN Population Statistics.

Table 16.2 Old-age pension outlays in selected countries (% of GDP)

	2000	2050
Belgium	9.0	13.0
Canada	4.7	6.4
France	12.1	14.5
Germany	11.8	13.8
Italy	14.2	14.4
Japan	7.9	8.5
Netherlands	5.2	8.3
Sweden	9.2	10.8
Switzerland	7.2	10.8
UK	5.0	5.6
USA	4.4	6.2

Source: OECD (2005a).

pension-fund managers' competition, stimulated by career concerns (Besley and Prat, 2004; Greco, 2005).[4]

As a result of this market opening, the weight of pension funds in the economy and financial markets has considerably increased in recent years.

Table 16.3 Weight of pension funds in the economy and financial markets in selected countries

Countries	Share of GDP (%)		Share of market capitalization (%)	
	2001	2002	2001	2002
Austria	3.9	4.4	29.7	26.8
Belgium	5.6	5.6	7.7	10.8
Canada	51.9	47.6	59.8	60.5
Denmark	27.0	28.6	50.6	64.3
France	3.6	4.0	4.4	9.8
Germany	3.4	3.8	5.8	11.0
Italy	1.8	2.0	3.7	5.1
Netherlands	106.0	99.6	157.4	133.9
New Zealand	14.8	15.1	42.8	41.2
Portugal	12.0	13.4	28.7	37.8
Spain	5.9	–	7.4	–
Sweden	3.8	4.2	3.6	5.7
Switzerland	109.4	125.5	43.0	61.4
UK	73.3	–	48.4	–
USA	66.3	56.9	48.2	53.7
OECD Average[1]	25.8	27.0	32.9	39.1

Note: [1] refers to a sample of 24 OECD countries.
Source: OECD (2005) *Global Pension Statistics Project*.

Table 16.3 shows that pension funds are particularly developed in the USA, the UK, Canada, the Netherlands and Switzerland, whilst they represent a very small share of market capitalization in France, Germany and Italy.

However, it should be stated that reform of the Italian pension system is still ongoing, and thus pension funds have a good development potential. Having this consideration in mind, this chapter aims at analysing the determinants of pension funds underwriting by actual workers and to draw some implications for portfolio management and financial market development. The chapter is organized as follows. In section 16.2 we present a brief outline of the most recent social security reforms in Italy. In section 16.3 an empirical analysis of the determinants of pension funds underwriting is reported, and in section 16.4 we propose some implications for portfolio management and prospects for market development. Finally, section 16.5 summarizes our findings as well as pathways for future reform.

16.2 SOCIAL SECURITY REFORMS IN ITALY

In recent years a number of countries have undertaken reforms to move towards more sustainable pension systems. As Table 16.4 shows, several system parameters have been adjusted in order to take into account the new demographic situation.

Changes have occurred in contribution rates, levels and indexation of benefits and in some cases private pension funds have been set up. Notice that contribution rates are very high in a number of countries, and are not likely to be raised without a reduction in the supply of labor. For this reason, the only credible option is the development of the private sector as discussed in the Introduction to this chapter.

The pension system in Italy was set up in 1969, when a reform turned the system from fully funded to PAYGO. In the late 1980s and the early 1990s, growing concern over the system imbalance led the Amato government to raise the contribution rate by 0.6 percent and to stop pension indexation for six months. The Amato reform also raised the statutory retirement age from 60 to 65 years for men and from 55 to 60 for women.

Later on, the Dini Reform in 1995 introduced the possibility for workers to underwrite pension funds and other forms of complementary pension systems.[5] Later, the Prodi reform abolished seniority pensions for workers having entered the labor force after 1997, and raised the minimum number of contribution years for almost all categories of workers. Finally, when this chapter was being written, the Italian government was to discuss a reform aiming at diverting the "Trattamento di Fine Rapporto – TFR" (a lump-sum transfer to workers at the time of retirement[6]) into pension funds in order to raise future pensions.

Few papers have studied the impact of these reforms on workers' welfare and on the whole economy. Attanasio and Brugiavini (2002) studied the impact of the reduction of pension wealth on private savings consequently to the 1992 reform, and found that the crowding-out effect is about 30–40 percent. Miniaci and Weber (1999) have also found that the 1992 reform magnified the effect of the 1993 recession as consumption fell excessively. Finally, Jappelli, Padula and Bottazzi (2003) carried out an extensive study on the impact of pension system reforms that occurred during the 1990s and found that no significant change occurred in the accumulation of private wealth. They argue that this could be due to the fact that people have not internalized the changes imposed by the reforms.[7]

The 1992 reform introduced tax incentives for contributions in life insurance. This policy innovation was meant to be particularly relevant because of the limited role of pension funds and other instruments to finance retirement and the relevance of life insurance as an investment opportunity for households. However, Jappelli and Pistaferri (2003), by using repeated

Table 16.4 Pension system reforms in selected countries

	Date of the last reform	Mandatory pensions		Public pension benefit[3]	Mandatory private regime	Last major reforms	
		Contribution rate[1]	Replacement rate[2]			Level of DB	Contribution rates
Belgium	1997	16.4	41	DB	No	↓	=
Canada	1997	9.9	43	DB, P	No	=	↑
France	2003	16.5	53	DB	No	↓	↑
Germany	2001	19.5	46	DB	No	↓	↑
Italy	2004	32.7	79	NDC	No	Abolished	=
Japan	2004	18.3	50	DB, NF	No	↓	↑
Netherlands	2004	28.1	68	DB	Quasi	↓	↑
Sweden	1998	18.9	65	NDC	Quasi	Abolished	=
Switzerland	2003	23.8	58	DB	Yes	↓	=
UK	2004	23.8	37	DB	No	=	=
USA	1983	12.4	39	DB, NF	No		=

Notes:[1] Employer's and employee's ones in percent of salary; [2] Gross replacement rate at average earnings in percent; [3] DB: Defined Benefit; NDC: Notional Defined Contribution; NF: Nominally Funded; P: Prefunded.
Source: OECD (2005a).

cross sections on household portfolio composition, could not find any evidence of an increase in the demand for life insurance.

This chapter aims at contributing to the debate on pension system reform in Italy from the viewpoint of pension funds development. To this extent, in the next section we provide some empirical evidence on the determinants of underwriting and on the development potential of those financial instruments.

16.3 EMPIRICAL EVIDENCE ON PENSION FUNDS UNDERWRITING

The data-set used in this chapter is the Survey of Household Income and Wealth (SHIW) published by the Bank of Italy and based on interviews in 2002. This data-set is representative of the Italian household population, and it was collected by stratifying the population into multiple strata paying particular attention to the quality of the data (Banca d'Italia, 2004). The 2002 data-set collects detailed micro data for about 8,011 households and 21,124 individuals on disposable income, consumption, labour market, monetary, financial and demographic variables. The SHIW also provides some sampling weights that reflect the stratification of the sample. At present it is the main data-set for economic analysis at the national level in Italy.[8]

The SHIW data-set is also useful for our aims, as in the questionnaire there is a specific question asking whether the interviewee thinks that the public pension she will receive after her retirement will be sufficient for personal and household needs. As this question is asked only to in-work people, we restrict our attention to this sub-sample only, which comprises 7,404 individuals. Nearly 50 percent of this sub-sample believes that the public pension will not be sufficient for their individual and household needs after retirement, and only 19 percent is instead optimistic about it (Table 16.5).

Table 16.5 "Do you think the public pension will be sufficient for your personal and household needs in the post-retirement period?"

Answer	Frequency	Percent	Cumulative
Yes	1,429	19.30	19.30
No	3,642	49.19	68.49
Don't know	2,333	31.51	100.00
Total	7,404	100.00	

Ideally it would be interesting to know whether interviewees are doing anything to integrate their public pension regardless of answers to previous questions; however SHIW focuses only on those who believe that public pensions will not be enough for future needs. Among these 3,642 individuals, a large portion is not doing or planning to do anything (30%) or is still undecided (21%). What will the remaining 49 percent do? A few of them will invest in real and financial wealth (8%), much more are considering working longer (21%), while the majority will consider joining a pension fund or increase payments to pension funds they have already joined (25%) (Table 16.6). By using the weights provided in SHIW, it is then possible to estimate that at least 4 million Italian workers are planning to invest in pension funds for integrating their public pensions (Table 16.7). This is clearly

Table 16.6 "What do you expect you will do or what have you done to increase your post-retirement income?" (more than one answer is possible)

Answer	Frequency	Percent	Cumulative
Join a pension fund	847	21.89	21.89
Boost payments to the pension funds he/she has already joined	113	2.92	24.81
Defer retirement	67	1.73	26.54
Work after retirement	551	14.24	40.79
Invest in real estate	108	2.79	43.58
Accumulate financial assets (government securities, mutual funds, shares,...)	193	4.99	48.57
Nothing	1,164	30.09	78.65
Don't know	826	21.35	100.00
Total	3,869	100.00	

Table 16.7 The potential demand of pension funds (figures grossed-up to population totals, using SHIW weights)

	Total
Investment in pension fund	2,398,554
Work more	1,660,972
Other real and/or financial investment	563,551
Nothing/other	5,773,390
Total	10,396,467

a conservative estimate, as it does not include those who are optimistic about future public pensions and might still consider investing in pension funds as they are not asked this question, and because some of those who answered "I don't know" might still consider investing in pension funds.

Our next step is to better characterize this potential demand for pension funds. By using SHIW we can provide a descriptive analysis of those who answered the previous questions. First of all, we are interested to understand whether we can draw a picture of those who are more likely to be optimistic about their future public pensions; for example, those who answered that they believe their public pensions will be enough to cope with their household's and their own needs after retirement. As longer contribution period and higher incomes (which imply larger social contributions paid) should be reflected into higher pensions and the public pension expenditure is highly concentrated in the North and in non-agricultural sectors, we might expect that those with higher incomes, longer social contribution history, living in the North and working in sectors other than agriculture would be more likely to be among the more optimistic ones. The model specification we use is as follows:

$$Pr(y = 1 \mid \boldsymbol{x}) = F(\boldsymbol{x}'\boldsymbol{b}) \tag{16.1}$$

where $Pr(y = 1 \mid \boldsymbol{x})$ is the probability that an individual is optimistic about the ability of her public pension to sustain her future needs after retirement ($y = 1$), conditional on individual and household characteristics and a constant ($\boldsymbol{x}$) and F is a given distribution. It is well-known that the model (16.1) can also be written as a latent variable model, where $y = 1$ if the latent variable $y^* = \boldsymbol{x}'\boldsymbol{b} + e > 0$ and $y = 0$ otherwise.[9] This model can provide us with an estimate of the magnitude of each individual and household variable we are considering. Moreover, it can provide an estimate of the effects of variables such as sex, role in the household or job qualification for which we have no clear *a priori* guess. Results are shown in terms of odds ratios, that is $Pr(y = 1 \mid \boldsymbol{x}) / Pr(y = 0 \mid \boldsymbol{x})$, to facilitate interpretation, where $y = 0$ means that the individual believes that her public pension will not be enough for her own and her household needs after retirement.

Assuming that the distribution of F is logistic, the model (16.1) can be easily estimated using SHIW data. Results shows that the spouse of the householder and householder's children are considerably more optimistic that the householder and that the degree of optimism decreases with age and increases with the level of education. The sex of the respondent is not a relevant variable to explain the personal opinion on adequacy of future pensions, and although the sign and magnitude of the area of residence coefficients is reasonable, they are not significantly different from zero at the 90 percent significance level. Sector of activity and job-qualification are indeed significant and consistent with our knowledge of the Italian context.

In particular, people employed in the agricultural sector have over 200 percent smaller probability of expecting a sufficient level of public pension income after retirement and blue-collars are considerably more concerned about their future pensions than better qualified employees. As sole proprietors, members of the arts and professions and other self-employed generally are small contributor to the public pensions systems their expectations are even smaller than blue-collars. Finally, it can be noted that while the number of income earner in the household and the size of the household are not significant variables, the probability of being optimistic about the future public pensions increases, *ceteris paribus*, by 6 percent for every additional year of contributions and by 70 percent for workers in the top income quintile (Table 16.8).

But let us now turn to those who joined a pension fund or are considering increasing their contributions to it. Who are they? It is important to have a better description of these individuals, as this might be useful for targeting future policies. As mentioned earlier, we only know what interviewees do or plan to do to integrate their future public pension provided they declared they expect an insufficient pension income after retirement. This is simply because this question was not asked of everybody in work. In principle, this is a typical problem of selection where only a part of the sample is asked a particular question. Hence, we run a selection model testing whether the outcome and selection equations had correlated error terms, where the selection model was as model (16.1) and the latent outcome equation $Pr(z = 1 \mid \mathbf{h}) = F(\mathbf{h}'\mathbf{g})$ can be interpreted as:

$$z^* = \mathbf{h}'\mathbf{g} + v \quad \text{and } z = 1 \quad \text{if } y^* > 0 \quad \text{and} \quad z = 0 \text{ otherwise} \qquad (16.2)$$

where $Pr(z = 1 \mid \mathbf{h})$ is the probability that an individual is a pension fund underwriter ($z = 1$), conditional on individual and household characteristics and a constant ($\mathbf{h}$) and v is a residual with logistic distribution. As the correlation coefficient of the two error terms, r_{ev}, is not significantly different from zero for any reasonable level of significance, the logit without sample selection delivers the same outcome as the logit with it. Hence, we present estimation results of model (16.2) using only the sub-sample of those who think their public pension will not be sufficient.

Table 16.9 shows that pension fund underwriter is more likely to be male, relatively young, and from the North. Although sector of activity is not a relevant variable, qualifications certainly are: qualified employees have about double the probability of underwriting a pension fund that blue-collars and other job-qualifications between 50 percent and 90 percent. People in two-income households have a significantly larger probability of being pension fund underwriters than one-person households and the larger the income the higher is the probability of being fund underwriters: 40 percent of richer people have a probability of pension fund underwriting that is larger by about 270 percent than the lower quintile.

Table 16.8 Who are those that think that their public pension will be sufficient for personal and household needs after retirement?

Logit estimates Number of observations = 4831

Wald chi2(25) = 353.21

Prob > chi2 = 0.0000

Log pseudo-likelihood = −2526.1798 Pseudo R = 0.1177

Variable	Odds ratio	Robust standard error	z	$Pr > \|z\|$	95% confidence interval	
Householder (HH)	omitted variable					
Spouse of HH	1.413	0.179	2.730	0.006	1.102	1.812
Son/daughter of HH	1.934	0.364	3.500	0.000	1.337	2.798
Other	1.114	0.364	0.330	0.741	0.587	2.114
Age	0.939	0.032	−1.840	0.066	0.879	1.004
Age^2	1.001	0.000	1.780	0.074	1.000	1.001
Education < = 8 yrs	omitted variable					
8 < educ < = 13 yrs.	1.292	0.158	2.100	0.036	1.017	1.641
educ > 13	1.667	0.304	2.800	0.005	1.166	2.384
Male	omitted variable					
Female	1.048	0.121	0.410	0.684	0.836	1.314
North	omitted variable					
Center	0.978	0.120	−0.180	0.855	0.769	1.243
South	0.821	0.099	−1.630	0.103	0.648	1.041
Agriculture	omitted variable					
Industry	2.303	0.555	3.460	0.001	1.436	3.693
Services	3.375	0.861	4.770	0.000	2.047	5.565
Other sector	1.980	0.488	2.770	0.006	1.222	3.208
Blue-collar worker	omitted variable					
Office worker or school teacher	1.421	0.198	2.520	0.012	1.082	1.868
Cadre or manager	2.236	0.496	3.630	0.000	1.447	3.454
Sole proprietor/member of the arts or professions	0.751	0.152	−1.420	0.157	0.506	1.116
Other self-employed	0.484	0.085	−4.120	0.000	0.343	0.684
1 income in household	omitted variable					
2 income in household	1.139	0.145	1.020	0.306	0.888	1.463
3+ income in household	1.009	0.165	0.060	0.954	0.733	1.390

Continued

Table 16.8 Continued

Variable	Odds ratio	Robust standard error	z	$Pr > \|z\|$	95% confidence interval	
Household size	1.096	0.052	1.950	0.051	1.000	1.202
Contribution years	1.060	0.009	6.960	0.000	1.043	1.078
1st income quintile	omitted variable					
2nd income quintile	1.075	0.170	0.460	0.649	0.789	1.464
3rd income quintile	1.302	0.205	1.680	0.093	0.957	1.773
4th income quintile	1.229	0.211	1.200	0.231	0.877	1.721
5th income quintile	1.757	0.349	2.830	0.005	1.190	2.594

Note: All estimates are weighted.

Table 16.9 The odds ratio for joining a pension fund or increasing the contribution to an already opened one

Logistic regression Number of observations = 3422

Wald chi2(26) = 281.18

Prob > chi2 = 0.0000

Log pseudolikelihood = −1691.2781 Pseudo $R2$ = 0.1411

Variable	Odds ratio	Robust standard error	z	$Pr > \|z\|$	95% confidence interval	
Householder (HH)	omitted variable					
Spouse of HH	0.942	0.144	−0.390	0.693	0.698	1.270
Son/daughter of HH	0.666	0.143	−1.900	0.058	0.437	1.014
Other	1.174	0.462	0.410	0.684	0.542	2.541
Eta	0.955	0.010	−4.550	0.000	0.936	0.974
Education < = 8 yrs	omitted variable					
8 < educ < = 13 yrs.	1.450	0.208	2.580	0.010	1.094	1.921
educ > 13	1.261	0.275	1.060	0.288	0.822	1.934
Male	omitted variable					
Female	0.851	0.115	−1.190	0.234	0.652	1.110
North	omitted variable					
Center	0.625	0.089	−3.290	0.001	0.472	0.827

Continued

Table 16.9 Continued

Variable	Odds ratio	Robust standard error	*z*	*Pr* > |*z*|	95% confidence interval	
South	0.344	0.056	−6.570	0.000	0.250	0.472
Agriculture	omitted variable					
Industry	1.613	0.431	1.790	0.073	0.956	2.723
Services	0.954	0.283	−0.160	0.873	0.533	1.707
Other sector	1.504	0.407	1.510	0.131	0.885	2.555
Blue-collar worker	omitted variable					
Office worker or school teacher	2.003	0.353	3.940	0.000	1.418	2.830
Cadre or manager	1.879	0.537	2.210	0.027	1.073	3.289
Sole proprietor/member of the arts or professions	1.893	0.408	2.960	0.003	1.241	2.887
Other self-employed	1.493	0.270	2.220	0.027	1.048	2.127
1 income in household	omitted variable					
2 income in household	1.664	0.264	3.210	0.001	1.219	2.271
3+ income in household	1.132	0.238	0.590	0.554	0.750	1.708
Household size	1.002	0.053	0.040	0.970	0.903	1.112
Household propensity to risk	1.079	0.044	1.870	0.061	0.996	1.169
Ownership share of dwelling	1.002	0.001	1.660	0.097	1.000	1.005
Contribution years	0.986	0.010	−1.500	0.134	0.967	1.004
1st income quintile	omitted variable					
2nd income quintile	1.554	0.286	2.400	0.016	1.084	2.228
3rd income quintile	1.650	0.318	2.600	0.009	1.131	2.407
4th income quintile	2.717	0.565	4.810	0.000	1.808	4.083
5th income quintile	2.698	0.610	4.390	0.000	1.732	4.202

Other household variables, such as its size, are not significant, as well as other household indicators (for example, propensity to risk, defined as financial wealth over real wealth; and ownership share of the dwelling; these are not so relevant and are insignificant).

Having shown the characteristics of potential underwriters and estimated that nearly 4 million workers (nearly 25% of the total working population) plan to underwrite a pension fund, in the next section we draw some implications for market development and asset management policies.

16.4 SOME IMPLICATIONS FOR PORTFOLIO MANAGEMENT OF PENSION FUNDS

Over recent decades, pension funds, mutual funds and insurance companies, that is institutional investors, have increased their share in household portfolios in industrialized countries. At present their share is nearly 40–45 percent on average, whilst in Italy this percentage is only 28 percent (Table 16.10). Notice that the portfolio of Italian households is equally balanced among deposits, bonds, equities and institutions, and that the main difference between Italy and other countries consists in the allocation of assets among bonds, equities and institutions. In particular, because of the lack of information and of the fact that households have not internalised changes in the pension system, saving is not channelled into pension funds but towards instruments such as bonds and equities offering short term return opportunities.

If we consider education to be a proxy of the financial education of an individual and of the information she is able to recover, we have from Table 16.9 that an individual with a university education is more likely to join a pension fund. Consequently, a relatively small percentage of individuals are able to behave in a non-myopic way and invest in pension funds rather than bonds and equities.

In the previous section we have shown that nearly 4 million workers are planning to join a pension fund, thus a considerable share of pension saving

Table 16.10 The composition of household portfolios in selected countries (2003; % of gross financial assets)

	Deposits	Bonds	Equities	Institutions[1]
Belgium	33	18	14	35
Canada	26	4	25	40
France	30	2	25	40
Germany	36	11	10	41
Italy	27	22	22	28
Japan	55	2	8	30
Netherlands	24	4	11	58
Sweden	30	5	18	54
Switzerland	23	8	15	54
UK	26	1	15	54
USA	16	6	18	38

Note:[1] "Institutions" refers to pension funds, insurance corporations and mutual funds.
Source: OECD (2005a).

is likely to be channelled into financial markets. However, as demonstrated by Khorana, Servaes and Tufano (2005) in the case of mutual funds, the increase in the size of the industry depends crucially on the institutional and legal framework, which, in Italy, is still being set up. Uncertainty over regulation and law will negatively affect the development of the sector, leading households to decrease their consumption and increase savings (Gale, 1998; Attanasio and Brugiavini, 2002).

A household's decision to invest in financial instruments is clearly driven by risk-and-return considerations. However, Guiso and Jappelli (2002) show that most of the action is in the decision on whether to invest or not; once the decision is made, the portfolio composition of Italian households accords to standard theories of constant relative risk aversion preferences. The authors argue that the binary decision could be a function of participation and management costs. On this point, Mitchell (1996) reports evidence that administrative costs are major determinants in private pension plan underwriting. Additionally, Besley and Prat (2005) call for an increase in the transparency on total management costs in the industry of pension funds. This point should be considered as of particular interest for Italy as in recent years, because of the Parmalat and Cirio financial scandals, increasing alarm towards banking operations transparency and costs has been expressed by households.

Concerning the risk and return profiles of pension funds, Table 16.11 shows that the structure of assets of Italian pension funds differs from others especially in the very low share of corporate bonds in portfolios and the relatively large share of land and buildings (through real-estate investment trusts and property companies). This implies a low risk–return profile embedded in the funds. Notice that the diversification of the portfolio is clearly a function of the quantitative regulation. As reported in Table 16.12, Italian regulation shows a schizophrenic path as there is no limit on equity and corporate bond investment, whilst a very strict regulation has been set up for real-estate investment and bank deposits. While the limit on bank deposits could be considered as a sort of precaution to avoid eventual underfunding problems (recall that bank deposit have very low or even zero interest rates), it does not seem to be any economic reason for not allowing direct investment in real estate.

Concerning strategic asset allocation, Campbell and Viceira (2005) provide convincing arguments on the fact that there are at least two peculiarities in pension fund asset management:

(a) special attention should be devoted to protect the value of the contributions;

(b) the existence of long-run liabilities should lead managers to measure financial risks over the long run rather than the short run.

Notice that, as a consequence of point (b), several authors and institutions predict an increase in the demand for long-term indexed bonds and annuities

Table 16.11 Structure of assets of pension funds in selected countries (2002; % of total assets)

OECD countries	Cash and deposits	Government bills and bonds	Corporate bonds	Loans	Shares	Land and buildings	Mutual funds	Unallocated insurance contracts	Other investments
Austria	2.0	74.5	–	0.5	13.4	0.4	–	–	9.2
Belgium	4.4	13.6	3.2	0.3	14.6	1.1	55.8	2.6	4.1
Canada	4.9	26.6	0.8	0.8	28.7	4.2	32.8	0.0	1.3
Denmark	0.4	26.8	40.0	0.4	20.0	2.8	6.6	–	3.1
France	–	–	–	–	–	–	–	–	–
Germany	2.3	41.4	–	25.6	15.8	6.4	8.1	–	0.4
Italy	9.1	33.0	0.5	–	5.8	16.4	4.3	15.0	15.9
Netherlands	3.0	0.0	44.0	8.1	37.0	5.0	0.0	0.0	0.0
Portugal	12.0	25.2	23.5	–	16.7	8.6	11.8	–	2.2
Spain[1]	4.7	37.2	20.9	0.0	19.6	0.2	4.3	0.0	13.0
Switzerland	7.1	26.8	–	4.9	26.5	10.5	15.2	–	8.9
UK[1]	2.6	14.5	4.7	0.5	53.8	4.3	11.4	6.2	2.0
USA	10.6	6.5	7.4	0.3	33.1	1.1	24.1	11.2	5.6

Note: [1] 2001 data.
Source: OECD (2005) *Global Pension Statistics Project*.

Table 16.12 Portfolio limits on OECD pension fund investment in selected countries

OECD countries	Equity	Real Estate	Bonds	Investment Funds	Loans	Bank deposits
Austria	50%	20%	No limit	No limit	No limit	No limit
Belgium	No limit (10% if not listed)	No limit	No limit	No limit	No limit	No limit
Canada	No limit	15% if in resource property 25% if real estate and resource property	No limit	No limit	No limit	No limit
Denmark	70%	No limit	No limit	70%	No limit	No limit
Germany	No limit	No limit	No limit	No limit	No limit	No limit
Italy	No limit	Direct investment not allowed	No limit	20%	0%	20%
Netherlands	No limit	No limit	No limit	No limit	No limit	No limit
Portugal	55% but maximum 15% joint limit in non-listed and non-OECD equities and bonds	50%	No limit, % but maximum 15% joint limit in non-listed and non-OECD equities and bonds	No limit	50%	No limit
Spain[1]	No limit	20%	No limit	No limit	20%	No limit
Switzerland	No limit	50% domestic and 5% foreign	No limit		75% mortgage	No limit
UK[1]	No limit	No limit	No limit	No limit	No limit	No limit
USA	No limit	No limit	No limit	No limit	No limit	No limit

Source: OECD (2005b).

(Brown and Poterba, 2004; OECD, 2005a) to support future liabilities with low risk exposure. On this point, the European Investment Bank has been asked by the European Parliament to create a bond having a 25-year maturity.

16.5 CONCLUSION

Social security and pension system reform is currently set on the political agenda of government in almost all industrialized countries. Population ageing and the PAYGO system are seen as the relevant reasons for a dramatic increase in public spending for old-age pensions.

The development of the private sector, as represented by the introduction of pension funds, is actually the most relevant policy option. In fact, the relevance of these institutional investors in terms of share of capital market capitalization is steadily increasing and is expected to increase even more in countries such as Italy, where pension reforms are still ongoing.

In this chapter we have provided some empirical evidence on the determinants of voluntary underwriting of pension funds relying on a large dataset of Italian households and individuals. We have found that the probability to underwrite such an instrument is positively correlated with education and negatively with the age of the worker. The fact that younger workers are more willing to join pension funds is crucial for portfolio management as this situation calls for a long-term investment horizon. The presence of liabilities (in terms of pensions) occurring in the long run will lead the market to demand new instruments, such as long-term indexed bonds, and for a portfolio composition reflecting the constant relative risk aversion of workers. However, tactical asset management is limited by the strict quantity regulation on fund investment, implying limited possibilities for rebalancing strategies over the short run. Notice that this situation could result in short-run underfunding during particular periods (depending on portfolio composition), thus the introduction of insurance instruments would be highly desirable to overcome liquidity problems.

There is substantial room for pension fund industry development and we feel that much work remains to be done in order to provide managers and analysts with appropriate tools for portfolio management and to promote the diffusion of information among workers.

NOTES

1. Besley and Prat (2003) show that in the case of complete contracting, governance is neutral, so that DB and DC private pension plans differ only on risk allocation. If instead, as it is likely, contracting is incomplete, DB should have strict funding requirements. The lack of regulation might be one of the causes of the underfunding of US pension funds in the 1990s (OECD, 2005a; Cooper and Ross, 2002).

2. Sinn (2000) argues that the PAYGO system is not more inefficient than other systems and that the causes of the current imbalance are to be found in the economic and demographic structures of industrialized countries.
3. James, Ferrier, Smalhout and Vittas (1999) conduct an extensive study on the most efficient system to set up and manage individual accounts through pension funds, and find that regulation is crucial for the efficiency of the system.
4. An interesting research topic in the economics of the pension fund industry concerns the role of trustees. Besley and Prat (2003) find that DB should rely less on trustees in the case of incomplete contracting. On the other hand, Kakabadse, Kakabadse and Kouzmin (2003) show that pension fund trustees have an effective and central role in shaping asset management policy and in determining returns.
5. For an analysis of the Dini reform, see Castellino (1995) and Fornero (1995).
6. It should be mentioned that part of pension contributions is channelled into the TFR throughout the working life of an individual.
7. Actually, another (perhaps, complementary) explanation could be the lack of information citizens have, as argued by Boeri and Tabellini (2005) and Boeri, Boersh-Supan and Tabellini (2002).
8. For an analysis of the SHIW and comparison with other Italian data-sets, see Brandolini (1999).
9. For example, see Greene (2003).

REFERENCES

Attansio, O. and Brugiavini, A. (2003) "Social Security and Households Savings", *Quarterly Journal of Economics*, 118(3): 1075–120.

Banca d'Italia (2004), *I bilanci delle famiglie italiane nell'anno 2002*, Vol. XII, *Supplementi al Bollettino Statistico. Note metodologiche e informazioni statistiche*, Banca d'Italia, Rome.

Banks, J. and Emmerson, C. (2000) "Public and Private Pension Spending: Principles, Practice and the Need for Reform", *Fiscal Studies*, 21(1): 1–63.

Besley, T. and Prat, A. (2003) "Pension Funds Governance and the Choice Between Defined Benefit and Defined Contribution Plans", London School of Economics, mimeo.

Besley, T. and Prat, A. (2005) "Credible Pensions", *Fiscal Studies*, 26(1): 119–35.

Boeri, T. and Tabellini, G. (2005) "Does Information Increase Political Support for Pension Reform?", Bocconi Unviersity, IGIER, mimeo.

Boeri, T., Boersch-Supan, A. and Tabellini, G. (2002) "Pension Reforms and the Opinion of European Citizens", *American Economic Association Papers and Proceedings*, 92(2): 396–401.

Brandolini, A. (1999) "The Distribution of Personal Income in Post-war Italy: Source Description, Data Quality, and the Time Pattern of Income Inequality", *Giornale degli Economisti e Annali di Economia*, 58: 183–239.

Brown, J.R. and Poterba, J.M. (2004) "Household Demand for Variable Annuities, Center for Retirement Research at Boston College", CRR Working Paper No. 2004–08.

Campbell, J.Y. and Viceira, L.M. (2005). "Strategic Asset Allocation for Pension Plans", chapter prepared for the *Oxford Handbook of Pensions and Retirement Income* (in press).

Castellino, O. (1995) "Redistribution Between and Within Generations in the Italian Social Security System", *Ricerche Economics*, 49(3): 317–27.

Cooper, R.W. and Ross, T.W. (2002) "Pensions: Theories of Underfunding", *Labour Economics*, 8(4): 667–89.

Diamond, P.A. (1977) "A Framework for the Analysis of Social Security", *Journal of Public Economics*, 8(3): 275–98.

Duesenberry, J.S. (1949) *Income, Saving, and the Theory of Consumer Behavior* (Cambridge, MA: Harvard University Press).

Feldstein, M. (2005) "Structural Reform of Social Security", *Journal of Economic Perspectives*, 19(2): 11–32.

Fornero, E. (1995) "Totally Unfunded vs. Partially Funded Pension Systems: The Case of Italy", *Ricerche Economiche*, 49(3): 357–74.

Gale, W.G. (1998) "The Effects of Pensions on Household Wealth: A Reevaluation of Theory and Evidence", *Journal of Political Economy*, 106(4): 706–23.

Greco, L.G. (2005) "The Optimal Design of Funded Pension Plans: Unbundling Financing and Investment", Econpubblica Working Paper No. 105.

Greene, W.H. (2003) *Econometric Analysis* (Upper Saddle River, NJ: Prentice-Hall).

Guiso, L. and Jappelli, T. (2002) "Household Portfolios in Italy", in L. Guiso, M. Haliassos and T. Jappelli (eds), *Household Portfolios* (Cambridge, MA: MIT Press).

Hall, R.E. (1978) "Stochastic Implications of the Permanent Income Hypothesis: Theory and Evidence", *Journal of Public Economics*, 96(2): 229–57.

Hines, J.R. and Taylor, T. (2005) "Shortfalls in the Long Run: Predictions About the Social Security Trust Fund", *Journal of Economic Perspectives*, 19(2): 1–9.

James, E., Ferrier, G., Smalhout, J. and Vittas, D. (1999) "Mutual Funds and Institutional Investments: What is the Most Efficient Way to Set Up Individual Accounts in a Social Security System?", NBER Working Paper No. 7049.

Jappelli, T. and Pistaferri, L. (2003) "Tax Incentives and the Demand for Life Insurance: Evidence from Italy", *Journal of Public Economics*, 87(6): 1779–99.

Jappelli, T., Padula, M. and Bottazzi, R. (2003) "Retirement Expectations and Pension Reforms", Università degli studi di Salerno, CSEF Working Paper No. 92.

Kakabadse, N., Kakabadse, A. and Kouzmin, A. (2003) "Pension Fund Trustees: Role and Contribution", *European Management Journal*, 21(3): 376–86.

Khorana, A., Servaes, H. and Tufano, P. (2005) "Explaining the Size of the Mutual Fund Industry Around the World", *Journal of Financial Economics*, 78(1): 145–85.

Miniaci, R. and Weber, G. (1999) "The Italian Recession of 1993: Aggregate Implications of Microeconomic Evidence", *Review of Economics and Statistics*, 81(2): 237–49.

Mitchell, O.S. (1996) "Administrative Costs in Public and Private Retirement Systems", NBER Working Paper No. 5734.

OECD (2005a) *Ageing and Pension System Reform: Implications for Financial Markets and Economic Policies* (Paris: OECD).

OECD (2005b) *Survey of Quantitative Investment Regulation of Pension Funds* (Paris: OECD).

Sinn, H.-W. (2000) "Why a Funded Pension System Is Useful and Why It Is Not Useful", *International Tax and Public Finance*, 7(2): 389–410.

CHAPTER 17

Managerial Response to Mutual Fund Performance in the Spanish Market: An Agency Approach

Begoña Torre-Olmo, Carlos López-Gutiérrez and Sergio Sanfilippo Azofra

17.1 INTRODUCTION

The mutual fund market has grown so much over the last decade that we now have a real need for a criterion to evaluate portfolio managers. The mutual fund environment is characterized by asymmetric information, which makes analysing performance difficult, and promotes conflicts of interests about the use of market signals and control mechanisms to minimize agency costs.

In this context, an agency approach makes it possible to study how the positive relationship between fund returns and inflows is affected by an incentive system for managers to maximize participant wealth. Such a mechanism could generate moral hazards in the manager–investor relationship. For example, there might be incentives for managers to increase portfolio risk because they are rewarded on the basis of a fund's year-end return, which is compared to the relative return of the fund globally and its competitors in general.

So in this chapter we study the moral hazards in mutual funds, hazards that determine manager activity in terms of risk-taking behavior, window-dressing, or follow-up of active or passive management strategies. The chapter is organized as follows. Section 17.2 describes the core issue, agency problems between managers and investors. Section 17.3 describes the databases and methodology that we use; section 17.4 presents the results, and section 17.5 concludes.

17.2 AGENCY PROBLEMS ASSOCIATED WITH INFORMATION ASYMMETRIES BETWEEN MANAGERS AND MUTUAL FUND INVESTORS

The continual uncertainty about where information is lacking is the main cause of problems between economic agents. Conflicts of interests can crystallize before or after contract signing.

In the mutual fund market, asymmetric information between managers and participants makes it difficult to evaluate portfolio performance. The degree of competitiveness is also problematic, leading to the introduction of numerous products in the same hazard category, which can cause adverse selection and moral hazard. These problems can be solved by sounding out signals that the market can interpret and accept as control mechanisms.

A peculiar characteristic of mutual funds is the separation required between ownership (the participant) and control (the manager), particularly with respect to limited companies. Mutual funds are not comprised of shares of common stock. Rather, the funds are made up of participants whose objective is to obtain the advantages of collective and professional management, usually a managerial company established as a limited company.

Mutual fund participants hold a co-ownership right, or a series of economic and political rights. The former includes participating in profits derived from portfolio investment, but does not bestow voting rights or the ability to call a board meeting. In other words, if investors disagree with the manager, their only option is to sell their shares.

But the advantage of being able to remove political rights, or attempting to obtain reimbursement with the guarantee of a speedy cash flow, is not sufficient to avoid adverse selection problems. Participants still need to ensure the quality of investments *a priori* in order to minimize agency costs.[1] Here, the imbalances in the financial markets make it difficult to ensure the continuous, generalized presence of quality products. In addition, to evaluate management properly, it is essential to have a great deal of data.

Reduction of agency costs has been fully analysed in the financial literature, as well as the control mechanisms and market signals that act as disciplinary systems and contribute to maximizing asset value. But it is also possible to find these systems in collective investment. Investor decisions can be thought of as signals to the market of management quality, and they can be used, if necessary, as alternatives to knowledge and a thorough, constant monitoring of manager decisions (Ippolito, 1992).

Based on the efficiency hypothesis, it is possible for participants to distinguish between high-quality funds, and low-quality funds. When information is free, the theory of market efficiency implies that the price already incorporates all the information available (Fama, 1970). But if obtaining and applying information is costly, investor transactions occur at prices sufficiently different to compensate them for the cost of acquiring the information (Grossman, 1976; Grossman and Stiglitz, 1980). In this manner, mutual fund returns should at least make up for the commissions and associated costs that a benchmark incurs to be considered a high-quality fund (it would otherwise be considered low-quality).

The development is as follows:

$$E(R_{it}) - R_{ft} = \alpha + \beta(E(R_{mt}) - R_{ft}) + \varepsilon_{it}$$

where $E(R_{it})$ = the expected return of fund i at time t; R_{ft} = the return of the risk-free asset; $E(R_{mt})$ = the expected performance of the benchmark during the period in question; β = the measurement of systematic risk of the mutual fund; α = the parameter that makes it possible to measure portfolio manager skill; and ε_{it} = the residual component of the model.

In this case, Jensen's alpha (α) is a performance measurement. If it is positive and significant, the return obtained by the managers is higher than the return corresponding to the given levels of risk and the sums of commissions charged. If it is negative and significant, the return will be less than we would expect in a balanced state.

The signals that participants send via investment decisions with higher alphas substantiates Ippolito's (1992) hypothesis that the control role played by investors is vital for keeping markets balanced. In theory, this externality also ensures that the lowest-quality portfolios will systematically fall, because it will be impossible to obtain market quotas. This is an illustration of how markets act more or less efficiently and provide the best products over the long term.

Empirical evidence, however, highlights several important issues about the actual behavior of participants. Numerous articles have shown the existence of asymmetric behavior decisions. This means that investors are not penalized quantitatively, by means of capital outflows, to the same extent that they are rewarded via higher levels of investment to the funds that are ranked the highest (Sirri and Tufano, 1993, 1998).

Such behavior worsens the moral hazard problem between managers and participants. Once the fund is undersigned, participants have no way of knowing what actions the manager is taking, apart from whatever information is legally stipulated. Investor action becomes limited to analysing results, and this creates incentives for managers to take on excessive risk. For example, returns for getting the right strategy may be high, but the risk assumed in the event of losses (measured in reimbursements required by the investors) tends to be far less, partly because mutual fund participants on the whole are cautious and resistant to change. Thus if we see that more risky investing has increased during the final months of the year, it may confirm our hypothesis that managers with below-average relative returns in the sector tend to manage risk differently than portfolio managers with higher-than-average returns.

Brown, Harlow, and Starks (1996) analysed the monthly returns of 334 funds from 1976–91. They found that managers who were losers in the first half of the year tended to increase risk in the second half of the year to a greater extent than those considered winners. The authors determined this was done to gain position in the yearly rankings, since this information, and not performance, is what determines the demand for mutual funds in the same given risk category.

Within this context, we can see how managers are motivated to window-dress portfolios, or to take on indiscriminate risks. Likewise, managers may opt to underuse information and resources, and make decisions depending on what the majority do, or attempt to maximize power and prestige by increasing the size of the fund, even if it sacrifices investor objectives (see Table 17.1).

There are several mechanisms by which to minimize the divergence of interest between owners and managers, however. In the literature, they are classified into two groups: those that are internal to the company, and those that are external. The former include manager compensation systems, mutual control systems, and the board of directors and decision-making hierarchies. The latter include independent councils, capital markets, the company control market, and the markets for debt, managers, products and services.

When evaluating mutual fund managers, the underlying problems of moral hazard are no less serious than in any other type of contractual relationship. However, the possibilities of conflict are more limited, which lessens the need to analyze all the aligning mechanisms we refer to here (Berkowitz and Kotowitz, 1993).

The absence of debt, for example, restricts analysis of the relationship between investor and manager, thus removing the possibility of controlling manager behavior in terms of the capital structure. On the other hand, the relationship of the manager as a limited company, with investors and rights, is exclusively that of managing a collective patrimony. But share concentration or alignment of interests is not achieved by means of wages or of shares or options, since, legally, those are restricted activities.

Table 17.1 Conflict of interest between managers and investors in mutual funds

Conflict	Description	Contributions
Assuming excessive risk	Managers who find that their portfolios are low ranking in the initial return analyses tend to take on greater risks in the latter months to compensate	Berkowitz and Kotowitz (1993) Brown, Harlow, and Starks (1996) Chevalier and Ellison (1997) Busse (2001) Taylor (2003)
Actions en masse, or herd mentality	Because reputation is so important in the market, managers tend to imitate other managers' investment decisions, even to the extent of ignoring private information they may have that might increase asset value	Scharfstein and Stein (1990) Lakonishok, Shleifer, and Vishny (1992) Zwiebel (1995) Grinblatt, Titman, and Wermers (1995)
Window-dressing	Managers seek to "window-dress" the portfolio at year-end in order to maintain their reputation and take advantage of market seasonality	Haugen and Lakonishok (1988) Lakonishok, Shleifer, Thaler and Vishny (1991) Amutio (1995)
Size effect	Using the scale economy argument, managers tend to increase portfolio size	Gorman (1991) Alvarez (1995) Jans and Otten (2005)

One arm of the financial literature analyses the influence a compensatory incentive system can have on returns.[2] A contract between a principal and an agent under an incentives system that establishes a delegation of power from the former to the latter ends up becoming, at least for portfolio management, a quasi-generalized formulization of the salary mechanism, as follows:

$$SALARY = K_f \mathrm{A} + K_v \mathrm{A}\,(R_p - R_I)$$

where K_f = the quota of the fixed salary; A = the asset on which the salary is based; K_v = the quota of the variable salary; R_p = the portfolio return; R_I = the benchmark return; and $(R_p - R_I)$ = the output.

The model proposed by Golec (1988) is applicable to mutual fund management given how costly it is to continuously monitor managers' actions and how difficult it can be to discern how much of the return is attributable to manager skill, and how much to luck. This difficulty may, in fact, limit the effectiveness of this type of wage system. For this reason, the variable remuneration plan depends not only on portfolio returns but also on comparison to a benchmark.

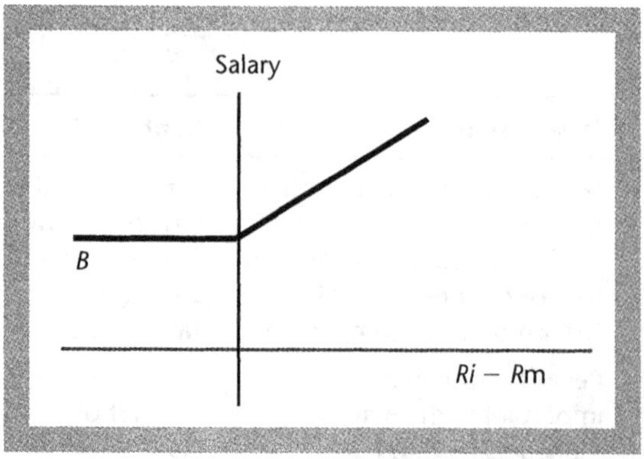

Figure 17.1 Salary of the manager as the value of a call
Source: Grinblatt and Titman (1989).

However, profit is not usually the only determinant of manager compensation. Many companies link remuneration to share price, and they deliver a part or options as an incentive to maintain their share price above a certain point for the financial year. In the case of mutual funds, it is also possible to relate managerial actions to options contracts. We assume that managers with the best past results will tend to receive higher capital flows even when they obtain worse results (for example, the market does not penalize the losers to the same degree that it rewards the winners). So the decisions made by a portfolio manager can be replicated with a liquidating mechanism on a purchase option where the wage system depends directly on the asset's return in terms of a benchmark (see Figure 17.1).

This similarity between manager salary and the value of a call option derives from the existence of a lower limit on the total salary, the base salary plus an "award" established in terms of the excess return obtained by the fund on the benchmark, so that:

$$SALARY = B + max\,[0, m(Ri - Rm)]$$

where B = base salary; m = percentage received by the manager as an award or bonus based on the difference between the mutual fund return and the benchmark return; R_i = the return of the portfolio that comprises the mutual fund; and R_m = the return of the benchmark.

In summary, this compensation mechanism can be compared to an option. The convexity of a lower limited salary mechanism provides incentives to managers to alter their portfolios' risk in order to maximize salary without considering investor preferences (see Grinblatt and Titman, 1987, 1989; Kritzman, 1987; Starks, 1987). For managers who have obtained poor partial results or simply wish to increase their variable wages, portfolio relative risk may be increased. Conversely, managers who have attained high returns tend to maintain or even reduce their volatility.

Following the variable wage trend, in the 1980s, a field of research came about under the agency theory on the underlying economic stimuli in certain sports competitions and the motivations they could generate in participants.[3] Many entrepreneurial organizations have committed themselves to similar salary-oriented mechanisms, where salary depends not only on skill, but also on relative return, the aim being to do it well, but also to do it better than the rest.

Similar studies based on Brown, Harlow and Starks (1996) have found differing results, especially in what is referred to as the tournament hypothesis in mutual funds (Jans and Otten, 2005). Busse (2001), using daily data from 1985–95 for 230 mutual funds, found that the funds ranked above the median increased in risk more than the below-median funds.

Taylor (2003) attempts to reconcile these seemingly contradictory results by introducing a more formal two-period tournament model. All previous studies assume that managers treat competing managers as exogenous benchmarks. Taylor (2003) extends this reasoning and hypothesizes that managers also consider the actions of other managers. The model is, therefore, based on strategic interaction between active fund managers. In this game, the winner expects the loser to increase risk (based on the tournament hypothesis), and the winner also increases risk to maintain the lead. Taylor (2003) shows that, in equilibrium, the winner is more likely to increase risk than the loser. Therefore, results that were previously interpreted as evidence against the tournament hypothesis may be explained as strategic behavior.

Recently, Goriaev, Nijman and Werker (2001, 2005) noted two potential biases that could influence all previous work: first-order autocorrelation, and the assumption that mutual fund returns are cross-sectionally independent. The authors found that tests of the tournament hypothesis using monthly data were more robust to autocorrelation than tests using daily data. Furthermore, they showed that cross-correlated fund returns did not necessarily invalidate the previous tournament tests. The idiosyncratic fund returns in a factor model should, however, be uncorrelated.

Nonetheless, the application of this method is not always possible, so it is necessary to study the conditions under which a salary-oriented system based on relative profitabilities can minimize the moral risk problems generated by the lack of control (Green and Stokey, 1983; Nalebuff and Stiglitz, 1983). These conditions include the existence of a high number of agents whose actions are not observable, and a common component that generates results. These features are satisfied by the investment fund market, where a group of portfolio managers competes to attain maximum profitability in a common scenario, the economic environment, and with the same transaction mechanisms and capital markets where financial assets are negotiated.

In effect, mutual fund management is an ongoing competition, given the frequency of publications and rankings. These become qualifying heats in a tournament, where funds compete in a common economic environment, and where, at the end of the year, it is possible to rank results. The winning funds end up garnering more investment in the future.

Apart from the internal supervisory mechanisms based on incentives, though, there is also a series of external mechanisms that can reduce managerial discretion. For example, in the labor market, the fee that managers earn depends on their prestige (Fama, 1970). In the capital market, share prices remove the possible consequences of managerial actions (Fama and Jensen, 1983a and 1983b). The consumer market can be seen as a mechanism that hinders the survival of companies that do not offer their clients the most sought-after products.

In the mutual funds market, the aim of the managing company is acquisition, ownership, administration, and transfer of goods, values, and other financial assets. So the labor market is therefore the most important, since the rotation of managers serves a disciplinary function as well as a vital information function.

Our hypothesis is whether a direct relationship exists between the profitability obtained by a portfolio manager and his job security. This hypothesis is contrasted by Khorana (1996), who found that managers attained below-average profitability for an average of two years before being replaced. Nevertheless, we consider the return immediately prior to the month the manager is replaced to be the most significant determinant.

Given the relationship between performance and losing one's job, we posit that managers who have performed poorly during the year may be motivated to alter the makeup of their portfolio toward the end of the year in an attempt to increase their performance. In doing so, they may be motivated to churn assets and temporarily conceal low portfolio yields by window-dressing. This behavior may in fact seem logical if a portfolio manager is evaluated in relationship to a group of managers. As the theory of herd mentality notes, managers may tend to imitate other managers' investment decisions from a desire not to stand out. They may even end up ignoring valuable private information they may have that could increase asset value (see Table 17.1).

We find that portfolios whose managers have recently been replaced often have a very high asset rebalancing rate in proportion to the total sample. Inevitably, they also have high management costs. Furthermore, we still theorize that managers approaching their evaluation may take on excessive levels of risk by leveraging their portfolios, in a last effort to generate positive returns and compensate for accumulated losses.

In summary, based on the theoretical background outlined above, our hypothesis for the Spanish market is: The existence of asymmetric information leads to indiscriminate risk-taking by mutual fund managers as a response to regular evaluations of mutual funds.

Table 17.2 Growth in the number of funds

Year	Number of funds
1992	84
1993	98
1994	95
1995	144
1996	174
1997	200
1998	304
1999	414
2000	493
2001	622
2002	653
2003	620

17.3 DATA AND METHODOLOGY

Our empirical data cover the period 1992–2003 for a sample of growth-oriented funds, including portfolios that have maintained a more risky style each year (Table 17.2). We obtain the availability of net asset values and size from the Madrid Stock Exchange and the National Values Market Commission.

Our hypothesis is expressed as follows:

$$(\sigma_{2L}/\sigma_{1L}) > (\sigma_{2W}/\sigma_{1W}) \tag{17.1}$$

$$RAR_L > RAR_W$$

where RAR = the risk adjustment ratio between the second and third period of the year; L = the partial losers; W = the partial winners; σ_1 = the volatility in the first period; and σ_2 = the volatility in the second period.

In order to verify equation (17.1), we define the following variables. First, for each year studied, we create subgroups of partial winners and losers in accordance with the relative return of each mutual fund between January and month M (June and September[4]). In particular, for each fund "j" in year "y," we calculate the cumulative monthly yield as follows:

$$RTN_{jMy} = [(1 + r_{j1y})(1 + r_{j2y})\ldots(1 + r_{jMy})] - 1 \tag{17.2}$$

where r_j = the return of fund j (measured by the difference of net asset values, including dividends); and M varies between June and September, for example, the accumulated return (RTN_{jy}) for six and nine months.

We classify winners or losers depending on whether their returns lie above or below the RTN average.[5] We next construct a ratio to measure the relationship of the volatility of each investment j for each year y before and after the "first partial" (RAR_{jy}):

$$RAR_{jy} = \sqrt{\frac{\sum_{m=M+1}^{12} \left(r_{jmy} - \bar{r}_{j(12-M)y}\right)^2}{(12-M)-1}} \div \sqrt{\frac{\sum_{m=1}^{M} \left(r_{jmy} - \bar{r}_{jMy}\right)^2}{M-1}} \qquad (17.3)$$

Empirically, we expect RAR_{jy} to be greater for funds classified as losers in month M than for winners. Once the variables are calculated, we create a pair (RTN_{jy}, RAR_{jy}) for each fund and each year. We then create a contingency table to examine the relationship.

17.4 RESULTS

In accordance with our initial aim, we relate the returns (RTN_{jy}) of the funds in the sample, where we can assess the first partial results, with managers' tendency to take on more risk to compensate for adverse historic returns and obtain higher year-end rankings. Each fund is classified as a winner or a loser depending on (1) whether its accumulated daily return (RTN_{jMy}) until June and September is above or below average, and (2) whether it is high volatility or low volatility, depending on whether the adjusted portfolio risk between the first and second periods of the year exceeds the average of the sample (RAR_{jy}).

We therefore expect a negative relationship between the loser funds in accumulated profitability at the end of June and September, and the risk taken on by these portfolios. The contrast of Pearson's chi-square allows us to note whether the relationship between RTN_{yt} and RAR_{yt} is statistically significant. The results are shown in Table 17.3.

In summary, for our study period of 1992–2003, we confirm the existence of a significant relationship in June and September between the return of the initial months and the risk taken on by the managers in the latter part of the year (that is, the tournament hypothesis). In the temporary analyses, however, we note some differences.

For September, the relationship is clear from 1996 to 2000, years of high growth in risky funds in Spain. This period also saw an increase in competition, which coincided with an upward trend in the stock market. This

Table 17.3 Contrasts between chi-square and Spearman's rho

	Sample frequency					
	Low RTN		High RTN			
	Low RAR	High RAR	Low RAR	High RAR	Chi square	Spearman's rho
			Panel A: June			
All years	***30.1***	***19.7***	***24.5***	***25.8***	***21.526****	***−0.117****
1992	19.05	47.62	13.10	20.24	0.392	0.002
1993	30.61	15.31	18.37	35.71	19.492***	−0.052***
1994	26.32	22.11	20.00	31.58	4.795**	−0.036
1995	27.08	31.94	25.69	15.28	5.15**	−0.032
1996	38.51	13.79	11.49	36.21	19.119***	−0.053**
1997	31.4	19.6	27.5	21.6	101.023***	−0.071**
1998	20.9	29.6	27.0	22.6	1.949	0.130
1999	31.4	18.8	33.8	15.9	68.002***	−0.057***
2000	30.2	19.8	25.0	25.0	2.756*	−0.105*
2001	24.4	25.7	22.8	27.0	0.264	−0.029
2002	28.0	20.8	31.1	20.1	0.362	0.034
2003	40.5	9.7	10.4	39.5	110.771***	−0.599***
			Panel B: September			
All Years	***26.8***	***23.2***	***24.1***	***25.9***	***4.479****	***−0.053****
1992	7.14	45.24	13.10	34.52	1.496	−0.059
1993	31.63	11.22	15.31	41.84	6.416**	−0.058**
1994	30.53	22.11	23.16	24.21	1.699	−0.030
1995	28.47	26.39	27.08	18.06	2.272	−0.113**
1996	28.74	27.59	18.97	24.71	11.815***	−0.282***
1997	21.2	28.8	26.9	23.1	90.063***	−0.631***
1998	26.7	23.3	33.6	16.4	2.306	0.141
1999	36.5	13.5	17.8	32.2	29.471***	−0.376***
2000	19.8	30.2	33.1	16.9	17.621***	−0.267***
2001	24.4	25.7	22.8	27.0	0.264	−0.029
2002	17.1	32.9	30.2	19.8	22.617***	−0.263***
2003	38.1	11.9	16.5	33.5	58.399***	−0.434***

Notes: ***Denotes significance at the 1% level; **denotes significance at the 5% level; and *denotes significance at the 10% level.

explains the results obtained for 1993, a year that coincided with a general rise in the stock exchange (from October 1992 to January 1994), and, more recently, for the two-year period of 2002–03.

For these years, the chi-square values are high, with bilateral significance greater than 1 percent. This leads us to reject the null hypothesis and accept the alternative hypothesis of a statistically significant relationship between fund returns in the first part of the year, and volatility in the second part of the year.

Nevertheless, we find that 1998 was an anomalous year, with an upward trend during the final quarter, following the national and international debt crisis. Managers appear to have safeguarded returns accumulated in the first part of year, without taking on excessive risk. Therefore, we reject the alternative hypothesis, and accept the null hypothesis regarding the lack of relationship between the *RTN* and *RAR* variables.

Note also the loss of significance in 1995, which is confirmed in June. Despite a market recovery, the appearance of guaranteed funds (which guarantee participants a preset return) influenced the demand toward these portfolios.

For June, the results are less uniform, and the tournament hypothesis is confirmed in some years but not in others. This generally coincides with the stock market results. In 1992, 2001 and 2002, the contrast is barely significant, which confirms the significance of the market trend followed by portfolio managers in assuming risks (the Spanish market was falling until August 2002). Under adverse conditions, it is easier for managers to find low-risk investments, since their focus is more on mitigating losses in a downward-trending market than on beating the competition.

In 1994, a marked decrease occurred in both the debt markets and the stockmarket. This had repercussions for fund development, and changed the increasing trend because of its size and return. The change was more notable for variable-income and fixed-income investors, as in Table 17.1. Such results explain the reduction in fund size from the second half of 1994. Although the market began to recover after mid-1995, investors reacted by shying away from risky investments.

Finally, in 1992, the chi-square statistic was very low, which indicates the minimum probability of finding values lower or equal to the value obtained in our sample. Therefore, we should accept the null hypothesis of the lack of any relationship between *RTN* and *RAR*. This lack of connection may be because this was the beginning of our analysis, and it coincided with the beginning of the explosive growth in the mutual fund market. It may be that the higher interest rates, lower competition from collective investment, lack of awareness of these financial instruments, and even lack of attractive stocks available on the exchange at the time justified the fact that risk was not a differential factor in manager behavior.

Nevertheless, the chi-square contrast only shows whether the relationship between the variables is statistically significant. It does not provide the sign. In order to verify whether the relationship between the first partial return of the year and risk in the second part of the year is positive or negative, we apply the correlation coefficient between Spearman ranges that responds to the following formula. The null hypothesis refers to the non-association between the variables:

$$r = 1 - \frac{6\sum_{i=1}^{n} D_i^2}{N(N^2 - 1)} \tag{17.4}$$

where N = the number of pairs of observations; and D = the difference between the degrees of corresponding values of the related variables.

The value of this coefficient varies in the same manner as the linear correlation coefficient, from -1 to 1. A positive value indicates a relationship in the same sense between the variables. A negative value indicates an inverse relationship.

The results show an inverse, significant relationship in almost all the comparisons, except for those months where the relationship between *RTN* and *RAR* was not significant by contingency analysis. This confirms our hypothesis about the possibilities of moral hazard in the manager-participant relationship in mutual funds. The latter, in the case of loser funds or those with below-average initial returns, tended to increase risk in the second part of the year.

17.5 CONCLUSION

The dramatic growth of the investment fund market can create conflicts of moral risk in the manager–investor relationship. Managers may fail to provide adequate portfolio management because their success or failure does not depend on their own actions but rather on relative returns in terms of the market. In this regard, we hypothesize that managers who realize that their year-end results will be below average have an incentive to increase portfolio risk indiscriminately. This may be manifested by more volatility in the second part of the year for funds with below-average partial results.

Our results confirm that the loser funds tended to show an increase in volatility, and were subsequently ranked high volatility. This trend, however, is seen more clearly during the upward-trending periods in the Spanish stockmarket, during the period we analyse and as the number of risky funds increased. Thus competition has been increased by capturing market quotas, and by endeavoring to obtain maximum returns even at the expense of satisfying investor objectives. The September results are also more relevant, and, generally, the analyses are similar to those noted for other markets.

This managerial behavior is caused by the need to achieve the best results. Participants tend to choose funds in terms of their most recent profitability. Note also that manager prestige, a part of their wages, and even their job security depends on market reactions.

However, managers may be tempted to take on risk indiscriminately because of the asymmetrical behavior that we find characterizes mutual fund participant decisions. In effect, higher-returning funds are rewarded by higher future levels of investment. But the reverse does not occur to the same degree for lower-returning funds. Thus managers are already aware that participants tend not to penalize for increasing risk if the strategy fails to the same extent they will reward if it is successful.

NOTES

1. In Spain, these agency costs have increased because of the provisional "captivity" to which mutual fund participants have been subject if they wish to enjoy the tax advantages of this type of product. According to current legislation, Law 35/2003, 4 November, however, this captivity has disappeared.
2. See Kritzman (1987), Starks (1987), Grinold and Rudd (1987), Grinblatt and Titman (1987 and 1989), Cohen and Starks (1988) and Golec (1992).
3. Concentration of awards is a way of solving the problem of moral hazard in some elite sports competitions. The process is a long one, the hurdles must be overcome one by one, and the best performers must be encouraged to continue to try their hardest. It is important that the incentive is representative (the yields should be on the rise), so as to compensate for the additional risk (effort). If the awards are shared equally, once a very high level of effort is reached, there would naturally be a downward trend. See Lazear and Rosen (1981), Nalebuff and Stiglitz (1983), Green and Stokey (1983), Dye (1984), Rosen (1986), Bull, Schotter and Weigelt (1987), McLaughlin (1988) and Ehrenberg and Bognanno (1990).
4. The National Values Market Commission draws up the Quarterly Reports on the Collective Investment Institutes from data sent by the managing companies the month following the close of each natural quarter. These reports are included in the Register and are available to the public, which is a further protection for investors, because this official body oversees the quarterly reports before they are included in the register. If any irregularities are found, the managing company must provide clarification. Therefore, investors have reliable information on investment growth at the end of March, June, September and December. We choose June and September to calculate the partial profitability results because (1) June is the halfway point, and (2) September is the last month for which data are officially published before annual closures, and there are still three months to make portfolio corrections.
5. Similar articles have classified funds in other ways besides "winners"or "losers". In order to provide more information and verify other hypotheses such as the influence of size or the age of the fund in more or less aggressive manager behavior, Brown, Harlow and Starks (1996) segment samples into quartiles depending, for example, on size. The more classification intervals there are, however, the broader-based the samples need to be to ensure the contingency tables contain enough events to guarantee the reliability of the analysis.

REFERENCES

Alvarez, J. (1995) "Análisis de los Fondos de Inversión de Renta Fija en España", *Investigaciones Económicas*, 19(3): 475–88.

Amutio, G. (1995) "Puede el Maquillaje de Carteras Explicar el Efecto Enero?", *Análisis Financiero*, 66(1): 20–34.

Berkowitz, M.K. and Kotowitz, Y. (1993) "Incentives and Efficiency in the Market Form Management Services: A Study of Canadian Mutual Funds", *Canadian Journal of Economics*, 26(4): 850–66.

Brown, K., Harlow, W. and Starks, L. (1996) "Of Tournaments and Temptations: An Analysis of Managerial Incentives in the Mutual Fund Industry", *The Journal of Finance*, 51(1): 85–110.

Bull, C., Schotter, A. and Weigelt, K. (1987) "Tournaments and Piece Rates: An Experimental Study", *Journal of Political Economy*, 95(1): 1–33.

Busse, J.A. (2001) "Another Look at Mutual Fund Tournaments", *Journal of Financial and Quantitative Analysis*, 36(1): 53–73.

Chevalier, J. and Ellison, G. (1997) "Risk Taking by Mutual Funds as a Response to Incentives", *Journal of Political Economy*, 105(6): 1167–200.

Cohen, S.I. and Starks, L.T. (1988) "Estimation Risk and Incentive Contracts for Portfolio Managers", *Management Science*, 34(9): 1067–79.

Dye, R. (1984) "The Trouble with Tournaments", *Economic Inquiry*, 22(1): 147–9.

Ehrenberg, R. and Bognanno, L. (1990) "Do Tournaments Have Incentive Effects?", *Journal of Political Economy*, 98(6): 1307–24.

Fama, E. (1970) "Efficient Capital Markets: A Review of Theory and Empirical Work", *Journal of Finance*, 25(1): 383–417.

Fama, E. and Jensen, M.C. (1983a) "Separation of Ownership and Control", *Journal of Law and Economics*, 26(2): 301–25.

Fama, E. and Jensen, M.C. (1983b) "Agency Problems and Residual Claimants", *Journal of Law and Economics*, 26(2): 327–49.

Golec, J.H. (1988) "Do Mutual Fund Managers Who Use Incentive Compensation Outperform Those Who Don't?", *Financial Analysts Journal*, 44(6): 75–8.

Golec, J.H. (1992) "Empirical Tests of a Principal–Agent Model of the Investor–Investment Advisor Relationship", *Journal of Financial and Quantitative Analysis*, 27(1): 81–95.

Goriaev, A.P., Nijman, T.E. and Werker, B.J.M. (2001) "On Empirical Evidence of Mutual Fund Strategic Risk Taking", *Center for Economic Research*, Discussion Paper 09: 1–13.

Goriaev, A.P., Nijman, T.E. and Werker, B.J.M. (2005) "Yet Another Look at Mutual Fund Tournaments", *Journal of Empirical Finance*, 12(1): 127–37.

Gorman, L. (1991) "A Study of the Relationship Between Mutual Fund Return and Asset Size, 1974–1987", *Akron Business and Economic Review*, 22(4): 53–61.

Green, J.R. and Stokey, N.L. (1983) "A Comparison of Tournaments and Contracts", *Journal of Political Economy*, 91(3): 349–64.

Grinblatt, M. and Titman, S. (1987) "How Clients Can Win the Gaming Game", *Journal of Portfolio Management*, 13(4): 14–20.

Grinblatt, M. and Titman, S. (1989) "Adverse Risk Incentives and the Design of Performance-Based Contracts", *Management Science*, 15(7): 807–22.

Grinblatt, M., Titman, S. and Wermers, R. (1995) "Momentum Investment Strategies, Portfolio Performance, and Herding: A Study of Mutual Fund Behavior", *American Economic Review*, 85(5): 1088–105.

Grinold, R. and Rudd, A. (1987) "Incentive Fees: Who Wins? Who Loses?", *Financial Analysts Journal*, 43(1): 27–38.

Grossman, S. (1976) "On the Efficiency of Competitive Stock Markets Where Traders Have Diverse Information", *Journal of Finance*, 31(2): 573–85.

Grossman, S. and Stiglitz, J. (1980) "On the Impossibility of Informationally Efficient Markets", *American Economic Review*, 70(3): 393–408.

Haugen, A. and Lakonishok, J. (1988) *The Incredible January Effect: The Stock Market's Unsolved Mystery* (New York: McGraw-Hill).

Ippolito, R.A. (1992) "Consumer Reaction to Measures of Poor Quality: Evidence from the Mutual Fund Industry", *Journal of Law and Economics*, 35(1): 45–70.

Jans, R. and Otten, R. (2005) "Tournaments in the UK Mutual Fund Industry", *EFMA Annual Meeting 2005.*

Jensen, M.C. (1968) "The Performance of Mutual Funds in the Period 1945–1964", *The Journal of Finance*, 23(2): 389–416.

Khorana, A. (1996) "Top Management Turnover: An Empirical Investigation of Mutual Fund Managers", *Journal of Financial Economics*, 40(3): 403–27.

Kritzman, M. (1987) "Incentive Fees: Some Problems and Some Solutions", *Financial Analysts Journal*, 43(1): 21–6.

Lakonishok, J., Shleifer, R., Thaler, R. and Vishny, R. (1991) "Window Dressing by Pension Fund Managers", *American Economic Review*, 81(2): 227–32.

Lakonishok, J., Shleifer, A. and Vishny, R. (1992) "The Impact of Institutional Trading on Stock Prices", *Journal of Financial Economics*, 32(1): 23–43.

Lazear, E. and Rosen, S. (1981) "Rank Order Tournaments as Optimum Labor Contracts", *Journal of Political Economy*, 89(3): 841–64.

Mclaughlin, K. (1988) "Aspects of Tournament Models: A Survey", *Research in Labor Economics*, 9(1): 225–56.

Nalebuff, B. and Stiglitz, J. (1983) "Prizes and Incentives: Towards a General Theory of Compensation and Competition", *Bell Journal of Economics*, 14(1): 21–43.

Rosen, S. (1986) "Prizes and Incentives in Elimination Tournaments", *The American Economic Review*, 76(4): 701–15.

Scharfstein, D. and Stein, J.C. (1990) "Herd Behavior and Investment", *American Economic Review*, 80(3): 465–79.

Sirri, E. and Tufano, P. (1993) "Buying and Selling Mutual Funds: Flows, Performance, Fees, and Services", Working Paper, Harvard University.

Sirri, E. and Tufano, P. (1998) "Costly Search and Mutual Fund Flows", *The Journal of Finance*, 53(5): 1589–622.

Starks, L. (1987) "Performance Incentive Fees: An Agency Theoretic Approach", *Journal of Financial and Quantitative Analysis*, 22(1): 17–32.

Taylor, K. (2003) "Risk-Taking Behaviour in Mutual Fund Tournaments", *Journal of Economic Behaviour and Organization*, 50(3): 373–83.

Zwiebel, J. (1995) "Corporate Conservatism and Relative Compensation", *Journal of Political Economy*, 103(1): 1–25.

CHAPTER 18

Analysis of Mutual Fund Demand in the Spanish Market

Begoña Torre-Olmo, Carlos López-Gutiérrez and Sergio Sanfilippo Azofra

18.1 INTRODUCTION

The globalization of today's economy has led to a renewed interest in financial systems that can explicate the differences in the evolution of market-based and bank-based systems.[1] In market-based systems, a legal separation is made between the typical commercial banking activity of resource-building, loan-granting and credit risk, and the development of activities such as stock-brokerage operations, wealth management, and assessing takeovers and acquisitions, which are carried out by other entities known as business or investment banks.

In contrast to the market concept of financial intermediation, which is predominant in the USA and the UK, another idea has emerged: the universal bank, in which one institution provides all the services. Within this bank-based system, any specialization that exists is not a consequence of legislation, but rather of the banking entity's own strengths and preferences.

The evolution of financial systems over the last few decades is closely linked to financial innovation, one of the most important phenomena seen in financial activity over the last twenty years. This process has manifested itself in the creation of new products, in the development of new processes, and in the appearance of new intermediaries and markets.

The papers published on this subject[2] have attempted to explain the factors that have given rise to it, and its effects on the stability and efficiency of the financial system. Two main perspectives prevail. One suggests that the desire to avoid banking regulations and fiscal pressure has motivated financial innovation (Silber, 1983; Miller, 1986 and 1991). The other suggests that the introduction of financial instruments is the essence of the innovation, because they can distribute risk between participants and the market more efficiently.

In this sense, financial innovation takes place as a response to the profit opportunities arising from the inadequacy of the existing financial intermediation and/or an incomplete market (Van Horne, 1985). But the relationship between innovation and the evolution of the most representative financial systems needs to be verified. Thus, the main underlying message (see for example Boot and Thakor, 1993b, 1996) is that when financial activity is aimed at the market, new innovations are looked on more favorably than when the allocation of resources is intermediated.

This is because the two types of financial systems are based on different philosophies of how risk is distributed among investors. Models with a greater level of intermediation are characterized by a better distribution over time because they can buffer the consequences of sudden market changes. However, in systems aimed at the capital markets, it is possible to distribute this risk more widely, depending on how great the opportunities are for diversification and distribution. This promotes innovation and the development of new markets.

The clearest recent manifestations of this financial innovation are found in deregulation and disintermediation. Deregulation can both hinder and encourage the growth of new financial alternatives. Excessive regulation may on the one hand prevent the development of innovations in the financial system. But, in an attempt to avoid restrictions, it may give rise to innovations as byproducts of the legislation.

This is what has happened with the development of off-balance-sheet services, which account for a great number of financial innovations and are a sign of the new composition of the banking business. Among the off-balance-sheet services provided, mutual funds have made especially large contributions to efficiency improvements in financial systems by allowing a reduction in transaction costs.

The recent boom in mutual funds has highlighted the need to demarcate and compare explanatory models of investor behavior in these financial instruments. Mutual funds can be studied from either a macro- or a microeconomic viewpoint. The macroeconomic approach views mutual fund demand as the choice of one financial instrument over the other available alternatives; the microeconomic approach focuses on how funds compete with each other to attract investor savings. In order to examine this phenomenon more fully, we aim to determine what factors are most important to investors when they decide to participate in mutual funds in the Spanish market.

A priori, we consider that the decision criteria should center on rational capital market principles, so that investment strategies can be in line with the binomial of risk-adjusted return. In this regard, most research is focusing on the issue of mutual funds, and on analysing evaluation techniques in portfolio management and the problems that may arise.[3] The results, to a large extent, point to the need for efficient markets, and do not justify an active portfolio management strategy, since, in global terms; funds are incapable of overcoming the yields of an index portfolio. Such results contrast with the growth in size of these financial instruments, leading to what Gruber (1996) has termed the puzzle of mutual funds.

It is obvious that the advantages of collective investment for the small investor come from combining resources to set up a portfolio that is large enough to be efficiently managed by a team of professionals. The greater volume is what makes it possible to diversify risk and take advantage of scale economies. Large-scale investors gain access more easily and at a lower cost.

However, why are certain investment products continually chosen over others? This is particularly puzzling against the background of the theory of market efficiency, since there may be similar-risk products available with more active management backed by past successes. In this regard, research has analyzed investor behavior when determining their demand for mutual funds. Note that investor attitudes do not always respond to the criteria of economic rationality, since investors often appear to pay more attention to the potential return than to any risk involved. The appearance of emotional factors or non-rational responses implies that portfolios with higher yields and higher periodic return rankings are compensated for by greater future demand.[4] As Fama (1998) notes, it is essential to incorporate the tenets of behavioral finance in these analyses.

We continue as follows. Section 18.2 outlines the role of mutual funds in the disintermediation process, and section 18.3 explains the theoretical state of the art. Section 18.4 contrasts our results with the Spanish market, and section 18.5 provides some relevant conclusions.

18.2 THE ROLE OF MUTUAL FUNDS IN THE FUTURE OF FINANCIAL ACTIVITY

The deregulation and disintermediation processes are fundamental to explaining how the functioning and behavior of financial markets and entities has changed. As we noted earlier, the rise of off-balance-sheet products like mutual funds is one of the most obvious signs of disintermediation, which has been linked to the liberalization of financial markets and the introduction of financial innovations. Analysing the behavior of these collective investment products will help to clarify the current and future standing of financial intermediation and the development of capital markets.

Because collective investment has had such an influence on the structural changes taking place in financial intermediation, and because mutual funds allow savings to be transformed into investments, these instruments introduce a component of competition into the financial system. There are two important implications of the increasing role of mutual funds in the development of financial systems: (1) they contribute to an increase in efficiency, reducing the transaction costs of investors and companies, and (2) the volume of trade has affected the relationship between money and economic activity by competing with banks in their role of intermediaries between lenders and borrowers (Mack, 1993).

Indeed, the consolidation of collective investment, and in particular of mutual funds as the standard-bearer, is a key component of the expansion of financial markets, whose development has led to easier access for smaller investors. The immediate consequence has been the appearance of a great number of collective investment societies who are competing with the traditional financial intermediaries in offering smaller investors investment opportunities suited to their needs (almost hand-made portfolios) with ever-decreasing costs.

This has been one of the reasons for the success of this alternative in recent years. Their swift development has generated a tendency in the finance literature to posit that these institutions may become the banks of the future (Gorton and Pennacchi, 1993). The commonly cited hypothesis is that advances in information technology will reduce transaction costs, alter the make-up of traditional banking, and promote the separation between loan services and purely transactional services. This would make it possible to test whether these institutions can compete with financial intermediaries in creating liquidity. However, the monetary authorities will, of course, have the final say in this matter.

The debate about the possibility of financial intermediaries being supplanted by collective investment societies, which are subject to less regulation, is centered on external motives, which have led to periods of panic in the banking world (Diamond and Dybvig, 1983). However, if the separation of loan services and liquidity creation is produced by the high cost of banking regulations rather than by increased efficiency, this substitution would prove inefficient. Any alternative institution would be equally prone to situations of panic, and therefore would also require regulation.

This is the point of view expressed in much of the finance literature when it attempts to explain the shift away from traditional financial activity toward off-balance-sheet types of activity, whether the commercialization of mutual funds, the designation of shares, or operations in unofficial markets. These non-traditional products allow financial intermediaries to generate income without the financial burden imposed by solvency regulations, even though the credit entity must continue to supervise itself, as it is still exposed to risk.

The panic over mutual funds and the subsequent desire to establish control over them has been a topic of much discussion since the financial crash of 1998. The bankruptcy of some of the best-known high-risk funds in the USA led to a questioning of the US financial system's stability. These high-end funds enjoyed special advantages such as the flexibility of the management of their shares, which are usually not subject to any specific investment coefficient. Fund managers were able to invest in highly speculative stocks using "financial engineering" techniques, high leverage and arbitration techniques. Their headquarters were usually in tax havens or offshore, so they would not be subject to national economic or tax authorities.

The existence of asymmetrical information is the main cause of banking panics, but at the same time, such information can also act as a control mechanism and thus fulfill a useful function. In fact, the impossibility of the efficient supervision of the agent by the manager (whether it be borrower-lender or participant-handler) may lead to situations of uncertainty during periods of recession, for example, when depositors may be incapable of gauging which banks will go bankrupt. This asymmetry of information has also led to the provision of private regulation, audits, and insurance.

The same is true for mutual fund societies, however, which means that the argument for an efficient substitution of banks by collective investment societies does not hold. The truth is that some mutual fund managers exercise some functions similar to those of traditional banks, so that the solution to the problem of moral risk might serve to readdress the problem of regulation and the guarantees demanded in both types of financial intermediaries.

It certainly seems that, in traditional banking at least, the problem is aggravated by specific regulations. Because deposits are guaranteed by the central or main bank, depositors have less motivation to supervise the managers. Moreover, in comparison with funds, banks are less transparent entities. Investments in funds, on the other hand, are constantly revalued according to their market price, and their progress can be observed at all times. For banks, there are no objective criteria for evaluating all their investments. One must simply trust in the reputation of the bank and its directors.

The controversy between banks and collective investment institutions has focused more on the theory that the functions of liquidity creation and loan-granting should be separated than on actual practice. In fact, in order for non-bank financing to be underwritten by mutual funds, there must be guarantees from financial entities, so the hypothetical competitiveness by non-bank entities is still no more than an idea.

It is clear, however, that banks have responded to the growing presence of these alternative entities by increasing their intervention of them, whether by offering more services in the values market, or by distributing disintermediated products. In Spain, for example, banks are increasingly present in the placement and insurance of the values issued by other agents. Their presence in the options and futures market has increased considerably because of the need to cover risks. For mutual funds, the need to compete with other managing agents has led to the issuing of negotiable liabilities, and the mobilization of certain banking assets by means of temporary loans or through securitization.

The volume of savings administered by mutual funds does require an in-depth analysis of this market. Improving the management of fund portfolios and of the information provided to the participants is necessary for this sector to develop and function efficiently. It is also important to establish mechanisms to assess and control these portfolios better. Investors, who have become increasingly knowledgeable about finance, are demanding more information and better performance management.

In short, if the managing societies can earn the confidence of the investing public, it will positively influence the future development of the sector. Much of the research into mutual funds is dedicated to these matters.

18.3 THE INFLUENCE OF BEHAVIORAL FACTORS IN INVESTOR DECISIONS TO CHOOSE MUTUAL FUNDS

Our analysis of the demand for mutual funds focuses on what leads investors to choose one investment over another. In a market where increasing competition means investors must choose among a large number of quasi-equivalent portfolios, managers need to determine which attributes investors' value. Thus, acquiring abnormal returns, any associated costs, and position in the market (Sirri and Tufano, 1993, 1998) have all become factors.

In this manner, despite the fact that financial variables are the most relevant, they are not sufficient to explain the decision-making. Other factors taken into consideration relate to market configuration and the services provided: the reputation of the manager and his ratings, the investment publication rankings, recommendations from friends, technological advancements, and distribution mechanisms (Capon, Fitzsimons and Prince, 1996;[5] Del Guercio and Tkac, 2002).

It appears that the promise of higher returns is essential to the decision-making. It is interesting to note that one branch of research says that markets are efficient, rendering active management unnecessary;[6] but another branch corroborates the phenomenon of the persistence of results according to past yields that make it possible to predict future returns.[7]

Conversely, the presence of anomalies in the capital markets makes it necessary to broaden the analysis. Once some of the CAPMs restrictive criteria have been relaxed, it is possible that another type of factor besides binomial risk/return would suggest that historical returns influence investment flow into certain portfolios.

Recent financial literature has found that behavioral theories may explain the emotional components of the decision making process (Fama, 1998). More recent research into the field of anomalies has begun to incorporate psychological factors on the basis of human behavior theories. Any overreaction or underreaction of economic agents is ascribed to new information in the markets that generate correlations between asset prices and make it easier to develop active management strategies that take advantage of such price dysfunctions.

In fact, investors tend to overreact at the appearance of new information, for example they respond with an exaggerated price increase and show excessive enthusiasm or fear. Later, they may appraise the information more carefully, and adjust by moving share prices in the opposite direction. The market is such that good news can lead to over-inflated prices, but bad news can push prices to extreme lows.

One of the most influential papers in this line of research is by De Bondt and Thaler (1985), who examined the directional changes in economically significant returns over long periods of time. They found that the stocks that experienced the lowest returns over the previous three- to five-year period tended to exceed higher performers over the subsequent three to five years. In accordance with this approach, the opposite strategy involves forming an arbitrage portfolio with long-term positions in the low-yield category, and short-term positions in the higher-yield category.

De Bondt and Thaler (1985) based their explanations on the results of Kahneman and Tversky (1982) who alluded to the phenomenon of cognitive dissonance[8] in order to highlight that individuals, when making decisions, tend to give greater weight to more recent information. This may cause prices to temporarily deviate from their basic values as a result of both excessive optimism and excessive pessimism.

On the other hand, behavioral patterns have also been noted that have kept returns down over the short term, for example, stocks that experienced high yields over the 12 months prior to the information tended to maintain their returns in the immediate future. In this context, a momentum strategy might be appropriate, for example, purchasing stocks with high past returns but lower recent yields.[9]

This type of action corresponds with the phenomenon of under-reaction, and can be explained by another aspect of human behavior, developed by Edwards (1968). This conservatism in decision-making, when investors are slow to react despite the appearance of new information, is also found in the financial markets. Investors tend to rely on the provisional nature of an event, and may underestimate the new information. Because the information is assimilated more slowly, there may be a positive correlation between short-term prices, which justifies a momentum strategy (Barberis, Shleifer and Vishny, 1998).

Both overreaction and underreaction are considered signs of investor irrationality, and are used to explain market anomalies. Their existence means we need a fresh approach to the issue of efficiency, since some investors can exploit market inefficiencies to obtain abnormal returns. In the case of mutual funds, a considerable part of the market uses relative resistance or momentum strategies. Since they tend to rely on the phenomenon of the persistence of results, the trend is toward purchasing shares whose price has increased during the most recent quarters of the year, with the aim of achieving extraordinary returns.

In this context, the positive relationship between stock returns and the choice of certain funds can be explained by the coexistence of rational and behavioral factors. Investors may not always behave in accordance with economic rationality; indeed, they may instead act according to behavioral arguments. The following may result:

- Demand that responds to mass movements (a herd mentality), and a status quo that is difficult to change (Samuelson and Zeckhauser, 1988; Patel, Zeckhauser and Hendricks, 1991 and 1994; Barberis and Thaler, 2003).
- A tendency to make decisions based on non-specialized information, such as publicity campaigns or temporary market movements (Capon, Fitzsimons and Prince, 1996).
- A tendency to bet on the winning horse, investing in funds that have performed the best in the most recent return rankings (Patel, Zeckhauser and Hendricks, 1991; Ippolito, 1992; Sirri and Tufano, 1993).
- An irrational asymmetry of behavior in terms of the previous tendency, since investors are not penalized for choosing poorer-performing funds to the same degree they will be rewarded for choosing higher-performing ones (Sirri and Tufano, 1993 and 1998; Goetzmann and Peles, 1997).

In short, analysing mutual fund choices is a multi-attribute function. Despite the fact that financial factors seem the most significant, we must also consider things like the representative variables of the structure and the manager's market position. These results will assist managers in establishing their strategies for activating and trading these financial instruments.

In accordance with the theoretical arguments put forth so far, investors not only attend to criteria of economic rationality when making investment decisions; they also place considerable importance on behavioral factors, particularly past returns.

18.4 EMPIRICAL ANALYSIS

18.4.1 Sample selection

Our empirical data cover 1997–2003 for a sample of growth-oriented funds, including portfolios that maintained more risky positions (Table 18.1). The

Table 18.1 The sample

Year	Quarter	Number of funds	Pure growth*	Non-pure growth**
1998	1	56	28	28
1998	2	56	28	28
1998	3	129	79	50
1998	4	129	79	50
1999	1	127	78	49
1999	2	127	78	49
1999	3	243	142	101
1999	4	244	142	102
2000	1	237	132	105
2000	2	237	132	105
2000	3	296	163	133
2000	4	296	163	133
2001	1	282	166	116
2001	2	282	166	116
2001	3	371	228	143
2001	4	371	228	143
2002	1	330	200	130
2002	2	329	199	130
2002	3	391	240	151
2002	4	391	240	151
2003	1	348	219	129
2003	2	348	219	129
2003	3	348	219	129
2003	4	348	219	129
Observations		6,316	3,787	2,529
Total number of funds		456	290	166

* Pure growth: funds with a higher than 70% component of variable income assets.
** Non-pure growth: funds with a variable income assets component of between 25% and 70%.

availability of net asset values and size are taken from the Madrid Stock Exchange and the Comisión Nacional del Mercado de Valores (CNMV).[10]

We only consider the mutual funds for which we have at least eight quarters of data to estimate the panel because of the problem of survivorship bias, as we explain more next (survivorship bias is a recurring problem in the performance of mutual funds). Despite the distortions this may cause for global fund sector results, some seminal articles such as Grinblatt and Titman (1989) note that survivorship makes little difference in average returns. They find less than a 1 percent per year difference between the average of survivors and an average designed to duplicate the entire population.

18.4.2 Model specification

For the empirical comparison, the first step is to construct a panel of data highlighting the specification of the model with cross-sectional and time series data for a large number of agents with the same investing commitment and other commonly observable parameters. Considerable divergences exist, because they have significant individual characteristics that need to be taken into account. To do this, controlling for non-observable heterogeneity allows for a more effective comparison, and is one of the advantages of the panel data methodology (Arellano and Bond, 1991).

We propose the following model:

$$
\begin{aligned}
Y_{Ft} &= \alpha + \beta X'_{Ft} + v_F + \varepsilon_{Ft} \\
F &= 1, \ldots, N \\
t &= 1, \ldots, T
\end{aligned}
$$

where Y_{Ft} represents the growth of investor demand for fund F in year t, α is the constant, and X'_{Ft} is the vector of explanatory variables. The random variable v_F covers the non-observable effects specific to each agent in the panel and is invariant over time. This therefore involves obtaining estimates for the model coefficients in the presence of these effects, which, as they are not observable, will become part of the term error in the estimated model.

We specify variables and descriptive analysis as follows:

$$
\begin{aligned}
INFLOW_{Ft} = \alpha &+ \beta_1 LAGRT_{Ft} + \beta_2 RISK_{Ft} + \beta_3 ALPHA_{Ft} + \beta_4 LNSIZE_{Ft} \\
&+ \beta_5 MARKET_{Ft} + \beta_6 GROWTH_{Ft} + v_F + \varepsilon_{Ft}
\end{aligned}
$$

The dependent variable is defined as the variation in demand for each mutual fund during the years analysed. We make an approximation based on the growth in volume of each fund managed by the investment fund managing companies ($INFLOW_{Ft}$), so that:

$$
INFLOW_{Ft} = \frac{PAT_{Ft} - PAT_{Ft-1}(1 + R_{Ft})}{PAT_{Ft-1}}
$$

where $INFLOW_{Ft}$ is the variation in demand for fund F in period t, PAT_{Ft} and PAT_{Ft-1} represent the size of fund F at the end and the beginning, respectively, of each year t, and R_{Ft} is the return of the fund net of deposit and management commissions.

Variability in demand depends on a series of explanatory variables. Higher returns are one of the determining factors in the movement of demand toward one mutual fund or another. In this regard, the relevant variables are:

- Lagged return ($LAGRT_{Ft}$).
- A dummy variable, with a value of 1 if the mutual fund has outperformed the market ($MARKET_{Ft}$).
- Excess return for the market ($EXCESS_{Ft}$).
- Fund position in the return ranking ($RANK_{Ft}$).
- Fund size ($LNSIZE_{Ft}$).

Based on net asset values, the yield for each mutual fund is obtained at a given moment in time (RT_{Ft}):

$$RT_{Ft} = \frac{NAV_{Ft} - NAV_{Ft-1} + Div_{Ft}}{NAV_{Ft-1}}$$

where NAV_{Ft} and NAV_{Ft-1} represent the net asset values net of management commissions and deposit of fund F at the beginning and the end of year t, respectively.

To determine whether the funds in our sample can outperform the market, and whether this is relevant for participants, we include a dummy variable $MARKET_{Ft}$ that takes a value of 1 if the fund obtains a higher than average return, and 0 otherwise. As an alternative, we include the difference in return of each portfolio with the benchmark, a variable we call $EXCESS_{Ft.}$

The increase in mutual funds has meant that return classifications are published even more frequently. Thus, including an explanatory variable of the position in the return ranking ($RANK_{Ft-1}$) of each fund comprising the sample at the end of the previous year is considered one of the factors that has caused increased demand for the higher-ranking funds.

To compare the positive relationship between fund size and increase in growth, we include the average size of each mutual fund for each of the years studied ($LNSIZE_{Ft}$) as one of the factors that may determine the inflow of demand toward larger portfolios.

In another category of variables, we find that those representative of the risk associated with each mutual fund and with the relationship between return and risk are:

- Mutual fund volatility ($RISK_{Ft}$).
- Risk-adjusted return, as measured by Jensen's alpha ($ALPHA_{Ft}$).
- A dummy variable ($GROWTH_{Ft}$) that indicates whether the investment fund in each quarter is more or less oriented towards risk in accordance with the definition given in Table 18.1.

Table 18.2 Statistics of the variables

Variable	Obs.	Mean	Std. Dev.	Min	Max
INFLOW	6316	0.0190927	0.1988709	−0.9879699	2.997014
LAGRT	6316	−0.0112892	0.1171355	−0.4554896	0.7192984
LNSIZE	6316	3.060889	1.518582	−4.60517	7.577818
RISK	6316	0.047072	0.0257771	4.89E-06	0.2018682
ALPHA	3697	−0.0018239	0.0074624	−0.0301142	0.0332825
EXCESS	6316	0.0158014	0.084218	−0.371194	0.7162615

In the analysis, the volatility ($RISK_{Ft}$) covering the return dispersion in terms of the measure of reference[11] is defined as a variable indicative of risk.

Nonetheless, Jensen's alpha (1968), which is based on the market model, is the most popular measurement for evaluating mutual funds. Jensen's alpha determines the risk premium for all portfolios, which, for a given systematic level of risk, practice a simple policy of purchasing and maintaining the assets. In this manner, $ALPHA_{Ft}$ is obtained as the constant term in the following regression equation:

$$(E(R_{Ft}) - R_f) = \alpha_F - \beta_F(E(R_m) - R_f)$$

where $E(R_{Ft})$ = the return expected from fund F at moment t; R_f = the return of the risk-free asset; α_F = the risk-adjusted return, the Jensen alpha; β_F = the portfolio systematic risk; and $E(R_m)$ = the expected return of the benchmark portfolio.

In line with the previous equation, whenever α_F takes positive significant values, it is interpreted as a positive mutual fund procedure because it has outperformed the market. If the constant α is negative and significant, the fund return is lower than what we would expect in equilibrium.

Table 18.2 summarizes the statistics of the variables (the number of observations, the mean, the standard deviation, the minimum, and the maximum). Table 18.3 gives the correlations between variables.

18.4.3 Empirical results

This section provides our main empirical results, which are shown in Table 18.4. According to the results of the Breusch and Pagan test, the hypothesis of no random effects is clearly rejected, and the Hausman test favors random effects. Therefore, all models are estimated using a random effects method. To make the most efficient possible use of the sample components, we have estimated six different models.

Table 18.3 Correlations

	LAGRT	*LNSIZE*	*RISK*	*EXCESS*	*RANK*	*MARKET*	*ALPHA*
LAGRT	1						
LNSIZE	0.0792	1					
RISK	−0.2477	−0.0051	1				
EXCESS	0.1123	0.027	−0.0545	1			
RANK	0.3566	−0.0515	0.0113	−0.0447	1		
MARKET	0.1908	0.0619	−0.0428	0.7496	−0.0643	1	
ALPHA	−0.0413	0.2037	0.0888	0.0785	0.0869	0.0677	1

We examine the following variables: lagged return (*LAGRT*), excess yield on the market (*MARKET*; *EXCESS*), position in the periodical return classifications (*RANK*), and the different measures used to measure risk and the return–risk combination (*RISK* and *ALPHA*). From these variables, we find that the investor overlooks the economic rationality criterion in return-risk, and is almost exclusively concerned with the fund's past returns, despite the premise of portfolio theory that past returns are not predictors of future returns.

We find a positive, significant correlation between the growth in mutual fund demand (*INFLOW*), and its returns, both in estimating the different panels. Note that the returns appear to be especially significant in all models considered.

Although investors do seem concerned about *RANK*, they are also interested in another type of publicity frequently aimed at variable and mixed income funds, such as the yields obtained beyond the market (*MARKET*; *EXCESS*). We might term this result the reputation effect, an attempt by investors to lessen their uncertainty over how to respond to new, potentially more profitable products about which there is little information available. It appears that investors are attempting to ensure that what is being offered ranks very highly, and, in the case of Spain, that it comes from a financial group.

GROWTH is another variable that turns out to be significant and positively related to the investing influx toward investment funds. *GROWTH* distinguishes between variable income funds with a greater or lesser risk capacity. Once investors have chosen this category, they appear to prefer more specialized products (portfolios with over 70% in shares). During upward-trending periods, when we see a notable increase in demand for this type of product, these portfolios obtain the highest yields and, therefore, the best return rankings. Both variables are determinants of future investment, and the hypothesis that we set out to verify.

Risk-adjusted return (*ALPHA*), which is a reliable measurement of whether the fund has outperformed the market, was not considered important in

Table 18.4 Estimation results (random effects panel data estimations)

	Model 1	Model 2	Model 3	Model 4	Model 5	Model 6
LAGRT	0.3631451	0.2362299		0.3627942	0.268933	0.1526426
	(9.33)***	(10.89)***		(9.38)***	(5.31)***	(5.55)***
RANK			0.0416649			
			(7.38)***			
LNSIZE	0.009365	0.0140353	0.0105727	0.0096181	0.0092292	0.0084399
	(3.86)***	(5.84)***	(4.26)***	(3.95)***	(3.12)***	(2.91)***
MARKET	0.0375376	0.0189044	0.0350818		0.0249444	0.0104839
	(5.7)***	(3.78)***	(5.33)***		(3.05)***	(1.75)*
EXCESS				0.3135918		
				(8.15)***		
RISK	0.2667578	0.3701847	0.1463438	0.2171416	0.3361101	0.0259192
	(1.87)*	(3.28)***	(1.02)	(1.52)	(1.77)*	(0.16)

GROWTH	0.0349823	0.0359671	0.0349132	0.0383878	0.0306309	0.0394046
	(4.35)***	(4.49)***	(4.26)***	(4.77)***	(3.13)***	(4.12)***
ALPHA					0.7439007	0.147357
					(1.46)	(0.33)
Time-dummy variables	Yes	No	Yes	Yes	Yes	No
Constant	−0.1013305	−0.0449538	−0.014416	0.1378368	−0.0556405	−0.0525549
	(−3.38)***	(−4.5)***	(−0.51)	(4.91)***	(−2.07)**	(4.03)***
Observations	6316	6316	6316	6316	3697	3697
Pseudo R^2	0.0726	0.0385	0.0689	0.0770	0.1173	0.0634
Breusch–Pagan	76.86***	61.73***	70.55***	77.08***	16.05***	16.71***
Hausman	309.39***	274.30***	296.88***	334.60***	296.61***	203.97***

Notes: Parameter estimation by random effects. *t*-values are in brackets. *** indicates significance at the 1% level, ** indicates significance at the 5% level, * indicates significance at the 10% level. Breusch-Pagan is a Lagrange multiplier test. Hausman refers to the Hausman specification test. Obs. is the number of observations.

any cases. However, in the second model, investors appear to ascribe importance to risk measured by volatility (*RISK*), but, contrary to our expectations, it is positive.

As far as investor irrationality, illustrated by ignoring Jensen's alpha, investors responded to the hypothesis about their behavior, an issue that is likely to continue to change in the future. The lack of information on risk-adjusted return (alpha or another performance measure) in the Spanish market until about 1997 has made it difficult for investors to learn about it. This has led them to make decisions using only the known variables published by official bodies.

In the case of mutual funds, the CNMV's quarterly Reports on Collective Investment Institutions provide data on returns, volatilities, size, commissions, and general market data, but not on performance measures. This issue has been changing in Spain over the last few years, however, especially since the new Law on Collective Investment Institutions was passed in November 2005. The appearance of new products such as hedge funds, and the increased competition, will cause the rating agencies to consolidate, which will offer investors additional information for their investment decisions.

Although it does not obtain high percentages, the size of the fund appears to be significant and has a positive sign in the six models estimated (*LNSIZE*). This means that investors overall tended to prefer larger funds. This is probably for economic reasons related to scale economies and lower costs, a theory not unanimously verified in the financial literature. However, we understand that the situation in the Spanish market justifies this result. Since the first regulation on these financial instruments in 1991, the investment funds market has been one of the cornerstones for what is known in Spain as the linked disintermediation process (Contreras, 1993).

The growth of off-balance-sheet operations, as we discussed earlier, has taken form in the Spanish financial system as bank and savings bank strategies to adapt to European competition following the liberalization process, especially since 1992. So the disintermediation occurring everywhere has been carried out by the universal bank, which currently in Spain holds over 70 percent of savings and investment captured through investment funds.

18.5 CONCLUSION

This chapter has attempted to illuminate the mutual funds market from the standpoint of how participants choose these financial products. We analyzed which factors are most important to investors, and found that financial factors and behavioral arguments must both be considered.

Participants use the historical return of the portfolio as the main reference variable when deciding whether to invest in certain funds. This coincides with conclusions in the literature on the influence of past returns on net flows of money and of participants in investment funds. As we noted, daily market movements show that the tenets of economic rationality are not always followed. Numerous academics have devoted their efforts over the years to determining which factors that affect investor decision-making do not maximize final expected wealth from a mathematical point of view. Behavioral finance is going even further in this regard, and some of the choices to date denote investor preferences. Although they are difficult to quantify for use in prediction models, they may be useful in fields such as the development of financial products.

We conclude that investor behavior is characterized by a series of distortions that cannot be explained without considering market faults and the lack of symmetric information, which call for the coexistence of rational and behavioral factors when defining the explanatory models.

NOTES

1. See Boot and Thakor (1993a, 1993b and 1996), Allen and Gale (1994 and 2000) and Allen and Santomero (2001).
2. See Silber (1983), Van Horne (1985), Miller (1986 and 1991), Finnerty (1988), Ross (1989 and 1991), Allen and Gale (1994) and Duffie and Rahi (1995).
3. For a more in-depth analysis of this issue in terms of the Spanish market, see Freixas, Marín, Martínez and Rubio (1997).
4. For a review of this issue, see, *inter alia*, Ippolito (1992), Sirri and Tufano (1993 and 1998), Rockinger (1995) and Goetzmann and Peles (1997).
5. These authors develop a research line related to consumer behavior and the most appropriate market strategies; their article entails segmenting the investment fund market into a series of relevant variables. The resulting stratification can be enormously useful to managers in designing their strategies.
6. See, *inter alia*, Jensen (1968), Ippolito (1989) and Carhart (1997).
7. Regarding this phenomenon, some papers find proof in the persistence of the results found in short-term funds, for periods of one to three years. This persistence is ascribed to what is referred to as hot hands, or common investment strategies (Hendricks, Patel and Zeckhauser, 1993; Goetzmann and Ibbotson 1994; Brown and Goetzmann, 1995; Wermers, 1996). Other research demonstrates the possibility of predicting the yield from more long-term investment funds, usually periods of five to ten years. This may be possible because of having different information than the managers and because of the quality of their asset selection ability (Grinblatt and Titman, 1992; Elton, Gruber, Das and Hlavka, 1993; Elton, Gruber, Das and Blake, 1996).
8. This theory was initially developed by Festinger (1957).
9. For mutual funds, this matter is discussed more fully in Jegadeesh and Titman (1993) and Chang, Jegadeesh and Lakonishok (1996).
10. The Comisión Nacional del Mercado de Valores (CNMV) in Spain is comparable to the SEC in the USA.
11. But its inclusion as one of the determining factors in fund demand is not justified by the data. Rather, this measure is generally accepted as making a mathematical representation of a fund for a given period. For the Spanish market, the CNMV requires managers to include it in the Quarterly Reports on Collective Investment Institutions. This means that the data on risk are one of the few pieces of information participants

receive directly. In this article, the standard deviation of monthly returns in the fund over the last six months is taken as a measurement of volatility.

REFERENCES

Allen, F. and Gale, D. (1994) *Financial Innovation and Risk Sharing* (Cambridge, MA: MIT Press).

Allen, F. and Gale, D. (2000) *Comparing Financial Systems* (Cambridge, MA: MIT Press, Massachusetts Institute of Technology).

Allen, F. and Santomero, A.M. (2001) "What Do Financial Intermediaries Do?", *Journal of Banking and Finance*, 25(2): 271–94.

Arellano, M. and Bond, S. (1991) "Some Tests of Specification for Panel Data: Monte Carlo Evidence and an Application to Employment Equations", *Review of Economic Studies*, 58(2): 277–97.

Barberis, N. and Thaler, R.H. (2003) "A Survey of Behavioral Finance", in G. Constantinides, M. Harris and R. Stulz (eds), *Handbook of the Economics of Finance* (Amsterdam: North-Holland), 1053–123.

Barberis, N., Shleifer, A. and Vishny, R. (1998) "A Model of Investor Sentiment", *Journal of Financial Economics*, 49(3): 307–43.

Boot, A. and Thakor, A. (1993a) "Security Design", *Journal of Finance*, 48(4): 1349–78.

Boot, A. and Thakor, A. (1993b) "Self-Interested Bank Regulation", *American Economic Review*, 83(2): 206–12.

Boot, A. and Thakor, A. (1996) "Banking Structure and Financial Innovation", in A. Saunders and I. Walter (eds), *Universal Banking: Financial System Design Reconsidered* (Irwing, NY: New York University Salomon Center): pp. 420–30.

Brown, S. and Goetzmann, W. (1995) "Performance Persistence", *Journal of Finance*, 50(2): 679–98.

Capon, N., Fitzsimons, G. and Prince, R. (1996) "An Individual Level Analysis of the Mutual Fund Investment Decision", *Journal of Financial Services Research*, 10(1): 59–82.

Carhart, M.M. (1997) "On Persistence in Mutual Fund Performance", *Journal of Finance*, 52(1): 57–82.

Chang, L., Jegadeesh, N. and Lakonishok, J. (1996) "Momentum Strategies", *Journal of Finance*, 51(5): 1681–713.

Contreras, C. (1993) "Un Balance de la Guerra de los Fondos de Inversión", *Papeles de Economía Española*, 54(1): 246–67.

De Bondt, W. and Thaler, R. (1985) "Does the Stock Market Overreact?", *Journal of Finance*, 40(3): 793–805.

Del Guercio, D. and Tkac, P.A. (2002) "The Determinants of the Flows of Funds of Manager Portfolios: Mutual Fund vs. Pension Funds", *Journal of Financial and Quantitative Analysis*, 37(4): 523–57.

Diamond, D. and Dybvig, P. (1983) "Bank Run Deposit Insurance and Liquidity", *Journal of Political Economy*, 91(3): 401–9.

Duffie, D. and Rahi, R. (1995) "Financial Market Innovations and Security Design: An Introduction", *Journal of Economic Theory*, 65(1): 1–42.

Edwards, W. (1968) "Conservatism in Human Information Procession", in B. Kleinmutz (ed.), *Formal Representation of Human Judgement* (New York: Wiley): pp. 17–52.

Elton, E., Gruber, M., Das, S. and Hlavka, M. (1993) "Efficiency with Costly Information: A Reinterpretation of Evidence from Managed Portfolios", *The Review of Financial Studies*, 6(1): 1–22.

Elton, E., Gruber, M., Das, S. and Blake, C. (1996) "The Persistence of Risk-Adjusted Mutual Fund Performance", *Journal of Business*, 69(2): 133–57.

Fama, E. (1970) "Efficient Capital Markets: A Review of Theory and Empirical Work", *Journal of Finance*, 25(2): 383–417.

Fama, E. (1998) "Market Efficiency, Long-Terms Returns, and Behavioral Finance", *Journal of Financial Economics*, 49(3): 283–306.

Festinger, L. (1957) *A Theory of Cognitive Dissonance* (Stanford: Stanford University Press).

Finnerty, J.D. (1988) "Financial Engineering in Corporate Finance: An Overview", *Financial Management*, 17(4): 14–33.

Freixas, X., Marín, J., Martínez, M. and Rubio, G. (1997) *La Evaluación de los Fondos de Inversión en España*, Editorial Civitas, Colección Economía.

Goetzmann, W. and Ibbotson, R. (1994) "Do Winners Repeat?", *The Journal of Portfolio Management*, 20(2): 9–18.

Goetzmann, W. and Peles, N. (1997) "Cognitive Dissonance and Mutual Fund Investors", *The Journal of Financial Research*, 20(2): 145–58.

Gorton, G. and Pennacchi, G. (1993) "Money Market Funds and Finance Companies: Are They the Banks of the Future?", in M. Klausner and L. White (eds), *Structural Change in Banking* (Business One Irwin, New York University Salomon Center).

Grinblatt, M. and Titman, S. (1989) "Mutual Fund Performance: An Analysis of Quarterly Portfolio Holdings", *Journal of Business*, 62(3): 393–416.

Grinblatt, M. and Titman, S. (1992) "The Persistence of Mutual Fund Performance", *Journal of Finance*, 47(5): 1977–84.

Gruber, M. (1996) "Another Puzzle: The Growth in Actively Managed Mutual Funds", *Journal of Finance*, 51(3): 783–810.

Hendricks, D., Patel, J. and Zeckhauser, R. (1993) "Hot Hands in Mutual Funds: Short-Run Persistence of Relative Performance, 1974–1988", *Journal of Finance*, 48(1): 93–130.

Ippolito, R.A. (1989) "Efficiency with Costly Information: A Study of Mutual Fund Performance, 1965–1984", *The Quarterly Journal of Economics*, 54(1): 1–23.

Ippolito, R.A. (1992) "Consumer Reaction to Measures of Poor Quality: Evidence from the Mutual Fund Industry", *Journal of Law and Economics*, 35(1): 45–70.

Jegadeesh, N. and Titman, S. (1993) "Returns to Buying Winners and Selling Losers: Implications for Stock Market Efficiency", *Journal of Finance*, 48(1): 65–91.

Jensen, M.C. (1968) "The Performance of Mutual Funds in the Period 1945–1964", *Journal of Finance*, 23(2): 389–416.

Kahneman, D. and Tversky, A. (1982) "Intuitive Prediction: Biases and Corrective Procedures", in D. Kahneman, P. Slovic and A. Tversky (eds), *Judgement Under Uncertainty: Heuristics and Biases* (New York: Cambridge University Press).

Mack, P. (1993) "Recent Trends in the Mutual Fund Industry", *Federal Reserve Bulletin*, 79(1): 1001–12.

Miller, M.H. (1986) "Financial Innovation: The Last Twenty Years and the Next", *Journal of Financial and Quantitative Analysis*, 21(4): 459–71.

Miller, M.H. (1991) *Financial Innovation and Market Volatility* (Cambridge, MA: Blackwell Publishers).

Patel, J., Zeckhauser, R. and Hendricks, D. (1991) "The Rationality Struggle: Illustrations from Financial Markets", *American Economic Review*, 81(2): 232–6.

Patel, J., Zeckhauser, R. and Hendricks, D. (1994) "Investment Flows and Performance: Evidence from Mutual Funds, Cross-Border Investments, and New Issues", in R. Sato, R. Levich and R. Ramachandran (eds), *Japan, Europe, and International Financial Markets: Analytical and Empirical Perspectives* (New York: Cambridge University Press).

Rockinger, M. (1995) "Determinants of Capital Flows to Mutual Funds", Working Paper HEC – School of Management.

Ross, S.A. (1989) "Institutional Markets, Financial Marketing and Financial Innovation", *Journal of Finance*, 44(3): 541–56.

Ross, S.A. (1991) "Innovation in the Financial Markets", in S.J. Khoury (ed.), *Recents Developments in International Banking and Finance* (IV–V), pp. 89–99 (Amsterdam: North-Holland).

Samuelson, W. and Zeckhauser, R. (1988) "Status Quo Bias in Decision Making", *Journal of Risk and Uncertainty*, 1(1): 7–59.

Silber, W.L. (1983) "The Process of Financial Innovation", *American Economic Review*, 73(2): 89–95.

Sirri, E. and Tufano, P. (1993) "Buying and Selling Mutual Funds: Flows, Performance, Fees, and Services", Working Paper, Harvard University.

Sirri, E. and Tufano, P. (1998) "Costly Search and Mutual Fund Flows", *Journal of Finance*, 53(5): 1589–622.

Van Horne, J.C. (1985) "Of Financial Innovations and Excesses", *Journal of Finance*, 40(3): 621–31.

Wermers, W. (1996) "Momentum Investment Strategies of Mutual Funds, Performance Persistence and Survivorship Bias", Working Paper, Graduate School of Business and Administration, University of Colorado at Boulder.

Index

CPSIA information can be obtained
at www.ICGtesting.com
Printed in the USA
LVHW081619121120
671523LV00010B/230